VISUAL BASIC 6

In Record Time

VISUAL BASIC® 6

In Record Time™

Steve Brown

SYBEX®

San Francisco • Paris • Düsseldorf • Soest

Associate Publisher: Gary Masters
Contracts and Licensing Manager: Kristine Plachy
Acquisitions Editor: Peter Kuhns
Developmental Editor: Kim Wimpsett
Editor: Davina Baum
Technical Editor: Scott Thompson
Book Designers: Franz Baumhackl, Patrick Dintino, Catalin Dulfu,
Robin Kibby
Graphic Illustrator: Tony Jonick
Electronic Publishing Specialist: Cyndy Johnsen
Production Coordinator: Jefferson McClure
Indexer: Matthew Spence
Cover Designer: Design Site
Cover Illustrator/Photographer: Adri Berger/Tony Stone Images

Screen reproductions produced with Collage Complete.

Collage Complete is a trademark of Inner Media Inc.

SYBEX is a registered trademark of SYBEX Inc.

In Record Time is a trademark of SYBEX Inc.

TRADEMARKS: SYBEX has attempted throughout this book to
distinguish proprietary trademarks from descriptive terms by
following the capitalization style used by the manufacturer.

Library of Congress Card Number: 98-86633
ISBN: 0-7821-2310-4

Manufactured in the United States of America

10 9 8 7 6 5 4 3

To my daughter McKenna...
"This!" book is for you!

Acknowledgments

Many people contributed a great deal to making this book a reality. Thanks to Peter Kuhns for asking me to work on this project. Kim Wimpsett and Davina Baum are the coolest editors to ever work in the Bay Area. Thanks for catching my goofs when the caffeine was running low. Scott Thompson: I have never worked with a better programmer in my life, and you made some really awesome suggestions during the technical editing process. Thanks also to Jefferson McClure, production coordinator, and to Cyndy Johnsen, electronic publishing specialist.

Kyle, Raffie, Alan, Cassie, and Bobby: Thanks for your support and friendship. May we all be successful on our ventures!

Extra special thanks go to my wife, Susan, and my daughter, McKenna, for putting up with my long hours. I'm on your time again! Finally, I want to thank my Lord, Jesus Christ, for sustaining me and my family in the slow times and blessing me with the knowledge and capacity to learn this computer stuff.

Contents at a Glance

Table of Contents

Introduction

Microsoft Visual Basic 6 is the newest version of the popular programming language. With its new features, Visual Basic is an even stronger contender in the enterprise application development arena than ever before.

The Visual Basic environment is great for creating almost any type of application you can think of. You can develop robust stand-alone applications, games, and utilities in less time than it takes in other languages. You can also use ActiveX technology to create Internet-enabled applications that are limited only by your imagination. When used in conjunction with the Windows API, you are armed with a serious programming tool for which you can do almost anything in your project development efforts.

Visual Basic 6 In Record Time is designed to help you quickly become proficient in Visual Basic. Not only will this book teach you how to use Visual Basic and the tools it comes with, it will teach you useful and practical development techniques that just aren't taught in the fast-paced world of rapid application development. Beginning programmers can be assured that the techniques learned in this book can be applied from language to language, platform to platform. You will learn the most important skills required to design, program, and distribute fully functional applications—without requiring you to study every aspect in detail. You are not required to have any prior programming experience; the only requirements are a basic familiarity with the Windows environment and a desire to learn. This book teaches you how to program, using Visual Basic as the primary language.

What Will You Learn from This Book?

This book aims to teach you everything you need to know about developing applications with Visual Basic, from start to finish, without requiring you to have any previous experience with Visual Basic or any other programming language.

The book is divided into skills that are designed to teach you specific aspects of the application development process. Each skill demonstrates a particular feature or programming method and offers you practical sample applications and routines. You do not need to read the book from cover to cover to learn a new skill. Simply jump to the skill you want to master and you are on your way!

In Skill 1, *Mastering the Integrated Development Environment (IDE)*, you will discover the tools that are essential to working in Visual Basic, and you will create your very first application. In Skill 2, *Working with Forms*, you'll understand and master the most basic element of application development. In Skill 3, *Selecting and Using Controls*, you'll become familiar with many of the components that you will use in almost all of your applications. Skill 4, *Working within Modules and Classes*, will help you to understand how and when to place procedures in code modules and class modules. You will learn how to create and link menus and toolbars, including the new CoolBar, as well as learn the basics of interface design in Skill 5, *Creating and Using Menus and Toolbars*. Skill 6, *Logic and Program Flow*, is particularly useful for readers who are learning to program for the first time. It covers Boolean and binary logic without making you feel like an algebra student in a calculus class. You will learn how to program your applications to make decisions.

In Skill 7, *Understanding Data Types*, you will take your programming knowledge a step further by learning how to manipulate memory objects, called *variables*, so your applications can perform useful tasks. Once you know how to work with variables, you can move on to Skill 8, *Storing and Retrieving Data*. Here you will learn how to store data to disk and how to retrieve it. You will also be introduced to Microsoft's new universal data access model called ActiveX Data Objects, or ADO. Skill 9, *Printing*, teaches you how to provide printing services in your application using Visual Basic's Printer object. Then you will learn how to integrate and use Crystal Reports Pro to develop sophisticated reports for your applications.

In Skill 10, *Using Dialog Boxes*, you will learn how to use the dialog boxes that are built-in to Visual Basic. Once you have mastered these, you will learn how to create your own reusable dialog boxes. Skill 11, *Working with the Mouse*, teaches you how to program the mouse to properly function in your application. You will learn how to detect mouse-clicks, mouse movements, as well as create a drag-and-drop application. You will also learn how to move data between applications using OLE drag-and-drop.

Skill 12, *Debugging Your Applications*, is another important chapter for beginners and experienced developers alike. You will learn how to effectively comment your source code to aid in the debugging process. These are two aspects of software development that programmers generally don't like to deal with. This skill makes debugging a familiar and useful process.

In Skill 13, *Creating and Using Help Files*, you will learn how to use the Help Compiler Workshop to design and build your own help files, as well as link them to your Visual Basic application. After you learn how to develop WinHelp-style help files, you will learn how to convert them to Microsoft's new HTML

Help system. This skill is a must for serious programmers! In Skill 14, *Compiling and Distributing Your Application,* you will learn how to compile your program and distribute it to others. This skill also covers some special considerations that you, as a programmer, must consider when entering the marketplace with your application.

The latter skills deal with the more advanced features of Visual Basic and application development. In Skill 15, *Learning and Using Object-Oriented Programming (OOP),* you will learn the basics of OOP and how to apply it in your application development efforts. It's easier than you think! Skill 16, *Extending the IDE with Add-Ins,* teaches you how to use the extensibility tools in Visual Basic to assist you when developing larger, more sophisticated applications. In addition, you will create three code documentation add-ins that you can use to create consistent, accurate comments in your code. In Skill 17, *Using ActiveX,* you will learn about the most common ActiveX technologies including how to create your own reusable ActiveX controls and documents. This skill will also prepare you for Internet development in Skill 18.

Skill 18, *Internet Development with Visual Basic,* will teach you how to develop Internet-enabled applications using several different tools and technologies. At the heart of this skill is the WebComm chat room utility that you will develop using three of Visual Basic's Internet tools to demonstrate their power and flexibility.

Finally, Skill 19, *Using DLLs and the Windows API,* teaches you how to use DLLs and the Windows API in your applications. You will learn how these tools can add elegance, sophistication, and power to your applications. Using Visual Basic with the Windows API gives you almost endless possibilities for program development.

I hope you will find this book to be a valuable resource that you will have by your side as you write your killer apps.

What This Book Assumes

This book assumes that you are familiar with the basics of the Windows environment:

- You know how to use Windows and navigate through its interface well enough to start an application.

- You know how to use the mouse and keyboard within Windows.

In addition, this book assumes that you have installed the sample applications and graphics from your Visual Basic CD. You will examine, as well as modify, some of these applications in this book.

Conventions Used in This Book

This book uses a number of conventions to convey more information accurately in a few pages:

- You will find Notes, Tips, and Warnings that can help you become more productive within the Visual Basic environment.

- The ➢ sign designates choosing a command from a menu. For example, "choose File ➢ Exit" means you should open the File menu and then choose Exit.

- The + sign indicates key combinations. For example, "press Ctrl+Alt+Del" means that you should hold down the Ctrl and Alt keys, and press the Del key.

- **Boldface** indicates items that you want to type in exactly as they are printed, or items that you should choose from a drop-down list.

- *Italics* are used to introduce new terms or information that may not be exactly the same from computer to computer, such as drive letters.

- A `monospaced` font is used to denote program code, object properties, as well as filenames and paths that you will load to run some of the examples in this book.

- An underscore character (_) in a code listing indicates that the line of code continues onto the next line. You should type these in as you see them in the book; Visual Basic recognizes them as continuations.

The VB6 Virtual CD

This book has a companion Web site that includes a number of helpful items to assist you in your application development efforts.

NOTE   Do you need some code? See the Sybex Web site to download all the lengthy code in this book. Go to http://www.sybex.com with your Web browser!

Code Lists   Some chapters in this book include large-scale tutorials that require you to create new objects and enter code for the objects. If you're in a hurry or don't really feel like entering a bunch of code, visit the companion Web site for complete code listings organized by chapter.

Job Links   When you're ready to take your knowledge out in the field and pursue the high-paying, high-tech jobs, check out the job links and special promotions Sybex has arranged with the industry's top Web employment services.

Special Offers   All work and no play? Well, check our site periodically for the latest and greatest offers.

Mastering the Integrated Development Environment (IDE)

- Introducing Visual Basic
- Learning the IDE features
- Using the Code window
- Working with multiple projects
- Customizing the IDE
- Creating an applet

Throughout the years the computer industry has seen some radical improvements in software development tools. In the early days of computers, when a computer took up an entire room, programmers flipped switches to make the machine perform simple addition. These complex machines were the cutting edge in technology. They could add two numbers! As technology progressed, punch cards provided more functionality by allowing programmers to punch an entire line of code on a single card. Large programs were developed using stacks of cards which were then fed into a reader that would interpret the holes and create programming code on mainframes. The next generation of programming tools were text-based editors and were used to write machine language, assembly language, and Beginners All-Purpose Symbolic Instructional Code: BASIC. Once considered a toy, the BASIC language has evolved into one of the most easy-to-use and powerful programming languages available. Microsoft's Visual Basic 6 is the newest addition to the long line of programming languages.

When using Visual Basic, the most important skill you need is to be adept at using the development environment. Without the integrated tools in the environment, Visual Basic programming would be much more cumbersome and difficult. All design would need to be done on graph paper and flow charts, and it would need to be typed in line by line. Fortunately, Visual Basic contains many integrated tools to make the application development process simpler. This collection of tools makes up the *Integrated Development Environment* (IDE). Before you jump ahead in this book, be sure to spend some time reading this skill. The skills you learn here will save you time developing applications in the future. Visual Basic gives you the tools, and this skill teaches you how to use them.

Introducing Visual Basic

Visual Basic version 6 is the newest addition to the family of Visual Basic products. It allows you to quickly and easily develop Windows applications for your PC without being an expert in C++ or other programming languages.

Visual Basic provides a graphical environment in which you visually design the forms and controls that become the building blocks of your applications. Visual Basic supports many useful tools that will help you be more productive. These include, but are not limited to, projects, forms, class objects, templates, custom controls, add-ins, and database managers. You can use these tools together to create complete applications in months, weeks, or even days; producing an application using another language can take much longer.

Version 6 of Visual Basic is specifically designed to utilize the Internet. It comes with several controls that allow you to create Web-based applications, called *ActiveX executables*. These work just like stand-alone Visual Basic applications, but they are accessed through the Microsoft Internet Explorer 4 Web browser. Using this new style of application, you can revise your existing Visual Basic applications and distribute them through the Internet. New to Visual Basic 6 are the ISAPI Application and Dynamic HTML project templates. These templates provide you with a framework to develop server-side components as well as "smart" Web pages and applications. We will discuss these features and more in detail in Skill 18, *Internet Development with Visual Basic*.

Visual Basic continues to sport the Explorer-style development environment, modeled after Windows Explorer. This makes it easy for a computer user to jump right into creating applications with Visual Basic. Almost all of the objects and tools on the screen can be manipulated through a right-click. You can set properties, add controls, and even view context-sensitive help with this single action.

When you start Visual Basic for the first time, the Project Wizard will open, and you will notice the New Project dialog box (see Figure 1.1).

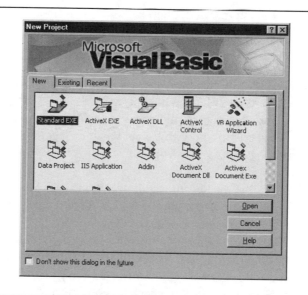

FIGURE 1.1: The Project Wizard's New Project dialog box

From this window, you can select from several types of *projects* that will give you a head start on developing your applications. This window has three tabs: New, Existing, and Recent.

By selecting a project template from the New tab, you let Visual Basic create the foundation of your application. This can save you a lot of time designing an application, especially if you are new to Visual Basic. The New tab presents you with several project templates:

- Standard EXE
- ActiveX EXE
- ActiveX DLL
- ActiveX Control
- VB Application Wizard
- Data Project
- IIS Application
- Add-In
- ActiveX Document DLL
- ActiveX Document EXE
- DHTML Application

You will learn to use some of these templates later in the book. For most of the skills in this book, you will use the Standard EXE template, but some of the ActiveX templates will be used in Skill 17, *Using ActiveX*.

The Existing tab allows you to select an existing project. This could be a sample project included with Visual Basic, or it could be a project you have worked on in the past. As you work more with Visual Basic, you will choose this tab more frequently.

Finally, the Recent tab allows you to select from the most recently used (MRU) projects. The tab is similar to the Existing tab, but it presents you with a list of the existing projects you have worked on recently, instead of *all* of the existing projects.

You can use any of these tabs to help get you started on a project in Visual Basic. You may also notice the small check box at the bottom of the form: "Don't show this dialog in the future." If you prefer not to be bothered with selecting a project type, you can check this box, and the window will not come up the next time you start Visual Basic.

 NOTE   Leave the "Don't show this dialog in the future" check box empty. We will be using project templates throughout this book. When you are more experienced, you can check this option if you do not want to use templates.

Now let's take a closer look at the Visual Basic Integrated Development Environment (IDE).

Learning the IDE Features

Behind the Project Wizard window lies the Integrated Development Environment (see Figure 1.2). The IDE is an important part of Visual Basic; it's where you put together your applications and where you'll spend much of your time when you're creating applications.

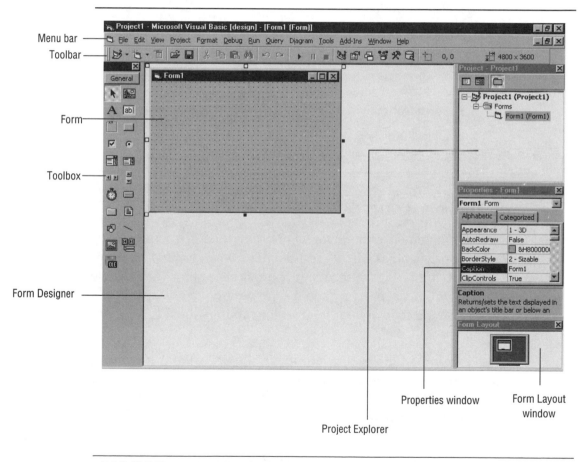

Menu bar

Toolbar

Form

Toolbox

Form Designer

Properties window

Form Layout window

Project Explorer

FIGURE 1.2: Visual Basic's Integrated Development Environment (IDE)

IDE is a term commonly used in the programming world to describe the interface and environment you use to create your applications. It is called *integrated* because you can access virtually all of the development tools you need from one screen, called an *interface*. The IDE is also commonly referred to as the *design environment*, the *program*, or just the *IDE*. We will use the latter term, so you can add your first programming buzzword to your vocabulary.

The Visual Basic IDE is made up of a number of components:

- Menu bar
- Toolbar
- Project Explorer
- Properties window
- Form Layout window
- Toolbox
- Form Designer
- Object Browser

THE ALL-IMPORTANT IDE

I cannot stress enough how important it is for you as a programmer to become familiar with your Integrated Development Environment (IDE). If you jump right into coding without becoming comfortable with your IDE, you may spend a good deal of your development time learning the editor and tools, rather than writing code—which is what programming is all about.

Take some time to play around in the IDE. Tweak settings, move windows, and adjust toolbars; just get comfortable. Not only will you be more productive, but your coworkers will sit in awe when you can be the first to show them all of the tricks you have learned.

After reading the next few sections and becoming familiar with Visual Basic's IDE, you'll be able to roll up your sleeves and get some bits and bytes under your fingernails!

The Menu Bar

The menu bar is the line of text that lies across the top of the Visual Basic window. It is very much like menus you may have seen in other Windows applications. The menu gives you access to many features within the development environment.

On the left is the File menu. From this menu you work with the actual files that make up your applications. You can create, open, print, and save projects. All of these menu options can also be accessed by right-clicking in the Project Explorer, explained later in this skill.

Next to File is the Edit menu. From here you can perform the standard Clipboard options such as cut, copy, and paste. You can use the functions to store controls as well as code. In addition, you can access the Find facilities in the IDE. You can use this menu to search for text throughout a procedure, a module, or an entire project. This feature will become handy as you start developing large Visual Basic applications.

From the View menu you can view various components and tools. You can view a form and a code module, as well as other utilities that help make your development time more productive. You will learn more about these tools in detail throughout the book.

The Project menu is the heart of your project. From here you can add to and remove forms, code modules, user controls, property pages, as well as ActiveX designers from your projects. In addition, you can add and remove custom controls and OLE references, discussed later. Many of these menu options can be accessed by right-clicking the Toolbox or Project Explorer.

The options on the Format menu deal specifically with the size and placement of controls and forms.

When you are debugging your applications, you will become really familiar with the Debug menu. From here you can start and stop your applications, set watches and breakpoints, and perform other tasks to help monitor your application's progress.

You will spend a great deal of time using the Run menu. From here you can start and stop your applications, as well as break in the middle of a program's execution, and then resume. Break and Resume are handy when it comes time to debug.

From the Tools menu you can add procedures and set procedure properties. In addition, you can access the Menu Editor, discussed in detail in Skill 5, *Creating and Using Menus and Toolbars*. You can also choose Options from the Tools menu to set preferences for your IDE.

The Add-Ins menu contains additional utilities called Add-Ins. By default you should have an option for Visual Data Manager, and another for the Add-In Manager. Visual Data Manager is a simple, but useful tool that allows you to design and populate a database in many popular formats including Microsoft Access. As you will learn in Skill 16, *Extending the IDE with Add-Ins*, the Add-In Manager allows you to select other Add-In utilities to be added to the Add-Ins menu.

The Window menu gives you options to tile and cascade windows within the IDE. You can also arrange the icons for minimized forms. However, perhaps the most important option is the window list at the bottom of the menu. This list allows you to quickly access open windows in the IDE.

The Help menu is your second stop when you get in a jam. This book, of course, should be your first.

The Toolbar

Immediately below the menu bar should be the Visual Basic toolbar (see Figure 1.3). If you can't see the toolbar, click View ➤ Toolbars ➤ Standard. You can control the whole Visual Basic environment from the menu bar, but the toolbar gives you easy access to the menu-bar commands you'll use most frequently.

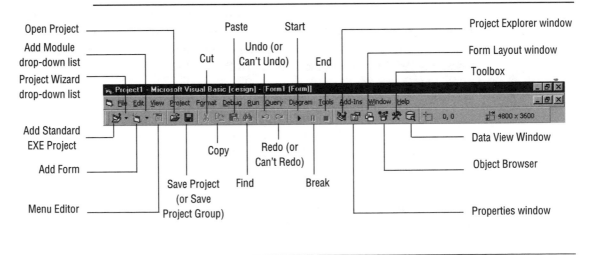

FIGURE 1.3: The Visual Basic toolbar

You will notice that when you move the mouse over the buttons they appear to raise themselves up from the toolbar. If you keep the mouse pointer over a button for a moment, you will see the *tool tip* for that button.

NOTE   A tool tip is a little cream-colored box that pops up and explains to you what the button's function is. You will most likely find yourself adding these helpful tips to your projects in the future.

One of the many features in the IDE is the provision of several toolbars. By selecting View ➢ Toolbars, you can also show or hide toolbars for the Edit, Debug, and Form Editor windows. If you are really finicky about your environment, you can even customize these toolbars to suit your preferences.

Moving a Toolbar Button

Let's say you want to move some buttons around on the Visual Basic toolbar to make them more accessible to you. You would follow these steps:

1. Right-click the menu bar or toolbar at the top of the screen.

2. Select Customize from the pop-up menu.

3. The Customize dialog box has three tabs: Toolbars, Commands, and Options. On the Toolbars tab, click the check box next to the toolbar you want to edit. (If the toolbar is already on the IDE like the Standard toolbar, you can go straight to it. If it is not already available, checking the toolbar option will bring up the newly selected toolbar.)

4. Click a toolbar button and hold the mouse button down. Now "drag" the button to a new position on the toolbar.

5. You will notice the I-bracket will move along the toolbar, under the button you are dragging. If the I-bracket is in the location where you want the button, let go of the mouse button and the toolbar button will "drop" into its new position.

TIP   You can move toolbar buttons to the menu as well. Just drag the button to the menu title. When the menu drops down, drag the button to a position on the menu.

If you decide you don't want to keep the changes you have just made, click the Reset button to restore the buttons to their default positions. Otherwise, click Close to save your modifications.

Removing and Adding a Menu Item

If a toolbar does not contain the shortcuts you want, or you want to add another menu item, you can customize them even further to get what you want. Try the following:

1. Right-click the menu bar or toolbar at the top of the screen.

2. Select Customize from the pop-up menu.

3. Select the Commands tab from the Customize dialog box.

4. In the Categories list, scroll down to the bottom and select Built-in Menus.

5. Now go up to the Help menu on the Visual Basic menu bar and drag it to the Commands list. Once the menu item is over the list, drop it. The Help menu has been removed from your menu.

6. Select Help from the Commands list and drag it back to the menu and drop it back in its original position.

7. Click Close to save your modifications.

Now you have a good foundation for customizing the menu bar and toolbars. Experiment and get your environment set up the way you want it.

 NOTE   The previous examples showed you a common Windows task called *drag-and-drop*. You will be using this frequently within the IDE, and you may even program this functionality in your own programs. See Skill 11, *Working with the Mouse*, for more information on the drag-and-drop technique.

The Project Explorer

Docked on the right side of the screen, just under the toolbar, is the Project Explorer window (see Figure 1.4). The Project Explorer is your quick reference to the various elements—forms, classes, and modules—in your project.

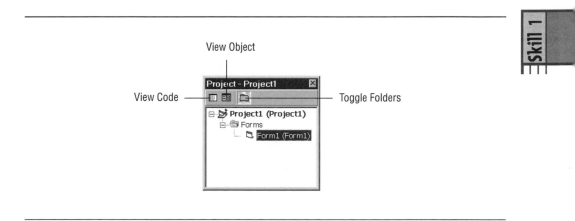

FIGURE 1.4: The Project Explorer window

The Project Explorer window is much like Windows Explorer in that it allows you to expand and collapse the subfolders.

All of the objects that make up your application are packaged in a project. If you save it for later use, testing, debugging, or improvement, Visual Basic provides the default file extension .VBP (Visual Basic Project) to the project.

A simple project will typically contain one *form*, which is the window used by your application. In addition to forms, the Project Explorer window also lists code modules and classes. We will learn more about these later in Skill 4, *Working within Modules and Classes.*

NOTE   Larger applications will often have a number of forms, modules, and classes. These too are listed in the Project Explorer window.

To view a form, select it in the Project Explorer and click the View Object button. (Any code associated with the form can be viewed in its own window by clicking the View Code button.)

If you right-click in the Project Explorer, you are presented with a pop-up menu that offers many options specific to that particular window. For instance, you can add, remove, and print forms and code modules from the pop-up menu.

If you want to remove an object from your project, right-click the name of the object in the Project Explorer window and select Remove. The name of the control will be listed after the Remove command.

TIP   Right-clicking objects in Visual Basic will expose object-specific pop-up menus. These menus will allow you to quickly access tools that you can use to operate directly on the active object. I recommend that you get used to doing this, because it will save time, as well as wear and tear on your fingers.

The Properties Window

Docked right under the Project Explorer window is the Properties window. The Properties window exposes the various characteristics (or *properties*) of selected objects. To clarify this concept, consider that each and every form in an application is an *object*. Each and every *control* (a command button, for example) that appears on a form is also an object. Now, each object in Visual Basic has characteristics such as color and size. Other characteristics affect not just the appearance of an object but the way it behaves, too. All these characteristics of an object are called its *properties*. Thus, a form has properties, and any controls placed on a form have properties, too. All of these properties are displayed in the Properties window (see Figure 1.5).

FIGURE 1.5: The Properties window

In the Properties window, you will see a list of the properties belonging to an object. There are quite a few of them, and you may have to scroll to see them all.

Fortunately, many of the properties are self-explanatory (`Caption`, `Height`, `Width`, and so on), but some of the others are rarely used. If you are not sure what a specific property does, you can highlight it and look at the brief description at the bottom of the Properties window. Besides scrolling to view properties, you can also view properties either alphabetically or by category, by clicking the appropriate tab. Whichever method you use is a matter of preference.

> **TIP**   If you're not sure of a property's purpose, click the property in the Properties window and press F1. This opens context-sensitive help on the highlighted property. This will give you a more in-depth description of the property and its use.

When a control (see Skill 3, *Selecting and Using Controls*) such as a command button, for example, is put on a form, the Properties window shows the properties for that control when it's selected. You can see the properties for different objects, including the underlying form, by clicking each object in turn. Alternatively, use the drop-down list at the top of the Properties window to select the control and display its properties. Most properties are set at design time, though many can be changed at run time.

Most of the time, you will set properties directly from the Properties window when you are creating an application. When you're working in the IDE, it is referred to as working in "design time" because you are still designing your program. Sometimes you will need to change properties while a program runs. You may want to disable a command button, for example. You can do this by writing code that changes the property. This is done at "run time," when your program is actually running.

> **NOTE**   When more than one control is selected on a form, you get to see only those properties shared by all the controls. Setting a property in those circumstances affects all the selected controls. Setting, say, the Top property of a number of controls simultaneously in this manner enables you to vertically align the controls. It's not possible to include the underlying form itself in a multiple selection.

The way to change a property setting depends on the range and type of values it can hold. Since the Visual Basic IDE is a visual environment, you will set most properties at design time. This technique saves you time by not requiring you to write the code to achieve the same results. Below are some examples of the most common types of properties and their uses.

To try these examples, start a new project by selecting File ➤ New Project from the menu. When the Project Wizard appears, select Standard EXE, and click the OK button to create a standard executable project.

Boolean Value Properties

To learn how to change a boolean value property, follow these steps:

1. Open Form1 by double-clicking it in the Project Explorer window.

    If the setting has a `True` or `False` value (called a *Boolean*), then you can change it by double-clicking the name of the property in the first column of the Properties window. Set the `MaxButton` property of Form1 to **False**.

2. Click Run ➤ Start. Your form will no longer have a Maximize button. This is handy if you don't want your application to cover the entire screen.

To stop the program, select Run ➤ End from the Visual Basic menu, press the End button on the toolbar, or click the [x] in the upper-right corner of Form1. This will bring you back into design mode.

Predefined Value Properties

If the setting has a number of predefined values (called an *enumerated list*), then double-clicking the property name cycles through all the permissible values. If there are a large number of options, then opening the drop-down list of values in the second column is probably quicker. To understand how an enumerated list works in the Properties window, you can experiment with the `BorderStyle` property of Form1.

1. Click Form1 to make it the active control.

2. In the Properties window, click the drop-down arrow to the right of the `BorderStyle` property. You will see a list of possible values for this property:

    *   Setting this value to `0-None` removes all borders from the form. This is commonly seen on splash screens.

    *   Setting `1-Fixed Single` allows you to create a thin border that cannot be resized.

- The default value of a form's `BorderStyle` property is `2-Sizable`. Use this setting if you want your users to be able to stretch the window to a different size.

- If you do not want your user to resize a dialog box for any reason, you can set the property to `3-Fixed Dialog`. Warning messages that you receive in Windows use this style of border.

- Finally, if you are creating a floating toolbar, also called a *tool window*, you can set the `BorderStyle` property to `4-Fixed Tool Window`, or `5-Sizable Tool Window`, depending on how you want the toolbar to behave.

3. Set the `BorderStyle` property to `3-Fixed Dialog`. This will prevent the user from resizing your form.

4. Select Run ➢ Start from the menu to test your form. You will notice now the form has no Minimize or Maximize buttons. In addition, the form cannot be resized by stretching its borders.

5. When you are done examining the form, click its Close button.

String Value Properties

Some properties require text, called *strings* in programmer jargon. Two of the properties you will encounter the most—`Name` and `Caption`—require strings. When the setting requires that you type an entry, then double-clicking the name is easier than clicking in the second column. The former highlights the entry (if any) in the second column so you can simply overtype instead of using the Delete or Backspace keys first. After you finish typing, it's safer to click back on the form or to press Enter—either of these removes the cursor from the settings box to prevent any accidental key presses from being added to the entry.

Let's change the name of the form and set a caption in the title bar of the form:

1. Click the form once to make it active.

2. In the Properties window, double-click the `Name` property. It is at the top of the properties list. The value Form1 should be completely highlighted.

3. Type **frmMain** in this field. Notice the old name was automatically deleted as you started typing.

TIP   Learning to overtype will save you time, not only in Visual Basic, but in other text applications as well. No longer do you have to continue hitting the Backspace key to edit text.

4. Hit the Enter key to set the Name property to **frmMain**.

5. Next, double-click the Caption property to highlight the text Form 1.

6. Overtype the words **I can overtype text.** in the Caption field.

As you work with Visual Basic, you will notice that you use these two proper-ties the most. The Name property identifies the form to the application, and the Caption property visually identifies the form to the user at run time.

Hexadecimal Value Properties

Some of the entries look quite unfriendly, such as BackColor and the other color settings. Fortunately, they're not as bad as they appear. A double-click on the prop-erty name in the first column opens a dialog box that contains two tabs. The Palette tab contains a color palette where you can choose a value by selecting its color, rather than by typing a hexadecimal code. The System tab allows you to select col-ors based on the color scheme defined in the Windows Control Panel. You can keep a color palette permanently visible by clicking View ➤ Color Palette. In this case, a single click on the setting followed by a click in the palette is enough. BackColor is a good one to try out for frmMain—the ForeColor and FillColor will have no effect at this stage.

1. Double-click the BackColor property in the Properties window to bring up the Color dialog box.

2. Select the Palette tab to show the color palette.

3. Click the red color to change the background of the form to red.

This looks pretty ugly, so change the color back to the default window color:

4. Double-click the BackColor property again and select the System tab.

5. Select Button Face as the color. If you select Window Background, the form will turn white. Because most controls in Windows are now 3-D controls, you can set the form's color to the same as the command button's color. This way it will be 3-D gray.

> **TIP** While this is an easy way to set colors on your forms, you will almost always want to stick with the system colors defined on the System tab. This will allow your application to inherit the colors your users prefer. Keep them happy.

Filename Properties

A couple of properties have the setting (None). These are the ones that require a file reference. To pick a file, double-click the property name. For example, the Icon property for a form determines the icon that is displayed if you minimize the form at run time. Under Windows 95 and Windows NT it also sets the icon that appears on the Taskbar and as the Control menu on the form. There are plenty of icons to evaluate in the \Graphics\Icons sub-directory of the Visual Basic directory. To reset one of these properties to (None), click once in the settings column and press Delete. To add an icon to the form:

1. Double-click the Icon property of frmMain. This will bring up the Load Icon dialog box.

2. Select Face02.ico from the \Graphics\Icons\Misc sub-directory. Click the Open button.

The icon for your application is now a little yellow smiley face.

Size Properties

Four properties—Left, Top, Width, and Height—appear on the toolbar as well as in the Properties window. You can, if you want, type the values directly into the second column of the Properties window. However, there's another, easier way: If you drag the form in the Form Layout window and release the mouse button, the Left and Top property coordinates are updated on the toolbar—they're also updated in the Properties window. When you drag one of the form's borders and release the mouse button, then the Width and Height property coordinates are updated. You can move and resize controls on the form as well, only this time the coordinates are updated as you drag.

The Form Layout Window

The Form Layout window is a simple but useful tool (see Figure 1.6). Its purpose is to simply give you a thumbnail view of the current form, showing you what it looks like and how it is positioned on the screen at run time.

FIGURE 1.6: The Form Layout window

The Form Layout window is useful for determining what screen real estate your form will use when your application is running. To use the Form Layout window, do the following:

1. Click the form in the Form Layout window and move it to the center of the monitor graphic in the middle of the window.

2. Run your program by selecting Run ➢ Start.

The Toolbox

As the name implies, the Toolbox contains the bits and pieces you need to build your application interface. All the tools shown in Figure 1.7, with the exception of the pointer at the top left, correspond to the objects, or items, you might want to place on a form in your application. These tools or objects are referred to as *controls*. Most of them are an intrinsic part of Visual Basic and are called *built-in* or *standard* controls. Some examples include the command button control and the text box control. Skill 3 covers these controls in more detail. Depending on your Visual Basic setup, there may be a few more controls in the Toolbox.

FIGURE 1.7: The Visual Basic Toolbox with the custom controls

Organizing the Toolbox

The Toolbox in version 6 is similar to the Toolbox in previous version of Visual Basic. It allows you to define tabs, which you can then use to organize your controls. You may want to organize your custom controls by category. For example, I like to keep all of my Internet custom controls on a separate tab.

To add a new Internet tab to your Toolbox, follow these steps:

1. Right-click a blank area of the Toolbox.

2. Select Add Tab from the pop-up menu.

3. When Visual Basic prompts you to enter a new tab name, type **Internet**.

4. Click the OK button.

5. Now that you can create a new Toolbox tab, you can drag whatever controls you'd like to the tab; for example, drag the image control to the Internet tab you just created. (You will not have any Internet-related controls on your toolbar at this time.)

6. To add custom controls—like those created by Microsoft and other third-party companies—right-click the Toolbox and select Components from the pop-up menu, or select Project ➢ Components.

7. Check the box next to the control you want to add from the list of available controls, in this case, Microsoft Internet Controls.

8. Click the OK button to add the controls to the toolbox.

The names of the tabs and the categories you define are strictly a matter of your personal preference. Create tabs you are comfortable with, and organize your controls the way you like them.

Removing a Toolbox Control

To remove a control, simply turn off the appropriate check box in the Custom Controls dialog box. Be aware that you can't add or remove the built-in controls from the toolbox, so controls such as the command button will always be present. To remove the Internet controls:

1. Right-click the Toolbox.

2. Select Components from the pop-up menu.

3. Just as you added the components in the previous exercise, you remove them by removing the check from the box next to the control. Remove the check next to Microsoft Internet Controls.

4. Click the OK button.

The Form Designer

In the center of the screen, you will see the Form Designer. This is the workspace where you actually design the visual layout of the form and the controls that lie on it.

In the Visual Basic IDE, you will see either one form at a time, or the Code window, in this space. (The Code window is discussed in the next section.)

Notice in Figure 1.8 that the form has little black dots in the center of each side. These boxes are called anchors. You can drag an anchor with the mouse to resize the form.

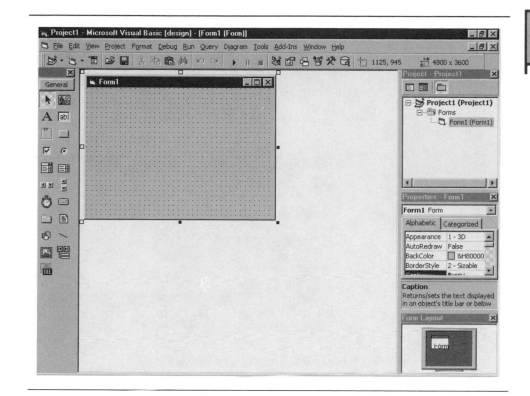

FIGURE 1.8: The Form Designer

TIP

If you want to make a form that is larger than the Form Designer window, you can stretch the border over the Project Explorer and Properties windows and Visual Basic will resize it accordingly. The form will then lie under the Project Explorer and Properties windows. You can use the scroll bars at the right and bottom of the Form Designer to uncover the hidden portions of the form.

The Object Browser

The Object Browser, shown in Figure 1.9, allows you to browse through the various properties, events, and methods that are made available, or exposed, to you. You can access it by selecting Object Browser from the View menu, or by pressing F2. We will cover the Object Browser in more detail in Skill 15, *Learning and Using Object-Oriented Programming (OOP)*.

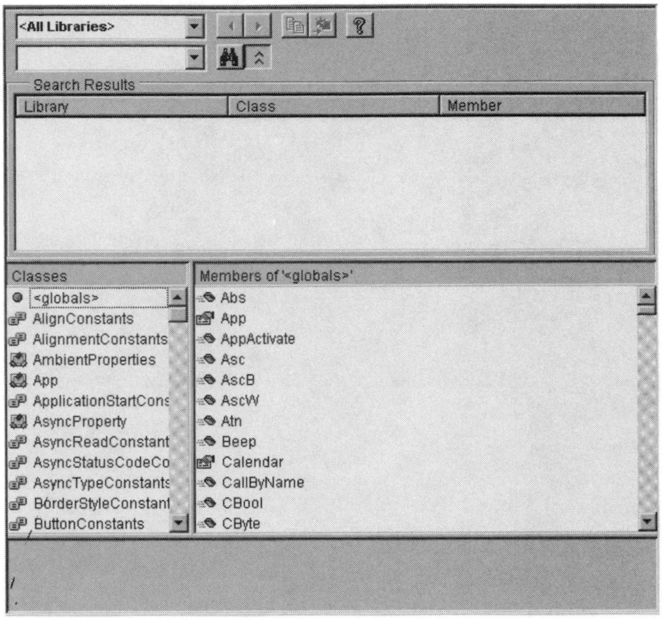

FIGURE 1.9: The Object Browser

Know Your Visual Basic Editor, and Know It Well

My Unix instructor's first words to the class were "Know your editor!" If you have ever had the dubious pleasure of working with the Unix's Vi Editor, you know exactly what he meant. These words have proven their meaning over and over to me during my years of programming.

In Visual Basic, the editor is called the *Code window* (see Figure 1.10). It's actually a turbo-charged text editor with many productivity tools built in. Regardless of what you want to call it, this is the window where you will do most of your work.

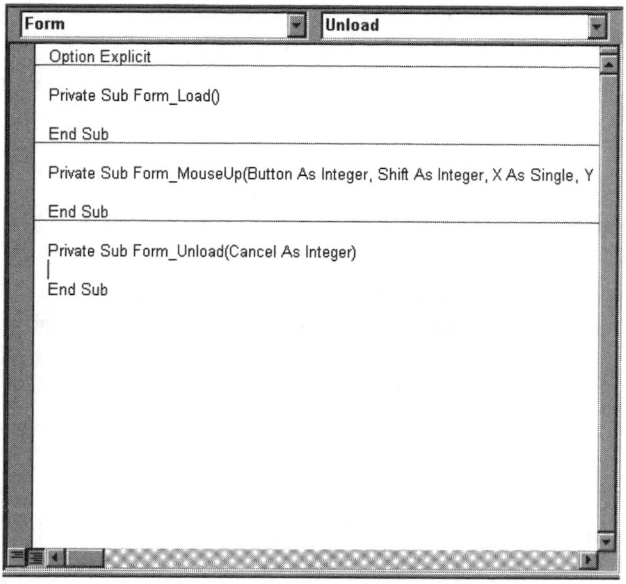

FIGURE 1.10: The Visual Basic Code window

You can open the Code window by double-clicking a form or control in the Form Layout window. If you double-click a form, you will be taken to a *procedure* for the form. Open the form by double-clicking in the Project Explorer window, or select the View Code button in the Project Explorer. If you double-click a control, you will be taken to a procedure for that control. Once the Code window is open, you can go to any procedure for any object on the selected form.

> **NOTE**   A procedure is a collection of lines of code that are grouped together to perform a set of related tasks. We will cover these in detail in Skill 4.

Like I said, you should get *real* familiar with your editor. Learn as much about its features as possible. Learn all of the shortcuts and keystrokes. Set your fonts and colors exactly the way you want them. Becoming as comfortable as possible now with the Visual Basic editor will save you time later.

Depending on how you set your IDE options, you can have your Code window display multiple procedures at one time, as described in the next section. In addition, it can display object properties as you type, as well as give you visual cues as to the state of your code. We will cover these features in more detail later in this skill.

Working with Multiple Projects

Visual Basic allows you to work on multiple projects simultaneously. The Project Explorer window shows you the projects and their components in a tree view. If you are a beginner, you may not have an immediate need to open multiple projects at one time. However, when you start creating ActiveX objects (as you will do in Skill 17, *Using ActiveX*), you may want to open one project for the object and another to test the object.

If you have not already done so, you need to install the sample applications that come with Visual Basic. To install them, follow these steps:

1. Start the MSDN Library - Visual Basic 6 Setup program by selecting Add/Remove Programs from the Windows Control Panel.

2. Click the Add/Remove button to start the installation process.

3. When the MSDN Library - Visual Studio 6.0 dialog box appears, press the Add/Remove button.

4. Once the MSDN Library - Visual Studio 6.0 - Custom dialog box appears, check the box next to VB Product Samples. If the check box is grayed, press the Select All button.

5. Press Continue to finish the setup process.

Once you have installed the sample applications that come with Visual Basic, then you can try the following example to open multiple projects:

1. From the Visual Basic IDE select File ➢ Add Project.

2. In the Add Project dialog box, click the Existing tab.

3. Select `FirstApp.vbp` from the `\MSDN98\98vs\1033\Samples\VB98\Firstapp` sub-directory.

4. Click the Open button. This will add the FirstApp project to the IDE.

5. Select File ➤ Add Project to add another project.

6. Again, click the Existing tab in the Add Project dialog box.

7. Select `Controls.vbp` from the `\MSDN98\98vs\1033\Samples\VB98\Controls` sub-directory. This will add the Controls project to the IDE.

That's all there is to opening multiple projects. You can add more projects if you wish, but it will be very rare that you will need to do so. You will most likely start working with multiple projects when you start creating ActiveX servers and clients.

> **NOTE**   Working with multiple projects is a skill you will perfect with experience. However, throughout most of this book, we will only open one project at a time.

Customizing the IDE

While version 6 of Visual Basic has many productivity features in the IDE, you may still want to customize the IDE to suit your preferences. You can define the number of spaces of a tab, change the color of your Code window, dock your toolbars, and much more. If you want to change any settings within the IDE, select Tools ➤ Options. The tabs of the Options dialog box categorize many IDE options you will become familiar with.

The Editor Tab

The first tab of the Options dialog box to be examined is the Editor tab, shown in Figure 1.11. Many of these options may be unfamiliar to you if you are new to Visual Basic, but as you become more comfortable, you can use the Editor tab to customize your working environment.

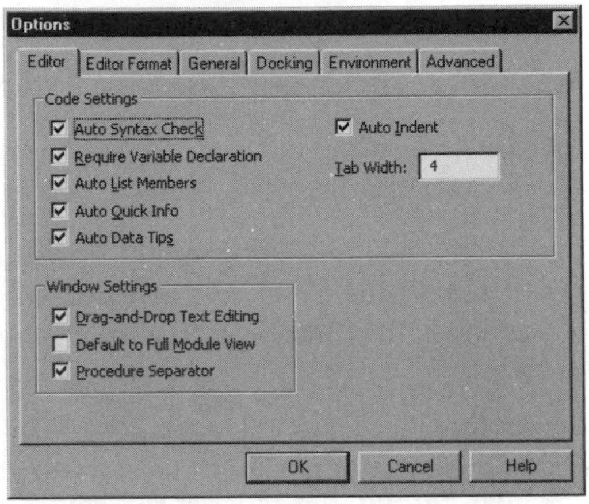

FIGURE 1.11: The Editor tab

Within the Code Settings frame are the options that will affect your editor. After selecting Tools ➢ Options, experiment with these choices:

- Check the Auto Syntax Check box to force the editor to check your code for errors during design mode. Keep this setting enabled so you won't program errantly only to discover you have an error in your code.

- Check the Require Variable Declaration box to force you to declare all variables before using them in your code.

TIP　　You should check Require Variable Declaration when you customize your IDE. This will make Visual Basic place one line—Option Explicit—in the General Declarations portion of every form, module, and class. This will save you many hours of frustration when you start debugging larger applications. As you gain programming experience, you will discover that most of your errors will be the result of incorrect variable types and miscalculations. Setting variables to the appropriate type will minimize these types of errors. If you have not developed the habit of using this feature, take time to do so now.

- Check the Auto List Members box to have the editor display a list of members belonging to the object, which you can easily reference as you type. As you type, the properties and methods are automatically listed at the cursor point. All you need to do is click the desired property or method.

- Check the Auto Quick Info box to show or suppress information about functions and their parameters. This is a useful setting if you are new to Visual Basic; by enabling this, Visual Basic will make recommendations to you as you type in the Code window.

- Check the Auto Data Tips box to toggle the display of the value of a variable under the cursor. This option is especially helpful when you are debugging your applications.

- Check the Auto Indent box to automatically indent your code a number of spaces. This is good for structured code. Neat code is easier to read, which is very helpful during the debugging process. As you read through the examples in the skills to follow, you will see what structured code looks like.

- Use the Tab box to set the number of spaces the editor will insert when you press the Tab button. The default is four spaces. Although this is the default, you may desire to have more or less spaces. What you choose is a matter of preference.

Within the Window Settings frame you can experiment with three options:

- Check the Drag-and-Drop Text Editing option if you want to drag text within the Code window.

- Check the Default to Full Module View if you want to see all of the procedures within an object in the editor. If you prefer viewing one procedure in the editor at a time, disable this option.

- Check the Procedure Separator option if you are in Full Module View mode and want a visual separator between your procedures. If you choose to view code in Full Module View, I recommend checking this box.

The Editor Format Tab

As you can see in Figure 1.12, you use this tab to set your color and font preferences for your editor. Because this tab is self-explanatory, I will not cover it in detail.

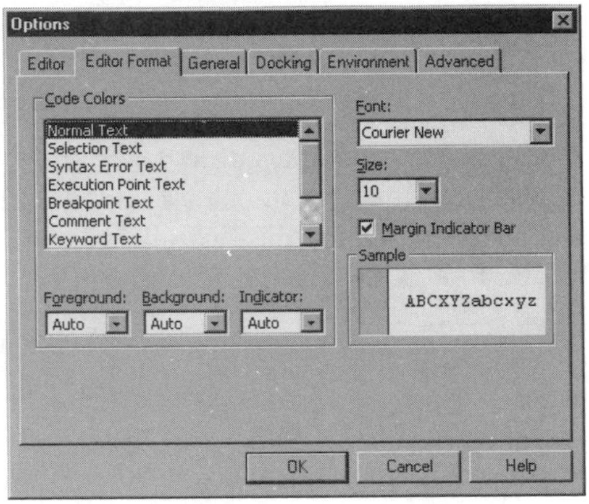

FIGURE 1.12: The Editor Format tab

The General Tab

The General tab, shown in Figure 1.13, allows you to fine-tune various aspects of the IDE, such as the gridlines on forms, error trapping, and compiling. Don't worry if some of these terms are unfamiliar to you at the moment. These terms will be explained throughout the text as you hone your Visual Basic programming skills.

- You can set the grid-spacing units in the Form Grid Settings section. You use these lines to align controls on the form. Usually, the default settings will be sufficient.

- The Error Trapping section allows you to set the sensitivity of error trapping. You can have your application break on all errors, break in class modules, or break on all unhandled errors. Unhandled errors are errors that may be encountered that you have not written an error-trapping function for. Leave this option at its default, Break in Class Module.

The Compile section contains the following options:

- Set Compile on Demand to allow Visual Basic to compile your code as you write your code. This helps your program start sooner when you select Run ➢ Start. This setting is enabled by default.

- Enable Background Compile to allow yourself to continue working in Visual Basic while it compiles your application. This setting is enabled by default.

Checking Show ToolTips will allow Visual Basic to show you tool tips that describe the control under the mouse pointer. This is a helpful feature, especially if you are new to Visual Basic. Finally, selecting Collapse Proj. Hides Windows will collapse the associated windows of a project when a project is collapsed in the Project Explorer window.

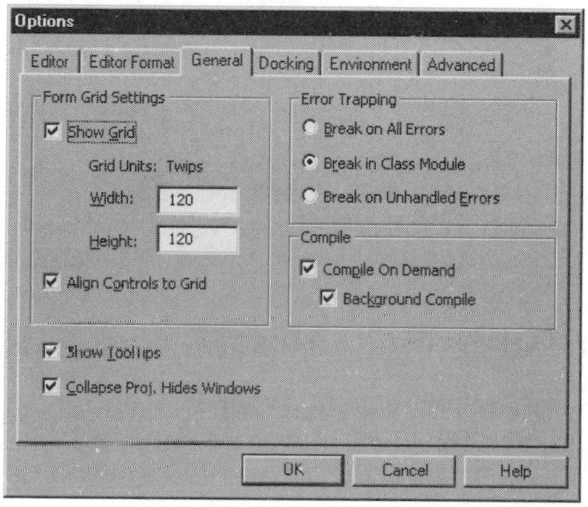

FIGURE 1.13: The General tab

The Docking Tab

By selecting the Docking tab shown in Figure 1.14, you can determine which windows within the IDE are dockable. These are self-explanatory.

NOTE   *Docking* allows windows to physically position themselves along borders of the screen or other objects and lock themselves into place. This is another feature that allows you to keep various windows out of your way.

FIGURE 1.14: The Docking tab

The Environment Tab

The Environment tab is perhaps the most important place to customize settings within the IDE (see Figure 1.15).

FIGURE 1.15: The Environment tab

If you decide you do not want the Project Wizard window disturbing you when you create a new project, you can deselect the Create Default Project option in the When Visual Basic Starts frame. However, leave this option checked for now. You will be using the Project Wizard window throughout this book.

In addition, if you do want the Project Wizard window but you want to remove some of the templates from the window, you can select and deselect them in the Show Templates For frame.

The most important settings, perhaps in the whole IDE, are the ones listed in the When a Program Starts frame. When you are involved in serious project development, you will want to save your work often. The best way to do this is to check the Prompt to Save Changes option. This will cause Visual Basic to ask you to save your project just before your application is run from the IDE.

I find that the Don't Save Changes option is helpful when I am experimenting or demonstrating a series of programs that I do not want to keep. You can choose this option if you wish, but if you want to keep the projects you work on in this book, I recommend that you check Prompt to Save Changes.

The Advanced Tab

Finally, the Advanced tab (Figure 1.16) has a few options that you will not need to worry about at this time, but I will briefly discuss them here.

- Selecting the Background Project Load option will force Visual Basic to load projects while you continue working. This is useful because it allows you to continue working while a project loads. This option is set by default.

- Leave the Notify When Changing Shared Project Items option checked. Some Visual Basic projects can use shared objects such as forms or modules. If you load multiple projects that use the same objects and change one of the shared objects, Visual Basic will notify you that a shared object has been changed. Although you will not use shared objects within this book, you may do so as you become more proficient with Visual Basic.

- The SDI Development Environment option allows you to change your IDE from a multiple document interface (MDI) to a single document interface (SDI). All of the projects and examples used in this book were created in an MDI environment, so leave this option unchecked.

- Finally, Visual Basic 6 adds some more Internet functionality. If you are familiar with Hypertext Markup Language, or HTML, you may find yourself designing Web pages from within VB. You can select your Web editor from the External HTML Editor field.

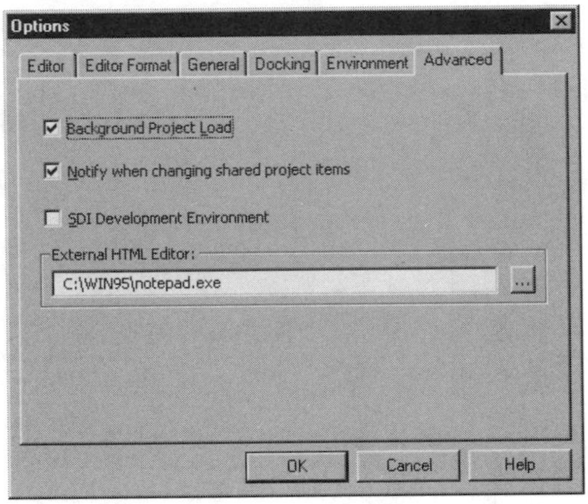

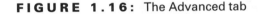

FIGURE 1.16: The Advanced tab

TIP   Because we cannot possibly cover every aspect of the IDE in this skill, I recommend you take some time to snoop through each menu option and experiment with what it does. As I mentioned earlier, get to know the Code window—as well as the whole IDE. With practice, using the IDE will become second nature to you, and your efforts will be spent on coding rather than fumbling through the IDE.

Creating Your First Applet

Now that you have had a chance to get familiar with the IDE and its new-and-improved tools, it's time to put all this knowledge to work by creating a simple application. You might not know it, but most programmers' first "real" application is the little Hello World program.

The Hello World program is historically the first application when one learns a new programming language. While very simple, it gives you tangible results with a minimal amount of coding, and it will give you a feel for working with Visual Basic and using the IDE environment. So let's continue and you can join the legions of programmers who have tackled the Hello World application.

Hello World!

To create the Hello World application, follow these steps:

1. Click File ➤ New Project. You might be asked to save changes to the current project if you've been experimenting. If so, click the No button; if you want to keep your work, then click Yes.

2. If it is not already visible, open the Form Layout window by selecting View ➤ Form Layout Window.

3. Right-click the form in the Form Layout window. Select Startup Position ➤ Center Screen from the pop-up menu.

TIP   You can move the form by dragging it around in the Form Layout window. The pop-up menu also offers positioning options.

4. Resize the form by dragging its borders until it's about 3 inches wide and 2 inches high.

5. Double-click the Command Button control in the toolbox to create a command button of default size in the center of the form. Drag the button near the bottom center of the form.

6. Double-click the Label control in the toolbox to create a label on the form. Drag the label so it sits just below the top of the form. Resize the label so it is roughly the height of one line of text and wide enough to contain the text "Hello World." Your form should now look similar to the one shown here.

7. Now, click the form once to select it. You can tell that the form (as opposed to any of the controls) is selected because its properties are listed in the Properties window. If you can't see the Properties window, press F4.

8. Set the following two properties for the form by typing in the text under the Setting column in the appropriate property field:

Property	Setting
Caption	My First Application!
Name	frmHelloWorld

The Caption property setting appears in the title bar of the form. The Name property is a very important one and is used to refer to the form in program code. In Skill 3, I'll have a lot more to say about the Name property. For now, take it on faith that frmHelloWorld is a better name than the default one of Form1, which is the same as the default Caption property. The same applies to the Name property of the controls in this application. In each case, the default Name property has been changed.

9. Now, click the label and set the next two properties:

Property	Setting
Name	lblHelloWorld
Text	Hello World.

10. Click the Command button and set its properties as follows:

Property	Setting
Name	cmdOK
Caption	&OK

This time the Caption property shows as the text on the button. The ampersand character (&) before the first letter adds an underline to the letter *O*; this provides a quick keyboard alternative to a mouse-click to activate the button (here it's Alt+O). Happily, you can make many of your shortcut keys a mnemonic (*O* for *OK*, in this example).

11. Now double-click the cmdOK button. Double-clicking a control (or a form) opens the Code window at the default event for the control. The default event for a command button is the Click event. You should be looking at a procedure template or *stub* for cmdOK_Click, as in Figure 1.17. You can afford to ignore the Private Sub prefix for now; the important point is the name of the procedure: cmdOK_Click. This means that any code entered in the procedure will be executed when the user clicks the cmdOK button.

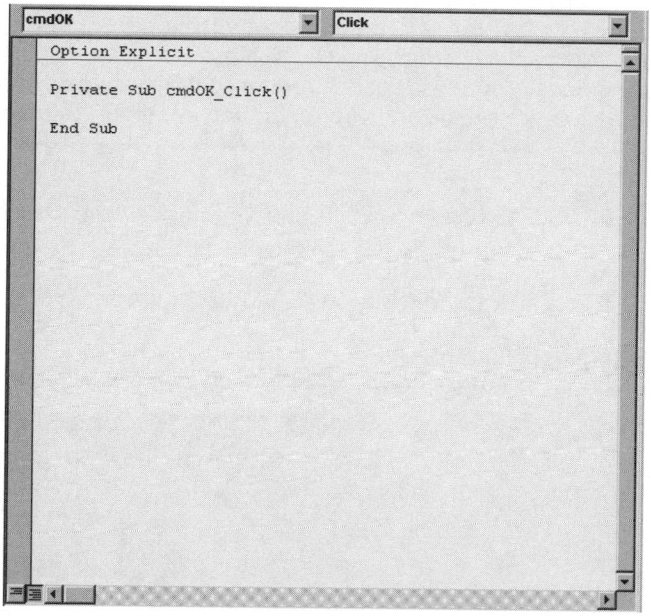

```
cmdOK                          ▼   Click                    ▼

  Option Explicit

  Private Sub cmdOK_Click()

  End Sub
```

FIGURE 1.17: The procedure in the Code window

12. Type the following line of code between the Private Sub and End Sub lines:

```
Unload Me
Set frmHelloWorld = Nothing
```

When the user clicks the cmdHelloWorld button, the cmdOK_Click event occurs. This event tells the form to unload itself. Because this is the only form in the application, it also tells the application to end.

13. Click File ➤ Save Project. Enter **frmWorld.frm** as the name of the form and **HelloWorld.vbp** as the name of the project. Before a project as a whole is saved, all the individual component files are saved. In this application there is one form and therefore one file corresponding to the form. The project file is basically a list of the component files.

NOTE   Notice that the form now has three descriptors—the Name property (frmHelloWorld), the Caption property (My First Application), and the filename (frmWorld.frm). It's vital that you understand the difference between these three descriptors. The Caption property appears in the title bar of the form, the Name property is used to reference the form in code, and the filename is used by the project file and your operating system to reference the form.

14. Click Run ➤ Start. If you've followed the directions correctly, you should see a form, similar to the one in Figure 1.18, that simply says "Hello World."

15. Click the OK button to end. If things go wrong, check through the previous steps to find your mistake.

FIGURE 1.18: Your first application—the Hello World applet

You've just created your first application! Congratulations—you're well on your way to being a master Visual Basic programmer.

Creating this simple applet was an example of how you will be working in the Visual Basic IDE. Although the Hello World applet was very easy, it allowed you to get a feel for working in Visual Basic. The following skills will present you with more information about the various tools you will be working with to build your killer app.

Are You up to Speed?

Now you can...

- ☑ use Visual Basic to create your own applications
- ☑ use the Project Wizard to help you get your application started
- ☑ right-click objects to expose their properties
- ☑ effectively use the Code window
- ☑ work with multiple projects in the IDE
- ☑ customize the look and feel of the IDE to suit your preferences
- ☑ write a simple applet

SKILL 2

Working with Forms

- Introducing forms
- Creating a form
- Changing a form's properties
- Becoming familiar with form events
- Understanding form methods
- Creating multiple document interface (MDI) forms
- Adding forms to your projects
- Using the Form Wizard

This skill will focus on laying the foundation for your Visual Basic programming. In Visual Basic, the Form object is the foundation of any application that presents an interface. This is the main control that will allow you to place other controls on top of it to create a window, called an interface, that the user can see on the screen.

You will learn about the various parts of the form that you can manipulate to get the style of form you desire for your application. In addition, you will be introduced to menus as well as more complex interfaces using Multiple Document Interfaces, or MDIs.

The Anatomy of a Form

The most basic object you will be working with in Visual Basic is the *form* object, which is the visual foundation of your application. It is basically a window that you can add different elements to in order to create a complete application. Every application you can see on the screen is based on some type of form. Before delving into the details of application development, let's take a look at the basic form object that you will probably use the most often in your projects: the single form.

As you learn Visual Basic, most of your applications will only have one interface, which is the single form. When you become more experienced and start writing larger, editor-styled applications like Notepad or Microsoft Word, you will want to use multiple forms, often referred to as *documents*. We will introduce these types of forms toward the end of this skill (see "Working with Multiple Document Interface (MDI) Forms"). To create a new form, open Visual Basic and select File ➢ New Project; you'll then see the various parts of a single form object, as shown in Figure 2.1. In the following sections, we will go through each of the parts that make up this object so you can become familiar with what forms are and how you will use them.

All of these elements should be familiar to you if you have spent any time using the Windows operating systems. Let's take a look at how these features are referenced in Visual Basic.

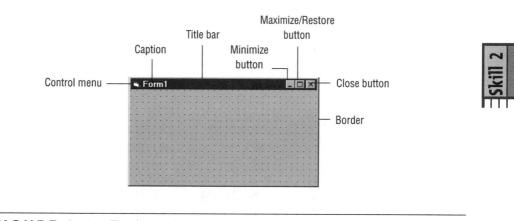

FIGURE 2.1: The form object

The Border

The form's border is what gives the form its elasticity. Depending on the type of form you want to display, you can program the border to be fixed, sizable, or even nonexistent. These features can be set with the BorderStyle property.

The Title Bar

The title bar is the colored bar on the top of most forms. If your desktop color scheme is set to the Windows default scheme, this bar will be blue. You can use the title bar to drag the window around the screen. In addition, double-clicking it will alternately maximize and restore the form.

The Caption

The form's caption is the text you see in the form's title bar. It can be used to identify the name of the application, the current function of the form, or as a status bar. What you put in the caption depends on what your program is trying to achieve.

If you set a form's BorderStyle property to None, then the caption (along with the whole title bar) is hidden. You can set the caption to display the text you want by setting the form's Caption property in the Properties window.

The Control Menu

The Control menu is a simple menu that allows you to restore, move, resize, minimize, maximize, and close a form. To enable this button on your form, set the form's ControlBox property to True in the form's Properties window.

The Minimize Button

The Minimize button is used to minimize the current form, that is, move it out of the way, to the Windows Taskbar. To enable this button on your form, set the form's MinButton property to True in the form's Properties window.

NOTE   In MDI forms, minimized forms move to the lower-left corner of the MDI parent. Apps initiated from the System Tray get minimized back to the tray.

The Maximize/Restore Button

The Maximize button has two purposes. If the form is in its normal state, that is, its normal size, you can click the Maximize button to automatically expand the current form to the size of the screen or container of the form. A form's *container* is also known as a multiple document interface (MDI) form, which is described in "Working with Multiple Document Interface (MDI) Forms" later in this skill. If the form is maximized, you can click this button again to restore the form to its original size. To enable this button on your form, set the form's MaxButton property to True in the Properties window.

The Close Button

The Close button's sole purpose is to close the current window. In Visual Basic, you can control whether the Close button is visible to the user with the ControlBox property. The Close button will not be visible if the Control box is not visible. If you decide not to enable the Close button or the Control box, then you must provide a way for the form to unload. This can be done automatically, or by using a menu or a button to close the form. You will learn more about this in the next section.

Working with Form Properties

As you learned in Skill 1, properties describe the characteristics of an object. They can be used to manipulate the identity of an object, its appearance, or even its behavior. Every Visual Basic object has at least one property, but most have many more. Certainly the form is no exception. The following shows the properties for a form object:

ActiveControl	DrawWidth	HelpContextID	NegotiateMenus
ActiveForm	Enabled	HWnd	Picture
Appearance	FillColor	**Icon**	ScaleHeight
AutoRedraw	FillStyle	Image	ScaleLeft
BackColor	Font	KeyPreview	**ScaleMode**
BorderStyle	FontBold	**Left**	ScaleTop
Caption	FontItalic	LinkMode	ScaleWidth
ClipControls	FontName	LinkTopic	**ShowInTaskbar**
ControlBox	FontSize	**MaxButton**	Tag
Controls	FontStrikethru	MDIChild	Top
Count	FontTransparent	**MinButton**	Visible
CurrentX	FontUnderline	MouseIcon	WhatsThisButton
CurrentY	**ForeColor**	MousePointer	WhatsThisHelp
DrawMode	HDC	Moveable	**Width**
DrawStyle	**Height**	**Name**	**WindowState**

If you glance at the list of properties for a form in the Properties window, you'll see there are quite a lot of them. Fortunately, only a few of the properties are used frequently—these are boldface in the above list—the rest you'll probably only use occasionally. It's important to note that these properties are specific to the Form object. As you will soon learn in Skill 3, many objects share many of the same properties, but each property is specific to the control it belongs to. For example, a person could be described using properties. My Name property would be set to Steve and my EyeColor property would be set to Blue. However, my wife's Name would be set to Susan and her EyeColor property would be set to Brown.

TIP

You won't see all these form properties in the Properties window. If you can't see a certain property, it means it's a run-time–only property and can't be set at design time (see "Tweaking a Form's Properties" later in this chapter for more information).

HELP IS JUST A BUTTON AWAY

You can get help with a property at any time. Just highlight it in the Properties window and press the F1 function key. For example, highlight the Caption property in the Properties window, and you will see a screen similar to the one shown below.

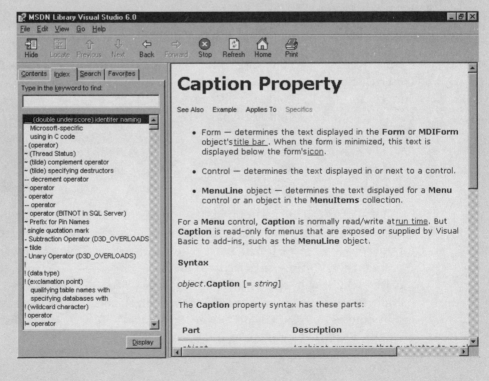

continued ▶

You can scroll through the information or click links (text that is under-lined) to find related information. The tabs at the top of the screen—Contents, Index, Search, and Favorites—offer you more options for finding help with Visual Basic topics.

You may notice that the Help window does not look like the familiar Windows Help style that has been used in the past. With version 6, Microsoft has started using the Microsoft Developer Network, or MSDN, using the HTML Help system, to provide extensive online help facilities. We will look at this in more detail in Skill 13, *Creating and Using Help Files.*

Let's take a closer look at some of the properties that are used most often (the next sections are listed alphabetically to act as a quick reference; the properties also appear in the Properties window in alphabetical order).

The *BackColor* Property

The BackColor property sets the background color of the form. You briefly met this property in Skill 1. You can set a form's background color to any color on the palette. When you double-click BackColor in the Properties window or click the drop-down arrow next to the color selection, the Properties window will display a dialog box containing a color palette and a system color palette.

Usually you would not want to set a form's background color because this prevents the user from utilizing their own color scheme, which they may have defined in the Control Panel. In fact, it is required that you do not set it if you want the "Designed for Windows" logo on your software.

The *BorderStyle* Property

The BorderStyle property determines how the border of a form behaves. A form can have fixed borders that cannot be stretched or sizeable borders that can be stretched by dragging them with the mouse. Table 2.1 shows each option for the BorderStyle property.

T A B L E   2 . 1 :   BorderStyle Settings

Setting	Description
0 - None	Selecting this setting means the form can't be resized or moved. The Control menu, Close button, Maximize and Minimize buttons, and the form's title bar are all suppressed. Although you will not use this setting often, it is useful for making splash screens and screen savers.
1 - Fixed Single	This setting means the form can't be resized by dragging its borders. However, you can use the Maximize and Minimize buttons.
2 - Sizable	This is the default setting for Visual Basic forms and for most other Windows applications windows. The user can resize the form by dragging the form borders or by using the relevant buttons on the title bar.
3 - Fixed Dialog	As its name implies, this is usually the setting chosen for forms that act as dialog boxes. The user can't resize the form—the only options are to move or close it. If you want to force the user to interact with the form, you can set the ControlBox property to False. This prevents users from even closing the form. All they can do is to move the form by dragging its title bar. In that situation you would probably place one or more command buttons on the form—the Click events containing a line of code to close the form (for example, frmFormName.Hide).
4 - Fixed ToolWindow	This acts the same as the Fixed Dialog setting, but with the addition of a Close button (the caption in the title bar is also shown in a smaller font). The form will not appear on the Taskbar.
5 - Sizable ToolWindow	This is just the same as the Sizable style but does not include a Maximize or Minimize button. Under Windows 95 it shows the Close button but doesn't appear on the Taskbar.

Try out these options—you can use the form in the Hello World application that you created in Skill 1 to do this. Open the frmHelloWorld project from Skill 1 by selecting File ➢ Open Project. Select the project you saved in Skill 1.

1. In the Form Designer, click the form once to make it the active control.

2. Because the Hello World form acts more as a dialog box than a useful form, set its BorderStyle property to **3 - Fixed Dialog**.

3. Run your modified Hello World program by selecting Run ➢ Start.

Notice that the form doesn't stretch. Now you have created a true dialog box.

The *Caption* Property

A caption is the text that appears on the title bar of the form. If you set the Border-Style property to None, then the caption (along with the entire title bar) is hidden. You can read more about changing the Caption property in "Tweaking a Form's Properties" later in this chapter.

The *ControlBox* Property

The True and False settings determine whether the Control menu is visible. Keep in mind that the settings for BorderStyle, ControlBox, MaxButton, and MinButton are interdependent. For example, if you turn off the Maximize button and have the Control menu visible, the latter will not contain an option for maximizing the form. Or, to look at another example, if you set the BorderStyle to FixedToolWindow, then this turns off the ControlBox even if you explicitly turn it on.

Stop your Hello World application if you have not already done so. In design mode, do the following:

1. Make the form the active control by clicking it.

2. In the Properties window, set the ControlBox property to False.

3. Run the program again (Run ➤ Start).

Notice this time there is no Control menu on the left side of the title bar or a Close button on the right side. The only way to close this form is to click the OK button.

The *ForeColor* Property

This doesn't affect the color of objects you place on a form, though it does affect the color of text you print to a form. For example, if you wanted to print red text directly on the form, you would set the form's ForeColor property to red. Whenever you print text directly on the form using the Print method, it would be red. Don't worry too much about printing text directly on a form. It is very rarely used. Remember the color of the form itself is set through the BackColor property.

Let's try adding a command button (described in detail in Skill 3) to a form and changing the color of the text and the form itself:

1. Start a new project by Selecting File ➤ New Project.

2. Add a command button to Form1 by double-clicking the command button control in the Toolbox.

3. Once the button is on the form, double-click it to open the button's Click() event.

4. In the Click event procedure for the command button, enter the following line:

```
Print "Hello World"
```

Now experiment by changing the BackColor and ForeColor properties at design time using the Properties window. You can see how these properties work together. If you want to hide the text, you can set the BackColor and ForeColor properties to be equal. For example:

```
BackColor = ForeColor
```

The *Height* Property

Use this property to change the height of a form. You can also set the height by dragging the form's borders in design view. The default units for measuring the Height property (as well as for the Width, Left, and Top properties) are *twips*. Don't worry too much about the units of measurement right now. These are more important when you become more skilled in Visual Basic. If you require precise measurements for a form, or any other control for that matter, you can set its size in the Height and Width properties.

Using your form from the previous example:

1. In the Properties window, set the Width property to **3600**.

2. Set the Height property to **3600**.

Notice that even without running the program, the form has been resized in the Form Designer. This is not much use to you at this time, because you can visually size the form by dragging its borders in the Form Designer. You will find that the dimensions of a form will be set in code at run time. Try this example to see what I mean:

1. Double-click the form to open the Code window. The two boxes at the top of the Code window, called drop-down list boxes, should say Form and Load respectively. This means you are currently in the Form's Load event. Don't worry too much about the details of an event. We will cover these in Skill 4, *Working within Modules and Classes*.

2. Scroll down the list on the right until it says Resize. This will take you to the form's `Resize` event.

3. In the `Resize` event, type the following line of code:

    ```
    Width = Height
    ```

4. Select Run ➤ Start to run the project.

Resize the form by dragging the top or bottom border. Notice how the form automatically resizes itself to a perfect square? This is an example of setting properties at run time.

Try dragging the left or right border. The form does not resize, but it instead snaps back. This happens because the width will always equal the height, according to the code you entered. The width cannot change unless the height changes.

The *Icon* Property

Select an icon by double-clicking this property. The `Icon` property determines the icon to display on the Taskbar when the form is minimized at run time. This property has no effect if you can't minimize the form—you may have set its `BorderStyle` to Fixed Dialog.

If you installed all of the options for Visual Basic, then there are a large number of icons in the `\Graphics\Icons` folders—if they're not there, they'll always be found in the same directory on your Visual Basic CD-ROM. Helpfully, Windows 95 lets you preview the icons before choosing one.

The *Left* Property

The `Left` property functions much like the `Height` and `Width` properties you learned about earlier. The difference is this property determines the distance of the form from the left of the screen. This property is commonly used in conjunction with the form's `Top` property, which sets the vertical spacing of the form. Try this example that centers the form on the screen:

1. Stop the program if you have not already done so.

2. Double-click the form to get back to the form's `Resize` event.

3. Add these two lines of code to the `Resize` event, below the `Width = Height` statement:

    ```
    Left = (Screen.Width - Width) / 2
    Top = (Screen.Height - Height) / 2
    ```

4. Run the program.

This time, the form will not only resize itself, but it will center itself as well. If you want to see a cool elastic-style form, then change the last statement in the `Resize` event to:

```
Width = (Screen.Height - Height) / 2
```

The *MaxButton* Property

By setting this property to `True`, your form will show the standard Maximize button on the right side of the title bar. If you do not want your users to maximize the form, set this property to `False`.

The *MinButton* Property

By setting this property to `True`, your form will show the standard Minimize button on the right side of the title bar. If you do not want your users to minimize the form, set this property to `False`.

> **TIP**   There may be instances when you do not want your users to resize the form. For example, you may have a graphic that must keep the same proportions on the form. Setting the MaxButton and MinButton properties to False will prevent this.

The *Name* Property

The `Name` property is the single most important property in Visual Basic. This is the name of a control that Visual Basic refers to when the program runs. In order to know exactly what your forms are, you should give them a descriptive name and prefix it with the letters `frm`. If you look back at your Hello World application in Skill 1, you will notice you named the form "frmHelloWorld." Although it is not so important to give a descriptive name in that particular application, imagine if you had 20 or 30 forms in your program! You wouldn't want to have to remember their names as `Form17` or `Form20`; names like `frmLogon`, `frmLogoff`, and `frmChangePassword` are more descriptive. Descriptive names make it easier for you to identify forms and controls in your code.

As you read Skill 3, you will learn how to apply more three-letter prefixes called *naming conventions* to your controls.

The *ScaleMode* Property

Although the `Height`, `Width`, `Left`, and `Top` properties of a form are in twips, you have a choice of scales for any controls you place on a form. If you wanted to set the size and position of a command button using the more familiar system of pixels, then set the `ScaleMode` property for the form to **3 - Pixel**.

The *ShowInTaskbar* Property

This property is interesting, because it allows you to hide the form from the Taskbar. If you write an application that you want to reside in that little box in the right side of the Taskbar, called the *System Tray*, or you just don't want your program noticed by the user, you will need to set this property to `False`. You can do this at run time in the form's `Load` event, as shown below:

```
Private Sub Form_Load()
    ShowInTaskBar = False
End Sub
```

The *Width* Property

This specifies the width of the form in twips. This is similar to and is commonly used in conjunction with the `Height` property.

The *WindowState* Property

The `WindowState` property is responsible for how the form starts up. There are three options; the following shows you what each option does:

You type...	Option	Effect
0	Normal	The form will open in its normal state.
1	Minimized	The form will open, but it will be minimized.
2	Maximized	The form will be maximized when it opens.

Tweaking a Form's Properties

Now that you are familiar with several of the form properties, let's manipulate them so you can see how they work. Many properties can be set at run time as well as design time. A few can be set only at design time (for example, Border-Style), and one or two can be set or read only at run time. Those that are only available at run time (for instance, a property called hWnd) do not appear in the Properties window at design time.

> **NOTE** To set properties at design time, you use the Properties window. To set them at run time, you set the properties through code.

One property you can easily change at run time is the Caption property. Here's a hands-on example to show you how to change "Hello" to "Bye." Afterward, you'll see how to extend the code slightly, and you'll learn to change the caption of an object on a form, too.

1. Start a new project (File ➢ New Project) and set the Name property of Form1 to **frmForm1** in the Properties window. Also set the Caption property to **Hello**.

2. Double-click the command button in the Toolbox to add a button to the form. Set its Name property to **cmdHello** and set its Caption property to **&Hello** in the Properties window.

3. Double-click the command button on the form to display the cmdHello_ Click event procedure. Add the following lines to the procedure (as shown in Figure 2.2):

```
If frmForm1.Caption = "Hello" Then
    frmForm1.Caption = "Bye"
Else
    frmForm1.Caption = "Hello"
End If
```

> **NOTE** If-Then-Else statements allow your program to make decisions. They operate much like they sound: *If* condition1 is true, *then* do something, or *else* do something else. We will cover logic and program flow extensively in Skill 6.

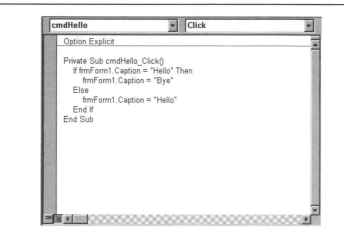

```
cmdHello                          ▼   Click                          ▼

  Option Explicit

  Private Sub cmdHello_Click()
      If frmForm1.Caption = "Hello" Then
          frmForm1.Caption = "Bye"
      Else
          frmForm1.Caption = "Hello"
      End If
  End Sub
```

FIGURE 2.2: Adding lines to a procedure

4. Run the application (Run ➤ Start) and click the command button.

All the code does is to check the current Caption property of the form. As you can see in Figure 2.3, if the caption is "Hello" when you click the button, then it gets set to "Bye." If it's set to "Bye" (that's the meaning of the Else statement), then it gets set back to "Hello."

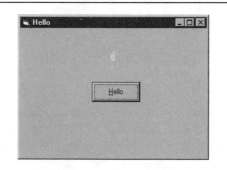

FIGURE 2.3: Caption manipulation

Extending the Code

The second example takes this a step further. Double-click the command button to open the Code window for the command button's `Click` event. Amend the code to read the following:

```
If frmForm1.Caption = "Hello" Then
    frmForm1.Caption = "Bye"
    cmdHello.Caption = "&Hello"
Else
    frmForm1.Caption = "Hello"
    cmdHello.Caption = "&Bye"
End If
```

NOTE When you set string properties in code, you must surround them in quotes. This lets the compiler know the properties are being set to actual values, rather than referencing the names of variables. When setting string valued properties in the Properties window, no quotes are necessary.

Fixing a Bug

As shown in Figure 2.4, the code now contains two additional lines that set the `Caption` property of the command button at run time:

```
cmdHello.Caption = "&Hello"
    .
    .
    .
cmdHello.Caption = "&Bye"
```

If you're using Windows 95, watch how the entry in the Taskbar is updated to reflect the current caption of the form. Also note there's something wrong with the application—when it first starts, the caption of the button is "Hello" when it should be "Bye." Of course, this is fixed by simply altering the `Caption` property of the button at design time, but there's also another way of doing it.

To fix the small bug in the code:

1. Double-click the form in the Form Designer to see the `Form_Load` event procedure.

2. Add the next line

    ```
    cmdHello.Caption = "&Bye"
    ```

to that procedure (between the Private Sub and End Sub lines, as shown in Figure 2.5).

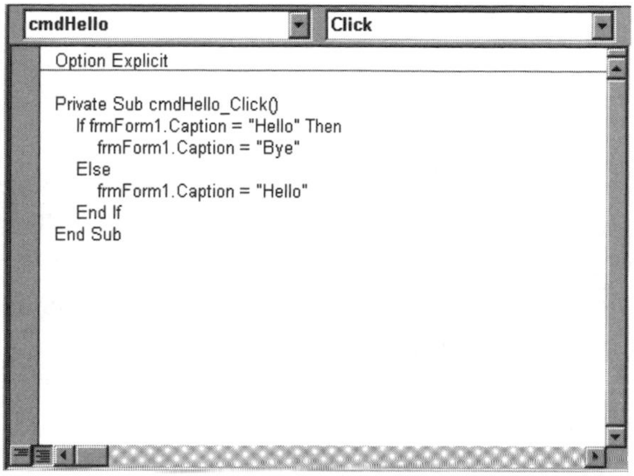

```
cmdHello                    ▼   Click                    ▼

   Option Explicit

   Private Sub cmdHello_Click()
       If frmForm1.Caption = "Hello" Then
           frmForm1.Caption = "Bye"
       Else
           frmForm1.Caption = "Hello"
       End If
   End Sub
```

FIGURE 2.4: Setting the Caption property

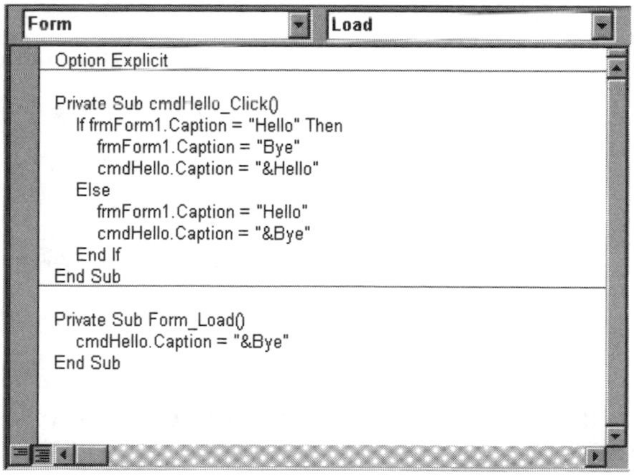

```
Form                        ▼   Load                     ▼

   Option Explicit

   Private Sub cmdHello_Click()
       If frmForm1.Caption = "Hello" Then
           frmForm1.Caption = "Bye"
           cmdHello.Caption = "&Hello"
       Else
           frmForm1.Caption = "Hello"
           cmdHello.Caption = "&Bye"
       End If
   End Sub

   Private Sub Form_Load()
       cmdHello.Caption = "&Bye"
   End Sub
```

FIGURE 2.5: Adding another line of code

3.   Now run the application (Run ➤ Start) and all is well.

What you did here was to use one of the events associated with a form. In the event procedure you changed one of the control properties at run time. Now let's look at some of those events. Don't be concerned about the `Private` prefix to the `Form_Load` event procedure—the meaning of the prefix will become clear in Skill 4.

Introducing Form Events

Before looking at the events for a form, let's learn what an event actually is. Windows is an *event-driven* operating system. This means it utilizes system events to react to the environment. Events are triggered by messages. Whenever you click a button, move the mouse, resize a form, or anything else, Windows will generate a message that describes your action. This message then gets sent to the message queue. From here the message is sent to the appropriate control—for example, a form. When the control receives this message, it then generates an appropriate event. You can write your own code in an event to force a control to react precisely the way you want it to. You will learn more about events in this skill, and in the ones to follow. The more you program, the more familiar you will become with events. Now let's look at a form's events:

Activate	KeyDown	LostFocus	OLESetData
Click	KeyPress	MouseDown	OLEStartDrag
DblClick	KeyUp	MouseMove	Paint
Deactivate	LinkClose	MouseUp	QueryUnload
DragDrop	LinkError	OLECompleteDrag	**Resize**
DragOver	LinkExecute	OLEDragDrop	Terminate
GotFocus	LinkOpen	OLEDragOver	**Unload**
Initialize	**Load**	OLEGiveFeedback	

Just like properties, there are only a few of a form's events that are used a great deal of the time. The ones you will use most often are shown in boldface type. Many of the events are rarely used, unless you're building a very complex application. The best way to view the events associated with a form is to double-click the form in design view to display the Code window. The form is already given in the Object drop-down box, so all you have to do is open the Proc drop-down list associated with it, shown in Figure 2.6.

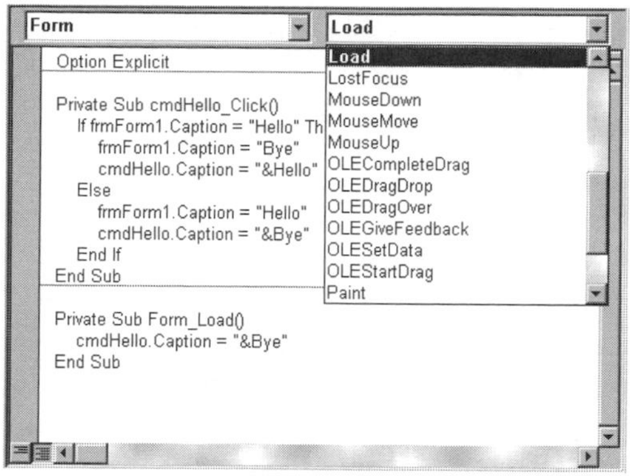

FIGURE 2.6: Form events appearing in a drop-down list

GETTING ONLINE HELP FOR EVENTS

To find out what different events are, click a form in design mode to remove the focus from any other objects or windows. Then press F1 to show the Help window for the form object, as shown below.

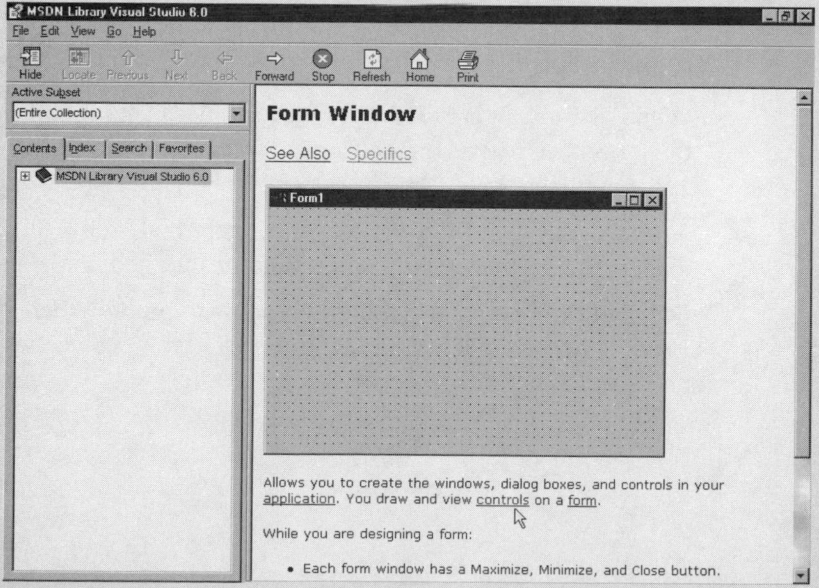

continued ▶

Just below the form click the controls link—the link has a solid underline and is usually blue on a color monitor. This jumps to a window that defines a Visual Basic control.

The list of events is quite long, and some of them may appear to be fairly similar to their names—for example, the `Activate` event sounds similar to the `Load` event. You might think that a form can be displayed by activating it. However, the form must be loaded into memory before it can do anything. Once it is loaded, it can be activated and deactivated as needed. It all depends on the exact nature of the applications you want to create, but it's a fairly safe bet that, rather than using the less popular events, you'll want to use the ones described in the following sections.

The *Activate* Event

You may think that activating a form and initializing a form are the same things, but they are not. A form is actually activated *after* it is initialized. The form then receives the focus after it has been activated.

These subtle differences appear between all of them. The most important difference is the order in which they occur in an application. The order is as follows:

`Initialize`   This event is triggered when a form is being configured before it is loaded.

`Load`   This event is called after the form has been initialized, and before the form is displayed on the screen. You can type code in a form's `Load` event to further tailor the appearance or behavior of the form.

`Activate`   The `Activate` event is triggered when the form has been loaded into memory and when it becomes the active form.

`GotFocus`   If it occurs at all, this event is triggered when the form gets the focus, either when it is loaded or when a user accesses the form with a mouse-click.

Skill 2

Once a particular form is open, only the Activate and possibly the GotFocus events can occur from these four events—though the Initialize event can occur in certain special circumstances.

The Initialize event happens when Visual Basic first becomes aware of the form. At run time, this happens just as you click Run ➤ Start. This is followed by the Load event, as Visual Basic reads the form from disk to memory, or from a disk cache in memory. Once the form is loaded, then the Activate event occurs as the focus shifts to the form—in other words, as the form becomes active. This happens a millisecond or so before the GotFocus event. The GotFocus event, however, can only take place if there are no visible controls on the form. If there's a visible control, then the control receives the focus rather than the form itself, and the form's GotFocus event is bypassed—though there will be a GotFocus event for the control.

In normal circumstances, then, there's always a Load event followed by an Activate event for the first form in the application when the application is started up. Of course, the application may have other windows. When the user or program switches back to the first window, it receives another Activate event, so this time there's no Load event. However, there *is* a Load event if the form has been unloaded in the meantime.

To summarize, there's a Load event followed by an Activate event when the application starts. As the focus moves to other forms and back to the first form (provided it hasn't been unloaded), then the Activate event occurs without a preceding Load event. As a beginning Visual Basic programmer, don't be too concerned with the Activate event yet. You can initialize your forms using the Load event.

The *Deactivate* Event

The Deactivate event is the converse of Activate. The Deactivate event occurs when the form ceases to be active. Depending on your Windows color scheme, you might see the title bar of the form turning a different color (or becoming fainter) as it deactivates and stops being the active form.

The *DragDrop* Event

This event takes place when a dragged control is dropped onto a form. When you run the Hello World application, you'll find if you attempt to drag a command button, nothing appears to happen. To enable the DragDrop event, you must have something to drag and drop on the form in the first place. A fuller discussion of drag-and-drop comes later in Skill 11, *Working with the Mouse*; but if you want a quick teaser, follow these steps:

1. In the Properties window, set the DragMode property of the command button to **Automatic**.

2. Optionally, select an icon for the DragIcon property by double-clicking the DragIcon property in the Properties window.

3. Double-click the form to open the Code window.

4. Select the DragDrop event from the event drop-down list at the top of the Code window.

5. Finally, add the following statement to the DragDrop event procedure for the form:

```
Private Sub Form_DragDrop(Source As Control, _
 X As Single, Y As Single)
    Print "Dropped"
End Sub
```

NOTE   The DragDrop event can only happen if you have a "draggable" control to drag and drop. Some objects are not usually dragged around a form. For example, you would not drag a command button around. Other objects lend themselves to being dragged, such as picture boxes containing icons, or elements within list boxes. If you are unfamiliar with drag-and-drop controls, you can examine other Windows applications and see how drag-and-drop behaves in them.

The *Load* Event

The Load event comes after the Initialize event, but it comes before the Activate event as a form is loaded into memory from disk or from a disk cache in memory. The Load event is a particularly important one and is the one most frequently used. It's extremely handy for specifying some of the contents of the form—for example, it's often used to center a form on the screen.

WHEN TO USE *LOAD/UNLOAD* OR *ACTIVATE/DEACTIVATE*

Before a form is visible on screen, it needs to be loaded into memory. When this happens, Windows sends a message to the form and a Load event is generated by the form. If you decided you wanted to perform checks for your program or wanted to change the position of your form, you would place the code to do so in this event.

For example, if you wanted to center your form before it was displayed, you would write the following code:

```
Private Sub Form_Load()
    Move (Screen.Width - Width) / 2, (Screen.Height - Height) / 2
End Sub
```

Once the form is loaded, it gets activated because it becomes the active window. As a result, it generates an Activate event. In addition, this event is generated whenever an inactive form is acted upon. A good example of when to use the Activate event is in an e-mail program. You could write code in the Activate event that checks for new mail. As a result, every time you start working with the program, it will check for new mail for you.

The Deactivate event is generated when another form or application receives the focus. You could possibly use this event to minimize your application when you go to another program.

Finally, the Unload event is important, because this is your last chance to perform any "housekeeping" for your form. You will want to close any open databases or files in this event. This ensures that memory is not wasted when the form is removed from memory.

Skill 2

The *Resize* Event

When the user or the program code alters the size of a form, the `Resize` event occurs. This has two main uses:

- You can resize the controls on the form (in the event procedure) with code.

- You can set the form back to its original size.

To do these you employ the `Height` and `Width` properties of objects. You can examine the code in the example dealing with the `Height` and `Width` properties.

> **NOTE** You can't resize a form that has been maximized or minimized. To prevent either of these from happening, the easiest solution is to set the MaxButton and MinButton properties to `False`.

The *Unload* Event

The `Unload` event is, logically, the opposite of `Load`. The most popular choice for an `Unload` event procedure is one that asks the user if they're sure they want to close the form (though another event procedure, `QueryUnload`, is a little more flexible in this respect). If you look at the `Unload` event in the Code window, you can see it's a little different from some of the others you've met. It has (`Cancel As Integer`) after the name of the procedure. You can use this argument to cancel the unloading of the form. You can see this in action with the following example:

1. Start a new project (File ➤ New Project), and select Standard EXE.

2. Double-click Form1 in the Form Designer to open its Code window.

3. Select the `Unload` event from the Events drop-down list box.

4. Add the following code:

```
Private Sub Form_Unload(Cancel As Integer)
    If MsgBox("Are you sure?", vbYesNo, _
"Quit?") = vbYes Then
        Unload Me
        Set Form1 = Nothing
    Else
        Cancel = 1
    End If
End Sub
```

5.   Close the Code window and run the program by selecting Run ≻ Start.

6.   You should see a plain form on the screen. Click the Close button on the form. This will generate an Unload event.

> **NOTE**   The MsgBox function is used to display a dialog box, called a *message box*, to the user. You can learn more about this function in Skill 10, *Using Dialog Boxes*.

Because you added the code to the Unload event, Visual Basic executes this code, which asks you if you really want to exit. If you click the Yes button, the form will close. However, if you click No, the program sets the Cancel parameter to 1, which notifies Visual Basic not to unload the form.

> **TIP**   If you are creating an editor-style application—like a word processor or paint program—you should ask the user if they are sure about closing an application if they have not saved their edits and changes. You can place warning code, similar to the code in the previous example, in the form's Unload event.

Introducing Form Methods

Before we look at a form's methods, let me take a minute to explain what a method does. A method is a command that allows you to tell an object what to do. In plain English, a method is the equivalent of a verb. For example, you can tell a form to unload itself by calling the Unload method. The following are a form's methods:

Circle	Move	PSet	TextHeight
Cls	PaintPicture	Refresh	TextWidth
Hide	Point	Scale	**Unload**
Item	Print	SetFocus	Zorder
Line	PrintForm	**Show**	

Show, Hide, and Unload are the three most popular methods to apply to a form. These are put into practice in the next section.

Working with Multiple Document Interface (MDI) Forms

Another breed of the form object is the multiple document interface (MDI) form. An MDI lets you open windows within a *parent container* window. If you look at a typical word processor—Word for Windows is a classic example—you can have many documents open simultaneously within the main window (see Figure 2.7). This main window serves as the container—it contains multiple forms. The MDI application was originally developed back when previous versions of Windows were predominant. The multiple document nature allowed users to open more than one file at a time, without having to open several copies of the program itself. This not only saves time, but it also saves memory.

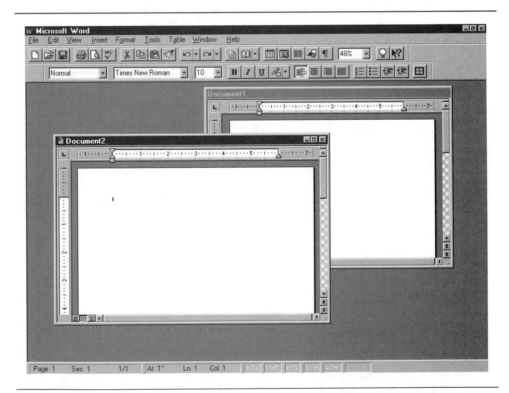

FIGURE 2.7: Multiple documents open simultaneously within a parent container window.

MDI interfaces are more commonly used for *document-centric* applications, like word processors and paint programs. A program is said to be document-centric when the main objects that you work on are documents. If you plan to allow your users to work on several similar forms at one time from within an application, you should use the MDI model. Visual Basic makes it very simple to create an MDI application.

Creating an MDI

To create an MDI application, you need at least two forms in the application. One is the *parent*, or *containing* form, and the second is the *child*, or *contained* form. To have more than one type of child form, you can add further forms to the project. But you only need one child form for the simplest of MDI projects. Here's how it's done:

1. Start a new project by selecting File ➤ New Project. Select Standard EXE as the project type if you have the Project Wizard enabled.

2. You will already have a form in the project. Set its Name property to **frmChild** and its Caption property to **MDI Child**.

3. To create the MDI parent form, right-click the Forms folder in the Project Explorer and select Add ➤ MDI Form. If the Form Wizard appears, select MDI Form.

4. Set the Name property to **frmMDI**, and the Caption property to **MDI Parent**.

5. Right-click Project1 in the Project Explorer, and select Project1 Properties from the pop-up menu. Set the Startup Object list to frmMDI. If you omit this, the application will start with the child form showing.

6. Select frmChild from the Project Explorer. Set the form's MDI Child property to True. This will cause this form, which is the child, to rest inside of the MDI Parent container.

7. Select frmMDI from the Project Explorer.

8. Start the Menu Designer by selecting Tools ➤ Menu Editor. You will see a window like the one in Figure 2.8.

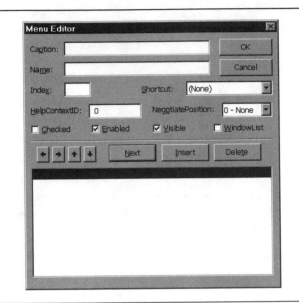

FIGURE 2.8: The Menu Editor

Now that you have created a MDI child form to reside inside the MDI parent window, let's create a simple menu for the form. Don't worry about the details of creating a menu now. We will cover menus in detail in Skill 5, *Creating and Using Menus and Toolbars*.

1. Type **&File** in the Caption field.

2. In the Name field, type **mnuFile**.

3. Click the Next button.

4. Click the right arrow button. This will indent this menu item.

5. Enter **&New Form** in the Caption field.

6. Type **mnuFileNew** in the Name field.

7. Click the OK button to close the Menu Editor.

8. The frmMDI form should now have a File menu on it. Select File ➤ New from the MDI menu. This will open up the Code window.

9. In the `mnuFileNew_Click()` event, type the following lines of code:

    ```
    Dim frm As New frmChild
    frm.Show
    ```

10. Save and run the project. You should now see the MDI shown here.

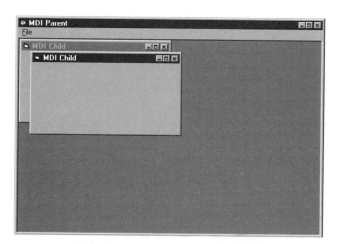

The code creates (or *instantiates*) new copies of `frmChild` and shows them. It does this each time you click File ➢ New. Try opening and closing a few child windows. You should have a functioning MDI application.

Improving the MDI

But there are a few additions to make before it really resembles a commercial Windows MDI application. For example, each child form has the same caption, so it's impossible to tell them apart. Let's fix that. It would also be nice to tile or cascade the children. Further, it's normal to have a menu option (called a *window list*), which lets you switch easily to children that get hidden behind other children.

1. Open the Menu Editor and add a **&Window** menu title to the MDI parent, frmMDI. Turn on the check box for `WindowList` in the Menu Editor as you do so.

2. Using the same methods as in steps 5 and 6 in the previous section, add a **Tile** and a **Cascade** item to this menu title. Name them **mnuWindowTile** and **mnuWindowCascade**, respectively.

3. Click OK to close the Menu Editor.

4. Enter this code for the Click event of the mnuWindowTile object:

    ```
    frmMDI.Arrange vbTileHorizontal
    ```

5. Enter this line for the mnuWindowCascade item:

    ```
    frmMDI.Arrange vbCascade
    ```

    The vbCascade and vbTileHorizontal terms are built-in Visual Basic constants. These can be obtained from Visual Basic's online help.

6. Change the code for the mnuFileNew menu item so that it looks like this:

    ```
    Private Sub mnuFileNew_Click()
        Static Counter As Integer
        Dim frm As New frmChild
        Counter = Counter + 1
        frm.Caption = "MDI Child" & Counter
        frm.Show
    End Sub
    ```

Now save and run the application, and notice the difference in Figure 2.9.

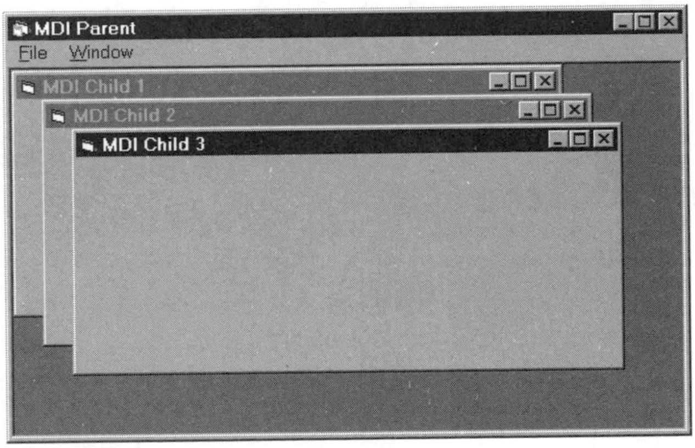

FIGURE 2.9: The improved MDI application

Deciphering the Code

The code you typed in the previous example may look like Greek to you, but don't worry. Many of the statements are explained in later skills in this book. But let's take a quick look so you can get an idea of what's actually going on when you type in code.

The first line (`Static Counter As Integer`) tells Visual Basic to create a variable called `Counter`. The `Static` keyword tells Visual Basic to remember the value of `Counter` every time this procedure is called. This allows `Counter` to count the forms as they are created.

The second line (`Dim frm As New frmChild`) uses a `Dim` statement to "dimension" a variable. In this case, it is dimensioning a variable called `frm` and this variable will be based on, or derived from, the frmChild form. The `New` keyword tells Visual Basic this will be a new form, not one of the others created by this procedure.

Because `Counter` remembers its value, it can increment itself with the line:

```
Counter = Counter +1
```

In effect, if `Counter` was equal to the number 3, then it would say that `Counter` equals the value of `Counter`, three for example, plus one. The result would be that `Counter` equals three plus one, or four. Because `Counter` is a `Static` variable, it will remember this value, so it will be five the next time this procedure is called, six the next, and so on.

The next statement (`frm.Caption = "MDI Child" & Counter`) just changes the `Caption` property of the form to the text "MDI Child" and the number stored in `Counter`. For example, the second form would have the caption "MDI Child 2."

The last statement brings the child to life, so to speak. It tells the child form to show itself. Because you now understand how a form comes to be, you know the first event of a form is the `Load` event. Once the form is loaded, it is activated and then displayed on screen.

Using the Form Wizard

As you work with Visual Basic more often, you will find yourself adding forms to your projects. You have just done this in the multiple document interface (MDI) example. Because a single document interface (SDI) form cannot perform the functions of an MDI form very well, a special MDI form was created to handle the task. When you start writing your own applications, you may find that a single form is not enough to complete the task. At this point you will need to add a new form and customize it to do the task you need. With Visual Basic 6 it is easy to include a form; you can use the Form Wizard to select the style of form you would like to add to your project. Just right-click in the Project Explorer and select Add ➤ Form and the Form Wizard will display the Add Form dialog box (see Figure 2.10).

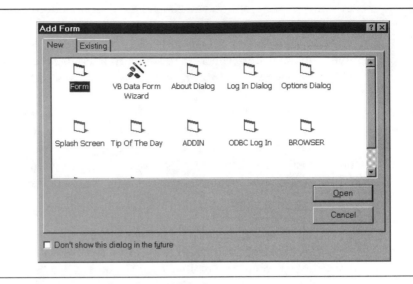

FIGURE 2.10: The Form Wizard

As you can see, you have many form choices to choose from, including About Dialog, Splash Screen, Tip of the Day, and even a Web browser! When you select a form from the Wizard, Visual Basic will create a template complete with graphics and code and add it to your project. You will find that the Form Wizard can be a real time-saver, because it writes the code for a form automatically.

TIP   If you want to have standard-looking forms and do not want to code them yourself, you can use the Form Wizard to do the work for you.

Let's use the Form Wizard to add one last form to your project to spice it up a little.

1. To bring up the Form Wizard, right-click in the Project Explorer and select Add ➤ Form from the pop-up menu.

2. Add another form to your project by selecting About Dialog in the Add Form dialog box. The form will automatically name itself frmAbout.

3. Make the multiple document interface (MDI) form active by double-clicking frmMDI in the Project Explorer.

4. Go back to the Menu Editor, and add another menu by clicking the blank space directly under the &New Form caption. There should be no ellipses (the three dots) in this space. If there are, click the left arrow button to remove them. Now set its Caption property to **&Help**, and its Name property to **mnuHelp**.

5. Click the Next button to add another menu item.

6. Under the mnuHelp menu, add a menu item by clicking the right arrow once. Set the Caption property to **&About**, and its Name property to **mnuHelpAbout**. Be sure to indent this menu item once by clicking the right arrow in the Menu Editor. This will ensure that this will be a menu item of the Help menu. Click OK to close the Menu Editor.

7. Right-click Project1 in the Project Explorer and select Project1 Properties.

8. When the Project Properties dialog box comes up, click the Make tab.

9. Change the Title field to **A Sample MDI**.

10. In the Version Information frame, click Company Name in the Type list, and type your name or your company name in the Value field.

11. Scroll down to the Product Name entry in the Type list, and enter **A Sample MDI**. Click OK when you are done.

12. Select Help ➢ About from the menu on your MDI form to open the Code window.

13. In the mnuHelpAbout_Click() sub, type the following line of code:

    ```
    frmAbout.Show vbModal
    ```

14. Run your application and check out the About dialog box (shown in Figure 2.11).

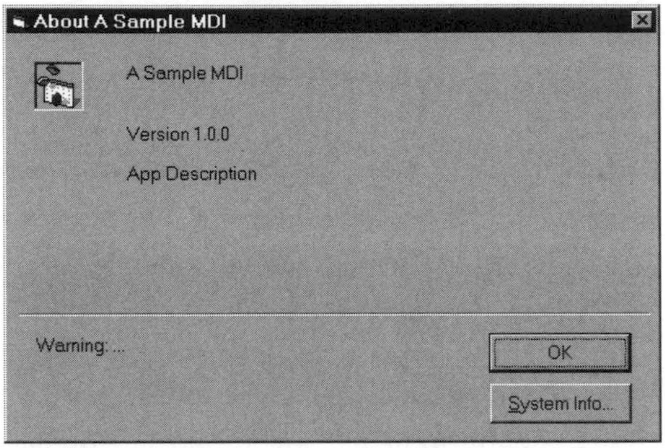

FIGURE 2.11: The About dialog box created by the Form Wizard

Now that you have tried this example, let's look at the keyword vbModal. As you will learn in Skill 4, *Working within Modules and Classes*, you will learn about passing parameters to procedures. In this case, the vbModal keyword is a parameter passed to the form's Show method. This tells Visual Basic to show the About dialog box in a modal state. A *modal* form gains the exclusive attention of the user. A user cannot access any other forms within an application until the modal dialog box has been addressed. This technique is used in many ways. You would most certainly want to make a login dialog box modal, because you do not want your users to gain access to a program without first being properly validated by the login process.

In addition to a simple modal form, you can also have *system modal* forms. These forms require the attention of the user and do not allow any other applications to be accessed until the dialog box has been addressed. A good example of a system modal dialog box is a screen saver. No applications can be accessed until the proper password is entered. This provides a small amount of security for your applications. (A full discussion of system modal dialog boxes is beyond the scope of this book; see *Mastering Visual Basic 6*, by Evangelos Petroutsos (Sybex, 1998), for more information.)

TIP   If you find your Visual Basic design window becoming cluttered with lots of forms, close them. The quickest way to redisplay a form is to double-click its name in the Project Explorer.

Are You up to Speed?

Now you can...

- ☑ create a new form
- ☑ work with forms in Visual Basic
- ☑ use the most important properties and methods to display your forms
- ☑ give your application some life by placing code in a form's events
- ☑ create a multiple document interface (MDI) application with working menus
- ☑ use the Form Wizard to add specialized forms to your application

Skill 2

SKILL 3

Selecting and Using Controls

- Introducing controls
- Learning about the Toolbox
- Using controls
- Grouping controls with frames
- Adding other controls to the Toolbox
- Designing Windows 95–style interfaces

As you learned in the previous skill, the form object is the foundation of your Visual Basic application. Almost every application you develop will have a form in it, and on these forms will be controls. Controls are the building blocks of your application. They give your application the enhanced functionality and personality that is required for your user to interact with your application. In this skill, we will discuss the most common and useful controls that come with Visual Basic 6. While we cannot discuss every control in detail, those discussed in this skill will be the ones you will work with the most. But don't worry! We will cover some more controls in later skills.

Introducing Controls

Custom controls are the building blocks of a Visual Basic application. Controls allow your form to do more than just sit empty on a screen. Some controls, such as labels or list boxes, give users feedback, while others, like command buttons and text boxes, elicit responses. Other controls sit quietly, invisible to the user, and perform some of the grunt work that makes your application useful. The timer control is one example of an invisible control. Controls are easy to use and, when used properly, can add significant functionality to your programs. To add a control to a form you simply double-click the control you want to add, or you can "draw" the control on a form by clicking the control and then dragging the mouse around the area on the form where you want the control to be. After you add some controls, you can set most of their properties in the Properties window. You simply click the control to make it active and change the appropriate properties in the Properties window.

The Toolbox is the containing window that holds the custom controls for your applications (see Figure 3.1). In this skill, we are going to take a look at some of the basic controls you can use to get your applications up and running.

There are also several advanced controls that come with Visual Basic 6, many of which have been enhanced since the previous version. Some controls work with multimedia, such as the Multimedia control, and others—Winsock and Internet Transfer controls—utilize the Internet. There are also several new data-aware controls that help you work with databases. In addition, you can develop your own ActiveX custom controls and add them to your Toolbox, or you can distribute your custom controls to other developers through a variety of methods.

For more information about creating and distributing these kinds of controls, see Skill 17, *Using ActiveX*.

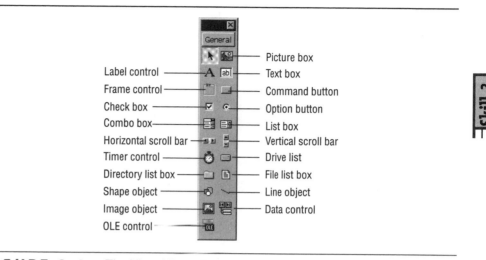

Label control ——— A

Frame control ———

Check box ———

Combo box———

Horizontal scroll bar ———

Timer control ———

Directory list box ———

Shape object ———

Image object ———

OLE control ———

——— Picture box

——— Text box

——— Command button

——— Option button

——— List box

——— Vertical scroll bar

——— Drive list

——— File list box

——— Line object

——— Data control

FIGURE 3.1: The Visual Basic Toolbox

Using Command Buttons

A command button control (shown here) is one of the most common controls found in Windows applications. Visual Basic is no exception. You can use a command button to elicit simple responses from the user or to invoke special functions on forms. You have surely encountered command buttons before: Every time you click the OK button on a dialog box you click a command button.

In the following sections we will look at some of the most important properties, methods, and events of this simple but powerful control. In "Command Button Methods" you will learn how a command button control works; follow along with the exercise to get some hands-on experience.

NOTE   Remember that properties describe the characteristics of an object. Methods are actions that you can tell the object to perform, and events are triggered when a control does something.

Command Button Properties

Below is a list of the properties of a command button. The most commonly used properties appear in boldface. If you are interested in any properties not discussed below, you can select it in the Properties window and press the F1 key to get online help.

Appearance	**Enabled**	hWnd	**Style**
BackColor	Font	Index	**TabIndex**
Cancel	FontBold	Left	**TabStop**
Caption	FontItalic	MaskColor	Tag
CausesValidation	FontName	MouseIcon	ToolTipText
Container	FontSize	MousePointer	Top
Default	FontStrikethru	**Name**	UseMaskColor
DisabledPicture	FontUnderline	OLEDropMode	Value
DownPicture	ForeColor	Parent	Visible
DragIcon	Height	**Picture**	WhatsThisHelpID
DragMode	HelpContextID	RightToLeft	Width

The two most important properties of command buttons are Name and Caption. The Name property is used to give the control its own identity. This name is used by your code and Visual Basic to distinguish it from the rest of the controls. I will be discussing the Name property often throughout this book. The Caption property determines the text that appears on the command button. Placing an ampersand character (&) in the caption gives a keyboard-access key alternative (called a *hotkey*) to a mouse-click. You access these controls by holding the Alt key down while you press the underlined letter of the control you wish to access. The user could also tab to the command button and press the spacebar to simulate a mouse-click on the button.

TIP   Access keys, also called *hotkeys*, are important to understand because not all users like to use the mouse. Users who write for a living, for example, don't like it when they have to move their hands off of the keyboard to change a font, and then resume typing. You should provide hotkeys whenever possible to make using your software easier on your users.

Two other useful properties are Cancel and Default. Setting the Default property to True means the user can simulate a click on the button by pressing Enter. Setting Cancel to True means the user can close a form by pressing Esc.

Skill 3

NOTE   When you add command buttons to a form, only one button can have its Default property set to True at a time. This button becomes the default button for the form. Likewise, only one command button can have its Cancel property set to True.

By setting the Style property, you can make the button contain text only, or you can add a picture to the button. If you want the button in its normal, unpressed state to have a picture, you can specify the picture's filename in the Picture property. You can also place other graphics on the button by setting them using the DisabledPicture and DownPicture properties.

Two properties can stop the user from accessing a command button—Enabled and Visible. If either is set to False, the command button will be unusable. Disabling a command button is a handy technique if you want to force the end user to complete certain actions (such as filling in text boxes) before clicking the next button in the process.

TIP   When you want a button to be disabled, you should set the Enabled property to False rather than setting the Visible property to False. This lets the user know a control is available under certain conditions, rather than completely hiding the functionality of your program.

If the user moves around the form with the Tab key, you can determine the order in which they visit controls by specifying the TabIndex property. A control with a TabIndex of 0 (zero) is the first to receive the focus on a form, provided it's not disabled or invisible. If you alter the TabIndex of one control, the other controls' orders adjust to accommodate the new order. When you want to prevent a user from tabbing to a control, set its TabStop property to False. This does not prevent a mouse-click on a control—to stop that, use the Enabled or Visible properties described previously.

Command Button Events

Without a doubt, the most frequently coded event procedure for a command button corresponds to the `Click()` event; the other events for a command button are listed here:

Click	KeyPress	**MouseUp**	OLESetData
DragDrop	KeyUp	OLECompleteDrag	OLEStartDrag
DragOver	LostFocus	OLEDragDrop	
GotFocus	**MouseDown**	OLEDragOver	
KeyDown	MouseMove	OLEGiveFeedback	

In your first programs, the `Click()` event is probably the only event in which you'd be interested. It's the most commonly used event on a command button. You won't use many of the other events until you become more proficient in Visual Basic. However, you can also use the `MouseUp()` event in place of the `Click()` event. Many Windows 95 applications use this event because it gives the user a chance to back out without firing a `Click()` event.

Command Button Methods

Listed below are the methods for the command button. The most commonly used method is `SetFocus`.

Drag	OLEDrag	**SetFocus**	ZOrder
Move	Refresh	ShowWhatsThis	

The `SetFocus` method is sometimes used to place the focus on a particular button. This comes in handy if you want the user to return to a default button after editing a text box on a form. If that were so, the code for the focus button looks like this:

```
cmdMyButton.SetFocus
```

and it might be placed in the `Change()` event procedure for a text box.

Experimenting with a Command Button

Let's put the command button to use.

1. If you installed the sample applications from the Visual Basic CD, then open the project \MSDN98\98vs\1033\Samples\VB98\Controls\Controls.vbp.

(This directory may be slightly different, depending on how you installed your sample applications.)

NOTE If you haven't already installed the sample applications, take a moment to refer back to the section "Working with Multiple Projects" in Skill 1. It covers how to install the sample applications. You will need to have these installed to do many of the exercises in this skill.

2. Click Run ➢ Start from the Visual Basic menu to run the application. From the Control Examples dialog box, click Test Buttons. You will see a form like Figure 3.2.

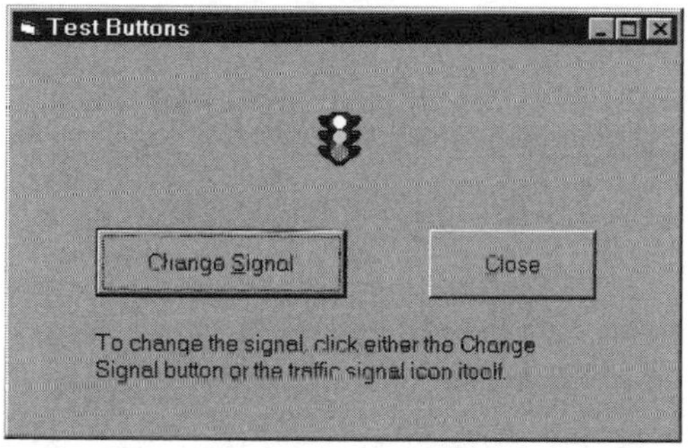

FIGURE 3.2: Testing the command button

3. Click the Change Signal button to watch the signal lights change. When you are done testing the buttons, click the Close button.

With the command button control, you can enhance this form by placing the signal directly on the Change Signal button.

4. Stop the application by selecting Run ➢ End from the Visual Basic menu.
5. Make the Test Buttons form active by double-clicking frmButton in the Project Explorer.
6. Stretch the Change Signal button so it can fit an icon the size of the signal on it. In the Properties window, change the button's `Style` property to **1 - Graphical**.

7. Set the Visible property of the controls imgGreen, imgYellow, and imgRed to False.

8. Add the following code to the form's Load() event:

```
Private Sub Form_Load()
    cmdChange.Picture = imgGreen.Picture
End Sub
```

9. Now change the ChangeSignal procedure to the following code:

```
Private Sub ChangeSignal()
    Static signal As Integer

    signal = signal + 1
    If signal > 3 Then signal = 1

    Select Case signal
        Case Is = 1
            cmdChange.Picture = imgYellow.Picture
        Case Is = 2
            cmdChange.Picture = imgRed.Picture
        Case Is = 3
            cmdChange.Picture = imgGreen.Picture
    End Select
End Sub
```

10. Run the program again (Run ➤ Start). Click Test Buttons again to get to the Test Buttons dialog box. When you click the Change Signal button, the signal icon on the command button will change in the same manner that the signal image did previously.

Although not sophisticated, this example shows you how the command button works. You can place other commands in the Click() event so the button will perform any tasks you want it to. If you wanted the button to close your application, you could change the Click() event procedure to:

```
Private Sub cmdChangeSignal_Click()
    End
End Sub
```

TIP To add a graphic to your command buttons, set the Style property to **1 - Graphical**. Then add the graphic by setting the Picture property to the filename of the graphic you want to use.

Using Text Boxes

[ab|]

Nearly every Visual Basic project involves at least one text box control (shown here). Text boxes are commonly used for accepting user input or for entering data. Their properties are, of course, specifically designed for these purposes. If you only want the simplest of user responses, you might consider using an InputBox instead. The InputBox displays a dialog box and prompts the user to enter something and returns this to the application. The Visual Basic InputBox and the converse MsgBox (message box) are discussed in Skill 10, *Using Dialog Boxes*. A MsgBox is used for displaying simple messages to the user.

Skill 3

Text Box Properties

Here is the list of properties for the text box control. Again, the most important properties appear in boldface:

Alignment	Font	LinkItem	RightToLeft
Appearance	FontBold	LinkMode	**ScrollBars**
BackColor	FontItalic	LinkTimeout	**SelLength**
BorderStyle	FontName	LinkTopic	**SelStart**
CausesValidation	FontSize	**Locked**	**SelText**
Container	FontStrikethru	**MaxLength**	**TabIndex**
DataChanged	FontUnderline	MouseIcon	TabStop
DataField	ForeColor	MousePointer	Tag
DataFormat	Height	**MultiLine**	**Text**
DataMember	HelpContextID	**Name**	ToolTipText
DataSource	HideSelection	OLEDragMode	Top
DragIcon	HWnd	OLEDropMode	Visible
DragMode	Index	Parent	WhatsThisHelpID
Enabled	Left	**PasswordChar**	Width

As always, the property you set first is the Name property. By convention this begins with the txt prefix. Notice that there is no Caption for a text box. Instead the text shown in the text box is determined by the Text property. You can provide a default entry in the text box by setting the Text property accordingly. It's possible you don't want any value in the text box—you want the user to enter something from scratch. In that case, delete the Text property setting and the text box appears blank. The MaxLength property is handy for limiting the user to a specified number of characters. This is often used in conjunction with the PasswordChar property. The latter is valuable for showing a default character (the asterisk character—*—is the best choice) when the user is entering a password. MaxLength and Password-Char properties are often employed for a text box on a logon form.

The MultiLine property lets the user type more than one line of text into the text box. If MultiLine is used with the ScrollBars property, you can make a simple text editor with no coding—though you would need a couple of lines of code to save the user's typing.

The SelLength, SelStart, and SelText properties are useful for dealing with text appropriately. For example, the SelText property returns the text in the text box that the user selected with the mouse or arrow keys. From there it's easy to copy or cut the selected text to the Clipboard.

Note that the ReadOnly property from previous versions has been replaced by the Locked property. Setting the Locked property to True will cause the text box to display data, but will permit no editing. You may have noticed this type of text box on license agreement dialog boxes that appear during program installations. You can select and copy text, but you cannot type or delete text from the box.

To change the order in which the user tabs around the text boxes (and other controls) on a form, change the TabIndex setting. If you don't want the user to tab into a text box, set its TabStop property to False. To prevent a user from clicking in the text box with the mouse, set the Enabled property to False. There may be some situations where you would want to prevent the user from accessing a text box. For example, the user is not allowed to enter a message in an e-mail program until an address has been entered in the address text box. You will discover other examples of why you would want to use this feature as you become more proficient with Visual Basic.

Text Box Events

The text box control supports a few events that are listed in the table here:

Change	KeyDown	LinkOpen	OLEDragDrop
Click	KeyPress	LostFocus	OLEDragOver
DblClick	KeyUp	MouseDown	OLEGiveFeedback
DragDrop	LinkClose	MouseMove	OLESetData
DragOver	LinkError	MouseMove	OLEStartDrag
GotFocus	LinkNotify	OLECompleteDrag	Validate

The Change() event occurs every time the user inserts, replaces, or deletes a character in a text box. You can perform some elementary validation of user entry in the Change() event. You can even use it to restrict entry to certain characters only. However, you may find that the Masked Edit control or one of the Key events is more suitable for this purpose. The Microsoft Masked Edit control lets you specify entry templates or masks. It's a custom control that you need to add to the Toolbox if you want to use it. There's a full reference for all the custom controls bundled with Visual Basic in the Microsoft Developer Network, included on your Visual Basic CD.

Text Box Methods

Here is the list of methods supported by the text box control:

Drag	LinkRequest	OLEDrag	ShowWhatsThis
LinkExecute	LinkSend	Refresh	ZOrder
LinkPoke	Move	SetFocus	

Most of the methods here are not used very frequently, though the Link methods are necessary if your text box is involved in a DDE (Dynamic Data Exchange) conversation. DDE allows one application to communicate with another. As the user interacts with one application, it sends data automatically to the other application. Unfortunately, it is beyond the scope of this book to cover DDE in detail. If you are interested in pursuing it further, check the online help.

The SetFocus method, though, is a boon in data-entry applications. When the user clicks a command button (say, an Update button), the focus remains on that button. If the last statement in the Click() event for the command button is a SetFocus method, you can force the focus back to the data-entry text boxes. This saves the user from an extra mouse-click or excessive use of the Tab key just to get back into position. The syntax is:

```
txtMyTextBox.SetFocus
```

Experimenting with Text Box Controls

To see the SetFocus method in action, try the following example:

1. Open the project \MSDN98\98vs\1033\Samples\VB98\Controls\
   Controls.vbp if it is not already open.

2.   Select Run ➣ Start to run the application. From the Control Examples dialog box, click the Text Box button. You will see a form similar to the one shown in Figure 3.3.

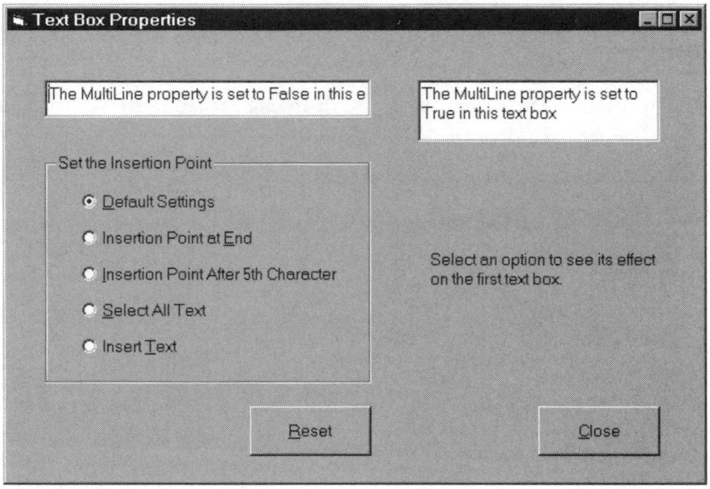

FIGURE 3.3:   Testing text box controls

The text box on the left of Figure 3.3 can be changed by selecting the options within the frame. The text box on the right has its MultiLine property set to True, as the text in the box indicates. Text editing applications often exploit the MultiLine and ScrollBars properties of a text box. Make the text box as large as the form and keep the form fixed in size (BorderStyle property). If you want the user to resize the form, or it's a multiple document interface (MDI) child form, you have to resize the text box dynamically as the user alters the size of the form. One way of doing this is to add the following code to the form's Resize event procedure:

```
txtText1.Top = frmForm1.ScaleTop
txtText1.Left = frmForm1.ScaleLeft
txtText1.Width = frmForm1.ScaleWidth
txtText1.Height = frmForm1.ScaleHeight
```

The Scale properties refer to the internal dimensions of a form. Thus a form's Height property is different from its ScaleHeight property. The latter makes allowances for title bars and borders.

3.   Next, stop the application and make frmText active in the Form Designer.

4. Double-click the Insertion Point After 5th Character option to expose its procedure code, which looks like this:

```
Private Sub optInsert_Click()
    ' place the insertion point after 5th char
    txtDisplay.SelStart = 5

    ' set the focus to the text box so we can see
    ' the result of our settings
    txtDisplay.SetFocus
End Sub
```

The SelStart property is used to select the starting position, in characters, of a selection within a text box. Here it is set to the fifth position. The Set-Focus method sets the focus of the application back to txtDisplay.

5. Open the procedure for the Click() event of optSelect:

```
Private Sub optSelect_Click()
    ' place the insertion point at the beginning
    txtDisplay.SelStart = 0
    ' find the length of the string and
    ' select that number of characters
    txtDisplay.SelLength = Len(txtDisplay.Text)

    ' set the focus to the text box so we can see
    ' the result of our settings
    txtDisplay.SetFocus
End Sub
```

This code shows how you can select all of the text within a text box. So if you had a Select All menu option, you would call a procedure similar to this example. If you want to check the text that is highlighted, you can check the SelText property.

6. Replace the code in the cmdClose_Click() event with the following:

```
Private Sub cmdClose_Click()
    If txtDisplay.SelLength > 0 Then
        MsgBox "You selected " & txtDisplay.SelText
    End If

    Unload Me        ' Unload this form.
End Sub
```

7. Run the application. In the Text Box Properties dialog box, select the word MultiLine and click the Close button. You will see something like Figure 3.4.

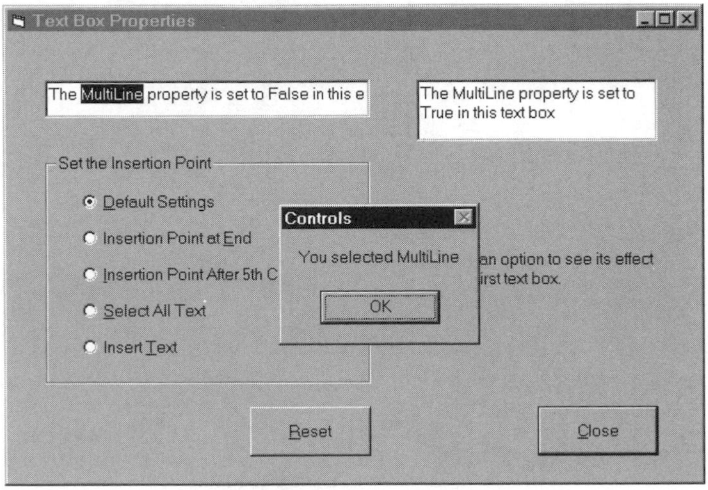

Text Box Properties

The MultiLine property is set to False in this e

The MultiLine property is set to True in this text box

Set the Insertion Point

◉ Default Settings

○ Insertion Point at End

○ Insertion Point After 5th C

○ Select All Text

○ Insert Text

Controls

You selected MultiLine   an option to see its effect
                          irst text box.

[OK]

[Reset]   [Close]

FIGURE 3.4:   The SelText property contents

Using Labels

A label control (shown here) is similar to a text box control in that both display text. The main difference, however, is that a label displays read-only text as far as the user is concerned, though you can alter the caption as a run-time property.

The property of interest in a label control is the Caption property, as opposed to a text box's Text property. Labels are often used for providing information to the user. This can be in the form of a message shown on the form itself or a prompt. The prompt is usually combined with a text box, list box, or other control. It gives the user an idea of the nature of the referenced control. For example, if you had a text box that allowed the user to enter the data for a customer's name, then you might place a label to the left or above the text box with its Caption property set to Customer Name.

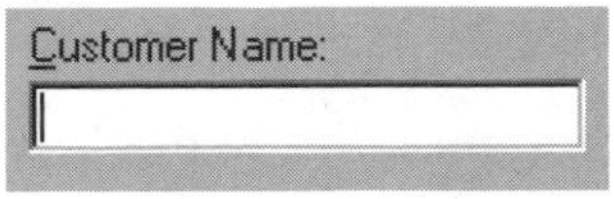

Customer Name:

SETTING ACCESS KEYS FOR A LABEL CONTROL

Access keys, also known as *accelerators*, are actually Alt+key combinations that allow the user to access a control by holding down the Alt key while pressing the underlined letter of a text-type control. Access keys can only be set for controls that have a `Caption` property—for instance, command buttons and menu controls. Many controls, text box controls for example, do not have a `Caption` property, so it's impossible for a keyboard user to jump straight to the control—unless they press the Tab key and the control just happens to be next in the tab order.

The workaround is to place a label control before the control in question. Then you set the `TabIndex` property of the label to one less than the `TabIndex` of the control the label is describing. Include an ampersand character (&) in the `Caption` property for the label to define the access key.

Let's try an example to give you an idea of what's required:

1. If it's not already open, open the `Controls.vbp` project from the previous example.

2. Double-click frmText in the Project Explorer to make it the active form.

3. Click txtDisplay, the text box control on the upper-left side of the form, and examine its `TabIndex` property in the Properties window. It should be set to **0**. This makes this control the first tabstop on the form.

4. Add a label control to the form and place it above txtDisplay. Set its `Name` property to **lblDisplay** in the Properties window. Set its `Caption` property to **Dis&play**. Be sure to place the ampersand before the letter *p*.

5. The `TabIndex` property of lblDisplay should be 11. Change it to **0**.

6. Run the program by selecting Run ➢ Start.

continued ▶

Skill 3

7. From the Control Example form, click the Text Box button.

8. From the Text Box Properties form, click the Reset button to move the focus away from txtDisplay.

9. Now, hold down the Alt key and press the letter **P**.

Now pressing the Alt key with the underlined letter moves the focus to the label. But if you look at the properties, events, and methods of a label (described shortly), you see that there's no TabStop property; no GotFocus or LostFocus events; and no SetFocus method. What this means is a label can never receive the focus—so moving the focus to a label with an access key will move the focus to the next control in the TabIndex property order.

Label Properties

You have already worked with some of the properties of a label control. Here is the complete list of properties for this control:

Alignment	DataSource	Height	Parent
Appearance	DragIcon	Index	RightToLeft
AutoSize	DragMode	Left	**TabIndex**
BackColor	Enabled	LinkItem	Tag
BackStyle	**Font**	LinkMode	ToolTipText
BorderStyle	FontBold	LinkNotify	Top
Caption	FontItalic	LinkTimeout	**UseMnemonic**
Container	FontName	LinkTopic	Visible
DataChanged	FontSize	MouseIcon	WhatsThisHelpID
DataField	FontStrikethru	MousePointer	Width
DataFormat	FontUnderline	**Name**	**WordWrap**
DataMember	ForeColor	**OLEDropMode**	

As a reminder, the most important property at the outset is—once again—the Name property. For labels the prefix is normally lbl. The Caption property determines the text shown in the label. If you incorporate an ampersand (&) character in the caption, an access key is defined. This raises an interesting question: What happens if you want to show an actual ampersand in the caption? An ampersand does not display; instead, it remains hidden and causes the subsequent character to appear underlined.

> **TIP**   If you do want an ampersand character to appear in a label, set the UseMnemonic property to False, because by default it's True. A mnemonic is an abbreviation or shorthand—in this context it means an access key, or accelerator.

You define the size of the label at design time. At run time you might wish to alter the Caption property, only to find it's too big to fit within the label control. You could calculate the length of the caption and adjust the label size accordingly, but this is messy and there's a danger of an enlarged label obscuring other controls. To simplify matters, use the AutoSize and WordWrap properties, either by themselves or in conjunction. That way the caption will fit and you can control whether the label expands vertically rather than horizontally.

One more interesting label control property is BorderStyle. This is not related to the form property of the same name—there are only two choices. But by setting BorderStyle to 1 - Fixed Single and the BackColor to white (or whatever), the label looks exactly like a text box, except that it's read-only. Labels were often used in this fashion in prior versions of Visual Basic to show data for browsing purposes only.

Label Events

The label control has many of the same events as any other controls:

Change	LinkClose	MouseMove	OLEGiveFeedback
Click	LinkError	MouseUp	OLESetData
DblClick	LinkNotify	OLECompleteDrag	OLEStartDrag
DragDrop	LinkOpen	OLEDragDrop	
DragOver	MouseDown	OLEDragOver	

Most of the standard events are supported. But note the absence of any Key() events. This is consistent with a label not being able to receive the focus. The Mouse() events are there, because there's nothing to stop you from clicking a label at run time. The ability to click a control does not indicate it must necessarily receive the focus. The Link() events are not shared by many other controls (with the exception of text boxes and picture controls). These events are concerned with DDE (Dynamic Data Exchange) conversations. The Key() and Mouse() events are discussed later in Skill 11, *Working with the Mouse*.

Label Methods

The label control also has methods, but you will probably not use them very often in your applications. The following shows the methods supported by the label control:

Drag	**LinkRequest**	OLEDrag	ZOrder
LinkExecute	LinkSend	Refresh	
LinkPoke	Move	ShowWhatsThis	

The label methods are not particularly useful, although the LinkRequest method is sometimes used to update a nonautomatic DDE link.

Experimenting with a Label Control

Although there is not much that can be done to show you how a label works, we will add a label to the main form in the Controls project that you have been working with in previous examples:

1. Make frmMain the active form in the Form Designer by double-clicking frmMain in the Project Explorer.

2. Add a label on the bottom of the form. Stretch it so it is almost the width of the form.

3. Set its Name property to **lblHelp** and set the Caption property to **Click a button to see how a control works**.

4. When you run the application, the main form should look like Figure 3.5.

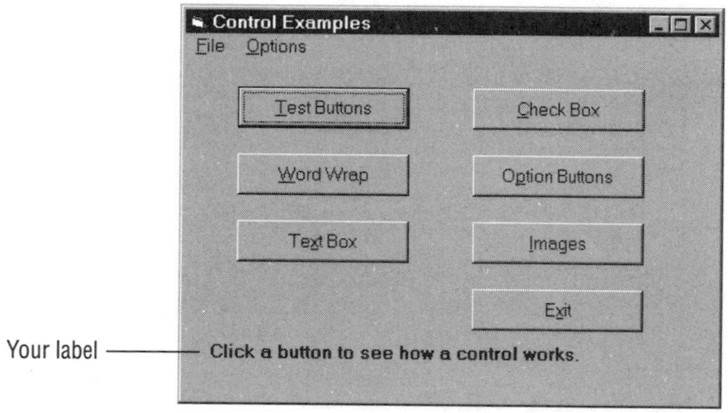

Your label ─────

FIGURE 3.5:   Your label added to the form

Using Option Buttons

Option button controls, also called radio buttons, (shown here) are used to allow the user to select one, and only one, option from a group of options. Usually option buttons are grouped together within a frame control (described later in this chapter), but they can also be grouped on a plain form, if there is to be only one group of option buttons. Thus, if you had a frame specifying a delivery method, you might have one button for UPS (United Parcel Service) and another for Courier delivery. Products can only be shipped by *one* of these methods (not both—and not none). In contrast, option buttons representing, say, bold and italic settings for text would not make sense. Text can be both bold *and* italic, or neither (none).

Option Button Properties

The option button supports many properties which are shown in the table below:

Alignment	FontSize	Picture
Appearance	FontStrikethru	RightToLeft
BackColor	FontUnderline	**Style**
Caption	ForeColor	TabIndex

CausesValidation	Height	TabStop
Container	HelpContextID	Tag
DisabledPicture	hWnd	ToolTipText
DownPicture	Index	Top
DragIcon	Left	UseMaskColor
DragMode	MaskColor	**Value**
Enabled	MouseIcon	Visible
Font	MousePointer	WhatsThisHelpID
FontBold	**Name**	Width
FontItalic	OLEDropMode	
FontName	Parent	

Once again the Name property is the one to set first; option buttons have an opt prefix by convention. The Caption property helps the user determine the purpose of an option button. The other popular property is Value. This is invaluable at both design time and run time. At run time you test the Value property to see if the user has turned on (or off) the option button. The property has two settings, True and False. At design time you can set the Value property to True for one of the buttons if you wish—the default setting is False. This means that the option button (and only that option button in a group) is pre-selected when the form opens. If you try to make Value for another button in the group True, then the previous one reverts to a False setting.

A new property added in version 6 is the Style property. The default setting of 0 - Standard will draw a normal option button, as shown at the beginning of this section. However, by setting this property to 1 - Graphical, you can make the option button look just like a command button, but it allows only one selection to be made within a group. It works much like the old memory preset buttons on the old stock car radios.

TIP   If you want to present your users with multiple buttons, but only allow them to select one, then you can set the Style property of the option button control to 1 - Graphical. In addition, you can set the Picture property if you want to display a picture on the button.

Option Button Events

The option button control has a few events, but only the Click() event is really used:

Click	KeyDown	MouseMove	OLEGiveFeedback
DblClick	KeyPress	MouseUp	OLESetData
DragDrop	KeyUp	OLECompleteDrag	OLEStartDrag
DragOver	LostFocus	OLEDragDrop	Validate
GotFocus	MouseDown	OLEDragOver	

The typical way of dealing with option buttons is to test the Value property at run time to see if they're selected. Your code then initiates actions accordingly. It's common to test for the Value property in the Click() event procedure for a command button that's clicked after the user has selected the option button of interest. This allows you to check for a condition before the next procedure is called. You test the Value property in an If ... End If or Select Case ... End Select construct. But there may be occasions when you want to initiate an action immediately after the user makes a choice. Then you may want to trap the option button's Click() event. Try this example to see what I mean:

1. Run the Controls project by selecting Run ➢ Start.

2. Click the Option Buttons button on the Control Examples form.

3. Click any of the option buttons and watch the label at the top of the form. The Click() event of each option button is used to change the Caption property of the label.

4. When you are done watching the results, click the Close button to close the dialog box.

5. End the application by clicking the Exit button on the Control Examples form.

If you want to see the code that makes this example work, follow these steps:

1. Double-click frmOptions in the Project Explorer to make it the active form.

2. Double-click the option button next to 486 to open its Code window. You will see the following code:

```
Private Sub opt486_Click()
    ' assign a value to the first string variable
    strComputer = "486"
    ' call the subroutine
    Call DisplayCaption
End Sub
```

Notice that the `Click()` event sets the value of `strComputer` to 486. Then it calls another procedure to change the caption.

3. Select (General) from the left pull-down menu, called the *object pull-down*, at the top of the Code window. Then select (DisplayCaption) from the procedure pull-down on the upper right of the Code window. This will display the code for the `DisplayCaption` procedure:

```
Sub DisplayCaption()
    ' concatenate the caption with the two string
    ' variables.
    lblDisplay.Caption = "You selected a " & _
      strComputer & " running " & strSystem
End Sub
```

Notice how the `Caption` property of lblDisplay is set in this procedure, which is called in every `Click()` event of every option button. That's all there is to it!

Option Button Methods

The methods for the option button are of little use in the Visual Basic environment:

Drag	OLEDrag	SetFocus	ZOrder
Move	Refresh	ShowWhatsThis	

Therefore, we will not deal with their explanations here.

Open and start the Controls sample application. Click the Option Buttons button to bring up the Options dialog box (see Figure 3.6).

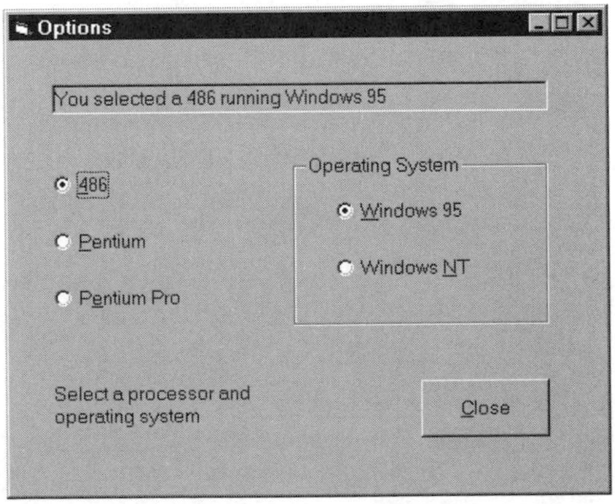

FIGURE 3.6:   The Options dialog box

The five option buttons are actually in two groups. The options labeled 486, Pentium, and Pentium Pro are in their own group directly on the form. The Windows 95 and Windows NT options are in a separate group on the Operating System frame. This frame then rests on the form and separates the two groups of option buttons. If you click an option button, you will notice the other option buttons in the same group become deselected. Only one option can be selected in any particular group at one time.

Using Check Boxes

A check box control (shown here) is rather similar to an option button, which was described in the last section. Both often partake in groups, and the Value property is tested to see if a check box is on or off. But there are two fundamental differences between check boxes and option buttons: Check boxes are valid as single controls—a single option button is probably counter-intuitive. Check boxes (even when in a group) are not mutually exclusive. Finally, check boxes have three possible settings for the Value property.

An option button is either on or it's off. Therefore, Value can be either True or False. Check boxes can be in one of *three* states—on, off, or grayed. Grayed (dimmed) does *not* mean the same as disabled in this context—a grayed check box is neither on nor off, though the user can change its setting. If the check box were disabled, the user wouldn't be able to turn it on or off. A grayed check box is used to signify that some, but not all, options on another dialog box are selected. If you look at the dialog box in Figure 3.7, you will notice two of the check boxes are grayed. If you have installed Windows 95, then you understand what the grayed check box means. The Accessories check box is gray because I installed some, but not all, of the accessories for Windows 95.

Check Box Properties

The following table lists the properties for the check box control:

Alignment	DownPicture	Height	RightToLeft
Appearance	DragIcon	HelpContextID	Style
BackColor	DragMode	hWnd	**TabIndex**
Caption	**Enabled**	Index	**TabStop**
CausesValidation	**Font**	Left	Tag
Container	FontBold	MaskColor	ToolTipText
DataChanged	FontItalic	MouseIcon	Top

DataField	FontName	MousePointer	UseMaskColor
DataFormat	FontSize	**Name**	**Value**
DataMember	FontStrikethru	OLEDropMode	Visible
DataSource	FontUnderline	Parent	WhatsThisHelpID
DisabledPicture	ForeColor	Picture	Width

Again, as with option buttons, the three most popular properties are Name, Caption, and Value. When setting the Name property it's conventional to use a chk prefix.

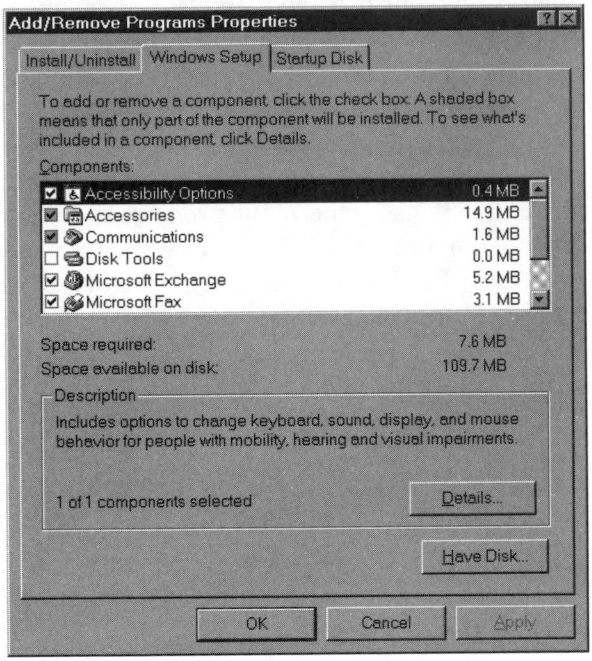

FIGURE 3.7:   Grayed or "dimmed" check boxes

Check Box Events

The following table shows you that the check box has similar events to the option button control:

Click	KeyPress	MouseUp	OLESetData
DragDrop	KeyUp	OLECompleteDrag	OLEStartDrag

DragOver	LostFocus	OLEDragDrop	Validate
GotFocus	MouseDown	OLEDragOver	
KeyDown	MouseMove	OLEGiveFeedback	

To carry out further processing as soon as the user has clicked the check box, use the Click() event. Normally, though, if you do not put code directly within the Click() event, you will have another procedure that will ascertain the value of a check box by retrieving its Value property.

Check Box Methods

Like the events of the check box control, its methods are similar to those for the option button control:

Drag	OLEDrag	SetFocus	ZOrder
Move	Refresh	ShowWhatsThis	

Like option buttons, the methods for the check box control are non-vital to the operation of the control.

If you want to test the functionality of the check box control, start the Controls application and click the Check Box button. The Check Box Example dialog box has two check boxes that manipulate the text box at the top (see Figure 3.8).

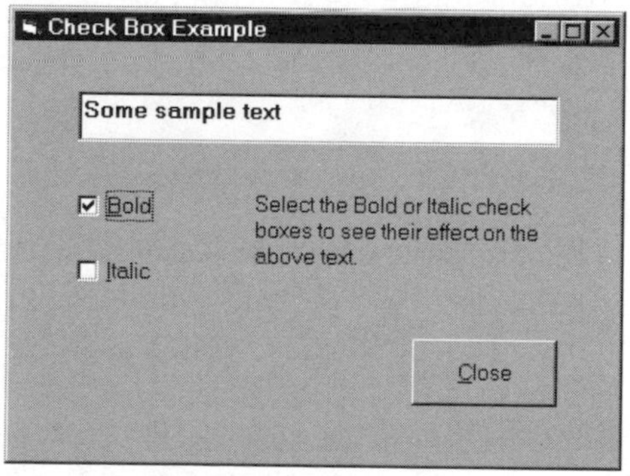

FIGURE 3.8:   The Check Box Example dialog box

Clicking the Bold check box turns the text bold, and the Italic option italicizes the text within the box. In the procedure below you can see how the FontBold property for the text box is modified in the Click() event.

```
Private Sub chkBold_Click()
```

```
' The Click event occurs when the check box changes state.
' Value property indicates the new state of the check box.
If chkBold.Value = 1 Then      ' If checked.
    txtDisplay.FontBold = True
Else                               ' If not checked.
    txtDisplay.FontBold = False
End If
End Sub
```

Experimenting with Check Box Controls

Try this example to see the check box work in all three of its states:

1. Start a new project by selecting File ➤ New Project.

2. In the Properties window, change the Name property of Form1 to **frmMain**.

3. Add a check box control to the form. Set its Name property to **chkOptions**, and its Caption property to **What do you want on your sandwich?**

4. Double-click chkOptions to open the Code window. Select the (General) (Declarations) section from the object and procedure drop-down lists. Add the following code:

    ```
    Public PeanutButter As Boolean
    Public Jelly As Boolean
    ```

5. Add the following code to the MouseUp event of chkOptions:

    ```
    Private Sub chkOptions_MouseUp(Button As Integer, _
    Shift As Integer, X As Single, Y As Single)

        frmOptions.Show vbModal

        If PeanutButter And Jelly Then
            chkOptions.Value = 1
            Exit Sub
        End If

        If PeanutButter Or Jelly Then
            chkOptions.Value = 2
            Exit Sub
        End If

        If Not PeanutButter And Not Jelly Then
            chkOptions.Value = 0
            Exit Sub
        End If
    End Sub
    ```

6. Right-click the Project Explorer and select Add ➤ Form from the pop-up menu. Select Form from the Add Form dialog box.

7. In the Properties window, set the Name property of the new form to **frm-Options**. Set its Caption property to **Set Options**.

8. Add a check box control to frmOptions. Set its Name property to **chkPeanut-Butter** and its Caption to **Peanut Butter**.

9. Add another check box control. Set its Name property to **chkJelly** and its Caption to **Jelly**.

10. Double-click frmOptions to open the Code window. Add the following code to the Load() event of the form:

```
Private Sub Form_Load()
    If frmMain.PeanutButter Then
        chkPeanutButter.Value = 1
    Else
        chkPeanutButter.Value = 0
    End If

    If frmMain.Jelly Then
        chkJelly.Value = 1
    Else
        chkJelly.Value = 0
    End If
End Sub
```

11. Add the following code to the Click() event of chkPeanutButter:

```
Private Sub chkPeanutButter_Click()
    If chkPeanutButter.Value = 1 Then
        frmMain.PeanutButter = True
    Else
        frmMain.PeanutButter = False
    End If
End Sub
```

12. Add the following code to the Click() event of chkJelly:

```
Private Sub chkJelly_Click()
    If chkJelly.Value = 1 Then
        frmMain.Jelly = True
    Else
            frmMain.Jelly = False
    End If
End Sub
```

13. Select Run ➤ Start to start your application.

Skill 3

If you click the check box on frmMain, you are presented with a dialog box offering you peanut butter and jelly. Some people like both, while others may like only one or the other. If you check both and close the dialog box, you will see the check box is solid. If you only select peanut butter or jelly, but not both, then the check box will be grayed. If you don't want either, the check box will be unchecked.

Using Frame Controls

When used by itself, the frame control (shown here) is not particularly useful. The controls normally placed in a frame are option buttons and check boxes. This has the effect of grouping them together so that when the frame is moved, the other controls move too. For this to work you can't double-click a control (say, an option button) to add it to the form, and then drag it into position within the frame. Instead, you must single-click the control in the Toolbox and drag a location for it inside the frame. Then all the controls move together.

In addition, the option buttons function as a group—that is, if you select one at run time, the others become deselected. If you simply scatter option buttons randomly on a form, then they all function as one large group. To create separate groupings of option buttons, you place them in frames. The button items within each frame act as a self-contained group and have no effect on the option buttons in other frame groups.

Although a frame is often used as a container for check box groups too, each check box is completely independent. Thus the setting for one check box has no effect on the setting for the others in the same group. This is the behavior you would expect of check boxes. Check boxes are not mutually exclusive. This contrasts with option buttons, where the buttons within a single group should be mutually exclusive. The reason then for placing check boxes in a frame is to enable you to move the group as a whole, when you reposition the frame at design time. The frame also serves as a visual grouping for the check boxes. For example, the check boxes relating to a particular feature can be in one frame and those pertinent to another feature in another frame.

A frame is usually given the prefix fra. You place the frame on the form before you place the controls it's going to contain.

Frame Properties

The frame control has several properties, listed below:

Appearance	**Enabled**	Height	Parent
BackColor	Font	HelpContextID	RightToLeft
BorderStyle	FontBold	hWnd	TabIndex
Caption	FontItalic	Index	Tag
Container	FontName	Left	ToolTipText
ClipControls	FontSize	MouseIcon	Top
Container	FontStrikethru	MousePointer	Visible
DragIcon	FontUnderline	**Name**	WhatsThisHelpID
DragMode	ForeColor	OLEDropMode	Width

After the Name property, perhaps the single most important property is Caption. You use this to give a meaningful title to the frame on the form. Then it's clear to the end user which feature the option buttons (or check boxes) in the frame refer to. To provide a clue as to how each option button affects the feature, you use the Caption property of the buttons. For example, in an order dispatch system you might have a frame with the caption Delivery. And within that frame you might have two option buttons, with the captions Normal and Express.

Frame Events

The frame control only supports a few events:

Click	MouseMove	OLEGiveFeedback
DblClick	MouseUp	OLESetData
DragDrop	OLECompleteDrag	OLEStartDrag
DragOver	OLEDragDrop	
MouseDown	OLEDragOver	

The frame control events are only rarely used. In an application that uses drag-and-drop, however, the DragDrop() event is sometimes used to initiate actions when the user drops an object into a frame area. Drag-and-drop is covered in Skill 11.

Frame Methods

A frame object supports only a few methods. None are very helpful and they're hardly ever seen in Visual Basic projects:

Drag	OLEDrag	ShowWhatsThis
Move	Refresh	ZOrder

As you can see in Figure 3.9, a frame control serves as a container for other controls. You can group option buttons to separate them from other groups, or you can group other controls to provide visual organization to your form. Set the Caption property of the frame to the description of the functionality that the contained controls provide. In this example, the Caption is set to Set the Insertion Point.

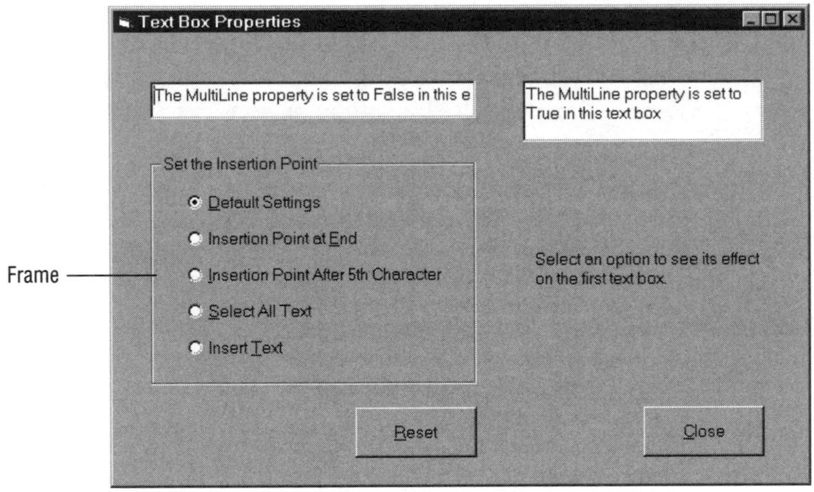

FIGURE 3.9: A frame control

Using List Boxes

If you're a regular user of Windows, then you're familiar with list box controls (shown here). A list box is an ideal way of presenting users with a list of data. Users can browse the data in the list box or select one or more items as the basis for further processing. The user can't edit the data in a list box directly—one way around this is to use a combo box instead; combo boxes are discussed next. When the list of data is too long for the list box, Visual Basic will add a vertical scrollbar. Let's examine most of the important list box control properties, events, and methods.

List Box Properties

Many of the list box properties are shared by a combo box control, and some of them are essential for getting the best from the control:

Appearance	FontBold	**List**	**Style**
BackColor	FontItalic	**ListCount**	TabIndex
CausesValidation	FontName	**ListIndex**	TabStop
Columns	FontSize	MouseIcon	Tag
Container	FontStrikethru	MousePointer	Text
DataChanged	FontUnderline	**MultiSelect**	ToolTipText
DataField	ForeColor	**Name**	Top
DataFormat	Height	**NewIndex**	TopIndex
DataMember	HelpContextID	OLEDragMode	Visible
DataSource	hWnd	Parent	WhatsThisHelpID
DragIcon	Index	RightToLeft	Width
DragMode	IntegralHeight	SelCount	
Enabled	ItemData	**Selected**	
Font	Left	**Sorted**	

The Columns property lets you create a multicolumn list box. Unfortunately, the columns are of the snaking, or newspaper, type. There's no direct support for the multiple columns of an Access-style list box where different data items are displayed in separate columns. Instead Visual Basic wraps the same type of data items from column to column.

TIP You can't have a true multiple-column list box in Visual Basic. One workaround is to concatenate (join) the different data items into one string and add that string to a single-column Visual Basic list box. To line up the columns, you can embed spaces or tab characters (Chr(9)) in the concatenated string. Alternatively, use fixed-length strings to hold the items to be concatenated. However, this does not work when you're using a proportional font.

The List property sets or returns the value of an item in the list. You use the index of the item with the List property. The index positions of items in a list box start at 0 (zero) and run to 1 less than the total number of items in a list. Thus, if you had 10 items in the list box, the index positions run from 0 to 9.

 NOTE   Don't confuse the index *position* in a list box with the Index *property* of a list box. The latter is displayed in the Properties window—the index position is not shown anywhere. The Index property is used when you create a control array of list boxes.

You use the List property to get the value of any item in the list. For example, to return the value of the third item in the list, use the following:

```
lstList1.List(2)
```

To get the value of the currently selected item in the list, simply use the Text property of the list box. The ListIndex property sets or returns the index position of the currently selected item—if no item is selected, the ListIndex property is -1.

 NOTE   lstList1.List(lstList1.ListIndex) and lstList1.Text are the same.

You can pick up the index position of the last item added to a list (see the Add-Item method shortly) with the NewIndex property. The ListCount property returns the number of items in a list box. Confusingly, this is always 1 greater than the value returned by the NewIndex property—this is because the index positions count from 0 (zero) while the ListCount property starts counting from 1 for the first item. ListCount returns 0 if the list box is empty.

The MultiSelect property determines whether the user can select one item or whether they can select more than one. List boxes support both a simple and an extended multiple selection. A simple multiple selection allows the user to select contiguous items—usually accomplished with the mouse and the Shift key. An extended multiple selection lets the user select contiguous and noncontiguous items—usually done by mouse clicks in conjunction with the Ctrl and/or Shift keys.

The Selected property is a Boolean property and is a run-time property only. A Boolean property is one that can take only a True or False setting. The following line preselects the third item in a list box:

```
lstList1.Selected(2) = True
```

Note the use of index position (2) to reference the *third* item in the list.

The final property that we're going to consider is the `Sorted` property. This is one of those properties that you can set only at design time. You can read it, or return it, at run time (that is, see if it's `True` or `False`) but you can't set it (that is, change an unsorted list into a sorted one or vice versa). When you set the `Sorted` property to `True` at design time, any items you add to a list box (typically, with the `AddItem` method) are sorted in alphabetical order. The sort can only be in ascending order and it's not case-sensitive.

List Box Events

The list box control supports a few events, shown here:

Click	KeyDown	MouseUp	OLEStartDrag
DblClick	KeyPress	OLECompleteDrag	Scroll
DragDrop	KeyUp	OLEDragDrop	Validate
DragOver	LostFocus	OLEDragOver	
GotFocus	MouseDown	OLEGiveFeedback	
ItemCheck	MouseMove	OLESetData	

Perhaps the most commonly used event for a list box is `DblClick()`. This coincides with the normal operation of list boxes in Windows applications. The first thing to do with a list box is usually to fill it with items for the list. The `AddItem` method can be used to do this (see "List Box Methods"). You can then, if you want, preselect one of the items in the list by setting the `Selected` property to `True`. The user either accepts the default selection or chooses another item with a single-click. Then clicking an OK command button carries out a process using the `Text` property, which returns the value of the selected item. However, a popular shortcut is to double-click the item in the list—that way, the user can both select an item and initiate a process based on that item in a single action. Many Windows applications adopt this technique to copy one item from a list box into another list box.

List Box Methods

The list box has many of its own methods, as well as some common to the other controls discussed so far:

AddItem	Move	SetFocus
Clear	Refresh	ShowWhatsThis
Drag	**RemoveItem**	ZOrder

There are three methods here worthy of note—AddItem, Clear, and Remove-Item. AddItem, as already indicated, is for adding items to a list box control. The RemoveItem method, as you might expect, removes items from a list box. To remove all the items in one fell swoop, use the Clear method.

An example of the simplest syntax for the AddItem method is:

```
lstList1.AddItem "Hello"
```

This adds the word "Hello" to the list box. Often you employ a number of AddItem methods, one after the other, to populate (fill in) a list box. Many developers place the AddItem methods in a Form_Load() event procedure so the list box is filling as the form loads. You can specify the position that an item will take in a list by specifying the index position:

```
lstList1.AddItem "Hello", 3
```

This places the text "Hello" at the *fourth* position in the list. If you omit the index position, the item is added to the end of the list—or if the Sorted property is set to True, the item is placed in the correct sorted order.

WARNING   Be careful when using the AddItem method with a specified index position in a sorted list box. The Sorted property automatically calculates the index position of added items. If the position you specify does not match the one generated by the Sorted property, then the results will be unpredictable.

Experimenting with List Box Controls

Now that you have read about what makes a list box work, try this example to see it in action:

1. Start a new project by selecting File ➤ New Project. Select Standard EXE from the Project Wizard.

2. Add two list box controls to Form1.

3. Place one list box on the upper half of the form, and the other on the lower half of the form. Size both list boxes until they are almost as wide as the form.

4. Double-click the form to open the Code window. Add the following code to the Load event:

```
Private Sub Form_Load()
    List1.AddItem "Nuts"
    List1.AddItem "Bolts"
```

```
            List1.AddItem "Nails"
            List1.AddItem "L-Brackets"
            List1.AddItem "Hammers"
            List1.AddItem "Saw"
            List1.AddItem "Drill"
            List1.AddItem "File"
            List1.AddItem "Sandpaper"
            List1.AddItem "Planer"
        End Sub
```

5. Add the following code to the DblClick() event of List1:

```
        Private Sub List1_DblClick()
            'Add the item to the other list
            List2.AddItem List1.Text

            'Remove the item from this list
            List1.RemoveItem List1.ListIndex
        End Sub
```

6. Add the following code to the DblClick() event of List2:

```
        Private Sub List2_DblClick()
            'Add the item to the other list
            List1.AddItem List2.Text

            'Remove the item from this list
            List2.RemoveItem List2.ListIndex
        End Sub
```

7. Finally, run the program by selecting Run ➤ Start.

You can double-click any product to move it to the opposite list box. If you look at the code in steps 5 and 6, you will notice the item is added to the other list box before it is removed from the current one. The AddItem must be called *before* the RemoveItem method because the AddItem needs to know what to add to the other list. If you call RemoveItem first, then the wrong list item will be added to the opposite list. You will learn more about lists in the next section.

Using Combo Boxes

The name combo box comes from "combination box"; the control is shown here. The idea is that a combo box combines the features of both a text box and a list box. A potential problem with list boxes—in some situations anyway— is that you're stuck with the entries displayed. You can't directly edit an item in the list or select an entry that's not already there. Of course, if you *want* to restrict the user, then a list box is fine in this respect. A combo box control (at least in two of its styles available in Visual Basic) allows you to select a predefined item from a list *or* to enter a new item not in the list. A combo box can also incorporate a drop-down section—that means it takes less room on a form than a normal list box. In all, there are three types of combo boxes to choose from at design time: a drop-down combo, a simple combo, and a drop-down list. You can specify the type by setting the Style property.

Apart from the Style property, the properties, events, and methods of combo boxes are very similar to those of list boxes, described shortly. However, the Text property is different. With a list box, the Text property returns the text of the currently selected item at run time. With a combo box, on the other hand, you can assign a value to the Text property at run time—in effect, you can set the text, even if the item is not already in the list. The results of choosing a different Style property are covered in the next section.

Note that the combo box discussed here is the built-in combo box control. There's also another combo box (DBCombo, or the data-bound combo box). This has a few more features that let you work with data from databases.

Combo Box Properties

These are the properties for the combo box control:

Appearance	FontItalic	**ListCount**	**Style**
BackColor	FontName	**ListIndex**	TabIndex
CausesValidation	FontSize	Locked	TabStop
Container	FontStrikethru	MouseIcon	Tag
DataChanged	FontUnderline	MousePointer	Text
DataField	ForeColor	**Name**	ToolTipText
DataFormat	Height	**NewIndex**	Top
DataMember	HelpContextID	OLEDragMode	TopIndex
DataSource	hWnd	Parent	Visible
DragIcon	Index	RightToLeft	WhatsThisHelpID
DragMode	IntegralHeight	**SelLength**	Width
Enabled	ItemData	**SelStart**	
Font	Left	**SelText**	
FontBold	**List**	Sorted	

The List, ListCount, ListIndex, NewIndex, and Sorted properties are identical to those for a list box. The property that's different, and that consists of one of the fundamentals of designing combo boxes, is the Style property. There are three settings for Style, and the behavior and appearance of the combo box are determined by the setting you choose. The styles are numbered from 0 to 2 and represent, in order, a drop-down combo, a simple combo, and a drop-down list:

- The drop-down combo looks like a standard text box with a drop-down arrow to the right. Clicking the arrow opens a list beneath the text box. The user has the choice of selecting an item from the list, which places it in the text box, or of entering their own text in the text box. In other words, this is the true combo box.

- The simple combo is a variation on this theme—the only difference being that the list is permanently displayed. This one's an option if your form is not too crowded.

- The final style, the drop-down list, is really a type of list box rather than a combo box. It looks identical to a drop-down combo but, as the name suggests, the user is confined to selecting a predefined item from the list. The advantage of this latter style is that it takes up less space than a conventional list box.

Combo Box Events

Here are the events for the combo box:

Change	**DropDown**	LostFocus	OLESetData
Click	GotFocus	OLECompleteDrag	OLEStartDrag
DblClick	KeyDown	OLEDragDrop	Scroll
DragDrop	KeyPress	OLEDragOver	Validate
DragOver	KeyUp	OLEGiveFeedback	

Most of the events for a combo box control are the standard ones. However, the DropDown() event is specific to combo boxes—though not supported by the simple combo box, which is already "dropped-down."

The Change() event is not supported by the drop-down list (style 2), because the user can't change the entry in the text box section. To see if that type of combo box has been accessed by the user, try the Click() or the DropDown() event procedures.

The DblClick() event is only relevant to the simple combo box, for it's the only one where the user can see the full list by default. Usually, the DblClick()

event procedure calls the `Click()` event for a command button. This means the user can simply double-click an item in the list, rather than using a single-click to select followed by a click on a command button to carry out some processing based on the user selection.

Combo Box Methods

The methods you can apply to a combo box control are the same as those for a list box:

AddItem	Move	**RemoveItem**	ZOrder
Clear	OLEDrag	SetFocus	
Drag	Refresh	ShowWhatsThis	

Again, the important methods are `AddItem`, `Clear`, and `RemoveItem`. And, just as with a list box control, it's common practice to populate a combo box with a series of `AddItem` methods in the `Load` event of a form.

Incidentally, especially if you've worked with the database application Microsoft Access, you may be wondering about the flexibility of list and combo boxes. What do you do if the predetermined items in the list continually change? Do you continually have to re-code the `AddItem` methods? How can you do this anyway in a stand-alone `.EXE` you generate from your project? Another concern of yours could be regarding the actual tedium of typing long series of `AddItem` methods.

All of these questions are easily resolved if you exploit the `RowSource` and `ListField` properties of a data-bound list or data-bound combo box. Even more flexibility is provided by these data-bound versions of those two controls (DBList and DBCombo). For more information on these and other data-bound controls, consult the Microsoft Developer Network online help.

Often you want the user first to select an item from a list box and then to click a command button. The button initiates an action using the selected item. An accepted alternative is for the user to simply double-click the item in the list. This both selects the item and carries out the action. To do this, you can call the button's `Click()` event procedure from the list box's `DblClick()` event procedure, as shown below:

```
Private Sub cboItems_DblClick()
    cmdAdd_Click
End Sub
```

The code listed below populates the list and combo boxes in Figure 3.10. The following example will show you the difference between a list and a combo box by simulating a grocery list. In the list I added some fruits. The combo box lists different types of bread. Because I obviously haven't covered all of the different types of bread, you can type another kind of bread in the combo box to add it to your list.

```
Private Sub Form_Load()
    'Add items to list box
    lstItems.AddItem "Apples"
    lstItems.AddItem "Oranges"
    lstItems.AddItem "Grapes"
    lstItems.AddItem "Tangerines"
    lstItems.AddItem "Lemons"
    lstItems.AddItem "Bananas"

    'Add items to combo box
    cboCombination.AddItem "Wheat"
    cboCombination.AddItem "White"
    cboCombination.AddItem "Rye"
    cboCombination.AddItem "Sourdough"
    cboCombination.AddItem "French"
    cboCombination.AddItem "Pita"
End Sub
```

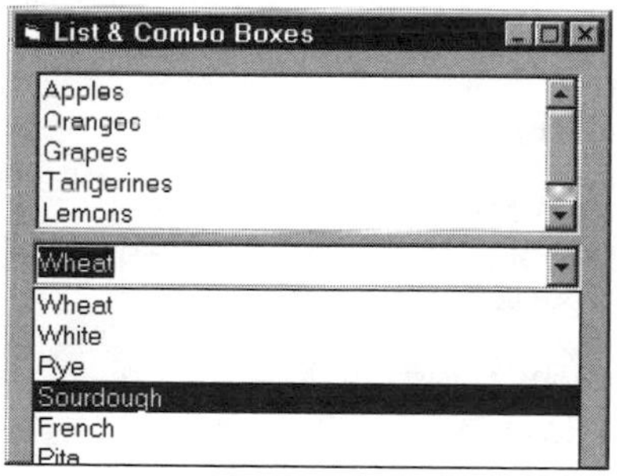

FIGURE 3.10:   The list and combo box

Experimenting with List and Combo Box Controls

Let's modify this form to function like a grocery list. You code the form to allow you to select items from the combo box and add them to your grocery list box.

1. Start a new project and add one list box to a form and set its Name to **lstGroceries**.

2. Add a combo box below the list box and set its Name to **cboProducts**.

3. Add two labels to a form. Place the first label above the list box and set its Caption property to **Grocery List**.

4. Place the second label between the list box and the combo box. Set its Caption to **Store Items**.

5. Add a command button to the bottom center of the form. Set its Name property to **cmdAdd**, and its Caption to **&Add**.

6. Modify the Form_Load() event as follows:

```
Private Sub Form_Load()
    'Clear the list box
    lstGroceries.Clear

    'add items to combo box
    cboProducts.AddItem "Wheat"
    cboProducts.AddItem "Cereal"
    cboProducts.AddItem "Steak"
    cboProducts.AddItem "Pasta"
    cboProducts.AddItem "Candy"
    cboProducts.AddItem "Soda"
End Sub
```

7. Add the following code to the cmdAdd_Click() event:

```
Private Sub cmdAdd_Click()
    lstGroceries.AddItem cboProducts.Text
End Sub
```

8. Run the program. You can select a product from the combo box. If you want to add it to the grocery list, click the Add button.

9. Notice that this store doesn't carry any ice cream. You can type this in the combo box and click the Add button. The store will have to special order it for you.

 TIP To call the event procedure for another control, you type the name of the procedure, as in cmdListAdd_Click. But to initiate a command button's Click() event there's an alternative method. You can set the Value property of the button to True, as in cmdListAdd.Value = True.

Using Image Objects

The image control (its prefix is often img) is a lightweight equivalent of the picture box control, which is described in a later section. But unlike the picture control, the image control can't act as a container for other objects. In some of its other properties it's not as versatile, but it's a good choice if you simply want to display a picture on a form. Image controls consume far less memory than picture controls.

The image control that comes with Visual Basic can now display bitmap (.BMP), icon (.ICO), metafile (.WMF), JPEG (.JPG), and GIF (.GIF) files. This makes it easier to display graphics from the World Wide Web, as well as graphics from other popular graphics program.

Image Properties

The image control utilizes several properties, but fewer than the picture box, discussed later.

Appearance	DragIcon	MousePointer	Tag
BorderStyle	DragMode	**Name**	Top
Container	Enabled	OLEDragMode	Visible
DataField	Height	OLEDropMode	WhatsThisHelpID
DataFormat	Index	Parent	Width
DataMember	Left	**Picture**	
DataSource	MouseIcon	**Stretch**	

As with most other graphical controls, you add the graphic by setting the Picture property. Perhaps the most interesting property here is Stretch. This is a Boolean property—meaning it takes only the values True or False. When Stretch is set to False (the default), the control resizes to the size of the picture placed inside it. If you later resize the control, then the loaded picture either is cropped or has empty space showing around it, or both, depending on the relative directions of horizontal and vertical resizing. But if you set Stretch to True, the picture resizes with the control. Thus you can make the enclosed picture larger or smaller, or fatter or thinner, by resizing the control after the picture is loaded. A picture control has no Stretch property. Its nearest equivalent is the AutoSize property. When AutoSize is set to True for a picture box, then the control adapts to the size of the loaded picture. However, unlike an image control with `Stretch` turned on, if the picture box is resized the enclosed picture remains the same—the picture does not "stretch" with the picture box control.

Image Events

The image control doesn't use many events, and of those, you may only use a few if any.

Click	MouseDown	OLEDragDrop	OLEStartDrag
DblClick	MouseMove	OLEDragOver	
DragDrop	MouseUp	OLEGiveFeedback	
DragOver	OLECompleteDrag	OLESetData	

Image controls are sometimes handy as drag-and-drop destinations. This is because you can have a picture inside that gives an indication of the results of dropping onto the control. Drag-and-drop is discussed later in Skill 11.

Image Methods

The following are properties of an image control:

Drag	OLEDrag	ShowWhatsThis
Move	Refresh	ZOrder

You will most likely not use any of these methods in your applications.

TIP   There's a catalog of bundled icons included with your Visual Basic documentation. They can be found in the \Graphics\Icons subdirectory of Visual Basic as well as on the CD.

Experimenting with Image Controls

Let's take a look at some image controls in action.

1. Open the Controls project from earlier in the \MSDN98\98vs\1033\Samples\VB98\Controls subdirectory.

2. Run the program and click the Images button.

As you can see in Figure 3.11, you can click one of the four card icons and the program will notify you that it is selected. The code listed below is fairly straight-forward.

FIGURE 3.11:   The image control

```
Private Sub imgClub_Click()
    shpCard.Left = imgClub.Left
    picStatus.Cls
    picStatus.Print "Selected: Club"
End Sub

Private Sub imgDiamond_Click()
    shpCard.Left = imgDiamond.Left
    picStatus.Cls
    picStatus.Print "Selected: Diamond"
End Sub

Private Sub imgHeart_Click()
    shpCard.Left = imgHeart.Left
    picStatus.Cls
    picStatus.Print "Selected: Heart"
End Sub

Private Sub imgSpade_Click()
    shpCard.Left = imgSpade.Left
    picStatus.Cls
    picStatus.Print "Selected: Spade"
End Sub
```

The card outline is actually a shape control that is moved off the left side of the form. This is done in the Form's Load() event by setting the shape's Left property to -500. This achieves the same results as hiding a control by setting its Visible property to False.

Using Picture Boxes

As you might expect, picture boxes (shown here) often display graphics (for example, bitmaps, icons, JPEGs, and GIFs). In this role, picture boxes are similar to image controls. However, picture boxes and images have slightly different properties and therefore behave differently. If you just want to show a picture, then an image control is usually a better choice than a picture box. An image control takes up less memory and is a lightweight version of the picture box control. However, if you want to move the graphic around the form, a picture box produces a smoother display. In addition, you can create text and use graphics methods in a picture box at run time. The graphics methods enable you to draw lines, circles, and rectangles at run time. But, most importantly for this application, picture boxes can act as containers for other controls. Thus, you can place a command button within a picture box. In this respect, picture boxes function as "forms within forms."

Picture Box Properties

The table below lists the properties for the picture box control. Notice that there are many more properties for this control than there are for the image control.

Align	FillStyle	MousePointer
Appearance	Font	**Name**
AutoRedraw	FontBold	OLEDragMode
AutoSize	FontItalic	OLEDropMode
BackColor	FontName	Parent
BorderStyle	FontSize	**Picture**
CausesValidation	FontStrikethru	RightToLeft
ClipControls	FontTransparent	ScaleHeight
Container	FontUnderline	ScaleLeft
CurrentX	ForeColor	ScaleMode
CurrentY	HasDC	ScaleTop
DataChanged	hDC	ScaleWidth
DataField	Height	TabIndex
DataFormat	HelpContextID	TabStop
DataMember	hWnd	Tag

DataSource	**Image**	ToolTipText
DragIcon	Index	Top
DragMode	Left	Visible
DrawMode	LinkItem	WhatsThisHelpID
DrawStyle	LinkMode	Width
DrawWidth	LinkTimeout	
Enabled	LinkTopic	
FillColor	MouseIcon	

Quite a lot of properties this time! When you put a picture into a picture box, it appears at its normal size. If it's too big for the picture box, the graphic is clipped. Setting the AutoSize property to True causes the picture box to resize to match the size of the graphic. The graphic displayed in the picture box is determined by the Picture property—you can change this property at both design time and run time. There's a similar-sounding property—the Image property. This one's only available at run time, and it's used to make a copy from one picture box to another. The syntax for doing this is:

```
Picture2.Picture = Picture1.Image
```

You can place this line of code in any event where it is relevant. For example, maybe you want to change the picture in a picture box when the user selects a different record in a database.

The line above places a copy (image) of the picture in the first picture box into the second picture box (using its Picture property). You can even change the picture directly at run time. The syntax is:

```
Picture1.Picture = LoadPicture ("filename")
```

To empty a picture box, use the Visual Basic LoadPicture function with no parameter:

```
Picture1.Picture = LoadPicture()
```

Picture Box Events

The picture box events are listed in the following table:

Change	KeyPress	MouseDown	OLESetData
Click	KeyUp	MouseMove	OLEStartDrag
DblClick	LinkClose	MouseUp	Paint

DragDrop	LinkError	OLECompleteDrag	Resize
DragOver	LinkNotify	OLEDragDrop	Validate
GotFocus	LinkOpen	OLEDragOver	
KeyDown	LostFocus	OLEGiveFeedback	

Two of the popular events for picture boxes are the Click() and DragDrop() events. The Click() event is, with any luck, self-explanatory by now. The Drag-Drop() event is discussed in detail in Skill 11, later in the book.

Picture Box Methods

The picture box control supports more methods than its counterpart, the image box. The most important ones are listed in boldface in the following table:

Circle	LinkRequest	**PSet**	TextHeight
Cls	LinkSend	Refresh	TextWidth
Drag	Move	ScaleX	**ZOrder**
Line	OLEDrag	ScaleY	
LinkExecute	**PaintPicture**	SetFocus	
LinkPoke	Point	ShowWhatsThis	

The Circle, Cls, Line, PaintPicture, and PSet methods are all used when drawing graphics or text in the picture box at run time—Cls (like the old DOS command for "clear screen") is actually used to erase entries. The ZOrder method is the run-time equivalent of Format ➤ Order ➤ Bring to Front or Format ➤ Order ➤ Send to Back. You can use ZOrder to determine which controls overlap other controls. However, you should be aware that there are three layers on a form—ZOrder only works within the layer that contains the control. All the non-graphical controls except labels (for example, command buttons) belong to the top layer. Picture boxes and other graphical controls (as well as labels) belong to the middle layer. The bottom layer contains the results of the graphics methods—for instance, a circle drawn with the Circle method is on the bottom layer. This contrasts with a circle drawn with the Shape control, which is in the middle layer. What all this means is that you can't position a picture box over a command button with ZOrder—the picture box is permanently relegated to the layer behind. The ZOrder method is for rearranging objects *within* one layer.

NOTE   ZOrder determines the relative positions of objects within the same layer or level of a form. In design view, use Format ➤ Order ➤ Bring to Front, or Format ➤ Order ➤ Send to Back to change relative positions. At run time you can use the ZOrder method.

Using Timers

The timer control (shown here) is one of the few controls always hidden at run time. This means you don't have to find room for it on a form—it can go anywhere, even on top of existing controls. The timer basically does just one thing: It checks the system clock and acts accordingly.

Timer Properties

The timer control does not have many properties, as you can see in this table:

Enabled	Left	Tag
Index	**Name**	Top
Interval	Parent	

Apart from the Name property (a tmr prefix is recommended), there are only two important properties for the timer control—the Enabled property and the Interval property. Indeed, you have to set these properties to get the timer to do anything at all (assuming the Enabled property is at its default, True). The Left and Top properties are virtually superfluous—it makes little difference where you put a timer on a form.

The Interval property is measured in milliseconds. This means if you want to count seconds, you have to multiply the number of seconds by 1,000. Once an interval has elapsed (provided the timer is enabled), the timer generates its own Timer event. It does this by checking the system clock at frequent intervals.

TIP   The Interval property is measured in milliseconds. If you want to count the number of seconds elapsed, you have to set the Interval property to the number of seconds multiplied by 1,000. Keeping this in mind, the Interval property is limited to values between 0 (the timer is disabled) and 65,535 (65.5 seconds).

The Timer Event

The timer control has only one event called, appropriately, a `Timer()` event. As already stated, this event takes place every time an interval elapses. The interval is determined by the `Interval` property. To stop the `Timer()` event from occurring, you can set the timer's `Enabled` property to `False` at run time.

Timer Methods

The timer control does not support any methods at all.

Experimenting with a Timer Control

To give you an idea of how the timer works, let's create a Caption Bar clock:

1. Start a new project by selecting File ➤ New project. Select Standard EXE as the project type.

2. Set the `Name` property of Form1 to **frmMain**. Set its `Caption` property to **Application Time**.

3. Add a timer to the frmMain. Set its `Name` property to **tmrTimer**.

4. Set the timer's `Interval` property to **500**. We want to have the clock check itself every half-second. We do this because the timer control is not as precise as other timer-type controls, but it will perform well for this example.

5. Add the following code to the `(General)(Declarations)` procedure for frmMain:

    ```
    Option Explicit
    Private OldCaption As String
    ```

6. Add the following code to the `Form_Load()` event:

    ```
    Private Sub Form_Load()
        OldCaption = Me.Caption
    End Sub
    ```

7. Now add the following code to the `Timer()` event of the timer:

    ```
    Private Sub tmrTimer_Timer()
        Dim msg As String

        msg = OldCaption & ": " & Time$
        Caption = msg
    End Sub
    ```

8. Save and run the application by selecting Run ≻ Start. Your Caption Bar clock should now look like Figure 3.12.

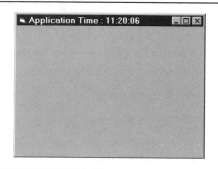

FIGURE 3.12:   The Caption Bar clock

You may notice that the caption flickers a bit. You can minimize this by changing the code in the `Timer()` event to minimize the number of refreshes to the Caption:

```
Private Sub tmrTimer_Timer()
    Dim msg As String

    msg = OldCaption & ": " & Time$
    If msg <> Caption Then
        Caption = msg
    End If
End Sub
```

The `If...Then` statement checks to see if the time, returned through `Time$`, has changed. If the `msg` string is different than `Caption`, then you update the `Caption` property to reflect the time change. Otherwise you do nothing to cause a refresh on the `Caption`. The flicker will go away.

> **TIP**   You can use the `Format` function to change the format of the display. `Format` accepts many named parameters as well as ones you define yourself. You can use the function to format the display of numbers and strings—it's not just confined to date and time. To see some of the possibilities, search the Microsoft Developer Network help for the `Format` function. Once you reach the topic entitled *Format Function*, click the See Also pop-up text at the top of the window.

Using Scroll Bars

A scroll bar control (shown here) on a form is not to be confused with a scroll bar on a large text box or list box. The scroll bar controls are completely independent objects that exist without reference to any other control (this is not the case with large text boxes or list boxes). The horizontal scroll bar and the vertical scroll bar are identical except for their orientation. Both controls share the same properties, events, and methods. When the term "scroll bar" is used in this section it means both the horizontal scroll bar and the vertical scroll bar.

A scroll bar control is typically employed to increase or decrease a value. For example, you may want to change a color setting, a number, or the volume of a digital audio device. The scroll bar acts as a sliding scale with a starting point and an ending point, including all the values in between. If you simply want to increment or decrement a number, then you should also take a look at the spin button custom control.

One problem with a scroll bar is that once it is used it retains the focus and may flicker on screen. To circumvent this you can change the focus to another control.

TIP To avoid scroll bar flicker, add a SetFocus method on another control as the last statement in the scroll bar control's Change event procedure.

Scroll Bar Properties

The scroll bar control has a few properties worth noting:

CausesValidation	hWnd	MousePointer	Tag
Container	Index	**Name**	Top
DragIcon	**LargeChange**	Parent	**Value**
DragMode	Left	RightToLeft	Visible
Enabled	**Max**	**SmallChange**	WhatsThisHelpID
Height	**Min**	TabIndex	Width
HelpContextID	MouseIcon	TabStop	

The most useful scroll bar properties are the Max, Min, LargeChange, and SmallChange properties. The Min and Max properties determine the limits for the Value property of the scroll bar. You can set the Min property to the lowest value allowed, for example 0. Then you would set Max to the maximum allowed value. For example, the following code could be used to define the lowest and highest volume allowed by your application:

```
Private Sub Form_Load()
    hscVolume.Min = 0      'The lowest volume
    hscVolume.Max = 255    'The maximum volume
End Sub
```

The LargeChange property determines how much the Value property changes when the user clicks in the scroll bar. The SmallChange property sets the amount the Value property changes when the user clicks one of the scroll arrows at either end of the scroll bar. You don't have to worry about the direction of the change, only the amount; Visual Basic figures out whether it's an increase or decrease, depending on where you click. There is no property setting to correspond to the user dragging the scroll box (also called *thumb* or *elevator*) within the scroll bar. This is because there's no way of predicting how far the scroll box will be dragged. However, it automatically updates the Value property. You can ascertain the new Value in the Change event procedure for the scroll bar. The Value property can also be set at design time to place the scroll box at a certain point within the scroll bar. For example, if you wanted the volume in the previous example to be set half way, you would use the following code:

```
Private Sub Form_Load()
    hscVolume.Min = 0      'The lowest volume
    hscVolume.Max = 255    'The maximum volume
    hscVolume.Value = 128  'Set the volume half way
End Sub
```

The Value, LargeChange, and SmallChange property settings must lie within the range dictated by the Min and Max properties. Value is usually set equal to Min or Max so the scroll box is at one end of the scroll bar. LargeChange is ordinarily some integral multiple of SmallChange. Max can be less than Min, which is often counter-intuitive. Max and Min, or both, can also be negative.

Scroll Bar Events

This is the list of events supported by the horizontal and vertical scroll bars:

Change	GotFocus	KeyUp	Validate
DragDrop	KeyDown	LostFocus	
DragOver	KeyPress	**Scroll**	

There are two vital events here—Change() and Scroll(). The Change() event occurs whenever the Value property of the scroll bar is altered at run time. The Value property, in turn, is changed whenever the user clicks a scroll arrow (Small-Change), clicks in the scroll bar to one side of the scroll box (LargeChange), or stops dragging the scroll box along the scroll bar. The latter induces a Value change depending on the length of the drag—though the Value change can never be greater than the difference between the Min and Max properties.

Although the Change() event is generated when the user stops dragging the scroll box, it does not occur during the drag. If you want to generate the Change() event *as the user drags,* then you must call it from the Scroll() event. The Scroll() event is continually triggered as the user drags the scroll box. By calling the Change() event from the Scroll() event, you can continually generate a Change() event. If you don't, you have to wait until the user stops dragging to ascertain the results of the action. On the other hand, any kind of click on the scroll bar produces an immediate Change() event.

Scroll Bar Methods

The following scroll bar methods are not terribly important and are rarely beneficial.

Drag	Refresh	ShowWhatsThis
Move	SetFocus	Zorder

Experimenting with Scroll Bar Controls

To see how a scroll bar works by adding a horizontal scroll bar to a project, follow these steps:

1. Start a new project by selecting File ➢ New Project.

2. Add a horizontal scroll bar to Form1 and set its Name property to **hscVolume** in the Properties window.

3. Set the Min property of hscVolume to **0**. Set its Max property to **100**. Set its Value property to **50**.

4. Set the SmallChange property to **1**, and the LargeChange property to **10**.

5. Add a label control to the top of the form and set its Name property to **lblVolume**. Set its Caption to **50**.

6. Click Font in the Properties window to set the Font Size property of the label to **24**.

7. Set the AutoSize property of the label to True. Center the control on the form above the scroll bar.

Your form should now look similar to Figure 3.13.

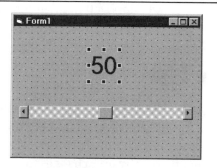

FIGURE 3.13:   The scroll bar demo

8. Double-click the scroll bar to open the Code window.

9. Add the following code to the Change() event of the scroll bar:

```
Private Sub hscVolume_Change()
    lblVolume.Caption = Trim$(Str$(hscVolume.Value))
End Sub
```

10. Finally, select Run ➢ Start.

The program is very simple. It just displays the volume setting, which you control by moving the slider within the scroll bar. You can move it by clicking either of the direction arrows, by dragging the slider, or by clicking between the slider and an arrow.

Perhaps the parts of the program that deserve the most attention are the Trim$ and Str$ functions. First, the Str$ function is used to convert a numeric value to a string. You need to make this conversion because the Caption of lblVolume expects either a string or a variant. However, the Value property of the scroll bar is an integer. So, the value returned by the function:

```
Str$(hscVolume)
```

will be suitable for the Caption property. The Trim$ function trims the leading and trailing spaces from a string. When you convert a number to a string, the string result will contain leading spaces. So to keep the formatting neat, you can use the combination:

```
Trim$(Str$(hscVolume))
```

If this were a true volume control applet, you would put code that would call the volume control application programming interface (API), and set the volume this way.

Using Drive Lists

The drive list box control (or just *drive*), which is shown here, is normally used in conjunction with the directory list and the file list controls. At its most fundamental, these three controls allow the user to select a file in a particular directory on a particular drive. The user changes to another drive via the drive control. They switch directories with the directory control, and they select the file from the file control. You can also use the drive and directory controls to let the user choose a destination for a file they wish to save. Although a common dialog control is better suited for retrieving filenames, we will look at these three controls in the following sections. You will be able to find other uses for them as you develop your skills.

Drive List Box Properties

The following table lists the many properties for the drive list box control:

Appearance	FontItalic	List	Tag
BackColor	FontName	ListCount	ToolTipText
CausesValidation	FontSize	ListIndex	Top
Container	FontUnderline	MouseIcon	TopIndex
DragIcon	ForeColor	MousePointer	Visible
DragMode	Height	**Name**	WhatsThisHelpID
Drive	HelpContextID	OLEDropMode	Width
Enabled	hWnd	Parent	
Font	Index	TabIndex	
FontBold	Left	TabStop	

For the Name property a drv prefix is normally adopted. Apart from the Name, the single most important property is Drive. This is a run-time property only, which is used to return the drive the user has selected in the drive control. Your application could retrieve this value and use it to synchronize the directory for file list controls explained later. The Drive property is invariably accessed in the Change event procedure for the drive control (see the next section).

Drive List Box Events

The drive list box has a few events, but few are useful to the beginning programmer.

Change	KeyDown	OLECompleteDrag	OLESetData
DragDrop	KeyPress	OLEDragDrop	OLEStartDrag
DragOver	KeyUp	OLEDragOver	Scroll
GotFocus	LostFocus	OLEGiveFeedback	Validate

The Change() event is the most popular event to trap. It is triggered whenever the user makes a selection of a drive in the drive control. The Drive property of the control is used to update the display of directories in the directory list control. Thus, the directories shown are always those on the currently selected drive. A fuller discussion of how to do this appears under the section on the file control, which follows shortly.

Drive List Box Methods

Below is the list of methods for this control.

Drag	OLEDrag	SetFocus	ZOrder
Move	Refresh	ShowWhatsThis	

These methods are rarely used.

Using Directory List Boxes

As already stated, the directory list box (or simply *directory*) control, which is shown here, is used in conjunction with the drive control, described earlier, and file control. The user can select a directory on the current drive from the directory list. However, it's important to update the directories displayed when the user changes drives in the drive control. It is also important to update the files shown in a file control, too. To do these, the directory's Path property and Change() event are used.

Directory List Box Properties

The following are the directory list box properties:

Appearance	FontName	List	TabIndex
BackColor	FontSize	ListCount	TabStop
CausesValidation	FontStrikethru	ListIndex	Tag
Container	FontUnderline	MouseIcon	ToolTipText
DragIcon	ForeColor	MousePointer	Top
DragMode	Height	**Name**	TopIndex
Enabled	HelpContextID	OLEDragMode	Visible
Font	hWnd	OLEDropMode	WhatsThisHelpID
FontBold	Index	Parent	Width
FontItalic	Left	**Path**	

A directory control is often given a Name property with a dir prefix. The Path property is a run-time property that sets or returns the path to the directory in the directory list. It's usually accessed in the Change event for the *drive* control—where it updates the list of directories to match the drive selected by the user. The Path property is also used in the *directory* control's Change event procedure to update the list of files in a file control when the user changes directories or drives.

Directory List Box Events

The table below shows the events used by the directory list box.

Change	GotFocus	LostFocus	OLECompleteDrag
Click	KeyDown	MouseDown	OLEDragDrop
DragDrop	KeyUp	OLEDragOver	OLEStartDrag
DragOver	MouseMove	OLEGiveFeedback	Scroll
KeyPress	MouseUp	OLESetData	Validate

Although you may use the Click() event in your code, the Change() event procedure is where you will place code to update the files in a file list control.

Directory List Box Methods

You probably won't be working with the following directory list box methods too often:

Drag	OLEDrag	SetFocus	ZOrder
Move	Refresh	ShowWhatsThis	

Using File List Boxes

The File List Box control (shown here) comes at the end of the drive-directory-file chain. It is used to list the actual filenames that are in the directory specified by the Path property, as shown in Figure 3.14.

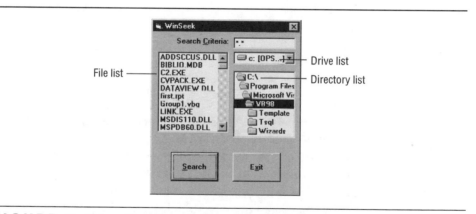

FIGURE 3.14:   The drive, directory, and file list controls

To reiterate, the file control should be updated in the directory Change() event. The directory control itself is updated when the user selects a directory in the directory control—it's also updated when the user selects a new drive in the drive control. For these links to work you must code *two* Change() event procedures correctly (this is explained in the example coming up in the next section).

File List Box Properties

File list boxes have a lot of properties—and many of them quite valuable:

Appearance	FontName	ListCount	ReadOnly
Archive	FontSize	ListIndex	**Selected**
BackColor	FontStrikethru	MouseIcon	**System**
CausesValidation	FontUnderline	MousePointer	TabIndex
Container	ForeColor	MultiSelect	TabStop
DragIcon	Height	**Name**	Tag
DragMode	HelpContextID	**Normal**	ToolTipText
Enabled	**Hidden**	OLEDragMode	Top
FileName	hWnd	OLEDropMode	TopIndex
Font	Index	Parent	Visible
FontBold	Left	**Path**	WhatsThisHelpID
FontItalic	List	**Pattern**	Width

Let's concentrate on just a few. The Path property is vitally important. It's a run-time property and is often both set and returned. When the Path property is returned, Visual Basic is aware of the path to the currently selected file in the file control. To ascertain the path and the filename together (sometimes called a *fully qualified path*), you have to concatenate the Path property with the FileName property. The fully qualified path can then be used as a basis for opening files.

Saving files is not quite so straightforward—you'll also need to provide a text box for the user to enter a new filename rather than writing over the selected file. An alternative approach is to generate the filename for a saved file automatically and use the controls to determine only the drive and directory for the file. In that case, you might want to disable the file control by setting its Enabled property to False, or make it invisible by setting its Visible property to False.

The Path is set in response to the user changing the drive (in a drive control) or the directory (in a directory control). You must code the series of possible events correctly for this to work. The following steps give you an idea of how this works:

1. In the Drive1_Change() event, you would add a line like this:

    ```
    Dir1.Path = Drive1.Drive
    ```

    This line updates the directory list to reflect the selected drive. The fact that the directory Path property changes in code generates a Change() event for the directory control as well. And the same event is generated if the user manually changes directories in the directory control.

2. You now code the Change() event for the directory as follows:

```
File1.Path = Dir1.Path
```

This ensures that the files displayed (governed by the file control's Path property) reflect both the currently selected drive and the directory. Changing a drive automatically selects a new directory.

The Pattern property can be set at design time—it can also be changed at run time. By default the Pattern property is *.*, which shows all files in the file control. You can narrow down the list of files by providing a suitable filter, for example, *.txt to display just your text files.

The Archive, Hidden, Normal, ReadOnly, and System properties can all be used to further narrow or expand the list of files. Hidden and System are False by default—ideally, you wouldn't want the end user even to be aware that hidden and system files exist.

TIP   If you're designing a project for a system administrator or a network manager, you may want the hidden and system files to be visible. To do this, set the Hidden and System properties to True.

By using the above code, you will also synchronize the controls when the application begins.

File List Box Events

This is the list of events supported by the File List Box control.

Click	KeyPress	OLECompleteDrag	**PathChange**
DblClick	KeyUp	OLEDragDrop	**PatternChange**
DragDrop	LostFocus	OLEDragOver	Scroll
DragOver	MouseDown	OLEGiveFeedback	Validate
GotFocus	MouseMove	OLESetData	
KeyDown	MouseUp	OLEStartDrag	

In a sense, the events for a file list control are similar to those of an ordinary list box. The standard approach is to have a command button's Click() event procedure carry out some processing based on the Path and FileName properties of the file control. However, it's often helpful to give the user a double-click alternative. The way to do this, if you recall from an earlier discussion on list boxes, is to code the file control's DblClick() event procedure to call the command button's Click() event.

Two events that are specific to a file control are PathChange() and Pattern-Change(). The PathChange() event occurs when the file's Path property alters. Similarly, the PatternChange() event occurs when the Pattern property is changed in code. It's common practice to let the user enter a pattern in a text box and set the Pattern property to the value of the Text property of the text box at run time. You can then use the PatternChange() event procedure to reset the Pattern if the user has entered a pattern that might be dangerous, for example, *.ini.

File List Box Methods

This control only supports a few methods, listed in the table below. None of them are particularly useful for the operation of the control.

Drag	OLEDrag	SetFocus	ZOrder
Move	Refresh	ShowWhatsThis	

Experimenting with File List Box Controls

To get a look at the Drive, Directory, and File List Box controls in action, let's experiment with the WinSeek.vbp sample project. This program will simply search the current drive and directory for files matching a file specification, such as an .AVI extension (see Figure 3.15).

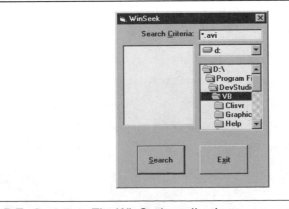

FIGURE 3.15: The WinSeek application

1. Load and run the WinSeek project by double-clicking WinSeek.vbp in the \MSDN98\98vs\1033\Samples\VB98\FileCtls\ subdirectoy.

2. Set the drive list control to C: if it has not defaulted to it already.

3. Set the directory list box to the root directory of the drive. You should be in the C:\ directory.

4. In the Search Criteria field, type a file specification (filespec) of a file type you want to search for, such as ***.AVI**. By entering an asterisk, the program will find any filename that ends with the .AVI extension.

5. Click the Search button and watch WinSeek find matching files. You will see search results similar to those in Figure 3.16.

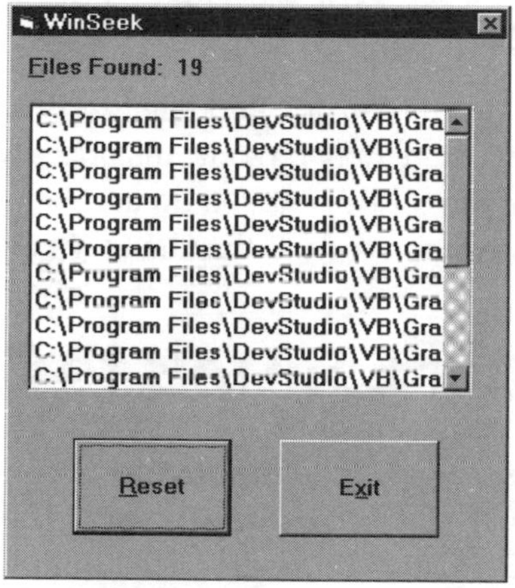

FIGURE 3.16: The WinSeek results

When you are done experimenting with the WinSeek application, stop it by selecting Run ➤ End from the Visual Basic menu. Double-click WinSeek to open its Code window. The procedures you want to examine are the Change() events for drvList and dirList. Let's start by looking at the drvList_Change() event:

```
Private Sub DrvList_Change()
    On Error GoTo DriveHandler
    dirList.Path = drvList.Drive
    Exit Sub

DriveHandler:
    drvList.Drive = dirList.Path
    Exit Sub
End Sub
```

The first thing you will notice is the On Error statement. The procedure calls an error-trapping routine because the drive list box is the most likely of the three controls to cause an error. The reason is the user could select a floppy drive that has no disk in it, which would cause an error. By trapping this error, the program can resume gracefully.

Also notice that this event triggers a Change() event in the directory list by setting the Path property. This, in turn, triggers a Change() event in the file list box. It is sort of like the domino theory. You trigger one event and it will trigger the next object and so on down the line. As you can see below, the directory list Change() event modifies the path of the file list box.

```
Private Sub DirList_Change()
    ' Update the file list box to synchronize with the directory list
    ' box.
    filList.Path = dirList.Path
End Sub
```

The Drive, Directory, and File List Box controls are almost always used together. However, there may be some instances where you will only need the functionality of one of the controls. If you do use them all together, you will place the relevant synchronization code in the Change() event of each control.

Adding Other Controls to the Toolbox

Before we move on to the next set of controls, you will need to learn how to add additional controls to your Toolbox. There are many more controls included with Visual Basic than those described in this skill. As you move through this book, you will continually learn more about these controls as well as the others not covered here.

You can add other controls by following a few simple steps:

- Add a tab to the Toolbox to keep it neat.

- Select the controls to add.

- Move them to the appropriate tab if necessary.

To teach you how to add controls to the Toolbox, let's add the controls used in the next sections.

1. Right-click the Toolbox to display its pop-up menu.

2. Select Add Tab from the pop-up menu.

3. When prompted for the tab name, type in **Common Controls** and click the OK button.

4. Now that the Common Controls tab has been added to the Toolbox, click it to make it the active tab.

5. Right-click the Toolbox and select Components from the pop-up menu.

6. From the Controls tab on the Components dialog box, click the check box next to Microsoft Windows Common Controls 6.0, as in Figure 3.17.

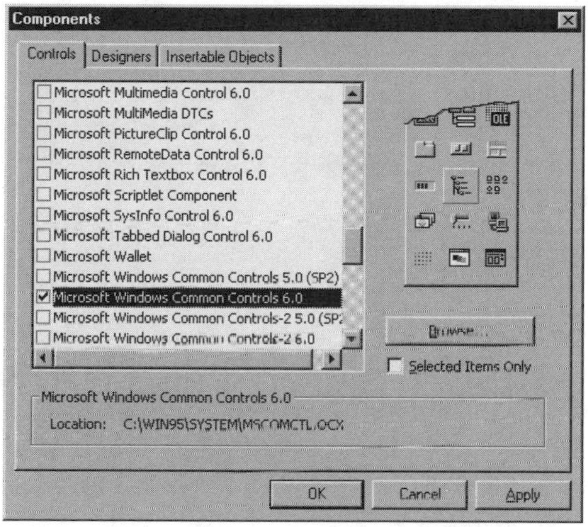

FIGURE 3.17: Adding new controls to the Toolbox

7. Click the OK button to add the controls to the tab.

If the controls don't "land" on the appropriate tab, you can move them by dragging them to the appropriate tab on the Toolbox.

You will notice that you may not be able to see "Common Controls" on the tab you just created. You can fix this by either stretching the Toolbox to the right to make it bigger, or you can rename the tab. To rename the tab:

1. Right-click in the Common Controls tab.

2. Select Rename Tab from the pop-up menu.

3. When the input box appears, rename the tab to Common.

4. Click the OK button to close the dialog box. When the dialog box closes the tab will be readable on the Toolbox.

That's all there is to adding controls to the Toolbox. Although it's not required, it is a good idea to create tabs that you can categorize your controls by. This will help make it easier for you to locate the control you need. Use the tabs to avoid Toolbox clutter.

Designing Windows 95–Style Interfaces

Now that you are familiar with the most common Visual Basic controls, we can learn how to design applications that look, feel, and behave just like the commercial applications written specifically for Windows 95 and Windows NT.

There are five controls that provide most of the functionality found in the most common Windows applications. These include the Tree View, List View, Image List, Status Bar, and Toolbar. We will cover the first four in the next sections. We will cover the Toolbar control in detail in Skill 5, *Creating and Using Menus and Toolbars*.

Figure 3.18 shows the Windows Explorer applet. It contains all of the controls that I have just described.

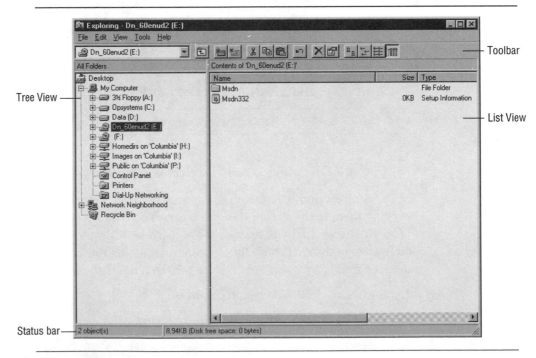

FIGURE 3.18:   Windows Explorer

At the top of the window, just below the menu, is the Toolbar control. It provides buttons that allow you quick access to the most commonly used functions, such as cut, copy, paste, and delete.

The pane on the left side of the window is a Tree View control. Its name describes its function: it displays items in a tree format, or tree view.

The pane on the right side is a List View control. Its purpose is to show a list of items. This control is most often paired with the Tree View control, and lists the contents of a selected folder in the Tree View.

At the bottom of the window is the Status Bar control. A status bar is used for many functions, including showing the number of selected objects, displaying the system date and/or time, and the amount of free disk space.

Now that you have an idea of what these controls do, and how they look, let's learn how to use them in our applications.

Using the Tree View Control

The Tree View control (shown here) provides a hierarchical view of folders or other items that can be neatly categorized in a tree-style layout. It is often used in conjunction with a List View control (explained in the next section), which is used to display the contents of the folder selected in the Tree View. Let's take a look at the Tree View's properties.

Tree View Properties

The Tree View control has a lot of properties—and many of them quite valuable:

Appearance	Height	MouseIcon	SingleSel
BorderStyle	HelpContextID	MousePointer	Sorted
CausesValidation	HideSelection	**Name**	**Style**
CheckBoxes	**HotTracking**	Nodes	TabIndex
Container	HWnd	Object	TabStop
DragIcon	**ImageList**	**OLEDragMode**	Tag
DragMode	**Indentation**	**OLEDropMode**	ToolTipText
DropHighlight	Index	Parent	Top
Enabled	**LabelEdit**	**PathSeparator**	Visible
Font	Left	**Scroll**	WhatsThisHelpID
FullRowSelect	**LineStyle**	SelectedItem	Width

Aside from the standard properties, there are some new ones that you must get familiar with to exploit the power of this control.

The Name property is the first property you should set when working with this control. The standard naming convention prefix is tvw. For example, if you had a tree view that contained the directory structure of your hard drive, you could name the control tvwDirectories.

If you double-click the Custom field in the Properties window, you can bring up a property page like the one in Figure 3.19 that exposes the most important properties.

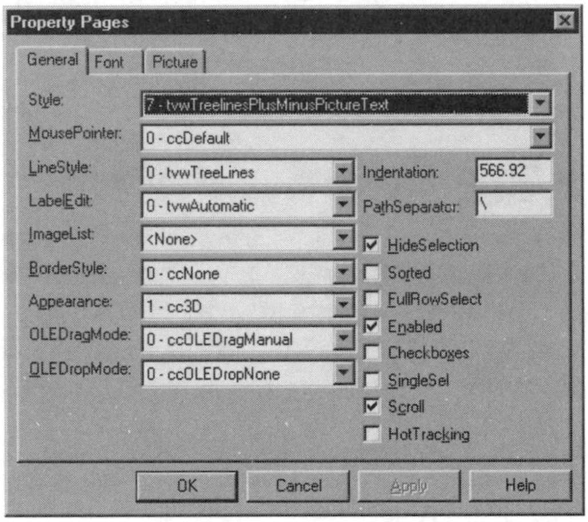

FIGURE 3.19: The Tree View's property pages

Of the three tabs displayed by the Tree View's property pages, the General tab is the one you will be most concerned with.

The General Tab

The Style property allows you to determine how you want the control to look and behave on the form. The possible values you can set this property to are:

Setting	Description
0 – tvwTextOnly	This setting shows only the text of the node.
1 – tvwPictureText	This setting shows the nodes icon and its text.

2 – `tvwPlusMinustext`	Use this setting if you want the collapse/expand symbol (the plus and minus signs) and the text of the node.
3 – `tvwPlusPictureText`	This setting displays the collapse/expand symbol, a small icon to the left of the text, and the text itself.
4 – `tvwTreelinesText`	If you want to have lines connect nodes that are related in the tree's hierarchy, you can use this setting to show the lines and the text for the node.
5 – `tvwTreelinesPictureText`	This setting displays a small icon to the left of the text, and connects related nodes.
6 – `tvwTreelinesPlusMinusText`	Pick this setting to show the collapse/expand symbol, connection lines, and the nodes text.
7 – `tvwTreelinesPlusMinus-` `PictureText`	If you want everything shown, choose this setting.

The `LineStyle` property is used to set the style of lines displayed between nodes. The possible values are:

0 – TreeLines

1 – RootLines

> **TIP** A node is an object that can contain both images and text. You will find that nodes are the data objects used in both the Tree View or List View controls.

The `LabelEdit` property is a Boolean property that allows you to enable or disable the automatic label-editing feature of the control. Windows Explorer demonstrates this feature when you single-click a folder or file name. It will turn into a miniature text box that will allow you to change the name. Set this property to `True` to enable label editing. Set it to `False` to turn it off.

If you want to have pictures in your Tree View control, you should set the `ImageList` property to the name of an existing Image List control, explained later in this skill.

The `BorderStyle` and `Appearance` properties are self-explanatory.

`OLEDragMode` configures the control for either manual or automatic dragging. You set this property to one of the following values:

> 0 – OLEDragManual
>
> 1 – OLEDragAutomatic

`OLEDropMode` configures the Tree View control to enable or disable OLE drop operations. The value of the property can be one of the following:

> 0 – OLEDropNone   When set to this value, the target component does not accept OLE drops and displays the No Drop cursor.
>
> 1 – OLEDropManual   The control will trigger the OLE drop events, allowing the programmer to handle the OLE drop operation in code.

The `Indentation` property determines the horizontal distance between nodes in the view. The lower the number, the closer the nodes are. If you prefer a tighter-looking interface, I have found that a value of 283 looks nice at run time.

The `PathSeparator` property allows you to set or retrieve the delimiter character used for the path returned by a node's `FullPath` property, as shown below:

```
Private Sub TreeView1_NodeClick(ByVal Node As Node)
    Dim rc as String
    rc = Node.FullPath
    MsgBox rc
End Sub
```

For example, you could set this property to a backslash (\) if you were showing a list of folders on your hard drive. Or, you could use a period (.) to designate an Internet-style path, as if you were mapping IP subnets on your LAN.

Set the `Scroll` property to `True` if you want the Tree View to show scroll bars; if there are more nodes than can be listed in the Tree View at one time, this may be necessary. Set it to `False` to disable scroll bars.

Finally, you can set the `HotTracking` property to `True` if you want the full name to be displayed in a tool tip–style box when the name does not fit horizontally within the view, as shown in Figure 3.20.

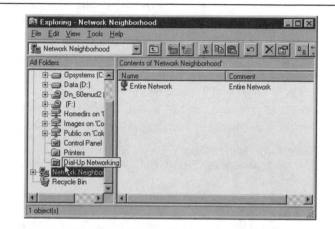

FIGURE 3.20:   Hot Tracking turned on

Tree View Events

This is the list of events supported by the Tree View control.

AfterLabelEdit	**Expand**	MouseMove	**OLEGiveFeedback**
BeforeLabelEdit	GotFocus	MouseUp	**OLESetData**
Click	KeyDown	NodeCheck	**OLEStartDrag**
Collapse	KeyPress	**NodeClick**	Validate
DblClick	KeyUp	**OLECompleteDrag**	
DragDrop	LostFocus	**OLEDragDrop**	
DragOver	MouseDown	**OLEDragOver**	

The AfterLabelEdit() event is triggered after you perform a label editing function on a node. This event is useful if you want to check the name of the node to make sure that it is valid. Its compliment, the BeforeLabelEdit() event, is triggered right before the node goes into edit mode.

The Collapse() event is triggered when a user collapses a branch of the tree. This can happen by double-clicking a root of a branch, or by clicking the minus sign next to the branch's root. You could place code in this event to remove items from the Tree View if you want to conserve memory.

The Expand() event is obviously the opposite of the Collapse() event. It is triggered when a user expands a branch of the tree by either clicking the plus sign next to the root of the branch, or by double-clicking the root of the branch. You could use this event to dynamically load data into the control when the node is expanded.

The NodeClick() event is one of the most important events that the Tree View provides. You can use this event to retrieve information about the node that was clicked, or any other function that your application requires. For example, the code

```
Private Sub tvwNodes_NodeClick(ByVal Node As ComctlLib.Node)
    MsgBox Node.FullPath
End Sub
```

will display a dialog box that shows the complete path to the node you clicked. If you used the backslash character in the PathSeparator property, with a root node named C: and the node clicked named Windows, the dialog box would display C:\Windows.

OLECompleteDrag() is triggered when OLE data is dropped on the control or the OLE drag-and-drop operation is canceled.

The OLEDragDrop() event is triggered when the OLEDropMode property is set to 1 – Manual, and OLE data is dropped on the control. You would place code in the event to determine what the control should do when data is dropped. You could place code in this event to make the control move data, but not copy it. Or you could have it copy the data, but not move it. The functionality depends on the needs of your application.

The OLEDragOver() event is triggered when OLE data is dragged over the control. After this event is triggered, Visual Basic will trigger the OLEGive-Feedback() event, which will allow you to check the data and provide feedback to the user.

The OLEGiveFeedback event is triggered after every OLEDragOver() event. It allows the Tree View control to provide feedback to the user, such as changing the mouse cursor to indicate what will happen if the user drops the object, or provide visual feedback on the selection (in the source component) to indicate what can happen.

The OLESetData() event is triggered when a target control executes the GetData method on the source's DataObject object.

Finally, the OLEStartDrag() event is triggered when a user starts dragging data from the control. If the OLEDragMode property is set to 1 – Automatic, the control will automatically start. You can use this event to populate data in the control's DataObject object. This will allow the destination control to read the data from the DataObject.

Tree View Methods

These are the methods exposed by the Tree View control:

Drag	Move	SetFocus	**StartLabelEdit**
GetVisibleCount	**OLEDrag**	ShowWhatsThis	ZOrder
HitTest	Refresh		

The GetVisibleCount method is used to retrieve the number of nodes that can be viewed in the Tree View at one time. This is not to be confused with the total number that the control can hold, but just how many can be viewed without scrolling vertically in the control. This method is useful if you need to ensure that a given number of nodes are visible at a time.

The HitTest method is used to determine if a node is available as a drop target. You can use this event during an OLE drag operation to highlight a node or change the mouse pointer when the OLE data is over a target that will allow it to be dropped.

The OLEDrag method is called to initiate an OLE drag operation. After this operation is initiated, the control's OLEStartDrag event is triggered, allowing you to supply data to a target component.

The StartLabelEdit method is used when you want to force a node into label edit mode. You can use this method in special circumstances, for example when you have set the LabelEdit property to False, but need to change the name of this one node. A good example of this can be seen again in Windows Explorer. You can change the names of folders and files within the tree, but you cannot change the names of built-in components, such as drives, Control Panel, or Network Neighborhood.

Before we create a sample application, let's take a look at the Tree View's counterpart: the List View control.

Using the List View Control

As mentioned previously, the List View control is often used in conjunction with the Tree View control. There are times when it will be used separately, but for this skill, we will use them together.

List View Properties

Below are the properties for the List View control:

AllowColumnReorder	Height	Parent
Appearance	HelpContextID	Picture
Arrange	HideColumnheaders	PictureAlignment
BackColor	HideSelection	**SelectedItem**
BorderStyle	**HotTracking**	**SmallIcons**
CausesValidation	HoverSelection	**Sorted**
Checkboxes	HWnd	**SortKey**
ColumnHeaderIcons	**Icons**	**SortOrder**
ColumnHeaders	Index	TabIndex
Container	**LabelEdit**	TabStop
DragIcon	**LabelWrap**	Tag
DragMode	Left	TextBackground
DropHighlight	**ListItems**	ToolTipText
Enabled	MouseIcon	Top
FlatScrollBar	MousePointer	Visible
Font	**MultiSelect**	WhatsThisHelpID
ForeColor	**Name**	Width
FontName	Object	**View**
FullRowSelect	OLEDragMode	
GridLines	OLEDropMode	

If you double-click the Custom field in the Property window for the List View control, Visual Basic will present you with the property pages for the control, as shown in Figure 3.21. These present the most useful, control-specific, properties that you could set to customize the look and behavior of the control.

Again, the first property you should set it the control's Name property. You can use a prefix like lvw. For example, if your control listed the files on your hard drive, you could name the control lvwFiles.

There are numerous tabs on the List View's property pages. You will be mostly concerned with the first four tabs.

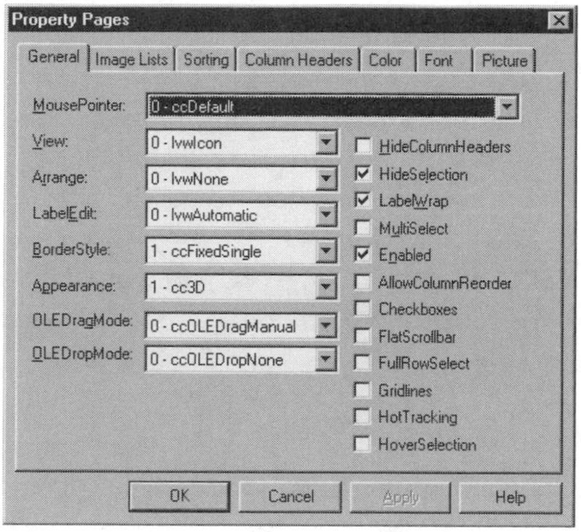

FIGURE 3.21:   List View property pages

The General Tab

The first tab on the property page, the General tab, contains many properties that control the layout of the List View control.

You can set the View property to make the List View display items in one of four different views:

> 0 - lvwIcon   Use this value to make the List View display large icons with text for each item in the list.

> 1 - lvwList   This value will list the items much like a List Box control.

> 2 - lvwReport   This setting is much like lvwList, but it will also show the subitems that belong to each item in the list.

> 3 - lvwSmallIcon   This setting is like lvwIcon, but it uses smaller icons.

The Arrange property allows you to set or retrieve the value that determines how the icons in the control's Icon or SmallIcon views are arranged. The possible values of this property are:

> 0 - lvwNone   This setting will not control how the items are arranged.

> 1 - lvwAutoLeft   This setting will make the control automatically arrange the items on the left of the control.

2 – lvwAutoTop   This setting will make the control automatically arrange the items on the top of the control.

The LabelEdit property is a Boolean property that allows you to enable or disable the automatic label-editing feature of the control. Windows Explorer demonstrates this feature when you click a folder or filename. It will turn into a miniature text box that will allow you to change the name. Set this property to True to enable label editing. Set it to False to turn it off.

OLEDragMode configures the control for either manual or automatic dragging. You set this property to one of the following values:

0 – OLEDragManual

1 – OLEDragAutomatic

OLEDropMode configures the List View control to enable or disable OLE drop operations. The value of the property can be one of the following:

0 – OLEDropNone   When set to this value the target component does not accept OLE drops and displays the "No Drop" cursor.

1 – OLEDropManual   The control will trigger the OLE drop events, allowing the programmer to handle the OLE drop operation in code.

The ColumnHeaders property is set to False when you check the box next to Hide Column Headers.

The LabelWrap property allows you to set or retrieve the value that determines if labels are wrapped when the List View is in Icon view. If this box is checked, then the property is set to True.

If you want to allow the user to select more than one item at a time, you can set the MultiSelect property to True. If you want to restrict the user to one selection at a time, set this property to False.

The FullRowSelect property is interesting, because it allows the List View control to behave much like a cell in a spreadsheet that can contain graphics. You can set this property to True to make the control highlight an entire row within a column, just as a spreadsheet will highlight the entire cell, rather than just the text of the item.

If you want to make the control look and behave like a spreadsheet even further, you can set the GridLines property to True. This will make the control draw horizontal and vertical lines between each row and between each column, yielding a grid.

To make the List View control behave like a spreadsheet, you can set the GridLines and FullRowSelect properties to True. Then you can set the List

View to display in Report view. For example, if you had a List View named lvw-Sheet, you would use the following code to make the spreadsheet:

```
With lvwSheet
        .View = lvwReport
        .GridLines = True
        .FullRowSelect = True
End With
```

You can set the HotTracking property to True if you want the full name to be displayed in a tool tip–style box when the name does not fit horizontally within the view.

The HoverSelection property allows you to set or retrieve a value that determines if an object is selected when the mouse pointer hovers over it. Set this property to True to enable hover selection, False to disable it.

The Image Lists Tab

The Image Lists tab contains the properties that enable the List View to use graphics. Normally, if you want to have pictures in your List View control, you should set the ImageList property to the name of an existing Image List control, explained later in this skill in the section "Using the Image List Control".

When you set the Small field to the name of an Image List, it will set the List View's SmallIcons property to the Image List control. When your List View is set to display small icons, the icons will be retrieved from the Image List specified in this property.

The ColumnHeader field will set the ColumnHeaders property to the Image List that contains the icons to be displayed in the Column Headers of the List View.

The Sorting Tab

The Sorting tab displays fields that expose the properties related to sorting data in a List View control.

The Sorted check box sets the Sorted property. If it is checked, then the List View will sort the data within it. If it is unchecked, then the Sorted property will be set to False.

If you want to specify how to sort the data within the List View, you can set the SortKey property. If you set it to 0, then the data is sorted by the item's Text property. If you set this property to a number higher than 0, then the List View will sort based on the text within the SubItems properties.

Skill 3

The `SortOrder` property determines whether the data is sorted in an ascending or descending fashion. Set this property to 0 to sort in ascending order. Set it to 1 to sort in descending order.

The Column Headers Tab

The Index field is incremented every time you add a `ColumnHeader` object to the List View Control.

When you fill in the Text field of this tab, Visual Basic will set the `Text` property of the `ColumnHeader` object with an index specified in the Index field above.

You can set the Alignment field to one of three values:

0 — `lvwColumnLeft`

1 — `lvwColumnRight`

2 — `lvwColumnCenter`

These determine the position of the text within the `ColumnHeader` object.

The value entered in the Width field will set the Column Header's `Width` property. This will set the width of the Column Header specified in the Index field.

The `Key` property determines the Column Header's unique key within the collection of Column Headers. This value can be either numeric or text. What you enter does not matter, as long as it is unique.

The `Tag` property sets the Column Header's `Tag` property. This property can contain any miscellaneous data that you want associated with the Column Header.

You set the IconIndex field to a number that indicates the index of the desired icon within the associated Image List control. For example, if you have three icons in an Image List, and you want the third icon to be displayed on this Column Header, you would set this field to 3.

List View Events

This is the list of events supported by the List View control.

AfterLabelEdit	DragOver	KeyUp	**OLEDragDrop**
BeforeLabelEdit	GotFocus	LostFocus	**OLEDragOver**
Click	ItemCheck	MouseDown	**OLEGiveFeedback**
ColumnClick	**ItemClick**	MouseMove	**OLESetData**
DblClick	KeyDown	MouseUp	**OLEStartDrag**
DragDrop	KeyPress	**OLECompleteDrag**	Validate

As you can see, many of the events for this control are the similar to those of the Tree View control.

Again, the `AfterLabelEdit()` event is triggered after you perform a label editing function on an object in the List View, called a *ListItem*. This event is useful if you want to check the name of the ListItem to make sure that it is valid. Its compliment, the `BeforeLabelEdit()` event, is triggered right before the ListItem goes into edit mode.

> **NOTE**
>
> A ListItem is the object inside a List View control. It is made up of text and the index of an associated icon. If the control is in report view, then this control also contains an array of strings, called *subitems*, that further describe the ListItem.

The `ColumnClick()` event is triggered when a user clicks one of the column headers. A column header is the button that sits at the top of a column, and describes the contents of that column. In report view in Windows Explorer, you can see that the column headers are labeled Name, Size, Type, and Modified. By inserting code in this event, you can make your List View control re-sort the data, or even re-order the columns.

The `ItemClick()` event is one of the most important events in this control. You can use this event to retrieve information about the ListItem that was clicked, or any other function that your application requires. It is used in much the same way as the Tree View's `NodeClick()` event.

`OLECompleteDrag()` is triggered when OLE data is dropped on the control or the OLE drag-and-drop operation is canceled.

The `OLEDragDrop()` event is triggered when the `OLEDropMode` property is set to `1 - Manual`, and OLE data is dropped on the control. You can place code in the event to determine what the control should do when data is dropped. You could place code in this event to make the control move data, but not copy it. Or you could have it copy the data, but not move it. The functionality depends on the needs of your application.

The `OLEDragOver()` event is triggered when OLE data is dragged over the control. After this event is triggered, Visual Basic will trigger the `OLEGiveFeedback()` event, which will allow you to check the data and provide feedback to the user.

The `OLEGiveFeedback()` event is triggered after every `OLEDragOver()` event. It allows the Tree View control to provide feedback to the user, such as changing the mouse cursor to indicate what will happen if the user drops the object, or provide visual feedback on the selection (in the source component) to indicate what can happen.

The `OLESetData()` event is triggered when a target control executes the `GetData` method on the source's `DataObject` object.

Finally, the `OLEStartDrag()` event is triggered when a user starts dragging data from the control. If the `OLEDragMode` property is set to `1 - Automatic`, the control will automatically start. You can use this event to populate data in the control's `DataObject` object. This will allow the destination control to read the data from the `DataObject`.

List View Methods

This control only supports a few methods, listed in the table below. None of them are particularly useful for the operation of the control.

Drag	**HitTest**	Refresh	**StartLabelEdit**
FindItem	Move	SetFocus	ZOrder
GetFirstVisible	**OLEDrag**	ShowWhatsThis	

The List View has many of the same methods as the Tree View.

You can call the `FindItem` method to find a ListItem within the control. You can make the control find exact matches or even partial matches.

Because you can have many more ListItems in the List View control than you can see at one time, you can call the `GetFirstVisible` method to determine which ListItem is at the top of the list within the view when it is in List or Report View.

The `HitTest` method is used to determine if a ListItem is available as a drop target. You can use this event during an OLE drag operation to highlight a target ListItem or change the mouse pointer when the OLE data is over a target that will allow it to be dropped.

The `OLEDrag` method is called to initiate an OLE drag operation. After this operation is initiated, the control's `OLEStartDrag()` event is triggered, allowing you to supply data to a target component.

The `StartLabelEdit` method is used when you want to force a node into label edit mode. You can use this method in special circumstances, for example when you have set the `LabelEdit` property to `False`, but need to change the name of this one node. A good example of this can be seen again in Windows Explorer. You can change the names of folders and files within the tree, but you cannot change the names of built-in components, such as drives, Control Panel, or Network Neighborhood.

Let's look at the Image List control before we work on our sample. That way we can add graphics to the controls, rather than using plain old text.

Using the Image List Control

The Image List control does not actually appear on a form at run time. Instead, it serves as a container for icons that are accessed by other controls, such as the Tree View, List View, and Toolbar controls. You may have several Image Lists on a form at a time. One could contain the large icons, another would contain small icons, and yet another could contain icons for the Column Headers of the List View control.

Image List Properties

The Image List control has only a few properties:

BackColor	**ImageWidth**	**MaskColor**	Parent
HimageList	Index	**Name**	Tag
ImageHeight	**ListImages**	Object	**UseMaskColor**

The first property to set is the `Name` property. You can use a prefix of `iml`. When I link an Image List to another control, I usually set the name to be the same as the other control. For example, if I link the Image List to a Toolbar control, I would name the Toolbar `tbrToolbar`, and the Image List would be named `imlToolbar`.

The `ImageHeight` property is used to set the height of all of the images within the Image List. `ImageWidth` is set to the width of all images in the list. It is important to know that all of the images must have the same dimensions. If you require images of different sizes, you must use multiple Image Lists.

To make the backgrounds of each image transparent, you need to set the `Mask-Color` property to the background color of the images within the control. Each image should use the same background color. Once the `MaskColor` property is set to the correct color, you can set the `UseMaskColor` property to `True`.

> **WARNING** All images within an Image List must be the same size. In addition, they should all use the same mask color.

Image List Events

The Image List control has no events, so let's look at its one and only method.

Image List Methods

The Image List has only one method: `Overlay`. You can use the `Overlay` method if you want to combine two images within an Image List. You can set the `Mask-Color` property to the transparent color of the top image, so the resulting image is a nice combination of the two. For example, the code

```
'This command will overlay image 1 onto image 2
Set Picture1.Picture = imlToolbar.Overlay(1,2)
```

will overlay the first image in the control with the second image.

Putting It All Together

Now is the time you have been waiting for. This example will combine the features of the Tree View, List View, and Image List controls. Let's see how they all work together.

1. In Visual Basic, start a new project by selecting File ➤ New Project from the menu, and select Standard EXE as the project type.

2. Left-click Project1 in the Project Explorer, then set the `Name` property of the project to **ObjectExplorer**.

3. Select Form1 and set its `Name` property to **frmMain**.

4. Set the `Caption` property to **Object Explorer**.

5. Right-click the Toolbox and select Components from the pop-up menu.

6. When the Components dialog box appears, scroll down and select Microsoft Windows Common Controls 6.0 from the list. Click OK to add the controls to your Toolbox.

7. Add an Image List to frmMain by double-clicking the Image List control in the Toolbox. When it is added to the form, move it to the lower-right corner of the form. Set its `Name` property to **imlCategories**.

8. In the Property window, double-click the Custom field to open the property page for the control.

9. Select the Images tab. Click the Insert Picture button to add an image to the list.

10. When the Select picture dialog box appears, select `Closed.bmp` from the `Common\Graphics\Bitmaps` directory. Click the Open button to add the file to the control, then click OK.

11.   Add another Image List to frmMain. Set its `Name` property to **imlItems**. Move it next to imlCategories.

12.   Using the same methods as described in steps 8–10, add the image `Leaf.bmp` to the control and click the Open button.

13.   Click the OK button to close the property page.

14.   Add a Tree View control to frmMain. Set its `Name` property to **tvwCategories**.

15.   In the Properties window, double-click the Custom property field. This will bring up the property page for the control.

16.   On the General tab of the property page, set the `Style` property to **7 – tvwTreeLinesPlusMinusPictureText**, set the `LabelEdit` property to **1 – Manual**, the `Indentation` property to **283**, and the `ImageList` property to **imlCategories**.

17.   Click the OK button to close the property pages.

18.   Move tvwCategories to the upper-left side of the form.

19.   Add a List View control to frmMain and set its `Name` property to **lvwItems**.

20.   In the Properties window, double-click the Custom property field. This will bring up the property page for the control.

21.   Set the `View` property to **3 – lvwReport**, the `Arrange` property to **2 – lvwAutoTop**, the `LabelEdit` property to **1 - Manual**, and the `OLEDropMode` property to **1 – OLEDropManual**.

22.   Click the Image Lists tab to make it the active property page.

23.   Set the `Normal` field to **imlItems**. This will link it to the Items Image List control.

24.   Click the Column Headers tab to make it the active property page.

25.   Click the Insert Column button. This will add the first Column Header object to the collection.

26.   Set the Text field to Control Name.

27.   Click the OK button to close the property pages.

28.   Move lvwItems to the upper-right corner of the form. The form should look like Figure 3.22.

29.   Save your work by selecting File ≻ Save Project from the Visual Basic menu.

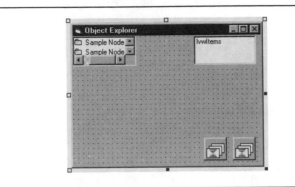

FIGURE 3.22:   The Object Explorer form under development

30.   Double-click frmMain to open its code window.

31.   Add the following code to the Form_Resize() event:

```
Private Sub Form_Resize()

    Dim mid1 As Integer
    Dim mid2 As Integer

    mid1 = (ScaleWidth / 2) - 50
    mid2 = (ScaleWidth / 2) + 50

    If WindowState <> vbMinimized Then
        tvwCategories.Move 0, 0, mid1, ScaleHeight
        lvwItems.Move mid2, 0, ScaleWidth - mid2, ScaleHeight
    End If
End Sub
```

The code for this example deserves some scrutiny. The first two statements dimension two variables, mid1 and mid2. The next two lines of code set these variables to values that indicate positions just to the left and right of the center-line of the form. By adding and subtracting 50 from these values, we can create a neat border between the two views.

The If…Then statement tells the program to execute the next lines of code only if the form is not minimized. If the form were minimized, then you would get an error when trying to move and size the controls. We will look at the If…Then statements in greater detail in Skill 6, *Logic and Program Flow.*

In the Form_Load() event, add the following code:

```
Private Sub Form_Load()
    Dim cat As Node

    'Add the nodes to the tree view
    With tvwCategories.Nodes
        Set cat = .Add(, , "root", "Objects", 1)
        Set cat = .Add("root", tvwChild, , "Intrinsic", 1)
        Set cat = .Add("root", tvwChild, , "Explorer", 1)
        Set cat = .Add("root", tvwChild, , "Internet", 1)
    End With
End Sub
```

The first line creates a Node-type variable. This will allow us to work with the Nodes collection inside of the List View control. The next line (With …) tells the Visual Basic compiler to work specifically with the Nodes collection of tvwCategories.

The first line of code under the With statement adds a node at the root level of the tree. We set its text value to "Objects" because that is what this tree contains. The following three lines of code add child nodes (tvwChild) to the root object. Each node has its own description, one for intrinsic controls, another for the Explorer-style controls, and finally some Internet controls. Remember that these nodes are actually categories. That means that they will "contain" other objects.

Add the following code to the (General)(Declarations) section of frmMain:

```
Option Explicit

Private Sub ListExplorer()
    Dim itm As ListItem

    With lvwItems.ListItems
        .Clear
        Set itm = .Add(, , "Tree View", 1)
        Set itm = .Add(, , "List View", 1)
        Set itm = .Add(, , "Image List", 1)
        Set itm = .Add(, , "Toolbar", 1)
        Set itm = .Add(, , "Status Bar", 1)
    End With
End Sub

Private Sub ListInternet()
    Dim itm As ListItem

    With lvwItems.ListItems
        .Clear
        Set itm = .Add(, , "Web Browser", 1)
```

```
                    Set itm = .Add(, , "Shell Folder View", 1)
                    Set itm = .Add(, , "Inet", 1)
                    Set itm = .Add(, , "Winsock", 1)
            End With
        End Sub

        Private Sub ListIntrinsics()
            Dim itm As ListItem

            With lvwItems.ListItems
                .Clear
                Set itm = .Add(, , "Picture", 1)
                Set itm = .Add(, , "Label", 1)
                Set itm = .Add(, , "Text Box", 1)
                Set itm = .Add(, , "Frame", 1)
                Set itm = .Add(, , "Command Button", 1)
                Set itm = .Add(, , "Check Box", 1)
                Set itm = .Add(, , "Radio Button", 1)
                Set itm = .Add(, , "Combo Box", 1)
                Set itm = .Add(, , "List Box", 1)
                Set itm = .Add(, , "Horizontal Scroll Bar", 1)
                Set itm = .Add(, , "Vertical Scroll Bar", 1)
                Set itm = .Add(, , "Timer", 1)
                Set itm = .Add(, , "Drive List", 1)
                Set itm = .Add(, , "Directory List", 1)
                Set itm = .Add(, , "File List", 1)
                Set itm = .Add(, , "Shape", 1)
                Set itm = .Add(, , "Line", 1)
                Set itm = .Add(, , "Image", 1)
                Set itm = .Add(, , "Data", 1)
                Set itm = .Add(, , "OLE", 1)
            End With
        End Sub
```

The first statement, `Option Explicit`, forces variable declaration within the project. The three subs are very similar. Each declares a ListItem variable, named `itm`. This variable is used to access the `ListItems` collection within lvwItems.

The `With...` statement tells the compiler to work with the ListItems collection of the List View control. The next command, `.Clear`, tells the List View to clear its `ListItems` collection. This removes other controls if any already exist within the collection. Finally, the next commands add ListItems to the collection.

Finally, add the following code to the `NodeClick()` event of tvwCategories:

```
        Private Sub tvwCategories_NodeClick(ByVal Node As ComctlLib.Node)
            Select Case Node
                Case Is = "Intrinsic"
                    ListIntrinsics
```

```
        Case Is = "Explorer"
            ListExplorer
        Case Is = "Internet"
            ListInternet
    End Select
End Sub
```

Save your project by selecting File ➤ Save Project from the menu. Press the F5 key to run the project.

The form should look like Figure 3.23. The window on the left side of the form is the Tree View, and the List View is on the right. Notice that if you resize the form, the windows will automatically resize as well. Double-click the Objects folder to expand it. Then, click any of the categories to view its contents.

FIGURE 3.23:   The Object Explorer in action

Don't worry about the OLE drag-and-drop procedures yet. We will build some more of your programming skills and then we will cover these in detail in Skill 11.

Using the Status Bar Control

The Status Bar control is the next important piece of the Windows Common Controls collection. It is used to report various bits of information to the user. It resembles the System Tray, found in the right side of the Windows Taskbar. It can also be found in Windows Explorer. It can reflect the system date and time, show icons, or display statistics related to other controls, for example the number of files listed in a List View control.

Status Bar Properties

This is the list of the status bar's properties:

Align	hWnd	OLEDropMode	Tag
Container	Index	**Panels**	ToolTipText
DragIcon	Left	Parent	Top
DragMode	MouseIcon	ShowTips	Visible
Enabled	MousePointer	**SimpleText**	WhatsThisHelpID
Font	**Name**	**Style**	Width
Height	Object	TabIndex	

The Name property should be set first. You can use the prefix sts. I prefer to name the status bar stsStatus.

The Panels property returns a reference to the collection of panel objects contained in the Status Bar control.

The Style property determines how the status bar is displayed. The allowed values are:

0 – sbrNormal   This setting shows multiple panels on the status bar.

1 – sbrSimple   This setting will show only one panel, which extends the width of the status bar.

The SimpleText property allows you to set or retrieve the value of the text in the panel when the Style property is set to 1 – sbrSimple.

Status Bar Events

This is the list of events supported by the Status Bar control.

Click	MouseDown	OLEDragDrop	OLEStartDrag
DblClick	MouseMove	OLEDragOver	**PanelClick**
DragDrop	MouseUp	OLEGiveFeedback	**PanelDblClick**
DragOver	OLECompleteDrag	OLESetData	

Since the status bar is used more to give you feedback, many of these events are not that important. The OLE drag-and-drop events will be covered in detail in Skill 11. So for now, let's look at the PanelClick() and PanelDblClick() events.

The `PanelClick()` event is triggered when the user clicks a panel. So what is a panel, you ask? A panel is a section of the status bar that contains either text or a bitmap, which may be used to reflect the status of an application. The `Panel-DblClick()` event is triggered when a user double-clicks a panel.

Neither of these actions is likely to occur, and so these events won't be used that often. However, everything a control does depends on the design of your applications.

Status Bar Methods

This control only supports a few methods, listed below. None of them are particularly useful for the operation of the control.

Drag	OLEDrag	SetFocus	ZOrder
Move	Refresh	ShowWhatsThis	

Experimenting with the Status Bar

Let's finish the Object Explorer example from the previous section. If you have not already done so, load the ObjectBrowser project by selecting File ➤ Open Project from the Visual Basic menu.

1. Add a Status Bar control to the bottom of frmMain. It will automatically stretch to fit the width of the form. Set its `Name` property to **stsStatus**.

2. Open the code window for the `Load()` event of frmMain.

3. Add the following line of code just below the `Dim cat as Node` line:

    ```
    Dim pnl As Panel
    ```

4. Add the following lines of code below the `With...End With` block:

    ```
    'Add two panels for time and date
    With stsStatus.Panels
        Set pnl = .Add(, , , sbrTime)
        Set pnl = .Add(, , , sbrDate)
    End With
    ```

5. Go to the `NodeClick()` event of tvwCategories and add the following line of code above the `Select Case` statement:

    ```
    Dim pnl As Panel
    Dim sts As String
    ```

Skill 3

6. Add the following lines of code below the `Select...End Select` block:

```
'Get the item count
sts = lvwItems.ListItems.Count & " Objects"

'Update the status bar
With stsStatus.Panels(1)
    .Text = sts
End With
```

7. In the `Form_Resize()` event, change the two lines of code with the Move statements to the following:

```
tvwCategories.Move 0,0,mid1,ScaleHeight-stsStatus.Height
lvwItems.Move mid2,0,ScaleWidth-mid2, ScaleHeight-stsStatus.Height
```

8. Save and run the project.

Figure 3.24 shows that there are three panels in the status bar. The leftmost panel shows how many objects are listed in the List View control. The middle panel displays the system time, and the right-most panel displays the system date.

You can use these same techniques to customize the Status Bar control in your own applications. You are only limited by your imagination!

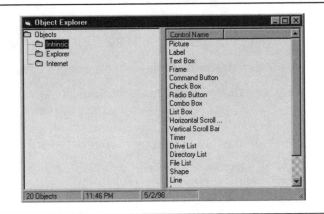

FIGURE 3.24: The status bar added to the Object Explorer

Moving On...

There are obviously too many controls to cover in this skill. To cover all of the controls would almost require a separate book. Fortunately, some of the other controls are covered throughout this book and provide sample code, so you can learn how to use each one. If you have read this entire skill, then you are more than ready to start using the controls covered here, as well as those that have not been covered yet. The nice thing about custom controls is that once you are familiar with one, it is easy to become familiar with others.

Are You up to Speed?

Now you can...

- ☑ understand when to use a control
- ☑ use the controls in the Toolbox
- ☑ group controls with frames
- ☑ coordinate the Drive, Directory, and File List Box controls
- ☑ add controls to the Toolbox
- ☑ use the Explorer-style controls

SKILL 4

Working within Modules and Classes

- Introducing code modules and classes
- Creating a code library
- Working with sub procedures
- Working with function procedures
- Passing parameters to functions and sub procedures
- Working with class modules
- Using the Class Builder

All the programming in this book so far has been fairly straightforward. The code you have worked with in previous skills has been entirely contained in the event procedures for forms. Now, to extend the capabilities of Visual Basic, it's necessary to move on from this rather limited approach. In particular, you'll learn how to create your own procedures and your own modules. You have already created a simple code module in the previous section, but you will soon want to add to it. This will allow you to extend your code library so you can spend more time designing rather than coding.

Introducing Code Modules and Classes

You have already worked with two major building blocks of Visual Basic in earlier skills: forms and controls. Now we're going to take a look at the next fundamental building block—the *code module*. Code modules are ASCII text files that contain sub procedures, functions, variables, and/or constants. You have already used code modules in the previous skills, but now you're going to get a detailed lesson on how they work.

Code modules are like the equivalent of an unorganized toolbox. Imagine if you had a hammer, a screwdriver, and a variety of nails and screws all stored in one box. The hammer and screwdriver are much like procedures in a code module. The nails and screws are much like the variables, or data. Now imagine if the nails were not stored in bags or boxes, but just thrown in the toolbox. That's much like how a basic code module is laid out.

> **NOTE** A code module is actually an ASCII text file that contains procedures of code. They are useful for combining related procedures that are available to your programs.

You can have many code modules in a project to compartmentalize your code. You could, for example, put the hammer and screwdriver in one box, and put the nails and screws in separate bags. Using this same sort of layout with your code will definitely make your code easier to organize and read.

This is nice, but imagine being a construction worker having to carry many toolboxes and bags of nails and screws to your job site. It would be much easier if you had a single toolbox that could hold the hammer and screwdriver, and that had separate compartments for each type of nail, and each type of screw. This would make your toolbox much more efficient. There is a way to mimic this same functionality in Visual Basic. To do this, you would use *class modules*, more commonly referred to as *classes*.

Classes are the fundamental building blocks to a style of programming called *object-oriented programming* (OOP), a programming model that allows you to think of your program in terms of objects. A class allows you to compartmentalize the functionality of a program into a single object, but extends the functionality of a basic module by allowing you to protect some portions of code, while making other portions visible to your application. This process is called *encapsulation*. OOP allows you to design code objects that are designed and behave much like real-world objects.

Much like the custom controls that you learned about in Skill 3, classes contain properties, methods, and events that all work together to perform a set of related operations. A well-designed class is a self-sufficient piece of code. This means that you can move the class from one project to another and it will work properly without any modification whatsoever. We will discuss objects and OOP in greater detail later in Skill 15.

Because code and class modules are actually separate files, you can include them in more than one project. This is a common method of writing reusable code. For example, I have several code modules with related procedures in them. One has many dialog box functions for use in my shareware programs. Another module has functions that make accessing multimedia devices much easier. By combining similar functions into one code or class module, you can create a *code library*. If you place these modules within one directory, or a logical set of subdirectories, you can reuse them in other projects.

Using a code library will save you time by not requiring you to write the same code more than once. Continuing the construction metaphor discussed previously, a code library is the equivalent of having a truck to carry your tools and supplies. It can hold many toolboxes that contain various tools. Maybe one toolbox holds the hammers and screwdrivers, while another holds the scrapers, paint rollers, and brushes. The bed of the truck could be used to transport the planks and plywood, much like a code module can be used to hold, and yet separate, different types of data.

Another benefit of using a code library is that after your code has been debugged, you will have a single, reliable function that you will almost never have to write again. That's like having a Craftsman hammer with a lifetime warranty. You won't have to go out and buy a new one for each job! Before we start working with modules and classes, let's create a code library where you can start collecting programming tools of your own.

Creating a Code Library

Before getting into the details of using code modules, let's create a place to store them. This will be your code library. You will put reusable code modules in this directory so that they can be used again in the future.

To create your own library, follow these steps:

1. From the Windows desktop or the Start button, open Windows Explorer.

2. Create a directory, also called a *folder*, named **CodeLib**. This folder must be in a location that is easy to find and back up. You don't want to accidentally delete this directory if you re-install software.

3. Close Windows Explorer.

 NOTE   In the Windows environment, the words folder and directory can be used interchangeably. The folder metaphor comes from the folder icons that you see in Explorer or My Computer. The word *directory* was used back in the days of DOS and Unix to indicate a distinct container that contained files and other directories, called subdirectories. In Windows, a directory and a folder point to the same location on your disks.

When you write code modules that are generic in nature, containing functionality that may be used in multiple separate applications, you can save them in your new CodeLib directory. When you need to use this code module in another project, just follow these steps:

1. In Visual Basic, right-click the Project Explorer.

2. Select Add ➤ Add Module from the pop-up menu.

3. In the Add Module dialog box, select the appropriate code module from your CodeLib directory.

Creating a Code Module

You can add your own procedures to modules by clicking Tools ➤ Add Procedure and selecting options in the Add Procedure dialog box (see Figure 4.1). This option is only available when the Code window is open.

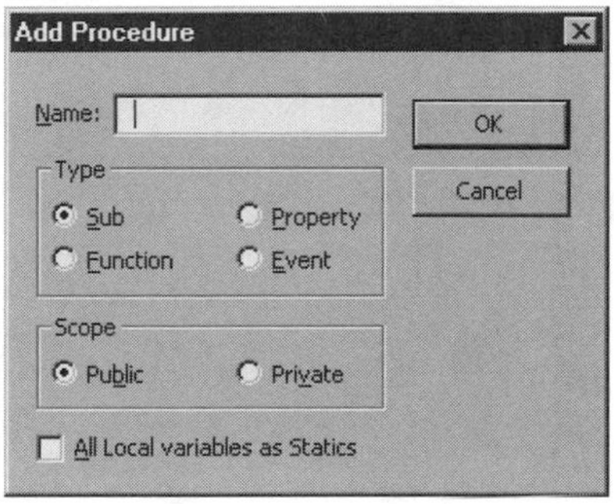

FIGURE 4.1: The Add Procedure dialog box

A QUICKER WAY TO ADD PROCEDURES

Instead of selecting Tools ➤ Add Procedure, a quick way to add a procedure is to follow these steps:

1. Type **Public Sub ProcedureName** on a blank line anywhere in the Code window.

You could also type **Private Sub ProcedureName** to make a private procedure, or you could just type **Sub ProcedureName**, which will automatically default to a public procedure.

2. Press Enter, and Visual Basic will create a procedure stub or template for you.

continued ▶

> For this example, Visual Basic's Code window will look like the one shown here.
>
> ```
> (General)                    ▼   ProcedureName            ▼
> ─────────────────────────────────────────────────────────
> Option Explicit
>
> Private Sub Form_Load()
>
> End Sub
>
> Public Sub ProcedureName()
>
> End Sub
> ```

Now that you have set up a code library directory, you can create your first reusable code module. We will add some functionality to this module in the next sections. Follow these steps to create the code module:

1. From Visual Basic, select File ➢ New Project to create a new project.

2. Right-click in the Project Explorer and select Add ➢ Module.

3. Select Module from the Add Module dialog box. Click the Open button to add a blank module to your project.

4. In the Properties window, set the Name property of the newly added module to **MyLibrary**.

5. Save the file by selecting File ➢ Save MyLibrary, or use the shortcut Ctrl+S. When the Save File As dialog box appears, save your file in the CodeLib directory you created in the previous section. This will start your code library.

Working with Sub Procedures

As you learned in previous skills, sub procedures, or just *subs*, are procedures that can accept arguments, execute code, and change the values of passed arguments. Arguments are variables that are passed to a sub so that the sub can process the data stored in the argument. For example, the `AddItem` method of the list box control accepts arguments to add data to the list and to set the position of the text within the list. The following line of code:

```
lstItems.AddItem "Widgets"
```

accepts the argument `"Widgets"` and adds this text to the bottom of the list. Note that an argument can be almost any data type. The type depends on what the sub expects to work with.

You will soon learn that subs are very useful for reusing code. Rather than typing the same lines of code to achieve the same functionality in multiple locations within a program, you can create one sub, and call it from those multiple locations in your program. Not only does this minimize your typing, but the sub will behave the same way every time it is called.

To give you a practical example of how to write and use a sub, we'll create a sub that changes the mouse pointer from an arrow to an hourglass. This routine can be called before your application performs a lengthy task behind the scenes. The hourglass gives the user a visual cue that the program is doing something and has not crashed.

1. If the project from the previous section is not already opened, then create a new project by selecting File ➢ New Project from the Visual Basic menu.

2. If the module `MyLibrary` is not in the project, then add it by right-clicking in the Project Explorer window, and select Add ➢ Module from the pop-up menu. When the Add Module dialog box appears, click the Existing tab. Then find the file `MyLibrary.Bas`, and click the Open button to add the code module to your project.

3. Double-click `MyLibrary.Bas` in the Project Explorer. This will open the code window for the module.

4. In the Code Window, add the following code:

```
Public Sub ShowHourglass()
    Screen.MousePointer = 11
End Sub
```

This procedure changes the mouse pointer to the hourglass. Now once the mouse pointer is changed, we need a way to get it back to normal again.

5. Add the following code to the module:

```
Public Sub ShowMousePointer()
    Screen.MousePointer = 0
End Sub
```

6. Select File ➢ Save MyLibrary from the Visual Basic menu.

The ShowHourglass and ShowMousePointer procedures are useful when you want to let the user know that a lengthy task is running. To use them, all you need to do is call ShowHourglass before the task you wish to perform, and call ShowMousePointer when the task is done. You would use code similar to the following:

```
ShowHourglass
    IndexLargeDatabase
ShowMousePointer
```

You can add more procedures to this code module in the future when you start writing your own useful procedures and functions. Now that you know the basics of writing a sub, let's look at another type of procedure, called a *function*.

Working with Function Procedures

Functions are much like subs, except they return a value to the calling procedure. They are especially useful for taking one or more pieces of data, called *arguments*, and performing some tasks with them. Then the function returns a value that indicates the results of the tasks completed within the function. This may sound a little bit confusing, but it's really not. Perhaps the best way to understand Function procedures is to try one out. Here's one that calculates the cube root of a number.

1. If the project from the previous section is not already opened, then create a new project by selecting File ➢ New Project from the Visual Basic menu.

2. If the module MyLibrary.Bas is not in the project, then add it by right-clicking in the Project Explorer window and selecting Add ➢ Module from the pop-up menu.

3. When the Add Module dialog box appears, click the Existing tab. Then find the file MyLibrary.Bas and click the Open button to add the code module to your project.

4. Double-click `MyLibrary.Bas` in the Project Explorer. This will open the code window for the module. Add the following code to the (`General`) (`Declarations`) section:

```
Public Function CubeRoot
```

This creates the following code:

```
Public Function CubeRoot()

End Function
```

5. Now alter the template as follows (see Figure 4.2):

```
Public Function CubeRoot(x As Double) As Double
    If x = 0 Then
        CubeRoot = 0
        Exit Function
    End If

    CubeRoot = 10 ^ ((Log(Abs(x)) / Log(10)) / 3)

    If x < 0 Then
        CubeRoot = - CubeRoot
    End If
End Function
```

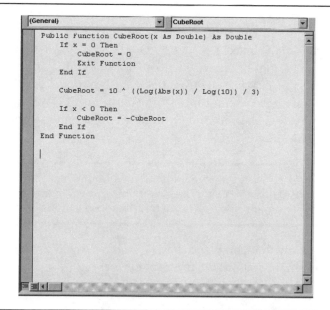

FIGURE 4.2: The Code window to calculate a cube root

6. Select File ➢ Save MyLibrary from the Visual Basic menu.

Before continuing with the example, let's briefly examine the code within the function. The function takes the value in the argument x and attempts to return the cube root of that value. You can specify the type of value that the function returns—here it's a Double (a numeric variable that can handle very large and small values as well as decimals)—by adding the statement As followed by the data type of the returned value. Another feature worth noting is that a function ends with the statement End Function, rather than End Sub. You will notice three separate instances where the variable CubeRoot is set to a value. When writing functions, you return the resulting value through a variable with the same name as the function, in this case CubeRoot. If you created a function called TimesTwo(), you would return the result by setting the variable TimesTwo to a value, for example TimesTwo = x*2.

Before we perform any functions on the argument, it is good practice to make sure that the function has some valid data to work with first. The first value we check for is 0. This is because we know that 0 x 0 x 0, or 0^3 is still 0. Based on this knowledge, we know that the cubed root of 0 remains 0. As a result, we can just set the return value, CubeRoot, to 0. Once we have the result, we can exit the function without processing the remaining code. We do this through the Exit Function statement.

The next possibility we check for is a value that is greater than zero. It is possible to extract a cubed root from a positive, nonzero value. The math involved here isn't important, but know that the combination of functions in the line CubeRoot = 10 ^ ((Log(Abs(x)) / Log(10)) / 3) returns the cube root of the argument x.

The final situation we must address is if the argument that is passed is less than zero. We know from basic algebra that a cube root cannot be a negative number, so we multiply the negative result by -1. In Visual Basic, we can accomplish this by preceding a variable with a minus sign. In this case we used the value -CubeRoot.

> **TIP** If you wish to leave a function without executing further instructions, you can use the Exit Function statement. This will cause the function to leave when the statement is executed, and further instructions are bypassed.

Now that you have a basic idea of what a function is made of, let's continue our example and put the function to work.

7. Double-click Form1 in the Project Explorer to show the form in the Form Designer window.

8. Set the Caption property of the form to **Code Library Demo**.

9. Add a command button to the form. Set its Name property to **cmdCubeRoot**, and its Caption property to **Cube Root**.

10. Double-click cmdCubeRoot to open its code window. You should be in the cmdCubeRoot_Click() event of the button.

11. Add the following code. When you are done, you should see something similar to Figure 4.3.

```
Dim Y As Double

Y = CubeRoot(27)

Print Y
```

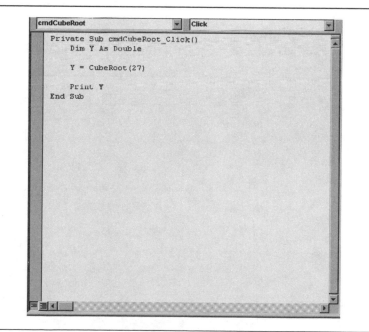

FIGURE 4.3: The code to call the Cube Root function

12. Now run the application and click the command button. You should see a form similar to the one shown in Figure 4.4. This code prints the return value straight onto the form.

Code Library Demo
3
Cube Root

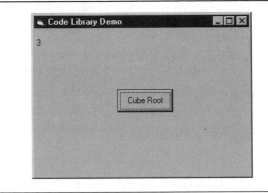

FIGURE 4.4: The function returns the value of 3.

Normally, you may want to assign the return value to a control on the form, such as a text box control like the one shown in Figure 4.5.

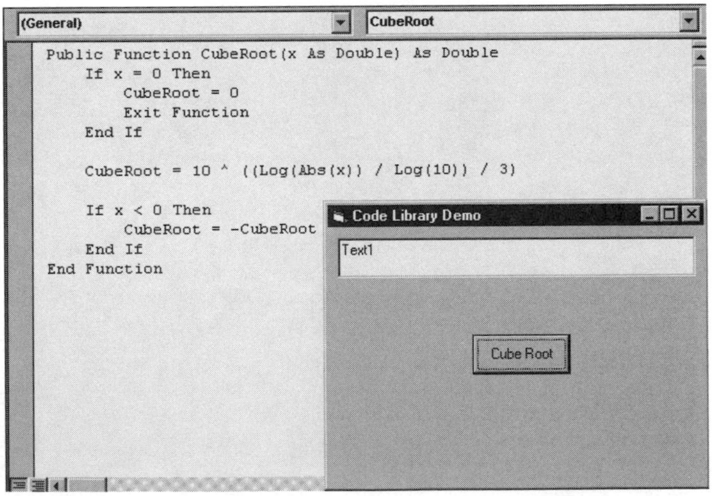

(General)
CubeRoot
Public Function CubeRoot(x As Double) As Double
If x = 0 Then
CubeRoot = 0
Exit Function
End If
CubeRoot = 10 ^ ((Log(Abs(x)) / Log(10)) / 3)
If x < 0 Then
CubeRoot = -CubeRoot
End If
End Function
Code Library Demo
Text1
Cube Root

FIGURE 4.5: The modified Code window and design form

13. Stop the program by clicking the close button (x) in the upper-right corner of the form. This will return you to the design environment.

14. Double-click Form1 in the Project Explorer to bring it to the Form Designer.

15. Add a text box to the form. Set its Name property to **txtText1**. Delete the contents of its Text property.

16. Modify the Click () event of cmdCubeRoot by removing the last line (Print Y) and replace it with the following:

    ```
    txtText1.Text = Y
    ```

The result is shown is Figure 4.6.

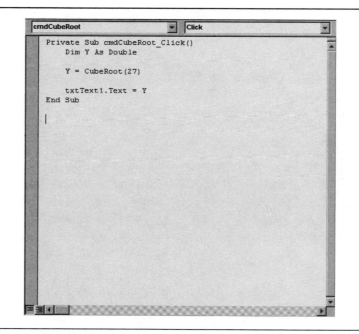

```
cmdCubeRoot                         ▼   Click                          ▼
    Private Sub cmdCubeRoot_Click()
        Dim Y As Double

        Y = CubeRoot(27)

        txtText1.Text = Y
    End Sub

```

FIGURE 4.6: The modified application

Alternatively, you can remove all of the lines of code in the event and replace it with this single line:

```
txtText1.Text = CubeRoot(27)
```

Here the return value is being assigned directly to a control.

NOTE   When you call a Function procedure, you must enclose the argument in parentheses.

TESTING FROM THE IMMEDIATE WINDOW

You can test both Sub and Function procedures from the Immediate window.

First, run your project. Then click Run ➤ Break. This usually brings the Immediate window to the front (shown below).

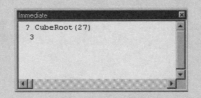

If you lose it, click View ➤ Immediate Window. You're now in Break or Debug mode. To run a Sub procedure from the Debug window, type the name of the procedure and press Enter. If the procedure accepts parameters, then add those too. For example:

```
AlterCaption "New Caption"
```

To run a Function procedure, you need to see its return value. You can do this by printing the return value to the Immediate window. For example:

```
Print CubeRoot(27)
```

or just:

```
? CubeRoot(27)
```

Updating Your Code Library

Let's add a useful function to your new library. The function is used to check if a file already exists on a disk. You would use this to check for a file before over-writing it. Or, you could call this function to ensure the existence of a file before attempting to open it.

1. If the project from the previous section is not already opened, then create a new project by selecting File ➢ New Project from the Visual Basic menu.

2. If the module MyLibrary.Bas is not in the project, then add it by right-clicking in the Project Explorer window and selecting Add ➢ Module from the pop-up menu.

3. When the Add Module dialog box appears, click the Existing tab. Then find the MyLibrary.Bas file and click the Open button to add the code module to your project.

4. Double-click MyLibrary.Bas in the Project Explorer. This will open the code window for the module. Add the following code to the (General) (Declarations) section:

```
Public Function IsFile(Filename As String) As Boolean
    If Len(Dir(Filename)) > 0 Then
        'The filename exists
        IsFile = True
    Else
        'The filename does not exist
        IsFile = False
    End If
End Function
```

5. Select File ➢ Save MyLibrary from the Visual Basic menu.

The bulk of the work is performed in the line with the code

```
If Len(Dir(FileName)) > 0 Then
```

The code actually consists of two functions that are used together to return a single value. The heart of this line is the Dir() function. As you can see, it accepts one parameter, Filename. The Dir() function checks for the existence of a file spec-ification, for example *.txt and returns the first matching file, if one exists. In this case, if you knew you had a file called FooBar.txt located in your My Documents folder, and you set the variable Filename to C:\My Documents\FooBar.txt, the

Skill 4

function would return the text `FooBar.txt`. If this file did not exist, then `Dir()` would return an empty value.

The next part of the line of code is the `Len()` function. You can pass an argument to `Len()`, and it will return the length of the text passed to it. For example, if you called the function `Len("abc")`, it would return the value 3, because `abc` is three bytes long. Since `Dir()` returns the name of a file that matches the argument passed to the function, the `Len(Dir())` functions would be the equivalent of calling `Len("FooBar.txt")`, which would return the value 10.

Finally, we check to see if the value returned by the `Len()` function is greater than zero. Since the length of the text `FooBar.txt` is 10, it is obviously greater than zero. As a result, we set the value of `IsFile` to `True`, indicating that the file actually exists. If the `Dir()` function returned an empty string of text, then the `Len()` function would return zero. Since zero is equal to, but not greater than zero, `IsFile` gets set to `False`, indicating that the file does not exist.

 TIP
When you place more complicated code, or combinations of code, into a single function, you are creating a *wrapper*. This is because your function wraps around the code within it. This is a useful programming technique, and is often used to simplify access to the Windows API. You will learn more about this in Skill 19, *Using DLLs and the Windows API*.

Now that you have your first reusable code module, you can include it in future projects to perform simple tasks. The `IsFile()` function is used to detect if a file exists on the hard disk. You will want to use this function before you attempt to open files in your programs. To use this function, simply call the function and pass it an argument using the following syntax:

```
If IsFile("C:\CONFIG.SYS") Then
    …Your code goes here…
End If
```

Passing Parameters to Functions and Sub Procedures

As you learned with functions, you can pass arguments, also known as *parameters*, to subs and functions. The reason for doing this with functions is obvious: you want the function to use your data to do something useful. This same concept applies to subs as well. The only difference is that subs do not return values back to the calling procedure. Parameter passing allows you to use a single function or procedure to perform the same tasks on different variables. This procedure can be used over and over, which is the first step to writing re-usable code.

To better understand how parameter passing works, think about a blender. The blender's sole purpose is to chop things up. What you put in the blender could be considered a parameter. If you put a carrot in the blender, the result will be carrot juice. If you put in celery, you get celery juice. So if you wrote a function called `Blender`, you could put something in it, the parameter, and it would work on it and return a type of juice, called the result.

The procedures, whether they are subs or functions, should be narrowed down to perform one discrete task. This task may consist of many subtasks, but they should all work neatly together to perform one desired result. For example, add the following code for a sub procedure to a form. This function will be used to change the `Caption` property of your form:

1. Start a new Standard EXE project.

2. Add a command button to Form1. Set its `Name` property to **cmdCaption**, and its `Caption` property to **Alter Caption**.

3. Add the following code to the (General)(Declarations) section of the form:

    ```
    Private Sub AlterCaption(X As String)
        Caption = X
    End Sub
    ```

When you run it, your application will look like Figure 4.7.

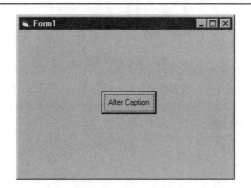

FIGURE 4.7: Running the sample application

This procedure has one argument, X. The name you give to the argument isn't important. However, in this case, the procedure will only work if you pass a string (text) value. You could create a string variable called MyTitleText and set it to **New Caption**. Then you could pass MyTitleText as the parameter to the procedure. Thus, you pass a string variable or the raw text enclosed in quotation marks, called a literal, to the procedure.

To call this sub procedure, try entering the following line of code (shown in the Code window below):

```
cmdCaption                    ▼   Click                      ▼
    Private Sub cmdCaption_Click()
        AlterCaption "New Caption"
    End Sub
```

The text after the procedure name is a string literal—note the use of quotes around a string literal. This text is the parameter that meets the argument X. To pass a string variable, try the following code (shown in the Code window following).

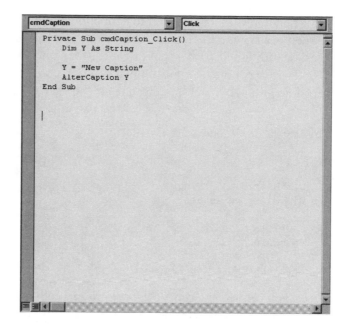

```
cmdCaption                          Click

Private Sub cmdCaption_Click()
    Dim Y As String

    Y = "New Caption"
    AlterCaption Y
End Sub
```

Note the lack of quotes this time. Also note the lack of parentheses around the parameter—though the argument it's passed to is surrounded by parentheses. When you run the program, click the button. Your form should look like the shown here in Figure 4.8.

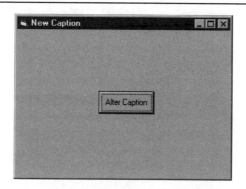

FIGURE 4.8: Changing the `Caption` property through code

When you pass a parameter to a function, you must enclose it in parentheses. When passing parameters to subs, you do not enclose the parameter in parentheses. In addition, if you are passing more than one parameter, you must separate each with a comma. For example, if you had a sub called `CreateUser`, you might want to pass it two parameters, one for the user's name, and another for the user's password. The code might look like this:

```
CreateUser "John Doe", "123456"
```

or,

```
Dim UserID as String
Dim Password as String

UserID = "John Doe"
Password = "123456"

CreateUser UserID, Password
```

As you can see, the code is very similar in both examples. The first passes the parameters directly. This technique is called *hard-coding*. Although it works, you would have to write many lines of code if you wanted to create many users. The alternative is to use variables and to set the values, and then call the sub once, as in the second example.

If you decide you want to verify the user, you could use a function to compare the user's ID with the user's password, and return a value indicating if the data is correct. The following code shows how you could do this:

```
Dim UserID as String
Dim Password as String

UserID = "John Doe"
Password = "123456"

If ValidUser(UserID, Password) = True Then
    'Do something useful here...
Else
    'Show an error message...
End If
```

Notice that the parameters are enclosed in the parentheses, and are separated by commas. The function declaration will determine how many parameters are required. Some will require many parameters, while others may not require any at all.

The *Optional* Keyword

When defining your own functions you can specify that a parameter be passed, but not be required. You would do this by using the Optional keyword in front of the parameter definition. For example:

```
Public Function CreateUser(UserID As String, _
          Password As String, _
          Optional Description As String) As Boolean
```

The third parameter, Description, is optional. This means that you can pass the user's description if you have it, but it is not required for the function to work successfully. The only caveat to passing optional parameters is that all subsequent arguments must be optional and declared using the Optional keyword.

There are three more prefixes that are allowed in front of the parameter declaration of a sub or function. These are ByRef, ByVal, and ParamArray.

The *ByRef* Keyword

The ByRef prefix indicates that the parameter is passed *by reference*, which is the default method in Visual Basic. When a variable is passed by reference, the memory address of the variable is passed to the function or sub. This allows the function or sub to modify the actual value of the variable. You can use this method as a makeshift way to pass multiple results in one function call. The syntax is:

```
Function FunctionName(ByRef AVariable As String) As Boolean
```

or

```
Function FunctionName(AVariable As String) As Boolean
```

> **TIP** Since ByRef is the default method of passing a parameter, you do not need to explicitly use the ByRef keyword in your function declaration. However, when working with DLLs, you will be required to use it more often.

The *ByVal* Keyword

The ByVal prefix specifies that a parameter is passed *by value*. Visual Basic will actually pass a copy of the contents of the variable, rather than the memory address of the variable. This prevents the function or sub from directly modifying the contents of the original variable. The syntax is:

```
Function FunctionName(ByVal AVariable As String) As Boolean
```

The *ParamArray* Keyword

The ParamArray keyword allows you to pass an undetermined number of parameters to a function. You could use this to pass a varying number of users to your CreateUser function. One requirement with the ParamArray keyword is that you must pass an array of data that is of the Variant type. The function declaration syntax is:

```
Function FunctionName(ParamArray AnArray() As Variant) As Boolean
```

You could access this function using code similar to the following:

```
Dim rc as Boolean

rc = FunctionName("John", "Jane", "Jim", "Jenny")
rc = FunctionName("James")
rc = FunctionName("Jerry", "Jackie")
```

Notice that the function can be called with any number of parameters but you do not need to make separate functions. ParamArray offers a flexible way to scale your functions, but does so at the expense of program execution speed, because variants are slower than other data types in Visual Basic.

Using *Private* and *Public* Sub Procedures

While working with code modules in previous examples and skills, you may have noticed that most procedures and functions are prefixed by the keyword Private or Public. Each of these defines the *scope* of the procedure. The Private keyword makes a procedure accessible only at the module level. That means only objects that reside in the same form or module can access the procedure. Procedures and functions declared as Public are available to the whole project. They have a global scope. Each of these scopes will have a significant impact on the design and functionality of your applications. Let's look further and see why.

Private Procedures

The code modules that make up forms consist of procedures that support the form and the controls on that form. While examining event procedures of forms in previous examples you may have noticed these procedures have the word `Private` in front of the Sub keyword. `Private` is an optional keyword that defines the procedure as being available only to other procedures in the form or module from where it is declared. These procedures are declared `Private` because they are private to the form—they cannot be called from outside that form.

If you open the controls sample application in the `\MSDN98\98vs\1033\Samples\VB98\Controls` directory, then a glance at the Project window shows a total of seven forms (see Figure 4.9). Each form file contains the design of the form and the controls on the form.

FIGURE 4.9: Seven forms in the Project window

Each form file also includes all the event procedures coded for the form, which is called *code behind forms* (CBF). This code behind the form is called a *form module*. A module is a self-contained collection of procedures. These procedures can be called by events on the form or from other procedures in the same module.

Each of the event procedures is preceded by the keyword `Private`. This indicates that the procedure can't be called from outside its own form module: Its scope is module-level, and it's not visible outside the form, meaning it's private or local. All form event procedures are `Private` by default. But you can add your own procedures to a form and make them application-level (public or global) by using the `Public` prefix, discussed next. Such procedures can be called from any other form (or standard module) in the project. If you leave out the `Private` or the `Public` prefix, the procedure is application-level by default.

Public Procedures

There may be times when you want to make a procedure available from outside the form. Perhaps you want to add buttons to a toolbox form in your own application. One way to do this could be to add a procedure to a code module, where every form, control, or procedure could access it. Another way is to write the procedure directly in the module it belongs to, and prefix the declaration with the keyword `Public`. By doing this, you can make the procedure available to other components within your application.

You can run a form's public procedure (or a private procedure) by typing the name of the procedure in another procedure behind the form. For example, if you have a procedure named `Test` you would enter the following line to run it:

```
Test
```

Strictly speaking, this is only true for sub procedures. As you learned previously, function procedures are dealt with in a slightly different manner. You will also see references to a third type of procedure, a property procedure. These are explained in the section "Working with Class Modules" later in this skill.

> **TIP** To call a public procedure in a form module (from outside the form) you must prefix the call with the name of the form. For example, to call a public sub procedure with the name `Test` in `frmForm1`, you type: `frmForm1.Test`.

Working with Class Modules

Another type of code module that deserves some discussion is the *class module*, or simply the *class*. Classes are the fundamental building blocks to object-oriented programming (OOP). You use these same objects throughout the entire project development process. You can learn more about OOP in Skill 13.

A class allows you to compartmentalize the functionality of a program into a single object, which helps make the program easier to design and develop. When you optimize your class objects, you minimize the risk of other portions of your application interfering with other pieces of code. In OOP, program objects are designed to mimic real-world situations.

In Visual Basic, you can insert classes into your projects, or you can compile them to make ActiveX controls, such as Dynamic Link Libraries (DLLs) and custom controls (formerly referred to as OCXs). When you make an ActiveX control, you can link it to your program or you can link or embed it into World Wide Web documents, commonly referred to as HTML documents. The sample application in Skill 10, *Using Dialog Boxes*, shows you how to create a custom dialogs class and compile it to an ActiveX DLL. Skill 17, *Using ActiveX*, presents you with more of the specific details of ActiveX. As you can see, classes are the becoming the framework for many of Visual Basic's new features. Although I won't go into detailed theory of how OOP works, I will discuss how to design and use class modules in your projects.

> **TIP**   A class module can be thought of as the blueprint of an object. The instantiated object is the actual product.

A class contains properties and methods that all work together to perform a set of related operations. The class is a self-sufficient piece of code, which means you can move the class from one project to another and it should work properly without any modification whatsoever. Visual Basic objects, the tangible objects that you access in your code, are derived from the class framework. For example, a command button object is actually created from a class object. The command button works by itself in any application you add it to, without modification. The classes you develop should be designed to do the same thing.

Much like a standard code module, a class is just a formless file, but it comes with two procedures, `Class_Initialize()` and `Class_Terminate()`:

- You use the `Class_Initialize()` procedure to set any properties to their defaults or configure anything the class requires before it is executed. For example, you can have a class check for the existence of a file before it is accessed, and create one if it does not exist. You could also have it check the registry to retrieve a default setting before the object runs.

- You can place code in the `Class_Terminate()` procedure that cleans up anything that needs it. For example, if your object created temporary files while it was in use, you could remove these files when the object is destroyed.

Methods

Adding a method to a class is just like adding a procedure to a code module. You can prefix the method name with `Private` or `Public`, depending on the scope of the method. `Public` methods serve as the interface to the programmer. Your program can access these without any problems. The class will use `Private` methods to hide functionality from the programmer.

A good example of a method that should be private is one that retrieves personnel information from a personnel database. You would not want to allow anyone access to this data, so it should be retrieved in a private method. Then you could write a public method that calls the private method behind the scenes. This shields you from the information and the data retrieval process altogether. Here is another example that shows how an ATM class could work:

```
Private Function GetBalance(AccountNo as String) as Double
    GetBalance = 10000
    'Don't we all wish we could have that much!
End Function

Public Function DisplayAccountInfo(AccountNo as String, PIN as _
        String) as Double
    If AccountNo = "123456" And PIN = "5551289" Then
        DisplayAccountInfo = GetBalance(AccountNo)
    End If
End Sub
```

The `GetBalance` function is declared private because we don't want just anybody looking at people's account balances. Imagine how many new relatives you would get if someone knew you had 10 million dollars in your account! To prevent this, we require the user to go through the `DisplayAccountInfo` procedure. Their account number and personal identification number (PIN) must be verified before the account balance is retrieved.

Properties

As you learned in Skill 3, properties are actually variables that are used to store and retrieve data from classes. Like procedures, properties can be `Public` and `Private` in scope. Properties that are declared as `Public` are said to be exposed. This means that data within the class can be accessed from another procedure outside the scope of the class. The exposed properties make up a portion of the class's *interface*. Private properties can be used to keep data and procedures hidden behind the interface. This prevents programs from directly or unintentionally modifying the contents of data required for the class to function properly. The only way to get to this data is through a `Public` interface.

Class properties are accessed through `Property Get`, `Property Let`, and `Property Set` statements. `Property Get` serves as the public interface to retrieve the values of variables inside the class that the program does not have access to. `Property Let` does just the opposite: It allows you to set the values of variables within the class. `Property Set` allows you to pass object by reference to the class. This is useful when you want a class module to directly manipulate an external control. You will see this in the next example. You can also create properties by declaring them as public within the class. The `Property Get` and `Property Let` statements create a sort of security model for the class properties.

Going back to our ATM example, two good properties would be `AccountNo` and `PIN`. You could rework the class so you set the properties and then call the methods without passing any parameters. For example:

```
Public AcctNo as String
Public PINNo as String

Private Function GetBalance() as Double
    GetBalance = 10000
    'Don't we all wish we could have that much!
End Function

Public Function DisplayAccountInfo() as Double
    If AcctNo = "123456" And PINNo = "5551289" Then
        DisplayAccountInfo = GetBalance()
    End If
End Sub
```

Here is the same code using the `Property Let` and `Property Get` statements:

```
Private AcctNo As String
Private PINNo As String

Public Property Let AccountNo(x As String)
    AcctNo = x
End Property

Public Property Let PIN(x As String)
    PINNo = x
End Property

Private Function GetBalance() As Double
    GetBalance = 10000
    'Don't we all wish we could have that much!
```

```
End Function

Public Function DisplayAccountInfo() As Double
    If AcctNo = "123456" And PINNo = "5551289" Then
        DisplayAccountInfo = GetBalance()
    End If
End Function
```

TIP   Use the `Private` keyword to encapsulate properties and methods within your classes. This helps protect the internals of your class from tampering by the calling program. Use the `Public` keyword to expose only the properties and methods that absolutely need to be accessed by the calling program.

Events

Events are the most interesting portion of the class model. They allow the class to communicate information back to an application when a set of conditions are met. This makes your application *event-driven*, meaning it relies on events to make the program operate. As a result, your program does not need to wait for a specific condition to be met. The application will let you know by firing an event.

All of the default procedures that are exposed in the code window are events. The procedure `Form_Load()` is an event.

To define an event in your class, you would use the keywords `Public Event` in the `(General)(Declarations)` section of the module. Here's the syntax:

```
Public Event EventName(parameters)
```

Notice that the statement is a declaration, not a procedure. To expose the event to your form you would use a syntax similar to the following:

```
Private WithEvents x As ClassName
```

For example, the code

```
Private WithEvents p as Person
```

would declare a private object, p, derived from the `Person` class. If our "person" could speak, it could have an event called `Speak`. The key to exposing the events is the keyword `WithEvents`. Without it, you could only access the `Public` properties and methods of the class, but not the events.

The reason that events are so powerful is that your application is not required to poll for data. *Polling* is the practice of checking a value over and over until a specific condition is met. The polling process is processor intensive, and makes it difficult for your program to run smoothly while it is in the loop. Using events, you or your application can continue doing something else until the appropriate event is fired.

These are the basics of class development. Forms, code modules, and controls are the building blocks of a Visual Basic application. Now that you understand the fundamentals, let's dig a little deeper to understand how to use these building blocks to create something useful.

> **NOTE** The interface of a class is the combination of public properties, methods, and events. They represent the portion of the class that can interact with the rest of the application. This is similar to a visual interface (a window for example). The visual interface is the only way you can interact with the application.

Creating a SmartForm Class

To help you understand class designs a little better, try the following example. I use the SmartForm class to store and retrieve the position and size information of forms. These forms "remember" their position and state between application executions. When you are done, you can add this class to your code library and use it in your own applications!

1. Start a new project by selecting File ➢ New Project from the menu, or by pressing Ctrl+N.

2. When the New Project dialog box appears, select Standard EXE.

3. Add a new class module to the project by right-clicking in the Project Explorer and selecting Add ➢ Class Module.

4. Select Class Module from the Add Class Module dialog box and click the Open button.

5. In the Properties Window, set the Name property of the new class to **SmartForm**.

6. Double-click SmartForm in the Project Explorer to open its code window.

7. Add the following code to the (General)(Declarations) section of the class module:

```
Option Explicit
```

```
'Private variables
Private mForm As Object
Private mLeft As Long
Private mTop As Long
Private mWidth As Long
Private mHeight As Long
Private mWS As Integer

Public Event ErrorMessage(Message As String)
```

These private variables are local to the class only. They will not be directly accessible from the application. Instead, they will be accessed through the class's interface. The `ErrorMessage` event is declared as `Public`.

8.   Add a property to the class by selecting Tools ➤ Add Procedure from the menu.

9.   When the Add Procedure dialog box appears, type **Form** in the Name field.

10. Click the Property option button, and leave the scope option button set to Public.

11. Click the OK button to create the property. Two property subs will be added to the code module: `Public Property Get Form()` and `Public Property Let Form(ByVal vNewValue As Variant)`.

12. In the line of code that reads:

```
Property Let Form(ByVal vNewValue As Variant)
```

change the keyword `Let` to `Set` so it reads as follows:

```
Property Set Form(ByVal vNewValue As Variant)
```

13. Add the following line of code to the `Property Get Form()` procedure:

```
Form = mForm
```

14. Add this line of code to the `Property Set Form...` procedure:

```
Set mForm = vNewValue
```

Since we have procedures that are defined as variants, let's use the search and replace features of the IDE to change these properties to Objects.

15. Press Ctrl+H to bring up the Replace dialog box.

16. Type the word **Variant** in the Find What field.

17. Type the word **Object** in the Replace With field.

18. If you were to perform a search and replace throughout the entire application, you would click Current Project. Since we are only concerned about the class module, make sure that Current Module is selected.

19. Click the Replace All button to change the properties to the `Object` data type. When the replace is complete, there should have been two replacements.

20. Click the Cancel button to close the dialog box.

TIP

As with any word processor or editor, the search and replace facilities in the Visual Basic IDE are extremely useful, and you should get familiar with them. They are particularly useful when you are changing the names of controls throughout a large project.

Skill 4

21. Add the following method to the (General)(Declarations) section:

```
Private Sub SaveSettings()
    Dim mAppName As String

        'Set the variable to the EXE filename
    mAppName = App.FXEName

        'We can only save information if we know
        'the app name and the form name...
    With mForm
        If .Name <> "" Then
            SaveSetting mAppName, .Name, _
                    "WindowState", Str$(.WindowState)

            If .WindowState = vbNormal Then
                SaveSetting mAppName, .Name, _
                        "Left", Str$(.Left)
                SaveSetting mAppName, .Name, _
                        "Top", Str$(.Top)
                SaveSetting mAppName, .Name, _
                        "Width", Str$(.Width)
                SaveSetting mAppName, .Name, _
                        "Height", Str$(.Height)
            End If
        Else
            'Trigger an ErrorMessage event
            RaiseEvent ErrorMessage("You must set "&_
                    "the form object!")
        End If
    End With
End Sub
```

The bulk of the work is done by the `SaveSetting` command. This command is intrinsic to Visual Basic and allows you to store values in the system registry without needing to use the Windows API.

22. Now add the following `GetSettings` method to the `(General)` `(Declarations)` section of the class:

```
Private Sub GetSettings()
    Dim mAppName As String

    'Set the variable to the EXE filename
    mAppName = App.EXEName

    With mForm
        If .Name <> "" Then
            mLeft = Val(GetSetting(mAppName, _
                     .Name, "Left", .Left))
            mTop = Val(GetSetting(mAppName, _
                     .Name, "Top", .Top))
            mWidth = Val(GetSetting(mAppName, _
                     .Name, "Width", .Width))
            mHeight = Val(GetSetting(mAppName, _
                     .Name, "Height", .Height))
            mWS = Val(GetSetting(mAppName, .Name, _
                     "WindowState", .WindowState))

            'Size the form
            .WindowState = mWS
            .Move mLeft, mTop, mWidth, mHeight
        Else
            'Trigger an ErrorMessage event
            RaiseEvent ErrorMessage("You must set "&_
                     "the form object!")
        End If
    End With
End Sub
```

We know that the purpose of this class is to remember the size and position of forms, so it can be assumed that forms can and will be resized. To allow our class to accommodate this we need to add a `Resize` method to the `(General)(Declarations)` section of the class module:

```
Public Sub Resize()
    'All we need to do is save the form's
    'coordinates
    SaveSettings
End Sub
```

23. Insert the following lines of code in the (General)(Form [Property Set]) section:

```
Public Property Set Form(ByVal vNewValue As Object)
    'Create a reference to the actual
    'form object
    Set mForm = vNewValue

    'Get the saved coordinates
    GetSettings

    'Do the first resize
    Resize
End Property
```

24. Finally, we need to make the class save its settings and destroy the link when the form object is unloaded. We can do this in the Class_Terminate() event by adding the following code:

```
Private Sub Class_Terminate()
    'Save the form's settings
    SaveSettings

    'Destroy the local object reference
    Set mForm = Nothing
End Sub
```

25. Now that you have added a significant amount of code, save the file by pressing Ctrl+S. When the Save File As dialog box appears, change the Save In field to the directory of your code library, if you created one.

26. Click the Save button to save the class.

Congratulations! You have just created a fully reusable class module. You can include this module in any of your projects that contain forms, and link it to your forms with a minimal amount of code. Let's see how.

1. Double-click Form1 in the Project Explorer to open the Code window for the form.

2. Add the following line of code to the (General)(Declarations) section of the form:

```
Option Explicit

Private WithEvents sf As SmartForm
```

Skill 4

Remember that the `WithEvents` keyword tells Visual Basic to expose the classes events in the code window. As a result, you can select `sf` in the Object drop-down combo box in the upper-left corner of the Code window.

3. Change to the `sf_ErrorMessage()` event and add the following code:

    ```
    Private Sub sf_ErrorMessage(Message As String)
        MsgBox Message
    End Sub
    ```

    The `MsgBox` command tells Visual Basic to create a message box dialog box to display a message. In this case, we pass it a parameter in the form of the variable `Message`.

4. In order to use the `SmartForm` (`sf`) object, we must instantiate it. That is, we must create an object based on the blueprint we designed in the class module. We can do this by adding the following lines of code to the `Form_Load()` event of Form1:

    ```
    Private Sub Form_Load()
        Set sf = New SmartForm
        Set sf.Form = Me
    End Sub
    ```

5. When the form is resized, we need to inform the `SmartForm` object so it can remember the form's size and position. Add the following lines to the `Form_Resize()` event:

    ```
    Private Sub Form_Resize()
        sf.Resize
    End Sub
    ```

6. Finally, we need to tell the SmartForm to close by setting the SmartForm to nothing, thus destroying the `sf` object. Add the following line of code to the `Form_Unload()` event:

    ```
    Private Sub Form_Unload(Cancel As Integer)
        Set sf = Nothing
    End Sub
    ```

7. Click `Project1` in the Project Explorer and set its `Name` property to **SmartFormTest**.

WARNING   It is important to make sure that you use a distinct project name whenever you use smart forms. This is because each form is tracked by its application name. Unpredictable results could occur if you make multiple projects with the same name and same form names.

Now that you have created a smart form, save and run the project. At first, the application is less than spectacular. Try resizing the form and moving it to a corner of the screen. When you are satisfied, click the Close button on the form to return to the IDE. Immediately re-run the application. If all goes well, the form should be the same size and located in the same position that you left it in when you closed the form. By using the same lines of code that you did in steps 1-5, you can add smart forms to your own applications. Now that you have created a class the hard way, let's look at a tool that makes it easy to visually design and create classes.

Using the Class Builder

When I created my first class, I kept thinking to myself, "There's got to be an easier way to do this!" Fortunately for you and me there is. Visual Basic comes with a tool to help you visually design your classes, called the *Class Builder*. Using the Class Builder, shown in Figure 4.10, you can graphically design the framework for your classes and it will add the skeleton code to your project.

The Class Builder is a utility that is designed as an add-in. It is called an add-in because the utility can be added in to the IDE. As you can see in Figure 4.10, the Class Builder is very much like Explorer, or the Project Explorer, displaying the current project name in the tree view window on the left side of the screen. The menu bar is fairly standard, as is the toolbar directly under it. Let's fire up the Class Builder and take it for a quick spin.

1. Select Add-Ins ➢ Add-In Manager from the Visual Basic menu.

2. When the Add-In Manager dialog box appears (Figure 4.11), double-click VB Class Builder Utility to load it into the IDE.

3. Click the OK button to close the dialog box.

Skill 4

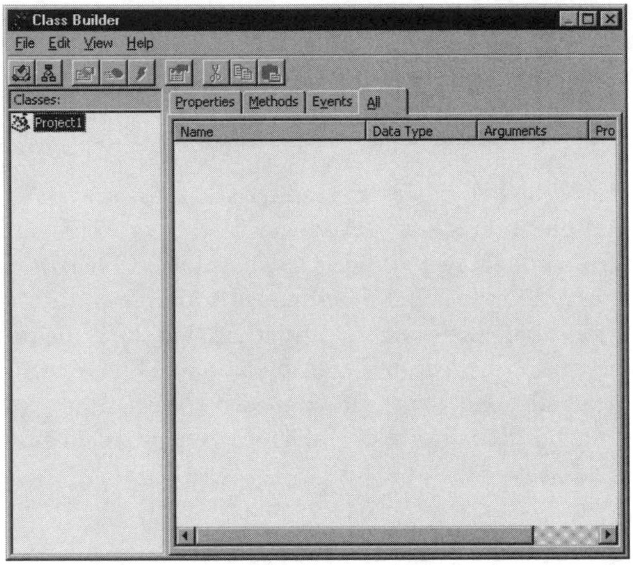

FIGURE 4.10: The Class Builder utility

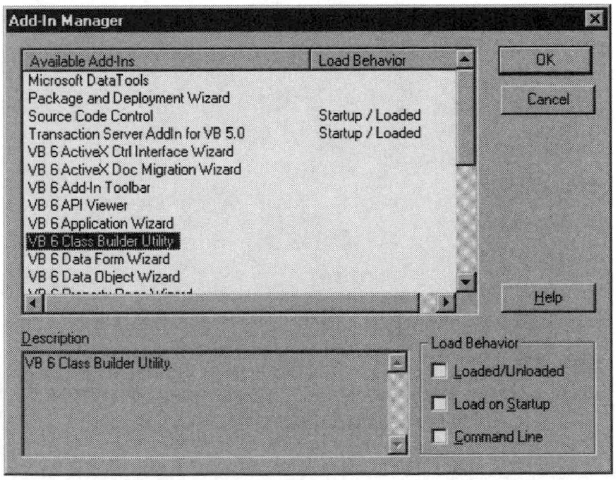

FIGURE 4.11: The Add-In Manager

> **NOTE**   You can learn more about add-ins in Skill 16, *Extending the IDE with Add-Ins.*

Now that you have the Class Builder added to the IDE, you can start using it to build your classes. The next example shows you how to use the Class Builder to create a simple class called `Person`. Although it is extremely simple, it will give you a good demonstration on how to use this useful utility. Let's try it!

1. Start a new project by selecting File ➤ New Project from the menu. Select Standard EXE from the New Project dialog box and click the OK button.

2. Start the Class Builder by selecting Class Builder Utility from the Add-Ins menu.

3. Create a new class by selecting File ➤ New ➤ Class from the Class Builder menu. This will bring up the Class Module Builder dialog box.

4. Type the word **Person** in the name field. Leave the Based On field set to (New Class). Click the OK button to create the class.

5. Using the toolbar, click the Add New Property to Current Class button. This will bring up the Property Builder dialog box shown in Figure 4.12.

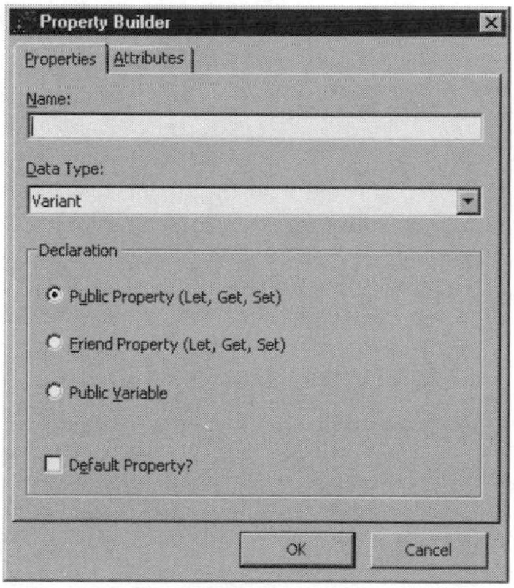

FIGURE 4.12: The Property Builder dialog box

6. Type **Name** in the Name field. We will use this property to identify our derived object later in the example.

7. Set the Data Type field to **String**.

8. Leave the Declaration option set to **Public Property (Let, Get, Set)**. This property must be public so we can access it through the class's interface.

9. Click the OK button to create the property.

10. Add an event to the Person class by pressing the Add New Event to Current Class button on the toolbar. This is the button with the yellow lightning bolt icon. You should see the Event Builder dialog box shown in Figure 4.13.

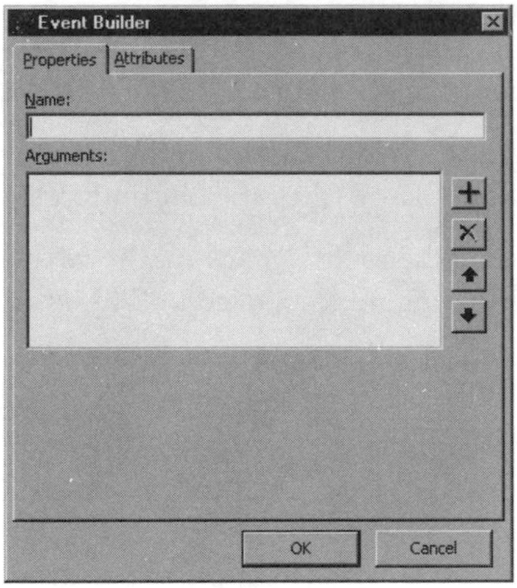

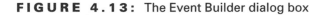

FIGURE 4.13: The Event Builder dialog box

11. Type the word **Say** in the Name field. Our person will actually "say" something, in computer terms of course!

12. We need to add a parameter so our person will know what to say. Do this by clicking the Add a New Argument button. This button has a plus sign icon on it.

13. Once again you will be presented with a dialog box, asking you for a name. We want to pass a parameter called Sentence. Type the word **Sentence** in the Name field.

14. Set the Data Type field to **String** and click the OK button to close the dialog box.

15. Click the OK button to close the Event Builder dialog box. The Say event should be added to your Person class.

16. Add a method to the class called **WhoAreYou**. This method will have no parameters.

17. Click the OK button to add the method to the class. Your Class Builder should look like Figure 4.14.

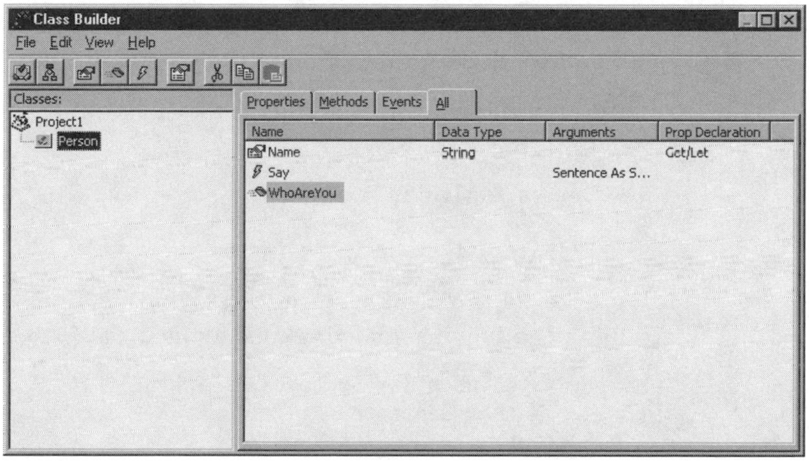

FIGURE 4.14: The Person class with properties, events, and methods

18. Now that you have designed the basic framework for the Person class, add it to the Visual Basic project by selecting File ➣ Update Project, or by pressing Ctrl+S.

19. Close the Class Builder by selecting File ➣ Exit.

After a moment, you will have a new class added to your project. Now all we need to do is add some code to the framework to make it functional. If you take a look at the Name property code (the Property Let and Property Get procedures), you will see that the Class Builder has actually completed the property code for us. All we need to do is write the code to make the person identify himself.

Add the following code to the WhoAreYou() procedure of the class:

```
Public Sub WhoAreYou()
    RaiseEvent Say("I am " & mvarName)
End Sub
```

Notice that there is only one line of code in this procedure. To fire an event, you must call the RaiseEvent command from within the class. In this case, we are firing the Say event. We could use a function to return a sentence, but I want you to get used to firing events. They will come in handy later on as you develop your own event-driven applications. Let's add some code to Form1 so we can test out the Person class.

1. Double-click Form1 in the Project Explorer to make it the active control. Then double-click the form to open its code window.

2. Add the following lines of code to the (General)(Declarations) section of the form:

```
Option Explicit

Private WithEvents p As Person
```

3. We are going to use a message box to make our person say something. Do this by adding the following code to the p_Say() event:

```
Private Sub p_Say(Sentence As String)
    MsgBox Sentence
End Sub
```

4. Now let's add the code to make our person come to life:

```
Private Sub Form_Load()
    Set p = New Person

        p.Name = "John Doe"
        p.WhoAreYou

    Set p = Nothing

    End
End Sub
```

Note that you can set p.Name to any name you like.

5. Give the program a try by pressing F5.

Of course there are more features available in the Class Builder utility, but most are self-explanatory, and you have used the important features. Take some time to practice creating your own classes. Create complex classes or simple ones. Just remember that practice makes perfect. We will continue developing other classes throughout this book.

You should now be familiar enough with modules and classes that you can create your own. It is important for you to master these concepts because code modules are the "glue" of your application. They combine forms and controls and make them do something useful. If you are still a little unsure about classes and objects, don't worry. We will discuss class objects and OOP in more detail in Skill 15, *Learning and Using Object-Oriented Programming (OOP)*.

Are You up to Speed?

Now you can...

- ☑ use code modules to write code behind your forms and controls
- ☑ create your own sub procedures and functions
- ☑ pass parameters to sub procedures and functions
- ☑ design a simple class object
- ☑ expose properties and methods using the *Public* keyword
- ☑ encapsulate properties and methods using the *Private* keyword
- ☑ start creating class modules
- ☑ use the Class Builder utility to develop your own classes

SKILL 5

Creating and Using Menus and Toolbars

- When to use menus and toolbars
- Creating and using menus
- Using the Menu Editor
- Considering a menu's design
- Creating toolbars
- Using toolbar custom controls
- Linking images with an image list
- Using the CoolBar control

Most Windows-based applications use menus and toolbars to offer the user a mechanism to take action on the program. Since these components are such a vital part of many applications, this chapter will take an in-depth look at how to create and use them.

When to Use Menus and Toolbars

By now you may have noticed that most applications written for Windows have a somewhat standard interface. Most of them have title bars, sizable borders, and Control Menu buttons. In addition, many have menus and toolbars to help you access special functions within the program. Visual Basic itself offers menus and toolbars to help make your job easier (see Figure 5.1).

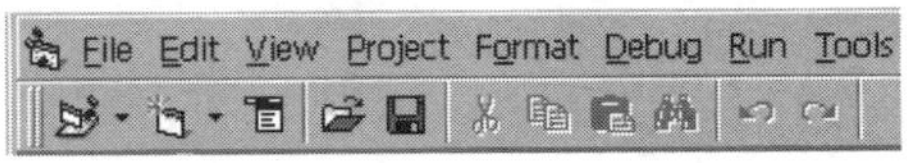

FIGURE 5.1: The Visual Basic menu and toolbar

Menus expose many of the underlying functions built into an application that are not necessarily obvious at first glance. Menu options can be enabled, disabled, checked, and even popped-up on an object. In addition, you can create a window list, which is a menu that has an option for each MDI child form within the form. As you have noticed in Visual Basic, menus can be docked to another control, be context-sensitive, and pop up directly on an object. You will create a menu later in this skill (see "Creating a Menu with the Menu Editor").

Toolbars, on the other hand, are used to provide quick access to the functions that are also available in menus. For instance, you have probably seen the Cut, Copy, and Paste buttons on menus and toolbars before. It is much easier and quicker for a user to press a button on a toolbar than it is to select Edit ➢ Copy from the menu. Toolbars are even more helpful if they expose functions that are buried under a menu of options or hidden deep in nested submenus. You will create a toolbar later in this skill (see "Creating Toolbars").

When you decide to create a large application, be sure to use menus and toolbars effectively. Make sure they conform to the Windows Graphical User Interface (GUI) standards (described in "Considering a Menu's Design" later in this chapter). Not only will this help reduce the learning curve of your application, it will make your application user-friendly and will be more likely to welcome new users.

Understanding the Menu Object

As stated in the previous section, a menu exposes functions to the user in a clean and, usually, user-friendly manner. To create a menu in Visual Basic, you will use the menu control. The menu control is just like any other control you add to a form, except the menu control does not appear in the Toolbox. Instead, you can start the Menu Editor from the Visual Basic menu or toolbar and create your menu from there.

A menu control has several properties and one event, but no methods. To place a menu control on a form, you set that particular form as the active control. With the desired form selected, click Tools ➤ Menu Editor, or use the toolbar alternative to open the Menu Editor (see Figure 5.2).

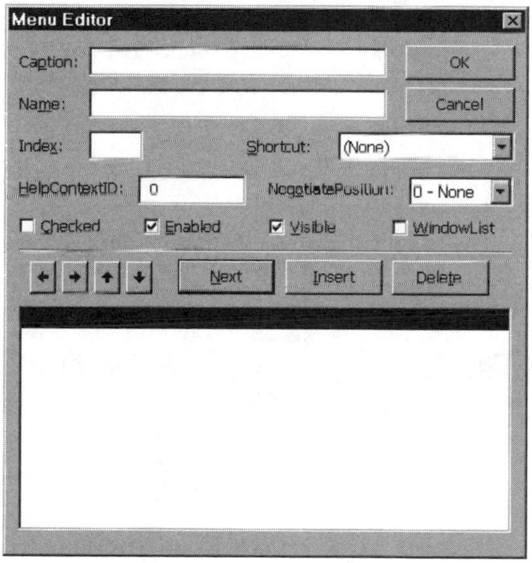

FIGURE 5.2: The Menu Editor

The Menu Editor is where you design your menu. A menu consists of one or more menu titles (for example, File) across the menu. Each menu title on the menu bar contains one or more menu items (for example, Exit). You can even include a separator to group related items together within one menu. You end up with a series of menu controls rather than a single control. Every menu title and menu item (including separators) is a distinct control with its own properties and Click() event.

Menu Properties

The design-time properties, which are listed below, are exposed in the Menu Editor rather than in the Properties window.

Appearance	Index	Tag
Caption	**Name**	**Visible**
Checked	NegotiatePosition	WindowList
Enabled	Parent	
HelpContextID	**ShortCut**	

The following explains some of the more important properties to remember:

- The Caption property determines the text you see in the menu. Using an ampersand (&) character gives an access-key alternative to the mouse.

- The Checked property places (or removes) a checkmark next to the menu item. This is handy for toggle items, and you can turn the checkmark off and on at run time by setting the Checked property appropriately.

- The Enabled property is sometimes set to False when the menu item is not relevant. For example, you may want to disable a Save item until the user has entered some data. Once again, you can reset the Enabled property at run time.

- A variation of the previous item is to use the Visible property and hide the item when it's not required—though it's less confusing for the user if you disable rather than hide items.

- The Name property is, as always, the first one to define—by convention, menu controls begin with the mnu prefix.

- The Shortcut property determines the keyboard alternative to the menu item. This is not quite the same as an access key (which is determined with the ampersand character). Usually, a shortcut is accessed through the Ctrl and Alt keys used in conjunction with another key, such as F1.

NOTE   A shortcut key immediately generates the Click() event for the menu control. With access keys, there are two actions to carry out: first, you press the Alt+key combination to open the menu, and then you press the key corresponding to the underlined letter in the menu caption. For example, you might press Alt+H to open a Help menu and then press C to see the contents page of the help file. With a shortcut key, all you have to do is press, say, F1 to see the same page.

You can open the menus created in the Menu Editor from the form when it is in design view. To see the code for the Click event procedure, you click the menu item in design view. Alternatively, choose the menu control's name from the Object drop-down list in the Code window. You can easily see the properties for a menu item by reopening the Menu Editor and selecting the menu item from the list at the bottom of the editor. You can also view menu control properties by selecting their names from the drop-down list at the top of the Properties window.

TIP   The properties are not displayed when you click the menu control in design view—this contrasts with all other controls. Usually, you set, review, and alter properties in the Menu Editor—but you may prefer to use the Properties window to make further changes.

The *Click()* Event

This is the only event for a menu control; this event is also generated when either access or shortcut keys are used. You place the code for the actions relevant to the menu item being selected in the Click() event procedure.

Each menu title has a Click() event, too. Usually, this event is ignored, as you don't want anything to happen if the user has merely opened the menu by clicking the menu title. However, advanced Visual Basic developers often use the Index property in conjunction with this event to dynamically add or remove items from the menu that is about to open. Dynamic menus are actually menu control arrays. Each menu item is similar, and resides in the same block of memory. Then rather than referring to the menu item by name, you refer to it by its index in the array. For more information on arrays, please refer to Skill 7, *Understanding Data Types*.

Menu Methods

There are no methods for Visual Basic menu controls, so let's move on and learn how to create your own menus.

Creating a Menu with the Menu Editor

The Menu Editor is where you will do most of the work designing menus for your applications. To define your first menu, open the Menu Editor by clicking

Tools ➤ Menu Editor (as shown previously in Figure 5.2). Notice the following items in the Menu Editor:

- As you might expect, you enter the Caption property and the Name property in the first two text boxes in the Menu Editor.

- You can also choose a shortcut key for the current menu control.

- Typically, leave the Checked, Enabled, and Visible property check boxes at their default settings.

- The left and right arrow buttons are for indenting and outdenting menu controls. A menu title must be flush with the left margin of the menu list box at the bottom. A menu item is usually indented once. You would indent a second time to create a submenu item (cascading menu) from the previous menu item.

- The up and down arrow buttons are for changing the order in which menu titles and menu items appear.

- You can type a number in the Index field to make the menu a control array. These are useful when you want to create a most recently used (MRU) files list like the ones you sometimes see at the bottom of the File menu in various applications.

- The HelpContextID field is used to link the Help menu to a help file through a unique identifier called a *help context*. For more information on linking to help files, refer to Skill 13, *Creating and Using Help Files*.

- Finally, the NegotiatePosition field is used to determine where a top-level menu will be positioned when an MDI child form is maximized, and both forms must share the menu bar of the MDI parent form.

To create a menu title or menu item, the minimum requirements are the Caption and Name properties. You create a title first, and then you add the items that are to appear under that title's menu. Each menu item must be indented once from the left. Then you add the next title and its items, and so on. To add each entry, click the Next button. If you leave out an entry, then either add it at the bottom and use the up arrow button, or select the one after the insertion point and click the Insert button. To remove entries, click the Delete button. If you want to have a separator bar in a menu, set its Caption property to a hyphen character (-). But you *must* give a separator a Name property. A separator must be at the same level of indentation as the items it's separating.

The accepted prefix for menu titles and menu items is mnu. For instance, a File menu title might have the name mnuFile. Any item under that title usually incorporates the title's name. For example, an Exit menu item in the File menu would have a Name property like mnuFileExit. A single separator in the File menu may have a name like mnuFileSep1. A Name property such as mnuExit is probably not sufficient for an Exit item. When you're reading code or debugging, it's not immediately apparent which menu this item belongs to. Instead, you might want to prefix Exit with File, so the Name would be mnuFileExit.

Let's create a simple menu so you can get some practice working with a menu object:

1. Start a new project using File ➢ New Project.

2. Select Standard EXE as the project type.

3. Click Form1 to make it active.

4. Open the Menu Editor by selecting Tools ➢ Menu Editor or selecting Ctrl+E.

5. Create the File menu by typing **&File** in the Caption field, and **mnuFile** in the Name field.

6. Click the Next button to start the next menu item.

7. You want to make this a menu item of the File menu, so click the right arrow button to indent this menu item.

8. Set the Caption property of the next item to **&Exit**. Set its Name property to **mnuFileExit**.

9. Now that you have created your first menu, finish making the Edit and Help menus by setting the properties below and clicking the Next button after you set each Name property:

    Edit Menu

Caption:	**&Edit**
Name:	**MnuEdit**

    Edit Menu Items

Caption:	**Cu&t**
Name:	**MnuEditCut**

Caption:	**&Copy**
Name:	**MnuEditCopy**
Caption:	**&Paste**
Name:	**MnuEditPaste**

Help Menu

Caption:	**&Help**
Name:	**MnuHelp**

Help Menu Items

Caption:	**&About...**
Name:	**MnuHelpAbout**

When you are done creating these menu objects, the Menu Editor should look like Figure 5.3. You can make any changes you may need to by clicking the appropriate menu item in the Menu Editor and changing its properties. When the menu looks like Figure 5.3, click the OK button.

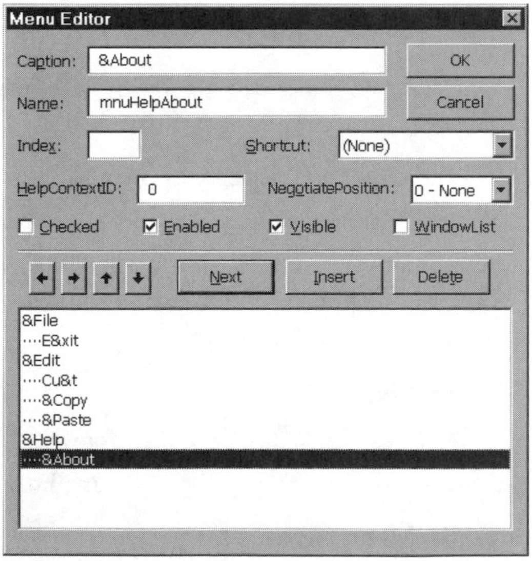

FIGURE 5.3: Creating a menu with the Menu Editor

Now you can see how your menu will look and behave. If you click the Edit menu, it will expose the Edit menu items (see Figure 5.4). If you click Paste, it will take you directly to the `mnuEditPaste_Click()` procedure in the Code window. You place your code to paste in the Code window.

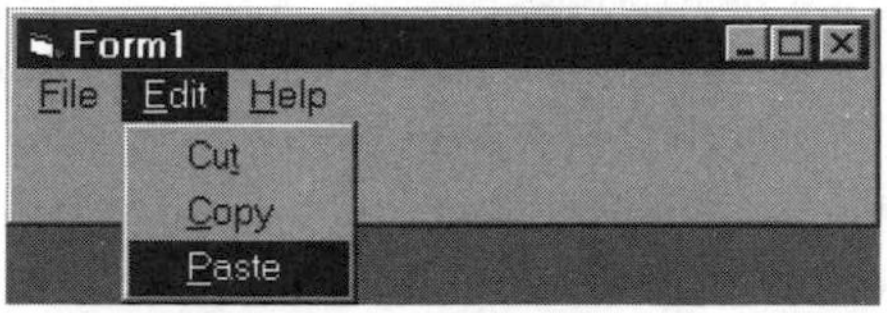

FIGURE 5.4: Your menu in action

Click File ➤ Exit on your newly designed menu so you can place code in the `mnuFileExit_Click()` procedure. Place the End statement in the procedure and run your application. All of the menus should expand and collapse properly. Clicking the Exit menu item should end your application.

Considering a Menu's Design

Windows is an operating system that uses a Graphical User Interface, or GUI. The reasoning behind the name is that you work more with graphics, forms, and icons, for example, than typing text. The GUI is what makes the environment and its programs user-friendly. Rather than trying to remember cryptic commands and their parameters, called *switches*, you can remember things easier with pictures. In order for the GUI to be effective, it must be standardized. All similar controls and forms should look alike and operate in pretty much the same fashion.

Before looking at toolbars, let's examine an often-overlooked aspect of Windows application design: standards. When you design your menus, you should strive to make them as standard as possible. While it is beyond the scope of this book to go into too much detail regarding GUI standards, it makes sense to get you started on the right track.

When you lay out your menus, try to make them as close to standard Windows applications as possible. While many applications have different menus and no two applications are exactly alike, you can duplicate the layouts of other menus to make yours standardized.

You may notice how the File menu is always the leftmost menu, and the Help menu is always rightmost. Make your applications the same way. The Edit menu is almost always to the right of the File menu, and the Window menu is to the left of the Help menu. If you incorporate Edit and Window menus, be sure to keep them in this order. Proficient Windows users get accustomed to moving the mouse in particular fashions to access menus. Don't throw them off by re-arranging your menus.

As menu layout is standardized, your shortcut keys should be standardized as well. Notice the letter *t* is underlined in the Cut menu option. Your first instinct might be to place the ampersand in front of the *C*, but when a user decides to copy something from the clipboard, they may be in for a shock when half of their document disappears! Many menu shortcuts are standardized. If you are in question as to what shortcuts to use, you can launch any of your other Windows applications and examine how they are designed.

Creating Toolbars

Toolbars are an extremely useful enhancement to menus. They provide mouse-driven shortcuts to menu options.

When designing toolbars, as with designing menus, it is important to consider design standardization. You may want to use standard-sized buttons or standardized icons so your users know exactly what a button does without having to depend on a manual or online help to navigate your application. You can duplicate toolbar designs from other applications in much the same way as you can with menus.

Let's create a toolbar to enhance the menu you just created in the section "Creating a Menu with the Menu Editor." Before you can work on the toolbar, you need to make sure it is added to your Toolbox.

1. If you need to add the Toolbar control, right-click the Toolbox, and click the Components menu item. When the Components dialog box appears, check the box next to Microsoft Windows Common Controls 6.0.

2. Add a Toolbar control to your form. Set its `Name` property to **tbrToolbar** and set its `Align` property to **1 - vbAlignTop**.

3. From the Properties window, select (`Custom`).

4. When the Property Pages dialog box appears, select the Buttons tab.

Notice how most toolbars are indented a bit from the left of the screen. To duplicate this you need to add a separator before you add your first button.

5. Click Insert Button to place the first button on the toolbar.

6. Click the Style drop-down list and select **3 - tbrSeparator** (see Figure 5.5).

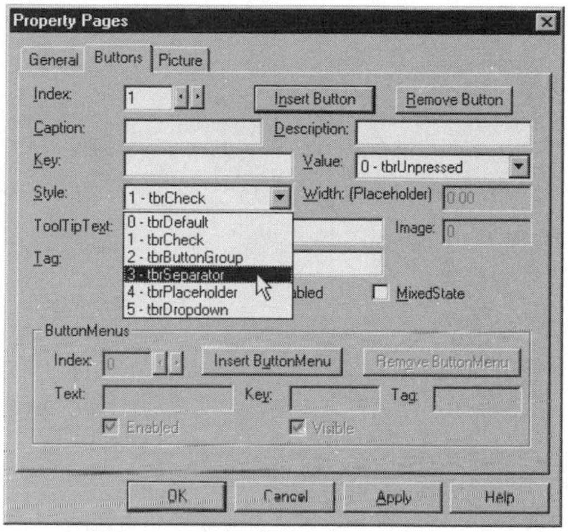

FIGURE 5.5: Setting the Style property

Adding Buttons to Toolbars

Now that you have added the Toolbar control to your form and inserted a separator, you can add some buttons to your toolbar:

1. Click Insert Button to add a new button. Set Key to **New** and Style to **0 - tbrDefault**.

2. Click Insert Button again to add another button. Set Key to **Open** and set Style to **0 - tbrDefault**.

3. Click Insert Button to add the last button. Set Key to **Save** and set Style to **0 - tbrDefault**.

4. Click the OK button to see what the toolbar looks like.

If you had no problems, your toolbar should now look like Figure 5.6. Again, notice the separator on the left of the toolbar that gives it the indent.

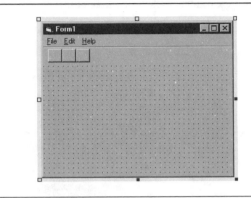

FIGURE 5.6:   A form with your toolbar

Adding Images to Toolbars

Now you need to add some images to the toolbar. Unfortunately, you cannot do it directly by setting a Picture property. Instead, you need to link the toolbar with an image list. Here's how to do it:

1. Add an image list to your form and set its Name property to **imlToolbar**. This control was added to your Toolbox when you added the Microsoft Windows Common Controls 6.0.

2. Open up the Property Pages by selecting Custom from the Properties window.

3. When the Property Pages dialog box appears, click the Images tab so you can add some images.

4. The first image you want to add is the standard blank page, which is used to represent a New file (i.e. File ➤ New). Click Insert Picture.

5. Select New.bmp from the Graphics\Bitmaps\Tlbr_w95 directory.

6. After the blank page appears, click it so the next image will be placed after it in the list.

7. Click Insert Picture. Select Open.bmp. When it is added, click the yellow folder.

8. Click Insert Picture one last time and select Save.bmp. Your Image List should look like Figure 5.7. Click the OK button to close the Property Pages dialog box.

TIP You can create your own Toolbar icons using Windows Paint. For small icons, set the dimensions of the icon to 16 pixels by 16 pixels, or 32 pixels by 32 pixels for large icons. You can set these dimensions by selecting Image ➢ Attributes from the Paint menu or by pressing Ctrl+E in Paint.

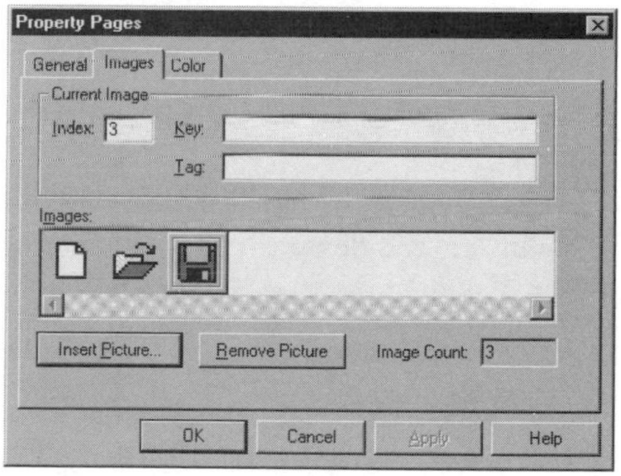

FIGURE 5.7: Inserting bitmaps in an image list

9. Select tbrToolbar and open its property pages again by selecting the Custom property from the Properties window.

10. On the General tab, set the ImageList property to **imlToolbar**, as in Figure 5.8.

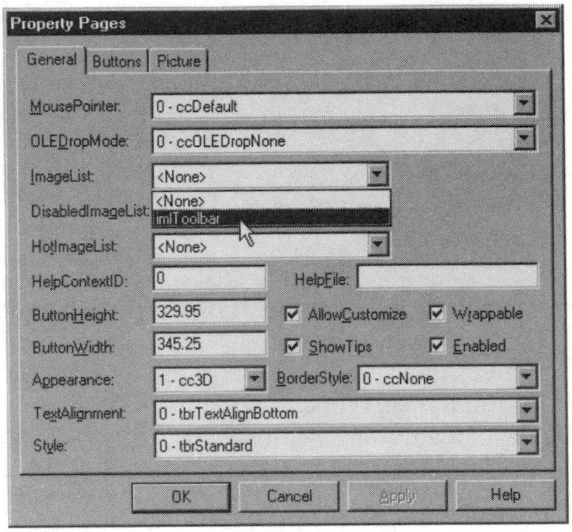

FIGURE 5.8: Linking the toolbar to the image list

11. Click the Buttons tab.

12. Set the Index property to 2, and set the Image property to 1. This will place the image in index position 1, the blank document, on the button in position 2. Remember that button 1 is actually a separator.

13. Set Index to 3 and Image to 2. This places the folder icon on the Open button on the toolbar.

14. Set Index to 4 and Image to 3. This puts the disk icon on the Save button on the toolbar.

15. When you are done, click the OK button. Your toolbar will look like Figure 5.9.

That's all there is to designing the layout of a toolbar and adding graphics to it, but the toolbar is not finished yet. You need to add code to the toolbar so it will know what button the user is pressing. Double-click the toolbar to open the tbrToolbar_ButtonClick() event. Notice that the Button parameter is passed to this event. This is actually the index value of the button that was clicked. You will use this index to help identify the button that was clicked.

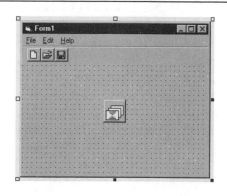

FIGURE 5.9: The toolbar with icons

Add the following code to the `tbrToolbar_ButtonClick()` event:

```
Private Sub tbrToolbar_ButtonClick(ByVal Button As ComctlLib.Button)
     Select Case Button.Key
     Case Is = "New"
          MsgBox "You clicked the New button."
     Case Is = "Open"
          MsgBox "You clicked the Open button."
     Case Is = "Save"
          MsgBox "You clicked the Save button."
     End Select
End Sub
```

Notice that you used a `Select…Case` statement to determine which button was pressed. This is like a supercharged `If…Then` statement. It allows us greater flexibility when dealing with multiple conditions. As you can see from the code above, you used three `Case Is` = statements rather than three separate `If…Then` code blocks. Also note that when using a toolbar, you need to be sure to set the `Key` property appropriately. You will need to reference this value to determine which button was clicked.

Now that you understand the basics of creating toolbars, you can use a new component that ships with Visual Basic 6: the CoolBar control. This is the same control that is used for Visual Basic's toolbar. Save your work from the previous steps and read on, and you can start using this cool tool in your applications!

Using the CoolBar Control

A new control that ships with Visual Basic 6 is the CoolBar control. You can see this control in action in the Microsoft Office suite (shown in Figure 5.10), Internet Explorer 4, and the Visual Basic IDE. The CoolBar is actually a dockable container that can hold other controls such as toolbars, combo boxes, and labels. Its most distinguishing characteristic is the Hot Image feature of the buttons. Hot Images are flat buttons that rise up when the mouse hovers over them, much like the hot tracking feature found in the Tree View and List View controls.

The CoolBar is made up of one or more bands which can contain a single control on each band.

FIGURE 5.10: The CoolBar

Unfortunately, Microsoft's documentation for this control was very sparse. However, I managed to find a way to make it easy for you to learn. Let's give it a try.

1. If necessary, open the project from the previous section. You will be updating it to use the CoolBar.

2. Right-click the Toolbox and select Components from the context menu. This will bring up the Components dialog box, where we can add the CoolBar control.

3. Scroll down and check the boxes next to "Microsoft Windows Common Controls 6.0" and "Microsoft Windows Common Controls-3 6.0." The CoolBar control is in Common Controls-3. We also need Common Controls 6.0 because it contains the Toolbar and ImageList controls.

4. Click the OK button to add the controls to your Toolbox.

5. Add a CoolBar control to frmMain.

6. Now click the Toolbar control to make it the active control.

7. Press Ctrl+X to cut the control from the form.

8. Click the CoolBar control and press Ctrl+V to paste the toolbar onto it.

9. In the Properties Window, set the CoolBar's Name property to **cbrCoolbar** and set the Align property to **1 – Align Top**.

10. Click the (Custom) property to bring up the property page for the CoolBar (Figure 5.11).

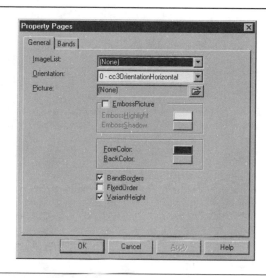

FIGURE 5.11: The General tab of the CoolBar's property page

11. There's not much for us to do on the General tab, so click the Bands tab.

Figure 5.12 shows the most common properties for the CoolBar control. In order for the toolbar to rest neatly in the CoolBar, you need to make it a child of the first Band object in the CoolBar.

12. Make sure the Index field is set to **1**, and set the Child field to **tbrToolbar**.

13. Click the OK button to close the property page.

Right now the toolbar in Figure 5.13 looks kind of funny. The toolbar appears to be on top of the CoolBar, rather than in it. In addition, the buttons are raised instead of flat. We need to change some properties in the toolbar to make it appear correctly.

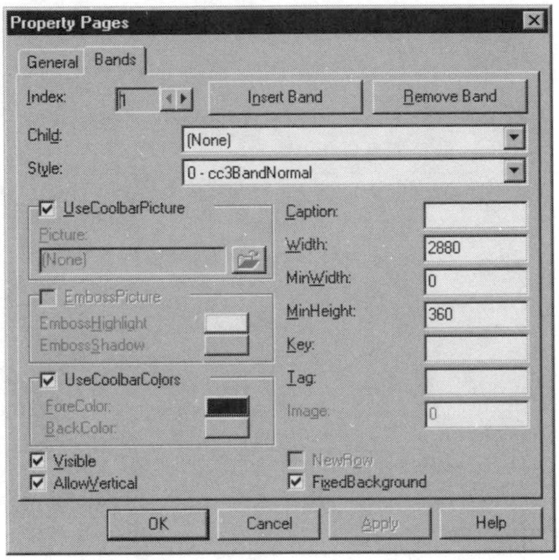

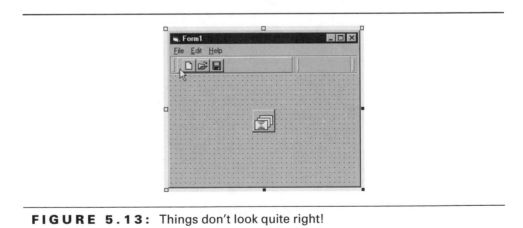

FIGURE 5.12: The Bands tab of the CoolBar's property page

FIGURE 5.13: Things don't look quite right!

14. Click a button on the toolbar to make it the active control.

15. Double-click the (Custom) field in the Properties window to open the property page for the control.

16. On the General tab, set the Appearance property to **0 – ccFlat**. Click the Apply button so you can see the toolbar "sink" into the CoolBar.

17. Now, set the Style property to **1 – tbrFlat**. Click Apply to see the buttons sink into the toolbar.

18. Click the OK button to close the dialog box.

TIP   You can set the HotImageList property to a separate Image List control if you want the button icons to change when the mouse moves over a button. This gives the effect of having animated buttons that react to your mouse! The only caveat to doing this is that the corresponding images in each Image List must have the same Index position, since the Toolbar control only allows for one index in the Image field.

19. Press F5 to run your project. Move your mouse over some buttons and watch them rise from the toolbar like in Figure 5.14.

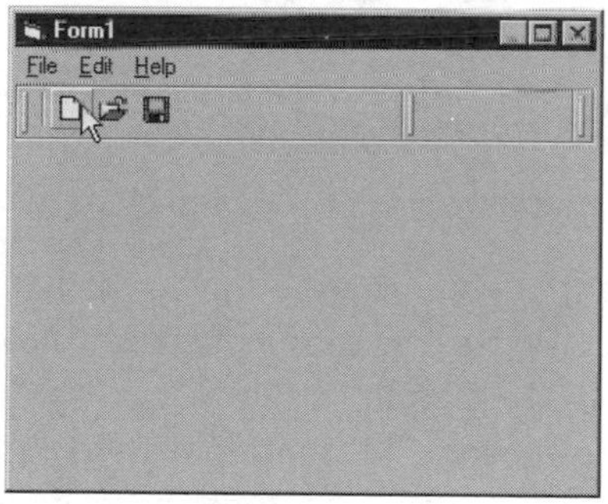

FIGURE 5.14: The CoolBar in action

You may notice that there are still two empty bands on the CoolBar. Since the CoolBar acts as a container for Band controls, and Bands can hold other controls, you can add more controls to your CoolBar!

1. Stop the project by selecting File ➢ Exit from the menu you created, or by clicking the Close button on the form.

2. Add a Combo Box control to the CoolBar control. Make sure that you draw the box on the CoolBar, and not the form.

3. Add a Check Box control to the CoolBar as well. Set its Caption property to **Check Me!**

4. Now, select cbrCoolbar and open its Property Page by double-clicking the (Custom) field.

5. Click the Bands tab and set the Index field to **2** by clicking the right-facing arrow to the right of the field. This sets the property page to the second band on the Coolbar.

6. Set the Child field to **Combo1**, and the Caption field to **Font**.

7. Click the Apply button to apply the changes.

8. Set the Index field to **3** to get to the third Band. Set the Child field to **Check1**.

9. Click the OK button to close the property page.

10. Run your project to see the changes.

Notice that you can grab the anchors (the vertical bars on the left side of each band) and resize and move the bands around. These are just a few of the cool features of the CoolBar control.

That's all there is to creating menus and toolbars! Remember that menus and toolbars offer simple and convenient ways to provide added functionality to your applications. By making your menus look and feel like other Windows-based applications, you will give your applications an advantage over poorly designed ones: Your application will be more useable than nonstandard applications, and users will thank you for it.

Are You up to Speed?

Now you can...

- ☑ determine when to use menus and toolbars
- ☑ create a menu using the Menu Editor
- ☑ design your menus to resemble those in other Windows apps
- ☑ create a toolbar using the toolbar control
- ☑ add images to the toolbar using an image list
- ☑ write code to make your toolbar function
- ☑ combine controls on a CoolBar

Skill 5

SKILL 6

Logic and Program Flow

- What makes a computer think?
- Understanding logical operators
- Making comparisons
- Evaluating conditions in code
- Performing repetitive tasks

Now that you have a good idea of how to piece together a visual application using the controls supplied with Visual Basic, it's time to learn how to tie these pieces together.

In this skill you will learn the basics of logic and how it is used to allow a computer to make decisions. You will then combine logic and conditional programming to develop more complex decision-making algorithms. Finally, you will learn how to program repetitive tasks using different types of looping algorithms.

What Makes a Computer Think?

A common misconception by people who are unfamiliar with computers is that computers are smart. Nothing could be further from the truth. Computers, at best, can only be as smart as their programmers. Computers can make decisions, but they need code to do it. In fact, the decision-making code is pretty much limited to the decisions that the programmer can address in the application.

Logical comparisons are required to make a computer perform useful tasks. They are required for code to run, to make error handlers, process files, and everything else you will do. A computer application makes decisions in much the same way a human does. It takes a condition and evaluates it to get a result. Then, it takes this result and compares it against a set of rules that the application knows how to handle. For example, an ATM machine needs to know how to decide if a PIN number is valid. It does this by comparing the PIN entered by the customer against a database of known PIN numbers. If the PIN is found and it matches the customer's profile in the bank's database, then the customer is granted access to the account. Almost all computer decisions are made in the same manner.

Understanding Logical Operators

The first step to giving your application "smarts" is to understand how the computer processes information.

Believe it or not, everything a computer does is actually processed in terms of ones and zeros, called *binary*. In binary language everything can be performed either mathematically or logically. Mathematically, the computer counts in base-2, meaning after a value is greater than one, it gets set back to zero, and the next bit is set to one. You and I think in terms of base-10 math, where when a number is greater than nine, the units digit is set back to zero and the tens digit is set to one, and so on.

Since a computer understands everything in terms of ones and zeros, it can use these numbers to represent on and off or true and false. A binary zero indicates a false condition, and one is used to indicate a true condition. This is how Boolean logic works. Using several combinations of expressions and logical operators, you can perform sophisticated tasks such as creating high-resolution graphics, special effects, and encryption algorithms. You will learn about five logical operators in the next sections: AND, EQV, OR, XOR, and NOT.

Logical *AND*

The Visual Basic operator AND is used to perform logical conjunctions between two expressions. In layman's terms, this means that the application tests for two expressions being True at the same time. Consider how an automated teller machine works. Assuming you actually have cash in your account, to get some from the machine you need two things: a valid ATM card and a valid PIN number. If either the card or the PIN number is invalid, you can't get any money. If both are valid, you can go to the store and buy some coffee and doughnuts.

The way logical AND works is simple. If both expressions evaluate to True, then the result is True. If either of the expressions is False, then the result is False. Table 6.1 shows several combinations of expressions and the results when they are ANDed together.

TABLE 6.1: The Results of Logical AND between Two Expressions

Expression 1	Expression 2	Result
True	True	True
True	False	False
False	True	False
False	False	False

Sophisticated graphics algorithms are processed using this logical operator as well. In bit-wise operations, when a bit is set, its value is one; that bit is said to be True. When it is zero, the bit is said to be False. When performing bit-wise logic, corresponding bits are logically compared, and the resulting bit values can be added together to form a number.

To better understand, take a look at Table 6.2. We take two values, 217 and 106, and AND them together. The bits in positions 128 through 1 correspond to the bits 7 through 0 in binary math. Since binary is actually base-2 math, we can say that the first bit is 2^0, or 1. The second bit is 2^1, or 2. Bit 3 is the equivalent of 2^2, the integer 4. You use this same math for each bit up to bit 7.

You may have noticed that the values are read from right to left, rather than the normal left to right. This is because in binary, the highest bit is always on the left, and the lowest on the right. In addition, the rightmost bit is called bit 0. Ordering the bits in the fashion allows you to count using as many bits as you need. The table shows 8-bit binary, which is what you will use most often. It consists of bits 0 through 7.

TABLE 6.2: ANDing Two Integers Together

Bit	7	6	5	4	3	2	1	0	
Binary	2^7	2^6	2^5	2^4	2^3	2^2	2^1	2^0	
Integer	128	64	32	16	8	4	2	1	Integer Value
Expression 1	1	1	0	1	1	0	0	1	**217**
Expression 2	0	1	1	0	1	0	1	0	**106**
Exp1 AND Exp2	0	1	0	0	1	0	0	0	**72**

If you were to add up all the bit values denoted by 1 in the third line of the table, 128+64+16+8+1, you would get a result of 217. The fourth line adds up to 106. If you AND the bit values together, you get the bit pattern in the sixth line of the table. By adding the bit values together, you get 72. Based on this table, 217 AND 106 = 72. To check the validity of the table, try the following example:

1. Open the Immediate window by pressing Ctrl+G.

2. In the Immediate window, type the following lines of code:

```
A=217: B=106
? A AND B
```

The result should be 72, just as the table showed.

3. Try some more ANDing with the following code:

```
? 163 AND 8
? 55 AND 12
? 37 AND 7
? 72 AND 255
? 255 AND 0
```

The results should be 0, 4, 5, 72, and 0.

You can duplicate the layout of Table 6.2 and insert bit values to test results. Try writing out the bit values in your own tables and test the results for yourself. This will help you get a solid grasp of binary logic.

Logical *EQV*

The Visual Basic operator EQV is used to test the equivalency of two expressions. If both expressions return the same Boolean value, then the result is True. If either expression is logically different, then the result will be False. Table 6.3 shows several combinations of expressions and their results.

TABLE 6.3: The Results of Logical EQV between Two Expressions

Expression 1	Expression 2	Result
True	True	True
True	False	False
False	True	False
False	False	True

As a beginning programmer, you will probably not use this operator.

Logical *OR*

When you want to test for one or more expressions that are True, you use the OR operator. When either expression is True, the result is True. If both expressions are False, then the result is False. Table 6.4 shows several combinations of expressions and their ORed results.

TABLE 6.4: The Results of Logical OR between Two Expressions

Expression 1	Expression 2	Result
True	True	True
True	False	True
False	True	True
False	False	False

Skill 6

You can OR two numeric values, just as you ANDed them in a previous example. Examine Table 6.5.

TABLE 6.5: ORing Two Integers Together

Bit	7	6	5	4	3	2	1	0	
Binary	2^7	2^6	2^5	2^4	2^3	2^2	2^1	2^0	
Integer	128	64	32	16	8	4	2	1	Integer Value
Expression 1	0	1	0	0	1	0	0	1	73
Expression 2	1	1	1	0	1	0	0	0	232
Exp1 OR Exp2	1	1	1	0	1	0	0	1	233

You can test the validity of the table with the following example:

1. Open the Immediate window by pressing Ctrl+G.

2. In the Immediate window, type the following line of code:

   ```
   ? 73 OR 232
   ```

   The result should be 233, just as the table showed.

3. Try making a table for each of the following expressions, and calculate the results on paper first. Then try validating them in the Immediate window:

   ```
   55 OR 12
   37 OR 7
   72 OR 255
   255 OR 0
   ```

4. Try validating the values in the Immediate window with the following lines of code:

   ```
   ? 55 OR 12
   ? 37 OR 7
   ? 72 OR 255
   ? 255 OR 0
   ```

   The results should be: 63, 39, 255, and 255. As you can see, anything ORed with 255 will be 255.

Logical *XOR*

If you want to test two expressions, and make sure that one and only one expression is True, you would use the *Exclusive Or*, or XOR operator. It is specifically used to check that only one expression or the other is True, but not both. You can see this from the results in Table 6.6.

TABLE 6.6: The Results of Logical XOR between Two Expressions

Expression 1	Expression 2	Result
True	True	False
True	False	True
False	True	True
False	False	False

Let's try XORing the same numbers that we ORed in the previous example. This will give you a clear idea of how OR and XOR differ. Examine Table 6.7.

TABLE 6.7: XORing Two Integers Together

Bit	7	6	5	4	3	2	1	0	
Binary	2^7	2^6	2^5	2^4	2^3	2^2	2^1	2^0	
Integer	128	64	32	16	8	4	2	1	Integer Value
Expression 1	0	1	0	0	1	0	0	1	73
Expression 2	1	1	1	0	1	0	0	0	232
Exp1 XOR Exp2	1	0	1	0	0	0	0	1	161

Again, verify these values for yourself:

1. Open the Immediate window by pressing Ctrl+G.

2. In the Immediate window, type the following line of code:

   ```
   ? 73 XOR 232
   ```

   The result will be 161, just as the table showed.

3. Try making a table for each of the following expressions, and calculate the results on paper first.

   ```
   55 XOR 12
   37 XOR 7
   72 XOR 255
   255 XOR 0
   ```

Skill 6

4. Try validating the values in the Immediate window with the following lines of code:

```
? 55 XOR 12
? 37 XOR 7
? 72 XOR 255
? 255 XOR 0
```

The results should be: 59, 34, 183, and 255.

Logical *NOT*

Logical NOT is used to return the opposite of the expression. This is useful when you want to test for the opposite condition that you expect. For example, consider the following code:

```
Dim Successful as Boolean

Successful = True

If Not Successful Then
    MsgBox "The operation failed."
End If
```

We declared a variable, Successful, as a Boolean data type. Then we said that we were, in fact, successful. Then using the If Not Successful... condition, we checked to determine if we were not successful. In your code, you could replace the variable Successful with a function that returns a True or False, and check the results accordingly. As you can see from Table 6.8, the result will always be the opposite of the expression.

T A B L E 6 . 8 : The Results of Logical NOT between Two Expressions

Expression 1	Result
True	False
False	True

For all practical purposes, you will use NOT when you want to check for the exception to the rule, often in error-checking code, as you will see later. For now, to see how Visual Basic uses the NOT command, try this easy example:

1. In the Immediate window, type the following line of code:

```
? NOT True
```

The result will be False.

2. Test for the opposite with this line of code:

```
? NOT False
```

Obviously, the result will be True.

Making Comparisons

In addition to using the logical operators to compare expressions, you can also use comparison symbols to compare two or more expressions. You can test for equality of numeric as well as text values, as well as how they relate to each other. Using the following operators, you can test data for values that lie within allowable tolerances, or test for values that lie outside those tolerances. You can compare words, names, PIN numbers, or anything else you can dream of. Let's see how its done.

Equality Comparisons

You will almost always need to compare two expressions for equality in your applications. To do this in Visual Basic you use the equal sign operator (=). If you have tried any of the examples in the book so far, you should be familiar with this operator. To check for equality, you could write code similar to the following:

```
If x = 3 Then
    MsgBox "The value of x is equal to 3."
End If
```

The beauty of BASIC is that it is almost like plain English. If this were Algebra 1, you could write out this as a word problem as such:

If the value of x is equal to 3, then display a message box.

You will often find that you will be doing just the opposite. You will convert word problems into code. Fortunately, the tangible results of program code are more rewarding than an answer on a piece of paper!

To see how to test for equality, you can try this example which checks the date, and displays an appropriate message.

1. Start a new project by selecting File ➤ New Project.

2. Select Standard EXE from the New Project dialog box. Click OK.

3. Set the Name property of Form1 to **frmMain**. Set its Caption property to **Pick a Number**.

4. Add two command buttons to the form.

5. Set the Name property of the first command button to **cmdGetSecretNumber**. Set its Caption property to **Get Secret &Number**.

6. Set the Name property of the second command button to **cmdGuess**. Set its Caption property to **&Guess**.

7. Double-click frmMain to open its Code window.

8. Add the following code to the Load() event of frmMain:

```
Private Sub Form_Load()
    'Get the scret number
    SecretNumber = GetSecretNumber()
End Sub
```

9. Now add the following line to the (General)(Declarations) section of frmMain:

```
Option Explicit

Private SecretNumber As Integer
```

10. Now you need to add the GetSecretNumber() function. This is one of the major components of the application. Add the following lines of code to the (General)(Declarations) section:

```
Private Function GetSecretNumber() As Integer
    'Think of a number between 1 and 10
    Randomize

    GetSecretNumber = Int(Rnd(1) * 10) + 1
End Function
```

11. Now, add the code to the Click() event of cmdGetSecretNumber:

```
Private Sub cmdGetSecretNumber_Click()
    'Get the secret number
    SecretNumber = GetSecretNumber()
End Sub
```

12. Finally, add the following code to the Click() event of cmdGuess:

```
Private Sub cmdGuess_Click()
    Dim guess As Integer
```

```
Dim msg As String
Dim cap As String

'Create the message
msg = "Enter a number between 1 and 10:"

'Get a number from the user
guess = CInt(InputBox(msg))

'Was it the right number?
If guess = SecretNumber Then
    'Yes! The user wins!
    msg = "You guessed the secret number!"
    cap = "Correct!"

    'Display the message
    MsgBox msg, vbExclamation, cap

    'End the game
    End
Else
    'No. Try again...
    msg = "You did not guess the correct number."
    cap - "Try again!"

    MsgBox msg, vbInformation, cap
End If
End Sub
```

This procedure is the most relevant for this example. The first "is equal to" operator is in the line msg = "Enter a number..." However, the "smarts" of the program lies in the line If guess = SecretNumber Then. This line of code actually checks to see if the value you enter is the same as the secret number.

13. Save the project. You will be modifying it through the next few examples.

14. Press F5 to run the project. Click Get Secret Number to make the application pick a number. Then click the Guess button and try to guess the secret number!

As you attempt to guess the secret number, you will prompted if the number is correct or not, as in Figure 6.1

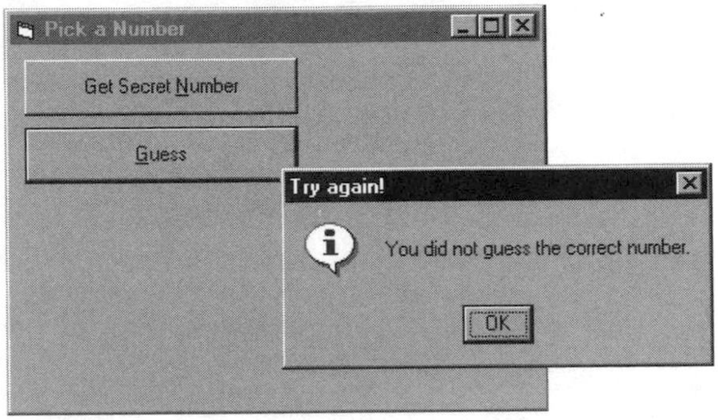

FIGURE 6.1: Guessing the secret number

Greater-Than Comparisons

Just as you did in algebra, when you need to test if a value is greater than another you use the greater-than symbol (>). This is apparent in the following code:

```
If x > 3 Then
     MsgBox "The value of x is greater than 3."
End If
```

Your applications may need to test for a value that is higher than another value. This is common when a value entered by the user must be between two values. The nature of the application will dictate how you use this operator.

Open the project from the previous example and continue with the following steps:

1. Open the Command window by double-clicking frmMain.

2. Modify the code for the Click() event of cmdGuess as follows:

```
Private Sub cmdGuess_Click()
    Dim guess As Integer
    Dim msg As String
    Dim cap As String

    'Create the message
    msg = "Enter a number between 1 and 10:"

    'Get a number from the user
    guess = CInt(InputBox(msg))
```

```
            'Was it the right number?
            Select Case guess
                Case Is = SecretNumber
                    'Yes! The user wins!
                    msg = "You guessed the secret number!"
                    cap = "Correct!"

                    'Display the message
                    MsgBox msg, vbExclamation, cap

                    'End the game
                    End
                Case Is > SecretNumber
                    'No. Try again...
                    msg = "No. You need to pick a lower number."
                    cap = "Try again!"

                    MsgBox msg, vbInformation, cap
            End Select
        End Sub
```

3. Save and run the project.

Try to guess the number. If the number you guess is greater than the secret number, then the program will let you know, as in Figure 6.2.

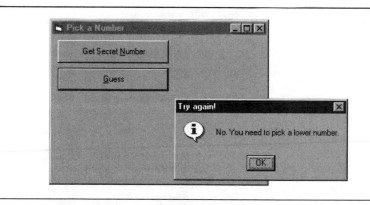

FIGURE 6.2: The results of guessing too high

The main modification to the code is in the block of code beginning with Case Is > SecretNumber. Here, the program evaluates the number being greater than SecretNumber. The next logical step is to check for values that are less than the secret number.

Less-Than Comparisons

If you need to test when a value is less than another, you use the less-than symbol (<) as shown in the following code:

```
If x < 3 Then
    MsgBox "The value of x is less than 3."
End If
```

This operator is the complement to the greater-than operator. You will often use them together to determine if an inputted value lies within a valid range of numbers. The following steps continue the previous example. Open the project from the previous example and continue with the following steps:

1. Open the Command window by double-clicking frmMain.

2. Modify the code for the Click() event of cmdGuess as follows:

```
Private Sub cmdGuess_Click()
    Dim guess As Integer
    Dim msg As String
    Dim cap As String

    'Create the message
    msg = "Enter a number between 1 and 10:"

    'Get a number from the user
    guess = CInt(InputBox(msg))

    'Was it the right number?
    Select Case guess
        Case Is = SecretNumber
            'Yes! The user wins!
            msg = "You guessed the secret number!"
            cap = "Correct!"

            'Display the message
            MsgBox msg, vbExclamation, cap

            'End the game
            End
        Case Is > SecretNumber

            'No. Try again...
            msg = "No. You need to pick a lower number."
            cap = "Try again!"
```

```
            MsgBox msg, vbInformation, cap
        Case Is < SecretNumber
            'No. Try again...
            msg = "No. You need to pick a higher number."
            cap = "Try again!"

            MsgBox msg, vbInformation, cap
    End Select
End Sub
```

3. Save and run the project.

Try to guess the number. If the number you guess is lower than the secret number, then the program will let you know, as in Figure 6.3.

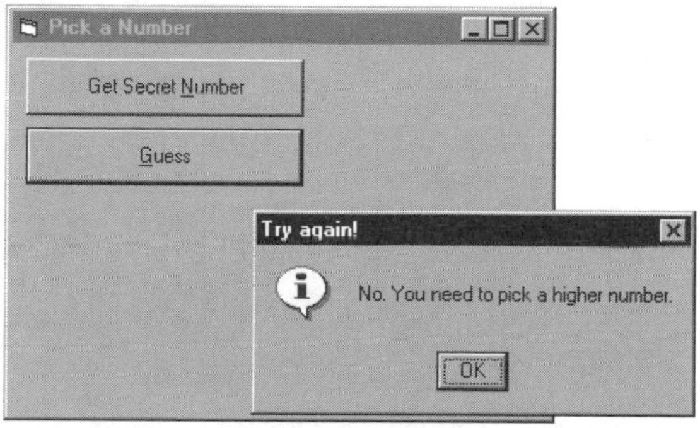

FIGURE 6.3: The results of guessing too low

Inequality Comparisons

When you want to test for a value completely different from another, you would use the greater-than and less-than symbols together (<>).

```
If x <> 3 Then
    MsgBox "The value of x is not equal to 3."
End If
```

This operator is especially useful when you want to make sure that a user entered a value. To understand why this would be important, run the previous example.

1. Click the Get Secret Number button to generate a random number between 1 and 10.

2. Click the Guess button to guess a number.

3. When the Input Box appears, click the OK or Cancel button.

As you noticed, you got a Type Mismatch error. Click the End button to stop the program. Without going too deep into the debugging process, the error was caused in the line:

```
guess = CInt(InputBox(msg))
```

The reason is the `CInt()` function requires data to convert to an integer. If it gets an empty string, then it generates an error.

To prevent this error, you can check to make sure that the user enters a value before attempting to check that value. The inequality operator is perfect for this! You can check for a value with the command:

```
If rc <> "" Then
```

Translated into English, this statement says: "If the value of guess is not equal to an empty string, then do something."

4. Modify the code for the `Click()` event of cmdGuess as follows:

```
Private Sub cmdGuess_Click()
    Dim guess As Integer
    Dim msg As String
    Dim cap As String
    Dim rc As String

    'Create the message
    msg = "Enter a number between 1 and 10:"

    'Get a number from the user
    rc = InputBox(msg)

    'Check to make sure a value was entered...
    If rc <> "" Then
        'Convert the number to an integer
        guess = CInt(rc)

        'Was it the right number?
        Select Case guess
            Case Is = SecretNumber
                'Yes! The user wins!
                msg = "You guessed the secret number!"
                cap = "Correct!"
```

```
                    'Display the message
                    MsgBox msg, vbExclamation, cap

                    'End the game
                    End
               Case Is > SecretNumber
                    'No. Try again...
                    msg = "No. You need to pick a " & _
                          "lower number."
                    cap = "Try again!"

                    MsgBox msg, vbInformation, cap
               Case Is < SecretNumber
                    'No. Try again...
                    msg = "No. You need to pick a " & _
                          "higher number."
                    cap = "Try again!"

                    MsgBox msg, vbInformation, cap
          End Select
     Else
          msg = "You must enter a value to play the game!"
          cap = "Give me a number!"

          MsgBox msg, vbCritical, cap
     End If
End Sub
```

5.   Save and run the project. Figure 6.4 shows you what happens when you fail
     to guess a number.

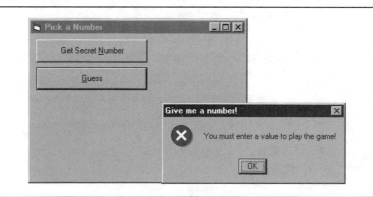

FIGURE 6.4: Checking for an empty string

Greater-Than or Equal-To Comparisons

Sometimes you want to check if a value is at least one number, but possibly more. You can do this using the greater-than or equal-to operator (>=) as shown in this example:

```
If x >= 3 Then
    MsgBox "The value of x is at least 3."
End If
```

The code is simple. If the value of x is equal to or greater than 3, then display a message box.

The use of this operator should be obvious to you by now. Suppose you were writing software to control avionics in a passenger jet. You would definitely need to warn the pilot if he or she were flying too fast. Doing so could overstress the aircraft, resulting in catastrophic structural failure. However, since your software is excellent (of course!) you check the airspeed to make sure the pilot flies under the maximum recommended airspeed, or redline. Let's start your aircraft software with the following example:

1. Start a new project by selecting File ➢ New Project from the Visual Basic menu.

2. Select Standard EXE from the New Project dialog box. Click OK.

3. Set the Name property of Form1 to **frmMain**. Set its Caption property to **VB Airspeed Indicator**.

4. Add a vertical scroll bar to frmMain and set its Name property to **vscThrottle**. Position it along the right side of the form and stretch it to the height of the form.

5. Set the Max property of vscThrottle to **100**.

6. Add a label control to frmMain and set its Name property to **lblAirspeed**. Set its Caption to **Indicated Airspeed:**.

7. Double-click frmMain in the Form Designer to open its Code window.

8. Add the following code to the (General)(Declarations) section of frmMain:

```
Option Explicit

Private Throttle As Integer    'Current throttle setting
Private Const VNE = 427        'Redline
```

9. Initialize the throttle by adding the following code to the Load() event of frmMain:

    ```
    Private Sub Form_Load()
        vscThrottle.Value = 100
    End Sub
    ```

10. Finally, add the following code to the Change() event of vscThrottle:

    ```
    Private Sub vscThrottle_Change()
        Dim ias As Integer   'Indicated airspeed

        'Let's reverse the value
        Throttle = 100 - vscThrottle.Value

        'Calculate the indicated airspeed against
        'the current power setting.
        ias = Throttle * 4.5

        'Update the airspeed indicator
        lblAirspeed.Caption = "Indicated Airspeed: " & _
            Trim$(Str$(ias))

        'Check the indicated airspeed to make sure
        'we are flying under the redline
        If ias >= VNE Then
            MsgBox "Power down!", vbCritical, "VNE Exceeded!"
        End If
    End Sub
    ```

The above code is worthy of a brief discussion. The first part, where we set the throttle, is necessary because the vertical scroll bar defaults to 0 when the elevator bar is at the top of the scroll bar. An airplane's throttle is at maximum power when it is pushed completely away from you. As a result, the code simulates a true aircraft throttle by making the scroll bar behave like a throttle.

The line that calculates the indicated airspeed (ias) is not accurate. Calculating indicated airspeed in a real aircraft is much more complex and is beyond the scope of this book. As a result, I just used a simple formula that allows the airspeed to go over 400 knots.

The warning system lies in these lines of code:

```
'Check the indicated airspeed to make sure
'we are flying under the redline
If ias >= VNE Then
    MsgBox "Power down!", vbCritical, "VNE Exceeded!"
End If
```

If the indicated airspeed is greater than or equal to the never exceed speed (VNE), then the warning is displayed.

11. Save and run the project. Slide the scroll bar up and watch the indicated airspeed climb. When you exceed VNE, the warning system will alert you, as shown in Figure 6.5.

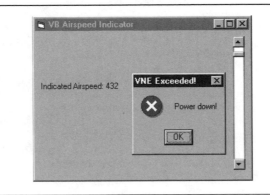

FIGURE 6.5: Exceeding VNE!

Less-Than or Equal-To Comparisons

Sometimes you want to check if a value is less than or equal to, but not greater than a specified value. To test this condition you can use the less-than or equal-to operator (<=). The following code shows how you can use it to test for this condition:

```
If x <= 3 Then
    MsgBox "The value of x is definitely not greater than 3."
End If
```

Let's use this condition in the previous example. When an aircraft flies too slow, it can stall and fall out of the air. It would be nice if the airspeed indicator would let the pilot know that they are flying dangerously slow. Continue the example as follows:

1. If it is not already opened, open the example from the previous section.

2. Add the following line of code to the (General)(Declarations) section of frmMain:

```
Private Const VSTALL = 73        'Stall Speed
```

3. Let's assume that you are flying, and the throttle is set to 77 percent. Modify the code in the `Form_Load()` event as follows:

```
Private Sub Form_Load()
    vscThrottle.Value = 23
    vscThrottle_Change
End Sub
```

4. Finally, modify the code in the `Change()` event of vscThrottle:

```
Private Sub vscThrottle_Change()
    Dim ias As Integer   'Indicated airspeed

    'Let's reverse the value
    Throttle = 100 - vscThrottle.Value

    'Calculate the indicated airspeed against
    'the current power setting.
    ias = Throttle * 4.5

    'Update the airspeed indicator
    lblAirspeed.Caption = "Indicated Airspeed: " & _
        Trim$(Str$(ias))

    'Check the indicated airspeed to make sure
    'we are flying under the redline
    If ias >= VNE Then
        MsgBox "Power down!", vbCritical, "VNE Exceeded!"
    End If

    'Make sure we don't stall
    If ias <= VSTALL Then
        MsgBox "Throttle up!", vbCritical, "Stall Warning!"
    End If
End Sub
```

5. Save and run your project. If you throttle down below stall speed, the airspeed indicator will warn you, as shown in Figure 6.6.

Now you know how to use the various operators to make decisions in your code. These are the basics of logic, and how a computer uses it. Next you will learn how to combine logic with program flow to program your application to make simple decisions.

Skill 6

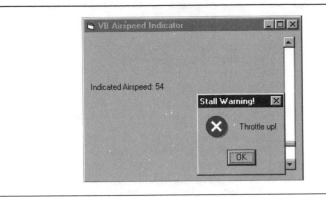

FIGURE 6.6: The stall warning

Evaluating Conditions in Code

Logic is only one half of a "thinking" application. You need a way to make your code use the logic in a useful manner. The code examples you used previously in this skill are good examples of how to evaluate conditions through code.

If...Then...Else Statements

If...Then...Else statements are the simplest, but most common condition-testing statements in Visual Basic. The syntax for using the If...Then statement is:

```
If Expression1 Operator Expression2 Then
     'Do Something...
End If
```

In the above example, the parameter Operator is any of the operators that you learned about previously in this skill: AND, OR, =, <>, and so on. Expression1 and Expression2 are variables or constants that can be compared using the given operator. For example, to compare to strings you could use code similar to the following:

```
PIN = "123456"
.
.
.
If PIN = "123456" Then
     MsgBox "The PIN is valid."
End If
```

In this case the value of PIN is compared against a known value, "123456." If the comparison is True, then a message box is displayed.

Handling only one condition at a time may be what's called for in some situations, but often you will want to handle the exception as well. You can use Visual Basic's Else statement to handle the exceptions. The syntax is:

```
If Expression1 Operator Expression2 Then
     'Do Something...
Else
     'Do Something Else...
End If
```

All you need to do is place the Else statement after the first block of code to be executed. Then you place the next block of code to be executed between the Else and End If statements. This block of code will handle the exception to the condition. So if you wanted to handle the exception to the previous example, you could code this:

```
PIN = "654321"
.
.
.
If PIN = "123456" Then
     MsgBox "The PIN is valid."
Else
     MsgBox "Invalid PIN number!"
End If
```

Now you have code to handle both the successful condition as well as the exception to the condition. This is a useful programming technique that will help minimize the number of bugs introduced into your code.

If you want to evaluate more than one condition, you can insert one set of If...Then...End If statements between another set. This is called *nesting*. You might want to nest If...Then statements to check for a series of conditions in a given order. For example:

```
If ValidUserID(UserID) Then
     If ValidPassword(UserID, Password) Then
          MsgBox "Invalid Password!"
     Else
          MsgBox "Login Successful!"
     End If
Else
     MsgBox "Invalid UserID!"
End If
```

The first step is to check if the user entered a valid UserID. This would be validated in the `ValidUserID()` function. If the function returned `True`, indicating a valid User ID, then the code would attempt to validate the password. Otherwise, it would notify the user that he or she entered an invalid User ID.

If the `ValidPassword()` function returns `True`, then we can let the user into the system. Otherwise, their login attempt fails.

Yet one more method of nesting `If...Then` statements is to use the `ElseIf` statement, as in:

```
If x = 1 Then
    'Do something...
ElseIf x = 2 Then
    'Do something else...
End If
```

The method you use is a matter of preference and/or habit. Either method works equally well.

The *IIf* Function

The *immediate if*, or `IIf`, function can be used in place of an `If...Then...Else` block. The only difference, however, is that both return expressions are evaluated. Look at the following code:

```
Function TasteIt (Food As String) As String
    CheckIt = IIf(Food = "Sushi", "No thanks.", "Yummy!")
End Function
```

The second and third parameters, `"No Thanks."` and `"Yummy!"`, will be evaluated regardless of which value is returned from the `IIf` function.

TIP   It is important to understand that the IIf() function evaluates both expressions before returning a result. This may not be a problem when executing the command once, but it may make your program run slower if it is executed repeatedly.

The function `TasteIt()` is very simple. It just checks to see if Food = `"Sushi"`. If it does, then `TasteIt()` returns `"No thanks."` Otherwise it returns `"Yummy!"`

You can use discreet values or expressions as possible return codes from the `IIf` function.

Select Case...End Select Statements

When you want more sophisticated processing, especially when there are more than one or two conditions, you can use the `Select Case...End Select` block of statements. Its syntax is simple:

```
Select Case x
    Case Is = 3
            'Do something
    Case Is > 17
            'Do another thing
    Case Else
            'No explicit condition was met.
End Select
```

For every `Select Case` statement, you must have a corresponding `End Select` statement. You can nest as many `Case` statements between the `Select Case...End Select` block as you like.

For every condition you want to evaluate, you add a corresponding `Case` statement to the block. If you want to handle all exceptions to the block of conditions, you use the `Case Else` statement. It acts very much like the `Else` statement in an `If...Then` statement.

You can use `Case` statements to evaluate string literals, variables, and ranges of values. For example, if you wanted to check for a number between 1 and 10, you could use the following code:

```
Select Case guess
    Case 1 to 10
            'Valid guess
    Case Else
            'Invalid guess
End Select
```

The statement `Case 1 to 10` checks to see if the value stored in the variable `guess` falls between 1 and 10. The `Case Else` statement handles every other possibility.

You can also evaluate strings using `Select Case...End Select` commands. You could use code similar to the following:

```
Select Case x
    Case Is = "3"
        'Do something
    Case Is > "17"
        'Do another thing
    Case Else
        'No explicit condition was met.
End Select
```

As you can see, you place the code you want to execute under the Case statement. You can call many lines of code in a Case statement, as you saw in the "Pick a Number" example discussed earlier. Notice that there is no corresponding End statement after each individual Case block. This illustrates why it is important to write structured code using tabs and whitespaces. You can visually separate blocks of functionally related code in this manner. This not only makes your code easier to read, but helps minimize bugs as well.

> **TIP**
>
> You can learn more about how to write structured code in Skill 12, *Debugging Your Applications*.

One thing to remember when evaluating strings is that your user may type results in uppercase, lowercase, or mixed case. As a result, you must write code in your program to accommodate for these situations. You can do this by nesting two functions to yield one result. First, you must remove any leading and trailing spaces from the string. There may be times when the user accidentally presses the space bar before typing, or possibly after. You can remove them by passing the text to the Trim$() function. Then, you must force the text to be either all uppercase or all lowercase. You can do this using the UCase$() or LCase$() functions. To evaluate the data, you could use either of the following styles:

```
If Trim$(UCase$(txtInput.Text)) = "ADMINISTRATOR" Then
    'Do something...
End If

If Trim$(LCase$(txtInput.Text)) = "administrator" Then
    'Do something...
End If
```

Both If...Then statements are functionally equivalent, but notice that the string on the right side of the expressions must be the same case that the expression on the left expects.

Performing Repetitive Tasks

A computer's power can best be seen when it is used to perform many tasks over and over and over. Since a computer can perform calculations faster than the human brain, it makes sense to have the computer do as many calculations as possible when time is of the essence. This is one example of what truly makes a computer a tool.

For...Next Loops

The most basic type of loop in Visual Basic is the For...Next loop. You use it to loop through a specific number of iterations. This is most useful for counting, or in situations when you know exactly how many times you need to iterate. The syntax for the For...Next loop is:

```
For Counter = StartingNumber To EndingNumber
    'Do something several times
Next Counter
```

Although it is very simple, there are several things to note about this block of code:

- The *Counter* argument is a numeric (Integer or Long) variable that you specify (I, for example).

- *StartingNumber* is the number or variable that you want to start counting from.

- *EndingNumber* is the number or value you want to stop counting at.

So, if you wanted to use a variable x to count from 1 to 5, you would replace *Counter* with x, *StartingNumber* with 1, and *EndingNumber* with 5.

> **NOTE**   You do not have to specify the variable for the counter after the Next statement. You can simply end the For...Next code block with Next. In fact, benchmarks have proven that your code will run faster if you omit the variable after the Next statement. It is important to keep your code structured so you can match For and Next statements.

There is another keyword that you can add to the end of the first line of code in the For...Next loop. By adding the keyword Step, you can count in intervals. For example, if you wanted to count by threes, you would end the For statement with Step 3. To count by twos, you would use Step 2. The following code shows how you would count from 10 to 100 in increments of five:

```
For I = 10 to 100 Step 5
    'Place your repetitive code here...
Next
```

> **TIP**   By default, a For...Next loop counts in increments of one. You can count in other increments by using the keyword Step, followed by the value of the increment you wish to use.

Skill 6

It is even possible to count backward. You can do this by setting Starting-Number to a number greater than EndingNumber and using a negative interval after the Step keyword. For example, if you wanted to count from 10 to 1, you would use this code:

```
For I = 10 To 1 Step -1
        'Place your repetitive code here…
Next
```

If you wanted to count from 100 to 0 in decrements of 10, you would use:

```
For I = 100 To 0 Step -10
        'Place your repetitive code here…
Next
```

If you decide you want to break out of the loop before it has reached the EndingNumber, then you can use the command Exit For. The following code shows you how you can break out of a loop:

```
For I = 1 to 100 Step 5
    X = I * 10
    If X > 100 Then
            Exit For
    End If
Next
```

You will notice that many of the examples in this book use the For…Next construct to perform looping operations. You will use it frequently as well.

Do…Loop Loops

Another looping technique can be achieved through the Do…Loop construct. This construct is useful when you don't know exactly how many times you need to repeat a task, or you need to wait until a specific condition is met. For example, you may want to iterate through every record returned in a recordset from a database. Naturally, you will most likely not know how many records will be returned, but you do know how to check if you've reached the end of the recordset. Do…Loop handles this nicely.

To make an infinite loop, you would write code like the following:

```
Do
    'Do something repetitive
Loop
```

If you want to add a condition so your program can exit the loop, you could use code similar to the following:

```
Do While X < 10
     X = X + 1
Loop
```

The code above will continue looping until X is 10. Since X is not initialized to any other value, you can deduct that this code will loop 10 times. You can also use the Until keyword instead of While. The same code could be re-written:

```
Do Until X = 10
     X = X + 1
Loop
```

The condition that you use to break out of the loop can be almost any logical condition you can write in Visual Basic. You can use any of the logical or comparison operators, as well as Boolean values, to determine the condition that allows the program to exit the loop.

TIP   You can also break out of the loop by using the Exit Do command within the loop, particularly within an If...Then statement.

While...Wend Loops

Another looping construct that is similar to the Do...Loop construct is the While...Wend loop. It will execute a series of commands while the specified condition is true. For example, the code:

```
While X < 10
     X = X + 1
Wend
```

will loop until X reaches 10. Since the While...Wend loop is similar to the Do...Loop construct, determining which construct to use is a matter of preference.

Looping through Collections

There is another type of looping mechanism in Visual Basic that allows you to iterate, or step, through each control in a *collection*. You can do this using For Each...Next loops. This technique is extremely useful when you don't know the exact number of items in the collection.

NOTE   A collection is an object that contains a set of related objects.

You can loop through all items in the collection using code similar to the following:

```
Dim cmd As CommandButton

For Each cmd In Form1
    With cmd
        If .Index <> Index Then
            MsgBox "Button " & Trim$(Str$(.Index)) & _
                " was not pressed."
        End If
    End With
Next
```

The first line dimensions an object of the `CommandButton` class. The next line tells Visual Basic to iterate through every `CommandButton` object of `Form1`. The `With cmd` statement on the next lines tells Visual Basic to use the current object in the collection set to `cmd`.

Looping through collections is useful for many tasks including iterating through items in TreeView and ListView controls, child forms in an MDI application, and objects in a Dynamic HTML document (discussed in Skill 18, *Internet Development with Visual Basic*).

Experimenting with Loops

To see exactly how loops, conditions, and logic work together to do something useful, try the following example. It shows the contents of several text boxes using the various looping techniques discussed previously. While the program is not particularly useful as an application, it is a good example of how the various looping constructs work.

1. Start a new project by selecting File ➢ New Project from Visual Basic.

2. Select Standard EXE from the New Project dialog box and click OK.

3. Set the `Name` property for Form1 to **frmMain**. Set its `Caption` property to **Loops**.

4. Open the Menu Editor by pressing Ctrl+E.

5. Create a top-level menu by setting the Caption field to **&Loop**. Set the Name field to **mnuLoop**.

6. Add a sub-menu to mnuLoop by clicking the Next button in the Menu Editor.

7. Click the right-arrow directly above the menu list, shown in Figure 6.7, to indent the menu one level. This will make this entry a menu item belonging to the top-level menu.

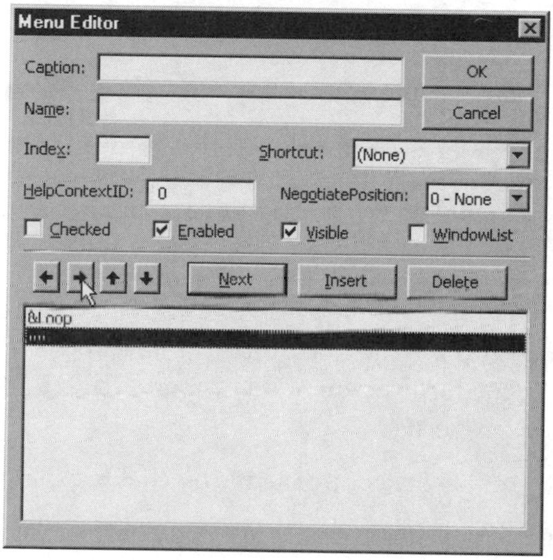

FIGURE 6.7: Creating a menu item

8. Set the Caption field to **&For...Next** and the Name field to **mnuLoopForNext**.

9. Click the Next button to add another menu item. Notice that it is already indented, so you don't need to click the right-arrow button.

10. Set the Caption field to **&Do...Loop** and the Name field to **mnuLoopDoLoop**.

11. Click the Next button to insert another menu item. Set its Caption field to **&While...Wend** and the Name field to **mnuLoopWhileWend**.

12. Click the Next button to insert another menu item. Set its Caption field to - (a hyphen) and the Name field to **mnuLoopSep1**.

TIP When you set the Caption of a menu item to the hyphen character (-), you will create a separator bar in the menu, so you can visually group menu items. For more information on creating menus, refer to Skill 4, *Using Menus and Toolbars*.

13. Insert another menu item and set its Caption field to **&Clear** and the Name field to **mnuLoopClear**.

14. Click the OK button to close the menu editor.

15. Save your project by selecting File ➢ Save Project from the Visual Basic menu.

WARNING You should save your work frequently when working on tasks that are lengthy or complex. If the program crashes, you will lose only a minimal amount of work. Save often!

16. Add a TextBox control to frmMain. Position it near the upper-left corner of the form. Set its Name property to **txtTextBox**. Delete the contents of its Text property.

17. Make the control active by clicking txtTextBox in the Form Designer.

18. Press Ctrl+C to make a copy of the control on the Clipboard.

19. Now click frmMain to make it the active control

20. Press Ctrl+V to paste a copy of the TextBox on the form. A dialog box will appear similar to the one shown in Figure 6.8, asking you if you want to create a control array. Click the Yes button.

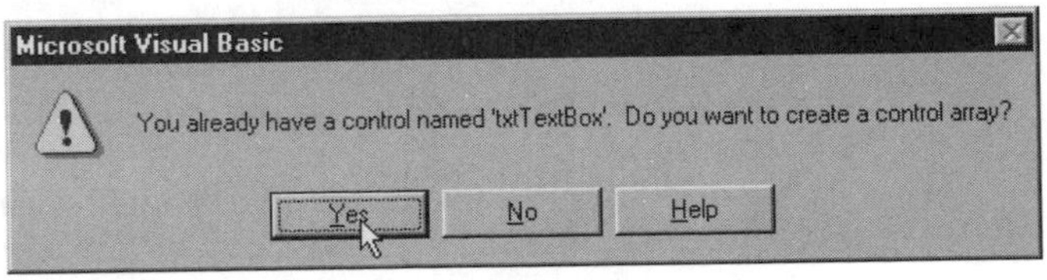

FIGURE 6.8: Creating a control array

21. When the TextBox is created, drag it to the right of the first TextBox you created.

22. Click the form again to make it the active control. Press Ctrl+V to paste another TextBox on the form. Position it to the right of the one you created in steps 20 and 21.

Now that you have a row of three TextBox controls, continue pasting copies of the control on the form. Lay them out in rows of three wide, and five down. You will have 15 TextBox controls on the form arranged like Figure 6.9.

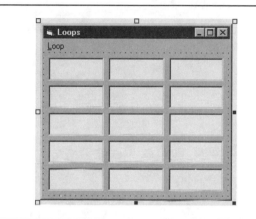

FIGURE 6.9: The form with an array of TextBox controls

23. Select For…Next from the Loop menu on frmMain. This will open the Code window for the `mnuLoopForNext_Click()` event.

24. Add the following code to the event:

```
Private Sub mnuLoopForNext_Click()
    Dim i As Integer

    'Set the text of the text boxes using
    'the For...Next loop
    For i = 0 To 14
        txtTextBox(i).Text = "i = " & Trim$(Str$(i))
    Next
End Sub
```

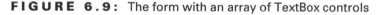

25. Now go the `mnuLoopDoLoop_Click()` event and add the following code:

```
Private Sub mnuLoopDoLoop_Click()
    Dim i As Integer

    'Set the text of the text boxes using
    'the Do...Loop loop
    i = 0
    Do While i < 15
        txtTextBox(i).Text = "i = " & Trim$(Str$(i))
        i = i + 1
    Loop
End Sub
```

26. Add the following code to the `mnuLoopWhileWend_Click()` event:

```
Private Sub mnuLoopWhileWend_Click()
    Dim i As Integer

    'Set the text of the text boxes using
    'the While...Wend loop
    i = 0
    While i < 15
        txtTextBox(i).Text = "i = " & Trim$(Str$(i))
        i = i + 1
    Wend
End Sub
```

27. Add the following code to the `Click()` event of `mnuLoopClear`:

```
Private Sub mnuLoopClear_Click()
    Dim x As Control

    'Iterate through each text box in the form,
    'and clear its contents...
    For Each x In frmMain.Controls
        If UCase$(Left$(x.Name, 3)) = "TXT" Then
            x.Text = ""
        End If
    Next
End Sub
```

28. Save and run the project.

To try this example, select a looping method from the Loop menu. Watch how the text boxes change. Each looping algorithm achieves the same results, but in a different manner, shown in Figure 6.10. You will find that in programming, there is almost always more than one way to accomplish the same task. After you watch the application loop, select the Clear menu item from the Loop menu. This will iterate through each object on the form and clear the Text property of each text box. As you start writing your own applications, keep this skill handy. You will be using many of the techniques before you know it!

> **TIP** If you are a beginning programmer, or are new to Visual Basic, take some time to go through the sample projects. Run them to see what they do, and then look at the code to see how it is done. Studying code from other programs is the best way to learn how to program!

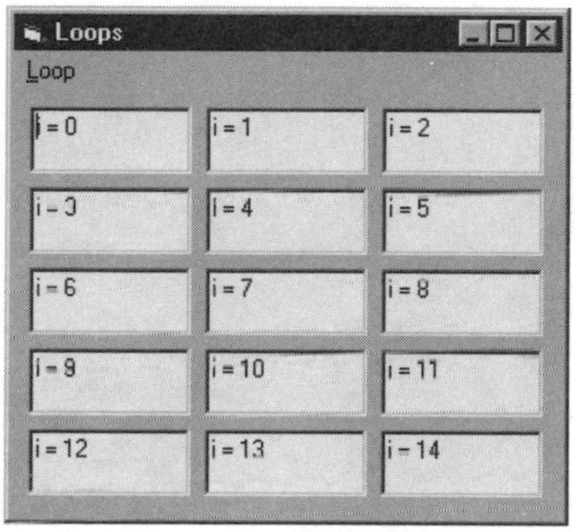

FIGURE 6.10: The results of the looping example

Are You up to Speed?

Now you can...

- ☑ understand how binary logic works
- ☑ use Visual Basic's logic operators to manipulate data
- ☑ use conditional statements to evaluate expressions
- ☑ use different looping techniques to perform repetitive tasks
- ☑ combine the techniques in this skill to make your applications "think"

SKILL 7

Understanding Data Types

- Understanding variable types
- Using variables
- Using arrays
- Using constants

Every application you design will depend on one or more forms of data. As a result, it is important for you get familiar with what they are and how to use them. This skill will introduce you to how data is stored in a computer's memory, and how to access that data using several data types, including variables, arrays, and constants. You will learn which data type to use for a specific task, as well as how to dynamically add data and to define constants that help make your applications easier to manage.

Introducing Variables

No matter what language you program in, you must learn how to use the various data types employed by a language. These include, but are not limited to, variables, arrays, and constants. These elements are crucial to making your application run. So what is a variable? A *variable* is an area in memory that stores values. As its name implies, a variable can change its value; in other words, it can vary.

What Is Memory?

To better understand how variables work, you must understand a little bit about memory first. To get a visual picture of memory, consider a piece of graph paper. Each square is .0625 square inches in size, or ¼ inch wide by ¼ inch high. If the piece of graph paper represented a computer's memory, then each square would be the equivalent of one byte of memory. One kilobyte of memory, which is equal to 1,024 bytes, would cover a piece of graph paper 8 inches by 8 inches. That may not seem like much, but imagine how large a megabyte would be. One megabyte equals 1,024 kilobytes, so one megabyte would cover a sheet of graph paper 21.33 feet by 21.33 feet in size, or 5,461.33 square feet. Now that's one large piece of graph paper! Assuming your computer has 16 megabytes of memory, the sheet of graph paper would be 87,381.33 square feet, or approximately 85.33 feet wide and 85.33 feet high. That's almost one-third the area of a football field!

Imagine how big it would be if you actually broke down each byte into bits. Because a byte is made up of eight bits, the graph paper would almost be the size of three football fields; fortunately, you don't need to use bits at this beginning level. Now that you have a general idea of what memory looks like, you can start to understand how the different variable types work.

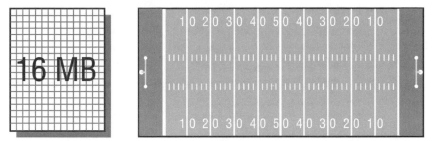

Variable Types

When you start presenting, retrieving, and storing data in your applications, you will invariably start using variables, arrays, and constants. These are fundamental coding tools designed to hold temporary values in memory. Not only will you use these tools in Visual Basic, you will most certainly use them in other languages as well. Let's look at variables in a little more detail.

A variable is a name that references an area of memory which holds a temporary value. This value can change while an application is running. Variables are used in an unimaginable variety of tasks, most of which you will learn through experience. There are several types of variables, called *data types*, in Visual Basic. Each data type has its own characteristics, which you can see in Table 7.1.

TABLE 7.1: Data Types for Variables and Constants

Data Type	Purpose
Integer	A numeric variable, holds values in the range -32,768 to 32,767
Long	A numeric variable with a wider range than Integer
Single	A numeric variable, holds numbers with decimal places
Double	A numeric variable with a wider range than Single
Currency	For holding monetary values
String	For holding text or string values
Byte	A numeric variable with a range of 0 to 255, even less than Integer
Boolean	For holding True or False values
Date	For holding date values
Object	For holding references to objects in Visual Basic and other applications
Variant	A general-purpose variable that can hold most other types of variable values

Skill 7

As you can see from Table 7.1, there are lots of different variable types. For the scope of this book, you will only need to learn about some of the most common variable types: bytes, strings, integers, booleans, variants, and objects.

The object type can be further subdivided into types such as form, control, printer, and so on. The variant type is quite clever in that it can hold all the other types but can cause headaches when debugging larger applications. You will learn more about these intricacies in Skill 12, *Debugging Your Applications*.

Using Byte-Sized Variables

No pun intended, but the most basic type of variable is a byte. A byte can only hold one value at a time. Without getting too involved in the complexities of binary math, take my word that a byte's value must always be between 0 and 255. If you look at Figure 7.1, you can see how a byte fits into the larger memory scheme.

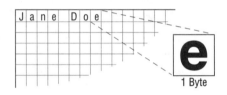

FIGURE 7.1: The byte data type

A byte is useful for dealing with smaller-sized numbers. They are particularly useful when working with the ASCII character set and binary data. Try the following example to learn how the byte works:

1. Start a new project by selecting File ➤ New Project.

2. From the Project Wizard, select Standard EXE.

3. After Visual Basic creates the project, remove Form1 from the project by right-clicking Form1 in the Project Explorer. Select Remove Form1 from the pop-up menu.

4. If Visual Basic asks you to save Form1, click the No button.

5. Right-click in the Project Explorer and select Add ➤ Module from the pop-up menu.

6. Select Module from the Add Module dialog box. This will add a blank code module to your project.

7. If it is not already open, double-click Module1 in the Project Explorer to open its Code window.

8. Add the following code to the module:

```
Option Explicit

Private Sub Main()
    Dim b As Byte
    Dim text As String

    Debug.Print "ASCII Table Example"
    For b = 0 To 63
        text = Str$(b) & "   " & Chr$(b)
        text = text & Chr$(9) & Chr$(9)
        text = text & Str$(b + 64) & "  " & Chr$(b + 64)
        text = text & Chr$(9) & Chr$(9)
        text = text & Str$(b + 128) & " " & Chr$(b + 128)
        text = text & Chr$(9) & Chr$(9)
        text = text & Str$(b + 192) & "  " & Chr$(b + 192)

        Debug.Print text
    Next

    End
End Sub
```

9. Select Run ➢ Start to run the program.

After a brief moment you will see a list of numbers and characters scroll by in the Immediate window. This list is known to programmers as an *ASCII table*. It consists of a list of values between 0 and 255, which fit neatly into a byte data type. Next to each number is the corresponding ASCII character for the number. You can use these numbers to add nonprintable and other special characters to your code. For example, the code contains several references to Chr$(9). The value of nine represents the ASCII tab character. Because you cannot print this character directly in your text, you must use Chr$(9). The Debug.Print command allows you to print directly to the Immediate window. You can learn more about this in Skill 9, *Printing*.

TIP   If you want to add a character to your text that cannot be accessed from the keyboard, look up the character in an ASCII table and use the function Chr$() with the ASCII value of the character between the parentheses.

Working with a String: The Byte's Big Brother

Now that you understand how a byte works, let's look at a more useful method of using them. A string-type variable, called a *string*, is made of up several consecutive bytes in memory that can contain letters and numbers. When used together, these bytes can form mnemonics, words, and even sentences. Figure 7.2 shows you a simple string in memory. Notice that it is actually 11 bytes long, with each byte consisting of one ASCII character.

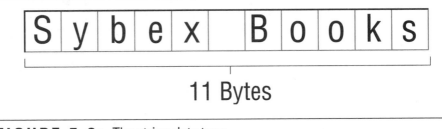

11 Bytes

FIGURE 7.2: The string data type

A couple of the properties you have already worked with are actually string variables. The Name and Caption properties require alphanumeric values. To use a string variable, you must do a couple of things:

- Pick a name for the variable

- Dimension the variable as a String data type

- Give the variable a value

Let's create a simple string variable called strName. The str naming convention is used to denote that the variable is a string type. This is useful when you are debugging and are not sure what data type a variable is.

The next step is to dimension the variable as a string. This is done using Visual Basic's Dim keyword:

```
Dim strName as String
```

Once the variable is declared, an area in memory is set aside for it. Visual Basic will allocate enough memory for the proper type of data to fit in it. Finally, you can set the string to a value, as shown below:

```
strName = "Jane"
```

When you assign values to a string, you must enclose the value in quotes. If you don't, then `strName` would assume that its value can be found in the variable named `Jane`.

Once you assign a value to the variable, you can use that value as a basis for further processing. For example, you can pass the value as a parameter to a procedure or assign the value to a control on a form:

```
Form1.Caption = strName
```

To give you a better idea of how this works, try the following example:

1. Start a new project using File ➢ New Project.

2. Double-click Form1 in the Form Designer to open the Code window.

3. Select the form's `Click()` event from the Events drop-down list in the Code window.

4. Add the following code to the `Click()` event:

    ```
    Private Sub Form_Click()
        Dim msg As String

        msg = "Ooh. That tickles!"
        Caption = msg
    End Sub
    ```

5. Run the project by selecting Run ➢ Start.

6. Click the form once and watch the caption change.

This is a very simple example of how you can use string variables in your applications. As you continue to work through this book, you will see many more examples that demonstrate how strings work.

It can sometimes get quite difficult to remember to dimension your variables, so you can force explicit declaration by typing **Option Explicit** in the `(General)` `(Declarations)` section of your form's Code window. You can put this in the same section for every form and in the same section for any standard .BAS or class modules you create.

Skill 7

TIP   To force explicit declaration of variables in all modules, click Tools ≻ Options on the Visual Basic menu. Select the check box for Require Variable Declaration in the Editor tab of the Options dialog box (see Figure 7.3). Once you've done this, Visual Basic will add an `Option Explicit` line in the `(General)` `(Declarations)` section of every module.

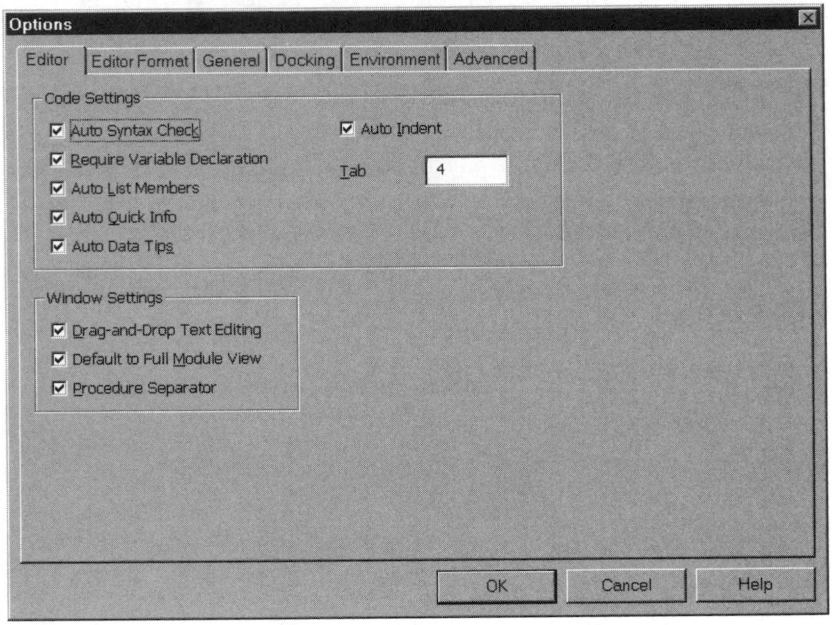

FIGURE 7.3: The Options dialog box

Using Integers

Another fundamental data type is the integer. An integer is a numeric data type much like a byte data type except that it can be *signed* (be positive or negative) and can hold a minimum value of -32,768 and a maximum value of 32,767. Integers are useful for simple mathematics where you know that values are not going to exceed the integer's range. Integers are also useful when used as counters.

To see an integer data type in action, try this example:

1. Start a new project.

2. Add a command button to the form. Set its Name property to **cmdPush**. Set its Caption to **Push**.

3. Double-click the command button to open the Code window.

4. Add the following code to the command button's Click() event:

    ```
    Dim A As Integer
    Dim B As Integer

    A = 2
    B = A + 1
    Print B
    ```

5. Run the project and click the button.

Figure 7.4 shows a snippet of code using integer variables.

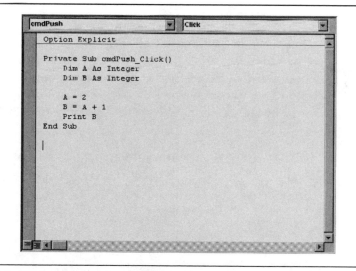

FIGURE 7.4: The Code window for the sample application

The last line of code prints the value contained in the variable B (which should be 3) on the current form (see Figure 7.5).

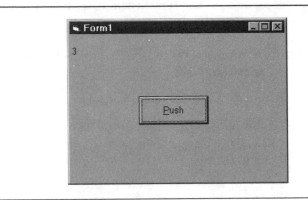

FIGURE 7.5: Running the sample application

You will see more examples of integers in this skill as well as throughout the rest of this book.

Using Boolean Variables

The boolean data type can be set to a value of either True or False. This value is often used to determine the "on" or "off" status of something within a program. Booleans are useful as return codes for wrapper functions. You can set the return code to True if the function was successful, or to False if the function failed. Let's use the Boolean data type to create a wrapper function that determines the existence of a file on the hard disk:

1. Start a new project by selecting File ➤ New Project.

2. For the project type select Standard EXE from the Project Wizard.

3. Add a Text Box control to Form1. Set its Name property to **txtFilename**.

4. Blank the Caption property of the Text Box by double-clicking the Caption property in the Properties window and deleting Text1.

5. Add a command button to the form. Using the Properties window, set its Name property to **cmdSearch** and its Caption to **&Search**.

6. Double-click Form1 to open the Code window.

7.   Type the following code in the Code window to create a wrapper function called IsFile():

```
Private Function IsFile(Filename As String) As Boolean
    If Len(Dir$(Filename)) > 0 Then
        IsFile = True
    Else
        IsFile = False
    End If
End Function
```

8.   Select cmdSearch from the object drop-down list (on the top left of the Code window). The event will set itself to Click().

9.   Add the following code to the Click() event of cmdSearch:

```
Private Sub cmdSearch_Click()
    Dim filename As String
    Dim rc As Boolean

    filename = txtFilename.Text
    rc = IsFile(filename)
    If rc = True Then
        MsgBox "File exists!"
    Else
        MsgBox "File not found!"
    End If
End Sub
```

10.   Run the project.

To test the wrapper function, type the name of a file in the text box. If the file exists, then the wrapper IsFile() will return a boolean value of True. Otherwise it returns a False. Notice that the IsFile() function also uses a string variable, filename, passed to it as a parameter. The value of filename is set in the Click() event of cmdSearch.

Skill 7

TIP   If you want to test the existence of a file, you can use the Dir$() function nested within a Len() function, for example Len(Dir$(filename)). This will yield an integer value greater than zero if the file exists or a zero otherwise. To make this function a little simpler, you could use a wrapper function much like IsFile() in the previous exercise.

Variants: The Bane of a Programmer's Existence

A variant is a general-purpose data type that can take any value—whether it be an integer, byte, string, or boolean—and convert it to another type without requiring you to keep track of the variable. If you use a variable implicitly, without dimensioning it with the Dim statement, Visual Basic will treat the variable as a variant.

The variant data type may sound handy, but heed my warning: Don't use a variant unless you have absolutely no other option. Visual Basic will attempt to convert the data type when necessary. Variants are slower because of the overhead that Visual Basic requires to interpret them, and they waste memory because they allocate enough memory to hold strings, when all you may require is a byte of memory.

> **WARNING** Don't use a variant unless you absolutely have to. You can lose track of a data type and crash your program. Variants also make debugging more difficult.

Determining the Scope of a Variable

The explicit variables discussed so far are all declared with the Dim (short for "dimension") statement. You use Dim to declare variables in a procedure. However, you can only access that variable from the same procedure. In other words, you can't assign it a value or read its value from any other procedure, whether in the same form, or in another form, or in a standard code module.

The variable is a procedure-level (or local) variable. To make a variable visible throughout the whole module, you declare it slightly differently. First, you place the declaration in the (General)(Declarations) section of a form or standard module. Second, you declare it with Private rather than Dim (though Dim is still supported for compatibility with earlier versions of Visual Basic). The variable is now a module-level variable and can be accessed from any procedure in the module—its scope is larger than a procedure-level variable (see Figure 7.6).

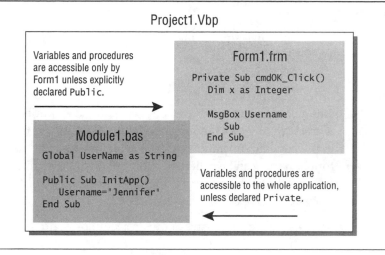

FIGURE 7.6: A variable's scope

You can also have a variable that is application-wide in its scope. These are often called *public* or *global* variables. To declare a public variable, you use Public rather than Dim or Private, and it must be declared in the (General)(Declarations) section of a module. It's common practice to add a standard .BAS module and place all your public variables together in its declarations section.

To better understand how the various scopes work, try this example:

1. Create a new project.

2. Select Standard EXE from the Project Wizard.

3. Add a code module to the project by right-clicking in the Project Explorer and selecting Add ➢ Module.

4. Select Module from the Add Module dialog box. This will also open the Code window for Module1.

5. In the Code window, add the following statements:

```
Option Explicit

Global UserID As String
Global ACL As Integer
```

6. Add the following procedure to Module1:

```
Public Sub InitApp()
    UserID = "Joe"
    ACL = 255
End Sub
```

Before you continue, let's look at the two previous steps. By declaring `UserID` and `ACL` as `Global`, they can be accessed and modified by any procedure in any module or form within the application. Because the function `InitApp()` resides in the code module and has the `Public` keyword in front of it, it becomes a global function that can be called from any procedure within the application. It will be called to initialize the application by setting the `UserID` variable to Joe and ACL to 255. Now let's create the logon form:

1. Double-click Form1 in the Project Explorer to make it the active control in the Form Designer.

2. In the Properties window, set the `Name` property of Form1 to **frmLogon**. Set the `Caption` property to **User Logon**.

3. Add a Label control to the form. Set its `Name` to **lblUserID** and its `Caption` to **User ID:**.

4. Add another Label control below lblUserID and set the `Name` property to **lblPassword** and the `Caption` to **Password:**.

5. Add a Text Box control to the right of lblUserID. Set the `Name` property to **txtUserID**.

6. Add another Text Box control to the right of lblPassword. In the Properties window set the `Name` property to **txtPassword** and the `PasswordChar` property to the asterisk character (*).

7. Add a Command Button to the bottom center of the form. Set its `Name` property to **cmdLogon** and the `Caption` to **&Logon**.

Once you have added all of the controls in the previous steps, your form should look like the one shown in Figure 7.7.

8. Next, double-click Form1 to open the Code window.

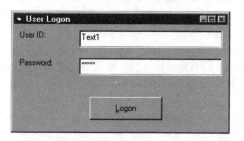

FIGURE 7.7: The logon form

9. Position the cursor to the left of `Option Explicit` in the `(General)` `(Declarations)` section of Form1.

10. Press the Enter key twice to insert two lines in front of `Option Explicit`.

11. Type the following line of code above `Option Explicit`:

    ```
    Private Password As String
    ```

12. Open the Load() event of the form and add the following code:

    ```
    Private Sub Form_Load()
        InitApp
        txtUserID.Text = UserID
        txtPassword.Text = ""
    End Sub
    ```

13. In the Code window, open the `Click()` event for cmdLogon and add the following code:

    ```
    Private Sub cmdLogon_Click()
        Dim msg As String

        UserID = txtUserID.Text
        Password = txtPassword.Text

        msg = "UserID: " & UserID & Chr$(13)
        msg = msg & "Password: " & Password & Chr$(13)
        msg = msg & "ACL: " & Str$(ACL)
        MsgBox msg
    End Sub
    ```

14. Run the project by clicking Run ➤ Start.

Notice that the User ID field has the name "Joe" in it. This value was retrieved from the global string variable named `UserID`. It was not declared in the `Form_ Load()` event but was declared global in Module1.

Also worth noting is the `Password` variable. This variable was declared in the `(General)(Declarations)` portion of the form. This allows any function within the form to access its value, but nothing else. This is important because you don't want code somewhere else in the program attempting to change the user's password. `Password` is said to be private to the form module. It is a module-level variable.

Next, type anything in the password field and click the Logon button. The code in the `Click()` event utilizes both module level and global variables to display your user information.

The *Static* Statement

There is one further way of declaring variables that's quite important and is used instead of `Dim` procedure-level variables. You use the command `Static`, as in:

```
Static X As Integer
```

This means the variable retains the last value assigned to it, even when the procedure has finished. `Static` variables are useful for accumulators, where you want to keep a running tally. If you omit `Static` (and just use `Dim`), the variable is reset to zero (for integer and other numeric variables) each time the procedure runs.

Here's another example for you try. It shows a `static` variable in action. Visit the Sybex Coffee Shop and order all you want. Coffees are free, but I warn you there's no restroom! Follow these steps if you are thirsty or just need a good caffeine jolt:

1. Start a new Standard EXE project.

2. Set the `Caption` property of Form1 to **The Sybex Coffee Shop**.

3. Add a label control to the upper center of the form. In the Properties window, set its `Name` property to **lblQuantity**. Set its `Caption` property to **Coffees Ordered: 0**.

4. Add a command button below lblQuantity. Set the `Name` property to **cmdAdd** and the `Caption` to **&Give Me Another!**

5. Double-click cmdAdd in the Form Designer to open the Code window.

6. Add the following code to the Click() event of cmdAdd:

```
Private Sub cmdAdd_Click()
    Static count As Integer

    count = count + 1
    lblQuantity = "Coffees Ordered:" & Str$(count)
End Sub
```

7. Run the project and click the command button to order as many coffees as you want.

The count variable in the Click() event procedure is declared as Static. This allows the count value to remain the same between events. The result is a counter-style variable that remembers how many coffees you ordered.

> **TIP**
>
> To make all the Dim variables in a procedure static, you can leave them as Dim and preface the name of the procedure with the Static keyword, as in Private Static Sub cmdAdd_Click().

Using Arrays

Arrays are a form of variable, but you use them to hold more than one value at a time. For example, a spreadsheet is an array of cells, with each column or row belonging to a particular group. You may use arrays to hold red, green, and blue values (RGB) in a bitmap, or possibly as a small database in memory. While they are not used as often as other variable types, they do have an important role to play in program development. Let's look at an example of declaring an integer array and assigning values to the elements within the array:

```
Static X(2) As Integer

X(0) = 7
X(1) = 99
X(2) = 123
```

To process an array, use a For...Next loop that itself uses an integer variable as a counter (see Figure 7.8):

```
Dim Y As Integer

For Y = 0 To 2
    Print X(Y)
Next Y
```

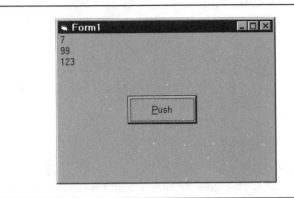

FIGURE 7.8: Using a For...Next loop

This prints the values of each element (0, 1, and 2 are the references to the three elements) in the integer array X to the current form.

To create a module-level array, declare it with Dim in the (General) (Declarations) section of a module. To have an application-level array, declare it with Public in the declarations section.

To understand better how to work with an array, try this example:

1. Start a new Standard EXE project.

2. Remove Form1 from the project by right-clicking Form1 in the Project Explorer and selecting Remove Form1 from the pop-up menu.

3. Add a code module to the project by right-clicking in the Project Explorer and select Add ➢ Module.

4. Select Module from the Add Module dialog box.

5. In the Code window for Module1, add the following procedure:

```
Sub Main()
    Dim x(7) As Integer
    Dim i As Integer
    Dim txt As String

    'Populate Array with Bit Values
    For i = 0 To 7
        x(i) = 2 ^ i
    Next

    'Print Array
```

```
        For i = 0 To 7
            txt = "Array Element" & Str$(i) & " = "
            txt = txt & Str$(x(i))
            Debug.Print txt
        Next
    End Sub
```

6. Run the program and watch the Immediate window.

The first block of statements dimension the required variables for this program. The array x is dimensioned to hold eight elements (0 to 7). I is the counter for the For...Next loops, and txt is a string that is used to format the output.

The first For...Next loop populates the elements in the array. Using the formula:

```
x(i) = 2 ^ i
```

each element is set to the corresponding decimal value for that bit. Don't worry too much about binary. You will not use it much, if at all, as a beginner. This is just used as an example.

The last For...Next loop formats the txt variable so it can be printed to the Immediate window. The command Debug.Print actually sends the value of txt to the window.

Dynamic Arrays

Often, you don't know how large (that is, how many elements) to make an array. If that's the case, then declare an empty array. An array that starts life with no elements is called a *dynamic array*. You declare it in the same way as a normal array, except that you can use Dim, as well as Static, in a procedure:

```
Dim Y() As Integer
```

It can be wasteful to allocate an array larger than you need. To prevent this, you can dimension the dynamic array with no elements (as shown above), and then add elements only when you need to. This technique is especially useful if you are working with a large number of elements.

Later you'll want to define some elements for the array to hold values. To do this, use ReDim, which can only appear in a procedure:

```
ReDim Y(5)
```

You can then assign values to elements within the array. You can also change the number of elements later, as in:

```
ReDim Y(7)
```

Skill 7

If you attempt that, then any values already in the array are lost. To keep existing values, use the `Preserve` keyword:

```
ReDim Preserve Y(7)
```

WARNING   When you work with arrays, be sure you know exactly what is going on. Arrays can consume a lot of memory if you are not careful, so plan accordingly.

Using Constants

Constants are nonvariable variables. They resemble variables in that they are declared and assigned a value, but unlike variables, the values they hold remain fixed while the application is running. These are commonly used to make coding easier. For example, it is easier to understand and debug a variable with the name vbModal, rather than to track down an integer one (1) coded somewhere in your application. You declare and assign values to constants on the same line, using the keyword `Const`:

```
Const conPi = 3.142
```

To see the value of a constant in action, see the code in Figure 7.9 and this code here:

```
Const conPi = 3.142
Dim Radius As Integer
Dim Area As Double

Option Explicit

Private Sub cmdPrintArea_Click()
    Radius = 3
    Area = conPi * (Radius ^ 2)
    Print Area
End Sub
```

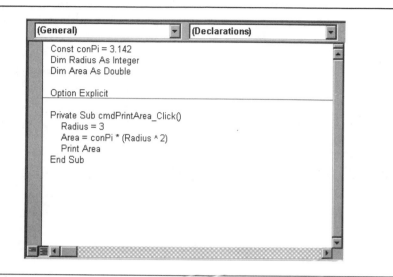

FIGURE 7.9: Using the value of a constant

This code calculates the area of a circle using a constant called conPi (the con prefix is optional, though recommended). It prints the area of the circle to the current form (see Figure 7.10).

FIGURE 7.10: Results of the area calculation

You can declare constants both in procedures and in the declarations section of modules. To create an application-wide constant, preface the declaration and assignment with the term `Global`, as in `Global Const Pi = 3.142`.

Choosing the right variable for the task at hand is of paramount importance. Not only will it will save you time debugging, it will help you create tighter code and will teach you good programming discipline. Construction workers don't build buildings with only a screwdriver. They use many tools, each with its own purpose. Variables are the same way. Remember to use the right tool for the job.

Are You up to Speed?

Now you can...

- ☑ use the appropriate variables for a given task
- ☑ use arrays to store information
- ☑ define and use constants in your programs

SKILL 8

Storing and Retrieving Data

- Working with ASCII files
- Understanding sequential mode
- Understanding random access mode
- Using binary access mode
- Using data controls
- Understanding the anatomy of a database
- Creating databases with Visual Data Manager
- Using ActiveX Data Objects (ADO)

Since computers are used to manage information, applications must have a convenient and reliable method to store and retrieve data. Arcade games store high scores in memory and keep them until they're unplugged. Fortunately, PCs have some sort of storage medium, such as a floppy disk, hard disk, tape, or optical disk. You can use any of these devices to permanently store information so it can be retrieved at a later time.

In this skill, you will learn many techniques to store and retrieve data including using ASCII files, databases, and database controls and tools. By the end of this skill, you will be able to select the best storage method for your application, and use it in your application.

Working with ASCII Files

When you use data in Visual Basic that was stored on a disk, it will come in one of two forms: a database or an ASCII file. You will probably spend most of your time working with database files (discussed later in this chapter), but it is important to learn how ASCII files work as well. ASCII files contain data of all types and can be formatted in a comma-separated values (CSV) list, otherwise known as a *delimited ASCII file* (see Figure 8.1). They can also be listed one item per line, or they can be formatted in any other layout you can think of. Understanding how to work with these files is important, because it allows you to work with almost any type of data. You can use your knowledge to retrieve information that describes your system from initialization files.

Keeping the data you enter into your applications is considered normal practice. For example, you might want to save to disk the entries you make in text boxes. Game programmers often save players' high scores so they can be loaded the next time a game is run. When you do need to retrieve this data, Visual Basic gives you many options. You can do it the hard way (which may be necessary in some cases) by hard-coding the writing and retrieving of data. For this purpose, you will need to create your own sequential, random, or binary files (described in the following sections). In addition, the code to explicitly read and write to only that file is added to the program. This *hard-coding* makes your code specific to the application, but sometimes that's all you need to complete the job.

```
Authors - WordPad                                    _ □ ✕
File  Edit  View  Insert  Format  Help

  □ ☞ 🖫   🖨 🖪   🗛   ✂ 🖹 🖺 ↶   🕮

"Au_ID","Author","Year Born"
1,"Jacobs, Russell",
2,"Metzger, Philip W.",
3,"Boddie, John",
4,"Sydow, Dan Parks",
6,"Lloyd, John",
8,"Thiel, James R.",
10,"Ingham, Kenneth",
12,"Wellin, Paul",
13,"Kamin, Sam",
14,"Gaylord, Richard",
15,"Curry, Dave",
17,"Gardner, Juanita Mercado",
19,"Knuth, Donald E.",
21,"Hakim, Jack",
22,"Winchell, Jeff",
24,"Clark, Claudia",
25,"Scott, Jack",
27,"Coolbaugh, James",

For Help, press F1                                    NUM
```

FIGURE 8.1: A delimited ASCII file

The first step in working with one of these types of files is to open it. In Visual Basic, you use the Open statement to do this. You use this command to open a specific file and prepare it for reading or writing. The minimum requirements for the Open statement are a filename, a mode to open the file, and a file number handle. The syntax is shown here:

```
Open filename For mode As fileno
```

You supply the name of a file in the filename parameter. The mode parameter specifies how you want to access the file. It can be set to Append, Input, Output, Binary, and Random. Finally, the fileno parameter specifies an integer, called a *handle*, that references the opened file. You use the handle to reference the file in your code. You will see this in the next section.

If the file specified by filename does not exist and you try to open the file in Append, Binary, Output, or Random modes, then Visual Basic will create an empty file for you. In addition, if you do not specify the mode parameter, the file will be opened in random access mode, which is the default. No particular file mode is better than the other. Each has its own specific advantages and they

Skill 8

should be selected based on the format of your data file. For example, you would not want to open a delimited ASCII file in binary mode because you would only read the data in one byte at a time. You would then need to write code to put the values back together into discreet strings. Input mode is better suited for these types of files.

When you are done working with the file, you need to close it with the `Close` statement. You just follow the `Close` statement with the handle of the file:

```
Close fileno
```

You will see more of this in the following sections. In the meantime, let's take a more detailed look at the different file-access modes.

Understanding Sequential Mode

When you want to store or retrieve data in Visual Basic, you may choose to create a *sequential file*. A sequential file is a series of lines of text in ASCII format, much like that shown in Figure 8.2.

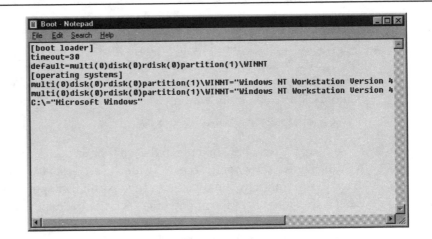

FIGURE 8.2: A sample sequential file

To write data to a sequential file, you open it for Output or Append. If the file doesn't exist, then Visual Basic creates it automatically. If the file *does* exist, then Output overwrites existing data, while Append adds it to the end of the file. In most cases you will append data, but there are times when you may create a file to serve as a temporary workspace. In this case it would be acceptable to over-write the contents of the file before each use. To read the data from a sequential file, you open it for Input. Whether you open for Input, Output, or Append, you must use a file handle (see below) with the file. In addition, you should always close the file when you're finished by using a Close statement with the appropriate file number. If you don't, your file may lose data, or be lost altogether! One way of writing to the file is to use the Print # statement (or Write #). One way of reading from a file is with the Line Input # statement (or Input # statement or the Input function).

Below is the code that you could write to create a file in the C:\Data directory with two names in it:

```
Dim FileNo As Integer

FileNo = FreeFile
Open "C:\data\test.txt" For Append As FileNo
    Print #FileNo, "John"
    Print #FileNo, "Doe"
Close FileNo
```

The FreeFile function returns the next available file handle. This file handle or file number is used in all the Open, Print #, and Close statements. After trying the above code, you can see the results in WordPad or Notepad, as shown in Figure 8.3. To overwrite rather than append data—in other words, to delete data in your file and substitute it with new data, rather than just adding to the file—you substitute the keyword Output for Append.

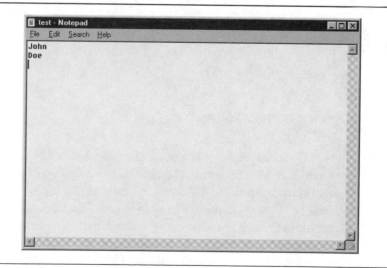

FIGURE 8.3: Viewing the results

One way of reading stored data is to read each line into an array. Just to refresh your memory, an array is a list of similar values that can be addressed using an index number with the variable name. You can learn more about these in Skill 7, *Understanding Data Types*. The following example uses an array to store the values retrieved from the file `c:\data\test.txt`:

```
Dim FileNo As Integer
Dim GetValues() As String
Dim Counter As Integer

'Initialize the counter
Counter = 0

'Get a unique finle number
FileNo = FreeFile

'Open the file
Open "c:\data\test.txt" For Input As FileNo
    Do Until EOF(FileNo)
        Counter = Counter + 1
        ReDim Preserve GetValues(Counter)
        Line Input #FileNo, GetValues(Counter)
    Loop
Close FileNo
```

The EOF function tests for the end of the file by detecting the End of File character. This is an ASCII character that is not displayed on-screen and is added when you create or append to a file. Once you have retrieved the data, you can loop through the GetValues array and assign the data to controls on a form, or print the data:

```
Dim J As Integer

For J = 0 To UBound(GetValues)
    Print GetValues(J)
Next J
```

This works better, with the earlier code that reads the data, if you have Option Base 1 in the (General)(Declarations) section of your form. This command will start the index of the array at 1 instead of the default 0. If you do that, change the For...Next to start at 1 rather than 0. The UBound() function returns the highest index in an array. You can use this function to determine how many elements are actually in the array, or to determine where the array stops. The LBound() function returns the lowest subscript in an array. Used with UBound(), it enables you to work out the size of an array. You can process every element in a one-dimensional array with the following code:

```
Dim J As Integer

For J = LBound(arrayname) To UBound (arrayname)
    'your code goes here....
Next J
```

Understanding Random Access Mode

Random access mode also works to retrieve data from ASCII files, but you have greater flexibility when you use it instead of sequential mode. Random access allows you to position yourself anywhere within the file at any time to get the data you need. As a result, this works more like a database than a sequential file. Random access is also faster at retrieving data than sequential mode, because you tell it explicitly where to position the file pointer within the file.

To open a file for random access, use the Random parameter by typing the following:

```
Open "c:\data\test.txt" for Random as FileNo Len=10
```

Before you specify the Len parameter, you should know the length of each line of data. You can do this by adding up the length of the line in ASCII characters. This line of data is called a *record*, just like a database record. For the purpose of this section, we will reference each line of data as a record.

Let's assume that each record will contain a last name, a first name, and a description of the person. We can concatenate all of these parameters together and write it to the file, but it would be cumbersome to retrieve the data in a useable format. For example, if we used the code:

```
Private Sub SaveFile()
    Dim FileNo As Integer
    Dim RecNo As Integer
    Dim FName as String
    Dim LName as String
    Dim LineOut as String

    FName = "Jane"
    LName = "Doe"
    Desc = "Wife of John Doe"
    LineOut = LName & FName & Desc

    RecNo = 1
```

Skill 8

```
        FileNo = FreeFile
        Open "c:\test.txt" For Random As FileNo
            Put #FileNo, RecNo, LineOut
        Close FileNo
    End Sub
```

our record would look like this when we retrieve it:

```
    DoeJaneWife of John Doe
```

Now that's ugly! It would be impractical to write code to extract the names from this, because different people would have names of different lengths. Instead, you could declare your own variable type for this situation using the Type…End Type construct.

The Type statement allows you to define your own variable type. This statement is especially useful in situations like the previous example. Before you can use the Type statement, however, you need to make sure there is a code module in the project. Visual Basic will not allow you to create a variable type within a form module. As a result, create the variable type within the (General) (Declarations) section of a code module. You could add the code:

```
    Type UserInfoRecord
        LName As String * 15
        FName As String * 15
        Desc As String * 50
    End Type
```

and change your procedure in the form to:

```
    Private Sub SaveFile()
        Dim FileNo As Integer
        Dim RecNo As Integer
        Dim usr As UserInfoRecord

        usr.FName = "Jane"
        usr.LName = "Doe"
        usr.Desc = "Wife of John Doe"

        RecNo = 1
        FileNo = FreeFile
        Open "c:\test.txt" For Random As FileNo Len = 80
            Put #FileNo, RecNo, usr
        Close FileNo
    End Sub
```

Let me explain the Type statement briefly. To create a variable type, you insert several variables and their declarations with the Type…End Type wrapping. In this example, we created a variable type that is broken into three separate string elements: LName, FName, and Desc. Notice that after they are declared, they are given a length. LName and FName are defined as strings with a fixed length of 15 characters each. Desc is defined to be 50 characters. If you add all of these lengths together, you get 80 characters. This is the total length of your variable, and because this is the only variable you write to the file, it also becomes your record length.

To use the variable, UserInfoRecord, you need to Dim it, just as you do with all variables, so Visual Basic knows what data type the variable is. Then you can access each of the elements within the variable using the variable name followed by the dot (.) operator and then the element name, much like accessing an object's properties. You can then pass a value to it, or retrieve a value from it using the Get# statement. When the previous code is run, it writes a record to a file. When viewed in Notepad, it looks like Figure 8.4.

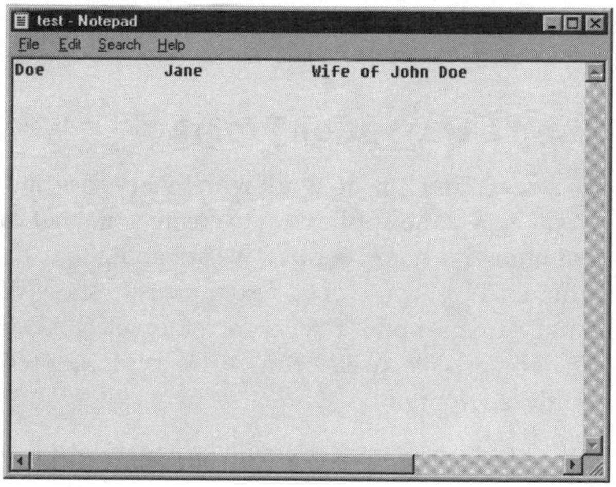

FIGURE 8.4: A record in a text file

Random access mode is good for working with lists of data supplied in an ASCII file. However, most files will not fit neatly into this format. They might have headers of different lengths or other inconsistencies within the file. You may find that a relational database will work better for you. We will discuss these after examining binary access mode.

Understanding Binary Access Mode

Binary access mode allows you the greatest amount of flexibility when working with files. When working with binary access mode, you retrieve data with the `Get#` command, and write data with the `Put#` command, just like you do with random access mode. The difference between binary and random access mode is that you cannot move around the file at random and get data. Instead, data is read sequentially and in chunks in the binary mode. The number of bytes read from the file equals the size of the string, in bytes, that you want to read data into. For example, the following statements read 10 bytes from a file:

```
Temp = String(10," ")
Get #FileNo, ,Temp
```

Notice that the `RecNo` parameter is missing. This is because binary files are read sequentially. Visual Basic remembers the current position within the file so you don't have to keep track of it. So without further delay, let's put this knowledge to use and write a file encryption program. I will describe the details of the program as we go along.

A Simple Encryption Program

To understand how to work with binary files, let's create an encryption program. Don't expect the application to create a file that cannot be hacked by a good programmer, however, because we are going to use the simplest of encryption algorithms. The purpose of this example is to show you how to work with a file in binary access mode. To encrypt a file, select Actions ➤ Encrypt from the menu. To decrypt a file, use Actions ➤ Decrypt. You will be asked to supply a text file for the encryption.

1. Start a new project. It will be a Standard EXE.

2. Make Form1 the active control and set its `Name` property to **frmMain**. Set its `Caption` property to **File Encrypter**.

3. Add a common dialog control to your form and set its `Name` property to **dlgFile**.

4. Open the Menu Editor and create the following menu objects:

> **File Menu**
>
> Caption: **&File**
>
> Name: **mnuFile**

File Menu Items

Caption: **E&xit**

Name: **mnuFileExit**

Actions Menu

Caption: **&Actions**

Name: **mnuAct**

Actions Menu Items

Caption: **&Encrypt**

Name: **mnuActEncrypt**

Caption: **&Decrypt**

Name: **mnuActDecrypt**

When you're finished, your form should look like Figure 8.5.

FIGURE 8.5: The encryption form

> **NOTE**
>
> The next step is to add the code behind the form. The only control used besides the menu is the common dialog control. The common dialog control is used to offer Open and Save dialog boxes, as well as font and printer settings. We will use it only to select a filename.

5. Next, open the Code window and set the object drop-down box to mnuFileExit.

6. Add an End statement to the `mnuFileExit_Click()` procedure.

7. You are going to add the encryption algorithm here, so open the `(General)(Declarations)` procedure and add the code below:

```
Function Encrypt(infile As String) As Boolean
    Dim fileno1 As Integer
    Dim fileno2 As Integer
    Dim outfile As String
    Dim xpos As Long
    Dim x As Byte

    'Show the hourglass
    MousePointer = vbHourglass

    xpos = 4
    outfile = "c:\temp.enc"
    fileno1 = FreeFile
    Open infile For Binary As fileno1
        fileno2 = FreeFile
        Open outfile For Binary As fileno2
            Put #fileno2, 1, 0
            Put #fileno2, 2, 128
            Put #fileno2, 3, 0
            Put #fileno2, 4, 128
            Do While Not EOF(fileno1)
                xpos = xpos + 1
                Get #fileno1, xpos, x
                Put #fileno2, xpos, x + 128
            Loop
        Close fileno2
    Close fileno1

    'Delete original file & replace with encrypted file
    Kill infile
    FileCopy outfile, infile
    Kill outfile
    Encrypt = True

    'Reset the mouse pointer
    MousePointer = vbNormal
End Function
```

This code deserves some scrutiny because it does most of the work for the program. You'll notice that instead of this procedure being a sub, it is a function. This is because the function will return a result code to its calling procedure. You should do this because you need to know if the process was successful before you actually notify the user or carry on with the program. This function simply returns a

True if the encryption is successful, or a `False` if the process was unsuccessful. Notice that we also pass the `infile` parameter to the function. This is the fully qualified path and filename of the file you wish to encrypt. `Infile` is retrieved through the use of the `GetFile()` function.

After bypassing the standard variable declarations, you will notice that the mouse pointer is set to an hourglass. This will inform the user to wait, because the program is processing. Because you will be reading the file byte by byte, it could possibly be a slow process, so you should display the hourglass.

> **TIP**
>
> When the program will take a while to process, you should show an hourglass. This will let the user know the program is working. Without one, a user will not know if the program is running or if it crashed. You can display the hourglass by setting the form's `MousePointer` property to vbHourglass.

As mentioned earlier, you use the `FreeFile` command to get the next available file handle. As I was creating this program, I had the two `FreeFile` statements next to each other in the code. I did this because I like to logically group commands whenever possible. When I ran the program, it kept giving me a File Already Open error. Why did it do this? I checked the values of `infile` and `outfile` in the debugger and they were both correct. Neither of the files were opened by any other applications, so they couldn't be locked or causing a sharing violation. After some more scrutiny, I realized that `FreeFile` did not allocate a file handle for me. The `Open` statement allocates the handle for us. `FreeFile` just tells us what handles are available. What I had done was return the same file handle for both `fileno1` and `fileno2`. Once I moved the `FreeFile` commands next to their corresponding `Open` statements, the program worked. The point is that you need to keep `FreeFile` as close to `Open` as possible, especially when you are working with more than one file in a procedure. Also, even the simplest programs may need to be debugged!

> **TIP**
>
> Keep the `FreeFile` command as close to the `Open` command as possible when working with multiple files in the same procedure. `FreeFile` will not lock the file handle but just inform you that it is available. Your best bet is to put the `Open` command right after the `FreeFile` command.

Before actually processing data, you'll want add a sort of digital signature to the beginning of the encrypted file. This signature is used in the decryption algorithm to determine whether the file is encrypted. The signature should be a sequence of bytes that are not likely to appear in a file. For this example, I used a four-byte signature that consists of 0, 128, 0, 128. This is the exact data and sequence expected by the decryption algorithm. You could enhance the Encrypt() and Decrypt() functions by creating another function that generates and uses its own signature.

Notice that x is dimensioned as a byte, and not an integer. The reason for this is that its maximum value can be 255. When you add another number to it that makes the total value of x greater than 255, the value of x rolls over to 0 and continues adding. So when you add 128 to 128 we get 256. Since 256 is greater than 255, the value of x rolls over to 0. This is the key to the encryption. When you go to decrypt the file, you use the same algorithm to bring back the original values. If you add 128 to 0, you get 128, which was your original value. As a result, the encrypted character is restored to its original state.

Just before the end of the function, you will notice some Kill statements. In Visual Basic, the Kill statement is the equivalent of delete. What this sequence of commands does is replace infile with outfile. This way you are left with one encrypted file and no temp file. Before you can rename a file, however, it must have a unique filename. This is why you delete infile before you rename outfile. Once the rename is successful, you delete outfile to clean up the mess.

Now that the function is complete, reset the mouse pointer to give the user a visual cue that the program is done running. You also want to send a True return code so the calling function can continue:

1. Now that you have written the meat of the program—the encryption function—you need a method to call it. You will do this through the mnuActEncrypt_Click() event:

    ```
    Private Sub mnuActEncrypt_Click()
        Dim filename As String

        filename = GetFile()
        If filename <> "" Then
            If Encrypt(filename) = False Then
                MsgBox "Error encrypting file!"
            End If
        End If
    End Sub
    ```

2. Before the menu command can call the Encrypt function, it needs to call GetFile() to retrieve a filename:

    ```
    Function GetFile() As String
        dlgFile.CancelError = True
    ```

```
'If the user clicks the Cancel button, then
'generate an error
On Error GoTo filerr

'Configure the dialog
dlgFile.DialogTitle = "Select a File..."
dlgFile.DefaultExt = "*.txt"
dlgFile.Filter = "Text Files (*.txt)|*.txt|" & _
    " All Files (*.*)|*.*"
dlgFile.FilterIndex = 1
dlgFile.MaxFileSize = 32767

'Show the dialog
dlgFile.ShowOpen

'Get the filename
GetFile = dlgFile.filename

'Bypass the error handler
Exit Function

filerr:
    GetFile = ""
End Function
```

The `GetFile()` function also deserves some examination. At the heart of this function is the common dialog control. This control provides all of the functionality you need to retrieve a filename. As you may have learned, the Open dialog box that you have seen in other applications does not actually open the file. Rather, it retrieves a filename and passes it back to the application. Then another procedure uses this filename and opens the file for processing. This is exactly what this program does as well.

The first action we take is to set the `CancelError` property to `True`. When this property is set to `True`, the dialog box will send an error message if the user clicks the Cancel button. We trap this error so that we do not process any code if the user wants to cancel. The `On Error` command is what actually tells the procedure to skip the encryption algorithm.

For aesthetic purposes, you set the `DialogTitle` property to `"Select a File..."`. This just makes the program a little more user-friendly. You can actually place any text here that you want.

Set the default extension to `*.txt`. For those of you familiar with DOS commands, the asterisk is a wildcard which tells the common dialog to filter out all files except those with a `.txt` extension. This makes it easier for the user to zero in on files of interest. When you work with the common dialog control in your own applications, be sure to make it easier for your users.

Next define filters by setting the Filter property. You do this by alternating a description and the actual filter. You separate these with the pipe symbol (|). There are multiple filters, which you may have seen in other applications. You just need to separate everything with the pipe symbols. We can access these filters using the FilterIndex property.

FilterIndex is the index number of the filter to be displayed in the dialog box. The first filter has an index of 1, the next is 2, and so on. When you set this property, it only sets the starting index. You can change the filter from the actual dialog box, as in Figure 8.6.

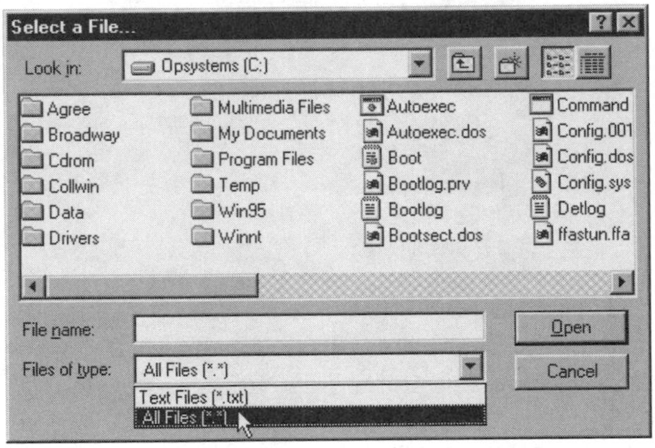

FIGURE 8.6: The common dialog box

Notice how I set the MaxFileSize property to 32767. Setting this property will cause the common dialog to only return filenames of files whose sizes are 32K or less. You can set this property to whatever you want, but it is important to make sure the files you open can fit into the controls you use. Since we don't use anything with a size limitation on it, this property doesn't really matter for this application.

> **TIP**
>
> You can use the MaxFileSize property in the common dialog control to filter filenames based on file size. This is a great error-checking feature to implement when you use controls that have memory limitations imposed on them, for instance, a text box control.

Finally, set the ShowOpen property to display the dialog box. If the user clicks the Cancel button, then the dialog box returns an error message, and the function cancels itself. Otherwise it sets the FileName property to the filename that the user selected. You then pass this value back through GetFile. If you don't get a filename, then you return an empty string to the calling procedure.

Let's add the decryption algorithm so we can get our file back:

1.   Add the following code:

```
Private Function Decrypt(infile As String) As Boolean
    Dim fileno1 As Integer
    Dim fileno2 As Integer
    Dim outfile As String
    Dim xpos As Long
    Dim x As Byte
    Dim t(3) As Byte

    'Show the hourglass
    MousePointer = vbHourglass

    xpos = 4
    outfile = "c:\temp.enc"
    fileno1 = FreeFile
    Open infile For Binary As fileno1
        fileno2 = FreeFile
        Get #fileno1, 1, t(0)
        Get #fileno1, 2, t(1)
        Get #fileno1, 3, t(2)
        Get #fileno1, 4, t(3)
        If (t(0) = 0 And t(1) = 128 And t(2) = 0 And_
        t(3) = 128) Then
            Open outfile For Binary As fileno2
                Do While Not EOF(fileno1)
                    xpos = xpos + 1
                    Get #fileno1, xpos, x
                    Put #fileno2, xpos - 4, x + 128
                Loop
            Close fileno2

            Decrypt = True
        Else
            Decrypt = False
        End If
    Close fileno1

    'Delete original file & replace with encrypted file
    If Decrypt Then
```

Skill 8

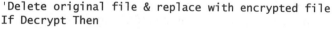

```
        Kill infile
        FileCopy outfile, infile
        Kill outfile
    End If

    'Reset the mouse pointer
    MousePointer = vbNormal
End Function
```

You will notice the code is almost identical to the encryption algorithm. However, before deciphering a file, you need to check to see if it is started with your signature, the 0, 128, 0, 128 sequence at the beginning. When a file is encrypted, the program inserts these four numbers in the beginning of the encrypted file. That way the program knows if a file is actually encrypted before it tries to decrypt it.

2. Now you need to add the code to call the Decrypt() function from the decrypt menu item:

```
Private Sub mnuActDecrypt_Click()
    Dim filename As String

    filename = GetFile()
    If filename <> "" Then
        If Decrypt(filename) = False Then
            MsgBox "Error decrypting file!"
        End If
    End If
End Sub
```

Now that you have all of the code added, save your project and give it a test run. Although it does not do anything spectacular, it's a good lesson on how files can be stored and retrieved from a disk. Now you have enough knowledge to start working with files and you should be able to incorporate them in your programs.

Using Data Controls

Many Visual Basic developers choose to keep data in Microsoft Access tables or other databases because Visual Basic provides database tools that make it relatively easy to access data within them. You can drop these controls onto a form, set a few properties, and work with almost any database! You can try this out by using the sample Access database supplied with Visual Basic—Biblio.mdb—it's in the VB98 directory by default. That database (and its component tables) is provided for you, but you'll probably need to create your own databases from time to time. To create an Access database, you could hard-code all the table, field, and index definitions, but that's not always very convenient. There are a couple of other avenues:

- If you already have Microsoft Access, you can use it to easily create databases that can be accessed by Visual Basic. This is the quickest and most efficient method of creating databases, but it is not the only solution.

- If you don't have Access, you can use the Visual Data Manager add-in of Visual Basic (see Figure 8.7). To start the Data Manager, select Add-Ins ➤ Visual Data Manager.

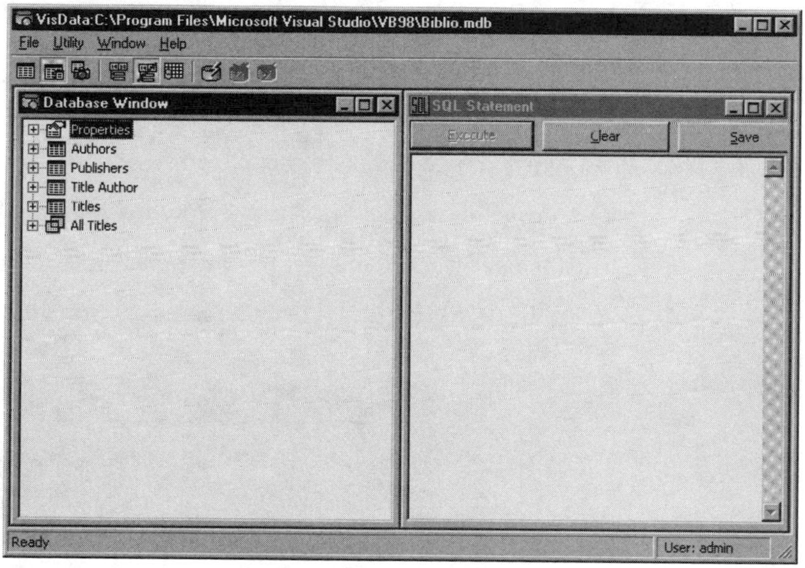

FIGURE 8.7: Visual Data Manager

Once you have a database, you need a way to access it from within Visual Basic. You have a few ways to do this:

- One way is to write code and use Data Access Objects (DAO), Remote Database Objects (RDO), or ActiveX Data Objects (ADO) to access your data. These are objects that allow you to access records, tables, and queries through code. ADO is new to Visual Basic 6, and it allows you to seamlessly access multiple databases through a single, consistent interface.

- You can also have an Access-style form wizard do all the hard work—the Visual Basic Data Form Designer. To install it, click Add-Ins ➢ Add-In Manager and select the Add-In from the list. Once it has been added, it will remain on the Add-Ins menu until you remove it through the Add-In Manager.

- The last method is to use the data controls that come with Visual Basic. This is the method that will be covered in this section.

Adding the Data Control

To get you started using a data control, try the following example, which allows you to browse through a table in a database. It requires no programming at all:

1. Press Ctrl+N in Visual Basic to start a new project.

2. From the New Project dialog box, select Standard EXE and click OK.

3. Add two text boxes to the top of a form.

4. Double-click the data control in the Toolbox to add it to the form.

5. Drag the newly added data control to position it below the two text boxes.

6. Widen the data control so you can see its caption (shown below).

7. Set the properties for the data control as follows:

Caption:	**Authors Table**
Connect:	**Access (default)**
DatabaseName:	**C:\Program Files\Microsoft Visual Studio\VB98\biblio.mdb** (amend the path if necessary)
RecordsetType:	**1 - Dynaset** (default)
RecordSource:	**Authors** (from drop-down list)

8. Set properties for the text box on the left as follows:

   DataSource: **Data1**

   DataField: **Author**

9. Set the properties for the text box on the right to:

   DataSource: **Data1**

   DataField: **Au_ID**

10. Run the program and scroll through the records with the navigation buttons on the data control. Note that any changes you make in the text boxes are written back to the database.

The following graphics show you some sample results that you may see when you browse through the database. If you go to the first record within the table, the author is Russell Jacobs. If you go to record 56, you will see Bradford Nichols.

11. Stop the program by clicking the close button (x) in the upper-right corner of the form.

12. If you want to add new records, then set the EOFAction property of the data control to **2 - Add New**.

> **NOTE** If you do not want to modify the original database, you can always make a copy of it from Explorer and reference the new database instead of the original.

13. Re-start the program. To add a record, scroll to the last record, and then click the next record navigation button.

14. Type the author name **Doe, John** in the first text box and move to another record. The new author name is appended to the database (shown below).

15. Stop the program once again.

16. If you want to delete a record, then add a command button to the form. Set its `Name` property to **cmdDelete**. Set its `Caption` property to **&Delete**.

17. Add the following code to the `cmdDelete_Click()` event:

```
Private Sub cmdDelete_Click()
    With Data1.Recordset
        .Delete
        .MovePrevious
    End With
End Sub
```

The above example gives you a simple, yet workable, database application. To repeat the process for another database, you need to be aware of some of the properties and what they mean.

The Data Control Properties

Let's start with the data control properties (see Figure 8.8). The Connect property specifies the type of database you want to use—the default is Access. The DatabaseName property specifies the actual filename of the database (strictly speaking, this is true only for Access databases; for non-Access databases you may have to set just the directory). The RecordsetType property determines whether the data you see is from a table, a dynaset, or a snapshot. Typically (though not always) a table is the most efficient if the data is from one table; a dynaset is needed if the data is a subset of a table or comes from more than one table, and a snapshot is sometimes best if the data is to be read only. In this example, the RecordsetType property could be any one of the three available. The RecordSource property corresponds to the table in the database you want to access (at least, it does in Access; for non-Access databases you may have to set this property to a filename). To access multiple tables in a dynaset, you have to enter an SQL statement or create the dynaset first in code or in Access.

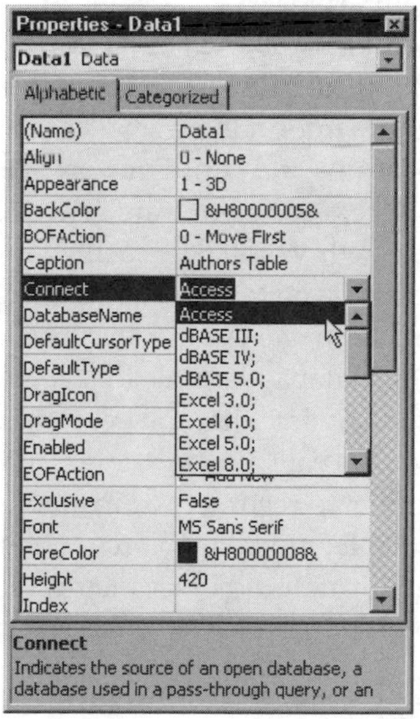

FIGURE 8.8: The data control properties

The data control does not actually display data—to do that, you must link another type of control to the data control. In the previous example, two text boxes were used. For each text box you set the `DataSource` property to the name of the data control (here it's Data1). Next you set the `DataField` property equal to the name of a field in the recordset returned by the data control's `RecordSource` property.

This ability of the data control to extract data is one of the strongest features of Visual Basic. It's possible to accomplish a great deal just through the data control. However, to get an even greater level of sophistication, you can write your own data access routines using Visual Basic code. This has been relatively easy in the past, but with the advent of ADO, data access has never been easier! We will cover ADO in detail later in the skill. In the meantime, you need to become familiar with database design.

Understanding the Anatomy of a Database

The possibilities for working with Visual Basic and Microsoft Access (`.MDB`) databases, and SQL Server and Oracle databases are manifold. While there are many methods of bringing data into Visual Basic, only a couple are touched on here (for more information, see *The Learning Guide to Access for Windows 95*, by Annette Marquis and Gini Courter (Sybex, 1997)). Fortunately, you don't need a copy of Access to begin using Access databases, because the Access Jet Engine is provided with Visual Basic. All you require is an Access `.MDB` file. Although using Access is a better solution to designing database files, you will use the Visual Data Manager Add-In for this skill because it comes with Visual Basic.

An Access database is a file that contains *tables*, *indexes*, and *queries*. A table is a collection of data that can be represented in rows and columns. In database terms, rows are called *records* and columns are called *fields*. An index is a linked list of pointers to records within a table. You use an index to rapidly search through a table, much like you use an index in a book to quickly find a page. Queries are Structured Query Language (SQL) statements that you write to extract specific records from a table.

Database Tables

If you've used SQL before, then you know what a table is. If you are moving to Visual Basic or Access from one of the traditional PC-based database applications, then you might need some practice. What xBase users refer to as a database is actually a table in Access. In Visual Basic and Access, the table is only one of potentially many components that will actually make up a database. A full-fledged Access database would typically contain other objects as well—other tables, queries, forms, and so on. A table is not saved as a separate file but rather is stored as an intrinsic part of a database. To open a table, you must open the parent database first. Tables are the starting point for any database, and they are where data is stored. If this is your first visit to the world of databases, but you have had experience working with spreadsheets, then think of a table as basically a worksheet. To extend the worksheet analogy, rows represent your records and columns your fields. I've reproduced a simple table here to illustrate this comparison.

TITLE	AUTHOR
C++ in 5 Easy Minutes	F. Bloggs
Astrophysics Simplified	J. Doe
How to Make a Billion	B. Gates

Apart from the column titles, there are three rows, each referring to a specific book. In other words, this table shows three records. Each record has various attributes or properties, in this case, title and author. These attributes are listed in columns, and each column represents a field. This table has only two fields—the title column and the author column. And that is all there is to a table—though, in reality, a table would typically include many more records than this one and possibly have more fields.

Without a minimum of one table, a database would contain no data and be totally meaningless. Therefore the first step in creating a database is to define a table and add some data to it. As your requirements develop, you'll probably find yourself creating more tables for the same database. For example, you might want a second table that lists publishers of the books in the first table. It *is* possible to append publisher details to the first table by adding extra fields—but if a publisher supplies more than one book, then you would want a second table. The reason for this has to do with data integrity and sensible database design.

Database Queries

A *query* is a way of inserting, extracting or changing table data. After you create the database, you pose a query to it, and (if you ask the question correctly) it comes up with an answer—saving you a good deal of time rummaging around for the answer by other means. There are additional methods of extracting data, but a query is a good place to begin. There are also alternatives for altering data—you could edit a table directly, although a query makes it easy to enact changes

Skill 8

on multiple records and fields simultaneously. Suppose you wanted to see which books were written by Stephen Blaha. In this case, you'd define a query that selected or filtered only the relevant records using Structured Query Language (SQL). Try this example:

1. Open the previous example from the "Adding the Data Control" section.

2. In the Properties window, change the `RecordSource` property to the following: **select * from [Authors] where [Author] = "Blaha, Stephen"**

3. Select Run ➤ Start to view the results.

The result of the query is shown here:

AUTHOR	AUTHOR ID
Blaha, Stephen	9033

This looks pretty much like a table, and in fact, it's a subset of the table. In Visual Basic and Access terminology it's called a *dynaset*. Dynaset means a "*dyna*mic *set* of records." The data in a dynaset does not actually exist—it's extracted from the underlying table or tables, and only the criteria for the query (here the criterion is books by the author Stephen Blaha) are saved. It's also dynamic in the sense that if you change the table, then different data could appear in the dynaset without your changing the query definition. Because it's a subset of an existing table, you can edit the data in the dynaset and this changes the original data back in the table. You should note that there are some restrictions on editing data in a dynaset—for example, you may not be able to edit data if it threatens referential integrity. For example, if you configure the table to only allow unique author names, then you could not add a new record for a book by the same author.

Queries are an extremely important part of Visual Basic and Access. Not only can you edit data directly in the dynaset, but you can then query the query itself, if you see what I mean. If the dynaset had included a number of separate titles by S. Blaha, then you could narrow this down further by specifying a couple of titles. This leads to an important observation on queries: Why not simply specify those titles in the first place and have just one query rather than two? That is, of course, perfectly possible and is often the approach to adopt. However, the great beauty of Access queries is that by querying another query you can progressively narrow down the dynaset and see the results of all intermediate queries. This allows a layered approach to queries and is sometimes exactly what's required.

You might raise another equally important point. Why bother to extract the data from the original table in the first place, when it's easy to spot the book by S. Blaha and all its details? With just three records, that might be a valid objection. But with tens, hundreds, or even thousands of records, the use of a suitable query lets you concentrate on only those records you want. Queries really come into their own when you add more than one table to the query definition—this allows you to view and edit data from related, though separate, tables from a Visual Basic form.

Creating Databases with Visual Data Manager

Databases provide a convenient method to store and retrieve data. They include tables, queries, and indexes that make record searching faster. Without these features, you would have to write your own code, which can be very difficult and impractical. Visual Basic and Access provide everything you need to make fast and efficient databases that can be used by your applications.

The first step in creating a database is to specify a filename. The database is saved as a single file with a .MDB extension. Once this is accomplished, you then go on to create the objects (tables, queries, and so on) that are going to be part of your database. As a reminder, these are held within the .MDB file and not as separate files.

Let's create a database designed for a bookstore named House of Books, which suggests a suitable name for the database.

Creating a database is straightforward; just follow these steps:

1. Select Tools ➤ Visual Data Manager to start Visual Data Manager.

2. Click File ➤ New ➤ Microsoft Access ➤ Version 7.0 MDB to see the Select Microsoft Access Database to Create dialog box.

3. Type in a name for your database; here let's use **HouseOfBooks** (the case is unimportant). There is no need to provide the .MDB extension, as Access does this for you automatically.

4. Click Save.

A database window will appear with the name of the database in its title bar. There are two windows that are visible right now. The left window is the Database window (see Figure 8.9), and the right window is the SQL Statement window. In the Database window is a list of the properties for the newly created database. There are no tables or queries defined in the database at this moment. The toolbar offers you some buttons to manipulate the database. The Dynaset button is pressed, but there are no tables listed in the Database window, indicating the database contains no tables at the moment.

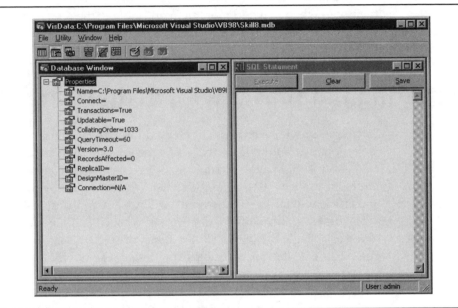

FIGURE 8.9: The Database window with properties expanded

Before adding the first table object to this database, let's see how to close and reopen it:

1. Click File ➢ Close. You could also use Close from the Database window's Control menu or double-click this menu. Double-clicking the Visual Data Manager Control menu not only closes your database but Visual Data Manager as well.

2. Click File ➢ Open Database ➢ Microsoft Access to see the Open Microsoft Access Database dialog box. In this dialog box, select HouseOfBooks.mdb and click Open. If you are not sharing your database across a network, then you can ignore the Open as Read-Only check box in the dialog box. You are back to the empty database window.

Now it's time to add the first object to the database.

Creating a Database Table

This section will use a bookstore metaphor to teach you how to create a database table. We will call the bookstore "House of Books." This bookstore carries hard-to-find books. But since you are going to create a well-written book location system, customers will come from all around to find that special book that they are looking for!

The sample table that you are going to create is simply a list of books. Each row (or *record*) in the table is to represent one book, though there may be more than one copy of an individual book in stock. The table is also to have three columns (or *fields*) to represent the properties of the books. To begin with, we only want to see the title and author of each book. Later you'll append more detail. Here's a table showing the books in stock:

TITLE	AUTHOR
A Philosophy of Solitude	John Cowper Powys
The Art of Growing Old	John Cowper Powys
Soliloquies of a Hermit	Theodore Francis Powys
Glory of Life	Llewelyn Powys
Windows—The Definitive Book	Emma Radek
Access—The Definitive Book	Emma Radek

This is fine as far as it goes. But book lists are often sorted by the author's last name. So you need to split the author field into two—last name and first name. Now the table looks like this, and this is how it's going to be entered:

TITLE	LASTNAME	FIRSTNAME
A Philosophy of Solitude	Powys	John Cowper
The Art of Growing Old	Powys	John Cowper
Soliloquies of a Hermit	Powys	Theodore Francis
Glory of Life	Powys	Llewelyn
Windows—The Definitive Book	Radek	Emma
Access—The Definitive Book	Radek	Emma

Before you can enter any data into the table, you must design the table. It's important to get the design stage right, though you can always modify the design later. There a few questions to ask before you begin the design. You must ask yourself what data you want to put in the table; in particular you must decide on the properties (fields) for the data. Once you've done this, the next question to ask yourself is what type of data is it. In the book list example the answers are quite straightforward. You need to have fields for the title of each book, plus two fields showing the last and first names of the author. These fields contain text, so the data type for all three fields is text.

Defining a Table

The table is part of the HouseOfBooks database, so make sure you can see the Database window (use File ➤ Open Database if necessary). As it stands, the window only has the properties list of the database. Select the Table button before creating a new table:

1. Right-click in the Database window and select New Table to begin a new table. You are presented with an empty table window in design view. This is where you specify your fields and the data type—it is not where you enter the actual data (see Figure 8.10).

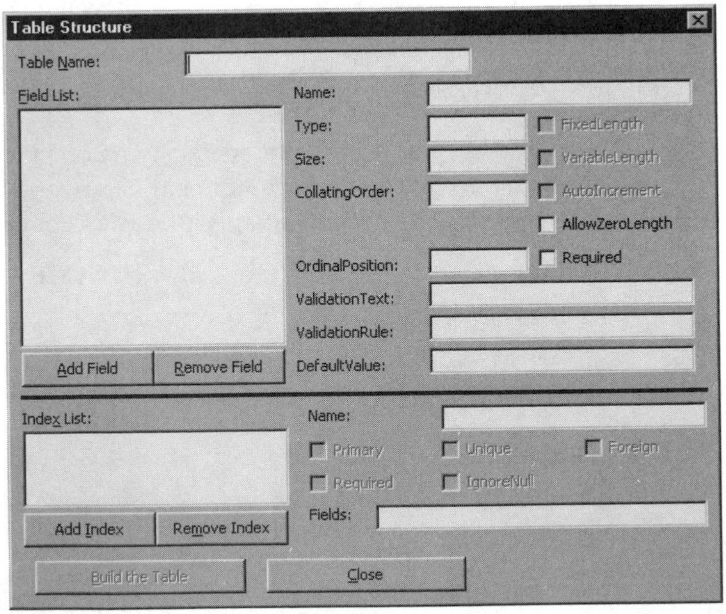

FIGURE 8.10: The Table Structure dialog box

The left side of the dialog box contains an empty list of cells. When you open a database that already has a table definition, you will see the database field names listed here. The right side contains the cells that describe the properties for each database field. Finally, the bottom of the dialog box contains the list of indexes within the database.

2. The field at the top of the dialog box is where you enter the name of the table. Enter **BookList** as the table name.

Adding Fields

Now you can add the three fields for this table:

1. Click the Add Field button to add the first field. You will see the Add Field dialog box shown in Figure 8.11.

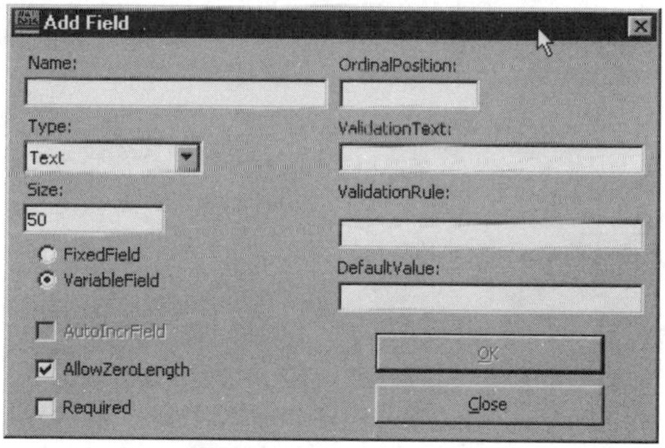

FIGURE 8.11: The Add Field dialog box

2. Type **TITLE** in the Name cell. The cursor should be in the Name cell by default—if you've been experimenting, click in this cell to reposition the cursor.

3. Press Tab to jump to the next cell. Note how Access inserts a default data type (Text) for you.

4. Press Tab to jump to the Size cell. Type **40** in this box.

5. Click the OK button to commit the field definition to the table.

6. Type **LASTNAME** for the second field name.

7. Press Tab twice to accept Text for the data type and type **20** for the field size.

8. Click the OK button to commit the field definition to the table.

9. Type **FIRSTNAME** as the next field name.

10. Press Tab twice to accept Text as the data type and enter **20** for the field size.

11. Click the Close button. The table design is now complete.

12. Click the Build the Table button in the Table Structure dialog box to have the Data Manager add the table structure to the database.

You have just added the first table to the database. From here you can re-open the table to modify it, or you can open it to add records. In addition, you can delete it, or you can copy the table's structure:

1. Right-click the BookList object in the Database window. Select Open from the pop-up menu. This displays your table in a row and column format ready for data entry—or editing or browsing if there were some data already there.

2. Close the Table Structure dialog box by clicking the Close button.

Entering Data

As you enter data into the BookList table, all the standard Windows editing techniques apply. The one you may not be familiar with is the F2 key, which selects all the data in a cell. You can, of course, simply double-click, but that only selects one word and is not enough if your field contains two or more words. But the first step is to re-open the table:

1. In the list of tables select BookList.

2. Right-click and select Open from the pop-up menu. A quicker way to open the table is to double-click the table name.

The cursor should be positioned ready for the first data in the first field of the first record.

Type the relevant data in each field and record. To move from field to field, click the desired field with the mouse. When you move the cursor to the next record, you will be asked if you want to commit the changes. Answer Yes to save the record. Here are the steps for the first record:

1. Click the Add button to add a new record to the database.

2. Type **A Philosophy of Solitude** as the Title for the first record and click in the LASTNAME field.

3. Type **Powys** as the last name and click in the FIRSTNAME field.

4. Type **John Cowper** in the FIRSTNAME field and click the Update button.

5. If you are prompted to save the new record, answer Yes.

The cursor is now in the first field of the record you just created. Click Add to add another record and continue data entry, using the rest of the data in the table below.

TITLE	SURNAME	FORENAME
The Art of Growing Old	Powys	John Cowper
Soliloquies of a Hermit	Powys	Theodore Francis
Glory of Life	Powys	Llewelyn
Windows—The Definitive Book	Radek	Emma
Access—The Definitive Book	Radek	Emma

As you click the Update button after the second entry for Emma Radek, you have finished populating the table.

As indicated earlier, a table is the basis for all the other objects in a database. We'll use this simple table to build a query. Later we'll go back and modify this table in order to look at some of the other features involved in constructing a table. For now, we'll base a simple query on this BookList table.

Skill 8

Creating a Query

A *query* is a SQL (pronounced *sequel*) statement that recalls a subset of records that match the criteria in the SQL statement. In this section you'll consider some very basic queries that filter the BookList table and carry out some sorting of data. Before running a query, however, you must define it first:

1. Right-click the Database window and select New Query from the pop-up menu. You could also select Utility ➢ Query Builder from the Visual Data

Manager menu. You will see the Query Builder dialog box shown in Figure 8.12.

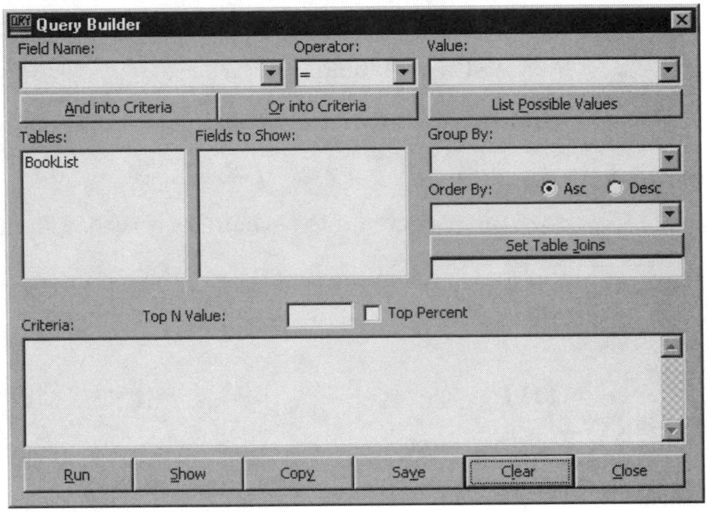

FIGURE 8.12:   The Query Builder dialog box

2. Select the BookList table from the Tables list in the dialog box. This will expose all of the fields within the table. Notice that the Field Name cell defaults to the first field in the table. Change this cell to **[BookList].LASTNAME**.

3. Leave the Operator cell intact. We are going to query on the authors' last names, so we want exact matches.

4. In the Value cell, you can type **Powys**, or you can click the List Possible Values button and select Powys from the list. This button queries all of the values entered in the selected field of the current table. This can be a time saver if you have many values to search through.

5. Select each field in the Fields to Show list by clicking each one. We want to show every field for any matching records.

6. You can preview the SQL statement by clicking the Show button. This will display a message box with the complete SQL statement required to extract all authors with the surname Powys from the BookList table.

7. Click the Add into Criteria button to add the SQL statement to the Criteria cell. You can continue making more queries to add to the current statement by clicking the And into Criteria or the Or into Criteria buttons. For this example, we just want to search for Powys.

8. To test the query, click the Run button. The Data Manager will ask you if this is a SQLPassThrough Query. (Click the No button. SQL Passthrough is used to access databases on SQL database servers such as Microsoft SQL Server.) If your query is built correctly, you will see a subset of records that all have the last name of Powys (see Figure 8.13).

9. After you have browsed the query results, click the Close button to close the dialog box.

10. Click the Save button on the Query Builder dialog box. You will be prompted to enter a query name. Type **Powys**. After a brief pause, the query will be added to the database.

11. Click the Close button to close the Query Builder.

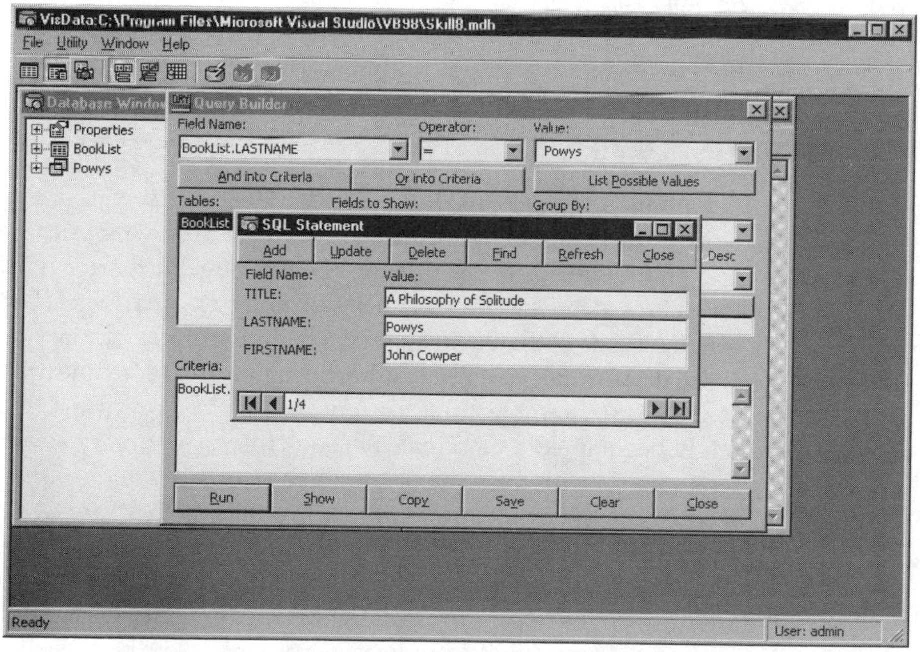

FIGURE 8.13: Query results

The query results are also known as a *dynaset*. The data is dynamic and can be edited—any changes are reflected in the underlying BookList table. There is little point, however, in designing a query like this—you can only see books from one author name. It would be impractical to create a separate query for every author in the database. As soon as you add a new author to the inventory, you would have to create a new query as well. Queries embedded within a database should be more general than this.

If you wanted a more generic query, you could use the Visual Data Manager to design the query. When you are satisfied with the query, you copy the SQL statement to your Visual Basic application. Using some string concatenation, you could selectively replace a value with that which was entered in a field by the user. For example, you could create a SQL query like this:

```
SQL = "Select * From [BookList] Where [BookList].LASTNAME = ' "
SQL = SQL & txtAuthorName.Text & "'"
```

Then you create a field on the form called txtAuthorName. The user can enter a value in this field, and when you call your query, it will extract the name entered in the field and place it in the SQL string. Then you just create a dynaset based on SQL.

Now let's consider what extra data the bookstore might find appropriate in the BookList table.

Primary Keys

A primary key is one that uniquely identifies each record in a table, such as a part number in a stock file. A primary key is advisable in tables, because it speeds up operations like searching, sorting, and filtering. Furthermore, if you want to relate two tables together, you must have a primary key in one of the tables. None of the existing fields in the BookList table would work as a primary key. A quick glance at the data reveals that both author surname and forename are duplicated across records—for example, there are four records for Powys and two for Radek. You might be tempted to nominate the book title as a primary key. However, two different books with the same title might be stocked. For example, if the bookstore were to expand on its Powys titles, it would find there are two books by John Cowper Powys called *The Art of Happiness*. And, given the nature of the bookstore, there is a further objection to using the title field as a primary key. Out-of-print and rare books (which the Powys books are) would warrant an entry for each individual copy (unlike modern computer books), because book collectors are concerned about the edition and condition of each book. For a bookstore, the ISBN

(International Standard Book Number, which uniquely identifies every book published) of each book might be an obvious candidate for a primary key. Unfortunately this bookstore stocks older, out-of-print books. This means many of its titles do not have an ISBN number. And it's no good simply leaving the ISBN entry for these books blank (a null value), for two blanks contravene the rule that every single entry in the primary key field must be unique. A solution to this problem is to create a counter field, described next.

Counter Fields

A counter field has two main benefits: It enables you to define a primary key when there is no other suitable candidate field and it automatically inserts data that increments by one for each record. The latter is ideal if you want to create part numbers (or invoice numbers and the like) in a table.

To create a counter field in Visual Data Manager, you first add a field and set its data type to Long. Then you check the Auto Increment option. Once the field is added, you need to create an index and set the field you added to Required and set it as the Primary Key. The result is each record has a unique value in the counter field.

In the BookList table a counter field is a viable alternative to an ISBN number, but it also assigns a unique identifier to all the books, not just those that are likely to have an ISBN. A suitable name for this counter is BOOK CODE. The information it contains is largely notional, and it's unlikely that the number would mean that much to employees. Still, you could argue that some customers might order books using this book code. In a real-world situation you would also include the ISBN number for the modern computer books, but you couldn't use it as a primary key. Here, we're dispensing with the ISBN altogether. However, the book code information is not notional to Access internally—it will speed up queries and so on, based on the table (the faster queries would be particularly noticeable with a larger table, though with the small amount of data in the BookList table, it's of little practical value here). The book code is also vital for relating tables together. When you design your own tables, it's good practice to have a primary key from the beginning—as your table grows, you'll reap the benefits.

Number Fields

The three existing fields in the BookList table are text fields. Such fields are not suitable for storing numeric values. With numeric values you may want to control how many decimal places are displayed and perform totaling and other calculations. A typical calculation is to add up the value of all items in stock for an inventory.

There are two distinct possibilities for numeric fields—the number of copies of each book, and the price. However, Access has a dedicated data type for prices, called a *currency field*. Therefore, you need only one numeric field—for the quantity in stock. This is particularly useful for the computer-book side of the business. When the quantities in stock begin to run a little low, it shows it's time to place fresh orders with publishers. The out-of-print side of the business is handled slightly differently. Here the quantity of each book is always one. Duplicate copies are given their own entries—each copy of the same book has a separate entry, as the price varies according to the edition and condition of the book. Thus the default number of copies is one. You'll instruct Access to enter this default amount for you shortly.

It's important to realize there are various subtypes to a number data type. These subtypes are defined in the Field Size row of the field's property sheet and include Byte, Integer, Long Integer, Single, and Double. The subtype you choose determines the range of values you can enter, the maximum number of decimal places the field can accommodate, and the amount of disk space (and hence processing time) the field requires. Here's a list of the number data type subtypes:

Field Size Property	Accepted Numbers	Decimal Places	Storage Requirements
Byte	0 to 255	0	1 byte
Integer	-32,768 to 32,767	0	2 bytes
Long Integer	-2,147,483,648 to 2,147,483,647	0	4 bytes
Single	-3.4×10^{38} to 3.4×10^{38}	7	4 bytes
Double	-1.797×10^{308} to 1.797×10^{308}	15	8 bytes

The list is in ascending size of the range, decimal places, and storage requirements of the subtype. If you can visualize your number fields holding decimal places, then you need to specify single or double (except for monetary values, which should be assigned to a separate currency data type field). Try to choose a subtype from as high up the list as possible, since this can cut down on disk space used to hold the data and thus improve processing times. In our example, the bookstore is never going to carry more than 255 copies of a book, so the byte subtype is fine. The field is called QUANTITY. For larger (or negative) whole numbers (integers), you should specify integer or long integer.

Currency Fields

Currency fields take as much room as double number fields. However, they're ideal for holding prices and values, for a number of reasons. They automatically display two decimal places for cents; they show a thousands separator for values of more than one thousand; they are right aligned; and finally, they are automatically prefixed with your default currency symbol, such as a dollar sign—you can simply type in the number during data entry. The BookList table would benefit from a field that gave the price of each book in stock. This, unsurprisingly, is to be called PRICE. As a safeguard, this field is going to be validated to prevent the possibility of entering negative prices—you presumably don't want the bookstore to pay its clients when they take a book!

> **TIP** You can use Currency fields if you want to add greater precision to the right of the decimal. This is useful for scientific calculations, or applications where mathematical tolerances must be minimal.

Yes/No Fields

Yes/No fields are sometimes referred to as Boolean or logical fields and contain only one of two possible values (typically Yes/No, True/False, or On/Off). The bookstore has two businesses—computer books and out-of-print rare editions. It would be nice to be able to distinguish the books at a glance. One way of doing this is to have a Yes/No field indicating if a particular book is (or is not) an out-of-print one. Using that field as a basis, it's then a straightforward matter to produce two separate book catalogs (by designing a query), one for computer book readers and another for out-of-print book readers. A good title for such a field might be RARE BOOK? (note the question mark).

Memo Fields

Memo fields are ideal for holding free-form text such as explanatory notes. This type of text often fits uncomfortably into normal text fields where there frequently are restrictions on the field length and formatting. In addition, it's difficult to apply validation to free-form text. If you want to validate normal text entries, then it makes little sense to place memo text in one of the normal text fields. The memo data type is specifically designed to accommodate free-form text. It allows you to input more characters than a text data-type field, but at the expense of more storage space on disk. The maximum capacity of a text field is 255 bytes (255 characters, or about 40 words), while a memo field holds up to 64,000 bytes.

A memo field would be ideal to hold information that describes in considerably more detail an out-of-print book. For example, you could mention whether it's a first edition, what its condition is, and whether it still has its original dust jacket or even an author's autograph. These are all of interest to the potential out-of-print book customer. The memo field is to be called NOTES.

Date/Time Fields

Date/Time fields are specifically designed to hold data that shows a date, or time, or both. Dates and times are stored internally by Access as numbers, making it possible to use them in calculations. However, both Visual Basic and Access display them as dates and times and both give you various formats from which to choose. There's also a degree of flexibility in how you enter dates. For example, to enter April 27, 1998, all the following are acceptable:

- 4 27 98
- 27 Apr
- April 27
- 04/27/1998

No matter how you enter the date, it always displays in the format you chose for the date field. Notice that omitting the year from the date results in the current year being stored and displayed. To enter April 27, 1989, you need to explicitly type 89 or 1989.

The BookList table might benefit from a date/time field. This is to hold the date when a book first arrived in stock—as a result, it only has to show the date and not the time. This information is more useful for the out-of-print business, because it lets you see how long you've been holding a particular item. Perhaps you might want to consider a price reduction for a rare book that's been sitting on the shelves for more than a year. You can ask Visual Basic or Access to list those books for you and to perform a price reduction automatically. The field is to be called ACQUIRED.

Modifying a Table

The preceding discussion suggested a number of fields and data types that would improve the usefulness of the BookList table. Here's a summary of those fields and the data types:

FIELD NAME	DATA TYPE
BOOK CODE	Counter (also to be a primary key)
QUANTITY	Number (Byte)
PRICE	Currency
RARE BOOK?	Yes/No
NOTES	Memo
ACQUIRED	Date/Time

To modify the table design to accommodate these new fields, follow these steps:

1. If you don't have the BookList table open in design view, right-click the BookList table and click the Design item on the pop-up menu.

2. Click the Add Field button to add another field. In the Name cell, type **BOOK CODE**. Press Tab to move into the Type cell. Open the drop-down list in the cell and select Long. To make this a counter field, click the check boxes next to **AutoIncrField** and **Required**. Click the OK button.

3. Type **QUANTITY** for the next field name and press Tab. This field is a number field. In the Type field, select **Byte**. Press the OK button to begin defining the next field.

4. Type **PRICE** in the Name field. Tab down to the Type list and type the letter **c**. This will select the Currency data type for this field. Click OK to save the field definition and start a new one.

5. For the next field type **RARE BOOK?**. Select **Boolean** for the field type. This is the equivalent of a Yes/No field. Again, click the OK button to save this definition.

6. The next field name should be labeled **NOTES**. Set the data type for this field to **Memo**. Click OK.

7. This is the last field for the table. Type **ACQUIRED** in the Name cell. Select **Date/Time** for the data type. Click OK to save. Click the Close button to close the Add Field dialog box.

8. From the Table Structure dialog box, click the Add Index button. Type **BOOK CODE** in the Name field. Click BOOK CODE in the Available Fields list to add the field to the Indexed Fields list.

Also notice that the Primary and Unique options are checked. This establishes BOOK CODE as the primary key field. In some cases you may not want to create a counter field to be the primary key field. In the absence of any other suitable field, you might want to nominate two or more fields as a single primary key.

For example, in a library neither the date of borrowing nor the book number is satisfactory. The date would be repeated (that is, not unique) for each reader borrowing books on the same day. The book number would be repeated, since the same book is borrowed on different dates. However, the two fields together are unique—this is assuming that the same book is not borrowed, returned, and borrowed again all in the same day.

To nominate a double-field primary key, click the names of the fields in the list to add them to the Index Fields list. With both fields selected, click the OK button to add this index to the database as the primary key. If you look at the Index properties in the Database window, you can see that the properties UNIQUE, PRIMARY, and REQUIRED are checked. The table is now indexed on the BOOK CODE field, and each entry into the field must be unique. With a counter field, each entry is automatically made by the Access engine, and you can be sure that they are all unique. With, say, a text field, you must make sure that you enter unique values into each record. If you don't, then Access won't let you save the duplicate record until you change your entry.

9. Now to index on some other fields. Type **TITLE** in the Name field and then click TITLE in the Available Fields list. Remove the checks from the Unique and Primary options. Clearing these two check boxes causes the index to allow duplicate values in the field—here it allows books with the same title to be entered. Click the OK button to save the index.

TIP　Setting an index, like a primary key, helps speed up many processes in any type of database. If you define a field with a unique index, then you're building in a form of validation—you can't enter duplicate values. A unique index is the same as a primary key except that a primary key is the controlling index for the table and can also be used to establish relations into other tables.

10. Repeat the previous step to index by last name—be careful, though, not to set a unique index.

11. When you are done adding the indexes, click the Close button to close the dialog box.

12. In the Field List, select QUANTITY to make it the current field. Enter **1** in the `DefaultValue` cell. This is the default number of books in stock.

    When you enter a new record, Access inserts this value automatically. This is handy for the out-of-print books that are usually bought and sold in single copies. When the bookstore acquires multiple copies of modern computer books, then the amount must be entered manually to override the default. Default values are very useful and can be used with all data types except counters and OLE objects.

13. In the Field List, select PRICE to make it the current field.

    As well as defaults, you can set validation rules for fields. One idea might be to validate the quantity field to ensure that negative amounts are not entered accidentally. However, the Byte subtype only accepts integer values between 0 and 255, so validation is not really necessary.

14. In the `ValidationRule` cell row type **>0 and <1000**. The price field requires a currency data type for each item. Therefore it's possible to enter negative prices.

    This validation rule prevents negative prices and at the same time stops the accidental entry of prices over one thousand dollars (or pounds, or whatever currency you're working in). This assumes that the bookstore is not going to stock books with a value of more than $1,000.

15. Click in the `ValidationText` cell and type **Price between zero and one thousand dollars**. If you try to enter a price that fails the validation rule, then a warning dialog box appears. This dialog box contains a message that tells you that your entry is not valid. However, to provide a more meaningful message (perhaps explaining which values are allowed), you make an entry under Validation Text.

16. Click the Close button to save the table definition.

When you're finished, try creating some Visual Basic projects that access your new database. From Visual Basic, you can click Add-Ins ➤ Data Form Designer to create an instantaneous form based on the table or one of the queries. Alternatively,

Skill 8

you can add a data control to a new form and add text boxes or any of the other data-bound controls to link to with the data control. The important properties for the data control are `DatabaseName`, which points to your Access `.MDB`, and `RecordSource`, which points to a table *or* a query in your `.MDB`. With text boxes, set the `DataSource` property to point to the data control and the `DataField` property to point to the fields in the table or query that's the `RecordSource` for the data control. For data-bound combo or list boxes, use the `RowSource` property (with `ListField`) to bring data from the data control. To write data back to the database, via the data control, use the `DataSource` property (and `DataField`) as well.

Using ActiveX Data Objects

If there was ever a promised land for seamless universal data access, *ActiveX Data Objects*, or ADO, is it! ADO is Microsoft's new universal data-access framework. It encompasses the functionality of Database Access Objects (DAO), Remote Data Objects (RDO), as well as almost any other data access method. You can use ADO to connect to Access, SQL, Oracle, MS Exchange, and many other data sources.

ADO uses a new database connection framework called OLEDB, which allows you faster, more flexible access to multiple data providers, and ADO wraps it all into one easy-to-use interface. What this means is you can write database applications that can scale easily from single-user databases such as Access to complex client/server systems using Microsoft's SQL Server, Oracle, or almost any other database that has either an OLEDB provider, or ODBC provider (See Figure 8.14).

As you can see from the figure, ADO can connect to any data source that uses an OLEDB provider. You may have noticed that you can use ADO to connect to Microsoft Exchange server. This is true, but unfortunately it is beyond the scope of this book.

Not only does the universal data-access model make a convincing case for ADO, but the ability to disconnect recordsets from the database so you can work with them offline and return them later is extremely beneficial in a client/server environment. When you disconnect a recordset, ADO maintains connection information such as the database name, the server the database resides on (if any), and user and password information, as well as other bits of information that are beyond the scope of this book. Because a disconnected ADO recordset remembers where it came from, you can update the data offline and send it back to the database at a later time by re-establishing the connection, minimizing the load on the server, which is a major concern as client/server applications grow.

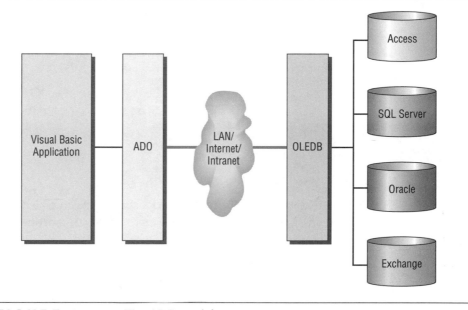

FIGURE 8.14: The ADO model

Visual Basic offers three tools that you can use to implement ADO in your applications. The first, and most simple is the ADO Data Control. There are also two ActiveX components called the ADO Connection Object and the ADO Recordset Object. We will take a look at all three in the next sections.

Using the ADO Data Control

The ADO Data Control is the simplest of the three ADO tools, but the others are not too complicated either. You will start with this control because it is very similar to the standard Visual Basic data control that you worked with earlier in this skill.

The ADO Data Control is very similar to the standard data control. You can set a few properties at design time and link them to any data-bound controls on the form. Rather than explain the theory, let's try it. You'll see how easy it is to use! This example will be the same as the first example you completed with the data control earlier, but you'll use the ADO Data Control instead.

1. Open the data control project you created earlier in this skill.

2. Click the data control on the form and press the Delete key on your keyboard. This will remove the control from the form.

Before you can use the ADO Data Control, you must add it to your Toolbox:

3. Right-click the Toolbox and select Components from the pop-up menu.

4. In the Components dialog box, select Microsoft ADO Data Control 6.0 (OLEDB), and click OK. This will add the control to the Toolbox.

5. Add the ADO Data Control to the bottom of the form, where the original data control used to be.

6. Set its `Caption` property to **Authors**.

7. Instead of using a `Database` property, ADO connects to databases through a Connection object. Click the `ConnectionString` property to bring up the property page for the control (Figure 8.15).

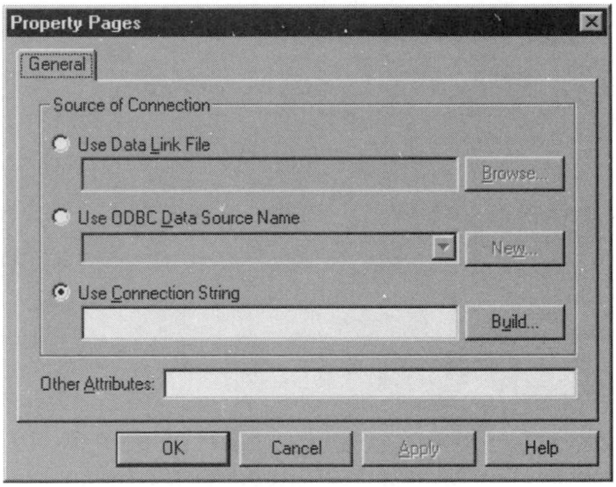

FIGURE 8.15: The ADO Data Control property page

The Use Data Link File and Use ODBC Data Source Name fields are used when you want to connect to an external data source, such as a database server. For this example, you want to connect to an Access table.

8. Click the Build button to start building a connection string.

9. From the Data Link Properties dialog box, shown in Figure 8.16, click Microsoft Jet 3.51 OLE DB provider to use this driver to connect to the database. Click the Next button.

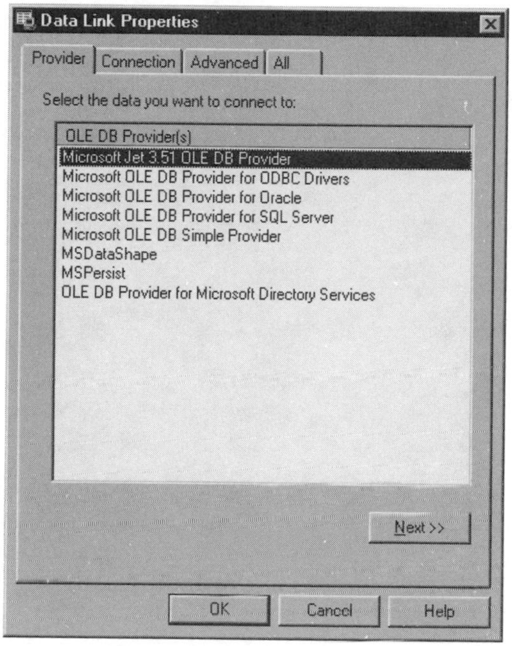

FIGURE 8.16: Selecting the database provider

10. Click the button to the right of the Select or Enter a Database Name field. Select the `Biblio.mdb` database from the `\Program Files\Microsoft Visual Studio\VB98` directory. Click the Open button to select the database. You will return to the Connection tab in Figure 8.17.

11. Click the OK button to create the connection string. Don't worry about the Advanced and All tabs. They are used for more advanced features. You may want to come back to it as you gain proficiency with ADO.

12. Click the OK button to close the property page. The `ConnectionString` property is now set.

13. Double-click the RecordSource property to specify the table you want to look at. You will see yet another property page like the one in Figure 8.18.

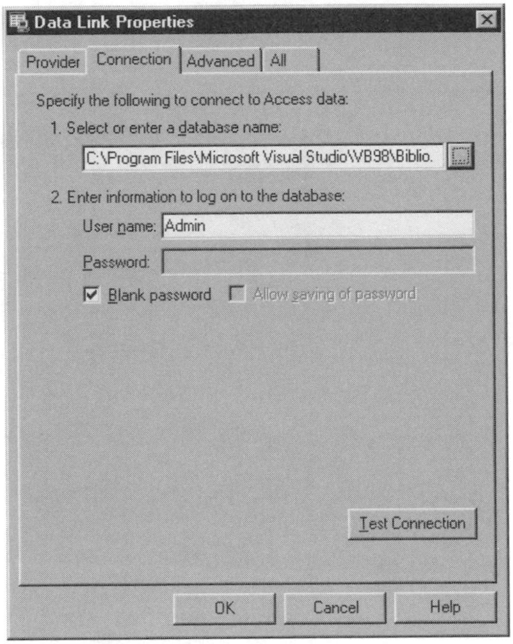

FIGURE 8.17: Selecting a database file

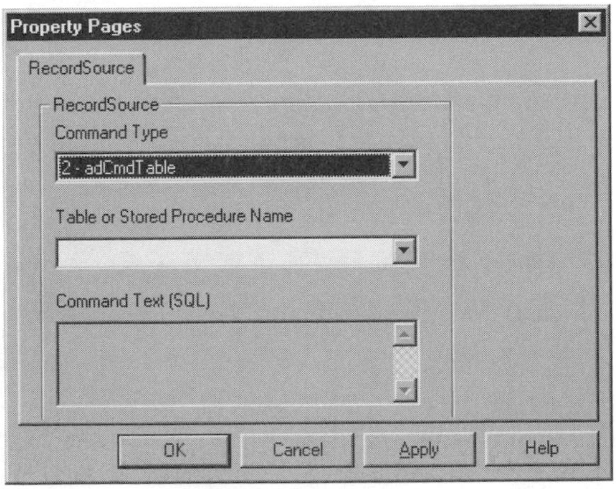

FIGURE 8.18: Setting the RecordSource

14. In the Command Type field, select **2 – adCmdTable**.

15. When the Table or Stored Procedure Name field appears, select Authors.

16. Click the OK button to close the dialog box.

Now that you have a live connection to the database, you need to bind the other controls to the ADO Data Control.

17. Click the Text1 control to make it the active control. Set its DataSource property to **Adodc1**. Set its DataField property to **Author**.

18. Click the Text2 control to make it the active control. Set its DataSource property to **Adodc1**. Set its DataField property to **Au_ID**.

19. Remove cmdDelete from the form

20. Finally, save and run the project.

After playing with the control for a while, you will notice that it works just as well as the standard data control. Although there were more steps to use this control, they were simple and consistent. You will use these same steps if you decide to connect to a database server, or other data format.

Using the ADO Connection and Recordset Objects

Now that you know the basics of how ADO works, you can start learning to write ADO code in your applications. Again, we will be using ADO to connect to the Biblio.mdb database, but it is more than enough to show you how to do it. Try this example, and we'll go over the code afterward:

1. Start a new project by select File ➢ New Project from the Visual Basic menu. Select Standard EXE from the New Project dialog box and click the OK button.

2. Set the Name property of the project to **ADORecordset**.

3. Set the Name property of Form1 to **frmMain**. Set its Caption to **Using ADO Recordsets**.

4. Add a listbox control to frmMain. Set its Name property to **lstAuthors**.

As I mentioned earlier, the ADO Data Control is an ActiveX control. It can be dropped on a form. The ADO Connection and Recordset objects are ActiveX DLLs. They can only be accessed through a reference to the *type library*.

NOTE   A *type library* contains all the component definitions that a component pro-vides, including properties, methods, events, and data types.

5. Selecting Project ➤ References from the Visual Basic menu to open the References dialog box.

6. Reference the ADO type library by checking the box next to Microsoft ActiveX Data Objects 2.0 library, as shown in Figure 8.19.

References - ADORecordset.vbp

Available References:

   ☐ Microsoft Access 8.0 Object Library
   ☐ Microsoft Active Server Pages Object Library
   ☐ Microsoft ActiveMovie Control
   ☑ Microsoft ActiveX Data Objects 2.0 Library
   ☐ Microsoft ActiveX Data Objects Recordset 2.0 Library
   ☐ Microsoft ActiveX Plugin
   ☐ Microsoft Add-In Designer
   ☐ Microsoft Agent Control 1.5
   ☐ Microsoft Agent Server 1.5
   ☐ Microsoft AutoFill Control
   ☐ Microsoft Binder 8.0 Object Library
   ☐ Microsoft Connection Designer Instance 1.0
   ☐ Microsoft Connection Designer v6.0
   ☐ Microsoft DAO 2.5/3.51 Compatibility Library

OK   Cancel   Browse...   Priority   Help

Microsoft ActiveX Data Objects 2.0 Library

    Location: C:\PROGRAM FILES\COMMON FILES\SYSTEM\ADO\MSADO15.
    Language: Standard

FIGURE 8.19: Referencing the ADO 2.0 type library

---

7. Click the OK button to reference the library and close the References dialog box. You can now access the ADO Connection and Recordset objects in your code.

8. Add the following declarations to the (General)(Declarations) section of the form:

```
Private cn As ADODB.Connection
Private rs As ADODB.Recordset
```

9. Add the following code to the Form_Load() event:

```
Private Sub Form_Load()
    Dim cmd As String
    Dim sql As String
    Dim cn As ADODB.Connection
    Dim rs As ADODB.Recordset

    'Create a connection string
    cmd = "Provider=microsoft.jet.OLEDB.3.51;" & _
        "Data Source=" & _
        "C:\Program Files\Microsoft Visual Studio" & _
        "\VB98\Biblio.mdb"

    'Establish a connection with the database
    Set cn = New ADODB.Connection
        With cn
            .ConnectionString = cmd
            .Open
        End With

        'create a query
        sql = "select * from authors"

        'Open the recordset
        Set rs = New ADODB.Recordset
            With rs
                .Open sql, cn, adOpenForwardOnly, adLockReadOnly
                    Do While Not rs.EOF
                        'Add the author to the list
                        lstAuthors.AddItem rs("Author")

                        'Move to the next record
                        rs.MoveNext
                    Loop

                'Close the recordset
                .Close
            End With
        Set rs = Nothing

    'Close the connection
    cn.Close

    'Destroy the connection object
    Set cn = Nothing
End Sub
```

Skill 8

10. Save and run the project.

This example simply accesses the `Biblio.mdb` database and lists the authors' names from the Authors table. It might appear to be a lot of code to do something so simple, but it is actually quite easy once you understand what's going on.

The first block of code dimensions two variables, `cmd` and `sql`. The variable `cmd` will be used to hold the ADO connection string used to connect to the database. `sql` will be used to store the SQL query.

The next block of code creates a connection to `Biblio.mdb` using Microsoft's new OLEDB provider. This is specified after the `Provider=` construct at the beginning of the string. If you wanted to connect to another type of data source, SQL Server for example, you would change the provider here. The second parameter in the string is the actual database name. The ADO `Connection-String` does most of the work, and will require the most attention when using ADO. By cleverly wrapping this code into a function, you could dynamically create multiple connection strings to connect to multiple databases (Access, SQL Server, and Oracle, for example). You could retrieve a parameter, pass it to the wrapper function, and retrieve a unique connection string. This will help make your ADO-based application scale well.

The next step is to establish the actual connection to the database. You did this by instantiating an `ADO.Connection` object, and then setting its `Connection-String` property equal to `cmd`. Then you issued the `.Open` method for the object. This method took the data stored in the `ConnectionString` property and used it to successfully connect to the database.

Once you have a successful connection to a database, you can open an `ADO.Recordset` object to retrieve records. However, before you can open a recordset, you must give it a SQL query to tell it what records to retrieve. This is accomplished in the statement:

```
sql = "select * from authors"
```

Without getting too involved in the details of SQL, the query simply states "get all (*) records from the table named 'Authors.'" As you saw in the example, that's exactly what it did.

Now that you have a query to pass to the recordset, you can create the actual recordset object using:

```
Set rs = New ADODB.Recordset
```

This command instantiates a new recordset object. It does not have any information in it because you have not told it to do anything yet. In the `With` block, you tell ADO to open the recordset using the command:

```
With rs
    .Open sql, cn, adOpenForwardOnly, adLockReadOnly
```

You may have noticed several parameters required to open the recordset. The first parameter passes the SQL query to the recordset. The second parameter, `cn`, tells the recordset to use the connection object `cn` to get to the database. The connection is like the road that the car takes to get the data. The recordset is the equivalent of the car. The next parameter tells ADO which type of database cursor to use on the recordset. ADO can use many types of cursors. The table below lists the possible options and what they do:

Cursor Type	Description
`AdOpenForwardOnly`	This type of cursor can only be used to move forward through the recordset. You cannot move backwards or jump around. However, this option is fast and is useful when you want to rapidly populate a list or combo box.
`AdOpenKeyset`	This is the best type of cursor to use when you expect a large recordset because you are not informed when changes are made to data that can affect your recordset.
`AdOpenDynamic`	This cursor allows you to see all of the changes made by other users that affect your recordset. It is the most powerful type of cursor, but because of that power, it is also the slowest.
`AdOpenStatic`	The static cursor is useful when you have a small recordset.

Finally, the last parameter tells ADO that you want the recordset to be read-only. You will not be adding data to this recordset. You can specify another lock type from the following table, but in this example we opted for speed.

Lock Type	Description
AdLocKReadOnly	Use this lock mode when you do not want to allow any additions, updates, or deletions from the recordset.
AdLockPessimistic	In pessimistic locking, the record is locked as soon as editing begins and remains locked until the editing is completed, or the cursor moves to another record.
AdLockOptimistic	Optimistic locking occurs when you issue the .Update method on the record. The record is still unlocked while you edit, but is temporarily locked when you want to save the changes to the database.
AdLockBatchOptimistic	This option allows you to perform optimistic locking when you are updating a batch of records.

If all of these parameters are correct, the recordset will be opened and you will have some data to work with.

The next block of code tells the application to loop through every record until the EOF (end of file) is reached. As the cursor moves to each record, you add the data in the Author field to the list using:

```
lstAuthors.AddItem rs("Author")
```

After you add the data to the list, you must move to the next record using the .MoveNext method, or else the loop will get stuck because the EOF will never be reached.

 WARNING   Whenever your are processing recordset data in a loop, be sure to include the .MoveNext method. It's easy to forget, and it will possibly hang your program. When you first create the Do While… statement, immediately write the Loop command. Then, immediately insert the .MoveNext method right above it. Then insert your code to retrieve the data. This will minimize your debugging time for sure!

Finally, it is always proper to close anything you open, and destroy objects that you have created when you are done with them. You do this by calling the

.Close method for the Recordset and the Connection objects. Then you set these objects equal to Nothing to prevent memory leakage in your application.

Adding Records

Although this example doesn't call for it, you will most certainly want to add records in your applications. This is easy to do with the ADO recordset object. To do so, you would use the .AddNew method in code similar to the following:

```
.
.
.
rs.AddNew
     rs("Author") = "Doe, John"
     rs("Au_ID") = 123456
rs.Update
.
.
.
```

The code is simple. When you want to actually add a new record, you issue the .AddNew method. This will create a blank record for your data. Then you insert data into the field. There are several techniques to achieve this including:

```
Rs("Author") = "Doe, John"
Rs!Author = "Doe, John"
Rs.Fields(1) = "Doe, John"
```

Each method is functionally equivalent, and the one you use is a matter of style. I prefer to use the first method because it is self-documenting. I know exactly what field I'm updating, and since the field name is enclosed in quotes, I can access field names with spaces in them.

After you added the data to the record, you issue the .Update method to update the data in the recordset.

Updating Records

Updating records is identical to adding records except you do not need to call the .AddNew method. You simply move the database cursor to the record you want to modify, change the data, and call the .Update method. For example:

```
Rs("Author") = "Brown, Steve"
Rs("Au_ID") = 373737
Rs.Update
```

Skill 8

Deleting Records

Deleting records is also easy to do in ADO. All you need to do is position the database cursor in the record you want to delete and call the `.Delete` method. This can be achieved with code similar to the following:

```
'Create a query
sql = "select * from authors where [Author] = 'Brown, Steve'"

'Open the recordset
Set rs = New ADODB.Recordset
    With rs
        .Open sql, cn, adOpenForwardOnly, adLockReadOnly
            If rs.RecordCount > 0 Then
                rs.Delete
            End If

        'Close the recordset
        .Close
    End With

'Destroy the recordset object
Set rs = Nothing
```

You now have experience creating Access databases and accessing them through a variety of methods. As you develop your applications, you can create new databases using the methods described in this skill. Although Visual Data Manager has many improvements over previous versions, you might want to consider purchasing Microsoft Access if you don't already have it. This application has many features that make database design even easier than what you have done to create the previous database. Access also has more features and functionality built into it that can further define your database. Best of all, the database will still be compatible with your Visual Basic application.

Now that you can work with files and databases, you can take the data from your applications and store it for retrieval, printing, or even use the data to store and retrieve application configuration settings. Spend some time experimenting with Visual Data Manager. There are many features that we have not covered in this skill (it could take another complete book to cover them!). You can use Visual Basic to access your database and can actually create some sophisticated applications when you couple these tools. The next skill deals with the third important feature of an application: printing.

Are You up to Speed?

Now you can...

- ☑ **open and work with an ASCII file**
- ☑ **work with files using sequential, random, and binary access modes**
- ☑ **use a data control to access information in a database**
- ☑ **use the Visual Data Manager**
- ☑ **create tables and queries**
- ☑ **understand and use ADO to access databases**

Skill 8

SKILL 9

Printing

- Making the best use of your data
- Understanding the *Print* method
- Printing to the Immediate window
- Understanding the *PrintForm* method
- Using the *Printers* collection
- Using Crystal Reports for Visual Basic
- Using a report in your application
- Printing your source code

To see the fruits of your programming labor, you may need to print information on your printer. When it comes to dealing with applications and programming, there are many things you may want to print. You might need a hard copy of your source code, a screen print of a form you're designing, or output generated from your application. Visual Basic has the capacity to do all these things and more!

In this skill you will learn how to use Visual Basic's `Printers` collection and the `Printer` object to print data to a form, a debugger, and a printer. In addition, you will learn how to use Crystal Reports Pro to design professional-looking reports that you can integrate directly into your own Visual Basic applications.

Making the Ultimate Use of Your Data

During the life of your project, you will input data, manipulate it in memory, and possibly store it on disk. These are all very important functions required by many applications, but it is perhaps most important to be able to print these values. In Visual Basic, you have many options to print. You can do any of the following:

- Print the current form
- Print line by line to a form or a printer
- Print to the Immediate window
- Print reports from Crystal Reports (bundled with Visual Basic)
- Print via another application, such as Word for Windows, using DDE or OLE Automation

Understanding the *Print* Method

The `Print` method is the first example you will examine in this skill. This method is handy for displaying the values contained in variables so you can examine how they've changed up until the `Print` statement. You can check the values printed to the Immediate window by breaking the project while it's running (with Run ➤ Break). The `Print` method also works for printing to both a form and a printer. To print to the printer, use `Printer.Print`; to print to the current form `Print` alone is sufficient, though it's good practice to preface the method with the object name (for example, `frmMyForm.Print`).

NOTE   If you want to clear the text on a form before printing to it, use the Cls method. Otherwise, a series of many Print methods causes the output to disappear off the bottom of the form.

When you do print to a printer, you have to tell the printer *when* to print. The Print method alone only places the output in memory—making it ready to print but not actually printing it. The reason for that is you may want to print a series of lines on a single page and, if Print caused the printer to start, you'd end up printing lots of pages with only one line on each one. To actually make the printer start printing you issue the Printer.EndDoc method. For multi-page documents the NewPage method is also available.

Try the following code (perhaps in a form's Click() event) to print a multi-page document:

```
Printer.Print "This is on page one"
Printer.Print "This is a second line on page one"
Printer.NewPage
Printer.Print "And this is on page two"
Printer.EndDoc
```

Viewing Values in the Immediate Window

While you are developing your application, you may find yourself spending time tracking down those pesky pieces of renegade code that programmers so fondly refer to as *bugs*. What you will find out when you are *debugging*—or fixing the erroneous code—is that you spend much of your time checking the values of variables. You have many options to display these values: You can place MsgBox commands strategically throughout your code, use trial and error (not a very efficient use of your time), or display values to the Immediate window.

A cumbersome, but operational way to view variables at run time is to place a message box in the code after the variable's value has been set. Then you tell the message box to display this value.

Although this works, it is bad practice because you must continually add the MsgBox statements in the code, re-run the application, stop it, debug the code, and then remove the MsgBox statements. This is an awful way to track down bugs and is time consuming.

Trial and error is basically experimenting with variables and their values until the program works. You can get an idea for where the program is causing problems and then try to fix that code, but often the data gets mangled long before it appears to the user or the application. These are the worst types of bugs to track down because they appear intermittently.

To print to the Immediate window, you need to use the Debug object. You simply tell Debug to print a value, like in the example below:

```
        .
        .
        .
x = x + 1
Debug.Print x
        .
        .
        .
```

This will display the current value of the variable x in the Immediate window. Although this is very simple code, it is also very powerful.

Viewing an Error in the Immediate Window

To give you a better idea of how you can implement this feature, let's create a small program with a bug in it; you can then use the Immediate window to view the error:

1. Start a new project by selecting File ➤ New Project. Select Standard EXE from the New project dialog box and click OK.

2. Double-click Form1 to open its Code window.

3. Add the following code to the Click() event for Form1:

```
Private Sub Form_Load()
    Dim x As Integer

    'Set an error handler
    On Error GoTo looperr

    'Loop until x = 100000
    Do While x < 100000
        x = x + 1
    Loop
```

```
        'bypass the error handler
        Exit Sub

looperr:
        Debug.Print "Error!"
        Debug.Print "x = " & Trim$(Str$(x))
End Sub
```

The program will create an error when you run it. Can you figure out what causes the error?

3. Run the code, click the form, and see what happens. You should see the results in the Immediate window, as shown in Figure 9.1.

FIGURE 9.1: The code returns an error in the Immediate window.

If you haven't read Skill 7, or if you are unfamiliar with the different variable types, the cause of the error will probably not be obvious to you. We caused an error by trying to force an integer to count beyond its own limitations. An integer can hold a value between -32,768 and 32,767. Since this example tries to count to 100,000 it will create an error when the value of the variable *x* equals 32,768. In a situation like this, it would be better for us to dimension the variable *x* as a long integer (Long).

Fixing the Bug

Once you find a bug, you need to fix it. You can fix this particular bug by following these steps:

1. Stop the program if you have not already done so.

2. In the Code window, change the Dim statement in the Click() event from:

    ```
    Dim x As Integer
    ```

    to:

    ```
    Dim x As Long
    ```

3. Run the program again (Run ➤ Start) and see what happens.

This time the program worked because a long integer can count much higher than a standard integer. Notice that the code is syntactically correct. Visual Basic recognizes all of the commands and even lets you try to run the program. Sometimes syntax is the cause of an error, and this is easy to fix. Unfortunately many bugs are the result of mismatched data types or invalid calculations. You can use the Immediate window to track the values of suspicious variables.

NOTE To learn more about debugging tools and the debugging process, read Skill 12, *Debugging Your Applications*.

Debugging is an important process to learn, and the `Print` method is a handy tool to use when checking the values of variables at run time. Not only is this method useful in debugging, but you can use it for prototyping programs as well as creating simple reports. Before your results can print to paper though, you must print the contents of the printer's buffer with the `PrintForm` method.

Understanding the *PrintForm* Method

The `PrintForm` method prints the active form, unless another form is explicitly named, to the default printer. It does this by sending a pixel-by-pixel image of a form object to the printer. This is a handy method if you want to make simple screen dumps.

If you add `Me.PrintForm` to the `Form_Click()` event in the previous example, the form picture will be sent to the printer before the error message is printed in the Immediate window. To explicitly name a form to be printed, name the form and call its `PrintForm` method as shown below:

```
frmReport.PrintForm
```

In this example, the code instructs Visual Basic to print the contents of `frmReport`. You could also specify names like `frmSplash`, `frmMain`, `frmAbout`, or any other form name in your project.

Using the *Printers* Collection

One of the many useful collections intrinsic to Visual Basic is the `Printers` collection. The `Printers` collection allows you to query the list of printer objects that are registered on your system. By querying the collection, you can change the default printer for the application, print something, and switch back to the normal printer.

Try this example to see how to query the collection and see what printers are installed on your system:

1. Start a new project by pressing Ctrl+N in Visual Basic.

2. Select Standard EXE from the New Project dialog box.

3. Set the `Name` property of the project to **PrintersCollection**.

4. Set the `Name` property of Form1 to **frmMain**. Set its `Caption` to **Printer List**.

5. Right-click the Toolbox and select Components from the pop-up menu.

6. Select Microsoft Windows Common Controls 6.0 from the Components dialog box. Click OK to close the dialog box.

7. Add a ListView control to frmMain. Set its `Name` property to **lvwPrinters**.

8. Double-click frmMain to open its Code window.

9. Add the following code to the `Resize()` event:

    ```
    Private Sub Form_Resize()
        'Stretch the listview
        lvwPrinters.Move 0, 0, ScaleWidth, ScaleHeight
    End Sub
    ```

10. Add the following code to the `Load()` event:

    ```
    Private Sub Form_Load()
        Dim p As Printer
        Dim x As ListItem

        'Set the listview to report view
        With lvwPrinters
            .View = lvwReport
            .ColumnHeaders.Add , , "Printer"
    ```

Skill 9

```
            .ColumnHeaders.Add 2, , "Driver"
            .ColumnHeaders.Add 3, , "Port"
        End With

        'List the printers on this system
        For Each p In Printers
            With p
                Set x = lvwPrinters.ListItems.Add(, , .DeviceName)
                    x.SubItems(1) = .DriverName
                    x.SubItems(2) = .Port
            End With
        Next
    End Sub
```

11. Save and run your project.

If you have any printers installed on your system, you will see them listed in the window (Figure 9.2).

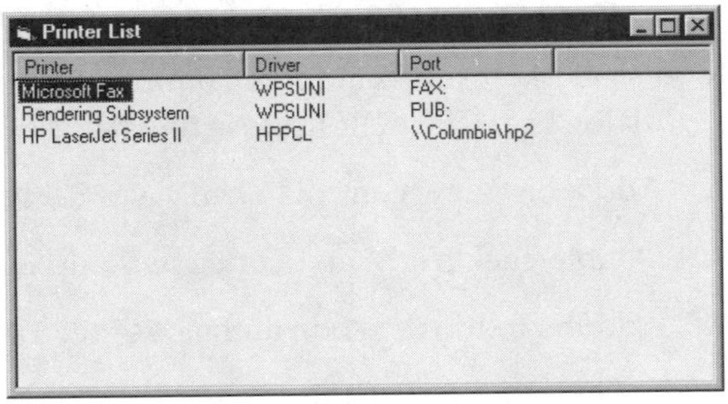

FIGURE 9.2: Enumerating the Printers collection

Using Crystal Reports for Visual Basic

Visual Basic comes with a companion product called Crystal Reports Pro. This powerful application allows you to visually design and lay out a report and then link it to your database. The result is a professional-looking report of the data you want to print.

Crystal Reports Pro follows Visual Basic's lead by presenting you with a Report Wizard (see Figure 9.3), much like the Project Wizard you are already familiar with.

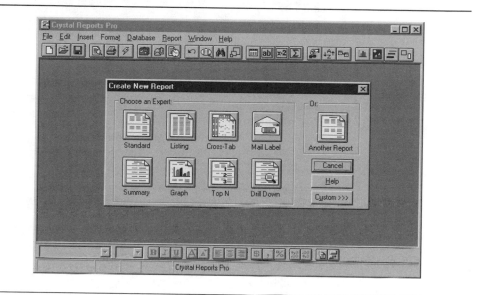

FIGURE 9.3: The Report Wizard in Crystal Reports

After you select a report type (the options are shown in Figure 9.3), Crystal Reports will guide you through a Wizard that allows you to select a database and choose the appropriate fields required to create a complete report. The final step in the Report Wizard allows you to select from a predefined layout for the report type. This feature is a great time-saver!

After you have defined your report, you can either preview the report or work with it further in Design view (see Figure 9.4). You can create, delete, and move the fields around the report to get the exact layout that you desire. After you test your report, you can save it so it can be called from your application.

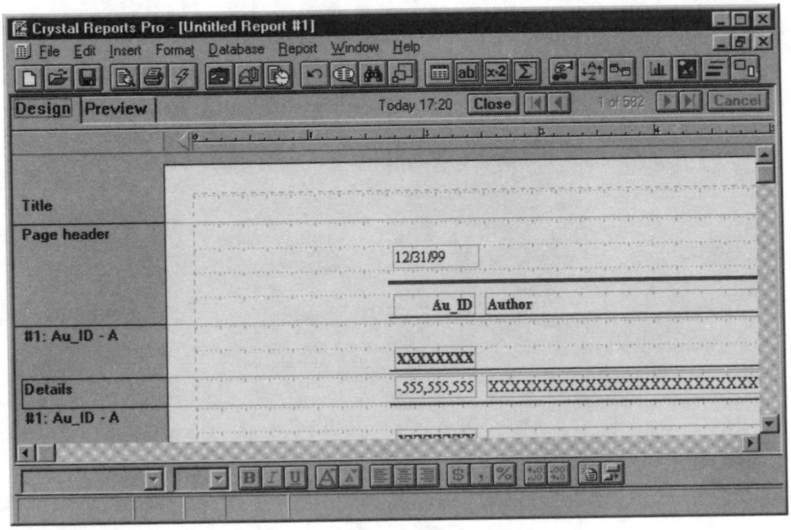

Crystal Reports Pro - [Untitled Report #1]
File   Edit   Insert   Format   Database   Report   Window   Help

Design | Preview | Today 17:20   [Close]   1 of 582   [Cancel]

Title
Page header

12/31/99

Au_ID   Author

#1: Au_ID - A

XXXXXXXX

Details   -555,555,555   XXXXXXXXXXXXXXXXXXXXXXXXXX

#1: Au_ID - A

FIGURE 9.4: Crystal Reports' Design view

Installing Crystal Reports Pro

If you want to use Crystal Reports Pro, you need to install it. Unlike previous versions of Visual Basic, Version 6 does not install it automatically. To install Crystal Reports Pro, follow these simple steps:

1. Insert your Visual Basic CD into your CD-ROM drive.

2. Change to the \Common\Tools\VB98\Crysrept folder on the CD.

NOTE   This directory may be different for you because at the time of this writing, directory layouts were changing.

3. Double-click the Cryst132.exe icon to start the installation process.

WARNING When installing applications, you should exit all running programs. If they are left running, some shared files may become locked and the installation program may not be able to update them properly. This could cause the installation to fail completely or may corrupt other applications installed on your system.

Creating a Report

Practice creating a report in Crystal Reports Pro by trying this example:

1. If you have not already done so, install Crystal Reports Pro using the steps listed above.

2. After Crystal Reports Pro is installed, launch Visual Basic 6.0.

3. If you are asked to select a project, select one from the New Project dialog box and click OK. The project you select is not important at this time. You just need to get into Visual Basic.

4. Launch Crystal Reports Pro by selecting Report Designer from the Add-Ins menu.

5. Create a new report by selecting File ➤ New from the Crystal Reports Pro menu.

6. Select Standard from the Create New Report dialog box.

7. From the Create Report Expert (Figure 9.5), click the Data File button to select a database.

8. Select `biblio.mdb` from the `\Program Files\Microsoft Visual Studio\` VB98 folder. Click the Add button to add the database to the report.

9. Click the Done button to close the dialog box.

As in Figure 9.6, you will see the Links tab of the Create Report Expert, and it will show you that each table is visually linked.

Skill 9

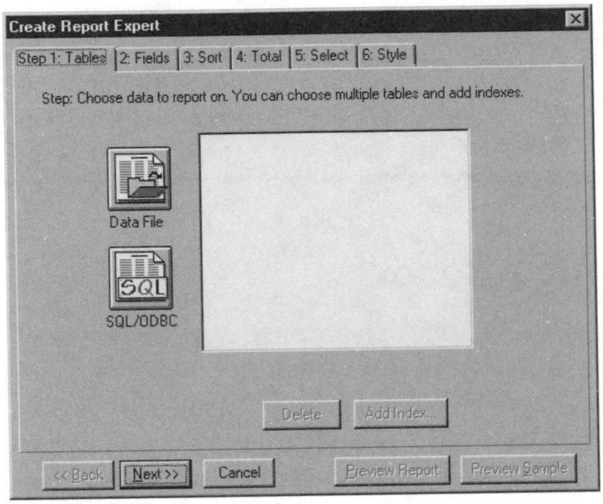

FIGURE 9.5: The Create Report Expert

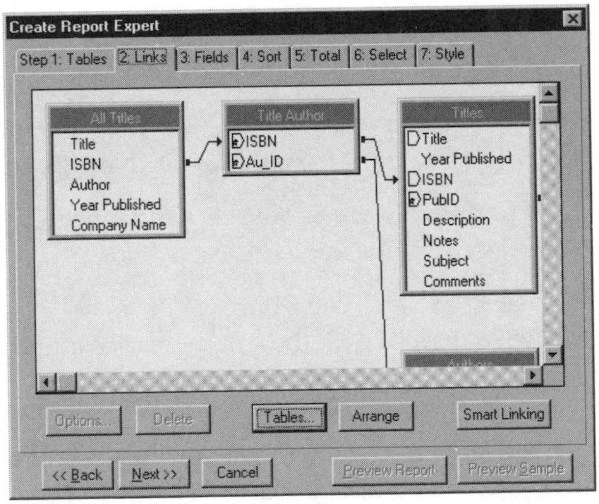

FIGURE 9.6: Linked tables

From the figure, you can see that the All Titles, Title Author, and Titles tables are linked together by the ISBN field of each table. In addition, the Title Author and

Authors tables are linked by the Au_ID field, and the Titles and Publishers tables are linked by the PubID field.

If you wanted to create or remove links between tables, you could do so in this tab. In the next step, you will remove the link between two tables.

10. Click the line (or link) connecting the Title Author table to the Authors table, and click the Delete button to remove the link.

11. Click the link connecting the Titles and Publishers tables and click the Delete button to remove the link.

12. Click the Next button to move to the next step in the expert.

The next tab is the Fields tab (Figure 9.7).

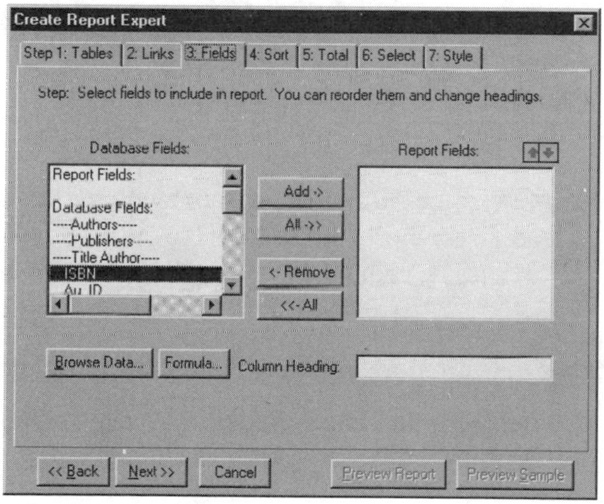

FIGURE 9.7: The Fields tab

13. Double-click the Au_ID field under the Title Author heading in the Database Fields list. This will add this field to the report.

14. Double-click the Title field under the Titles heading in the list to add it to the Report Fields list.

15. Click the Next button to go to the Sort tab show in Figure 9.8.

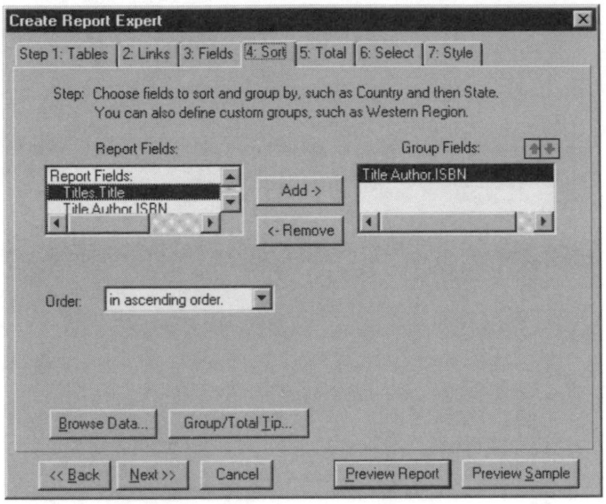

FIGURE 9.8: Choosing a field to sort by

16. Click Title Author.ISBN from the Report Fields list and click the Add button to sort the report on this field. Notice that the Order field appears and is set to ascending order. Leave this as is, and click the Next button.

The next tab is the Total tab shown in Figure 9.9. Although we will not be using totals in this report, you may want to experiment with these settings on your own.

17. Click the Next button to go to the Select tab.

From here you can select which field to use to filter the records. For example, you could tell the report to filter on the ISBN field.

18. Click Title Author.ISBN and click the Add button to filter this report on the ISBN field of the Title Author table.

19. Choose **is** from the drop-down list on the lower-left side of the tab.

20. In the next drop-down list, select **greater than**.

21. Now, click the next list and select **0-0307360-3-X** from the list. It is four items from the bottom of the list. The tab should look like Figure 9.10.

22. Now click the Next button to go to the Style tab.

23. In the Title field, type **My First Report!**

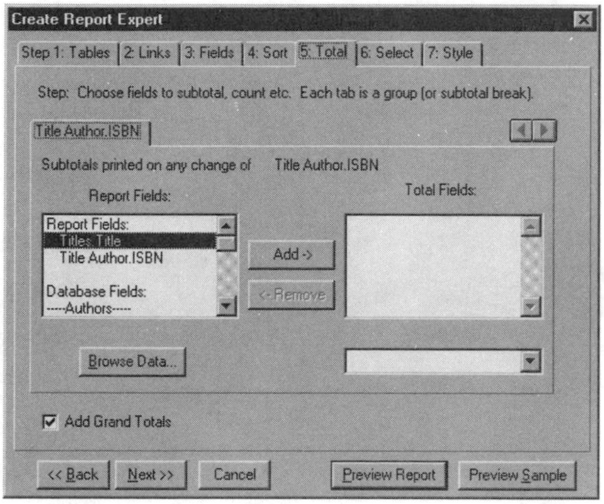

FIGURE 9.9: The Total tab

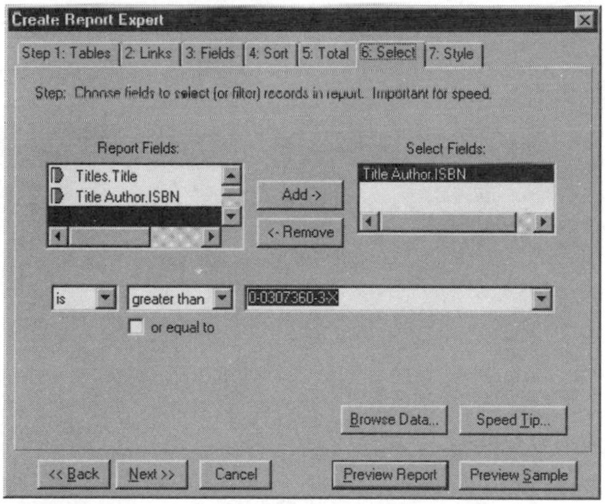

FIGURE 9.10: Filtering records in your report

24. In the Style list, select **Table**. The settings should look like Figure 9.11. This will set the style of the report to a simple table. When you are creating your own reports, you will select the style from this tab.

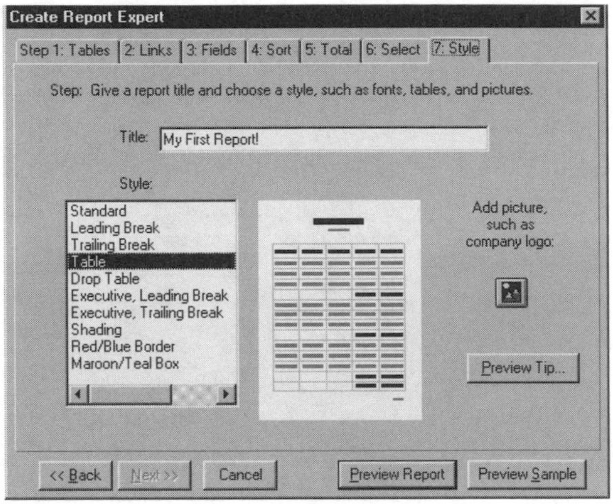

FIGURE 9.11: Setting the style of the report

25. Finally, click the Preview Report button to see how the report looks. As you can see in Figure 9.12, the report will look like a standard table, with several ISBN numbers and book titles.

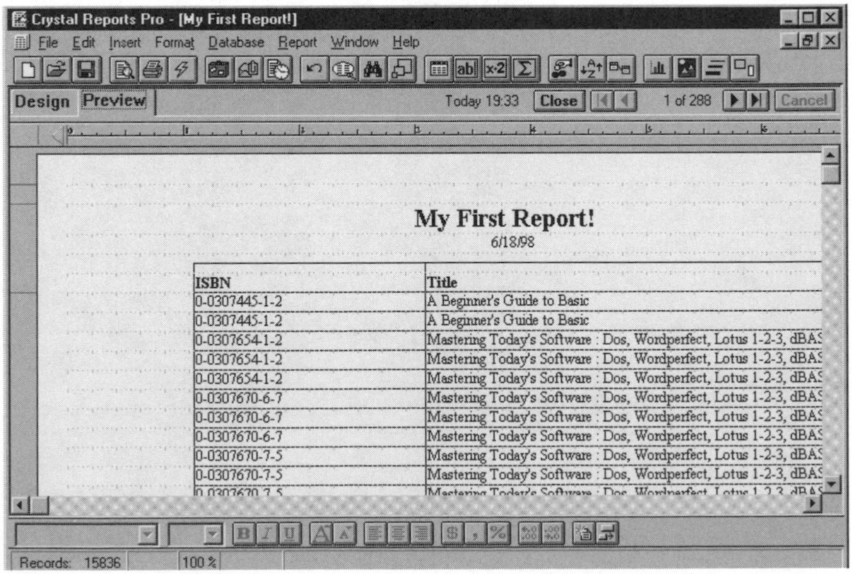

FIGURE 9.12: The generated report

Most likely, the report that is automatically created will not appear exactly the way you want it to look. Fortunately, you can go to Design view and rearrange the fields, change the fonts, add and remove fields, insert graphics, and do many, many more things. Unfortunately, it is beyond the scope of this book to cover every aspect of Crystal Reports Pro, so we will modify a couple of things, and then move on.

1. Click the Design tab just under the left side of the toolbar. This will take you to Design view.

In the Design view (Figure 9.13), you will see several sections that logically divide the report. The sections include, but are not limited to Title, Page header, Details, Page footer, and Summary. These sections are described in Table 9.1.

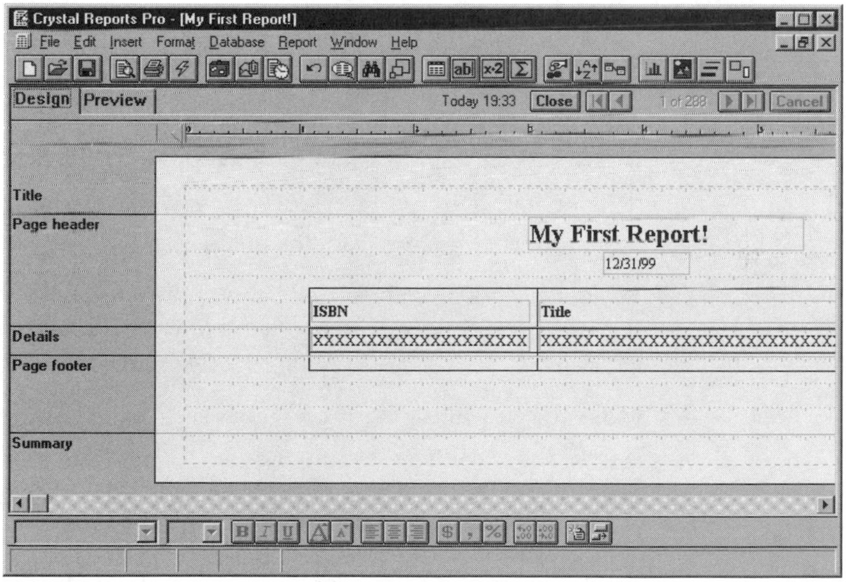

FIGURE 9.13: Design view

TABLE 9.1: Sections Available in Design View

Section	Description
Title	This section is where you can place text and/or graphics that will appear at the top of the first page of the report.
Page header	This section contains the information that you want displayed on the header section of each page within the report.
Details	This is where the bulk of the work is done. Crystal Reports will list all of the reports that match the filter, or selection criteria, that you specify for the report.
Page footer	This is where you place text that you want on the footer of each page in this section.
Summary	The summary section is where you view information that summarizes the details of the report. It will be displayed at the end of the report.

2. Press and hold the Ctrl key down on your keyboard and click the ISBN and Title field headers.

3. Now select Format ➢ Font from the Crystal Reports Pro menu. Set the font to **Arial**, **Bold**, **14pt**. Click the OK button to set the font and remove the dialog box.

4. Select Insert ➢ Picture from the menu.

5. When the Choose Picture File dialog box appears, select `beany.bmp` from the `\Program Files\Microsoft Visual Studio\Common\Graphics\Bitmaps\Assorted` folder. Click the OK button to close the dialog box.

6. Move the graphic to the Page header section, right next to the title of the report, as in Figure 9.14.

7. Select File ➢ Save As from the menu. Save the file as `First.rpt` in the VB98 folder.

8. Finally, click the Preview tab to see your updated report in action.

The examples you just completed are an introduction to designing and generating reports. Although they are simple examples, you can do many sophisticated things with Crystal Reports Pro. As you develop database applications, you will learn how to use the different reporting styles and techniques.

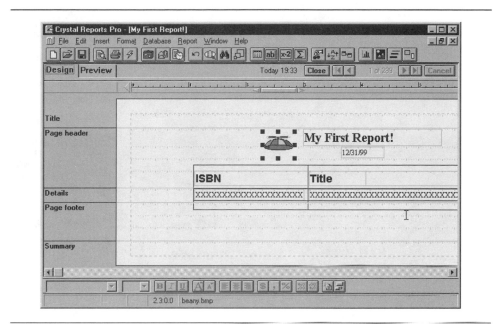

FIGURE 9.14: Your report in Design view

Using the Report in Your Application

To use the report created by Crystal Reports Pro in your application, you need to add the Crystal Reports custom control to your project. Once the control is added to the project, you can add the control to the form you want to print from.

If you are planning to use only one report and one database, you can probably get away with setting the report properties from the Custom property entry in the Properties window. Figure 9.15 shows you the Property Pages dialog box for the report control. By navigating through the tabs you can define what report to use with a database and where to print it. Notice that you can print to a window, a printer, a file, or even various e-mail systems such as MAPI, VIM, and Lotus Notes.

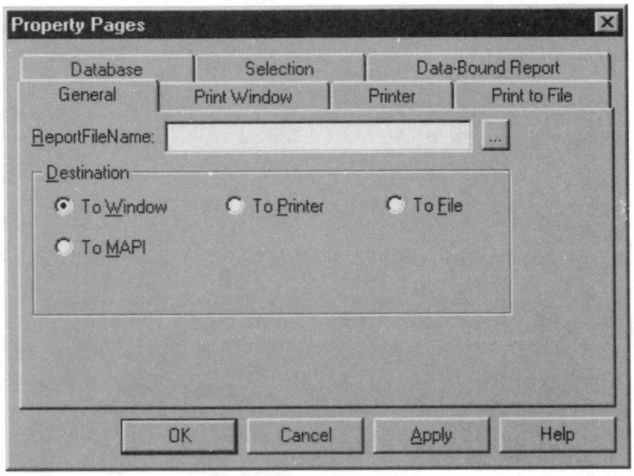

FIGURE 9.15: The Crystal Reports 4.6 Property Pages dialog box

To see how to use this control to print reports from your application, try the following example:

1. In Visual Basic, start a new project by selecting File ➢ New from the menu.

2. Select Standard EXE from the New Project dialog box. Click OK to close the dialog box.

3. Set the Name property of the project to **ReportDemo**.

4. Set the Name property of Form1 to **frmMain**. Set its Caption property to **Report Printing Demo**.

5. Right-click the Toolbox and select Components from the pop-up menu.

6. Select Crystal Report Control 4.6 from the Components dialog box, as shown in Figure 9.16.

7. Click the OK button to add the component to the Toolbox.

8. Add a Command Button to frmMain. Set its Name property to **cmdPrint**, and its Caption to **&Print**.

9. Add a Crystal Report control to the form and set its Name property to **rpt**.

10. Click the (Custom) property for the Crystal Report control to open its property page.

11. Click the button to the right of the ReportFileName field. Select the report you created in the previous example from the Choose Report dialog box. Click the OK button to choose the file.

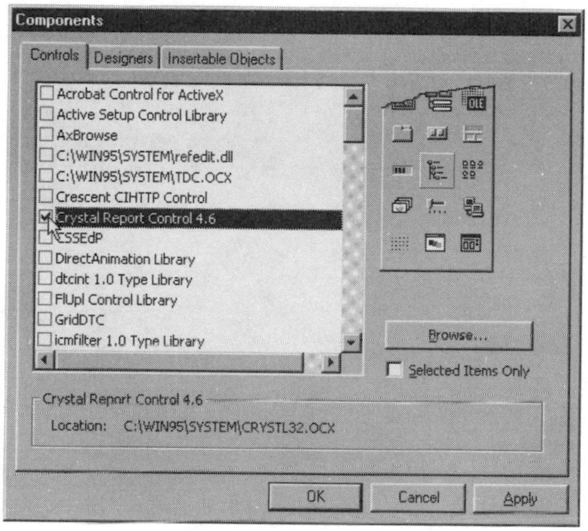

FIGURE 9.16: Adding the Crystal Reports control

12. Click the Print Window tab on the property page.

13. Type **Print Preview** in the Title field.

14. Click the OK button to close the property page.

Now that the report has been configured, let's write the code to print the report from your application.

15. Double-click cmdPrint to open its Code window.

16. Add the following code to the cmdPrint_Click() event:

```
Private Sub cmdPrint_Click()
    'Print the report
    rpt.PrintReport
End Sub
```

17. Finally, save and run the project.

Click the Print button to print the report to the screen. You will see the report printed like the one shown in Figure 9.17.

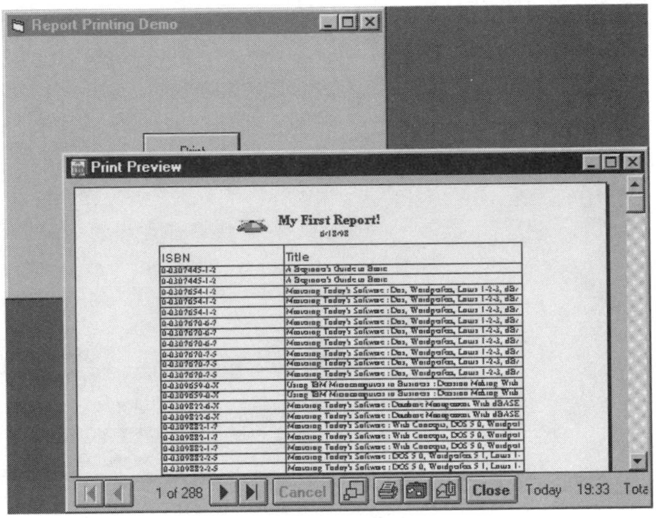

FIGURE 9.17: Printing from your application

As you can see, it's easy to print a report from your Visual Basic application. Simply remember these steps:

- Create the report.
- Add the Crystal Report Control 4.6 to the Visual Basic Toolbox.
- Add the Crystal Report Control to a form in your project.
- Set the properties to configure the report to display in the manner you wish.
- Add the code to the form to print the report.

As you develop your reports, be sure to read the online help for Crystal Reports Pro and the Crystal Report Control. There is so much useful information included that it would require a separate book to cover it all. Although this skill just scratches the surface of report generation and usage, it is more than enough to get you started developing your own reports. Make sure that you take time to practice creating reports and printing them from your applications. As you gain more experience, report generation will become second nature to you.

Printing Your Source Code

It can become quite hard to keep track of all the properties you've set for your forms and controls. To check all of them, you could open each form in turn and click each control with the Properties window open. But this would be very time consuming. Is there an easier way to keep a record of objects, properties, and code that's easy to read and check? By far the best way is to use File ➤ Print. This will open the Print dialog box (see Figure 9.18).

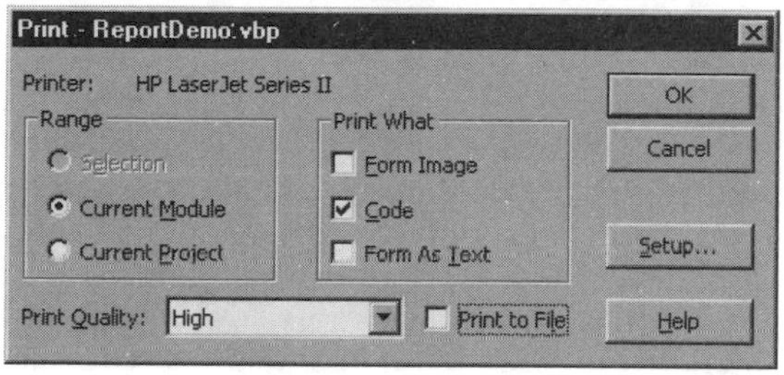

FIGURE 9.18: The Print dialog box

Using the Print Dialog Box

The Print dialog box contains a number of options in two main sections, Range and Print What. The Range options include Selection, Current Module, and Current Project; they are discussed next.

Selection   This only prints out code, and only the code you've selected in the Code window.

Current Module   This prints details of the form you're currently working on in the Design window. What details it actually prints depends on the settings in the Print What section (described shortly). There are other modules apart from form modules, and you can print their code if one of those modules is current.

Current Project   Choosing this option prints details of all the form modules in your project. It also prints details of other modules (standard and class modules). Again, the amount of data printed is determined by the settings in the Print What section.

The Print What section of the Print dialog box has three choices: Form Image, Code, and Form As Text; they are discussed in the following sections.

Form Image   This prints a bitmap of how the form will look at run time. You might want to use this option to produce a series of GUI screenshots for end-user evaluation. It also serves (together with the Form As Text option) as a way of documenting the whole of your interface design. It's not so handy as a method of producing a user manual—each form image prints on a separate page, and there's no easy way of inserting the form image into a document. All the screenshots of forms in this book were produced by a different method.

TIP   If you're interested—you might want forms to appear in a help file or in a manual you're preparing for users—the forms can be captured as Windows screenshots onto the Clipboard. You do this by holding the Alt button and pressing Print Screen. From there they can be pasted into the Clipboard and saved as .BMP files. Most word processing and DTP (desktop publishing) applications used for preparing manuals support the insertion of .PCX or .BMP files. To include the screenshot in a help file, you can simply reference the bitmap in your .RTF source file.

Code   Now we're getting closer to a traditional program listing. The Code option prints all the event procedures for a form and its controls. If you select Project under the Print Range section, it prints all the event procedures for all the forms and controls in your application. If you're debugging or documenting code for colleagues or for later referral, this is the one you want. The code is arranged form by form. Within each form code listing, the event procedures are arranged in the alphabetical order of the object Name property. Form event procedures always begin with Form, no matter how you change the Name property of the form. This means that it's unlikely that the form procedures are listed before those of all other controls on the form. For example, the event procedure cmdOK_Click() comes before that of Form_Load(). This assumes that you have a control called cmdOK and that you've entered code into both procedures. If an event procedure contains no code at all, then the blank procedure template is not printed. A Visual Basic application often includes other procedures apart from event procedures. These other procedures might be user-defined Sub and Function procedures that you've created in form or standard modules. These too will be in the printout.

Form As Text   This prints a listing of the properties of your form and the properties for all the controls placed on the form. As such, it's a valuable reference—it's actually easier to re-create and debug a Visual Basic application from a list of properties than it is by simply referring to a form image. Be aware that not every single property for every single object is listed. In a complex application, that could easily run into a hundred pages or more. The only properties listed are those you've changed from the defaults (typically, the Name and Caption properties), those that give an indication of the position and size of the object (Left, Top, Height, and Width), those that correspond to the internal measurements and measuring system of objects (Scale... properties), the TabIndex property if it's appropriate, and the LinkTopic property for forms. You can safely ignore the latter for now. The listing also contains the menu controls, detailing their Shortcut property as well as the expected Caption property.

COMMENTING YOUR CODE

Commenting your code is an important discipline to learn. Comments are lines of explanatory text preceded by an apostrophe; they are not actual program code. You should add comments to your programs when the code may be difficult to understand or when it requires special consideration during the development process. The comments in your source code are for the use of the programmer. Although Visual Basic ignores your comments when the application is running, commented code will print. It's often tempting to dispense with comments, because surely all the code *you* type is obvious! But will it be so to colleagues (or even to you) in a few weeks' time? Adding a few simple comments now could save hours of frustration down the road. Comments are especially important before and in between complex lines of code.

To place a comment in a procedure, type an apostrophe character (') at the start of the line. The following example is a comment:

```
'This line is a comment
```

You can also add comments at the end of a line, again preceded by an apostrophe:

```
cmdOK.Enabled = True      'Turns on the OK button
```

For more information of how you can comment you code, refer to Skill 12, *Debugging Your Applications*.

Skill 9

Viewing the Results

Another useful aspect of printing source code is that you might find it helpful to incorporate property or code listings in another document. Coming shortly is a sample property and code listing from Skill 4. It was not necessary to type all the listing out for the purposes of this book. Instead, a text file was created and inserted into the rest of this chapter text. To do this I chose to print to a file and used the Generic/Text printer driver supplied with Windows.

> **TIP** To create a text file containing properties and code for a project, first install the Generic/Text printer driver that comes with Windows 95 or NT. During the configuration, select FILE as the printer port. Then after selecting File ➤ Print in Visual Basic, check the Print to File check box. You can view the finished text file in WordPad. If you wish, you can incorporate this text file into a word processed document.

Below is the source code listing of the menu and toolbar example from Skill 4. Don't worry if your version is slightly different—some of the properties are not too important.

```
Form1 - 1

Option Explicit

Private Sub mnuFileExit_Click()
    End
End Sub

Private Sub tbrToolbar_ButtonClick(ByVal Button As ComctlLib.Button)
    Select Case Button.Key
        Case Is = "New"
            MsgBox "You clicked the New button."
        Case Is = "Open"
            MsgBox "You clicked the Open button."
        Case Is = "Save"
            MsgBox "You clicked the Save button."
    End Select
End Sub
```

Form1 - 1

```
VERSION 5.00
Object = "{6B7E6392-850A-101B-AFC0-4210102A8DA7}#1.1#0"; "COMCTL32.OCX"
Begin VB.Form Form1
   Caption        =   "Form1"
   ClientHeight   =   1572
   ClientLeft     =   3084
   ClientTop      =   2556
   ClientWidth    =   3744
   LinkTopic      =   "Form1"
   ScaleHeight    =   1572
   ScaleWidth     =   3744
   Begin ComctlLib.Toolbar tbrToolbar
      Align        =   1  'Align Top
      Height       =   336
      Left         =   0
      TabIndex     =   0
      Top          =   0
      Width        =   3744
      _ExtentX     =   6604
      _ExtentY     =   593
      ButtonWidth  =   487
      Appearance   =   1
      ImageList    =   "imlToolbar"
      BeginProperty Buttons {0713E452-850A-101B-AFC0-4210102A8DA7}
         NumButtons   =   4
         BeginProperty Button1 {0713F354-850A-101B-AFC0-4210102A8DA7}
            Key          =   ""
            Object.Tag   =   ""
            Style        =   3
            Value        =   1
            MixedState   =   -1  'True
         EndProperty
         BeginProperty Button2 {0713F354-850A-101B-AFC0-4210102A8DA7}
            Key          =   "New"
            Object.Tag   =   ""
            ImageIndex   =   1
         EndProperty
         BeginProperty Button3 {0713F354-850A-101B-AFC0-4210102A8DA7}
            Key          =   "Open"
            Object.Tag   =   ""
            ImageIndex   =   2
         EndProperty
```

```
            BeginProperty Button4 {0713F354-850A-101B-AFC0-4210102A8DA7}
                Key               =    "Save"
                Object.Tag            =       ""
                ImageIndex        =    3
            EndProperty
        EndProperty
        MouseIcon        =    {Binary}
    End
    Begin ComctlLib.ImageList imlToolbar
        Left             =    2520
        Top              =    720
        _ExtentX         =    804
        _ExtentY         =    804
        BackColor        =    -2147483643
        ImageWidth       =    16
        ImageHeight      =    16
        MaskColor        =    12632256
        BeginProperty Images {0713E8C2-850A-101B-AFC0-4210102A8DA7}
            NumListImages    =    3
            BeginProperty ListImage1 {0713E8C3-850A-101B-AFC0-
                    4210102A8DA7}
                Picture          =    {Binary}
                Key              =       ""
```

Form1 - 2

```
            EndProperty
            BeginProperty ListImage2 {0713E8C3-850A-101B-AFC0-
                    4210102A8DA7}
                Picture          =    {Binary}
                Key              =       ""
            EndProperty
            BeginProperty ListImage3 {0713E8C3-850A-101B-AFC0-
                    4210102A8DA7}
                Picture          =    {Binary}
                Key              =       ""
            EndProperty
        EndProperty
    End
    Begin VB.Menu mnuFile
        Caption          =    "&File"
        Begin VB.Menu mnuFileExit
            Caption      =    "E&xit"
        End
```

```
        End
        Begin VB.Menu mnuEdit
            Caption         =    "&Edit"
            Begin VB.Menu mnuEditCut
                Caption         =   "Cu&t"
            End
            Begin VB.Menu mnuEditCopy
                Caption         =    "&Copy"
            End
            Begin VB.Menu mnuEditPaste
                Caption         =    "&Paste"
            End
        End
        Begin VB.Menu mnuHelp
            Caption         =    "&Help"
            Begin VB.Menu mnuHelpAbout
                Caption         =    "&About"
            End
        End
    End
```

Deciphering the Code Listing

The code and properties of a form appear on separate pages. Each is headed by the name of the form and a page number. The latter is useful if a form's code or properties extend over more than one page. The code page is a listing of all the event procedures for that form module. The properties page lists all the relevant properties for the form and all the controls it contains. The separate pages have been run together for the purposes of this book. However, you can see a heading Form1 - 1 for the page of code for the Form1 form. There's also another Form1 - 2 for the first page of properties for that form.

The code pages are, I trust, straightforward. The property pages require a little by way of explanation: Each form starts with a Begin Visual Basic.Form and finishes with an End. Indented one level is a list of the form's properties and a number of further Begin...End blocks. Each of these indented Begin...End blocks corresponds to a control on the form. The Begin is followed by the object type, then by the Name property. Indented yet one more level are the properties for each control.

Now you have the basic foundation to print from your application. I encourage you to practice using Crystal Reports to design reports. It is a very powerful tool that can save you time and simplify your development efforts.

Skill 9

Are You up to Speed?

Now you can...

- ☑ use the *Print* method to send data to the printer
- ☑ display data in the Immediate window
- ☑ use the *PrintForm* method to print a form's image
- ☑ access the printers installed on your system through code
- ☑ use Crystal Reports to design your own reports
- ☑ use the Crystal Reports Control to include reports in your applications
- ☑ print out your source code

SKILL 10

Using Dialog Boxes

- Using predefined dialog boxes
- Creating your own dialog boxes
- Creating a dialogs class
- Using the dialogs class

Windows uses a special type of form, called a dialog box, to convey information to the user. This information can be as simple as an error message, or be as complex as a login screen. Dialog boxes are used to grab the user's attention and evoke a response. In this skill, you will learn how to use dialog boxes that are intrinsic to Visual Basic, as well as write and use your own reusable dialog boxes.

Using Predefined Dialog Boxes

Two dialog boxes are often used in Visual Basic projects: the message box and the input box. They are built into Visual Basic, and if you find that these built-in ones are adequate, you won't have to design your own forms as dialog boxes. A message box (`MsgBox`) allows you to provide the end user with simple messages. In contrast, an input box (`InputBox`) elicits information from the user.

Creating a Message Dialog Box

Here's a partial syntax for a message box statement:

```
MsgBox Prompt, DlgDef, Title
```

Prompt is the text the user sees in the message box. *Title* is the caption in the message box's title bar. The `DlgDef` parameter is used to set the Dialog Definition. That is, it defines which icons and buttons you will see on the message box. The following table lists the values and constants you can use to define your dialog box.

CONSTANT	VALUE	STYLE
vbOKOnly	0	Display OK button only
vbOKCancel	1	Display OK and Cancel buttons
vbAbortRetryIgnore	2	Display Abort, Retry, and Ignore buttons
vbYesNoCancel	3	Display Yes, No, and Cancel buttons
vbYesNo	4	Display Yes and No buttons
vbRetryCancel	5	Display Retry and Cancel buttons
vbCritical	16	Display Critical Message icon
vbQuestion	32	Display Warning Query icon
vbExclamation	48	Display Warning Message icon
vbInformation	64	Display Information Message icon

You can add these together to get the desired effect. For example, to see an OK and a Cancel button with an information icon, you would add the appropriate values in either format listed below:

```
DlgDef = vbOKCancel + vbInformation
DlgDef = 1 + 64
```

Then you would pass `DlgDef` to the `MsgBox` command.

The message box can also act as a function by returning a value that depends on the button clicked by the user. The syntax is virtually the same as for the message box statement:

```
Dim rc As Integer 'Return Code
rc = MsgBox(prompt, DlgDef, title)
```

Note the parentheses when it's a function. The possible values returned to `rc` are listed in the following table.

CONSTANT	VALUE	BUTTON CHOSEN
vbOK	1	OK
vbCancel	2	Cancel
vbAbort	3	Abort
vbRetry	4	Retry
vbIgnore	5	Ignore
vbYes	6	Yes
vbNo	7	No

Creating an Input Dialog Box

As with a message box, an input box can also be shown using a statement or a function. A partial syntax for it as a function is:

```
Dim rc As String
rc = InputBox(prompt, title, default)
```

There is no `DlgDef` parameter this time, but the additional default parameter lets you specify the default text to display in the entry text box. If the user clicks OK, any entry is returned to the variable (`rc` in the example). If the user clicks Cancel, a zero-length string is returned.

NOTE   Note that the `InputBox` function returns a string, while a `MsgBox` function returns an integer.

To try out the InputBox, try this example:

1. Start a new project by selecting File ➤ New Project.

2. Select Standard EXE from the Project Wizard.

3. Add a command button to Form1.

4. In the Properties window, set the Name property of the command button to **cmdTryMe**.

5. Set the Caption property of cmdTryMe to **&Try Me**.

6. Double-click cmdTryMe to open its Code window.

7. Add the following code to the Click() event of cmdTryMe:

```
Private Sub cmdTryMe_Click()
    Dim rc As String

    rc = InputBox("Enter your name below:")
    MsgBox "Hello, " & rc & "!"
End Sub
```

8. Run your project by selecting Run ➤ Start.

9. Click the Try Me button to test the InputBox dialog box.

10. When the InputBox appears, enter your name and click the OK button to see what happens.

This small example shows you briefly how an InputBox dialog box and a MsgBox dialog box work. If all goes well, you should be asked to enter your name in the InputBox dialog box. After you do that, Visual Basic should say "Hello, Steve!" (shown below) or whatever name you typed in the dialog box.

Creating Your Own Dialog Boxes

In addition to the MsgBox and InputBox, you may find that you want or need a custom dialog box of your own to include in several of your applications. In my software business, I have dialog boxes that I use to give all of my applications the same look and feel. In this section I will show you how to create your own dialog box objects that you can reuse in any of your applications.

If you do not remember all of the constants and parameters required to create your own dialog boxes, you can create simple functions, called *wrappers*, and put them in a separate dialogs code module. You can then include this module in your projects so you can call up the dialog boxes without having to remember too many specifics.

A wrapper is a function that encompasses one or more function and statement for the purpose of creating a simple and reusable module of code. You can call the wrapper function with all of the appropriate parameters and it will do most of your work for you. The beauty of a wrapper is that the code only needs to be written once. Afterward, the wrapper can be used over and over without you needing to rewrite its code for every program. Let's look at a quick example:

1. Open the Code window for the previous example.

2. Add the following code in the Code window:

    ```
    Private Sub LoginBox()
        Dim rc As String

        rc = InputBox("Enter your name below:")
        If rc = "ADMINISTRATOR" Then
            MsgBox "Welcome, master!"
        Else
            MsgBox "Hello, " & rc & "!"
        End If
    End Sub
    ```

3. Change the code in the Click() event of cmdTryMe:

    ```
    Private Sub cmdTryMe_Click()
        LoginBox
    End Sub
    ```

4. Run the application.

5. When the InputBox dialog box appears, type **ADMINISTRATOR** in the field and click the OK button.

Skill 10

Although much the same as the previous example, the dialog box code has been placed in a wrapper called LoginBox. Instead of placing all of the dialog code in the Click() event, you just call the LoginBox function and it performs the same tasks.

Notice that you also added another task to the function. It checks to see if the login name is *ADMINISTRATOR*. The LoginBox function checks for this name, and when it is entered Visual Basic greets the user appropriately. This is an example of how you can encapsulate all of the functionality necessary to perform a complete task within one logical function. You will learn to take this a step further in the next section, as well as in Skill 15, *Learning and Using Object-Oriented Programming (OOP)*.

If you want to take the use of wrappers a step further, you can combine this module with a class module and create your own dialogs class. However, this doesn't make sense unless you want to add custom dialog boxes that Visual Basic cannot provide. For example, much of the software I write is distributed as shareware. Because Visual Basic cannot provide the "nag" and registration code dialog boxes found in many shareware applications, I created a simple ShareLib class that I use in all of my shareware projects. In the next example, you will create a simple dialogs class that you can further modify to suit your needs.

TIP   If you have several tasks that you perform over and over within your programs, you can "wrap" them up in your own function, i.e., use a wrapper, and then call the wrapper function from your code. This not only saves you programming and debugging time, but it also saves memory!

Doing Dialog Boxes with Class

We are now going to create a simple dialogs class that you can use in your future projects. If you are confused as to the purpose of some of the properties and techniques, don't worry. We will cover object-oriented programming (OOP) and ActiveX in Skills 15 and 17.

To create a dialogs class, follow these steps:

1.   Start a new project by selecting File ➤ New Project.

2.   Select ActiveX DLL as the project type, and press OK.

3. Add a code module to your project and set its Name property to **modDialogs**.

4. Open the Code window for modDialogs and add the following procedure:

```
Sub Main()
    'No code is required here. However,
    'this sub is required for
    'the DLL to start.
End Sub
```

5. Double-click Class1 in the Project Explorer to make it active.

6. Set the following properties for the class:

    Name: **clsDialogs**

    Instancing: **5 - MultiUse**

The first dialog box you are going to add is a simple Yes/No dialog box. This type is handy for "Are you sure?" type questions. I use them before I ever call a critical piece of code, such as closing an app with unsaved data or formatting a disk. All you have to do is create a title and a message and pass them to the YNBox function. Then just check to see if the return code is vbYes or 6.

Open the Code window for clsDialogs and add the following function:

```
Public Function YNBox(title As String, msg As String) As Integer
    Dim rc As Integer
    Dim DlgDef As Long

    DlgDef = vbYesNo + vbQuestion
    rc = MsgBox(msg, DlgDef, title)
    YNBox = rc
End Function
```

The next subroutine we are going to add is an error message dialog box. You can call this from your error-trapping routines so your error messages have a similar look and feel.

Create the following sub:

```
Public Sub ErrMsg(title As String, msg As String)
    Dim rc As Integer
    Dim DlgDef As Long

    DlgDef = vbOKCancel + vbCritical
    rc = MsgBox(msg, DlgDef, title)
End Sub
```

To use this subroutine you just pass a title and a message, and the procedure will do the rest of the work for you.

The last function we are going to add is a login dialog box. I am not going to create a complex dialog box with password masking and UserID and password verification. This dialog box's only purpose is to prompt you to enter your UserID. However, at a later time, you can add a login dialog form with text boxes that mask password characters, check for password lengths, and any other rules you may define. Then you can call this form instead of calling the InputBox function.

1. Add the following code:

    ```
    Public Function LoginBox(title As String, msg As String, _
    default As String) As String
        Dim rc As String

        rc = InputBox(msg, title)
        LoginBox = rc
    End Function
    ```

2. Save your project as dialogs.vbp.

3. Open the Project Properties dialog box, and type **Dialogs** in the Project Name field. Then, type **A Sample Dialogs Class** in the Project Description field.

4. Select the Make tab and type 'Dialogs in the Application Title field. Click OK to close the dialog box.

5. Now that we have added the code to our dialogs class, we need to compile it so we can use it in our application. Select File ➤ Make Dialogs.Dll. Click the OK button.

After a short pause, you will have a fully compiled DLL that you can use in other programs. You will learn more about the details of using ActiveX DLLs in Skill 17. The next example shows you specifically how to use the dialogs class.

Using the Dialogs Class

In the previous example you created a simple dialogs class that you can reuse in your own applications. Once you work through the following example you will understand how to incorporate ActiveX DLLs in your applications. Then you can go back and tailor the dialogs class to meet your own needs.

Let's start a sample application to test our dialogs class:

1. Start a new project with File ➤ New Project. Select Standard EXE from the Project Wizard.

2. Set the following properties for Form1:

Name:	**frmDialogs**
Caption:	**Doing Dialogs With Class**

3. Add two labels to frmDialogs. Set their properties as follows:

Name:	**lblTitle**
Caption:	**Title Text:**
Name:	**lblMsg**
Caption:	**Message:**

4. Add two text boxes. Set their properties as follows:

Name:	**txtTitle**
Text:	**no text**
Name:	**txtMsg**
Text:	**no text**

5. Add three command buttons to your form. Set their properties as follows:

Name:	**cmdYN**
Caption:	**&Yes/No**
Name:	**CmdError**
Caption:	**&Error**
Name:	**cmdLogin**
Caption:	**&Login**

   Your form should now resemble the form displayed in Figure 10.1.

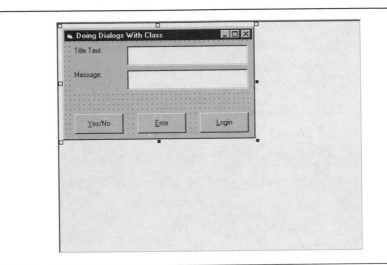

FIGURE 10.1: The sample dialogs class form

6.   Next, select Project ➤ References.

7.   Reference A Sample Dialogs Class by checking the box to the left of it, as shown in Figure 10.2; then click OK.

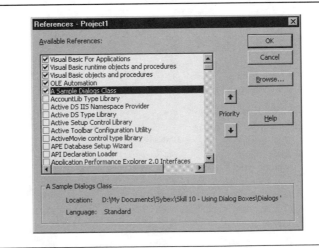

FIGURE 10.2: Referencing the dialogs class

8. Open the Code window and enter the following lines in the (General) (Declarations) sub:

```
Option Explicit
Private dlg As clsDialogs
```

9. The first thing you need to do to use the dialogs class is to create an instance of the dialogs object. You can do this by adding the following code to the Form_Load() sub:

```
Private Sub Form_Load()
    Set dlg = New clsDialogs
End Sub
```

10. Whenever you create an instance of an object, you must destroy it when you are done using it. Because you will use the dialogs class throughout the program, it would be best to destroy it when you exit the application. Add the following code to the Form_Unload() sub:

```
Private Sub Form_Unload(Cancel As Integer)
    Set dlg = Nothing
End Sub
```

11. Add the following code to test the Yes/No dialog box (YNBox):

```
Private Sub cmdYN_Click()
    Dim rc As Integer

    rc = dlg.YNBox(txtTitle.Text, txtMsg.Text)
    If rc = vbYes Then
        MsgBox "The user selected Yes"
    Else
        MsgBox "The user selected No"
    End If
End Sub
```

12. Add the following code to test the error dialog box (ErrMsg):

```
Private Sub cmdError_Click()
    dlg.ErrMsg txtTitle.Text, txtMsg.Text
End Sub
```

13. Add the following code to test the Login dialog box (LoginBox):

```
Private Sub cmdLogin_Click()
    Dim UserID As String
```

```
        UserID = dlg.LoginBox(txtTitle.Text, txtMsg.Text, "")
        If UserID <> "" Then
            MsgBox UserID & " logged in successfully!"
        End If
    End Sub
```

14. Save and run your project.

If you have no typos or errors in your code, you should be able to type text into the Title Text and the Message fields. To test the YNBox dialog box:

1. Type **Quit?** in the Title Text field.

2. Type **Wanna Quit?** in the Message field.

3. Press the Yes/No button.

You should see a dialog box similar to that shown in Figure 10.3.

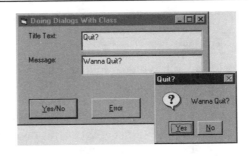

FIGURE 10.3: The YNBox dialog box

We will now use the ErrMsg to display a fake error message. You can call this dialog box from your error-trapping routines in your own applications. To test the ErrMsg dialog box:

1. Type **System Error** in the Title Text field.

2. Type **The Disk Cannot Be Formatted!** in the Message field.

3. Press the Error button.

You should see a dialog box similar to the one presented in Figure 10.4.

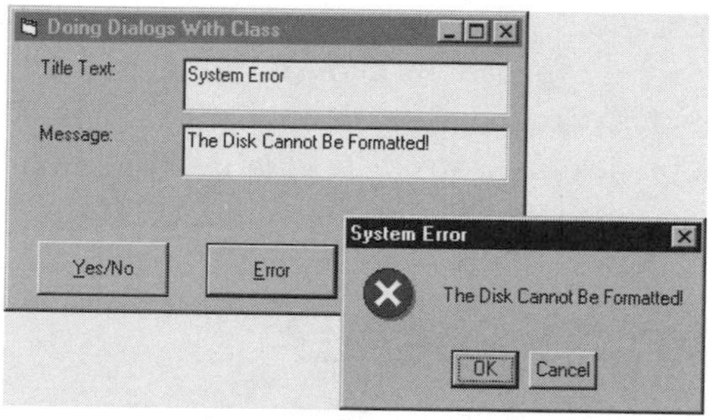

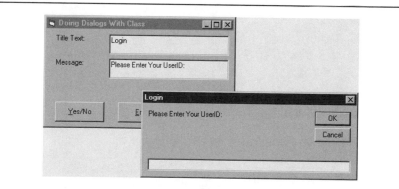

FIGURE 10.4: The ErrMsg dialog box

Although the LoginBox dialog box needs some serious improvements to be really useful, the simple test in this example will show you how the InputBox works. To test the LoginBox dialog box:

1. Type **Login** in the Title Text field.

2. Type **Please Enter Your UserID:** in the Message field.

3. Press the Login button.

You should see a dialog box similar to the one shown in Figure 10.5.

FIGURE 10.5: A sample Login dialog box

This is a simple example of how you can use a custom dialogs class in your applications. You can add many more dialog boxes as you develop more standardized applications in the future.

In this example, you not only learned how to use dialog boxes, but you got a brief taste of how to create your own object in Visual Basic. Again, we will cover objects in more detail in Skills 15 and 17.

Are You up to Speed?

Now you can...

- ☑ use the message box provided by Visual Basic to convey information to your users
- ☑ use the input box to receive simple information from the user
- ☑ create your own dialog boxes
- ☑ integrate a custom dialogs class into future applications

SKILL 11

Working with the Mouse

- Detecting mouse events
- Using drag-and-drop
- Using OLE drag-and-drop
- Creating an Easter egg

As users move to the Windows environment, they will almost certainly use a mouse to navigate through the operating systems as well as the applications that run in it. Your applications should be no exception.

Using a mouse is a fundamental skill and you need to learn how to program consistent mouse functionality in your programs as well. This skill will teach you how to respond to various mouse events and deal with them accordingly. By the end of this skill you will know how to respond to mouse clicks, generate context menus, and use drag-and-drop to enhance the functionality of your applications. You may even find some surprises along the way!

Detecting Mouse Events

So far you've met two mouse events, Click() and DblClick() (double-click). In this skill you'll learn there are many more mouse events that Visual Basic recognizes. These include the use of any button on the mouse, a movement of the mouse, and holding down the Shift, Alt, or Ctrl keys as a mouse button is pressed. The three event procedures you can use to carry out processing based on these actions are MouseDown, MouseUp, and MouseMove. The latter is handy for showing and hiding messages as the mouse passes over buttons on a toolbar.

Different controls have different mouse events. This skill will show you the basic events and how they are used. Then you will create a small drag-and-drop program sample. You will then have a good understanding of which mouse events to specify for your controls.

The *Click()* Event

The Click() event is generated when you click a control once. Almost all controls in Visual Basic that are visible at run time support the Click() event. You will use this event primarily for a command button control. You place code in the button's Click() event, and it is executed when you click the button with the mouse. For example:

```
Private Sub cmdOK_Click()
    Unload Me
End Sub
```

The *DblClick()* Event

The DblClick(), or double-click, event is called when you rapidly click a control twice in succession. The sensitivity of the double-click is set in the Mouse item of the Windows Control Panel. This event is useful for list boxes, enabling the user to view properties of an item, or to add or remove an item from the selection. For example:

```
Private Sub lstMembers_DblClick()
    Dim m as clsMember

    Set m = New clsMember
        m.MemberName = lstMembers.Text
        m.ShowMemberProperties
    Set m = Nothing
End Sub
```

Typically, you use this event to provide a quicker alternative to a command button or menu item that does the same thing.

The *DragDrop()* Event

The DragDrop() event is generated when you drop an object that was dragged from a form in the application. The DragDrop() event has the following syntax:

```
Private Sub target_DragDrop(Source As Control, X As Single, _
    Y As Single)
```

Notice that this event takes three parameters that you can check before you perform any actions. The Source parameter contains the name of the control that has been dropped on the current control. The parameters X and Y specify the coordinates of the mouse when the DragDrop() event was generated. You can use these to specify the placement of the control on its target. We will look at drag-and-drop functionality in more detail in the next section of this skill.

The *DragOver()* Event

The DragOver() event is generated when you drag an object over a control with your mouse. The syntax for this event is:

```
Private Sub target_DragOver(Source As Control, X As Single, _
    Y As Single, State As Integer)
```

Skill 11

Source is the name of the control being dragged over the target. The parameters X and Y are the coordinates of the mouse. State is an integer that represents the state of the control being dragged in relation to a target:

State	Purpose
0	The control is entering the boundary of the target.
1	The control is leaving the boundary of the target.
2	The control is being dragged within the target's boundaries.

This is a useful event if you want to show users when they can and cannot drop the item on a control. For example, you may not want your user to drop an object on a command button; when the command button's DragOver() event is generated, you can check the Source parameter and change the DragIcon property to a No Drop icon.

The *MouseDown()* Event

When you click a mouse button and hold it down, a MouseDown() event is generated. The MouseDown() event syntax is:

```
Private Sub target_MouseDown(Button As Integer, Shift As Integer, _
    X As Single, Y As Single)
```

As with other mouse events, the parameters X and Y are the coordinates of the mouse. The Button parameter is an integer that represents one of three values:

Button Parameter	Description
1	Left mouse button
2	Right mouse button
4	Middle mouse button

You can check this parameter to see which button was pressed. This is handy if you want to use one of the buttons to display a pop-up menu on a control. For example:

```
Private Sub lstMembers_MouseDown(Button As Integer, Shift As Integer, _
    X As Single, Y As Single)
    If Button = 2 then
        PopupMenu mnuMembers
    End If
End Sub
```

The Shift parameter contains an integer that describes which of the Shift, Ctrl, and Alt keys were pressed while the mouse button was held down. The values correspond to:

Shift Parameter	Key Pressed
1	Shift Key
2	Ctrl Key
4	Alt Key

The above values can be added together to indicate key combinations. For example, the integer 6 indicates the Ctrl and Alt keys were pressed simultaneously, while a 7 indicates all three keys were pressed simultaneously. You can also test the Shift parameter using the And keyword. You could embed commands to trap different keys using If…Then conditions. For example:

```
If Shift = 6 Then
    MsgBox "The Ctrl and Alt keys were pressed!"
End If
```

is equivalent to:

```
If Shift And 6 Then
    MsgBox "The Ctrl and Alt keys were pressed!"
End If
```

The *MouseMove( )* Event

The MouseMove() event is generated when you move the mouse over a control. You can use this event if you want to change the status of the control currently under the mouse. For instance, you can make a command button under the mouse turn green if it is enabled and the mouse is over it. The syntax is as follows:

```
Private Sub target_MouseMove(Button As Integer, Shift As Integer, _
    X As Single, Y As Single)
```

The parameters for this event are identical to those in the MouseDown() event. Here is a MouseMove() example that changes the form's caption if the mouse moves over the Exit button:

```
Private Sub cmdExit_MouseMove(Button As Integer, Shift As Integer, _
    X As Single, Y As Single)
    Me.Caption = "Click me to close the application"
End Sub
```

Skill 11

You can place a similar line of code in other controls' `MouseMove()` events to provide relevant captions for them. Before tool tips were readily available, I used this event to display status messages in the status bars of my applications.

The *MouseUp()* Event

When you release the mouse button on a control, it generates a `MouseUp()` event. The syntax for this event is:

```
Private Sub target_MouseUp(Button As Integer, Shift As Integer, _
    X As Single, Y As Single)
```

The parameters are the same as those for the `MouseDown()` and `MouseMove()` events.

Many of the Windows 95–compliant applications use this event, rather than the `Click()` event, to execute functions. For example, you can place the `End` statement in the `MouseUp()` event so the user has a chance to abort even after clicking the Exit button while the mouse button is still being pressed. Once the Exit button is clicked, the user can abort by moving the mouse away from the button and then releasing the mouse button. Then the `End` command is completely bypassed.

Using Drag-and-Drop Operations

Increasingly, drag-and-drop operations are used in Windows applications (to adjust the splitter bar in Windows Explorer, for example). They make many operations fast and simple. It is quite straightforward to add drag-and-drop capabilities to a Visual Basic application. Try the following small project to see how it's done:

1. Start a new project. Select Standard EXE for the project type.

2. Set the `Name` property of Form1 to **frmMain**. Set its `Caption` property to **Drag-N-Drop**.

3. Add two equally sized list boxes. Place one on the top of the form, and the other on the bottom of the form.

4. Set the `Name` property of the top list box to **lstA**. Set its `DragIcon` property to `\Graphics\Icons\DragDrop\Drag1pg.ico`.

5. Set the `Name` property of the bottom list box to **lstB**. Set its `DragIcon` property to `\Graphics\Icons\DragDrop\Drag1pg.ico`. Your form should look like the one displayed in Figure 11.1.

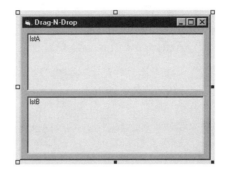

FIGURE 11.1: The Drag-and-Drop application

6. Add the following code to the Form_Load() event:

```
Private Sub Form_Load()
    lstA.AddItem "Apples"
    lstA.AddItem "Peaches"
    lstA.AddItem "Oranges"
End Sub
```

7. Now add the following code to the lstA_MouseDown() event:

```
Private Sub lstA_MouseDown(Button As Integer, Shift As Integer, _
        X As Single, Y As Single)
    If lstA.ListCount > 0 Then
        lstA.Drag 1
    End If
End Sub
```

8. Add this code to the lstA_DragDrop() method:

```
Private Sub lstA_DragDrop(Source As Control, X As Single, _
        Y As Single)
    If Source = lstB Then
        lstA.AddItem lstB.Text
        lstB.RemoveItem lstB.ListIndex
    End If
End Sub
```

9. Add this code to the lstB_MouseDown() event:

```
Private Sub lstB_MouseDown(Button As Integer, _
        Shift As Integer, X As Single, Y As Single)
    If lstB.ListCount > 0 Then
```

```
            lstB.Drag 1
        End If
    End Sub
```

10.   And, finally, add this code to the `lstB_DragDrop()` method:

```
Private Sub lstB_DragDrop(Source As Control, X As Single, _
        Y As Single)
    If Source = lstA Then
        lstB.AddItem lstA.Text
        lstA.RemoveItem lstA.ListIndex
    End If
End Sub
```

11.   Save and run the project.

The list box on the top of the screen will have apples, peaches, and oranges in it. You can click any of these items and drag it to the list box on the bottom. When the mouse pointer is over the list box, you can drop the item in it. You can also drag these items back to the top list box (see Figure 11.2).

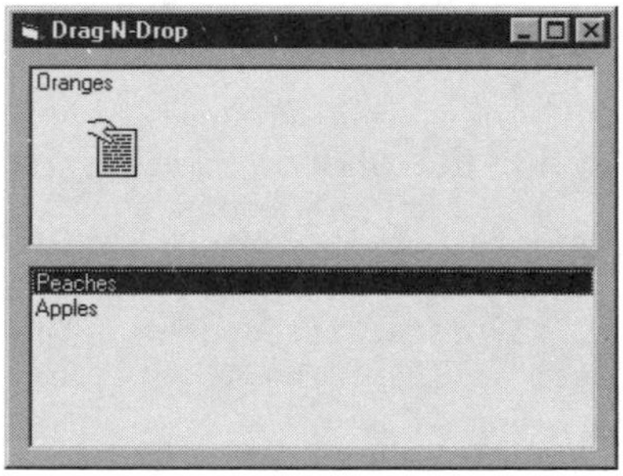

FIGURE 11.2: Dragging and dropping fruit

The key to this program is the `Drag` method. Notice that in the `MouseDown()` event we use the `Drag` method with the 1 parameter. The 1 tells the control to perform a manual drag. By coding a `Drag 0`, the object will stop dragging. In other words, if you want to drop a control, you set the `Top` and `Left` properties to the x and y coordinates of the mouse pointer, and add a `Drag 0` method. This will give the object the appearance of moving, whereas you actually perform the move in the `DragDrop()` event.

I'll leave you to have fun with this and to work out what's happening. You may want to adapt this approach for your own projects. Notice the `DragIcon` property for the source control—that is, the one being dragged. If you don't set DragIcon properties, then you see the outline of the control being dragged.

Using OLE Drag-and-Drop

With the arrival of Windows 95, a more versatile kind of drag-and-drop—called OLE drag-and-drop—was introduced. OLE stands for *Object Linking and Embedding*. It allows you to actually move text, files, and objects between OLE container controls, such as text, list, and picture boxes! Visual Basic's Code window has a feature called drag-and-drop text editing that uses OLE drag-and drop. When you move files from Windows Explorer to the Drive C folder in My Computer, you are performing OLE drag-and-drop operations.

OLE drag-and-drop works by setting a global data object equal to the data you wish to drag around. When an OLEDragDrop() event is fired, you can use code to retrieve the contents of the DataObject object. Let's take a closer look at the OLE methods and events.

The *OLEDrag* Method

The OLEDrag method is used to initiate an OLE drag operation. You can call this method when you want to copy or move OLE data between two OLE containers. The syntax is:

```
object.OLEDrag
```

where *object* is the OLE container object that acts as the source for the drag operation.

The *OLEDragMode* Property

The OLEDragMode property is used to determine if the object can act as an OLE drag source, and if the OLEDrag operation is performed manually or automatic. The allowable property values are:

vbOLEDragManual – 0	This is the default value. You use this setting when you want to write your own OLE drag handlers in your application.
vbOLEDragAutomatic – 1	Use this value when you want to let Visual Basic handle the OLE drag routines for you. This is the easiest way to enable your applications for OLE drag-and-drop.

Skill 11

The *OLEDropMode* Property

The OLEDropMode property is similar to the OLEDragMode property. You can set this property to determine how you want to process OLE drop events in your application. You can set this property to one of the following three values:

vbOLEDropNone – 0	This is the default value. It prevents the OLE container from allowing OLE drop events.
vbOLEDropManual – 1	You use this setting when you want to write your own OLE drop handlers in your application.
vbOLEDropAutomatic – 2	Use this value when you want to let Visual Basic handle the OLE drag routines for you. This is the easiest way to enable your applications for OLE drag-and-drop.

The *OLEDropAllowed* Property

You can use the OLEDropAllowed property to determine if an OLE container allows OLE drop operations. You can set this to:

True	Allow OLE drops operations on this container.
False	This is the default value. OLE drop operations are prohibited.

The *OLEDragDrop( )* Event

This event is fired whenever an OLE drop operation is performed on an OLE container that allows OLE drop operations. Its syntax is:

```
Private Sub object_OLEDragDrop(data As DataObject, effect As Long, _
        button As Integer, shift As Integer, x As Single, y As Single)
```

This event has many parameters that are important to understand. First, the data parameter is an OLE DataObject mentioned earlier. You can reference this object using the GetData method to retrieve the data being dropped in this event.

The `effect` parameter is used to tell the target component what action to perform on the data. This is where you can tell the OLE drag source what to do with the data, such as delete it from the source after it has been copied to the destination, effectively performing a move operation. The effect parameter can be one of the following:

`vbDropEffectNone - 0`	This setting indicates that the target cannot accept any OLE data.
`vbDropEffectCopy - 1`	This effect specifies that the data should be copied from the source to the destination.
`vbDropEffectMove - 2`	This effect specifies that the data should be moved from the source to the destination.
`vbDropEffectScroll` `-2147483648`	This value is a mask that indicates if the target has scrolled, or would scroll if the data were dropped onto it. This option is used rarely, and only in more complex applications.

The `button` parameter is used to identify which button on the mouse was pressed during the OLE drag operations. This can be one or a combination of the following values:

1	The left mouse button was pressed.
2	The right mouse button was pressed.
4	The middle button was pressed.

You can examine the value of the `shift` parameter to determine if the Ctrl, Shift, or Alt keys were held down during the drag operation. The value of in this parameter can be checked using the AND operator to check the bit fields, or you can check the integer value, as shown in the following table:

1	The Shift key was held down on the keyboard.
2	The Ctrl key was held down on the keyboard.
4	The Alt key was held down on the keyboard.

Skill 11

The x and y parameters indicate the current position of the mouse pointer. You can use these values if you require precision dropping within your target control.

The *OLECompleteDrag()* Event

The OLECompleteDrag event is fired when data has been dropped from the source control and it has either successfully performed a move or copy operation, or the operation was cancelled. It is the final event to be called in an OLE drag-and-drop operation. You can use it to inform the source control what operation the target performed so the source can act appropriately.

There is only one parameter to check in this event: effect. It has the same values as the effect parameter of the OLEDragDrop() event, except it does not check for vbDropEffectScroll.

The *OLEStartDrag()* Event

This event is fired when an OLE drag operation is performed when the source control's OLEDragMode property is set to manual. It is also fired when the source component initiates an OLE drag operation and the OLEDragMode property is set to automatic.

The data parameter is a DataObject object that contains the OLE data to be copied or moved, or the formats of the data that the source will provide later in the operation.

The allowedeffects parameter determines what drag operations are allowed by the OLE source of the OLE drag operation. This value can be one of the following: vbDropEffectNone, vbDropEffectCopy, or vbDropEffectMove.

The *OLEDragOver()* Event

This event is fired when the mouse is moved over an OLE container during an OLE drag operation. You can determine what to do by examining the parameters passed to this event. Its syntax is:

```
Private Sub object_OLEDragOver(data As DataObject, effect As Long, _
    button As Integer, shift As Integer, x As Single, _
    y As Single, state As Integer)
```

The first six parameters are functionally equivalent to those passed in the OLEDragDrop() event, discussed earlier. One additional parameter, state, is used to determine how the mouse pointer is moving through the control. This parameter has the same values as in the DragOver event discussed earlier in this skill.

The *OLESetData()* Event

The OLESetData() event is fired when the target component issues a GetData method on the source's DataObject. The syntax for this event is:

```
Private Sub object_OLESetData(data As DataObject, dataformat As
Integer)
```

This event has two parameters. The data parameter contains a DataObject object which will store the requested data. The dataformat parameter describes the format of the data stored in the data parameter.

The *OLEGiveFeedback()* Event

The OLEGiveFeedback() event is fired after every OLEDragOver() event. Its primary purpose is to give visual feedback indicating what is allowed when data is dragged over an OLE container. For example, you can put code into this event to change the drag icon or update a panel in a status bar.

Creating an OLE Drag-and-Drop Application

To give you a better idea of how the OLE drag-and-drop process works, try the following example:

1. Start a new project by selecting File ➢ New Project from the Visual Basic menu. Select Standard EXE from the New Project dialog box and click OK.

2. Set the Name property of Form1 to **frmMain**, and set its Caption property to **OLE Drag-N-Drop**.

3. Add two text box controls to the form. Size them so they fit side by side, and are approximately the height of the form.

4. Set the Name property of the text box on the left to **txt1**. Clear its Text property. Set its OLEDragMode property to **1 – Automatic**. In addition, set its MultiLine property to **True**. Set its ScrollBars property to **2 – Vertical**.

Skill 11

5. Set the Name property of the text box on the right to **txt2**. Clear its Text property. Set its OLEDragMode property to **1 – Automatic**. In addition, set its MultiLine property to **True**. Set its ScrollBars property to **2 – Vertical**.

6. Add the following code to the OLEDragDrop() event of txt1:

```
Private Sub txt1_OLEDragDrop(Data As DataObject, _
        Effect As Long, Button As Integer, Shift As Integer, _
        X As Single, Y As Single)
    If Shift > 0 Then
        Effect = vbDropEffectCopy
    Else
        Effect = vbDropEffectMove
    End If

    txt1.Text = Data.GetData(vbCFText)
End Sub
```

7. Add the following code to the OLEStartDrag() event of txt1:

```
Private Sub txt1_OLEStartDrag(Data As DataObject, _
        AllowedEffects As Long)
    Data.SetData txt1.Text, vbCFText
End Sub
```

8. Now you are going to add the same drag-and-drop functionality to txt2. Start by adding the following code to the OLEDragDrop() event of txt2:

```
Private Sub txt2_OLEDragDrop(Data As DataObject, _
        Effect As Long, Button As Integer, Shift As Integer, _
        X As Single, Y As Single)
    If Shift > 0 Then
        Effect = vbDropEffectCopy
    Else
        Effect = vbDropEffectMove
    End If

    txt2.Text = Data.GetData(vbCFText)
End Sub
```

9. Now, add the following code to the OLEStartDrag() event of txt2:

```
Private Sub txt2_OLEStartDrag(Data As DataObject, _
        AllowedEffects As Long)
    Data.SetData txt2.Text, vbCFText
End Sub
```

10. Finally, save and run the project.

Try typing some text into txt1. You can copy it or move it to txt2 using drag-and-drop. If you really want to see something cool, try opening WordPad or Microsoft Word, and try dragging the data from txt1 to either application. Do not mistake *Notepad* for *WordPad*. Notepad does not support OLE drag-and-drop operations. Try moving the text from WordPad to your application. You will see results similar to Figure 11.3.

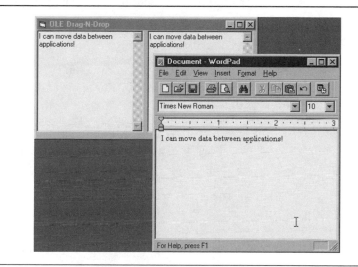

FIGURE 11.3: Dragging data between applications

Creating an Easter Egg

For our last sample application, we will create a simple Easter egg. If you are not familiar with what this signifies in computer terms, let me explain. Many Windows applications have hidden functions in them that display information or show a picture. The messages usually list the members of the programming team who worked on the program. Sometimes the Easter egg is a nasty animation about a competitor's product. Other times, the Easter egg will display a digitized photograph of the development team.

The reason they are called Easter eggs is because you have to hunt for them. They usually reside in a program's About dialog box and can only be discovered through a specific sequence of mouse clicks and key presses. We will use the About dialog box created by the Form Wizard and add a simple Easter egg to it. With a little clever programming, you can reuse this dialog box with the embedded Easter egg in other applications.

1. Start a new Standard EXE project.

2. Set the `Caption` property of Form1 to **Easter Egg**.

3. Add a simple menu to Form1. Set its `Caption` property to **&About**, and its `Name` property to **mnuAbout**.

4. Right-click the Project Explorer and select Add ➢ Form. When the Form Wizard appears, select About Dialog and click the Open button (see Figure 11.4).

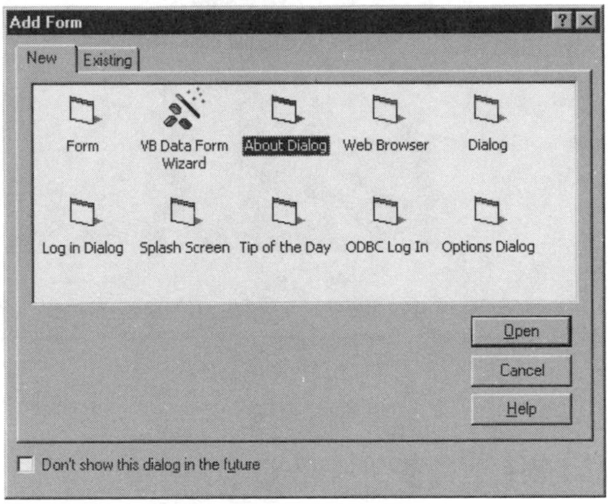

FIGURE 11.4: Adding a form to About Dialog

5. Double-click the icon in the upper-left corner of the About dialog box to open the Code window.

6. Select the `picIcon_MouseUp()` event in the Code window. Add the following code:

```
Private Sub picIcon_MouseUp(Button As Integer, _
      Shift As Integer, X As Single, Y As Single)
    If Button = 2 And Shift = 6 Then
        MsgBox "You found the Easter egg!"
    End If
End Sub
```

7. Double-click Form1 in the Project Explorer to open the Code window for Form1.

8. In the `mnuAbout_Click()` event, add the following code:

```
Private Sub mnuAbout_Click()
    frmAbout.Show vbModal
End Sub
```

9. Save and run the program.

10. Find the Easter egg by...

No, I won't tell you how to get to the Easter egg. If you understand the code in this example, it should be quite obvious. When you actually uncover the egg, you will see something like the Easter egg shown in Figure 11.5. This egg is actually quite boring. If you really want to razzle-dazzle your users, you can create a custom form with graphics and even sound. If you want to learn how to play a .wav file, read Skill 19, *Using DLLs and the Windows API*. It has all the code you will need.

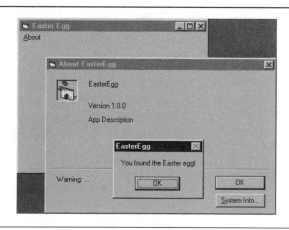

FIGURE 11.5: The Easter egg uncovered

Are You up to Speed?

Now you can...

- ☑ programmatically control the mouse
- ☑ add drag-and-drop functionality to your application
- ☑ use OLE drag-and-drop between applications
- ☑ create an Easter egg for your About dialog box

SKILL 12

Debugging Your Applications

- Documenting your code
- Using Visual Basic's debugging tools
- Developing testing utilities

Before you distribute your applications to other users, it's only common sense to test them and make sure you have eliminated as many bugs as possible. This skill will cover several techniques that will minimize the possibility of introducing bugs in your code, and track them down should any creep in. These techniques include customizing your environment, documenting your code with a liberal use of comments, using debugging tools, and developing your own testing utilities. By the end of this skill, you will be able to effectively document and debug your code so your programs can be virtually bulletproof.

Documenting Your Code

Before we delve into the details of how to use Visual Basic's debugging tools, let's take a look at what I call preventive medicine. It may not be obvious yet, but clear, concise, and consistent documentation is the foundation to well-behaved code.

> **TIP**
>
> The most important thing to remember when documenting your code is to be consistent. This means using the same commenting, naming, and code layout styles. If you learn to document and develop your applications proactively, you will cut down on the time spent debugging later.

Adding Comments to Your Code

Documenting your code with comments is almost as vital to your applications as the code itself. They can be use to identify the purpose of a line of code, a procedure, a module of code, and the entire application. If you have completed any of the examples in the other skills, then you have most certainly seen and used comments. The most obvious indicator of a comment is the apostrophe character. Any time this is inserted in the code (outside of a string), all of the text to the right becomes a comment, and the comment changes color. The default color is green.

How you use comments depends on your own personal style and habits, but the following sections will suggest some pointers to effectively document your code. Let's start by looking at how to document your code at the application level.

Application Level

I was recently presented with a problem by a co-worker. He wanted to know the best way to determine what third-party controls were required to make an application compile and execute properly. This question should have been easy to answer. After all, you wrote the application, right? In this situation, this was not the case.

Programmers were broken down into teams to develop separate projects, and each team used a single *build-system*. The build system is a central computer that has all of the third-party controls installed on it, as well as the various versions of Visual Basic.

The component requirement was especially important because the setup application could not always determine what resources are necessary, especially in a three-tier client/server architecture. As a result, we developed a single code module that contained nothing but comments about the project, using the following format:

```
'
'Application Name:
'Version:
'Copyrights:
'Trademarks:
'Author/Company:
'Purpose
'Requirements:
'
```

When the comment fields are filled in, the comments look something like this:

```
'
'Application Name:       Log File Interrogator
'Version:                1.1
'Copyrights:             1998 - ABC Software
'                        All Rights Reserved
'Trademarks:             None
'Author/Company:         Jane Doe / ABC Software
'Purpose:                This application reads and parses various
'                        log files using a single application. It can
'                        be used to "centralize" system log files into
'                        a single interface which can be accessed by a
'                        common set of tools.
'Requirements:
'            Client:     Windows 95 / Windows NT 4.0
'
'            Server:     MS SQL Server 6.5
'                        MS Transaction Server 2.0
'
```

Skill 12

This application-level comment file is included in the application; when anyone checks out the application, they can look at a project description file list to understand what is required to make the application compile and run properly. This file was originally created manually until I wrote an add-in to automate the task for me. You can see the code for this add-in in Skill 16, *Extending the IDE with Add-Ins*.

TIP   For applications that require third-party tools or have specific requirements (i.e., on a database server), it is wise to create a master comment file that can be included in the project. This file should always be named consistently, so all developers will know exactly where to go to retrieve application specifications.

Module Level

Describing the purpose of each module of code included in a project may just be more important than documenting the specific details and requirements of an application. This is especially obvious when multiple developers reuse centralized code modules that contain specific functions that are reused between applications.

Below is the style of comment code I prefer to use at the module level. It allows other programmers to know essentially all information required to use the module in their own applications, minimizing their development time and resulting in consistent, standardized applications.

```
'
'Filename:
'Author:
'Date:
'Description:
'Dependencies:
'Updates:
'
```

Here is a sample of the comment block filled in:

```
'
'Filename:        NetAPIs.cls
'Author:          Steve Brown
'Date:            June 6, 1998
'Description:     This library contains Win32 network API
'                 declarations and constants. In addition it
'                 wraps these in public properties and methods,
'                 eliminating the need for programmers to
'                 re-invent the ANSI to Unicode conversions.
```

```
'Dependencies:
'                   None
'Updates:
'          6-6-98   Created library.
'                   Added domain controller routines and
'                   global user and group functions.
'          8-14-98  Added local user account functions
'
```

TIP   If you or your team of developers reuse code, form, or class modules, you should add comments in the (General)(Declarations) section of the module that describes the procedures within the module, as well as requirements or dependencies for the module. This allows other programmers to identify exactly what they need to reuse your code in their applications.

Procedure Level

It is helpful to place comment blocks at the top of user-defined or non-obvious procedures and functions. These comments will help you or other programmers understand or remember exactly what the procedure does, and how it does it. For example:

```
'
'Procedure:      AddUser()
'Author:         Steve Brown
'Date:           January 6, 1998
'Description:    This function adds a global user to the domain.
'Requirements:   For this function to work, you must set the UserID
'                and Password properties first.
'
```

Notice that I included a field for the author's name. I prefer to include this because it lets others know who to come to if they find problems with the code. I can also use this to contact someone else for information regarding his or her code.

Code Level

Comments can be narrowed down to one more level. You can place comments directly inline with your code. This technique is useful if you have a line of code that needs special attention. Thanks to my co-worker Scott, I adopted an extended set of commenting techniques that ease the documenting and debugging processes, especially in a team development environment. The following table lists some of these comments:

Comment Code	Description
'	Generic comment. This can be used to note any comment that does not require special attention.
'???	Questionable code. This is especially useful in team development environments or when you are debugging someone else's code. This could possibly denote that code is questionable, unnecessary, or may require attention at a later time.
'!!!	Requires attention! This can be used to remind the programmer to take special care of the following code. This could be a reminder to debug or remove code, or restore it to a previous state.

The most basic of comment characters is the apostrophe. Whenever you place this character in a line of code, outside of strings, the text to the right of the apostrophe will be commented out. Knowing this, you can perform significantly flexible and reusable commenting techniques, as you will see next.

In its most basic form, you can place an apostrophe on a line by itself to give yourself a visual separation between comments or lines of code. This technique can be seen in the comment blocks shown previously in this skill. You can also add additional characters in some distinctive patterns to create your own custom commenting techniques, as shown in the table above.

The second and third comment styles shown in the table can be easily enhanced to work in a team environment. For example, you could add your initials to make it easy to go back and check code that you specifically need to address. If you had code you needed to remove for the final build, you could prefix the code with comments like:

```
'!!!-SB Remove the following code if the build is successful.
```

Now, all I would need to do is search the project for the pattern '!!!-SB to find all the code that I needed to address before the final compile process was executed.

Although these techniques are useful, they are certainly not the absolute only way to comment. You should use what you are most comfortable with. However, it is extremely important to be consistent to save time debugging your applications later!

Using Naming Conventions

In addition to writing comments in your code, you should use consistent naming techniques, called *naming conventions*, for your components. Naming conventions help make your source code more readable and obvious. You were introduced to some naming conventions back in Skill 3.

As you already know, each component in a Visual Basic project must be uniquely named. To ensure this, Visual Basic automatically names the components as they are added to the project. For example, the first form added to a project will be named Form1 by default. If you left the Name property set to Form1 and added another form, Visual Basic will automatically name it Form2. Another form will be named Form3, and so on. Controls are named in much the same manner.

While letting Visual Basic name your controls, imagine if you had a single form with twelve command buttons named Command1 through Command12. The program would run, but trying to remember the specific function of each button when you are writing your code would be difficult and confusing.

> **TIP**   The first thing you should do when adding a component to a project is to set its Name property to something descriptive. Your code will be more readable, and your development and debugging time will be decreased as a result.

Here are some general guidelines to developing and using your own naming conventions:

- Variables should be mixed case and contain no spaces (i.e., UserName)

- Constants should be all uppercase, and underscores should be used in place of white spaces (i.e., ACCESS_LEVEL_ADMIN)

Here is a short table of naming conventions that should be used for some of the most common Visual Basic controls:

Control	Prefix	Example
Form	frm	frmMain
Command Button	cmd	cmdOK, cmdCancel
Label	lbl	lblName
Text Box	txt	txtLastName
Combo Box	cbo	cboAccounts

Skill 12

List Box	lst	lstGroups
Frame	fra	fraOptions
Option Button	opt	optOn, optOff
Check Box	chk	chkTaxDeductible
Picture Box	pic	picWatermark
Image Box	img	imgSplashGraphic
Scroll Bars	scr	scrVolume
Timer	tmr	tmrCountdown
Drive List	drv	drvDisk
Directory List	dir	dirDirectories
File List	fil	filHiddenFiles
Line	lin	linSeparator
Shape	sha	shaCircle
Data Control	dat	datLogDatabase
OLE Control	ole	oleWordDocument
Tree View	tvw	tvwGroups
List View	lvw	lvwUsers
Image List	iml	imlGroups, imlUsers
Status Bar	sts	stsAccountStatus

As you start using more controls, you can use their recommended prefix, or you can develop your own three-letter prefix similar to those listed in this table.

Writing Structured Code

Besides commenting and naming conventions, another way to make your code easier to read and distinguish is to use tabs and spaces to visually separate your code in the Code Window. The default tab setting in Visual Basic is four spaces, but you can change this by Selecting Tools ➢ Options and selecting the Editor tab from the Options dialog box, as shown in Figure 12.1.

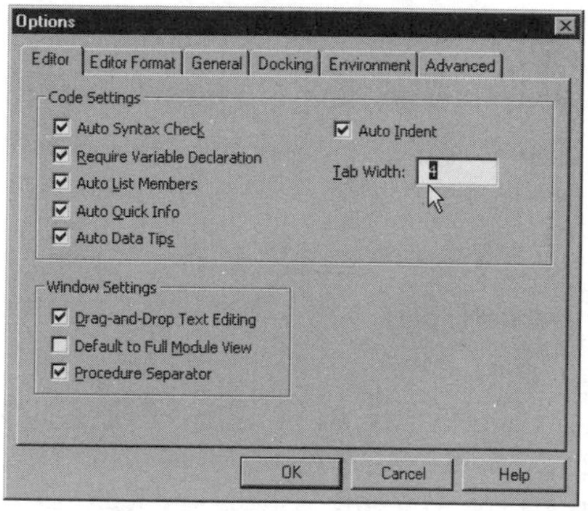

FIGURE 12.1: Setting the tabstops in the IDE

Many of the commands that you learned in Skill 6 should be blocked visually with tabs. For example, the following code:

```
Select Case x
Case Is = 1
'Do Option 1
Case Is = 2
'Do Option 2
Case Is = 3
'Do Option 3
Case Else
'Show an error message
End Select
```

would be much easier to read if you indented the nested code like this:

```
Select Case x
    Case Is = 1
        'Do Option 1
    Case Is = 2
        'Do Option 2
    Case Is = 3
        'Do Option 3
    Case Else
        'Show an error message
End Select
```

You should use this indenting style whenever your program changes state. For example, if you open a file, you indent the code that lies between the Open and Close commands. If you start a loop with the Do command, you should indent the code between the Do and the Loop commands, like the following:

```
Open filename For Input as fileno
    Do While Not EOF(fileno)
        Input #1, txt
        Debug.Print txt
    Loop
Close fileno
```

Doing this helps you to make sure that whenever you change a state in the code, you change it back. By indenting your code when a state changes, you can visually check to make sure that you haven't missed the closing statement. Indentation helps you both visually and logically write your code.

Setting Visual Basic Options to Optimize Accuracy

Some of the most useful preventative measures you can take to ensure accuracy in your code reside on the Editor tab of the Options dialog box (shown in Figure 12.2).

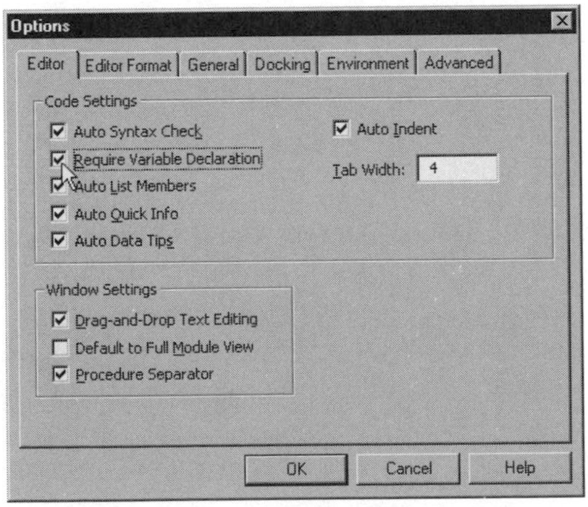

FIGURE 12.2: The Options dialog box

Check the Auto Syntax Check box to force the editor to check your code for errors during design mode. Keep this setting enabled so you won't program errantly only to discover later that you have an error in your code.

You can type the command `Option Explicit` at the top of each of your modules, and Visual Basic will force you to dimension your variables explicitly. You can also make Visual Basic automatically insert this code for you by checking the Require Variable Declaration box. This will force you to declare all variables before using them in your code.

Perhaps the most important rule to follow when programming in Visual Basic is to always explicitly dimension variables and objects with the `Dim`, `Public`, or `Private` commands. If you don't, Visual Basic will assume the variable is a `Variant`. Do not rely on Visual Basic's `Variant` data type to resolve variable formatting issues in your code. Although `Variants` are very flexible, they are inefficient and they make debugging extremely difficult. You should only use them if absolutely necessary.

TIP You should check Require Variable Declaration when you customize your IDE. This will make Visual Basic place one line—Option Explicit—in the (General)(Declarations) section of every form, module, and class. This will save you many hours of frustration when you start debugging larger applications in the future. As you gain programming experience, you will discover that most of your errors will be the result of incorrect variable types and miscalculations. Setting variables to the appropriate type will minimize these types of errors. If you have not developed the habit of using this feature, take time to do so now.

When you check the Auto List Members box, Visual basic will expose a list of properties and methods available to an object you are referencing in code. You can see this in Figure 12.3.

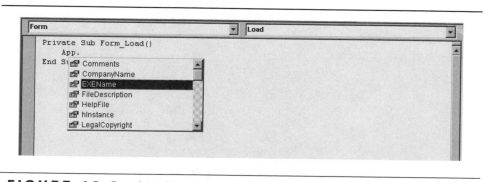

FIGURE 12.3: Auto Listing members of an object

Check the Auto Quick Info box to make Visual Basic display information about functions and their parameters as you type (Figure 12.4). This is a useful setting if you are new to Visual Basic; by enabling this, Visual Basic will make recommendations to you as you type in the Code window.

Check the Auto Data Tips box to toggle the display of the value of a variable under the cursor (Figure 12.5). This option is especially helpful when you are debugging your applications.

To aid in writing neatly structured code, you can check the Auto Indent box to automatically indent your code a given number of spaces.

TIP　　Remember that neat code is easier to read, and is extremely helpful during the debugging process.

As you learned previously, you can use the Tab box to set the number of spaces the editor will insert when you press the Tab button. The default is four spaces.

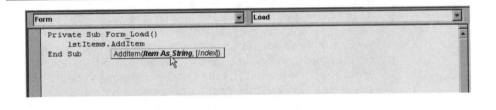

FIGURE 12.4: Auto Quick Info

As you can see, the Visual Basic editor offers many tools to get you started on the right track. I recommend that you enable these features so you can save yourself some time and frustration down the road when you start developing your own larger applications. Now let's look at some of the debugging tools that ship with Visual Basic.

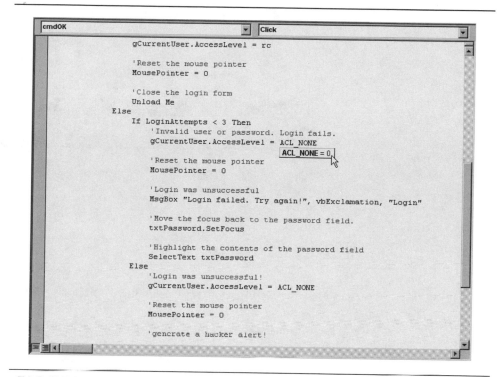

```
cmdOK                                  ▼    Click                           ▼

            gCurrentUser.AccessLevel = rc

            'Reset the mouse pointer
            MousePointer = 0

            'Close the login form
            Unload Me
        Else
            If LoginAttempts < 3 Then
                'Invalid user or password. Login fails.
                gCurrentUser.AccessLevel = ACL_NONE
                                        ┌─────────────┐
                                        │ ACL_NONE = 0 │
                                        └─────────────┘
                'Reset the mouse pointer
                MousePointer = 0

                'Login was unsuccessful
                MsgBox "Login failed. Try again!", vbExclamation, "Login"

                'Move the focus back to the password field.
                txtPassword.SetFocus

                'Highlight the contents of the password field
                SelectText txtPassword
            Else
                'Login was unsuccessful!
                gCurrentUser.AccessLevel = ACL_NONE

                'Reset the mouse pointer
                MousePointer = 0

                'generate a hacker alert!
```

FIGURE 12.5: Auto Data Tips

Using Visual Basic's Debugging Tools

Now that you know how you can write code in a structured fashion, you will help minimize the number of bugs introduced into your code. However, it is almost certain that a few bugs will creep in somehow. Fortunately, Visual Basic comes with many useful debugging tools to help you make your applications bulletproof. The debugging tools you will be using can be accessed through the Debug menu and the Debug toolbar, shown in Figure 12.6.

Skill 12

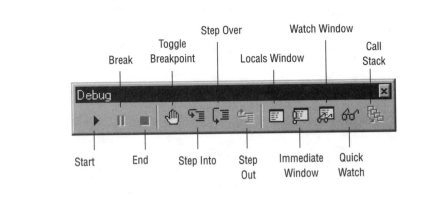

FIGURE 12.6: The Debug toolbar

You can view the Debug toolbar by selecting Toolbars ➤ Debug from Visual Basic's View menu.

As you have already learned in previous skills, the Start button is used to start the current project. In addition to using this button, you could Select Run ➤ Start, or press F5.

You can use the Break button to temporarily stop execution of a running application. This is useful if you want to check the values of variables or want to determine what state the program is in.

 TIP   If a project is in break mode, the Start button becomes a Resume button. You can press it to continue program execution from where the application was paused.

To stop a running application, you would press the Stop button.

The Toggle Breakpoint button is used to alternately set or remove (toggle) a breakpoint at the current line of code. A breakpoint is used to suspend execution of the application when program execution reaches the specified point. These are useful tools when you need to monitor the values of variables to determine if the application is performing as expected.

> **TIP** When you are finished debugging, you can clear all the breakpoints in the project by selecting Debug ➢ Clear All Breakpoints from the Visual Basic menu, or by pressing Ctrl+Shift+F9.

You can use the Step Into button to execute one line of code at a time. This is handy when you want to continuously monitor your application as you go through it line by line. You may want to use the F8 shortcut key to call this function because there will be times when you cannot access the Debug menu or toolbar when your application is running—for example, when the form is maximized.

The Step Over button allows you to step through a procedure or function call without having to single step through its individual lines of code. After calling this function, you are returned to the line after the procedure or function call. You will also want to use the Shift+F8 shortcut to call this function.

The Step Out button allows you to continue execution of the remaining lines of code within the procedure that the current execution point lies. Its shortcut key combination is Ctrl+Shift+F8.

By clicking the Locals Window button, you can display the Locals window shown in Figure 12.7, and automatically display all of the variables in the current stack and their values. The values in the Locals window are automatically updated every time you change from run time to break mode and every time the stack context changes.

> **TIP** The Locals Window is especially useful because not only does it show variables, but objects as well. You simply add an object to the window once, and all of its properties can be viewed as a result!

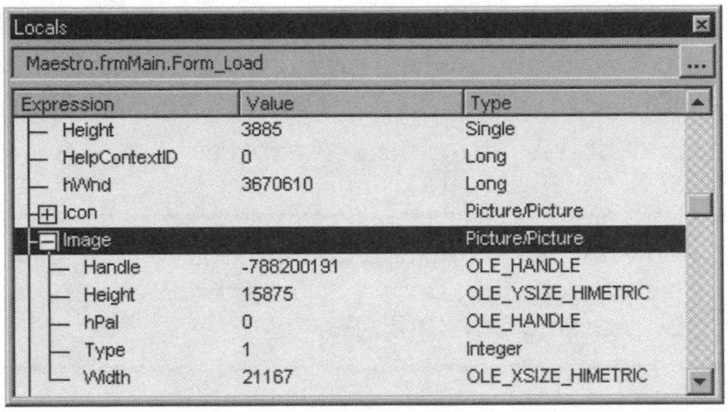

FIGURE 12.7: The Locals window

Press the Immediate Window button or Ctrl+G to show the Immediate window (See Figure 12.8). You can use the Immediate window to test functions and variables during design time as well as in debug mode.

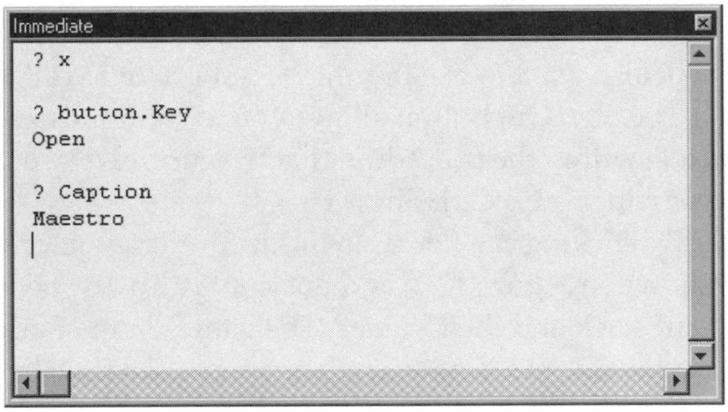

```
Immediate
? x

? button.Key
Open

? Caption
Maestro
|
```

FIGURE 12.8: The Immediate window

In debugging terms, a *watch* is a variable of object that is specifically monitored—or watched—in real-time as the program executes. You can view the properties of watches in the Watch window. The Watch window can be called up by pressing the Watch Window button or by adding a watch to the window. As you can see in

Figure 12.9, we are watching the `tbrToolbar` control as the application runs. As properties are set and buttons are pressed, you can see the Watch window update the watch for `tbrToolbar`.

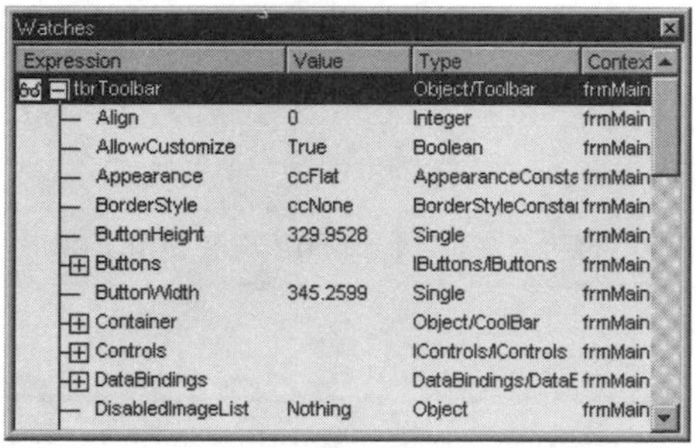

FIGURE 12.9: A Toolbar control in the Watch window

When you press the Quick Watch button, Visual Basic displays the Quick Watch dialog box (Figure 12.10) with the current value of the selected expression. From here you can add the watch to the Watch window so you can keep an eye on the watch for a longer duration.

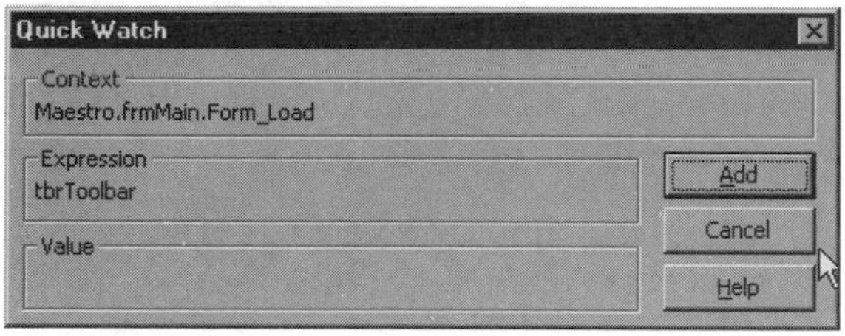

FIGURE 12.10: The Quick Watch dialog box

The Call Stack button opens a dialog box which displays all of the procedures that have been entered into, but not completed. As you can see in Figure 12.11, the `Form_Load()` event has been entered, as well as the `StartTimer` procedure.

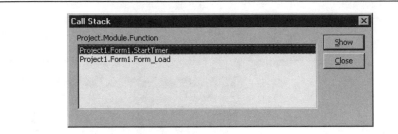

FIGURE 12.11: The Call Stack dialog box

TIP On the Debug menu is another useful function, called Run to Cursor, that allows you to run the application and have it go into break mode when the execution point is at the cursor. This is a handy method of getting directly to a point where you can start debugging. This might be the case when you know that your program runs perfectly up to a specific point, and then a bug occurs. You could place the cursor just before the point where you think the bug is and then step through the code and watch what happens. The shortcut key combination for this function is Ctrl+F8.

Stepping and Watching

Now that you know what debugging tools you have at your disposal, let's try some examples so you can get familiar with using the tools. Try this example:

1. Open the sample project MDINote.vbp from the \MSDN98\98vs\1033\ Samples\VB98\MDI\ directory.

2. Open the Code window for frmNotepad by clicking frmNotepad in the Project Explorer and selecting View ➤ Code from the menu.

3. Go to the Form_Load() event.

4. Set a breakpoint on the line

```
For i = 1 To Screen.FontCount - 1
```

by placing the cursor somewhere on the line and pressing the F9 key.

TIP   You can also set a breakpoint by clicking in the margin to the left of the line of code, as in Figure 12.12.

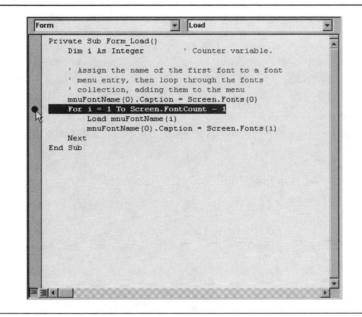

```
Private Sub Form_Load()
    Dim i As Integer          ' Counter variable.

    ' Assign the name of the first font to a font
    ' menu entry, then loop through the fonts
    ' collection, adding them to the menu
    mnuFontName(0).Caption = Screen.Fonts(0)
    For i = 1 To Screen.FontCount - 1
        Load mnuFontName(i)
        mnuFontName(0).Caption = Screen.Fonts(i)
    Next
End Sub
```

FIGURE 12.12: Setting a breakpoint

5. Run the application by pressing F5. The program should break at the line where you set the breakpoint.

6. Press F8 twice to single-step through two lines of code.

7. Using your mouse, highlight the text mnuFontName(0).Caption and press the Quick Watch button on the Debug toolbar.

8. When the Quick Watch dialog box appears, click the Add button to add the selected item to the Watch window. The dialog box will disappear.

9. Continue single-stepping through the loop while watching the value in the Watch window. You should see the value for the watch expression cycle through various Windows fonts.

Skill 12

10. After you have a good idea of how single-stepping works, press Ctrl+Shift+F8 to step out of the loop and the `Form_Load()` event. You should return to the `MDIForm_Load()` event.

11. Press the End button to stop the debugging process.

Working in the Immediate Window

You have just performed some of the most basic debugging techniques that you will use most often. But we're not done yet! Let's practice using the Immediate window.

1. Press Ctrl+G to open the Immediate window.

2. Clear all breakpoints in the project by pressing Ctrl+Shift+F9.

3. Double-click Module2 to open it in the Code window.

4. Go to the `OpenFile()` procedure.

5. Set a breakpoint on the line that says

   ```
   On Error Resume Next
   ```

6. Place the cursor in the Immediate window and type the following line:

   ```
   OpenFile "c:\config.sys"
   ```

7. Press the Enter key after you type the above line. This will execute the procedure `OpenFile()`.

You will notice that the IDE goes into break mode and the current execution point is where you set the breakpoint in step 5.

8. Continue pressing the F8 key to step through the procedure. You will notice that you will step into the `FindFreeIndex()` function.

9. When you step into the `FindFreeIndex()` function, click the Call Stack button on the Debug toolbar. You should see that both the `FindFree-Index()` and `OpenFile()` functions are currently running and have not been completed yet.

10. Click the Show button to return to the Code window.

11. Continue single-stepping through the remaining lines of code by pressing F8 for each step.

In the preceding example, you learned that you can call some procedures in your application without starting the program. This is a useful method of testing some functions, especially functions that are neatly contained and don't rely on `Public` or `Global` variables.

Let's try executing some simple Visual Basic functions in the Immediate window.

1. Click in the Immediate window to make it active.

2. Press Ctrl+A to select all the text, if any, in the window.

3. Press the Delete key to remove all the text. This will give you a clear window.

4. Type the following line of code in the window and press Enter:

   ```
   Print Mid$("The quick brown fox",7,3)
   ```

   The result should be `ick`.

5. Type this line of code and check the result:

   ```
   ? Format$(Date$,"mmmm")
   ```

   In this case, the `Format$()` function returned the value May. This will most certainly be different for you unless you happen to be doing the exercise in the month of May.

> **NOTE** The ? command is an abbreviation for the `Print` command. Both can be used interchangeably under most circumstances. The ? command is most commonly used in the Immediate window.

The best way to learn how to use these debugging tools is to use them to actually debug. As you develop your own applications, try developing the habit of using these tools to debug your applications. You will find that they will save you a great deal of time and frustration when your program doesn't work as expected.

Developing Your Own Testing Utilities

The debugging tools in Visual Basic provide a good way to hunt down and eradicate bugs that creep around in your applications. However, when you design larger applications, especially ones with re-usable code, it makes sense to write

Skill 12

your own testing applets that are designed specifically to give your code a work-out. Once your code has passed the test from your testing applet, you can add the code to the larger application with confidence that it should run properly. In this section, you will learn how to write your own testing utilities.

We will start by creating a simple interface like the one shown in Figure 12.13 that allows you to press buttons to test functions in modules. Well designed, self-sufficient functions should work well in this interface. You can add buttons to test the functionality of your own procedures. The name of the procedure, the input data, and results are all listed in the window at the top of the interface.

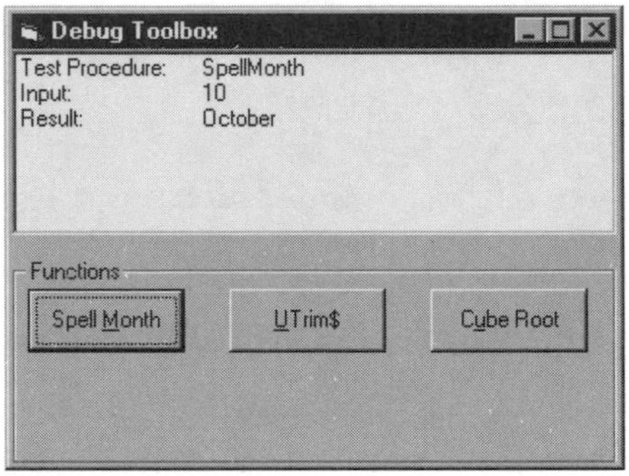

FIGURE 12.13: The Debug Toolbox application

Let's start creating the testing interface:

1. Start a new project by selecting File ➤ New Project from the Visual Basic menu, or by pressing Ctrl+N.

2. When the New Project dialog box appears, select Standard EXE as the project type, then click OK to close the dialog box.

3. In the Project Explorer, click Project1 to make it the active project.

4. Set the Name of the project to **DebugToolbox** in the Properties window.

5. Click Form1 in the Form Designer to make it the active control.

6. In the properties window, set its Name property to **frmMain** and its Caption property to **Debug Toolbox**.

7. Add a standard List Box control to the form. Move it to the upper half of the form and stretch it so it is roughly the width of the form, and half the height.

8. Set the Name property of the List Box control to **lstResults**.

9. Add a Frame control to frmMain. Set its Name property to **fraFunctions** and its Caption to **Functions**.

10. Position fraFunctions right under the lstResults and stretch it so it is approximately the width of the form, and one-half the width.

Now that we have the general layout of the form, let's add some buttons to the Functions frame. These are the buttons we will use to test some functions.

1. Using your mouse, "draw" a Command Button on the Frame control.

> **NOTE**   The Frame, much like a Form, is a container control. To add controls to it, you must draw them on the Frame control itself. Double-clicking the control in the Toolbox will add the control to the form, and not the Frame.

2. Set the Name of the Command Button to **cmdSpellMonth**. Set its Caption property to **Spell &Month**.

Instead of drawing another control on the Frame, we are going to copy the one just added. This will help you keep your buttons the same size and will simplify adding additional buttons on the container.

3. Click cmdSpellMonth to make it the active control.

4. Press Ctrl+C to make a copy of the control in the Windows Clipboard.

5. Click the Frame to make it the active control. Doing this will make it the target for the next paste operation.

6. Press Ctrl+V to paste a copy of the button on the frame. You will get a message saying there is already a control named cmdSpellMonth, as shown in Figure 12.14.

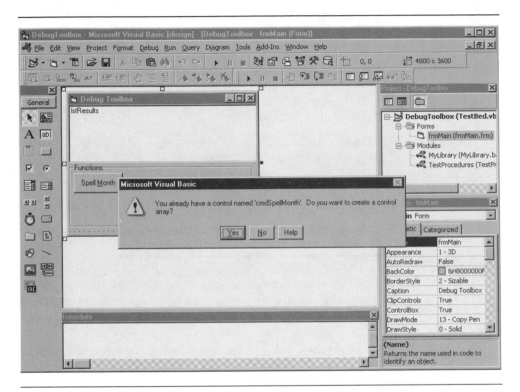

FIGURE 12.14: Do you want to create a control array?

7. Click the No button on the dialog box. You will be naming the buttons individually. The button will be added to the Frame control.

8. Move the new button to the upper-middle of the frame, so it is aligned with cmdSpellMonth.

9. Set the Name property of the new button to **cmdUTrim**. Set its Caption property to **Utrim$**.

10. Make cmdUTrim the active control and press Ctrl+C to copy it to the Clipboard.

11. Click fraFunctions to make it active and press Ctrl+V to paste a copy of the button on the frame. Answer No to the dialog box that asks you if you want to create a control array.

12. Move the newly added button to the upper-right corner of the frame, aligned with cmdUTrim and cmdSpellMonth.

13. Set the Name property of the new button to **cmdCubeRoot**. Set its Caption to **C&ube Root**. When you are done, the form should look like Figure 12.15.

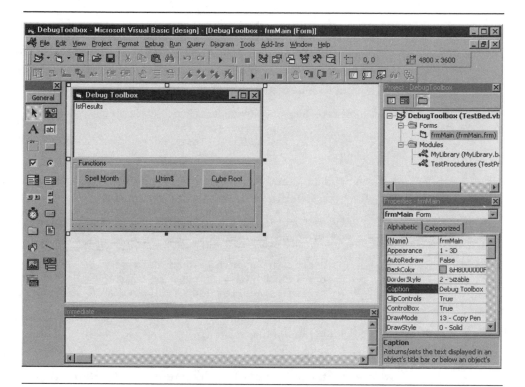

FIGURE 12.15: The Debug Toolbox in the Form Designer

Now that you have created the visual layout of the interface, save your project so you don't lose your work. We will be adding code next.

1. Add the following code to the Form_Resize() event of frmMain:

```
Private Sub Form_Resize()
    'Position the list in the upper-right
    'corner of the form. Stretch it to fit the
    'width of the form, and 1/2 the height of
    'the form.
    lstResults.Move 0, 0, ScaleWidth, ScaleHeight / 2
```

Skill 12

```
'Position the frame in the lower half
'of the form. Stretch it to fit the
'width of the form, and 1/2 the height of
'the form.
fraFunctions.Move 0, ScaleHeight / 2, ScaleWidth,_
        ScaleHeight / 2
End Sub
```

2. As you will see, the first thing that happens after a button is clicked is the name of the procedure being tested is added to the list. This is accomplished through the ShowProcedure() procedure. Add this procedure to the (General)(Declarations) section of frmMain:

```
Private Sub ShowProcedure(Proc As String)
    'Add the procedure to the list
    lstResults.AddItem "Test Procedure: " & vbTab & Proc
End Sub
```

3. We need a method to get input from the user. Add this function to the (General)(Declarations) section of frmMain:

```
Private Function GetInput(Msg As String) As Variant
    Dim rc As Variant

    'Prompt the user for input data
    rc = InputBox(Msg, "Input Test Data")
    lstResults.AddItem "Input: " & vbTab & vbTab & rc

    'Return the input value
    GetInput = rc
End Function
```

Notice that the GetInput() function returns a Variant. As you learned earlier in this skill, variants can cause some difficulties, and should be avoided unless absolutely necessary. This is a time when the Variant is the best choice for a data type, because GetInput() will be used to get text as well as numeric input, and both data types need to be passed back.

4. Again, add the following code to the frmMain:

```
Private Sub ShowResults(result As Variant)
    'Add the result to the list box
    lstResults.AddItem "Result: " & vbTab & vbTab & result
End Sub
```

5. Save your project so you don't lose your work.

Now that you have an interface to test procedures, you need to add procedures to the project.

1. Add a new code module to the project by right-clicking in the Project Explorer and selecting Add Module.

2. Set the `Name` property of the new code module to **TestProcedures**.

The first function you are going to add is called `SpellMonth()`. As you can probably guess, `SpellMonth()` is used to get the name of the month based on the month number. For example, if you pass the function the number 5, it should return the month `May`.

3. Add the following functions to the `(General)(Declarations)` section of the TestProcedures module:

    ```
    Public Function SpellMonth(MonthNumber as Integer) As String
        Dim rc As String

        'Extract the name of the month
        rc = Format$(MonthNumber & "/1/1998", "mmmm")

        'Return the month number
        SpellMonth = rc
    End Function
    ```

The next function you are going to add is called `UTrim$()`. It is a combination of Visual Basic's `UCase$` function, used to convert strings to uppercase, and the `Trim$` function, which is used to remove the leading and trailing spaces from a string. Logically speaking, `UTrim$()` is the equivalent of `UCase$(Trim$(txt))`. When used together, these functions provide a powerful and extremely useful data validation function. You should use it to compare to string values to ensure that the text is identical, excluding case. For example:

```
If UTrim$(MyInput) = UTrim$(DatabaseValue) Then…
    'The Data is Identical
Else
    'The Data is Mismatched
End If
```

4. Add the following code to add the `UTrim$()` function to your code module.

    ```
    Public Function UTrim(Txt As String) As String
            'Convert to upper case and trim off all leading
            'and trailing spaces.
            Txt = UCase$(Trim$(Txt))
    End Function
    ```

5. If you started the code library from Skill 4, add the module MyLibrary to the project and go to step 7. Otherwise continue with step 6.

6. Add the following function to the code module:

```
Public Function CubeRoot(x As Double) As Double
    If x = 0 Then
        CubeRoot = 0
        Exit Function
    End If

    CubeRoot = 10 ^ ((Log(Abs(x)) / Log(10)) / 3)

    If x < 0 Then
        CubeRoot = -CubeRoot
    End If
End Function
```

7. Save your project once again.

Now that we have some procedures to test, let's add the code to the interface to test them. You will notice as you enter the code that each set of code is very similar to the others. The basic functions are:

- Display the procedure name in the list
- Get input from the user
- Display the input in the list
- Pass the input to the procedure
- Display the results

Let's add the code to call the SpellMonth() function.

1. Add the following code to the cmdSpellMonth_Click() event:

```
Private Sub cmdSpellMonth_Click()
    Dim rc As Integer
    Dim result As String

    'Show the test procedure in the list
    ShowProcedure "SpellMonth"

    'Get the user input
    rc = GetInput("Enter a month number:")

    'Get the results
```

```
      result = SpellMonth(rc)

      'Show the results in the list
      ShowResults result
   End Sub
```

2. Now let's add the code to test the UTrim$( ) function:

```
   Private Sub cmdUTrim_Click()
      Dim rc As String
      Dim result As String

      'Show the test procedure in the list
      ShowProcedure "UTrim$"

      'Get the user input
      rc = GetInput("Enter a text string:")

      'Get the results
      result = UTrim$(rc)

      'Show the results in the list
      ShowResults result
   End Sub
```

3. Finally, add the code to test the CubeRoot( ) function:

```
   Private Sub cmdCubeRoot_Click()
      Dim rc As Double
      Dim result As String

      'Show the test procedure in the list
      ShowProcedure "CubeRoot"

      'Get the user input
      rc = GetInput("Enter a number:")

      'Get the results
      result = CubeRoot(rc)

      'Show the results in the list
      ShowResults result
   End Sub
```

4. Save and run your project.

Skill 12

It is always a good idea to save your work frequently. This is especially important after you have coded something that is vital to the application, or when the code you typed in would be difficult to re-enter should you lose it. Save your work often!

Now that you have a basic test interface and some calling functions, you can call each and test the results. The best way to do this is to determine some test input and manually calculate the results by hand. Then, you do the same using the computer. If the procedures you are testing are well designed and coded, the results from the computer will match those from your original calculations. Let's try some tests and you can see what I mean.

Before we test the SpellMonth() function, we need source data so we can verify the validity of the result data. We will do this by providing this simple table:

Month Number	Month Name
1	January
2	February
3	March
4	April
5	May
6	June
7	July
8	August
9	September
10	October
11	November
12	December

1. Click the Spell Month button. You will see that the words Test Procedure: SpellMonth appear in the list and an input box appears.

2. Type **10** in the Input Test Data dialog box and press OK.

The result, shown in Figure 12.16, shows that the SpellMonth function returns October. If you compare this with the table above, you will see that the tenth month corresponds to October. As a result, we can conclude that the function worked properly.

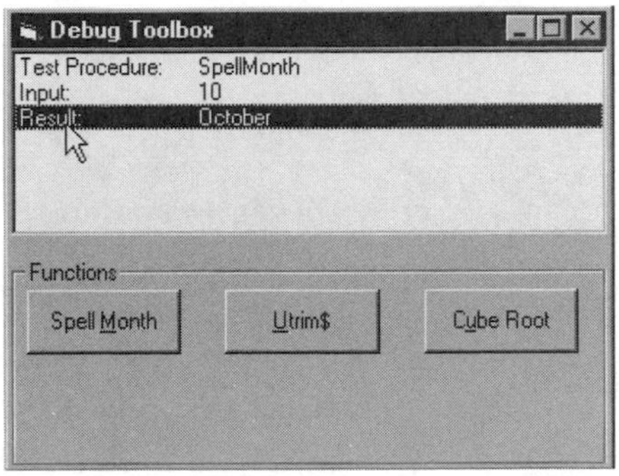

FIGURE 12.16: Testing the SpellMonth() function

3. Click the Spell Month button again.

4. Type **7** in the Input Test Data dialog and press OK. The result should be July.

5. Click the Spell Month button again.

6. Type **1** in the Input Test Data dialog box and press OK. This time the result should be January.

So far, the SpellMonth() function seems to be working properly. Let's try testing it one more time before we say that this function is finished.

7. Click the Spell Month button.

8. Type **15** in the Input Test Data dialog box and press OK.

Although there are only 12 months in a year, the function still passed a value back. In this case it was January. Would it be safe to assume that the fifteenth month should actually be 15-12, or the third month, March? Or would it be better to restrict the user to only values between 1 and 12, as we did with the table of test data? Let's add an If...Then...Else statement to the SpellMonth() function so we can restrict the allowed values.

9. Stop the Debug Toolbox application so you can fix the SpellMonth() code.

Skill 12

10. Modify the SpellMonth() function so the code reads as follows:

```
Public Function SpellMonth(MonthNumber As Integer) As String
    Dim rc As String

    'Make sure that MonthNumber is a value between
    '1 and 12.
    If MonthNumber > 0 And MonthNumber < 13 Then
        'Extract the name of the month
        rc = Format$(MonthNumber & "/1/1998", "mmmm")

        'Return the month number
        SpellMonth = rc
    Else
        'Return an error message'
        SpellMonth = "Error: Month value out of range!"
    End If
End Function
```

11. Now save and run your project again.

12. Click the Spell Month button.

13. Type **15** in the Input Test Data dialog box again and press OK. This time the result should be an error: Error: Month value out of range!

> **TIP**
>
> As you can see, it is important to test your functions repeatedly. If we had only tested one or two months, we may not have discovered the logical error in the SpellMonth() function. Make it a habit to test your procedures repeatedly before calling them bulletproof. Be sure to test for unexpected values as well. Undoubtedly, you will have a user who will try something crazy, and your application may crash if you don't prepare for it!

Now that you have successfully tested and fixed your SpellMonth() function, let's continue by testing the UTrim$() function. Let's create a table with some test values so we can compare the results. This time we will only test three values.

Unformatted String	Formatted String
This is a mixed case sentence	THIS IS A MIXED CASE SENTENCE
Here are some Leading spaces	HERE ARE SOME LEADING SPACES
DEBUGGING Your Applications is Fun!	DEBUGGING YOUR APPLICATIONS IS FUN!

1. Click the UTrim$ button to start testing the UTrim$() function.

2. Type the first sentence in the table, **This is a mixed case sentence**. The result should be THIS IS A MIXED CASE SENTENCE.

3. Click the OK button and see what you get.

4. As you can see in Figure 12.17, there was no result. Obviously the function did not work as expected. Stop the program and open the Code window for the UTrim$() function.

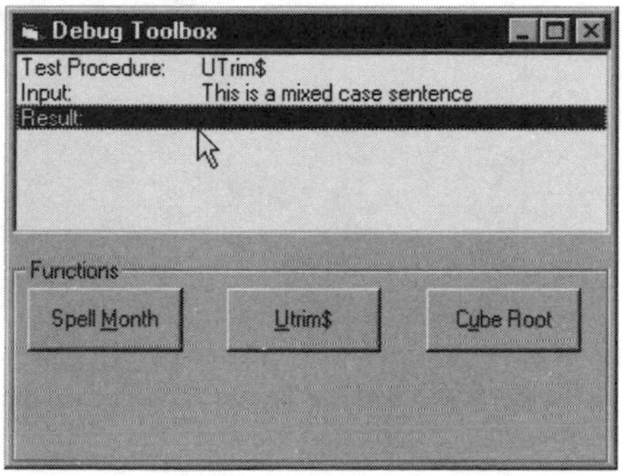

FIGURE 12.17: The UTrim$ function returns unexpected results

By examining the UTrim$() function code below, it appears that the function works. The variable Txt gets converted to UCase$(Trim$(Txt)).

```
Public Function UTrim(Txt As String) As String
    'Convert to upper case and trim off all leading
    'and trailing spaces.
    Txt = UCase$(Trim$(Txt))
End Function
```

After a little scrutiny, you may notice that we forgot to return the value of Txt through the UTrim$() function.

5. Change the last line of the function above End Function to the following:

    ```
    UTrim = UCase$(Trim$(Txt))
    ```

6. Now save your project once again and run it.

7. Click the UTrim$ button to resume testing the UTrim$() function.

8. Type the first sentence in the table, **This is a mixed case sentence**. The result should be THIS IS A MIXED CASE SENTENCE.

Skill 12

9. Click the OK button on the dialog box to see the results. Success!

10. Click the UTrim$ button again and type " **Here are some Leading spaces**" in the input dialog box. Do not type the quotation marks; they are in this step to show you to type in four or five spaces before you type the sentence, as you can see in Figure 12.18.

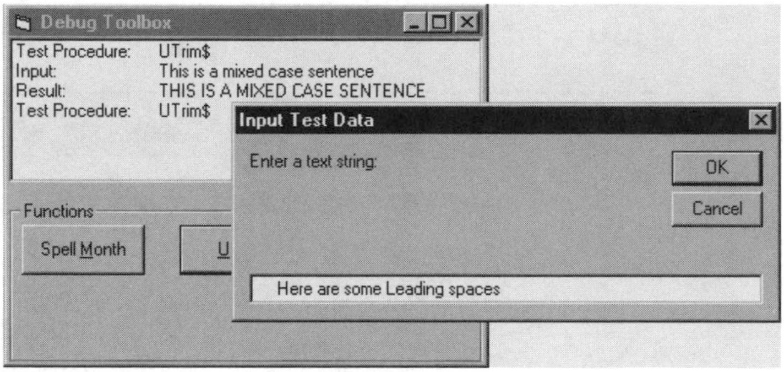

FIGURE 12.18: Typing the leading spaces

11. Click the OK button to see the results.

12. Click the UTrim$ button once more to pass our final test data to the UTrim$() function.

13. In the dialog box, type **DEBUGGING Your Applications is Fun!**

14. Click the OK button to see the results.

15. As you can see in Figure 12.19, once you fixed the bug in the function, UTrim$() seems to be working properly. Each of the three function calls returned the values we expected.

By now you should be seeing the importance of logically testing your functions before coding them. This technique provides a systematic way to test your procedures and compare the results.

We are near the final steps of testing your Debug Toolbox application. Now you need to test the CubeRoot() function. You may remember this function from Skill 4, when you learned about writing code modules and classes. Let's put this function to the test. Here is a table of test data. I took numbers at random and ran them through the cube root function of a calculator and noted the results.

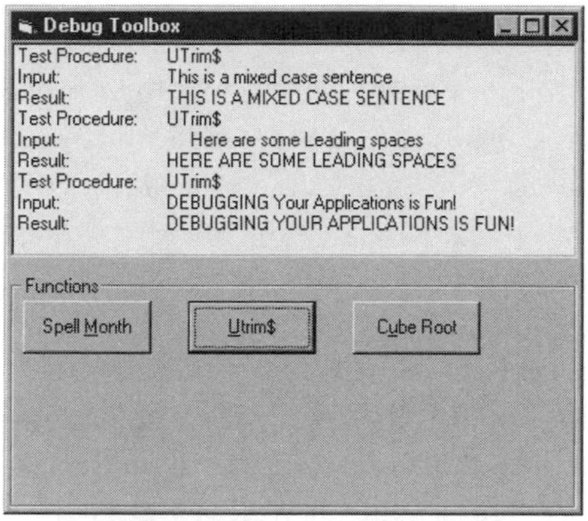

FIGURE 12.19: The results of the three UTrim$() tests

Find the Cube Root Of:	Anticipated Results
1	1
8	2
9	2.080083823
27	3
300	6.694329501

1. Click the Cube Root button.

2. Type **1** in the input box and click OK. The result should be 1.

3. Click the Cube Root button again.

4. Type **8** in the input box and click OK. The result should be 2.

5. Click the Cube Root button again to test the third value in the table.

6. Type **9** in the input box and click OK. The result should be 2.0800838230519.

7. Click the Cube Root button.

8. Type **27** in the input box and click OK. The result should be 3.

9. Finally, click the Cube Root button once more. This will be the last test.

10. Type **300** in the input box and click OK. The result should be 6.69432950082169.

As you can see, the results matched those I got from my calculator. As a result, it is fair to assume that the CubeRoot() function works properly, and it can be considered worthy of being stored in your code library. The other two functions, ShowMonth() and UTrim$() are also debugged and reliable. If you want, place them in your code library as well. These will become useful functions when you start comparing String data and working with dates.

Now that you have completed this skill, you are equipped with enough knowledge to successfully debug any application you develop. When designing your application, it is important to adequately document your code with liberal use of structured comments as well as hard copy notes (you do design your applications on paper first, don't you?!?!). Structured code helps make your code much easier to read, resulting in quicker development time and more reliable code. The comments and naming conventions you use will also greatly reduce your debugging time. Develop and practice your documentation and naming conventions now, and save yourself time and frustration in the future!

NOTE Debugging begins by taking preventative measures in your code. Consistency in your use of comments, code structure, and naming conventions is the key to simplifying the application development process. To quote an old construction term: "Measure twice; cut once!"

Are You up to Speed?

Now you can...

- ☑ **write well-documented code**
- ☑ **develop consistent coding habits**
- ☑ **utilize naming conventions**
- ☑ **use the debugging tools in Visual Basic**
- ☑ **write your own testing utilities**

Creating and Using Help Files

- Using help files in your applications
- Creating help files
- Designing and creating a contents file
- Writing topic files
- Creating help project files
- Linking your applications to your help files
- Converting your help files to HTML Help

One of the best things you can do to contribute to the success and usefulness of your application is to thoroughly document it so that your users have something to reference when they are having trouble. The simpler and more convenient you make your documentation, the easier it will be for your users.

There are two ways you can document your applications, and you should do both. The first is to create online help for the application. The application should be context-sensitive, so the user can get help from anywhere at any time. The second method requires writing hard-copy documentation: manuals. Although there are many ways you can write, print, and package written manuals, there are only a few techniques that you need to know to write online help. That's what you will learn how to do in this skill.

Using Help Files in Your Applications

Before you distribute your application, you should create an online help system to distribute with it. This is the user's first line of technical support if something about the application is unclear or needs explanation. Your help file should be well designed and should integrate well with your application. A context-sensitive help system allows the user to call up the online help from virtually any control on any form and display the help information for that particular control. In this skill, you will create a simple help file that explains how to create a help file. You can use this file as a reference when creating your own help files in the future.

Although there are numerous commercial and shareware applications available to create help files, for this skill you will use the tools that come with Visual Basic.

NOTE Contrary to popular belief, help files are not difficult to create. The difficult part is understanding the help documentation. As a result, this skill clarifies a lot of the gray areas of help-file creation.

To create a help file you will need a word processor that accommodates footnotes and can save .RTF (Rich Text Format) files. Many developers use Word for Windows for this purpose, and that is what we will use for the exercise in this skill. If you do not have Word, you can use another word processor. The methods for creating the files should be easy to understand and adapt to your personal

word processor. In addition, you will need a help compiler that generates a
.HLP file from a .RTF file (and from bitmaps if you wish). Fortunately, Visual
Basic comes complete with its own help compiler. We will use the Microsoft
Help Workshop found on the Visual Basic CD (see Figure 13.1).

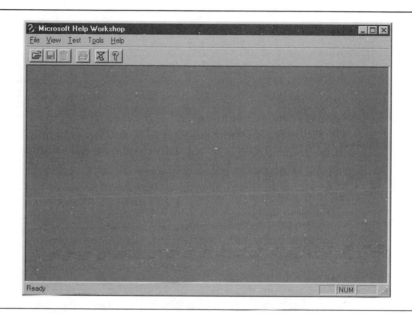

FIGURE 13.1: The Help Workshop

NOTE   In addition to this skill, see the Help Compiler Guide that is part of the Visual
Basic documentation set. This will provide you with additional information on
how to set up the .RTF files and how to make .HLP files.

Creating Your First Help File

To create any help file, you need to create a *contents file*, a *topic file*, and a *project
file*. The contents file is an ASCII file that defines the layout and appearance of the
Contents tab of the help file. The topic file is where you write the text and add the
graphics that make up the actual help document. Finally, the project file links the

topic and contents files, as well as other files that may be required to complete the project. It also defines the layout, appearance, and position of the help file when someone runs it. Figure 13.2 shows what a contents file looks like in a compiled help file.

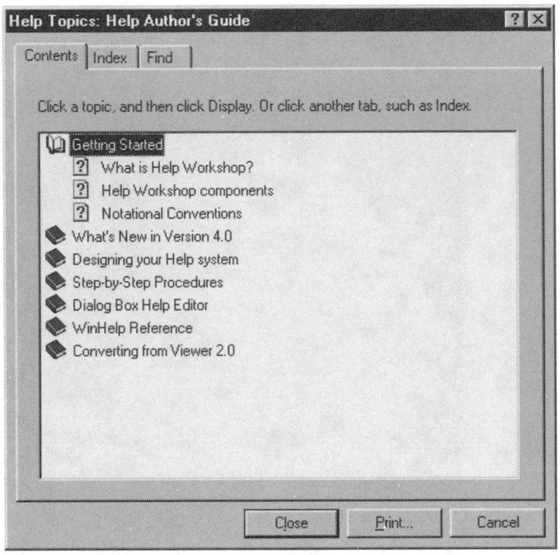

FIGURE 13.2: A sample help contents file

Designing and Creating a Contents File

Although many help manuals say to create the topic file first, I prefer to create a visual outline of the help system with the assistance of the contents file. I find it easier to create the outline on the computer because it allows you to easily make changes and it saves paper. After all, the computer is a tool, so let's use it as such. Fortunately, the Help Compiler Workshop provides a graphical layout of the topics within the project (see Figure 13.3), much like the Menu Editor in the Visual Basic IDE. During development it looks exactly like a normal Contents tab on other help files. It is a great way to lay out your help project.

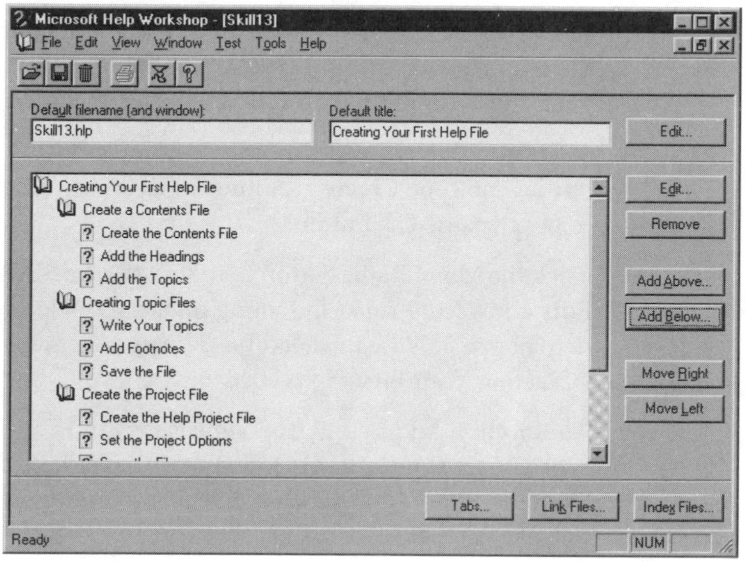

FIGURE 13.3: Creating a contents file

It is a good idea to write down the topic IDs and titles when you lay out your help contents file. Topic IDs are used by the Help Compiler to provide a numeric "hook" to your application. These will come in handy when you define the footnotes within your topic file. Let's start the help file project by creating the contents file:

1. If you have not already done so, install the Help Workshop, found in the \Common\Tools\VB\HCW subdirectory on the Visual Basic CD, to your hard disk.

2. Start the Help Workshop from the Windows Start menu.

3. Create a new contents file by selecting File ➤ New from the menu. Select Help Contents from the dialog box and click OK.

4. The first thing you want to do is define the name of the help file. Type **Skill13.hlp** in the Default filename field.

5. In the Default title field, type **Creating Your First Help File**.

6. The first step to creating your outline is to add a heading to the list. Click the Add Above button and select the Heading option. In the Title field, type **Creating Your First Help File**. Click OK to close the dialog box.

7. Click Add Below to add another heading below the first. Select the Heading option and type **Create a Contents File** in the Title field. When you are done, click the OK button.

8. Click the Move Right button to indent this heading. Much like the Menu Editor in Visual Basic, indenting makes the selected item a subitem of the item above it. Now the heading "Create a Contents File" is a subheading of "Creating Your First Help File."

9. Again, click Add Below. This time, select the Topic option. In the Title field, type **Create the Contents File**. In the Topic ID field, type **IDH_Create-ContentsFile**. Leave the Help File and Window Type fields blank. Click OK to close the dialog box.

10. Add the following topics using the topic text and topic IDs:

Topic ID	Topic Text
IDH_AddHeadings	**Add the Headings**
IDH_AddTopics	**Add the Topics**

11. Add another heading by clicking the Add Below button. Type **Creating Topic Files** in the Title field and click the OK button.

12. Add the following topics under the Creating Topic Files heading:

Topic ID	Topic Text
IDH_WriteTopics	**Write Your Topics**
IDH_AddFootnotes	**Add Footnotes**
IDH_SaveRTF	**Save the File**

13. Add the last subheading. Type **Create the Project File** in the Title field and click the OK button.

14. Add the following topics under the Create the Project File heading:

Topic ID	Topic Text
IDH_CreateProjectFile	**Create the Help Project File**
IDH_SetOptions	**Set the Project Options**
IDH_SaveRTF	**Save the File**
IDH_AddFiles	**Add Files to the Project**
IDH_DefineWindow	**Define the Help Window**
IDH_Compile	**Save and Compile Your Project**
IDH_Test	**Test Your Help File**

15. Save the file as Skill13.cnt.

Now that you have created your first contents file, you can start creating your topic file. I hope you wrote down the topic IDs and topic titles. You will need them when you add the footnotes to your topic file. If you didn't write them down, now would be a good time to do so.

Writing a Topic File

After you create the contents file, you can start writing the topic file. This is a Rich Text Format (RTF) document that contains the text, graphics, links, and macros that appear when you actually run the help file. For this example, I used Microsoft Word. If you don't use Word, you can read through and adapt the commands to work with your word processor.

1. The first step is to start your word processor and create a new document.

2. Take the first topic title you entered in the contents file and type it on the first line of the document: **Create the Contents File**.

3. Type the following text on the first page, under the topic title:

> **I believe that you should create the contents file first. I do this because the Help Compiler Workshop provides a graphical framework to do this. It is much like the Menu Editor in Visual Basic, allowing you to create a hierarchical list of headings and topics.**
>
> **From the Help Compiler Workshop, select File ➢ New.**
>
> **Select Help Contents and click the OK button.**

4. Before you can access this topic, you need to add a footnote. This footnote needs to be at the beginning of the topic. Place the cursor *before* the topic Create the Contents File.

5. Select Insert ➤ Footnote from the menu bar. In the numbering frame, select Custom Mark and enter the pound sign (#). Click the OK button to close the dialog box.

6. For the footnote text, type **IDH_CreateContentsFile**. This is the topic ID for this topic.

7. Next, add a topic title. This is the text that appears when you search through the help file. Position the cursor between the pound sign and the title at the top of the topic.

8. Insert another footnote by selecting Insert ➤ Footnote. Again, select Custom Mark. Enter a dollar sign ($) as the custom mark. Click OK.

9. When the word processor takes you to enter the footnote text, type **Create the Contents File**. This is the topic title for this topic.

10. Finally, add the browse sequence footnote. Place the cursor in between the dollar sign and the title text. Insert another footnote (Insert ➤ Footnote). Select Custom Mark and enter a plus (+) sign in the field. Click OK.

11. Enter **auto** as the footnote text. This will cause Windows Help to create an auto-browsing sequence throughout the help file.

12. If you have not already done so, you can enhance the title text at the top of the topic by raising the font size and adding a bold style to it. When you are done, your topic file should look similar to Figure 13.4.

Before continuing, let's take a look at what you did for this topic. The first thing you did was to add a title. This lets the user know what they are supposed to be reading about. In this case, the user is learning about creating the contents file. After you entered the title, you typed the body of the topic. Although you don't do it in this help file, you can add graphics and jumps to other topics. If you want to learn more about this, look at the online help for the Help Compiler Workshop. It gives you more information than you could ask for.

Finally, you added the footnotes. These are required for the help file to work properly when it is compiled. You used three footnotes, however, there are more that you can use. The first was the topic ID footnote. After that, you added the topic title footnote. Finally, you added the browse sequence footnote. If you think that you will have a difficult time remembering these footnote characters, remember that the topic ID comes first, and it is a pound sign (#). Most IDs that we think of are numbers. Even though the topic IDs in your help file are not numeric, remember that IDs are usually numeric. You used the dollar sign ($) for the topic title footnote. Obviously the topic title is, in programming terms, a string. You can use the dollar sign to represent strings in Visual Basic. Finally, you added the plus sign (+) as the footnote for the browse sequence. Just remember that since many programs use the plus and minus keys to navigate through numbers, you can use the plus symbol to navigate through the help file.

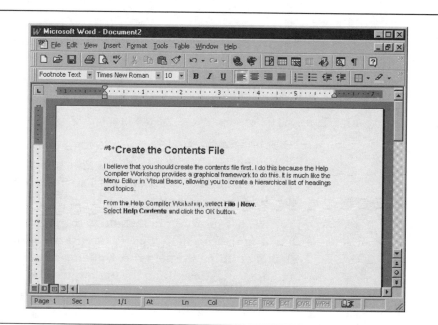

FIGURE 13.4: The first topic text

Here is a summary of how to add the appropriate footnotes to your help topics:

- Footnotes belong at the beginning of the topic, before any text.

- Add the topic ID footnote (#) first. Then type in the topic ID. This is required.

- Add the topic title footnote ($) next. Then type in the topic text. This is optional but recommended.

- Add the browse sequence footnote (+). Then you can enter a browse number or simply the word *auto* to let the help compiler worry about it.

Save your topic file as Skill13.rtf from your word processor. Make sure that the file type is Rich Text Format (RTF).

 WARNING Since you will be typing a lot of information, you should save your work between topics. There's a lot of information to be lost if you don't!

Now that you know the basics of creating a topic with footnotes, let's finish the topic file:

1. Add a hard page break by pressing the Enter key while holding down the Ctrl key at the bottom of the topic text. Before you can add another topic, you need to add a hard page break below the current topic. This makes the word processor keep topics on their own pages.

2. Type the following text as the next topic:

   Add the Headings

   You add the headings by clicking the Add Above and Add Below buttons. When the Edit Contents Tab Entry dialog appears, select the Heading radio button. Then enter the description of the heading.

   You can use headings to categorize the topics within the help file. For instance, this help file will have three headings, one for each step in building the help file. Under each of these headings, we will add the topics describing the operations that complete each step.

3. Create the following footnotes:

#	**IDH_AddHeadings**
$	**Add the Headings**
+	**auto**

4. Type the next topic:

   Add the Topics

   You create a topic for each subject you wish to discuss in the help file. This page you are typing is a topic within the help file.

   To add a topic, click either the Add Below or Add Above button and select the Topic radio button on the Edit Contents Tab Entry dialog box.

   For each topic, you need at least a Topic ID. The Help Compiler Workshop prefers to have Topic IDs prefixed with IDH_. Notice

that this is what we have been doing. This prefix makes it easier to compile the topic file.

In addition, you should give the topic a title. Enter this in the Title field. Don't worry about the other fields for this exercise. They are used when you execute help macros or utilize multiple help files within one contents file.

5. Add these footnotes:

    #   **IDH_AddTopics**

    $ **Add the Topics**

    +   **auto**

6. Type the next topic:

    Write Your Topics

    The next step to creating your help file is to write your help topics. You need a word processor that can save in Rich Text Format (RTF) to do this.

    Start by creating a new document.

    Write each topic on its own page. If you are writing multiple topic files, separate each with a hard page break. In Word, you do this by pressing Ctrl+Enter.

    When you are done, you can add the footnotes that link the topics together.

7. Add these footnotes:

    #   **IDH_WriteTopics**

    $ **Write Your Topics**

    +   **auto**

8. Type the next topic:

    Add the Footnotes

    After the topics have been created, you need to add the footnotes to each page. The only required footnote is the Topic ID. You define the Topic ID by inserting a footnote, and using the pound sign (#) as the footnote character.

    Add the Topic ID footnote

Go to the top of the topic page and click the mouse. The footnotes must be entered at the beginning of the topic. In Word, select Insert ➢ Footnote. Set the Custom Mark field to the pound sign. When you go to write the footnote text, type the Topic ID. This should be prefixed with the string IDH_. This helps the help compiler process the file.

9.   Add the footnotes:

   #   **IDH_AddFootnotes**

   $ **Add the Footnotes**

   +   **auto**

10.   Add the next topic:

   Save the File

   When you are done authoring your topics and defining the footnotes, you need to save the file as an RTF file. Then you can go back to the Help Compiler Workshop and start the project file.

11.   Add the footnotes:

   #   **IDH_SaveRTF**

   $ **Save the File**

   +   **auto**

12.   Add the next topic:

   Create the Project File

   The final element of the help file is the project file. This defines the characteristics of the help file, links to your topic file and contents file, and everything else that is needed to build the help file.

   From the Help Compiler Workshop, select File ➢ New.

   Select Help Contents and click the OK button.

   Type the name of the help file in the Help File field. For this example I used Skill13.Hlp**.**

13.   Add the footnotes:

   #   **IDH_CreateProjectFile**

$ **Create the Project File**

\+   **auto**

14.   Add the next topic:

Set Help File Options

Click the options button to set the project options.

General Tab

Set the Help Title to a description of the help file.

Compression Tab

Select Custom and Hall Compression. Selecting these allows your help file to perform keyword searches.

Files

Select the RTF topic file that you created. Set the contents file field to the name of the contents file you created for this project.

15.   Add the footnotes:

\#   **IDH_SetOptions**

$ **Set Help File Options**

\+   **auto**

16.   Add the next topic:

Add Files to the Project

Once you have set the project options, you add the topic file, graphics, and the contents file to the project.

17.   Add the footnotes:

\#   **IDH_AddFiles**

$ **Add Files to the Project**

\+   **auto**

18.   Add the next topic:

Define the Help Window Appearance

To allow your help window to have navigation buttons, you need to define a custom window style.

Click the Window button. In the Window Properties dialog box, click the Add button. Enter a name for the window style and base it on a standard procedure window.

Next, click the Buttons tab and check the Browse check box. This will allow the help window to display the browse buttons.

Finally, click the OK button to close the dialog box.

19. Add the footnotes:

    #   **IDH_DefineWindow**

    $ **Define the Help Window Appearance**

    +   **auto**

20. Add the next topic:

    Save and Compile Your Help File

    Before you do anything else, you need to save your project and contents files. You can do this by clicking the Save and Test button on the bottom of the project dialog box.

    The Help Compiler will process your topic, contents, and project files. Once they are processed, the results will be displayed in the window. If you have no errors, you can test the help file.

21. Add the footnotes:

    #   **IDH_Compile**

    $ **Save and Compile Your Help File**

    +   **auto**

22. Finally, add the last topic to your help file:

    Test Your Help File

    This is the last and most important step. Test your help file to make sure you can successfully navigate between topics. Check for typos and layout problems. Basically, test it like you would your application.

    When everything works, you can link the help file to your application!

23. Add the footnotes:

    #   **IDH_Test**

$ **Test Your Help File**

+   **auto**

You have just created your first topic file. Remember that this is a very basic topic file, but it shows you what you need to do. If you typed in every topic and footnote section, then this process should be stuck in your memory for quite a long time. After all, the best way to learn is to practice. Let's move on to the final stage of help file development: the project file.

Creating a Help Project File

Before you can link your contents and topic files together, you need to create a help project file:

1. If it is not already open, open the Help Compiler Workshop.

2. Create a new project file by selecting File ➢ New from the menu. Select Help Project and click OK.

3. When the Help Compiler asks you for a project name, type **Skill13** as the project name and click the Save button. You should see something like Figure 13.5.

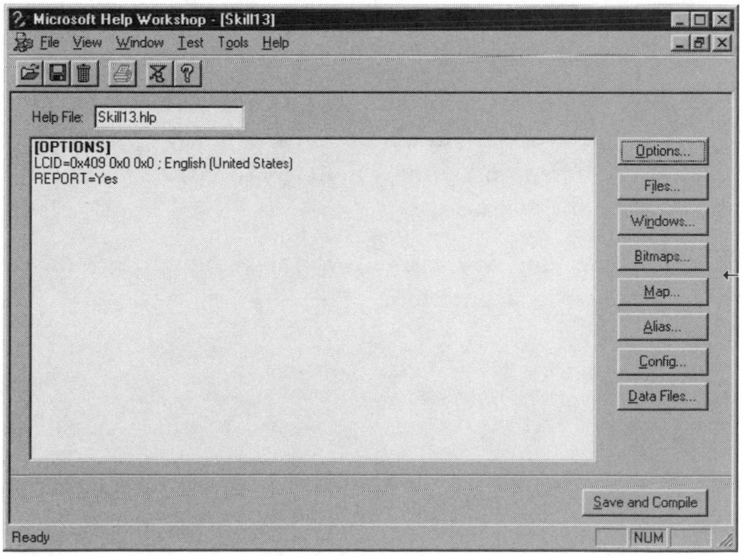

FIGURE 13.5: A new help project file

4. Click the Options button to open the Options dialog box.

5. When the Options dialog box appears, type **Creating Your First Help File** in the Help title field.

6. Click the Compression tab. Select the Custom option and check the box next to Hall Compression.

7. Select the Files tab. In the Help File field, type **Skill13.hlp**.

8. Click the Change button next to the RTF Files field.

9. When the Topic Files dialog box appears, click the Add button. Select `Skill13.rtf`. This adds your topic file to the help project. Click the Open button.

10. If `Skill13.rtf` is listed in the Topic Files list, click the OK button to close the Topic Files dialog box.

11. Click the Browse button next to the Contents field. Select `Skill13.cnt` from the dialog box. This binds the contents file you created to the project file.

12. Click the OK button to close the Options dialog box.

    You will notice there are several tabs in the Options dialog box (see Figure 13.6) that have not been selected. You can learn more about the options on the tabs from the online help for the Help Compiler Workshop.

13. Click the Windows button to bring up the Window Properties dialog box.

14. Before you can see window properties, you must create a window. Type **Main** in the Create a Window Named field. Set the Based on this Standard Window field to Procedure. Click the OK button when the options are set.

After you have created a window, the Window Properties dialog box will appear (see Figure 13.7).

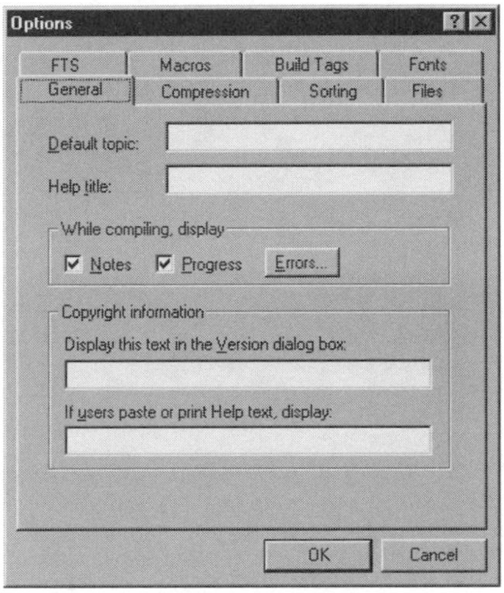

FIGURE 13.6: The Options dialog box

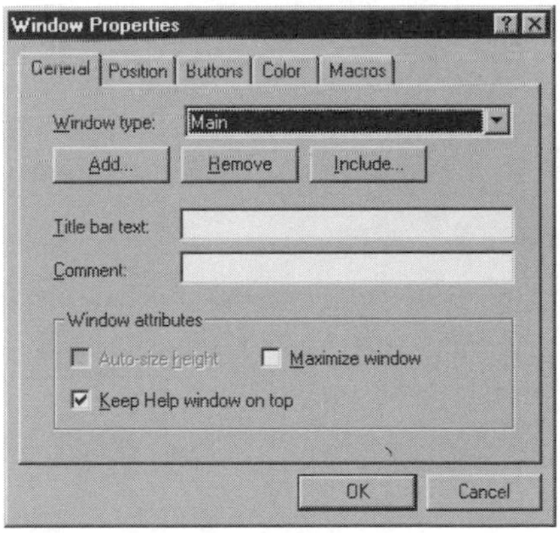

FIGURE 13.7: The Window Properties dialog box

15. Click the Buttons tab and check the Browse option. This adds the browse buttons to the help window. Leave the other options as they are.

16. Click the OK button to close the Window Properties dialog box. Your help project should look similar to Figure 13.8.

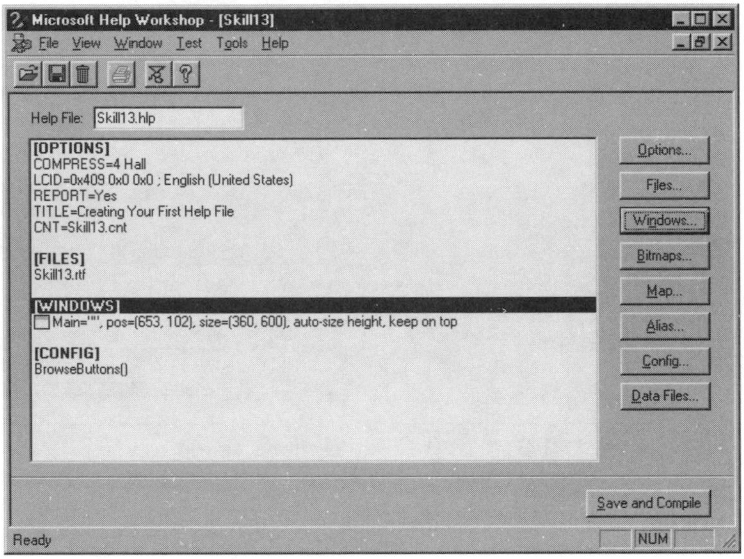

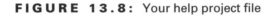

FIGURE 13.8: Your help project file

17. Click the Map button. From this dialog box, you will make your help context-sensitive.

18. For each of the topics below, click the Add button and enter the appropriate topic ID in the Topic ID field and the context ID in the Mapped Numeric Value field:

Topic ID	Context ID
IDH_CreateContentsFile	100
IDH_AddHeadings	200
IDH_AddTopics	300
IDH_WriteTopics	400
IDH_AddFootnotes	500
IDH_SaveRTF	600

IDH_CreateProjectFile	700
IDH_SetOptions	800
IDH_AddFiles	900
IDH_DefineWindow	1000
IDH_Compile	1100
IDH_Test	1200

19. After you have entered the values, click the OK button to close the dialog box.

20. Click the Save and Compile button. The Workshop will minimize while it compiles. If all goes well, the Workshop will restore itself and display the compiler results (see Figure 13.9).

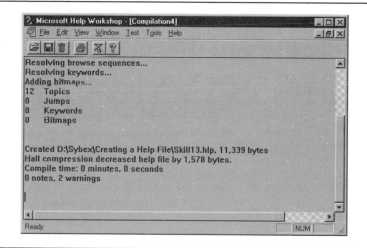

FIGURE 13.9: The compiler results for your project file

After making your complete help file, you'll want to test it right away to make sure it works. To do this, follow these steps:

1. To test the help file, click the Help button (the yellow question mark) on the toolbar.

2. When the View Help File dialog box appears, it should already be defaulted to Skill13.hlp. If it's not, click the Browse button and select Skill13.hlp. When this file is selected, click the View Help button.

3.   When you see the Contents tab of your help file, expand the headings to see how your help file looks. Click the topics to view them.

That's all there is to creating a simple help file. You now have a summarized version of this skill in help file format. You can open this file whenever you want to create a help file in the future. If you are adventurous, you can add updates to the topic file to explain other features of the help system, like jumps and graphics. If I were to explain all of the features and procedures to create a sophisticated help file, I would need to write another book on only that topic. So, I leave the rest up to you.

TIP   Be sure to check out the online help of the Help Compiler Workshop. It includes step-by-step instructions on implementing the other Windows help features.

Linking Your Application to Your Help File

Once you have a .HLP help file, there are a number of ways it can be used with your application. You can set a help file for the whole application, you can set up help files for each form, or you can set up context-sensitive help for forms and controls. To implement context-sensitive help, you must map Context IDs to the Topic IDs in your help project file.

You can set the help file for the whole application by opening the Project Properties dialog box and typing the name of the help file in the Help File field, or you can set the HelpFile property of the App (application) object at run time.

To access the help file from your code, you can use the Windows API or the Common Dialog control. We will use the latter for this example. If you want to learn how to use the Windows API functions for help, read Skill 15, *Learning and Using Object-Oriented Programming (OOP)*, to get familiar with accessing the API, and read the online documentation to learn the parameters and commands you must use. Aside from that, let's hook your help file to a sample application:

1.   Start a new project in Visual Basic. Select Standard EXE as the project type.

2.   Change the Name property of Form1 to **frmMain**. Set its Caption property to **My First Help Application**.

3. Right-click Project1 in the Project Explorer and select **Project1 Properties**.

4. From the Project Properties dialog box, set the Help File field to the help file you created in the previous exercise, then click the OK button.

5. Add a menu to the form. Define its menus and menu items as follows:

    ### File Menu

Caption:	**&File**
Name:	**MnuFile**

    ### File Menu Items

Caption:	**E&xit**
Name:	**MnuFileExit**

    ### Help Menu

Caption:	**&Help**
Name:	**MnuHelp**

    ### Help Menu Items

Caption:	**&Contents Files**
Name:	**MnuHelpContentsFile**
Caption:	**&Topic Files**
Name:	**MnuHelpTopicFiles**
Caption:	**&Project Files**
Name:	**MnuHelpProject**

6. When the menus are defined, click the OK button to close the Menu Editor.

7. Add a Common Dialog control to your project. Set its Name property to **dlgHelp**. This is what you will use to call up your help file.

8. Open the Code window and add an End statement to the mnuFileExit_ Click() procedure.

9. In the Form_Load() event, add the following line of code:

    ```
    dlgHelp.HelpFile = App.HelpFile
    ```

10. Add the following code to the mnuHelpContentsFile_Click() event:

    ```
    Private Sub mnuHelpContentsFile_Click()
        With dlgHelp
    ```

```
            .HelpContext = "100"
            .HelpCommand = cdlHelpContext
            .ShowHelp
        End With
    End Sub
```

11. Add the following code to the `mnuHelpTopicFiles_Click()` event:

```
Private Sub mnuHelpTopicFiles_Click()
    With dlgHelp
        .HelpContext = "400"
        .HelpCommand = cdlHelpContext
        .ShowHelp
    End With
End Sub
```

12. Add the following code to the `mnuHelpProject_Click()` event:

```
Private Sub mnuHelpProject_Click()
    With dlgHelp
        .HelpContext = "700"
        .HelpCommand = cdlHelpContext
        .ShowHelp
    End With
End Sub
```

13. Save the project and run it.

When you click a menu item, it will bring up the appropriate help topic from your help file. This is done because you mapped the topic IDs to context IDs. You told the Common Dialog which context to show by setting the `HelpContext` property to the corresponding context ID within the help file.

If you want to have context-sensitive help that is called up when you press the F1 key, you set the `HelpContextID` property in the Properties window or by code in run mode. Let's show you this in action:

1. Add a text box to frmMain. Set its `Name` property to **txtHelp**. Clear its `Text` property and set its `HelpContextID` property to **1200**.

2. Save and run the program.

3. Click the mouse in the text box to make it the active control. Press the F1 button.

If all goes well, you should see the topic Test Your Help File (see Figure 13.10).

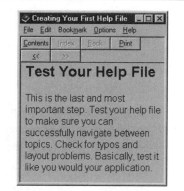

FIGURE 13.10: Your help file

Documentation for an application is just as important as the application itself. Fortunately, Windows provides an online help system that allows you to display your own help files from your application. The trick is writing the help file in the first place. Now you have enough information to start creating help systems for your applications.

Converting Your Help Files to HTML Help

As you know by now, Visual Basic's help system is different that the WinHelp system you just worked with. Visual Basic now uses the HTML Help system to provide online help. The Microsoft Developers Network also utilizes this new help system.

Well, you don't have to be left behind if you are up to giving HTML Help a try. Although it is beyond the scope of this book to go into the nitty-gritty details of HTML, you can use the HTML Help Workshop (shown in Figure 13.11) to convert your WinHelp projects to the new HTML Help system.

As you can see from the figure, the HTML Help Workshop is similar to its predecessor. Without going into the complexities of this new frontier of help systems, you will convert the help file from the previous example to the new HTML Help system.

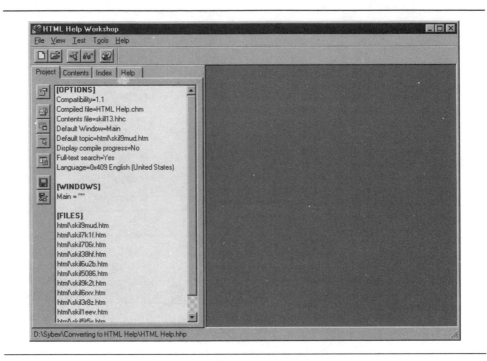

FIGURE 13.11: The new HTML Help Workshop

Before you can use the HTML Help Workshop, you need to install it. The setup program, called `htmlhelp.exe`, is located in the `\HTMLHelp` directory of your Visual Basic CD. If you have not already done so, double-click the file to start the installation process. The installation process is straightforward, so I will not cover it in detail.

After you have installed the HTML Help Workshop on your computer, try completing the following example so you can learn how to convert the help file you created earlier to HTML.

1. Start the HTML Help Workshop.

2. Select File ➢ New from the Help Workshop menu.

3. Select Project from the dialog box and click OK.

4. You will be presented with the New Project Wizard, shown in Figure 13.12. Make sure the Convert WinHelp project option is checked and click the Next button.

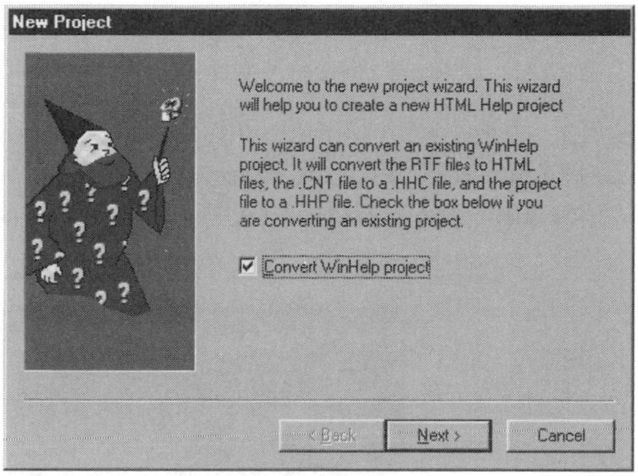

FIGURE 13.12: The New Project Wizard

5. In the next step (Figure 13.13), you will be prompted to enter the source and destination projects for the conversion. In the top field, select the Skill13.hpj help project that you created earlier in this skill. If you don't remember the location where you saved it, you can click the top Browse button and browse for the file.

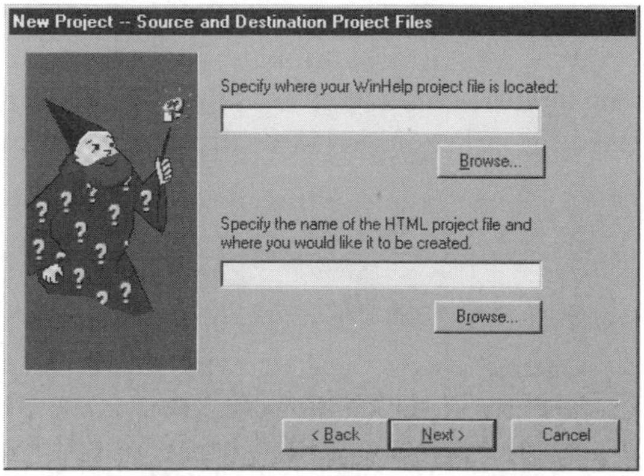

FIGURE 13.13: Choose a source and destination project.

6. After you have selected `Skill13.hpj`, click the Browse button below the lower field to select a directory to store the new HTML help file.

7. After you found a suitable directory, type **HTML Help** in the File Name field and click OK to close the dialog box.

8. After you have selected the source and destination projects, click the Next button to start the conversion.

9. You will be presented with a final screen, like Figure 13.14, that gives you a chance to go back and change options if you need to. When you are ready to start the conversion, click the Finish button.

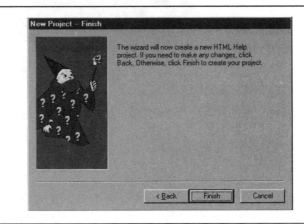

FIGURE 13.14: The Wizard is ready to convert your help file.

The Wizard will not take its time converting your help file. In almost the same instant that it started, your help file has been converted. However, you need to create an index file so the compiler will create the help file with no warnings. The index file is a list of keywords that you can browse to quickly navigate to a topic.

10. Click the Index tab in the Help Workshop. You will be asked if you want to create a new index file, or open an existing one.

11. Select Create a New Index File and click the OK button.

12. When the Save As dialog appears, type **Index** in the Filename field and click Save to create the index file.

13. Click the Project tab to make it active again.

14. Click the Change Project Options button, which is at the top of the leftmost toolbar. This will bring up the Options dialog box shown in Figure 13.15.

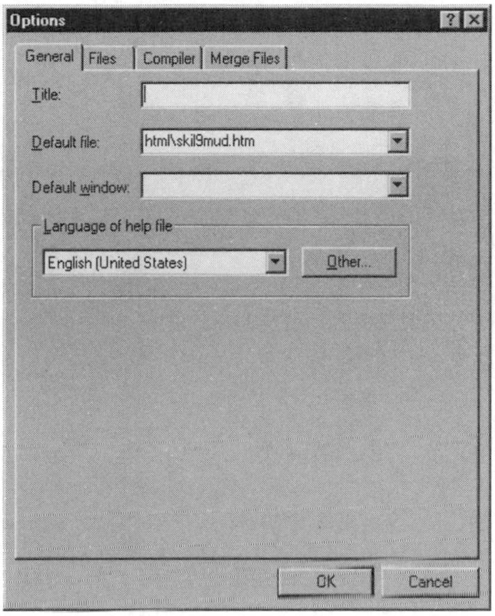

FIGURE 13.15: The Options dialog box

15. When the Options dialog box appears, click the Compiler tab.

16. Check the box next to Compile Full-Text Search Information and click the OK button. This will make the compiler read each topic and add the words to the search index.

17. Now click the Save All Project Files and Compile button, which is the bottom button of the toolbar on the left of the Project tab.

The compiler will process all of the files in the project and build a single compressed HTML file containing your help system. When the compiler is done, you will see the compile log in the right pane of the Help Workshop, like in Figure 13.16.

Now that you have a compiled HTML help file, click the View Compiled File button on the top toolbar. It's the button with the red sunglasses. When you are asked to select a compiled file, your compiled help file will already be selected in the Compiled File field. When you click the View button, you will see your help file (see Figure 13.17).

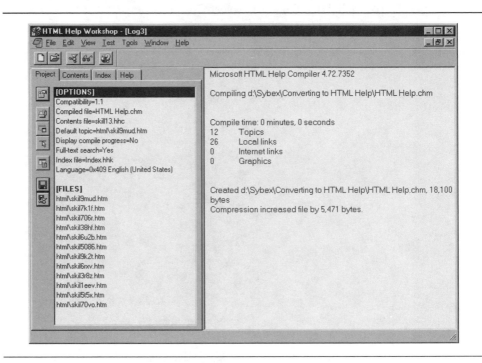

FIGURE 13.16: The compile log

FIGURE 13.17: The converted help file

Although you did not add any keywords into the index file, the compiler scanned your help files and built up a search facility that you can access through the Search tab. You can add keywords to your help files by inserting them on the Index tab and linking the keyword to the appropriate HTML file.

You have just created your first HTML help file. Since it is beyond the scope of this book to get to detailed with regards to HTML help, you should have enough familiarity to start experimenting with HTML help files on your own. Take some time to read the online help. It explains how to create entire HTML help projects from scratch.

As you get more proficient with HTML and Dynamic HTML, you will be able to create sophisticated help systems that can tie your applications to company intranets and even Web sites on the Internet. Once you accomplish that, your technical support options are endless!

TIP   HTML Help requires a subset of Microsoft's Internet Explorer to operate. If you decide to use HTML Help with your application, you should make sure that your users also install Internet Explorer, otherwise the help file will not function properly.

Are You up to Speed?

Now you can...

- ☑ **create help contents files**
- ☑ **create help topic files**
- ☑ **create help project files**
- ☑ **compile your contents, topic, and project files into a help file**
- ☑ **call a help file from your application**
- ☑ **use the HTML Help Workshop to convert WinHelp files to HTML Help files**

Compiling and Distributing Your Application

- Compiling your project
- Using the Make tab
- Setting the Compiler options
- Using the Package and Deployment Wizard
- Distributing your program

When you finish coding your application and writing that perfect help file, your job has just begun. Getting your application to your users is one of the most important aspects of software development. It may not seem like it at first, but your setup program is what gives your users their first impression of your product. If they can install your application smoothly, and their system doesn't crash, then they can fairly evaluate your application. That's great, but what happens if your application won't install? You could spend a great deal of time frantically answering help calls, dodging flaming e-mail, or losing the respect and loyalty of your customers. If they can't install your product, how can they be expected to use it?

Fortunately, this skill covers everything you will need to successfully compile your application and build a setup program that will get your applications where they need to be. Your users will be happy, and so will you.

Compiling Your Project

It's a great feeling when you finish your application. You may have spent hundreds of hours designing, coding, testing, and debugging. Everything appears to be in working order. The first step is to save your work! You should save your work as you go, but make sure you save this latest build. Your next step is to compile your project into an executable (EXE), dynamic link library (DLL), or ActiveX control (OCX). This will allow you or others to use your software without having to buy and install Visual Basic for themselves. For this skill, you will learn how to compile your project by working with the VB Terminal sample application.

When your program is compiled, you'll need to create a setup program to distribute your application and associated files. Fortunately, Visual Basic comes with the Package and Deployment Wizard. This handy utility allows you to build a fully functional setup program by answering a few simple questions. There are also other commercial as well as shareware utilities that allow you to build good setup programs, but for this example we will use Visual Basic's Package and Deployment Wizard.

Let's assume that you just finished your application and you want to compile it and start testing.

1. Open the VB Terminal project. It is saved as `Vbterm.vbp` and can be found in the `\MSDN\98VS\1033\Samples\VB98\MSComm` subdirectory. Then follow these steps:

2. Select File ➢ Make vbterm.exe from the Visual Basic menu.

3. When the Make Project dialog box appears, the File Name field should say `vbterm`. Click the Options button.

You will see a slim version of the Project Properties dialog box. It contains a Make tab and a Compile tab; each is discussed in the following sections.

Using the Make Tab

The Make tab of the Vbterm dialog box allows you to change various options that will affect how your program is built. You can change such options as version numbers, copyright information, and others. The Make tab is broken down into four sections: Version Number, Application, Version Information, and finally, two text boxes labeled Command Line Arguments and Conditional Compilation Arguments (see Figure 14.1). The Vbterm dialog box also includes a Compile tab, which provides you with options to compile your application to P-Code or Native Code. These functions are covered later, in the "Using the Compile Tab" section.

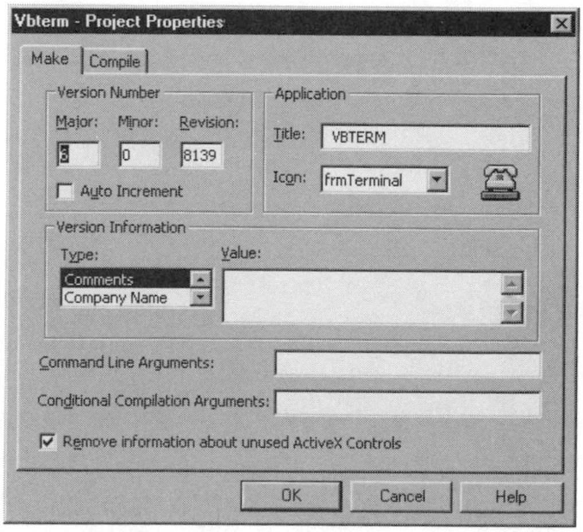

FIGURE 14.1: The Make tab of the Vbterm - Project Properties dialog box

Version Number

The Version Number frame contains three fields and one check box. In this section, you can set the version number of your application. A version number consists of a major version, minor version, and a revision number, otherwise known as a *build number*. When you set the version number for your application, you will usually start at version 1.0.0. This indicates the very first build of the first version. Notice that the Revision field in Figure 14.1 says 8139 by default. I doubt this sample application has had that many separate builds, but that's what the folks in Redmond typed in. By checking the Auto Increment check box at the bottom of the frame, you can have Visual Basic automatically increment the revision number of your application every time you compile it.

Version and revision numbers are important to include in your project. They enable you and your users to distinguish executables between builds. You can view these numbers and other program properties by right-clicking the executable in Windows Explorer, selecting Properties from the pop-up menu, and selecting the Version tab in the Properties dialog box. Revision numbers are especially useful when users call for technical support. If you have distributed several different builds to your users and each has its own set of bugs, you can check their revision number to determine if they have the latest bug-free build.

In addition to checking the Auto Increment box, I recommend you write down a description of program changes for each build. You might even be well served to put these change descriptions in a database and sort them by version and revision numbers. This will help you later on when you need to support your product.

> **TIP** Document the changes your program goes through between builds. You can refer back to this information when you are dealing with trouble calls, or when you want to implement new features. It is especially important to document changes when you are working with more than one developer on the same project.

Application

The Application frame contains two fields: Title and Icon. The Title field contains the name of the application. This will be the same as the name with which you saved the project. The Icon field is a list box that allows you to select a form from the project that has the icon you want to use to represent your application. You can set the application icon in the startup form, which by now you know I name frmMain. Then you set the Icon field to frmMain. When you choose a form containing the desired icon, the icon will be displayed to the right of this field.

Version Information

The Version Information section contains a Type list box and a Value text box. This is a very handy section because from here you can embed all of the legal notices and company information for your program. You can select from a number of options in the Type list and then you can type the text in the Value field. The Type list contains values for comments, company name, file description, legal copyright, legal trademarks, and the product name.

By selecting Comments from the Type list, you can enter any comments about the current version. Maybe you would include a notice that the program is a beta version. You could place any other information here not covered in the other sections. If you want to indicate the name of the company that wrote the application, you can select Company Name in the Type list and type the company name in the Value field. Select File Description to enter any information specific to the compiled file.

COPYRIGHTING YOUR APPLICATION

The Legal Copyright value is probably one of the most important properties of your compiled application. Let me first brief you on copyrights: When you create a work (in other words, a program, artwork, etc.) you have an automatic copyright to it. You can relinquish this copyright by explicitly stating that the work, in this case the application, is in the *public domain*. If you want further copyright benefits, you can register your application in the U.S. Copyright Office. It is beyond the scope of this book to discuss this much further, but if you are planning to sell your programs, you will want to pick up a book on copyrights and trademarks. It will serve you well to include a copyright notice in this property so users will know who owns the title to the product. For the copyright notice to be legal, you need to indicate the application name, the word "Copyright" (spelled out), and the year of first release. If you want to reserve copyright privileges overseas, you should also include the words "All Rights Reserved." For example, you could enter something like:

MyApp Version 1.0.5 Copyright 1998 - Steve Brown
All Rights Reserved

Again, don't just take my word for it; pick up some good literature on the copyright process or even consult a lawyer.

> **TIP** Be sure to include a copyright notice in your application. This will tell your users who owns the legal title to the application.

If your program contains any trademarks, for example a company logo, or any artwork that is known to represent you, your company, or your product, you should include these notices in the Legal Trademarks property.

Type the full name of your application in the Product Name property. For example, Vbterm is not very descriptive, so you could type in **Visual Basic Terminal** in the Value field. This is also a good way to distinguish between two applications of the same name. Maybe you have two applications named `Hello.exe`. The first one is the Hello World application that you created at the beginning of the book. The second application is a greeting program that plays an automated message when you boot up your computer. It is just called Hello. Hopefully, from this example, you can see the importance of spelling out the complete name of an application in this property.

When you re-compile your application, you do not need to continuously type text in these fields. Visual Basic will store them in the project file and use them for each compile. You only need to change the information in these fields when it is necessary to reflect the changes in the program's executable file.

Command Line Arguments

You can enter values in this field to trigger your application to perform special functions. As an example, some programs allow you to specify a filename after the program name, and the program will automatically load the file you specified. Entering a value in this field simulates typing a program name and filename in the Run dialog box from the Start menu. For example:

MyApp.Exe C:\Files\MyDoc.Doc

You can intercept any parameters passed to your applications through the reserved variable `Command$`. Anything typed after the program name will be passed to your application through this variable. You can then parse the information using functions such as `InStr()` and `Mid$()`. For example:

```
Private Sub Form_Load()
    If Command$ <> "" Then
        If InStr(Command$,"/?") > 0 Then
            ShowHelp
        End If
    End If
End Sub
```

The variable `Command$` is an intrinsic part of Visual Basic. It can only be used to retrieve the values passed to an application before it starts. You can check for these parameters by checking the value of `Command$` in the `Load()` event of the startup form or module.

The previous example first checks to see if any parameters were passed to the program. If there weren't any, then the `If...Then` command is bypassed and the program continues normally. If there is a parameter passed to the application, then the code checks to see what parameter was passed.

This sample only checks for the parameter /?, which you may be familiar with if you have ever tried to view online help for some DOS commands. By using multiple `If...Then` statements, you can check for any parameter that your application is designed to accept.

The `Instr()` function checks for the presence of a value in a string. If it finds the value, the `Instr()` returns the first position in the string where the value you're searching for occurs. So if you passed the parameter /? to this application, then `Instr()` would return a value greater than zero. From the code above, you can see that if this return code is greater than zero, then the `If...Then` condition is satisfied, and the program calls the `ShowHelp` procedure.

The Command Line Arguments option allows you to enter a parameter in the field, which will then be passed to your application when you run it. This allows you to test your code without performing a complete build on your application.

Conditional Compilation

You can use conditional compilation to make Visual Basic compile only specific portions of your code. This is commonly used when you are compiling a single application to run on multiple platforms, and when you want to remove debugging-specific code when you perform your final build. Look at this example and you will see what I mean:

```
Private Sub Form_Load()
    Dim platform As String

    #If WIN_NT Then
        platform = "Windows NT"
    #Else
        platform = "WIndows 95/98"
    #End If

    MsgBox platform

End Sub
```

If you wanted to build an executable to run on Windows NT, you could type:

```
WIN_NT=1
```

in the Conditional Compilation Arguments field. If you wanted a separate build for Windows 95 and Windows 98, you would type:

```
WIN_NT=0
```

in the Conditional Compilation Arguments field.

Another method you could use to achieve the same results is to place a #Const directive in the module you want to compile. You could use the command:

```
#Const WIN_NT = 1
```

You may have noticed that each statement is prefixed by a pound sign (#). This symbol is called a pre-processor directive. Commands to the right of each pre-processor directive are evaluated when the application is compiled, not when it is run. Visual Basic supports two sets of directives including the #Const directive, and the #IF…Then…#Else…#End If directives. You use #Const to define a pre-processor constant. Then you use the #If…Then…#Else…#End If directive to evaluate it.

Using the Compile Tab

The Compile tab contains the options available to you to compile your application (see Figure 14.2). You can compile your application using either *P-Code*, otherwise known as pseudo code, or *Native Code*, otherwise known as machine code or machine language.

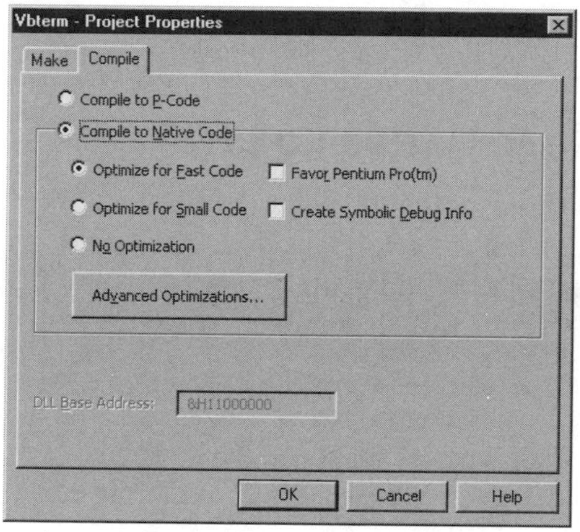

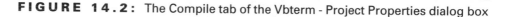

FIGURE 14.2: The Compile tab of the Vbterm - Project Properties dialog box

Compile to P-Code

When you select this option, Visual Basic will compile your application into an interpreted language called *pseudo code*. This is what the previous versions of Visual Basic have always done. Programs compiled in P-Code require a run-time interpreter to run, for example VBRUN300.DLL or VBRUN500.DLL. P-Code allows your program's executable file to be smaller, but it must be shipped with the interpreter DLLs and any other components. In addition, the program runs slower because each command in the application is interpreted to machine code before the processor executes the command. For example, if you run a P-Code application, then the runtime module VBRUN500.DLL will look at the first line P-Code. If it recognizes the code, it then compiles it to machine code on the fly, and then runs it. Any resulting values will then be converted back to P-Code for the next command to be executed. This means each line of code goes through a couple of conversions before it is even run. Then it is converted back. Native Code just runs the code without any conversion.

This does not mean that P-Code is not the best option. It works well for interfaces and other applications that are not processor-intensive. Database programs that depend on database engines to do most of the processing work well when compiled to P-Code. Simple utilities, such as data conversion utilities, will work well when compiled to P-Code. In addition, compiling to P-Code requires less compile time. So if you are in a hurry to try out your application, and speed is not a major concern, you can compile to P-Code.

Compile to Native Code

Selecting this option will make Visual Basic compile your program to machine code. You can compile your application to run without the requirement and overhead of other DLLs. If you select this option to compile your application, you can select from further compiler options listed below:

Optimize for Fast Code If you select Optimize for Fast Code, Visual Basic will attempt to maximize the speed of your application by trading off program size for speed. The result is a possibly bigger executable program size, but the code will run faster on the computer.

Optimize for Small Code Selecting this option will make Visual Basic trade off program execution speed for program size. Select this option if program size is a primary concern. If disk space is more of a concern than execution speed, this option will create a smaller executable file, but it could possibly run a little bit slower. You may want to use this option when compiling components that will be embedded in Web pages, or delivered over the Internet. This will minimize the download time, which is extremely important for users who dial in to the Internet using 28KB modems.

Favor Pentium Pro™ Selecting this option will make Visual Basic generate code for your program that utilizes the advanced features of the Pentium Pro processor. Don't select this option if your program is not specifically designed for the Pentium Pro. Your program can still run, but it will be slower overall.

Create Symbolic Debug Info This option will generate symbolic debug information about your program. If you use this option, your program can be debugged using Visual C++ or other debuggers that use the CodeView style of debugging. Visual Basic will create a .PDB file that can be used by CodeView-compliant debuggers.

No Optimization This option will make Visual Basic compile your program with no optimizations whatsoever. If you select this option, your compile time will be slightly shorter.

Advanced Optimizations Clicking this button will display the Advanced Optimizations dialog box (see Figure 14.3). Do not enable any of these options without checking the Visual Basic online help first. If you are a beginning Visual Basic programmer, you won't need to use any of these options.

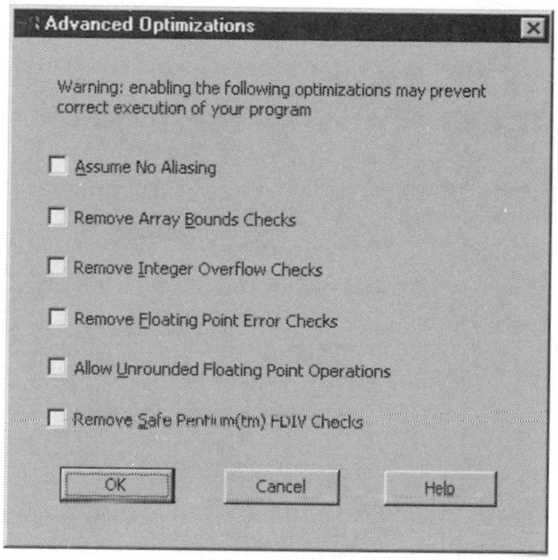

FIGURE 14.3: The Advanced Optimizations tab

Now that you know all of the compiler options available to you, you can tailor your program's executable to suit your preferences. For most of your applications, you will only need to set the options on the Make tab. You probably won't need to set anything on the Compile tab until it comes time to test and debug your application. After you have set all of the preferences for your application, you can click the OK button and finally build it. Now let's take a look at distributing your application with the Package and Deployment Wizard.

> **NOTE** Although Visual Basic can compile to Native Code, you still need to distribute the Visual Basic run-time libraries (VBRUN600.DLL) as well as other components. There are many OLE routines that are contained in these components that allow your application to run properly. The Package and Deployment Wizard utility, discussed next, automatically includes additional required files to your setup program.

Using the Package and Deployment Wizard

The Package and Deployment Wizard is new to Visual Basic 6. It is a far cry better than the Setup Wizard that shipped with previous versions of Visual Basic. It allows you to quickly and easily create setup programs to help distribute and install your application. When you start the Wizard, it will present you with an introduction dialog box (see Figure 14.4). From here you can decide which option you want to choose for your setup, including creating a standard installation to floppy or hard disk, an Internet download setup, or setup script generation.

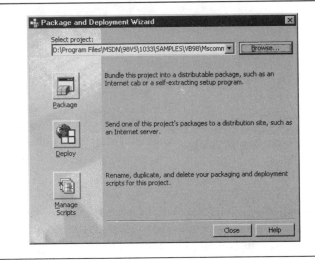

FIGURE 14.4: The Package and Deployment Wizard Introduction dialog box

For this example, you will compile and create a setup program for the VB Terminal application:

1. Close Visual Basic if it is open and start the Package and Deployment Wizard.

2. Click the Browse button to select the VBTerm project you opened in Visual Basic.

3. Select `VBTerm.vbp` from the `\MSDN\98VS\1033\Samples\VB98\MSComm` directory. Click the Open button to select the file.

4. Now that you have a project to deliver, click the Package button to start packaging the VBTerm application.

5. The Wizard will briefly examine the project and then ask you to select the deployment method you would like to use, as shown in Figure 14.5.

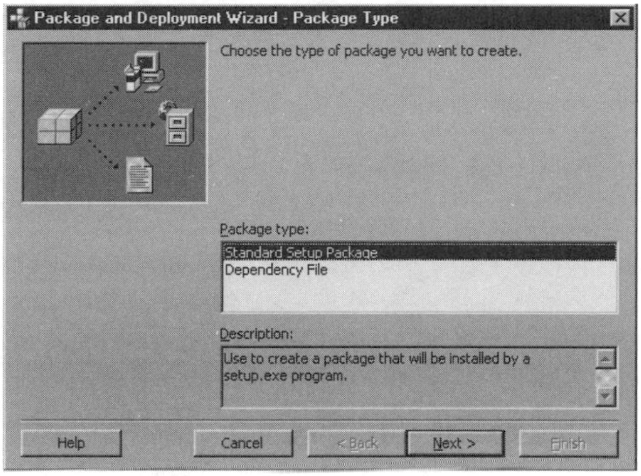

FIGURE 14.5: Selecting a package type

6. Click Standard Setup Package in the Package Type list.

NOTE If you wanted to see a list of components required for a successful installation, you could select Dependency File.

7. After you have selected the distribution method, click the Next button.

8. As you can see in Figure 14.6, the Wizard will ask you to specify a directory to store the setup program. The default is the project directory, but I don't recommend using it. Instead, create a Setup subdirectory under the project, or choose another directory that you prefer. After you have chosen a directory, click the Next button to continue.

The next screen (shown in Figure 14.7) allows you to see what files the Wizard has determined need to be distributed with your application. You can add additional files, such as databases, help files, and readme files here by clicking the Add button.

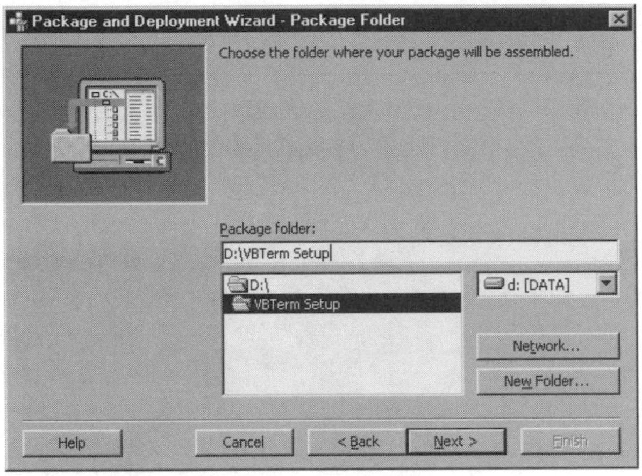

FIGURE 14.6: Choosing a setup directory

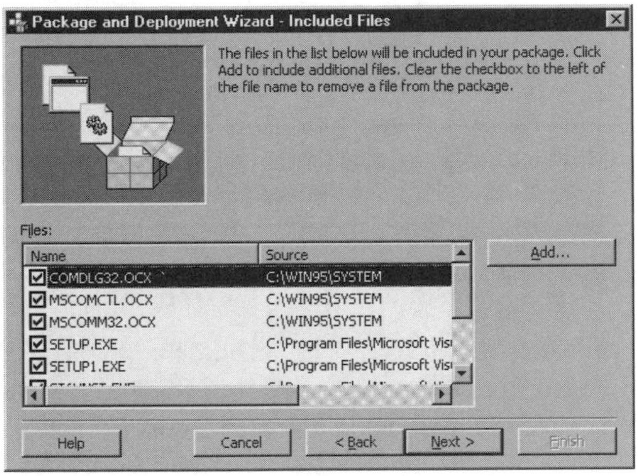

FIGURE 14.7: Included Files dialog box

9. Since you do not need any additional files, click the Next button to continue.

10. On the Cab Options dialog box, shown in Figure 14.8, you can choose between using a single or multiple Cabinet (.Cab) files. Leave the default option (Single cab) selected.

> **TIP**
>
> If you wanted to distribute your application on floppy disks, you would select Multiple cabs and then select a cab size that would fit on each floppy. If you wanted to ship your application on high-density floppy disks, you would select 1.44MB from the list.

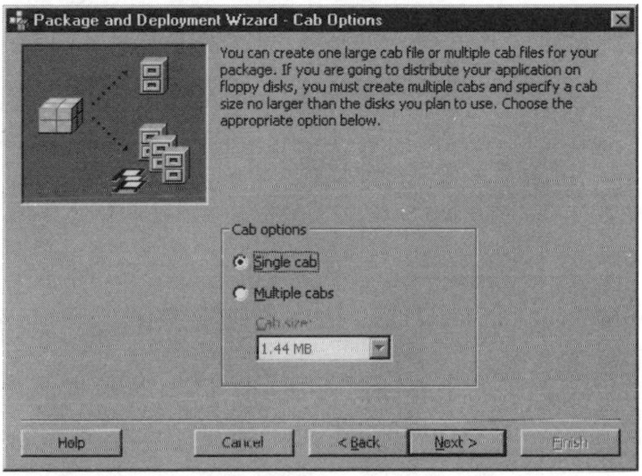

FIGURE 14.8: Selecting the Cabinet file type

11. Click the Next button. You can change the name displayed on your setup program by changing the value in the Installation title field on the Installation Title dialog box shown in Figure 14.9.

12. Type **Visual Basic Terminal** in the Installation title field and click the Next button to continue.

Figure 14.10 shows the long-awaited addition to the old Setup Wizard. The Package and Deployment Wizard allows you to define where you want the setup program to place the application's icons on the Start menu.

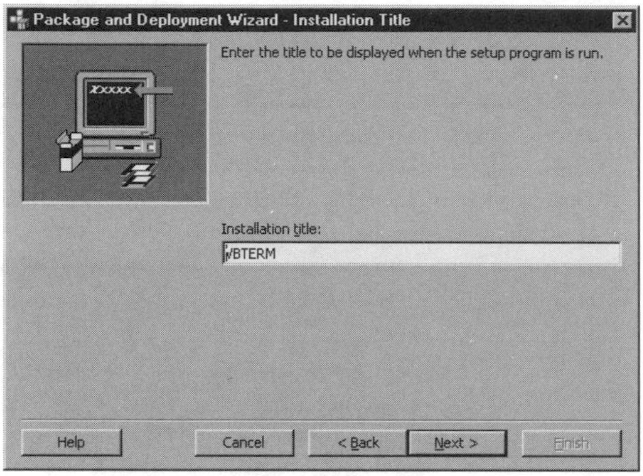

FIGURE 14.9: Changing the Installation title

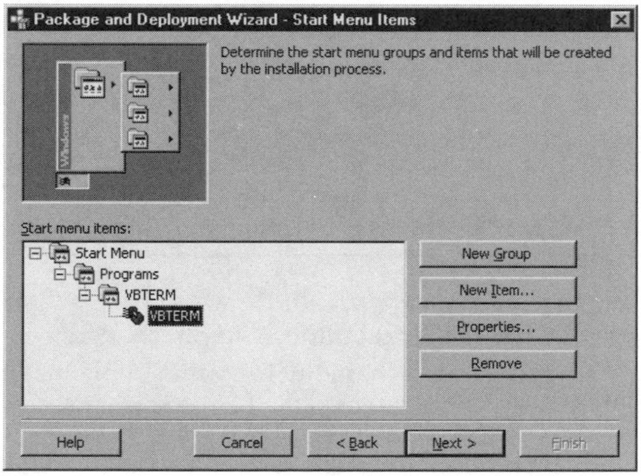

FIGURE 14.10: The Start Menu Items dialog box

13. Click the VBTERM program group and then click the Properties button. When the Start Menu Group Properties dialog box appears (Figure 14.11), type **Visual Basic Terminal** in the Name field. Click the OK button to commit the change.

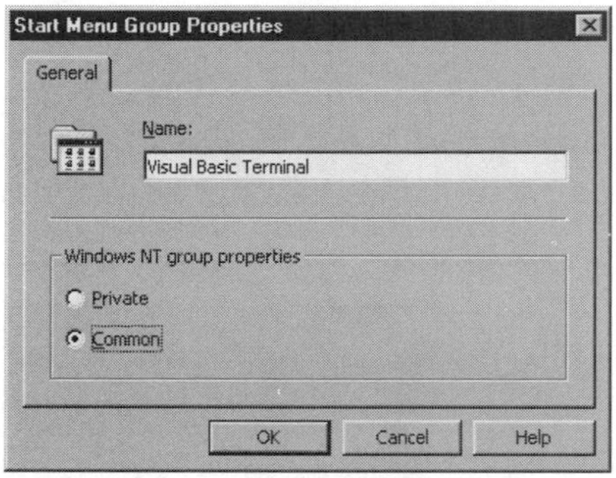

FIGURE 14.11: Changing the name of the application group

> **TIP**
>
> You will notice a Windows NT group properties frame on this dialog. By selecting between these options, you can tell the Wizard to create Program groups that are either private to the user installing the application, or common to all users using the Windows NT system.

14. Now click the VBTERM application icon and click the Properties button. When the Start Menu Item Properties dialog box appears (see Figure 14.12), type **Visual Basic Terminal** in the Name field to change the label of the application icon. When you're done, click the OK button to commit the change.

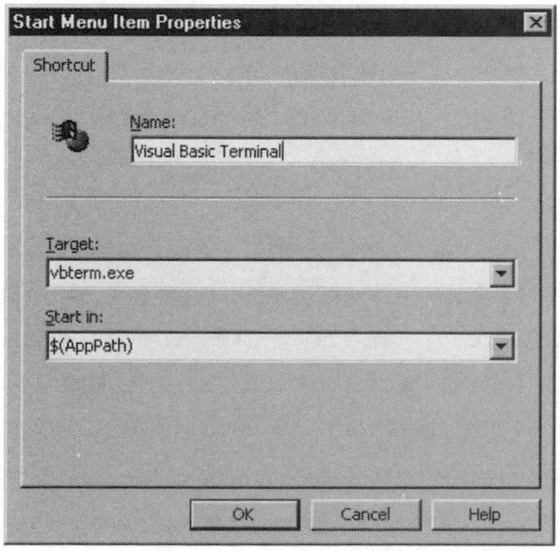

FIGURE 14.12: The Start Menu Item Properties dialog box

15.   Now that you've given the program group and icon more user-friendly names, click the Next button to go on to the next step.

Figure 14.13 shows the Install Locations dialog box. From here you can change the source or destination locations of the files in your setup program. For this example, none of these settings need to be changed.

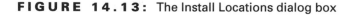

Package and Deployment Wizard - Install Locations

You can modify the install location for each of the files listed below by changing the macro assigned to the file in the table. If desired, you can add subfolder information to the end of a macro, as in $(ProgramFiles)\MySubFolder.

Choose the file you want to modify, then change the information in the Install Location column.

Files:

Name	Source	Install Locatic
COMDLG32.OCX	C:\WIN95\SYSTEM	$(WinSysPatl
MSCOMCTL.OCX	C:\WIN95\SYSTEM	$(WinSysPatl
MSCOMM32.OCX	C:\WIN95\SYSTEM	$(WinSysPatl
vbterm.exe	D:\Program Files\MSDN\98VS\1033\SAMPLES\VB98\Mscomm	$(AppPath)

Help   Cancel   < Back   Next >   Finish

FIGURE 14.13: The Install Locations dialog box

16.   Click the Next button to continue.

The Package and Deployment Wizard allows you to install components as shared components on the target computer (see Figure 14.14). This option is useful when you want to deploy ActiveX components that offer objects that can or will be used by other applications besides yours.

17.   You don't need to share this application, so click the Next button to continue.

Finally, you're at the last step in the Wizard! From the dialog box shown in Figure 14.15, you can specify the name of the setup script that will record all of the options you just configured. This script is important because the Package and Deployment Wizard will look for it the next time you want to build a setup program. Then you won't have to change every setting again. You only need to alter those that require modification!

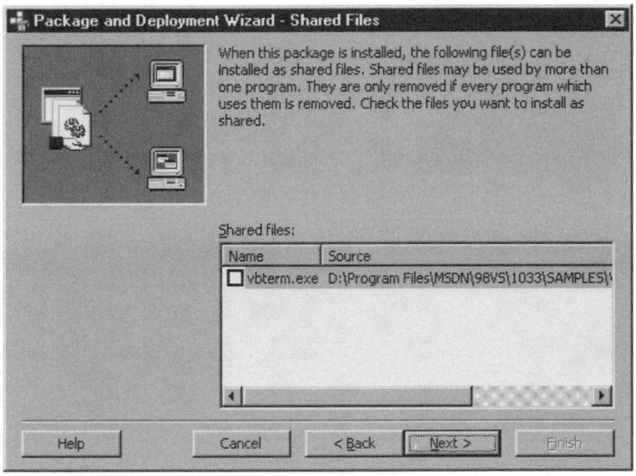

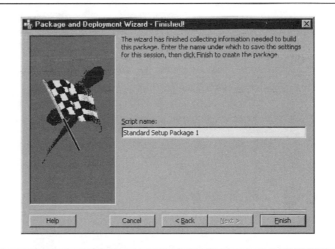

FIGURE 14.14: Selecting files to be installed as shared components

FIGURE 14.15: Saving the setup script

18.   Type **VBTerm Setup Script** in the Script Name field and click the Finish button.

After you click Finish, the Wizard will work its magic and combine all of the components into a nice self-contained package that you can distribute to your users. When all is complete, the Wizard will show you a packaging report (see Figure 14.16) that describes what the Wizard did, and tips for modifying the setup application. You can choose to save the report, or simply close the dialog box when you're done reading it.

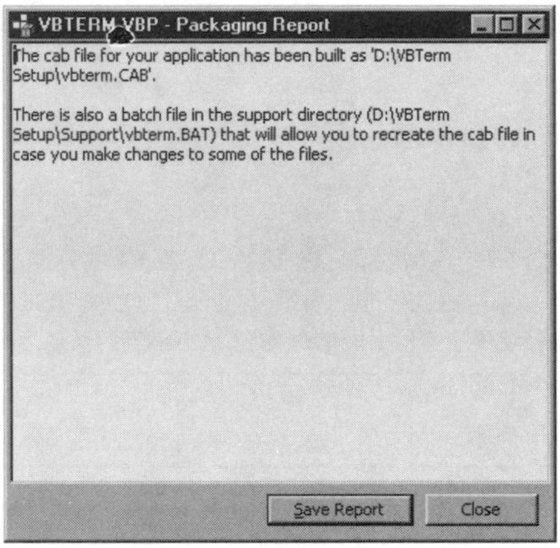

FIGURE 14.16: The packaging report

After everything is complete, the Wizard returns to the main dialog box, where you can build additional setup programs if you need to.

19. Click the Close button to quit the Package and Deployment Wizard.

Scanning for Viruses

Whenever you prepare to distribute your applications to others, you should scan your setup disks for viruses. This is an important warning and should not be taken lightly. Nobody wants to get infected setup disks. Remember that your application is the source of many duplicates. If your setup program, or the application itself, is infected, that virus will propagate to your users. Even worse, if your users give their friends or coworkers a copy of the setup program, then the virus will propagate even further!

After you have created a setup program and scanned it for viruses, you should test the installation on another computer that does not have Visual Basic 6 installed on it. If there are any glitches in the setup routine, you can go back and fix them. Make absolutely sure that everything works before you do a widespread distribution. It will save you a lot of headaches from trouble calls.

Although there are other setup programs available, the Package and Deployment Wizard is adequate for simple installations, and you can't beat the price. The best way to become proficient in the Package and Deployment Wizard, as with anything else, is to practice.

> **WARNING** Always scan your application and any dependent components before you embed them in a setup program. Then scan the setup program after it has been built. Clean, safe setup programs will definitely spare your reputation from unwanted criticism and mistrust!

Distributing Your Program

Once you have finished your setup program, you have a variety of methods to distribute your application. If the program is to be used throughout your company and you have a local area network, you can use the Package and Deployment Wizard to copy the disk images to a central file server that everybody has access to. Then each user can run the setup program from the server to install the program on their hard disks.

Another method is to distribute the application over the Internet. The Package and Deployment Wizard can do this as well. Unfortunately, not everybody has access to the Internet, or even to a Web site or FTP site where they can distribute their applications. As a result, I won't show you how to do it. But if you do have access to a Web server or FTP server, you should practice creating Internet setups on your own.

Finally, you can copy the individual disk images to floppy disks. This is still the traditional method, and you should do it for each setup program you create. Then you can archive these master disk sets in case you need them in the future. Again, be sure to scan them for viruses before you archive them.

Are You up to Speed?

Now you can...

- ☑ set compiler options for your applications
- ☑ understand the difference between P-Code and Native Code
- ☑ compile your application using P-Code or Native Code
- ☑ use built-in version and build numbers
- ☑ add copyright and trademark notices to your compiled files
- ☑ understand the various methods of software distribution
- ☑ use the Package and Deployment Wizard to distribute your applications
- ☑ understand why it is important to scan your media for viruses

Learning and Using Object-Oriented Programming (OOP)

- Defining OOP
- Why should you use OOP?
- Learning about inheritance, encapsulation, and polymorphism
- Writing reusable code
- Creating a Human Resources class
- Using the Human Resources class
- Using the Object Browser

Object-oriented programming, or OOP, is a programming technique that is gaining in popularity. Covering what was once the domain of C++ and SmallTalk, OOP has extended its reach to Visual Basic as well. This skill will cover the basics of OOP and how you can apply its fundamental concepts to your Visual Basic applications. You will soon understand why it is important for you to become familiar with using OOP.

Defining OOP

Object-oriented programming is a method of analyzing, designing, and writing applications using *objects*. So what is an object, you ask? An object is a piece of code, commonly referred to as a *class*, that contains properties and methods. Objects can mimic business rules, actions, or even physical objects.

People think of concepts in terms of objects. You think of baseball games as consisting of bats, balls, gloves, and players. You can think of your home entertainment center as a TV, VCR, and stereo. Using OOP, you can think of modeling your applications around objects, allowing your application to mimic tangible, real-world things. But that's not where OOP stops. You can use it to actually program using the same real-life metaphor you used to design the application!

OOP simplifies program development by encapsulating properties and methods within a simple security model. The security model of an object is defined by the keywords `Private`, `Public`, and `Friend`. If you want an application to be able to access your object, the object must be accessed through a `Public` property or method. Private properties and methods are used internally by the object itself. These object components cannot be seen or used by other procedures.

The most fundamental object in Visual Basic is the form object. Without it, your application would be hard pressed to be *visual*. The form has many properties, including `Appearance`, `BorderStyle`, `Caption`, `Name`, and `WindowState`. All of these properties are public and can be accessed by code that you write. The form also has many methods, including `Load`, `Unload`, `Show`, and `Hide`.

When you add a new form to your project, you are creating a "child" of the form class. It has the identical properties and methods as its parent form. However, as you change the properties and methods, it becomes its own form. This child form may perform many tasks similar to its parent, or it may not. That depends on how you program the form. You can add as many forms as your program can handle, and you can customize each of them differently. In essence, each form develops its own personality.

Why Should You Use OOP?

Why would a programmer want to use OOP to develop a project? Simply put, the programmer can compartmentalize the functionality of a program into discrete objects. This will help make the program easier to design and develop. When you optimize your objects, you minimize the risk of one piece of code interfering with another piece of code. Well-designed objects will mimic real-world situations. This design will be the same from the real-world situation, to the application design process, to the actual code you write.

Let's consider a large company with many departments. This company—we'll call it XYZ Corporation—will have an Administration department, a Human Resources department, an Information Technology department, and an Accounting department.

The Administration department is solely responsible to ensure that the other departments work together to produce the desired results. The employees in Administration are computer literate, but they are not computer-savvy enough to develop the company intranet. The administrators basically interact with the managers of different departments, but they do not directly deal with the rank-and-file employees within XYZ Corporation.

Human Resources (HR) is responsible for hiring, firing, and evaluating personnel within the company. HR manages several thousand personnel files that are considered confidential to other departments. Generally, people from other departments would not have free reign on the personnel files. A department must go through the proper channels to get the information required. Perhaps a manager will need to review an employee's file to determine eligibility for a promotion.

The Information Technology (IT) department makes sure all of the computer systems throughout the company function 100 percent of the time. The IT employees provide IT services to every other department within XYZ Corporation, as well as providing IT services that they need to do their job effectively.

Finally, the Accounting department handles all of the billing and invoicing for the company, maintains the inventory records, and balances the assets and liabilities. Some of the information that flows through Accounting deals with the financial situation of the company. This information is also highly confidential. If it got into the wrong hands, competitors could use it to gain an upper hand in the same market as XYZ Corporation.

Obviously, there are procedures to be followed for the departments to work together. If one department was to get hold of information it had no business seeing, it could cause turmoil within the company. If this turmoil got out of hand, it could possibly bring down XYZ Corporation as a whole.

As a result, XYZ Corporation has established policies dealing with who can get what information and for what reasons. Only managers are allowed to view personnel documents. In addition, they can only view documents of employees who work under them. They are not allowed to access files of personnel they have no business dealing with. To be allowed this level of access could possibly expose a person to undue scrutiny or treatment. This is why it is necessary to have these controls in place.

OOP works in much the same way by providing controls that determine what code is used by other pieces of code. Objects are designed to do their own thing and to interact with other objects only when necessary.

While OOP is a different approach to programming, it has definite utility to programmers. OOP allows you to apply a single representation of a piece of code from program analysis, to design, and to the actual program code. An object in the real world can be represented almost exactly the same way in code using OOP.

If your objects are designed well, your code becomes reusable. For instance, if you create an object that processes data according to a specific method that your company uses, this object can be reused in another application, or even a new version, and still provide the same results.

OOP requires a new method of thinking to be effective. You must learn to think of your programs as a collection of objects, and each component is an object itself. Fortunately, visual programming gives you a head start to this method of thinking. Just remember that you *can* understand OOP, and you have actually used objects before. If you have read this book up to this point then you are experienced at using objects. Now it is time to learn to design and create your own.

TIP   Learn to think of your programs as objects. If you study the way objects interact with each other, you will start understanding a more efficient way to engineer your applications.

Characteristics of an Object

An object has characteristics that make it a discrete entity in the programming world. An object consists of properties, methods, and events, just like other Visual Basic elements. However, objects are distinguished from procedures because OOP consists of three specific characteristics: inheritance, encapsulation, and polymorphism.

Visual Basic employs inheritance and encapsulation, but not polymorphism. So technically, Visual Basic is not an object-oriented language, but it still presents a good environment to learn the basics of OOP. Let's take a closer look at the internals of an object.

The Properties of an Object

Properties, as mentioned in Skill 1, describe an object. Every object you use or create will have a *class name* to distinguish it from other objects. Let's use properties to describe the Human Resources department mentioned earlier in this skill. First, you must be a manager in a department to access a personnel file. You can describe this with the following code:

```
Public IsManager as Boolean
```

In addition, a manager can only access personnel files of people within his or her department. Therefore, you need to define a property to describe the department:

```
Public Department as String
```

You also need to a way to tell the HR clerk who we want information on. We can do this by creating an `EmployeeID` property:

```
Public EmployeeID as Long
```

Figure 15.1 shows you an example of the HR class. Notice that the name and department lines are represented by their equivalent properties in the class. Properties alone will not make a good object. They need to be used by methods within the same object.

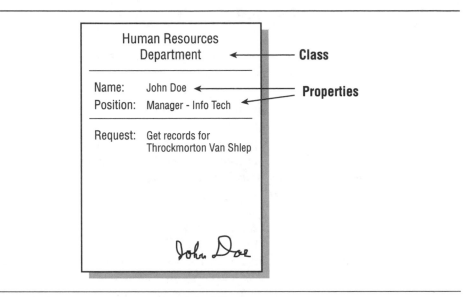

FIGURE 15.1: Properties of the HR class

The Methods of an Object

Methods are the actions that an object can perform. For example, a Window object can show itself, hide itself, and even resize itself. So what can the HR department do? A simple function is to retrieve a personnel file, as shown in Figure 15.2. However, before the clerk, our HR class, can retrieve a personnel file, the clerk must make sure the requester is a manager in the correct department. You can create the method using the following code:

```
Public Function GetFile() as String
    If IsManager and Department = "Administration" Then
        GetFile = "John Doe"
    Else
        GetFile=""
    End If
End Function
```

Within this method, you first check to see if it is even appropriate to give the personnel file to the requester. In this example, the requester must be a manager from Administration. Shop workers and propeller-heads are not allowed to gain access to personnel files.

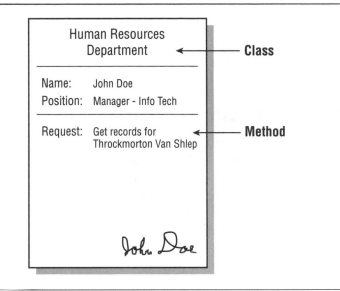

FIGURE 15.2: Methods of the HR class

The Inheritance Characteristic

Inheritance is the ability of an object to assume the same characteristics of its parent class. For example, when you create a new form object, it inherits the properties and methods of its parent class. It has a Name property, a WindowState property, and a BorderStyle property. In addition, it has the Load, Unload, and Hide methods.

In Visual Basic, you instantiate a new object by dimensioning an object of a particular class and then using the New keyword to create a new object. The new object will inherit the properties and methods of its parent.

If you look back at the dialogs class you created in Skill 10, you will see the methods contained in the clsDialogs object: YNBox, ErrMsg, and LoginBox. The sample application also showed you how to create a new dialog box.

First, you used Dim to allocate space for the object:

```
Dim dlg As clsDialog
```

Then you used the New keyword to create the object:

```
Set dlg = New clsDialog
```

The new object, `dlg`, has three members: `YNBox`, `ErrMsg`, and `LoginBox`. These are the same methods that were created in the original `clsDialogs` class.

Applying this same principle to your HR class, using the `New` keyword in Visual Basic is the equivalent of tearing off a form to fill out a request for the Human Resources Department.

The Encapsulation Characteristic

Encapsulation is a mechanism that hides data and methods from the programmer. It is used to shield the programmer from the complexities of the object. This is one of the major strengths of OOP.

Encapsulation is what prevents unauthorized employees from viewing personnel files. Each department encapsulates its business and only reveals it to the appropriate personnel under the appropriate conditions. Objects work the same way.

The Human Resources department encapsulates its personnel files by keeping them locked in a filing cabinet. The only way you can get access to them is to fill out the request form. In Visual Basic, encapsulation is performed using the `Private` keyword. You may have noticed that most procedures in code modules are prefixed with the word `Private`; this prevents these methods from being accessed by procedures in other forms and code modules. If you want to expose a particular procedure, prefix the `Sub` or `Function` statement with the keyword `Public` as in:

```
Public Function Format_Disk(Drive as String)
```

> **NOTE**   When creating an object, be sure to expose only the essential properties. Encapsulate everything that will not be manipulated by the programmer. This will help ensure that no bugs can be introduced into your object by another programmer.

The Polymorphism Characteristic

Polymorphism is the ability of an object to assume many forms. You know that objects can be derived from other objects. The new object inherits the methods and properties from the other. Using polymorphism you can add, modify, or even remove functionality from the derived object.

Suppose the IT department wanted to maintain its own Human Resources section. This section would follow many of the same rules as the HR department but would incorporate special policies used only in IT. For instance, HR likes to keep their files on paper, whereas Information Technology likes to maintain its personnel information on a computer. Perhaps the IT Department would give special awards to the programmers who meet deadlines on time. Maybe IT would informally handle disciplinary actions internally so they would not have to go to the company-wide HR department.

IT could create its own personnel request form based on the form used by HR. In OOP, this would be done by creating an instance of the HR class and modifying it to suit the needs of IT. Fortunately, the only difference is that IT stores files of only its employees, and on computers (see Figure 15.3). As a result, both IT and HR classes would have the same properties and methods, but if you asked HR to get a file, they would go pull it from their filing cabinet. If you asked for the same information from IT, someone would pull the information off a computer. Polymorphism is the vehicle by which this is achieved in OOP. In addition, when asked, a staff member in either department would automatically know which form to get when asked by a supervisor.

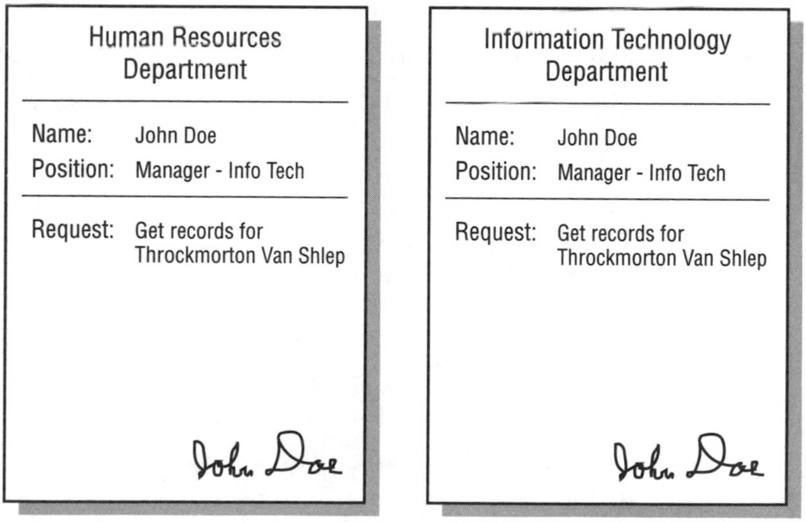

Human Resources Department	Information Technology Department
Name: John Doe	Name: John Doe
Position: Manager - Info Tech	Position: Manager - Info Tech
Request: Get records for Throckmorton Van Shlep	Request: Get records for Throckmorton Van Shlep
John Doe	*John Doe*

FIGURE 15.3: Polymorphism

Writing Reusable Code

Perhaps the biggest benefit of OOP is that you can write reusable code. Think of how you started writing in Visual Basic. Immediately you started working with objects, and you probably didn't even know it—which is exactly the point. You never touched the code to actually create a command button or a form. Visual Basic supplied you with objects and exposed only those properties and events you needed to make your application work. Visual Basic prevented you from dealing with the intricacies that lie deep within the bowels of the object. As a result you were spared from having to create your own command button from scratch!

Creating a Human Resources Class

To give you a taste of object design and development, let's create a more sophisticated version of the Human Resources class.

1. Start a new project and select Standard EXE as the project type.

2. Add a class module by right-clicking the Project Explorer and selecting Add ➢ Class Module from the pop-up menu.

3. In the Properties window, set the Name property to **clsHR**.

4. In the (General)(Declarations) section of the code window, add the following properties:

```
Option Explicit

Public Manager As Boolean
Public Dept As Integer
Public EmpID As Integer
Public EmpName As String
Public EmpDept As Integer
Public EmpPerformance As String
Public Reason As String
```

5. You want to be able to request personnel files, so add a public method to do this:

```
Public Function GetRecord() As Boolean
    If Manager = True Then
        If Dept = GetDept() Then
            EmpName = GetEmpName()
            EmpPerformance = GetPerfEval()
```

```
            Reason = ""
            GetRecord = True
        Else
            Reason = "You cannot access " _
& "files from another department."
            GetRecord = False
        End If
    Else
        Reason = "You must be a manager to " _
& "access personnel files."
        GetRecord = False
    End If
End Function
```

6. You must add a method to verify the department of the employee:

```
Private Function GetDept() As Integer
    Select Case EmpID
        Case Is = 1
            GetDept = 1
        Case Is = 2
            GetDept = 1
        Case Is = 3
            GetDept = 2
        Case Else
            GetDept = 0
    End Select
End Function
```

7. Add a method to retrieve the employee name:

```
Private Function GetEmpName() As String
    Select Case EmpID
        Case Is = 1
            GetEmpName = "John Doe"
        Case Is = 2
            GetEmpName = "Jane Doe"
        Case Is = 3
            GetEmpName = "Throckmorton Van Shlep"
        Case Else
            GetEmpName = ""
    End Select
End Function
```

NOTE   This is a rudimentary example of how you can use a class to restrict and permit the retrieval of data. You will probably want to access a database and compare the values in the fields rather than hard-coding data in the class itself.

Skill 15

8. Now you need to add a method to retrieve the performance evaluation.

```
Private Function GetPerfEval() As String
    Select Case EmpID
    Case Is = 1
            GetPerfEval = "I've seen better!"
        Case Is = 2
            GetPerfEval = "Works well with others."
        Case Is = 3
            GetPerfEval = "Satisfactory."
        Case Else
            GetPerfEval = "Unknown."
    End Select
End Function
```

9. Finally, you need to make sure the properties of this class are initialized. Add the code:

```
Private Sub Class_Initialize()
    Manager = False
    Dept = 1
    EmpID = 0
    EmpName = ""
    EmpDept = 0
    EmpPerformance = ""
    Reason = ""
End Sub
```

That is all that is required to create the HR class. You created seven properties: `Manager`, `Dept`, `EmpID`, `EmpName`, `EmpDept`, `EmpPerformance`, and `Reason`. `Manager` is a boolean value that determines if the requester is a manager. `Dept` is set to the department that the requester belongs to. You set the `EmpID` property to the employee ID of the employee whose file you want to retrieve. If the file is retrieved, `EmpName` gets set to the name of the employee. `EmpDept` is the department that the employee belongs to. `EmpPerformance` gets set to the performance of the employee requested. Finally, an error message and a reason are returned via the `Reason` property if the request fails.

In addition to the properties, you created four methods for the HR class. Notice that only the `GetRecord` method is public. We don't want anyone to access personnel files without going through the proper channels. The class object now has all of the functionality to be used by an application. Let's create the Human Resources interface.

Using the Human Resources Class

Now that you know how to build an object using OOP, try this example to use it.

1. Make Form1 the active form. Set the its `Name` property to **frmHR**. Set its `Caption` property to **Human Resources Dept.**

2. Add three labels and set their properties:

Name:	**lblDept**
Text:	**Department**
Name:	**lblManager**
Text:	**Are you a manager?**
Name:	**lblEmpID**
Text:	**Employee ID**

3. Add combo box and place it next to `lblDept`. Set its caption properties as follows:

Name:	**cboDept**
Style:	**2 - Dropdown List**

4. Add two option buttons and set their caption properties:

Name:	**optYes**
Caption:	**&Yes**
Value:	**True**
Name:	**optNo**
Caption:	**&No**

5. Now you need to provide a way to enter the employee ID. Add a text box control and set its caption properties.

Name:	**txtEmpID**
Text:	-

6. Finally, add the following command button:

Name:	**cmdGetPE**
Caption:	**Get Performance &Evaluation**

Arrange the controls so your dialog box looks like Figure 15.4.

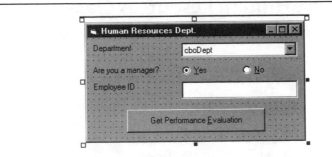

FIGURE 15.4: The Human Resources Dept. dialog box

7. Open the Code window for the form and place the following code in the (General)(Declarations) section:

```
Option Explicit

Private hr As clsHR
```

8. Add the following code to the Form_Load() event:

```
Private Sub Form_Load()
    'Instantiate HR Object
    Set hr = New clsHR

    'Add Departments to Combo Box
    cboDept.AddItem "1"
    cboDept.AddItem "2"
End Sub
```

Let's pause for a moment to examine the code in step 8. The New command is used to create a new instance of the clsHR class. In this single command, Visual Basic creates a new object of type clsHR, your Human Resources class. You must create a new instance of an object before you can start using it.

9. Proceed to the Form_Unload() event and attach the following code:

```
Private Sub Form_Unload(Cancel As Integer)
    Set hr = Nothing
End Sub
```

NOTE   Whenever you create an object, you must destroy it when you are done. You can do this by setting the object equal to Nothing, as you did in step 9. Forgetting to do so will leave the object in memory.

10. Add the code for the cmdGetPE button:

```
Private Sub cmdGetPE_Click()
    Dim rc As Boolean
    Dim msg As String

    hr.Dept = Val(cboDept.Text)
    hr.Manager = optYes.Value
    hr.EmpID = Val(txtEmpID.Text)

    If hr.GetRecord = True Then
        msg = "Employee ID: " & _
                Trim$(Str$(hr.EmpID)) & vbCrLf
        msg = msg & "Employee Name: " & _
                hr.EmpName & vbCrLf
        msg = msg & "Evaluation: " & _
        hr.EmpPerformance

        MsgBox msg
    Else
        msg = "I could not retrieve that " & _
                "record!" & vbCrLf
        msg = msg & hr.Reason

        MsgBox msg
    End If
End Sub
```

Save your project and give it a test run. You can select an employee number between one and three. If you want to see how the company's employees are doing, make sure you say you are a manager as well. Play with the parameters and check the results. You should see a dialog box that either says you have been denied access, or you will see the employee name and performance evaluation (see Figure 15.5).

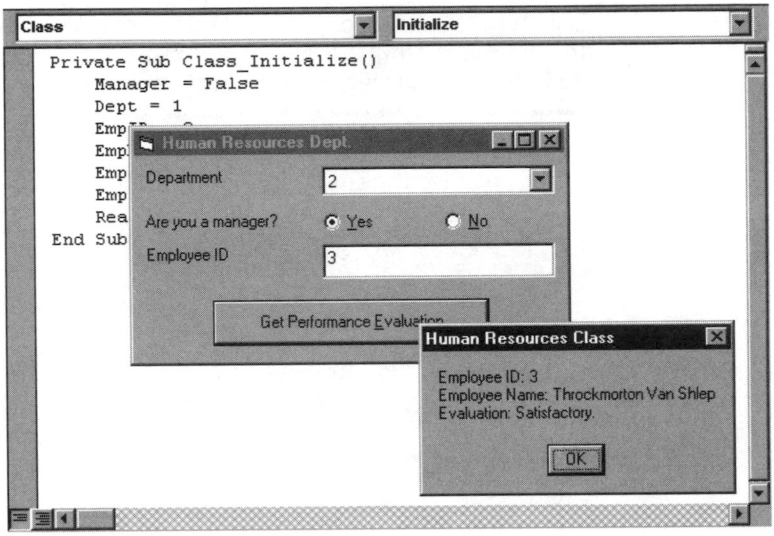

FIGURE 15.5: The HR class in action

Before we consider this example complete, I'm going to show you how to create an event, giving the class the ability to "talk back" to your application.

1. If you have not done so already, click the OK button to clear the message box, and stop the application by clicking the close button (x) in the upper-right corner of the form.

2. To create an event procedure, you must properly declare it in the class. You do this with the `Public Event` declaration. Add the following line of code to the `(General)(Declarations)` section of clsHR:

```
Public Event ShowEval(Eval As String)
```

Now that you have an event in the class, you need to call the event, sometimes called *triggering*, or *firing*, the event. You do this in Visual Basic using the `RaiseEvent` command.

3. Instead of returning a property, we are going to return the performance evaluation through an event. Remove the following line from the `(General)(Declarations)` section of clsHR:

```
Public EmpPerformance As String
```

4. In addition, remove the line:

    ```
    EmpPerformance=""
    ```

    from the (Class)(Initialize) event.

5. Go to the GetRecord() function and remove the existing code. Now add the
    following code:

    ```
    Public Function
    GetRecord() As Boolean
        Dim EmpPerformance As String

        If Manager = True Then
            If Dept = GetDept() Then
                EmpName = GetEmpName()
                EmpPerformance = GetPerfEval()
                Reason = ""
                GetRecord = True
            Else
                Reason = "You cannot access " _
                    & "files from another department."
                GetRecord = False
            End If
        Else
            Reason = "You must be a manager to " _
                    & "access personnel files."
            GetRecord = False
        End If

        RaiseEvent ShowEval(EmpPerformance)
    End Function
    ```

6. Open the Code window for frmHR.

7. In the (General)(Declarations) section, insert the WithEvents statement
    in the class declaration, so it reads:

    ```
    Private WithEvents hr As clsHR
    ```

    The WithEvents keyword tells Visual Basic that this class exposes events
    that can be accessed from the form.

8. To display the performance evaluation, we need to place code in the
    (hr)(ShowEval) procedure. Add the following code:

    ```
    Private Sub hr_ShowEval(eval As String)
        Dim msg As String
    ```

```
        If eval <> "" Then
            msg = "Employee ID: " & _
                Trim$(Str$(hr.EmpID)) & vbCrLf
            msg = msg & "Employee Name: " & _
                hr.EmpName & vbCrLf
            msg = msg & "Evaluation: " & eval
        Else
            msg = "I could not retrieve the " _
                & "evaluation you requested."
        End If

        MsgBox msg
    End Sub
```

Save and run your project. You will notice that it behaves the same way as before, but you used different code to achieve the same result. This is a handy technique to use when you are not sure how long a process will take. By utilizing events, you allow your application to continue running without having to wait for a response! Your class will let you know when it is ready.

TIP   To utilize events in your classes, you must first define the event using the `Public Event` *EventName()* statement in the `(General)(Declarations)` section of the class. Then you must trigger the event using the `RaiseEvent` command. Finally, you must dimension the object in your form using the `WithEvents` keyword.

You have created a simple object in Visual Basic. You will notice that the object itself is not visible, but you used an interface to make use of it. Some objects will have forms built into them, but most are formless. It is very easy to create a class as long as you take time to design it properly before you start coding.

Using the Object Browser

Now that you understand how objects are designed, you can start examining the characteristics of objects that ship with Visual Basic as well as objects that you create. As you progress as a developer, you will undoubtedly start searching for that perfect technique to write the procedure that will put your application over the top. Visual Basic's Object Browser (Figure 15.6) provides just the tool you need to examine the objects you plan to work with.

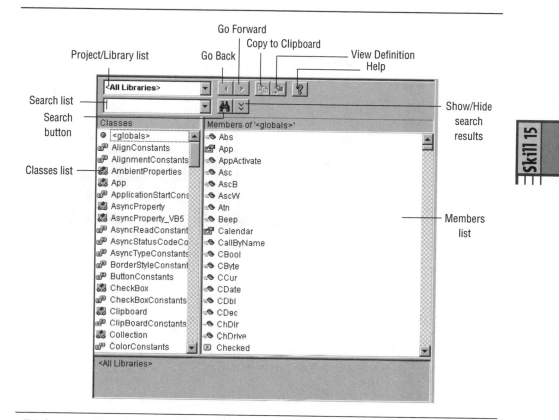

FIGURE 15.6: The Object Browser

To show the Object Browser, select View ➤ Object Browser from the menu, press the F2 key, or click the Object Browser button on the toolbar.

The left column in the Object Browser lists the objects and classes that are available in the projects you have open and the controls you have referenced in them. You can scroll through the list and select the object or class you wish to inspect.

After you pick an object from the Classes list you can see its *members* (the properties, methods, and events) in the right column. A property is represented by a small icon that has a hand holding a piece of paper. Methods are denoted by little green blocks, and events are denoted by the yellow lightning bolt icon.

Above the Classes list are Project/Library drop-down combo, a Search combo, and a toolbar. You can narrow down which parts of the project you want visible at a time by selecting it from the Project/Library combo.

If you are not sure which object you are looking for, but remember one of its components, you can type the name of the component in the Search combo and click the Search button to find it. The button to the right of the Search button allows you to display or hide the search results window, shown in Figure 15.7.

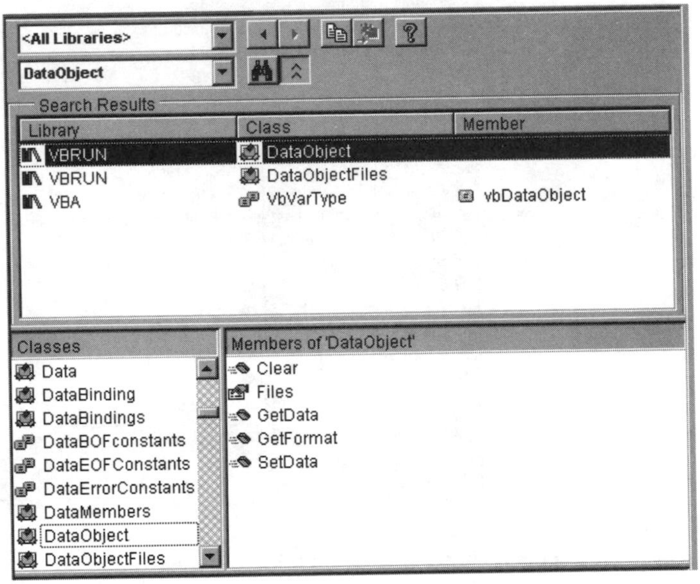

FIGURE 15.7: The Search Results window

As you use the Object Browser, take special note of the member names used by many classes and objects. As you develop more of your own classes, you should try to use the same types of names to describe members in your own classes. This will make it easier for you and others to get familiar and use the class with a minimal learning curve.

Are You up to Speed?

Now you can...

- ☑ understand OOP and its use
- ☑ create, use, and destroy objects
- ☑ design and create your own object classes in Visual Basic
- ☑ write reusable code using objects
- ☑ use the Object Browser to inspect classes and objects

SKILL 16

Extending the IDE with Add-Ins

- Loading add-ins into the IDE
- Using add-ins
- Creating your own add-ins

As you have learned by now, the Visual Basic IDE is full of useful features and utilities that assist you during the development process. Because Visual Basic is built around the Component Object Model, or COM, almost all of the components in the IDE can be accessed through code.

Since most components are exposed through COM, many third-party utilities, called *add-ins*, have been developed to simplify the development process. But the extensibility for the IDE is not limited to professional software companies. You can tap the powers of the IDE to write your own add-ins!

This skill will introduce you to add-ins and show you how to enable some of the add-ins that ship with Visual Basic. Then you will learn how to use a couple of the add-ins, so you can get a feel for how they integrate into the IDE. Once you are familiar with adding add-ins to the IDE and using them, you will develop some useful add-ins of your own.

Loading Add-Ins into the IDE

Add-ins are COM-enabled utilities that can be integrated into the IDE to provide more functionality than Visual Basic has out of the box. You can access utilities that help you create class modules, build data-aware forms, add toolbars, and manage source code through version control applications such as Microsoft Visual SourceSafe.

Before you can use add-ins, you need to connect to them first. You can do this using two different tools: the Add-In Manager and the VB6 Add-In Toolbar.

Using the Add-In Manager

The most basic method of connecting add-ins to the Visual Basic IDE is using the *Add-In Manager* (Figure 16.1). You can open it by selecting Add-Ins ➤ Add-In Manager from the Visual Basic toolbar. Its layout is simple. Under the left column of the list, you can see the add-ins that Visual Basic knows about. The right column tells you the load behavior of the selected add-in. As you select an add-in from the list, you can see its description in the field in the lower-left side of the dialog box. To the right of that field is a frame containing three check boxes that determine the load behavior of the add-in.

The first check box determines whether the selected add-in is loaded or unloaded. If this box is checked, the add-in is loaded and ready to use. The second check box determines if the add-in will be loaded when Visual Basic starts. If you have a favorite add-in that you want available at a moment's notice, then you can check this box. The third check box is checked if you want to use an add-in from the command line. If an add-in has an interface, then it cannot be run from the command line.

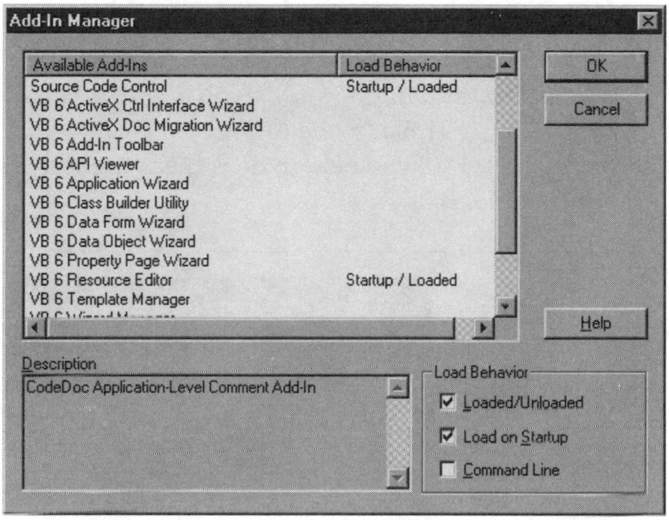

FIGURE 16.1: The Add-In Manager

There is an add-in in the list that makes it easier for you to use add-ins. It is called the VB6 Add-In Toolbar. Perform the following steps to load the toolbar:

1. Select VB 6 Add-In Toolbar from the list.

2. Make sure that the Loaded/Unloaded and Load on Startup check boxes are checked.

3. Click the OK button to close the Add-In Manager.

Using the VB6 Add-In Toolbar

The VB 6 *Add-In Toolbar*, shown in Figure 16.2, makes it easier for you to load and unload add-ins from the IDE.

FIGURE 16.2: The Add-In Toolbar

On the left of the toolbar is a white Add/Remove button with a +/- icon on it. By clicking this button, you can call up the Add/Remove Toolbar Items dialog box, which is similar to the Add-In Manager (see Figure 16.3). As it says on the top of the list, all you need to do is check the add-ins you want to show on the Add-In Toolbar.

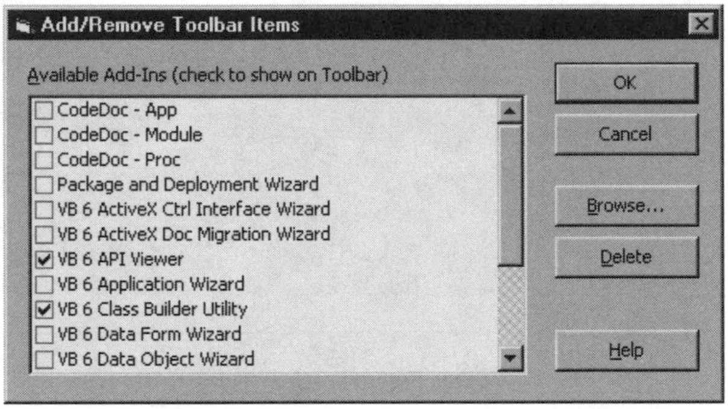

FIGURE 16.3: The Add/Remove Toolbar Items dialog box

This add-in surpasses the functionality of the Add-In Manager by offering two simple buttons. One allows you to browse for add-ins that are not registered with Visual Basic, and the other allows you to remove add-ins from the list. This is especially handy when you start experimenting with your own add-ins and they don't seem to work properly. This allows you a neat way to remove them from the clutches of Visual Basic.

Before you continue on to the next section, perform these steps to load a couple of add-ins into the Add-In Toolbar:

1. Click the Add/Remove button to bring up the Add/Remove Toolbar Items dialog box.

2. Load the VB6 Application Wizard by checking its box.

3. Load the add-in for the VB6 Data Form Wizard.

4. Click the OK button to close the dialog box.

 You should now have three buttons on the Add-In Toolbar, as shown in Figure 16.4. From left to right, the buttons are: the Add/Remove button, the VB6 Application Wizard, and the VB6 Data Form Wizard.

FIGURE 16.4: The Add-In Toolbar with add-ins loaded

Using Add-Ins

Now that you have some add-ins loaded into the IDE, let's try them out so you can see what they do and how they do it.

Using the VB6 Application Wizard

The VB6 Application Wizard is one of the most full-featured add-ins that comes with Visual Basic. It steps you through several options in Microsoft's traditional Wizard style and helps you quickly—and I mean quickly—lay down the foundation for a sophisticated application. To show you how fast it works, complete the following example to create the framework for a Windows Explorer-styled application.

1. Remove any projects you may have loaded in Visual Basic by selecting File ➤ Remove Project as many times as needed to give you a clean slate.

2. Click the VB6 Application Wizard button on the Add-In Toolbar. This will start the Wizard, as you can see in Figure 16.5.

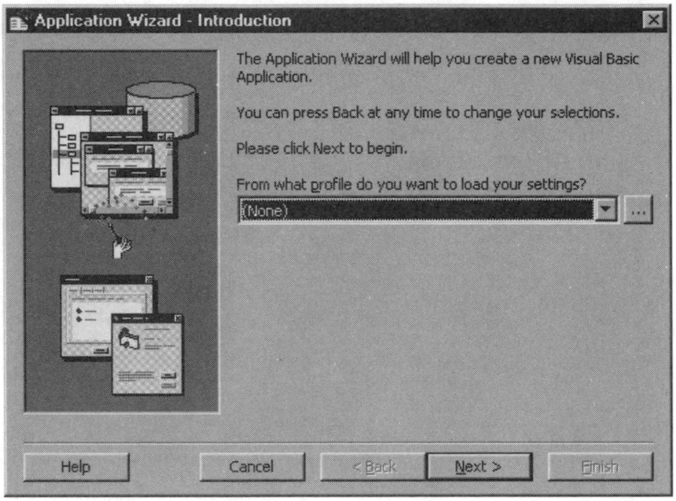

FIGURE 16.5: The VB6 Application Wizard

3. The first field allows you to select a project profile created from a previous session. Since you are creating an application from scratch, leave that field set to (None) and click the Next button to move on.

The next screen, shown in Figure 16.6, allows you to select from three basic project types including a Multiple Document Interface (MDI), a Single Document Interface (SDI), or an Explorer-style application.

4. Click the option next to Explorer Style and type **Explorer** in the field where you are asked to name your application. When you are done, click the Next button.

The screen shown in Figure 16.7 allows you to choose which menus and submenus you would like in your application. If you click a menu in the Menus list, you will see a list of available submenus for the menu you selected.

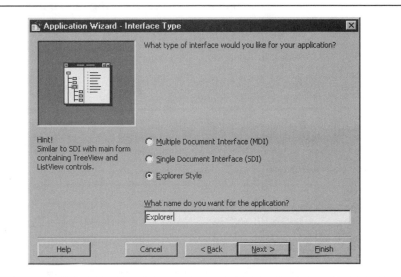

FIGURE 16.6: Selecting a project type

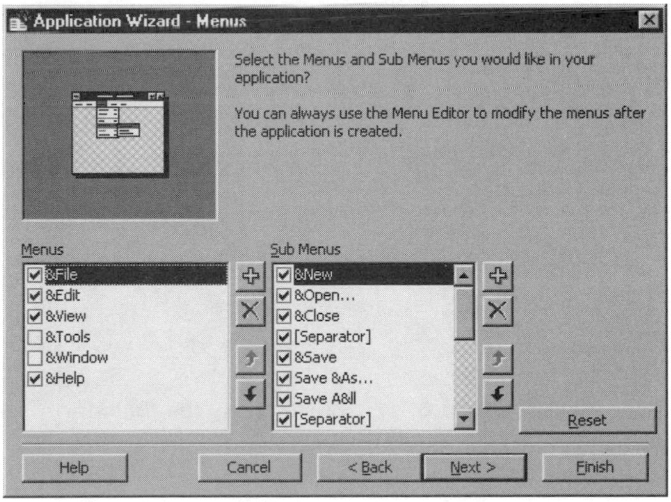

FIGURE 16.7: Selecting menus for your project

5. Click the File menu and uncheck the Find submenu.

6. Uncheck the first [Separator] submenu to remove it from the menu.

7. Remove the Send To submenu.

8. Remove the next [Separator] submenu.

TIP   If you need a menu or submenu that is not listed in either list, you can add it by clicking the appropriate add button next to the list you want to add the button to. In addition, you can move the submenu up or down by clicking the corresponding arrow button.

---

9. Click the Next button to move to the next step.

You can add, remove, or modify the toolbar using the form in Figure 16.8.

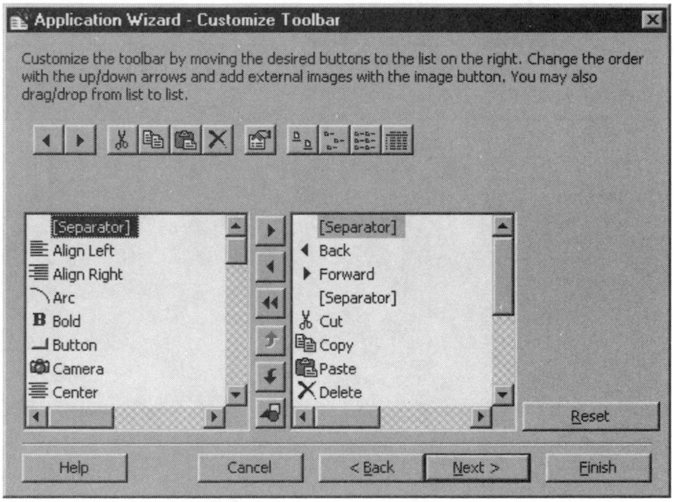

FIGURE 16.8: Customizing the toolbar

10. Remove the first three toolbar buttons corresponding to the first separator, the Back button, and the Forward button, by selecting each one and clicking the left button to remove it from the list.

11. Click the Next button to move to the next step.

12. From the form in Figure 16.9 you can include a *resource file* into your project. Since you don't have any resource files to include, click the Next button to move on.

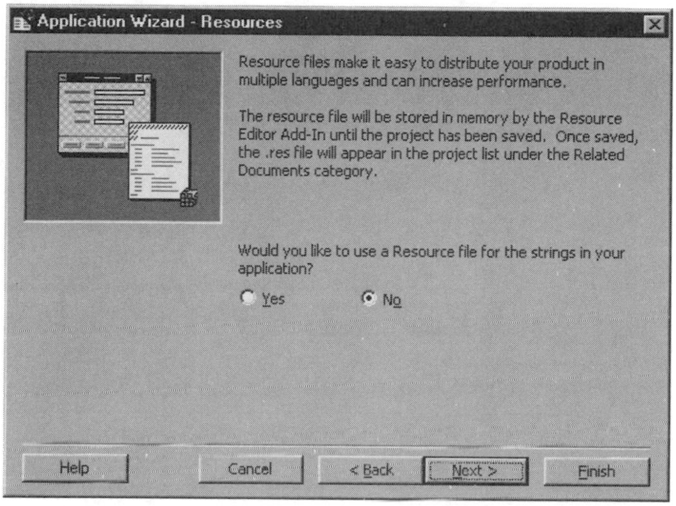

FIGURE 16.9: You can include a resource file if you want.

13. If you want to add a custom Web browser for your users, you could opt to include it on this form (shown in Figure 16.10). However, you won't need one for this example, so continue by clicking the Next button.

In addition to creating a standard application framework, the Application Wizard can even help you create a splash screen or an About dialog box, as well as other commonly used forms. You can see these options in Figure 16.11.

14. Click the Splash Screen and About Box options to include them in your project.

15. Click the Next button.

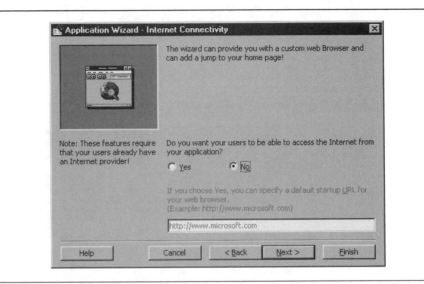

FIGURE 16.10: Do you want to add a custom Web browser?

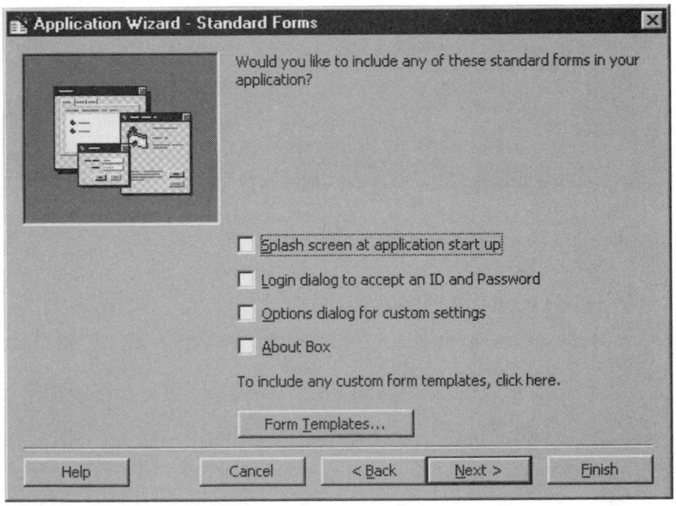

FIGURE 16.11: Selecting additional forms

16.   If you want to add a data-aware form, you could create one here, as shown in Figure 16.12. Click the Next button because this application won't connect to any databases.

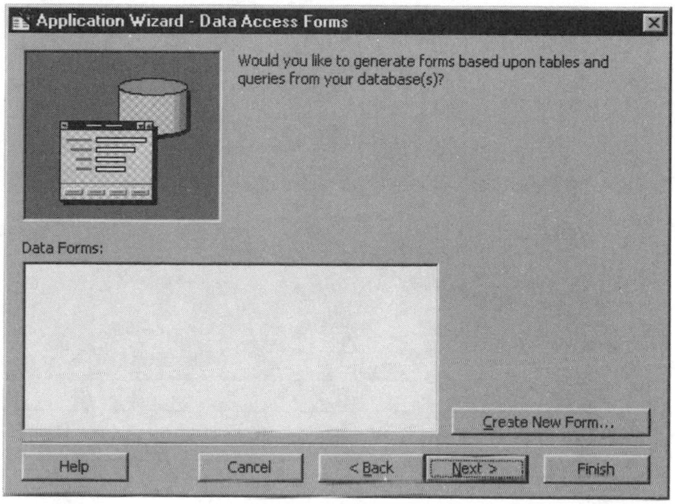

FIGURE 16.12: You can include Data Access Forms tool

Finally, you're at the point where the Application Wizard can take over and start building your application! If you want to save the settings you selected throughout the preceding process, you can click the ellipses button (...) and specify a filename for your setting file.

17.   When you reach the step shown in Figure 16.13, click the Finish button to let the Application Wizard start building the application.

After you click the Finish button, the Application Wizard will start creating forms and modules and adding them to a new project. When it is done, you will have a project framework where many of the features have been completed for you!

18.   Save and run the project to see what it looks like.

19.   When the Explorer is running, select the About submenu from the Help menu. You will see something like Figure 16.14.

Unfortunately, the Application Wizard cannot write all of the code for you. If it could, the information technology industry wouldn't need programmers like us. Now that you can see what the Wizard does, you can modify the project in any way you need to make your application perfect. I'll leave that up to you.

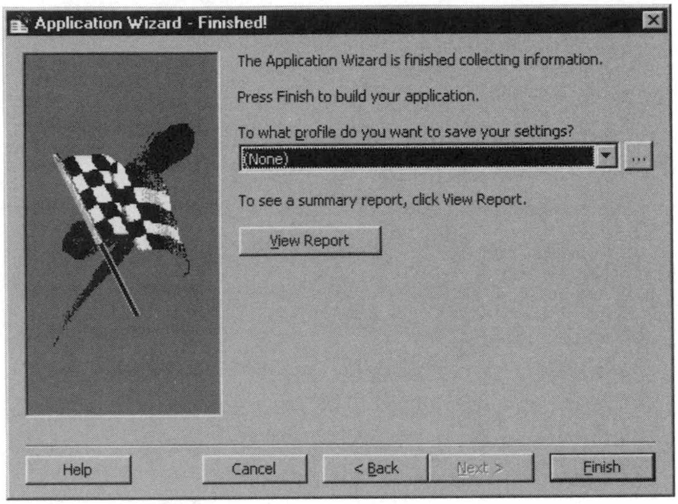

FIGURE 16.13: Build the application.

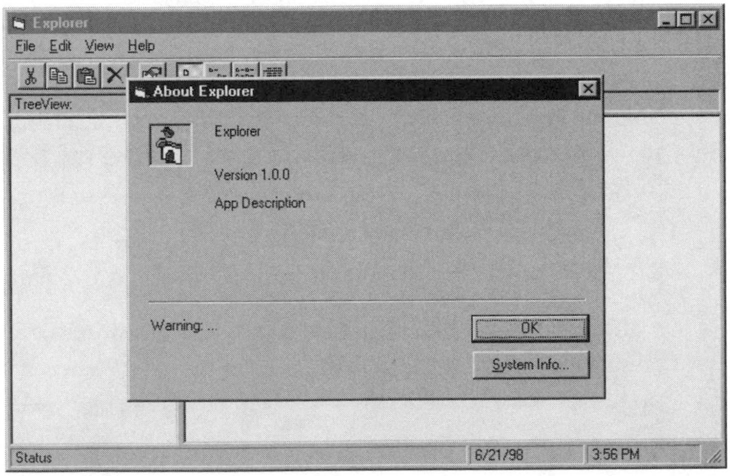

FIGURE 16.14: The About dialog box of the Explorer project

Using the VB6 Data Form Wizard

The next add-in that you're going to work with is the VB6 Data Form Wizard. You can use the Data Form Wizard to quickly create a data-bound form, allowing you to browse, add, and remove data from a database. In the next example, you will use the Data Form Wizard to create a data browser. By the end of the example, you will know how to use the Wizard well enough to create your own data-bound forms for your own applications.

1. In Visual Basic, start a new project by selecting New project from the File menu. Select Standard EXE from the New Project dialog box and click OK.

2. After the project is created, remove Form1 by right clicking it in the Project Explorer and selecting Remove Form1 from the pop-up menu.

3. Set the Name property of the project to **DataBrowser**.

4. Click the Data Form Wizard button on the VB6 Add-In Toolbar to start the Wizard. You will be presented with a dialog box like the one shown in Figure 16.15.

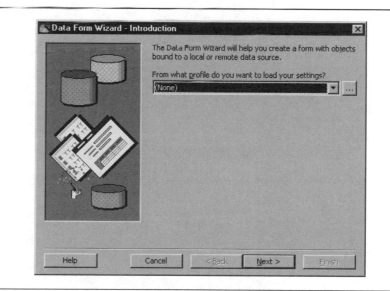

FIGURE 16.15: The VB6 Data Form Wizard

5. Just like in the Application Wizard, you can select a script saved from a previous session if you already have preferences saved to a file. Since you don't have any preferences saved yet, click the Next button to move on.

6. On the next screen (see Figure 16.16) you can select the type of database you want to connect to. You can select from Access or a remote database such as Microsoft SQL Server.

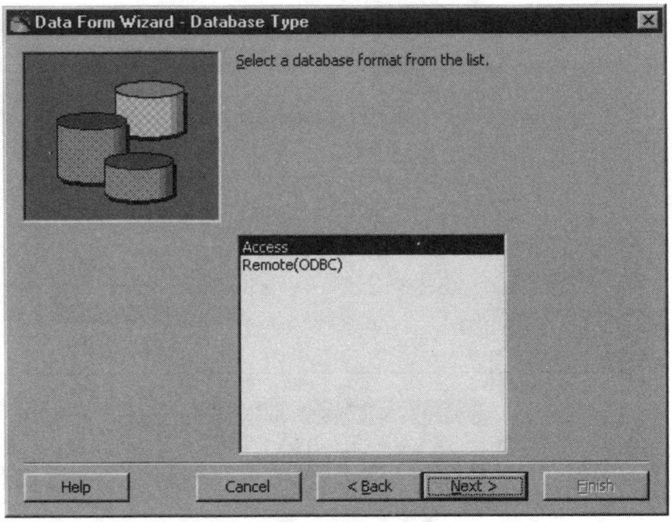

FIGURE 16.16: Selecting a database type

7. Select Access and click the Next button.

8. The screen shown in Figure 16.17 allows you to choose a database file. Click the Browse button to find the correct file.

9. Select `Biblio.mdb` from the `\Program Files\Microsoft Visual Studio\ VB98` directory. Click the Open button to select the database.

10. After you have selected the database, click the Next button to move on.

On the next screen (Figure 16.18) you can set the Name property of the form as well as the layout. You can select from a single record view, a grid, master/detail view, a Microsoft FlexGrid view, and a Microsoft Chart view.

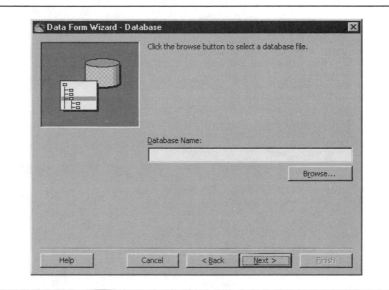

FIGURE 16.17: Selecting a database

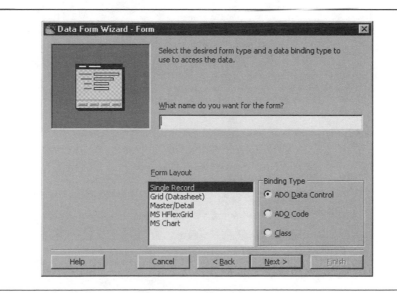

FIGURE 16.18: Defining the data form

11. Type **frmBrowser** in the field at the top of the dialog box. Select Grid (Datasheet) from the list of available layouts.

12. In the Binding Type section, select ADO Code. Selecting this option will make the Data Form Wizard write Visual Basic code to access the database using ADO. When you're done, click the Next button.

You can select the record source and fields you want to include on your form from the form in Figure 16.19.

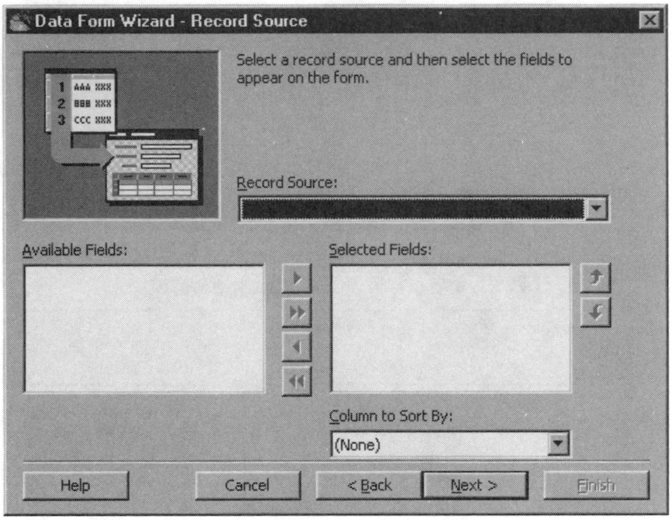

FIGURE 16.19: Selecting a record source

13. Select Titles from the Record Source combo box.

14. When the fields appear in the Available Fields list, click the Move All Fields to the Right button, indicated by double arrows pointing to the right. This will include all fields on your form.

15. In the Column to Sort By field, select the Title field. When you are done, click the Next button to continue.

16. In the Control Selection dialog box, shown in Figure 16.20, leave all of the options checked.

NOTE When designing your own data-bound forms, you can choose which buttons and features you want on your form from the Control Selection dialog box.

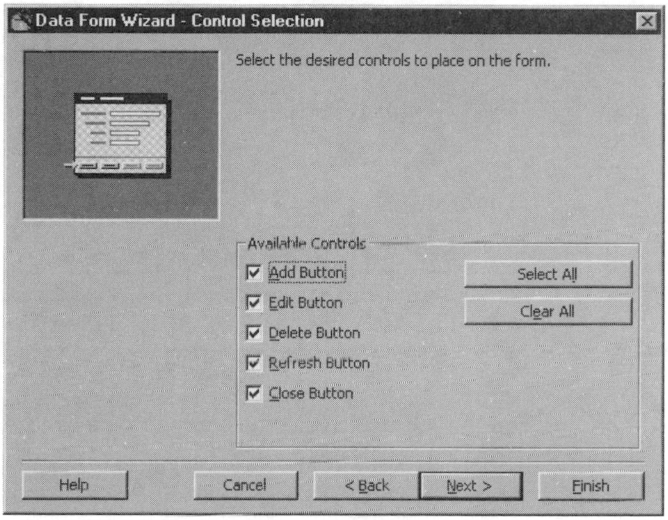

FIGURE 16.20: The Control Selection dialog box

17. Click the Next button to move on.

18. The final step of the Data Form Wizard, shown in Figure 16.21, allows you to save your selections in a script, so you can reuse them the next time you use the Wizard. You won't need to save these settings, so click the Finish button and let the Wizard work its magic.

19. For this project, you must set frmBrowser as the startup form for the project. Right-click DataBrowser in the Project Explorer and select DataBrowser Properties from the pop-up menu.

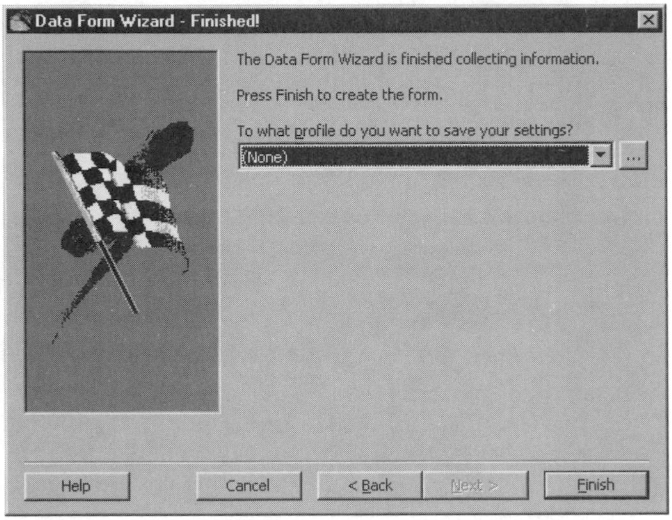

FIGURE 16.21: You're finished with the Wizard!

20. When the project Properties dialog box appears, select frmBrowser in the Startup Object field and click the OK button to close the dialog box.

21. Save and run your project.

When the project runs, you will see a form much like the one shown in Figure 16.22. You can navigate between records and fields, just like you can in Microsoft Access or other grid-based data browsers. If you click the Edit button at the bottom of the form, you can edit the contents of the current field and click Update to commit the changes. This form is much easier to use for data entry than those contained in Visual Data Manager, discussed in Skill 8. With a little work, you could write your own database administration application!

By now you should have a good idea of how add-ins compliment the Visual Basic IDE to simplify your development efforts. There are many more add-ins available, both in Visual Basic, and from third parties. If you are looking for that perfect add-in, and haven't found it yet, read the next sections. They show you how you can write your own add-ins to fill in the gaps of the Visual Basic IDE.

Comments	Description	ISBN	Notes	PubID	Subject
HF5548.4.L67A52 1989	29.95	0-8802234-6-4	650.0285536920	45	
{}	29.95	1-5676127-1-7		192	Book&Disk
HF5548.4.L67A178 199	39.95	0-8802280-4-0	650.0285536920	45	Book&Disk
HF5548.4.L67L84 1991	49.95	0-5533496-6-X	650.0285536920	139	Bk&Disk
HF5548.4.L67F689 199	39.95	0-8802262-5-0		45	Bk&Dsk
{}	39.95	1-8780587-3-8		19	Book&Disk
QA76.9.D3T6787 1994	0	1-5676123-0-X	005.756520	192	
QA76.9.D3T6787 1994	10.95	1-5676145-0-7	005.756520	192	
{}	12.99	0-7897055-5-9		45	
{}	10.99	1-5676153-9-2		192	
QA76.9.D3M83 1994 {9	10.99	1-5676140-7-8	005.756520	192	
HF5548.4.L692B37 199	10.95	1-5676117-6-1	650.02854620	192	
QA76.9.D3D88 1992 {9	10.95	1-5676102-7-7	005.756520	192	
{}	10.95	1-5676149-4-9		192	
QA76.9.D3A99 1991 {9	0	0-6722283-2-7	005.36920	721	
QA76.9.D3A99 1991 {9	10.95	0-6723003-5-4	005.36920	721	
{}	29.95	1-5608711-3-X		635	
{}	11.16	0-0280074-8-4		175	2nd
{}	0	0-0706146-6-0		175	2nd
QA76.9.D3C366 1993 {	9.95	0-8745528-7-7	005.756520	278	
QA76.9.D3I534 1984 {8	19.95	0-1363489-0-4	001.64219	715	

FIGURE 16.22: The running data form

Creating Your Own Add-Ins

If you think that add-ins are cool, then you will really like these next sections. If you have read Skill 12, then you understand why consistently commenting your code is important. You may have also noticed that the techniques I used required a bit of typing. Well now it's time to simplify that process. You will be creating three add-ins that you can use to consistently add comments to your modules, and document your applications. When you are done creating these add-ins, you will be able to use them with all of your other projects. In addition, you will have a good idea of how to access the IDE so you can create even more add-ins if you wish.

The three add-ins are components of what I call CodeDoc, which is short for Code Documentation utilities. The first add-in automatically summarizes the entire scope of your application and places the summary into a separate code module called `AppSpecs.bas`. If you need to determine what is required to make an application operate properly, you can open this file and the information is there!

The second add-in adds a comment block at the top of the current module. You can fill in the blanks of the comment block so you can have consistent comments between forms, classes, and `.bas` modules.

The last add-in is much like the second, except it inserts a comment block at the beginning of the current procedure. Then you can fill in the blanks to describe the procedure.

Although they may seem trivial, these add-ins will greatly ease the burden of documenting your code. If there are features you think would be useful, you will have the source code and can modify your add-ins to get the exact functionality you want. Let's get started.

Creating an Application-Level Comment Utility

The add-in you are about to create is called CodeDoc – App. You can use this add-in to summarize the details of your application. It can document the project properties; list the forms, modules, and classes in the project; and list the project's references. Instead of dealing with all of the complexities of the add-in object, let's use Visual Basic's Add-In project template. This will greatly reduce your development efforts. You can always go back and look at the source code after the project is finished to see how it does what it does.

1. Start a new project by selecting File ➤ New Project from the Visual Basic menu.

2. Select Add-In as the project type, as shown in Figure 16.23, and click the OK button to create the project.

3. After the project is created, set its `Name` property to **CodeDocApp**.

4. Open the Designers folder in the Project Explorer and double-click Connect to open it. You will see the design for the add-in object shown in Figure 16.24.

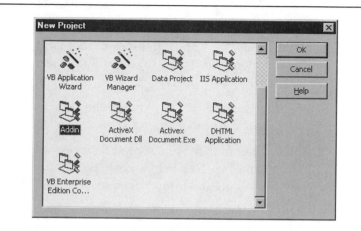

FIGURE 16.23: Selecting the Add-In project template

FIGURE 16.24: The add-in designer

5. In the Add-In Display Name field, type **CodeDoc – App**. This is the name that will appear in the Add-In Manager or the Add-In Toolbar.

6. Type **CodeDoc Application-Level Comment Add-In** in the Add-In Description field. This is the description that will appear in the Add-In Manager.

7. Select Visual Basic in the Application field, and Visual Basic 6.0 in the Application Version field.

8. Select Startup in the Initial Load Behavior field. Make sure the Addin is Command-Line Safe field is unchecked. Since the add-in displays an interface, it will not run from the command line.

9. Open the Code window for the designer by right-clicking the Connect object and selecting View Code from the pop-up menu.

10. About half-way down the `AddinInstance_OnConnection()` event, change the line that reads:

    ```
    Set mcbMenuCommandBar = AddToAddInCommandBar("My AddIn")
    ```

    to:

    ```
    Set mcbMenuCommandBar = AddToAddInCommandBar("CodeDoc - App")
    ```

11. Remove the code from the `AddToAddInCommandBar()` function and replace it with the following:

    ```
    Function AddToAddInCommandBar(sCaption As _
            String) As Office.CommandBarControl
        Dim cbMenuCommandBar As Office.CommandBarControl
        Dim cmd As Office.CommandBarButton
        Dim cbMenu As Object

        'If we have an error, bypass all code
        On Error GoTo AddToAddInCommandBarErr

        'See if we can find the Edit command bar
        Set cbMenu = VBInstance.CommandBars("Edit")
        If cbMenu Is Nothing Then
            'not available so we fail
            Exit Function
        End If

        'Add it to the command bar
        Set cbMenuCommandBar = cbMenu.Controls.Add(1, , , 11)
    ```

```
        'Reference the button so we can
        'customize it...
    Set cmd = cbMenuCommandBar
        'Copy the button image from the add-in form
        Clipboard.SetData frmAddIn.picButton.Picture

        'Paste the button image from the clipboard
        cmd.PasteFace

        'Give it a user-friendly tooltip
        cmd.ToolTipText = "Document the Application"
    Set cmd = Nothing

        'Return the reference to the new button
        Set AddToAddInCommandBar = cbMenuCommandBar

    AddToAddInCommandBarErr:

    End Function
```

12. Save your project so you don't lose your work.

13. Close the Code window for the Connect designer.

14. Open frmAddIn by double-clicking it in the Project Explorer.

15. Add a label control to the upper-left corner of the form. Set its `Name` property to **lblDescription**, and set its `Caption` to **Description goes here…**

16. Stretch the label so its right edge is one grid line away from the OK button. Stretch it vertically so its bottom edge is aligned with the bottom edge of the Cancel button.

17. Add a frame control to the form. Set its `Name` property to **fraOptions**. Set its `Caption` property to **&Options**.

18. Position the frame so it is one grid line below the label and away from the left edge of the form.

19. Stretch the frame so its right edge and bottom edge are one grid line away from the right and bottom edges of the form.

20. Add a check box control to the frame. Set its `Name` property to **chkProject-Summary** and set its `Caption` property to **List Project &Summary**.

21. Add another check box below the first one. Set its `Name` property to **chkComponents** and set its `Caption` property to **List Com&ponents in Project**.

22. Add another check box below the previous one. Set its Name property to **chkReferences** and set its Caption property to **List Project &References**.

23. Place a picture box control on the right side of the frame. Set its Name property to **picButton**. Set its Visible property to False.

> **NOTE** The picture box is used as a container to hold the button icon for the add-in. Since the Control object of the CommandBar does not have a specific Icon or Picture property, you must use its PasteFace method to paste the icon onto the object. Before it can be pasted, however, you must copy a button image onto the Clipboard using Visual Basic's Clipboard object. The picture box will serve as the source for the copy/paste operation.

You can select a graphic from those that shipped with Visual Basic, or you can create your own using the Paint utility that comes with Windows. If you want to use the custom graphic for this add-in, you can download the graphic CodeDocApp.bmp from the Sybex Web site at www.sybex.com.

24. Double-click the Picture property of the picture box control in the Properties window.

25. Select a graphic to act as your toolbar button for the add-in. You can choose from any of the toolbar graphics located in the \Program Files\Microsoft Visual Studio\Common\Graphics\Bitmaps\Tlbr_Win95 directory.

26. Save your project once again so you don't lose your changes.

27. The form should look similar to Figure 16.25.

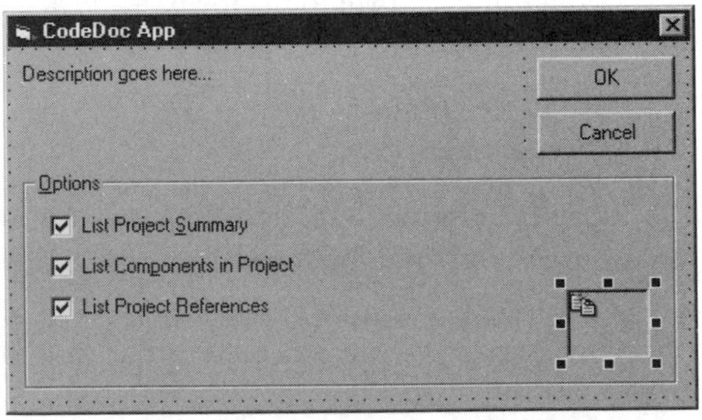

FIGURE 16.25: The CodeDoc – App form in design view

28. Change the Name property of the OK button to **cmdOK**.

29. Change the Name property of the Cancel button to **cmdCancel**.

30. Double-click cmdOK to open its Code window.

31. Add the following code to the cmdOK_Click() event:

```
Private Sub cmdOK_Click()
    'Add a new code module
    AddModule

    'Document the application
    DocumentApp

    'Remove the dialog
    Connect.Hide
End Sub
```

32. Add the following code to the Load() event of the form:

```
Private Sub Form_Load()
    Dim msg As String

    msg = "CodeDoc-App allows you to " & _
            "select project-wide options " & _
            "options and creates adds a " & _
            "single application-wide " & _
            "code module that lists " & _
            "the project's dependencies."

    lblDescription.Caption = msg
End Sub
```

33. Create a procedure called DocumentApp() and add the following code:

```
Public Sub DocumentApp()
    Dim X As String
    Dim msg As String

    If chkProjectSummary.Value = 1 Then
        'Summarize the project
        X = ListSummary()
    End If

    If chkComponents.Value = 1 Then
        'List the components used in the project
        X = X & ListComponents()
    End If
```

```
If chkReferences.Value = 1 Then
    'List the references used by the project
    X = X & ListReferences()
End If

'Add the comments to the top of the module
With VBInstance.ActiveCodePane.CodeModule
    .InsertLines 1, X & "'"
End With

'Let the user know we're done
msg = "Project documented successfully!"
MsgBox msg, vbInformation, "Complete!"
End Sub
```

The preceding code is used to determine what items to document. As you can see, it checks what options were checked and calls the appropriate functions to create the comments. Now let's add the functions so you can see how the add-in works with the IDE.

1. Add the following procedure to the (General)(Declarations) section of the form:

```
Private Sub AddModule()
    Dim ndx As Integer
    Dim i As Integer

    With VBInstance.ActiveVBProject
        'Does the module exist?
        For i = 1 To .VBComponents.Count
            'If so, then don't add the module.
            If .VBComponents(i).Name = "AppSpecs" Then
                'Activate the module so we can add to it
                .VBComponents(i).Activate

                'We don't need to add new file
                Exit Sub
            End If
        Next

        'Add a new code module
        .VBComponents.Add vbext_ct_StdModule
        ndx = .VBComponents.Count

        'Rename it
        .VBComponents(ndx).Name = "AppSpecs"
    End With
End Sub
```

2. The next function you are going to add is responsible for listing all of the forms, modules, classes, and designers that make up your project:

```
Public Function ListComponents() As String
    Dim i As Integer
    Dim X As String

    With VBInstance
        'Add the section header
        X = "'" & vbCrLf & "'Components in Project:" & _
                vbCrLf

        If .ActiveVBProject.VBComponents.Count > 0 Then
            'Add the components to the list
            For i = 1 To _
                    .ActiveVBProject.VBComponents.Count
                X = X & "'" & vbTab & _
                    .ActiveVBProject.VBComponents(i). _
                        Name & vbCrLf
            Next
        Else
            'There are no components
            X = X & "'" & vbTab & "None."
        End If
    End With

    'Return the list of components
    ListComponents = X
End Function
```

The next function lists all of the type library references required to make the application run properly. This is useful to know when a team of developers share code and download it to different machines. By examining the References section of the AppSpecs file, a developer can make sure he or she has the required components installed before trying to open the project.

3. Add the following function to the form:

```
Public Function ListReferences() As String
    Dim i As Integer
    Dim X As String

    With VBInstance
        'Add the section header
        X = "'" & vbCrLf & "'References:" & vbCrLf

        If .ActiveVBProject.References.Count > 0 Then
```

```
                    'List the references
                    For i = 1 To .ActiveVBProject.References.Count
                        X = X & "'" & vbTab & _
                        .ActiveVBProject.References(i). _
                            Description & vbCrLf
                    Next
                Else
                    'There are no references
                    X = "'" & vbTab & "None."
                End If
            End With

            'Return the list of references
            ListReferences = X
        End Function
```

4. Finally, add the `ListSummary()` function to the `(General)(Declarations)` section as follows:

```
Private Function ListSummary() As String
    Dim X As String

    'Create the comments
    X = "'" & vbCrLf & _
        "'Project Name: " & vbTab & vbCrLf & _
        "'Version: " & vbTab & vbTab & vbCrLf & _
        "'Company: " & vbTab & vbTab & vbCrLf & _
        "'Copyright: " & vbTab & vbCrLf & _
        "'Trademarks: " & vbTab & vbCrLf & _
        "'Description:" & vbTab & vbCrLf

    'Return the list of ActiveX controls
    ListSummary = X
End Function
```

5. Save your project again.

Before you can use the add-in, you need to compile it so that it will register itself with Visual Basic. This will put the add-in's name and startup information to the VB.INI file, which is referenced by both the Add-In Manager and the VB6 Add-In Toolbar.

1. Compile the add-in by selecting File ➤ Make CodeDocApp.dll from the Visual Basic menu.

Before you can use the add-in, you need to make sure that the Edit toolbar is visible. The CodeDoc add-ins automatically add themselves to the Edit toolbar.

2. If the Edit toolbar is not visible, select View ➤ Toolbars ➤ Edit to show it.

3. Select Add-Ins ➤ Add-In Manager to launch the Add-In Manager.

4. When the Add-In Manager is visible, select CodeDoc – App and check the Loaded/Unloaded check box as shown in Figure 16.26. You will notice that the description you typed in the designer is visible in the Description box.

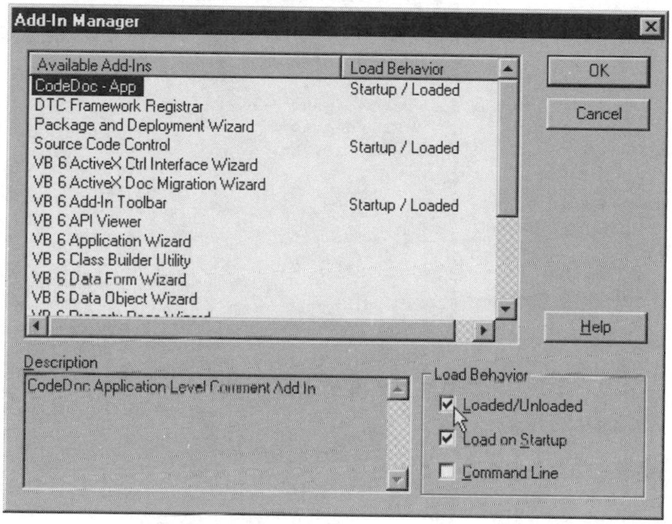

FIGURE 16.26: Loading the add-in

5. Click the OK button to load the add-in.

6. When the add-in loads, you should get a new toolbar button added to the middle of the Edit toolbar, like the one shown in Figure 16.27.

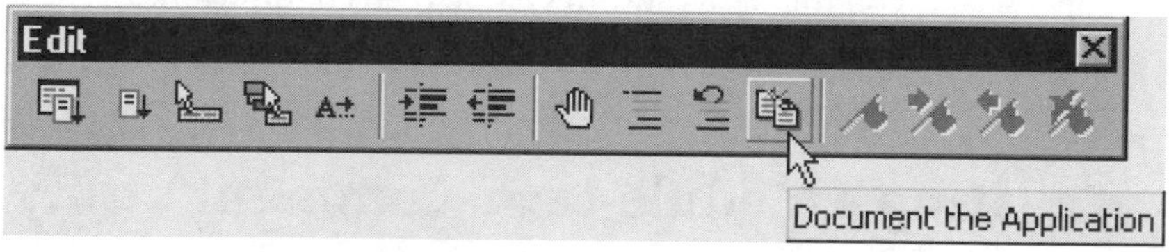

FIGURE 16.27: The application-level add-in on the Edit toolbar

7. Give the add-in a test spin by clicking the newly added button. Leave all of the options checked and click the OK button.

If you pay attention, you will see Visual Basic add a new module to your project and type some comments in it. You should see something like Figure 16.28.

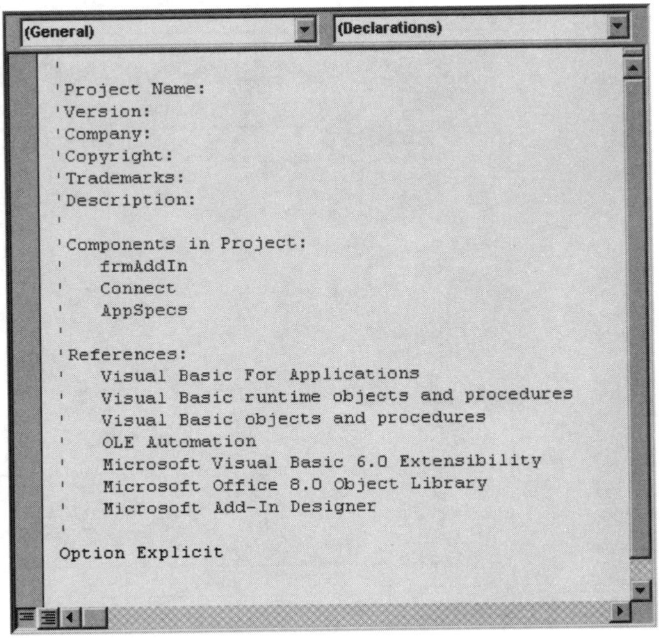

```
(General)                                (Declarations)

'
'Project Name:
'Version:
'Company:
'Copyright:
'Trademarks:
'Description:
'
'Components in Project:
'    frmAddIn
'    Connect
'    AppSpecs
'
'References:
'    Visual Basic For Applications
'    Visual Basic runtime objects and procedures
'    Visual Basic objects and procedures
'    OLE Automation
'    Microsoft Visual Basic 6.0 Extensibility
'    Microsoft Office 8.0 Object Library
'    Microsoft Add-In Designer
'
Option Explicit
```

FIGURE 16.28: The contents of the AppSpecs file

Although you need to fill in the blanks with the pertinent information, CodeDoc has laid the groundwork for you, greatly simplifying the code documentation process.

If you think this add-in is cool, then continue on. There are two more add-ins you can write that add similar comments to the beginning of the current module, and the current procedure.

Creating a Module-Level Comment Utility

The next add-in you will be creating is called CodeDoc – Module. As you can deduce, this add-in helps you comment the current code module. Without any further explanation, let's get started!

1. Start a new project by selecting File ➤ New Project from the Visual Basic menu.

2. Select Add-In as the project type and click the OK button to create the project.

3. After the project is created, set its `Name` property to **CodeDocModule**.

4. Open the Designers folder in the Project Explorer and double-click Connect to open it.

5. In the Add-In Display Name field, type **CodeDoc – Module**. This is the name that will appear in the Add-In manager or the Add-In Toolbar.

6. Type **CodeDoc Module-Level Comment Add-In** in the Add-In Description field. This is the description that will appear in the Add-In Manager.

7. Select Visual Basic in the Application field, and Visual Basic 6.0 in the Application Version field.

8. Select Startup in the Initial Load Behavior field. Make sure the Addin is Command-Line Safe field is unchecked. Since the add-in displays an interface, it will not run from the command line.

9. Open the Code window for the designer by right-clicking the Connect object and selecting View Code from the pop-up menu.

10. In the `(General)(Declarations)` section, remove the line that reads:

    ```
    Dim mfrmAddIn As New frmAddIn
    ```

11. Remove the lines from the `AddinInstance_OnDisconnection()` event that read:

    ```
    Unload mfrmAddIn
    Set mfrmAddIn = Nothing
    ```

12. About half-way down the `AddinInstance_OnConnection()` event, change the line that reads:

    ```
    Set mcbMenuCommandBar = AddToAddInCommandBar("My AddIn")
    ```

    to:

    ```
    Set mcbMenuCommandBar = AddToAddInCommandBar _
    ("CodeDoc - Module")
    ```

13. Remove the code from the `AddToAddInCommandBar()` function and replace it with the following:

    ```
    Function AddToAddInCommandBar(sCaption As _
            String) As Office.CommandBarControl
        Dim cbMenuCommandBar As Office.CommandBarControl
    ```

```
        Dim cmd As Office.CommandBarButton
        Dim cbMenu As Object

        'If we have an error, bypass all code
        On Error GoTo AddToAddInCommandBarErr

        'See if we can find the Edit command bar
        Set cbMenu = VBInstance.CommandBars("Edit")
        If cbMenu Is Nothing Then
            'not available so we fail
            Exit Function
        End If

        'Add it to the command bar
        Set cbMenuCommandBar = cbMenu.Controls.Add(1, , , 11)

        'Reference the button so we can
        'customize it...
        Set cmd = cbMenuCommandBar
            'Copy the button image from the add-in form
            Clipboard.SetData frmAddIn.picButton.Picture

            'Paste the button image from the clipboard
            cmd.PasteFace

            'Give it a user-friendly tooltip
            cmd.ToolTipText = "Add Module Summary Template"

        Set cmd = Nothing

        'Return the reference to the new button
        Set AddToAddInCommandBar = cbMenuCommandBar

    AddToAddInCommandBarErr:

    End Function
```

14. Save your project so you don't lose your work.

15. Replace the code in the Show() procedure of the designer with the following:

```
    Sub Show()
        Dim filename As String
        Dim x As String

        'Get this module's name
        filename = VBInstance.SelectedVBComponent. _
            Name

        'Create the comments
        x = "'" & vbCrLf & _
```

```
            "'File:" & vbTab & vbTab & vbTab & _
            filename & vbCrLf & _
            "'Author:" & vbTab & vbTab & _
            "Type your name here" & vbCrLf & _
            "'Created:" & vbTab & vbTab & _
            Format$(Date$, "mm-dd-yyyy") & _
            vbCrLf & "'Description:" & _
            vbCrLf & "'" & vbTab & vbTab & _
            vbTab & vbTab & "Type the " & _
            "description of this module " & _
            "here." & vbCrLf & "'Updates:" & _
            vbCrLf & "'" & vbTab & vbTab & _
            vbTab & vbTab & "None" & _
            vbCrLf & "'"

        'Insert the comments above all procedures and declarations
        With VBInstance.ActiveCodePane
            .CodeModule.InsertLines 1, x
        End With
    End Sub
```

16. Remove the code from the Hide() procedure.

17. Open frmAddIn by double-clicking it in the Project Explorer.

18. Remove the OK and Cancel buttons from the form.

19. Add a picture box control to the form. Set its Name property to **picButton** and its Visible property to False.

> **TIP**
>
> You can select a graphic from those that shipped with Visual Basic, or you can create your own using the Paint utility that comes with Windows. If you want to use the custom graphic for this add-in, you can download the graphic CodeDocModule.bmp from the Sybex Web site at www.sybex.com.

20. Double-click the Picture property of the picture box control in the Properties window.

21. Select a graphic to act as your toolbar button for the add-in. You can choose from any of the toolbar graphics located in the \Program Files\Microsoft Visual Studio\Common\Graphics\Bitmaps\Tlbr_Win95 directory.

22. Save your project once again so you don't lose your changes.

Now that you have built the add-in, compile it and use the Add-In Manager to load it into the IDE as you did with the previous add-in. After the add-in is loaded into the IDE, your Edit toolbar should look like Figure 16.29

Edit
Add Module Summary Template

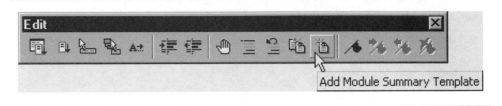

FIGURE 16.29: The module-level add-in on the Edit toolbar

To try this add-in, follow these simple steps:

1. Open the Code window for the module that you want to add comments to. For this example, use the Code window for the Connect designer.
2. Click the CodeDoc – Module button on the Edit toolbar.
3. After you run the add-in, the comment block will be added automatically. You should see something like Figure 16.30.

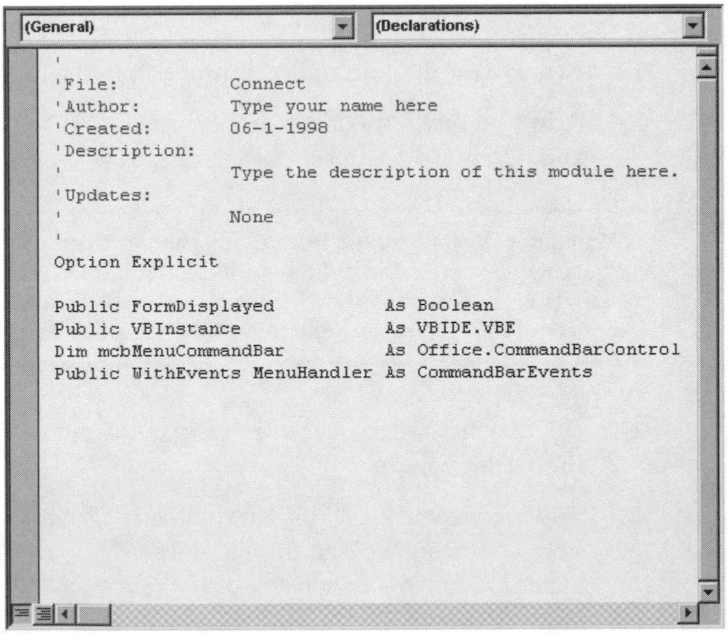

(General)
(Declarations)
'
'File: Connect
'Author: Type your name here
'Created: 06-1-1998
'Description:
'   Type the description of this module here.
'Updates:
'   None
'
Option Explicit
Public FormDisplayed   As Boolean
Public VBInstance   As VBIDE.VBE
Dim mcbMenuCommandBar   As Office.CommandBarControl
Public WithEvents MenuHandler As CommandBarEvents

FIGURE 16.30: The module-level code block

Now you just need to fill in a couple of lines, and you have laid the groundwork for a living block of comments. As changes are made to the module, all you need to do is add a description of the changes you made. I prefer to include the date, my name, and a detailed description of the changes I made. You can see what I mean in Figure 16.31.

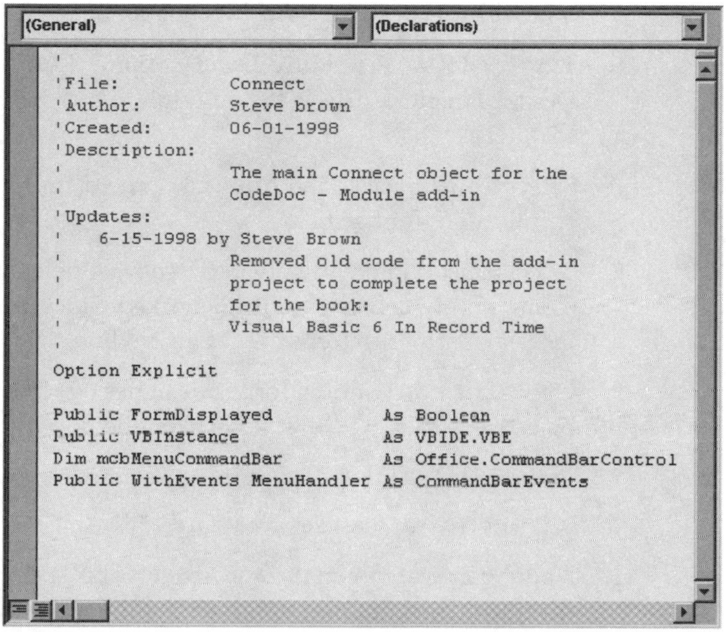

FIGURE 16.31: Describing changes to the module

You now have two add-ins under your belt! Continue with the next section so you can complete your suite of source code documentation utilities.

Creating a Procedure-Level Comment Utility

The final add-in you will be creating assists you in documenting your code at the procedure level. I call it CodeDoc – Proc.

1. Start a new project by selecting File ➢ New Project from the Visual Basic menu.

2. Select Add-In as the project type and click the OK button to create the project.

3. After the project is created, set its `Name` property to **CodeDocProc**.

4. Open the Designers folder in the Project Explorer and double-click Connect to open it.

5. In the Add-In Display Name field, type **CodeDoc – Proc**. This is the name that will appear in the Add-In manager or the Add-In Toolbar.

6. Type **CodeDoc Procedure-Level Comment Add-In** in the Add-In Description field. This is the description that will appear in the Add-In Manager.

7. Select Visual Basic in the Application field, and Visual Basic 6.0 in the Application Version field.

8. Select Startup in the Initial Load Behavior field. Make sure the Addin is Command-Line Safe field is unchecked. Since the add-in displays an interface, it will not run from the command line.

9. Open the Code window for the designer by right-clicking the Connect object and selecting View Code from the pop-up menu.

10. In the `(General)(Declarations)` section, remove the line that reads:

    ```
    Dim mfrmAddIn As New frmAddIn
    ```

11. About half-way down the `AddinInstance_OnConnection()` event, change the line that reads:

    ```
    Set mcbMenuCommandBar = AddToAddInCommandBar("My AddIn")
    ```

    to:

    ```
    Set mcbMenuCommandBar = AddToAddInCommandBar _
            ("CodeDoc - Proc")
    ```

12. Remove the lines from the `AddinInstance_OnDisconnection()` event that read:

    ```
    Unload mfrmAddIn
    Set mfrmAddIn = Nothing
    ```

13. Remove the code from the `AddToAddInCommandBar()` function and replace it with the following:

    ```
    Function AddToAddInCommandBar(sCaption As _
            String) As Office.CommandBarControl
    ```

```
Dim cbMenuCommandBar As Office.CommandBarControl
Dim cmd As Office.CommandBarButton
Dim cbMenu As Object

'If we have an error, bypass all code
On Error GoTo AddToAddInCommandBarErr

'See if we can find the Edit command bar
Set cbMenu = VBInstance.CommandBars("Edit")
If cbMenu Is Nothing Then
    'not available so we fail
    Exit Function
End If

'Add it to the command bar
Set cbMenuCommandBar = cbMenu.Controls.Add(1, , , 11)

'Reference the button so we can
'customize it...
Set cmd = cbMenuCommandBar
    'Copy the button image from the add-in form
    Clipboard.SetData frmAddIn.picButton.Picture

    'Paste the button image from the clipboard
    cmd.PasteFace

    'Give it a user-friendly tooltip
    cmd.ToolTipText = "Summarize Procedure"

Set cmd = Nothing

'Return the reference to the new button
Set AddToAddInCommandBar = cbMenuCommandBar

AddToAddInCommandBarErr:

End Function
```

14. Save your project so you don't lose your work.

15. Replace the code in the Show() procedure of the designer with the following:

```
Sub Show()
    Dim proc As String
    Dim x As String
    Dim l As Integer

    'Get the procedure name
```

```
    proc = GetProcedureName()

    With VBInstance.ActiveCodePane.CodeModule
        'Get the top line of this procedure
        l = .ProcStartLine(proc, vbext_pk_Proc)

        'Create the comments
        x = "'" & vbCrLf & _
            "'Author:" & vbTab & vbTab & _
            "Type your name here." & _
            vbCrLf & "'Created:" & _
            vbTab & vbTab & _
            Format$(Date$, "mm-dd-yyyy") & _
            vbCrLf & "'Description:" & _
            vbCrLf & "'" & vbTab & vbTab & _
            vbTab & vbTab & "Type the " & _
            "description of the " & _
            "function here." & vbCrLf & _
            "'Updates:" & vbCrLf & _
            "'" & vbTab & vbTab & vbTab & _
            vbTab & "Type any updates " & _
            "here." & vbCrLf & "'"

        'Insert the line above the procedure declaration
        .InsertLines l, x
    End With
End Sub
```

16. Remove the code from the Hide() procedure.

17. Now add the GetProcedureName() function as listed:

```
Public Function GetProcedureName() As String
    Dim currentline As Long
    Dim a As Long
    Dim b As Long
    Dim c As Long

    With VBInstance.ActiveCodePane
        'Get the current line of the cursor
        .GetSelection currentline, a, _
            b, c

        'Pass that line number to the
        'ProcOfLine() function
        GetProcedureName = .CodeModule. _
            ProcOfLine(currentline, _
            vbext_pk_Proc)
    End With
End Function
```

18. Open frmAddIn by double-clicking it in the Project Explorer.

19. Remove the OK and Cancel buttons from the form.

20. Add a picture box control to the form. Set its Name property to **picButton** and its Visible property to False.

TIP   You can select a graphic from those that shipped with Visual Basic, or you can create your own using the Paint utility that comes with Windows. If you want to use the custom graphic for this add-in, you can download the graphic CodeDocProc.bmp from the Sybex Web site at www.sybex.com.

---

21. Double-click the Picture property of the picture box control in the Properties window.

22. Select a graphic to act as your toolbar button for the add-in. You can choose from any of the toolbar graphics located in the \Program Files\Microsoft Visual Studio\Common\Graphics\Bitmaps\Tlbr_Win95 directory.

23. Save your project once again so you don't lose your changes.

Now that you have built the add-in, compile it and use the Add-In Manager to load it into the IDE as you did with the previous add-in. After the add-in is loaded into the IDE, your Edit toolbar should look like Figure 16.32.

FIGURE 16.32: The procedure-level add-in on the Edit toolbar

To try the add-in, follow these simple steps:

1. Open the Code window for the module that you want to add comments to. For this example, use the Code window for the Connect designer.

2. Select a procedure to add comments to by clicking the mouse within the body of the procedure. For this example, select the function GetProcedureName().

3.   Click the CodeDoc – Proc button on the Edit toolbar.

4.   After you run the add-in, the comment block will be added automatically. You should see something like Figure 16.33.

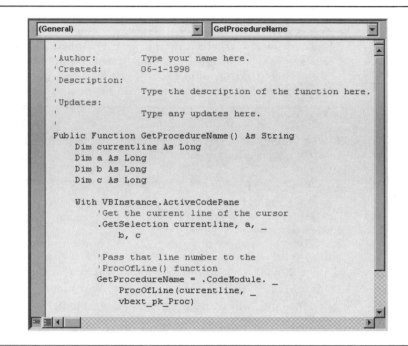

```
(General)                              ▼   GetProcedureName                    ▼
 '
 'Author:        Type your name here.
 'Created:       06-1-1998
 'Description:
 '               Type the description of the function here.
 'Updates:
 '               Type any updates here.
 '
 Public Function GetProcedureName() As String
     Dim currentline As Long
     Dim a As Long
     Dim b As Long
     Dim c As Long

     With VBInstance.ActiveCodePane
         'Get the current line of the cursor
         .GetSelection currentline, a, _
             b, c

         'Pass that line number to the
         'ProcOfLine() function
         GetProcedureName = .CodeModule. _
             ProcOfLine(currentline, _
             vbext_pk_Proc)
```

FIGURE 16.33: The procedure-level code block

Now you just need to fill in a couple of lines, and you have laid the groundwork for a living block of comments. As changes are made to the procedure, you can update the comment block by adding a description of the changes you made.

Good commenting techniques are vital to the life and durability of your code. Not only do they make it easy to understand your code, they are especially useful when you are working in a team development environment. Even if you don't work in that kind of environment, the comments are still important. You just might need them a year from now when you have to make that inevitable update or bug fix. Would you still understand your source code or logic after you haven't seen the code for that long?

Are You up to Speed?

Now you can...

- ☑ use add-ins to help you in your development efforts
- ☑ use the Add-In Manager and Add-In Toolbar to connect add-ins to the IDE
- ☑ utilize the Add-In project template to write your own add-ins
- ☑ use your new CodeDoc add-ins to consistently document your source code

SKILL 17

Using ActiveX

- Understanding the Active Platform
- Understanding the role of ActiveX in software development
- Using ActiveX with Visual Basic
- Using ActiveX to automate Microsoft Word

ActiveX technology is by far one of the most important development paradigms to come out of Redmond, Washington. ActiveX empowers you with a set of re-usable components and a development framework that makes accessing these components simple and consistent.

ActiveX components are a piece of Microsoft's Component Object Model, know as COM. COM-enabled components can be accessed in the same manner whether they are running on the same machine, on separate machines running different operating systems, or on separate machines with different hardware and different operating systems. This extensibility model is awesome for programmers because now you can develop applications that run stand-alone, networked, or across the Internet, all as if they were right on your own computer!

ActiveX neatly wraps COM into an easy-to-use interface that is consistent among similar and disparate systems alike. This skill will introduce you to several ActiveX technologies and teach you how to use them. And if that's not enough, you will learn how to roll your own components! Let's dive in.

The Active Platform

Microsoft's *Active Platform* is a set of client/server development technologies used to integrate distributed systems, particularly the Internet and the PC, into one cohesive system. It consists of many separate technologies, including Remote Automation, ActiveX Documents, ActiveX Controls, Active Movie, Active Desktop, Dynamic HTML (DHTML), VBScript, Microsoft's Visual Basic scripting language, and Active Server Pages (ASPs). In other words, almost everything Microsoft is cranking out is a component of the Active Platform.

Since ActiveX is based on COM, its components can be reused and utilized by several applications. In particular, ActiveX uses Internet technology to assist in creating compact and reusable applications that can be deployed via the Internet or a corporate intranet.

If you have been following the examples throughout this book, then you have already been using ActiveX controls. You can use ActiveX to create fancy command buttons or specialized data-bound controls. The only limit is your imagination.

Although you have been using ActiveX, this skill will teach you how to design and create ActiveX components that you can reuse in your own applications, as well as offer to other programmers. Figure 17.1 shows an ActiveX document in Visual Basic, running in the Internet Explorer Web browser. You will create this application in the "Creating and Using ActiveX Documents" section later in this skill.

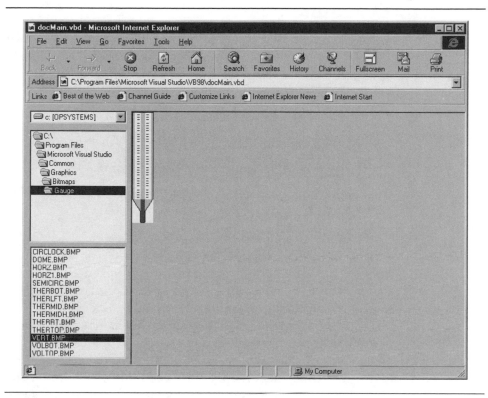

FIGURE 17.1: A sample ActiveX document

The Role of ActiveX

ActiveX leverages Internet technology for several reasons:

- It provides a familiar client/server infrastructure to run your applications.

- Stand-alone Visual Basic applications can be ported over to ActiveX documents so they can then be downloaded via Internet Explorer.

- You can use this same technology to update ActiveX programs on clients' computers: As the application runs from the browser, the document can be configured to request updates when they are available. Then the control can be automatically installed on the clients' computers.

- And, it's all done without disks and without installation programs.

ActiveX Requirements

So what about viruses? Is it possible to send nasty and destructive code to some-one's PC? Of course it is possible. If anyone is set on doing something destructive on a computer, they can do it. However, ActiveX takes steps to avoid guerrilla software. Here are some of the requirements:

- A digital signature is required.
- ActiveX components must be marked as safe for scripting and initialization.
- Each control must employ run-time licensing.
- ActiveX components must be packaged in a format that enables progressive downloading.

Let's look at the ramifications of these requirements.

First, each component must be digitally signed. This digital signature is received from an authorized certification company. When you distribute your control, the signature is embedded in the control so it can be reliably traced back to its origina-tor should something go terribly wrong on the installation PC.

Second, your code must be designated as safe for scripting. Since ActiveX con-trols are used in Web pages through scripts, people can inadvertently or inten-tionally write scripts that can cause damage to your system. Although a control may be harmless under proper usage conditions, a malicious programmer can use it to cause harm. Remember, it's not technology in and of itself that's bad, it's the misuse of technology that's bad. If your control is legitimate, but some-one uses it for malicious intent, the users will track you, the programmer, down. Remember that your control is digitally signed. Your recourse is to create con-trols that cannot be scripted in such a way that can cause harm on a user's com-puter. If you receive a control that has not been marked as safe for scripting, Internet Explorer will display a warning message stating so. It is then up to you to decide whether or not to accept the control.

Third, each control must employ run-time licensing. You must include a pointer to a license file on a server somewhere on the network. The reason this is done is because all of the code used to drive the control resides on the Web page. Any proficient Web surfer can view the source code of an HTML document and use your code. The pointer to the license file ensures users don't download your con-trol and create their own applications with it. This is very similar to how custom controls are licensed in Visual Basic. Controls are usually distributed with a license file that allows the control to work in the IDE. When an application is distributed, the license file does not go with the control. This way, users cannot use controls to develop applications in their own IDE.

Last, ActiveX controls must be packaged in a format that provides progressive downloading. This is basically using a Web browser as a replacement for an installation program. Let's look at how Web pages work within a browser. This will give you a better idea of how progressive download works.

How Web Pages Work

When you surf the Web and click a link, a Hypertext Markup Language (HTML) document is retrieved from the Web server. This document contains all of the information about the graphics, form layout, and content of the document. Before the page is displayed, the browser looks through a directory on your hard disk that maintains copies of Web pages, called a *cache*. The browser determines whether the page or any of its graphics have been loaded onto your computer in the past. If they haven't, the browser requests the graphics from the Web server and the browser will download them to your computer. The browser then takes these components and stores them in the cache. This allows the browser to get the information from your hard disk in the future, instead of from the Internet. The primary purpose for this is speed: It is much faster to load a Web page from your hard disk than it is to get one using a modem. Finally, the browser displays the Web page on your screen. The next time you visit the same site, it will appear on your browser much faster because the browser searches the cache first.

Progressive downloading uses this same type of process to prevent your browser from bogging down while online. This is especially important if you pay for your connect time by the hour! Instead of looking in a cache to see if a control exists, it compares the Class ID of an ActiveX control in the HTML document with the system registry. If the browser finds a match, then it knows your computer already has the control. If there is no match, then the browser starts the download and subsequent registration. Once the control is registered, the browser won't have to download it again.

These are some strict requirements for your ActiveX controls, but they are very important if you want to distribute your controls on a global basis. It should help you to sleep better at night knowing that this multilevel security model also protects you.

Skill 17

ActiveX in Software Development

Now that you understand how ActiveX fits into Microsoft's Internet strategy, you can start examining the tools Visual Basic gives us to utilize this technology. You can create sophisticated ActiveX controls that can be used in your Visual Basic applications, Web pages, and even in other Microsoft products such as Excel or Word. When you start up Visual Basic and examine the Project Wizard, you will notice several ActiveX component templates that you can choose from (see Figure 17.2). These include the ActiveX EXE, ActiveX DLL, ActiveX Control, ActiveX Document DLL, and ActiveX Document EXE. An ActiveX Control can be added to the Visual Basic Toolbox. From there, it can be added to your project just like any other control, and it will operate and behave the same way. When you add an ActiveX control to a program, it becomes part of the IDE and provides new functionality for your application. ActiveX documents are basically Visual Basic applications that run in a Web browser, Internet Explorer in particular.

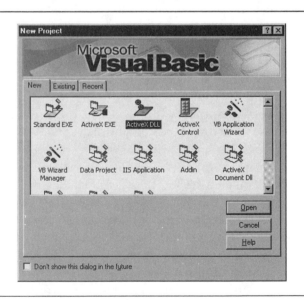

FIGURE 17.2: Available ActiveX components

Creating and Using ActiveX Documents

The ActiveX document allows you to bring the power of Visual Basic to the Internet or your own intranet. An ActiveX document is a Visual Basic application that utilizes Microsoft Internet Explorer 3 (or a newer version) as an application container. ActiveX documents allow you to create portable versions of your application that can be used on laptops, at remote offices, or even from your home. Everything runs from your browser. However, an ActiveX document is not a Web page, it is its own application. In addition, users can navigate between ActiveX documents and Web pages seamlessly through their browser.

When you design your application, you can use ActiveX documents on the front end to serve as the interface and ActiveX DLLs on the back end to do the processing.

To make the ActiveX document shown in the beginning of the skill, follow these steps:

1. Start a new project by selecting File ➤ New Project. Select ActiveX Document EXE from the Project Wizard.

2. In the Properties window, set the Name property of UserDocument1 to **docMain**.

3. Add a drive control to the upper-left corner of docMain. Place its upper-left corner on a grid line away from the top and left sides. Stretch the control so it is about 2 inches wide.

4. Add a directory list control to docMain, one grid line below the drive control. Stretch it so it is the same width as the drive control. Stretch it vertically so its bottom edge is about half-way down the document.

5. Add a file list control below the directory list control. Stretch it the same width as the directory list and stretch it down to one grid line above the bottom edge of docMain.

6. Now, add a picture box control to the document. Set its Name property to **picGraphic**.

7. Place picGraphic one grid line to the right of the edge of the drive control. Stretch it so its right edge is one grid line away from the right edge of the document. Drag the bottom of the picture box so its bottom edge is even with the bottom edge of the file list control. Your document should look similar to Figure 17.3.

Skill 17

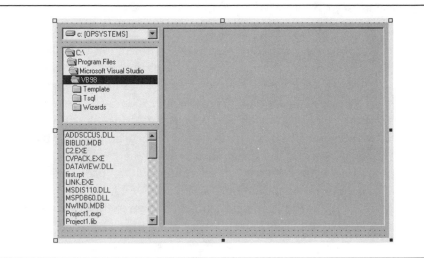

FIGURE 17.3: ActiveX document at design time

8. Double-click the drive control to open the Code window.

9. Add the following code to the Change() event of Drive1:

```
Private Sub Drive1_Change()
    'Synchronize directory with drive control
    Dir1.Path = Drive1.Drive
End Sub
```

10. Add the following code to the Change() event of Dir1:

```
Private Sub Dir1_Change()
    'Synchronize files with directory control
    File1.Path = Dir1.Path
End Sub
```

11. Add this code to the Click() event of File1:

```
Private Sub File1_Click()
    'Show the graphic
    picGraphic.Picture = LoadPicture(Dir1.Path & _
            "\" & File1.filename)
End Sub
```

Unlike forms, you initialize ActiveX documents in the `Initialize()` event. You can place code in this event to prepare the document before it is displayed.

12. We only want to view bitmap graphics for now. Add the following code to the `Initialize()` event of the UserDocument object (docMain):

```
Private Sub UserDocument_Initialize()
    'Show only BMP files
    File1.Pattern = "*.bmp"
End Sub
```

13. Add the last bit of code, listed below, to the `Resize()` event of the docMain:

```
Private Sub UserDocument_Resize()
    'Resize File List
    File1.Height = (ScaleHeight - File1.Top)

    'Resize Graphic Window
    picGraphic.Height = ScaleHeight
    picGraphic.Width = (ScaleWidth - picGraphic.Left)
End Sub
```

The previous code is responsible for making everything on the document look neat. Whenever you resize the browser, the document will resize itself. The code in the `Resize()` event will stretch the picture box control to fit the document. In addition, it will vertically stretch the file list control to be flush with the bottom of the document.

14. Run the project by selecting Run ➤ Start or by pressing F5.

15. You will be presented with a Debugging tab on a Project Properties dialog box. Notice that the Start Component field is set to docMain. Click OK to launch the document.

Notice that Internet Explorer automatically launches and displays the document for you. In the previous version of Visual Basic, you needed to manually run Internet Explorer and find the file yourself.

You have now completed your first ActiveX document. This program is a simple graphics viewer that runs in the browser. Now let's see the document work.

1. Using the drive and directory list controls, open the \Common\Graphics\ Bitmaps\Assorted directory.

2. Click any of the files in the file list box to view it in the picture box (see Figure 17.4).

Skill 17

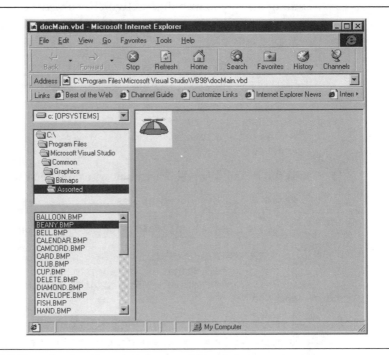

FIGURE 17.4: Running the graphics viewer

That's it for your first ActiveX document control. You can enhance this application or create your own. As time passes, you will see more and more ActiveX documents appearing on the Internet as well as intranets around the world. The possibilities are endless.

 NOTE   To learn more about creating ActiveX documents, search the Visual Basic Help Topics for *ActiveX document*.

Creating and Using ActiveX Controls

The ActiveX control is a custom control you create that can be added to the Toolbox and used in your applications. This type of control can then be used in other Visual Basic projects as well as other ActiveX-compliant programs such as Microsoft Excel. These controls can also be embedded and distributed through HTML Web pages.

To create an ActiveX control, start a new project and select ActiveX Control as the project type (see Figure 17.5).

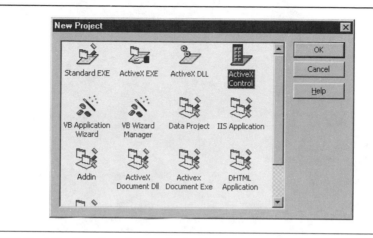

FIGURE 17.5: Creating an ActiveX control

Next you must create the interface. After you do this, you can use the ActiveX Control Interface Wizard to help you finish the job. Let's build a simple button control so you can see how its done:

1. Start a new project. Select ActiveX Control as the project type.

2. Set the `Name` property of the project to **ActiveXButton**.

3. Set the `Name` property of the User Control to **ctlExit**.

4. From the Toolbox, add a Command Button to the control designer. Position it so it is flush with the top-left corner of the control container.

5. Set the button's `Name` property to **cmdExit**. Set its `Caption` property to **E&xit**.

6. Set the `Style` property to **1 – Graphical**.

7. Now, to add a graphic to the button, set the button's `Picture` property to the `MsgBox01.Ico` icon found in the `\Common\Graphics\Icons\Computer` subdirectory.

8. Resize the container control (the gray flat form-like area that the button is sitting on) so it is the same size as the button, as in Figure 17.6.

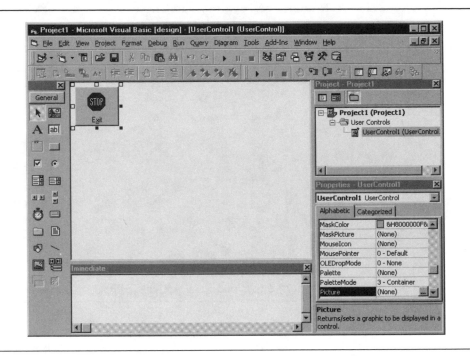

FIGURE 17.6: The custom button control

Adding the Code

Now you are finished with the interface to the control. The next step is to put some code behind it. You will use the ActiveX Control Interface Wizard to accomplish this:

1. Select Add-Ins ➢ Add-In Manager from the menu. This will bring up a dialog box similar to the Components dialog box in the previous exercise.

> **NOTE** For more information on add-ins, see Skill 16, *Extending the IDE with Add-Ins.*

2. Highlight VB6 ActiveX Ctrl Interface Wizard and check the boxes labeled Loaded/Unloaded, and Load on Startup, as shown in Figure 17.7. Click the OK button to close the dialog box. The wizard has now been added to the IDE.

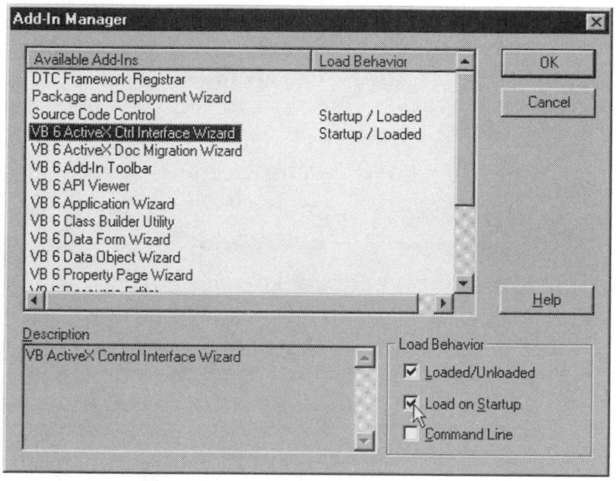

FIGURE 17.7: Adding the Control Interface Wizard to the IDE

3. Next, select Add-Ins ➤ ActiveX Control Interface Wizard from the menu to start the wizard.

4. When the Introduction dialog box appears (see Figure 17.8), read it and click the Next button.

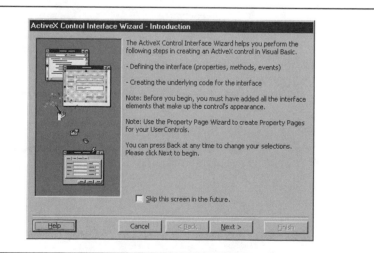

FIGURE 17.8: Starting the ActiveX Control Interface Wizard

In the next step, you determine which properties, methods, and events your control will need. If you think of your control as any other control and picture its properties in the Properties window, you can get an idea of what your control will need. This button is very simple, so you only need a few properties and only one event.

5. Remove all of the items from the Selected Names list except for those listed in Figure 17.9. Your object should have `Caption`, `Enabled`, `Font`, and one `Click` event. You will need to add the `Caption` property from the Available Names list. When all looks good, click the Next button.

6. The next dialog box will ask to create custom members. Since we have none, just click the Next button to move to the next step.

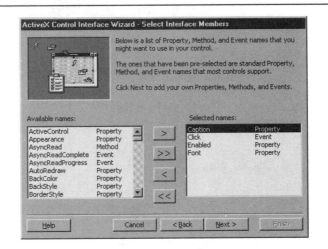

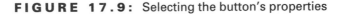

FIGURE 17.9: Selecting the button's properties

7. Now you need to map out the control's properties to the properties of its components: Click the `Caption` property and map it to the Exit button by selecting **cmdExit** from the Control drop-down list. The `Member` property should change to `Caption` (see Figure 17.10).

8. Click the `Click()` event and map it to the Exit button's `Click()` event.

9. Map your control's `Enabled` property to the Exit button's `Enabled` property.

10. Map the `Font` property to the Exit button's `Font` property.

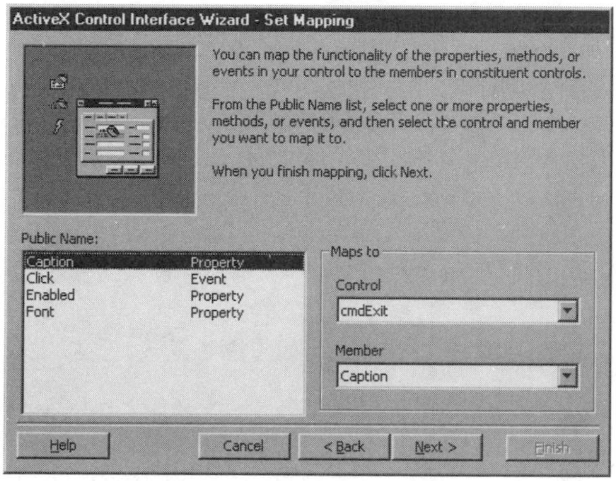

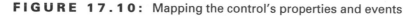

FIGURE 17.10: Mapping the control's properties and events

The next frame of the wizard will ask you if you want to view a summary report (see Figure 17.11). This report contains important information on how to utilize your control when it is finished. If you want to view the report, check the check box. If you do not want to view it, clear the check box.

11.   Click the Finish button.

12.   Save your project.

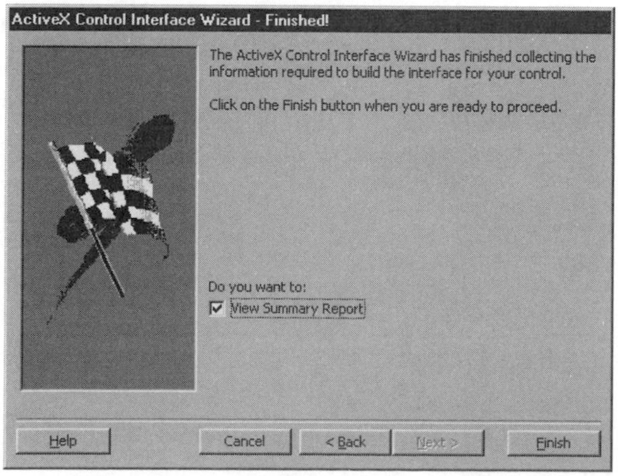

FIGURE 17.11: Finishing the control

You have just created your first ActiveX control. Although it seemed like a lot of steps for such a simple control, you will get used to it, and with practice you will be quickly creating ActiveX controls of your own.

You can compile this object to make a portable OCX control, or you can use it in its uncompiled form in the IDE. All you need to do is to close the object designer. It will automatically add itself to the Toolbox, where you can add it to a form in another project. In its compiled state, you can embed it into a Web document as well. You will learn how to embed ActiveX controls into Web pages in Skill 18, *Internet Development with Visual Basic*.

Creating and Using ActiveX DLLs

The ActiveX DLLs replace the components formerly known as OCXs. These components are especially useful when they are linked to databases and run on servers. These DLLs can be called from your browser or your custom Visual Basic front-end. In Skill 10, you created a very simple ActiveX DLL that displays several dialog boxes. Now it's time to create something a little bit more sophisticated, and yet practical enough for a beginner. In this example, you will create a line and page counting utility for Microsoft Word 97. The code here is a subset of a more sophisticated control I created a year ago.

To create an ActiveX DLL, follow these simple steps:

1. Start a new project.

2. Select ActiveX DLL as the project type from the Project Wizard (see Figure 17.12).

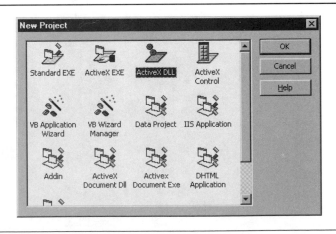

FIGURE 17.12: Selecting the ActiveX DLL project

3. Set the project Name to **WordHelpers**. The utilities in this control will be used to add some functionality to Microsoft Word 97.

4. Change the Name property of Class1 to **Counters**. You will be adding some counting functions in this class.

5. Select Project ➢ References from the Visual Basic menu. Add a reference to Microsoft Windows 8.0 Object Library and click OK to close the dialog box.

6. Double-click Counters in the Project Explorer to open the Code window.

7. Add the following function to the class. This is the function that dynamically calculates the line count of the active Word document:

```
Public Function LineCount(CharactersPerLine As Integer) As Long
    Dim x As Word.Application
    Dim cc As Long           'Character Count

    'Get a reference to the Document
    Set x = Word.Application

        'Get the total character count
        With x.ActiveDocument
            cc = .Characters.Count
        End With

    'Cleanup our mess
    Set x = Nothing

    'To get the total line count,
    'we need to divide the total
    'character count by
    'CharactersPerLine
    LineCount = Int(cc / CharactersPerLine)
End Function
```

8. Now add the following function. It will be used to retrieve the page count of the active document:

```
Public Function PageCount() As Integer
    Dim x As Word.Application

    'Get a reference to the Document
    Set x = Word.Application

        'Get the total character count
        With x.ActiveDocument
            PageCount = .BuiltInDocumentProperties("Number " & _
```

```
                    "of Pages")
             End With

         'Cleanup our mess
         Set x = Nothing
      End Function
```

9. Save the project so you don't lose any changes.

10. Compile the project as an ActiveX DLL by selecting Make WordHelpers.dll, as shown in Figure 17.13.

Once the DLL is compiled, you can access it by referencing its type library in the References Window in Word's Visual Basic Editor. After it's referenced, you can derive an object from the DLL and call its properties and methods just like any other object.

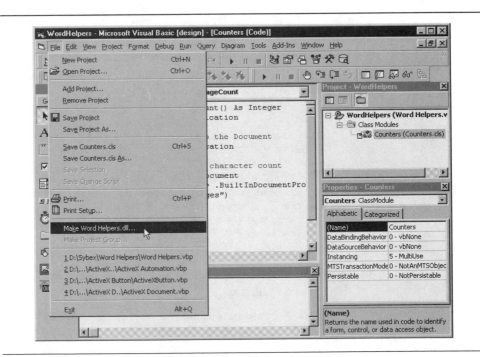

FIGURE 17.13: Compiling the DLL

You've completed one-half of the process to make this control do something useful. Now you need to write two macros in Word to access your control.

Fortunately, Word 97 uses Visual Basic for Applications, or VBA, as its scripting engine. In the future, most if not all Office applications will use VBA.

1. Start Microsoft Word 97.

2. Open the Visual Basic Editor for Word 97 by selecting Tools ➤ Macros ➤ Visual Basic Editor, or by pressing Alt+F11. If you have Visual Basic for Applications installed, you will see the Visual Basic Editor shown in Figure 17.14.

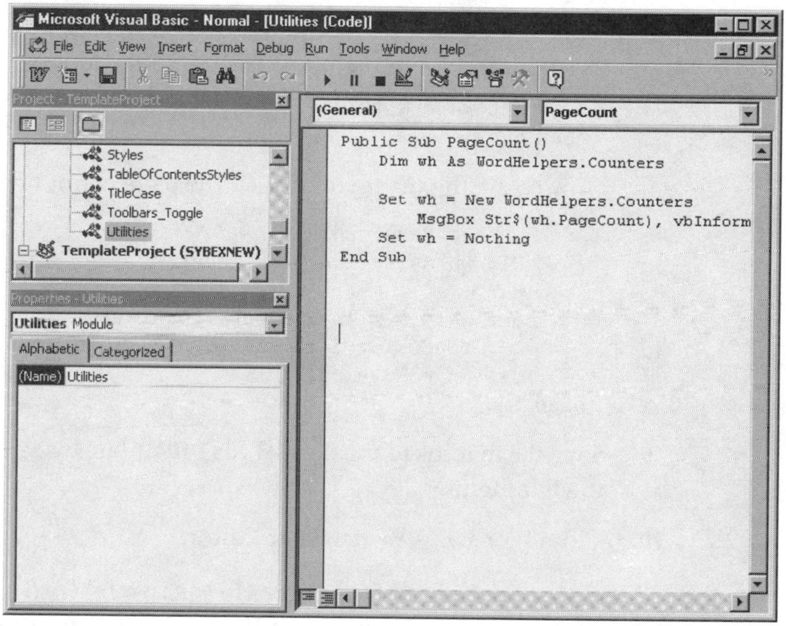

FIGURE 17.14: Word 97's Visual Basic Editor

3. Add a module to the Normal project by right-clicking the Project Explorer and selecting Insert ➤ Module from the pop-up menu.

4. Set the Name property of the new module to **Utilities**.

5. As you do in Visual Basic 6, you must reference the WordHelpers type library. Select Tools ➤ References to open the References dialog box.

6. Select WordHelpers from the list and click OK to close the dialog box.

TIP   Word's Visual Basic Editor is very similar to the Visual Basic 6 IDE, but some of the menu items have been moved around. The References menu item is on the Tools menu, rather than the Project menu.

7.   Add the following procedure to the module to create a line count macro:

```
Public Sub LineCount()
    Dim wh As WordHelpers.Counters

    Set wh = New WordHelpers.Counters
        MsgBox Str$(wh.LineCount(65)), vbInformation,_
            "Line Count:"
    Set wh = Nothing
End Sub
```

8.   Now create the macro to display the page count by typing this procedure:

```
Public Sub PageCount()
    Dim wh As WordHelpers.Counters

    Set wh = New WordHelpers.Counters
        MsgBox Str$(wh.PageCount), vbInformation, "Line Count:"
    Set wh = Nothing
End Sub
```

9.   Save the macros to the Normal.dot template by selecting Save Normal from the File menu.

10. Close Word 97's Visual Basic Editor.

Now you have added two macros to Microsoft Word 97. As you saw, the code is very similar, in fact identical, to Visual Basic code. The two procedures you added, LineCount and PageCount, are now stored as Word 97 macros in the global template. This means that they can be used on any Word document that you open. Try these steps to see what I mean.

1.   Open Microsoft Word 97 if it is not open already.

2.   Open any Word document you may have on your hard disk.

3.   Open the Macros dialog box by pressing Alt+F8. You will see a list of registered macros like those in Figure 17.15.

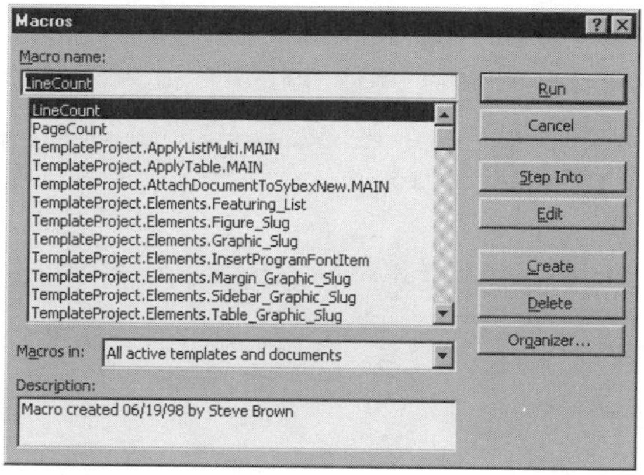

FIGURE 17.15: The Macros dialog box

Skill 17

4.   Select the LineCount macro from the list and click the Run button. You will see a small dialog box that shows the line count of the active document.

Using ActiveX to Automate Microsoft Word

Now that you have created an ActiveX DLL that you can use in Word 97, it's time to learn how to use Visual Basic to control Word. This process is called *automation*. If you have Microsoft Office, you can use Visual Basic and ActiveX to automate tasks in any Office application. You can create automation routines to calculate values in columns in an Excel spreadsheet or you can write your own line-counting routines for Microsoft Word. There is really no limit to what you can do—you just have to find a need.

Office automation is great because you can create utilities or complete third-party applications to fill in the gaps that Microsoft left in some of its applications. My first attempt to automate Word was when I had to write a line counting component that could be called from Word. It contained many user-customizable routines that could be called from VBA, the scripting language in Word. To give you an idea of how to use Visual Basic to control Microsoft Word 97, try this example. Even if you don't have Word 97, look through the steps and learn what's happening. It's useful, cool, and especially fun!

1.   Start a new project by selecting Ctrl+N in Visual Basic.

2. Select Standard EXE from the New Project dialog box. Click OK to create the project.

3. Set the Name property of the project to **ActiveXAutomation**.

4. Click Form1 to make it the active control. Set its Name property to **frmMain**. Set its Caption to **ActiveX Automation**.

5. Add a Command Button to frmMain. Set its Name property to **cmdCreate**, and set its Caption to **Create Some Documents**.

6. Before you can automate Microsoft Word, you need to reference its type library. Do this by selecting Project ➤ References from the Visual Basic menu.

7. In the References dialog box, select Microsoft Word 8.0 Object Library as shown in Figure 17.16, and click OK to reference its type library.

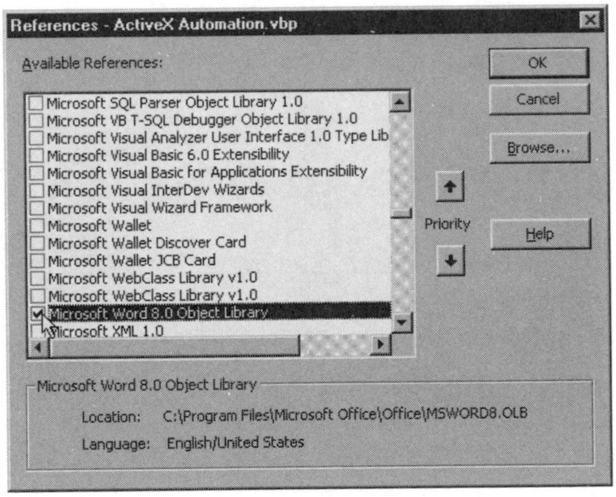

FIGURE 17.16: Referencing Word's type library

8. Double-click cmdCreate to open its Code window.

9. Add the following code to the Click() event of cmdCreate:

```
Private Sub cmdCreate_Click()
    Dim x As Word.Document
    Dim i As Integer

    'Loop 10 times
    For i = 1 To 10
        'Create a new word document
        Set x = New Word.Document

        'Type some text...
        With x.ActiveWindow.Selection
            .TypeText "This document was created using " & _
                "Visual Basic 6.0 "
            .TypeText "and Microsoft Office automation."
            .TypeParagraph
            .TypeParagraph
            .TypeText "This is document " & Trim$(Str$(i)) & _
                " of 10."
            .TypeParagraph
            .TypeParagraph
            .TypeText "Have a nice day!"
        End With

        'Now save and close it
        With x
            .SaveAs "c:\Visual Basic Created Me " & _
                Trim$(Str$(i)) & " times!"
            .Close
        End With

        'Destroy the object to release memory
        Set x = Nothing
    Next
End Sub
```

10. Save and run the project.

Before you click the Create button, make sure that you have Microsoft Word open. Close any documents and shrink its window. Place both applications side-by-side and watch what happens (see Figure 17.17).

Skill 17

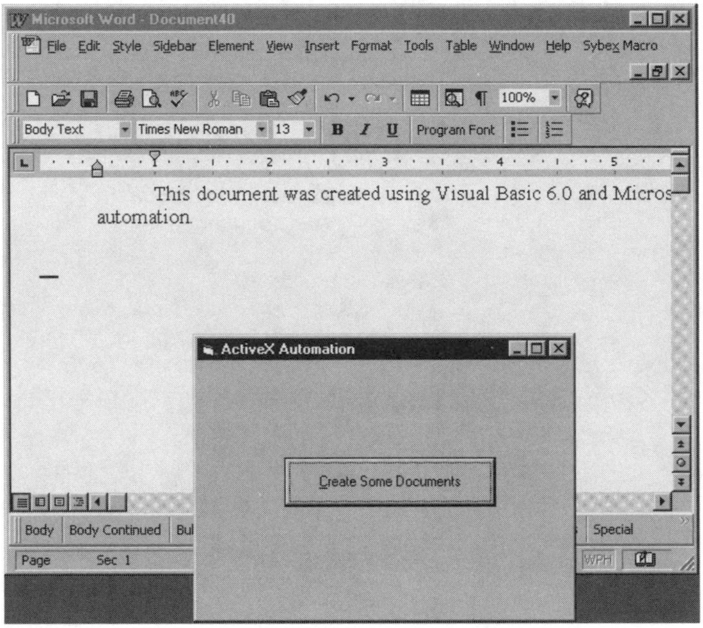

FIGURE 17.17: Holy automated scripts, Bitman!

If everything ran smoothly, you should have 10 new documents sitting in the root directory of your C: drive!

The key to this application is the object x. You will notice that first line of the Click() event defines a Word.Document object. This object is used to create, type, and save Word documents through OLE automation. After the Word.Document object is instantiated, it uses the .TypeText method to add text to the document. Once all of the text has been added, the document is saved using the .SaveAs method, and the document is closed with the .Close method. After that, the Word.Document object is destroyed so another can be created. All of these routines are nested in a For...Next loop that iterates 10 times, yielding 10 discreet documents.

There is almost no limit to what you can do now that you have the power of ActiveX at your fingertips! If you have Office 97, or even just Word 97, practice writing your own automation routines. If you are creative enough, you will probably create the next best helper-app. If it's good enough, you could probably sell it to others!

You can easily modify any class object in your Visual Basic projects to be its own stand-alone DLL or custom control. Which form you decide to create is dependent upon the design of your project. If you have not done so, look back at Skill 15. It teaches you the basics of object-oriented programming (OOP). This will help you to better understand class design and creation, which will in turn help you to create great controls.

You can use ActiveX to exploit the features of the Internet and to help you build robust client-server and Web-based applications from Visual Basic. ActiveX allows you to create your own custom controls that can be added to Visual Basic's Toolbox as well as be embedded in HTML documents. With a good understanding of OOP, client/server development, and the World Wide Web, you can create your own ActiveX controls to utilize the Internet as the foundation of your application.

Are You up to Speed?

Now you can...

- ☑ **understand the roles of ActiveX and COM in software development**
- ☑ **create ActiveX documents**
- ☑ **create ActiveX controls**
- ☑ **create ActiveX DLLs**
- ☑ **develop your own automation objects and use them in Microsoft Office**
- ☑ **control Microsoft Office from your own Visual Basic applications**

Skill 17

SKILL 18

Internet Development with Visual Basic

- Using the WebBrowser control
- Developing with Winsock
- Designing ActiveX Documents
- Using DHTML

Visual Basic offers many tools to help you develop applications for the Internet. You can create robust applications using any combination of static HTML, Dynamic HTML (DHTML), ActiveX documents, and Internet-aware ActiveX controls.

In this skill, you will learn about these Internet development tools and use them to build a Web-based chat room called WebComm. The entire application will consist of a custom Web browser that launches a DHTML start page, which in turn launches the WebComm client, which is actually a Visual Basic ActiveX document. The WebComm client utilizes the Winsock control to communicate with a centralized chat room server. The entire chat room is easy to develop and can be easily modified to accommodate more users or add functionality. By the end of this skill, you will be able to start developing your own Internet applications using Visual Basic!

Using the WebBrowser Control

As you can deduce, you use the WebBrowser control to add Web-browsing functionality to your Visual Basic application. Wouldn't it be nice to be able to show a Web page without having to launch a Web browser? A good example of this is Microsoft's new HTML Help System. Although it requires Microsoft Internet Explorer 4.01 to be installed on your computer, the help system never launches the browser. Instead it launches an application that wraps the WebBrowser control in its own interface (see Figure 18.1).

The example in this section shows how you can use Internet Explorer's Web-Browser control to write your own custom WebBrowser application. You are probably wondering why you would want to create another browser, especially one that requires the one you already use. The answer is simple: you can integrate specific Web sites, ActiveX documents, or other application-specific functionality that simply doesn't come with the browser. You'll see what I mean in a minute.

1. Start a new project in Visual Basic by pressing Ctrl+N. Select Standard EXE from the New Project dialog box and click OK.

2. Set the Name property of the project to **WebIndex**.

3. Set the Name property of Form1 to **frmMain**. Set its Caption to **WebIndex**.

4. Right-click the Toolbox and select Components from the pop-up menu. This will bring up the Components dialog box shown in Figure 18.2.

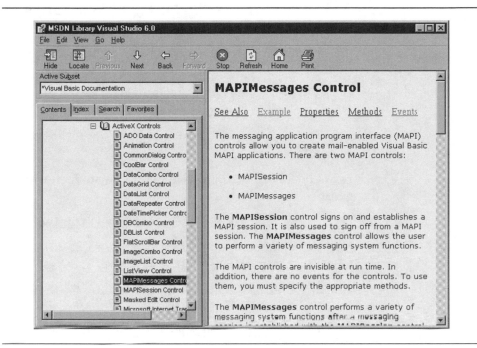

FIGURE 18.1: HTML Help uses a WebBrowser interface.

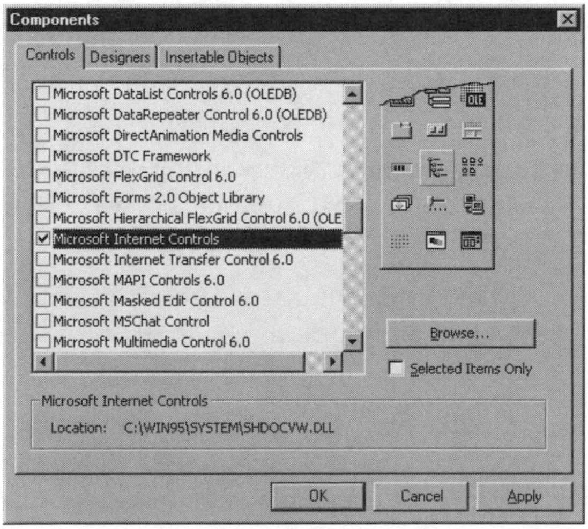

FIGURE 18.2: The Components dialog box

5. Add the WebBrowser control to the Toolbox by selecting Microsoft Internet Controls in the list.

6. Add the Microsoft Windows Common Controls 6.0 and Microsoft Windows Common Controls –3 6.0 by checking them in the list.

7. Click OK to close the Components dialog box. The components will be added to your Toolbox.

8. Add a CoolBar control to the top of frmMain. Set its Name property to **cbrCoolbar**.

9. Now add a Toolbar control to the cbrCoolbar. Be sure to drop it in the Coolbar, and not on the form.

10. Set the Name property of the Toolbar control to **tbrToolbar**.

11. Add a ListBox control to the left side of the form. Stretch it so it is about half the width of the form. Set the Name property of the list to **lstSites**.

12. Add a WebBrowser control to the right side of the form, under the toolbar. Set its Name property to **WebBrowser**.

13. Add an ImageList control to the form. Set its Name property to **imlToolbar**.

14. Save your project so you don't lose any changes. Your form should look similar to Figure 18.3.

15. Click the ImageList control and double-click the (Custom) field in the Properties window. This will open the property pages for the control.

16. Click the Images tab.

17. Click the Insert Image button to add an image to the list.

18. When the Select Picture dialog box appears, select Undo.bmp from the \Common\graphics\Bitmaps\Tlbr_Win95 directory and click the Open button to add the image to the control.

19. Click the Insert Image button again to add another image. Select Redo.bmp from the same directory in the previous step. Click OK to add the image to the list.

20. Click the Insert Image button again to add the last image. Select Find.bmp from the same directory in the previous step. Click OK to add the image to the list. The property pages should look like Figure 18.4.

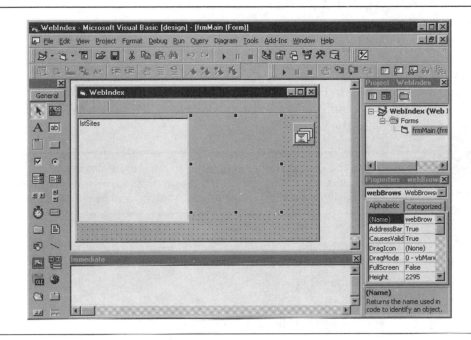

FIGURE 18.3: The WebIndex form in the Form Designer

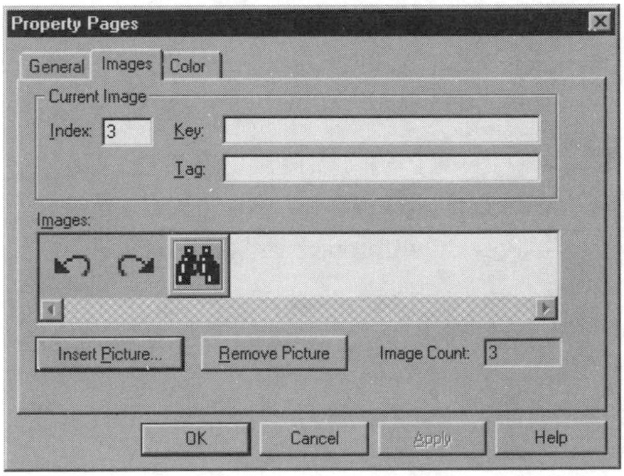

FIGURE 18.4: The images in the ImageList control

21. Click the OK button to close the property pages.

22. Click tbrToolbar in the Form Designer to make it the active control. Double-click the (Custom) field in the Properties window to open the property pages for the toolbar.

23. On the General tab of the property pages, set the Image List field to **imlToolbar**. Set the Style field to **1 – tbrFlat**. When you are done, click the Buttons tab.

> **TIP** As you develop larger applications with more buttons and graphics, you will want to consider adding and linking the graphics at run time using code. This will make it easier to add or remove graphics as you add new features to your applications.

24. Click the Insert Button button to add a button to the toolbar. Set the Key field to **Back** and the Image field to **1**. Click the Apply button to commit the changes.

25. Click Insert Button again to add another button to the toolbar. Set the Key field to **Forward** and the Image field to **2**.

26. Click Insert Button again and add another button to the toolbar. Set the Style field to **3 - tbrSeparator**.

27. Add another button. Set the Key field to **Search** and the Image field to **3**. Click the OK button to close the property pages for the toolbar.

28. Select the CoolBar control and open its property pages by double-clicking the (Custom) field in the Properties window.

29. When the property pages appear, click the Bands tab.

30. Keep clicking the Remove Band button until the index field says 1. This will leave you with one band on the Coolbar.

31. Set the Child property to **tbrToolbar** and click the OK button to close the dialog box. The form should now look like Figure 18.5.

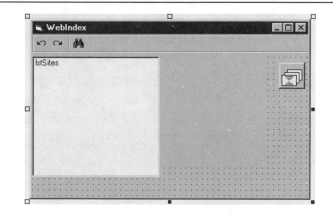

FIGURE 18.5: The visual design of the WebIndex application

Now that you have completed the visual design of the application, continue with the following steps to add code to the form.

1. Double-click frmMain to open its Code window.

2. Add the following code to the Load() event of frmMain:

```
Private Sub Form_Load()
    lstSites.AddItem "www.sybex.com"
    lstSites.AddItem "www.microsoft.com"
    lstSites.AddItem "www.myle.com"
End Sub
```

3. Add this code to the Form_Resize() event:

```
Private Sub Form_Resize()
    If WindowState <> vbMinimized Then
        'Stretch the Coolbar
        cbrCoolbar.Move 0, 0, ScaleWidth

        'Size the site list
        With lstSites
            .Move 0, cbrCoolbar.Height, .Width, _
                (ScaleHeight - cbrCoolbar.Height)
        End With

        'Size the browser
        With webBrowser
            .Move .Left, cbrCoolbar.Height, _
```

```
                        (ScaleWidth - .Left), _
                        (ScaleHeight - cbrCoolbar.Height)
                End With
            End If
        End Sub
```

The WebBrowser control loads Web pages by calling the Navigate method.
When you call this method, Internet Explorer's components will retrieve the
requested URL and display it on the WebBrowser control.

4.   To give the applications some navigational functionality, add this code to
     the Click() event of the lstSites control:

```
Private Sub lstSites_Click()
    'Jump to the selected site
    webBrowser.Navigate _
        Trim$(lstSites.Text)
End Sub
```

5.   Let's add some more navigational functionality to the browser. Add the
     following code to the ButtonClick() event of tbrToolbar:

```
Private Sub tbrToolbar_ButtonClick(ByVal Button As _
        ComctlLib.Button)
    'Skip error checking
    On Error Resume Next

    'What button was pressed?
    Select Case UCase$(Trim$(Button.Key))
        Case Is = "BACK"
            webBrowser.GoBack
        Case Is = "FORWARD"
            webBrowser.GoForward
        Case Is = "SEARCH"
            webBrowser.GoSearch
    End Select
End Sub
```

6.   Save the project once more so you don't lose any changes. When its saved,
     press F5 to run the application.

Click www.sybex.com to see the Sybex home page (Figure 18.6). You can click
any of the links in the page and the WebBrowser control will take you there. You
can even right-click the page and view the HTML code or print the page, just like
in Internet Explorer!

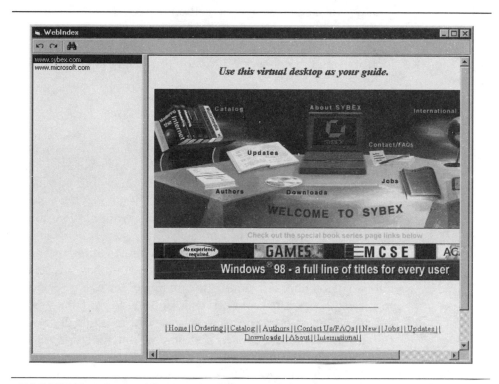

FIGURE 18.6: Viewing the Sybex Web site using the WebBrowser control

If you get too far into the Web site, you can always back out by clicking the Back button that you added on the toolbar. In addition, you can move forward, or you can go to Microsoft's Search Web page and search for another site. When you are done viewing some pages, close the application and return to Visual Basic.

Before you continue on with the next example, a few things are worth noting. First, the list of sites are added to the list in the Form_Load() event. You can add more sites to the list using the AddItem method of the list.

The heart of the work is completed in the Click() event of lstSites and the ButtonClick() event of tbrToolbar. As you know by now, you use the Navigate method to load a specific URL into the WebBrowser control. In addition, two methods are called in the ButtonClick() event.

The GoBack method is used to navigate backwards. You call this method from the Back button so the user doesn't get lost in *Web jail*. The GoForward method is used, obviously, to move forward through a list of recently navigated URLs.

Finally, you call the GoSearch method to navigate to the default search page that is defined in Internet Explorer.

Now that you have a good idea of how to make a Web-browsing client, let's look at using the Winsock control to utilize more low-level functionality.

Developing with Winsock

The Winsock control provides easy access to the Transmission Control Protocol (TCP), and User Datagram Protocol (UDP). You can use both of them in your applications to develop sophisticated communications applications and utilities. TCP requires an explicit *session*, while UDP is a *connectionless* protocol.

A *session* is a private logical link between two applications that allows both applications to communicate. You can think of a session as being like a telephone call. For both applications to communicate, one must request a connection from the other, like when you dial your friend's phone number. The server application is notified of a connection request (the ringing of the phone) and determines whether to answer it or not. Once the server accepts the request, the session is created and both the client and server can communicate bi-directionally. Both applications can communicate until either party disconnects from the session. This is like hanging up your phone.

UDP is *connectionless*. It functions more like a CB or other two-way radio. Instead of requiring an explicit session, both applications are made aware of each other. In UDP, this is achieved by specifying the host name or IP address and port number of the other application. Once both applications are "pointed toward each other," they can start communicating.

In this skill, you will be using TCP to develop a Web-based chat room application called *WebComm*. It can be used on your intranet, or on the Internet to bring people together to talk, collaborate on projects, or just goof off. No matter how you use the application, the development process will show you the details of communicating using TCP/IP.

Let's start building a chat room server using the Winsock control. Follow these steps. By the time you are done, you will have the completed the foundation for the WebComm application.

1. Start a new project by selecting File ➤ New project from the Visual Basic menu. Select Standard EXE from the New Project dialog box and click OK.

2. Set the Name property of the project to **WebCommServer**.

3. Change the Name property of Form1 to **frmMain**. Set its Caption property to **WebComm Server**.

4. Double-click the Icon property in the Properties window. Select W95mbx04.bmp from the \Common\Graphics\Icons\Computer directory. Click the Open button to add the icon to the form.

5. Open the Menu Editor by selecting Tools ➢ Menu Editor.

6. Add a top-level menu and set its Name property to **mnuFile**. Set its Caption to **&File**.

7. Add a submenu to mnuFile and set its Name property to **mnuFileExit**. Set its Caption to **E&xit**.

8. Click OK to close the menu editor.

9. Add a ListBox control to the form. Set its Name property to **lstMessages**.

10. Add a Timer control to the form. Set its Name property to **tmrTimer**, and its Interval property to **1000**.

11. Right-click the Toolbox and select Components from the pop-up menu.

12. Check the boxes next to Microsoft Windows Common Controls 6.0 and Microsoft Winsock Control 6.0. Click the OK button to close the Components dialog box. The controls will be added to the Toolbox.

13. Add a Winsock control to frmMain. For simplicity, set its Name property to **wsk**. Set its Index property to **0**. You will be creating a control array later. Don't worry about the other properties; they will be set at run time.

14. Add a StatusBar control to frmMain. Set its Name property to **stsStatus**. Make sure its Align property is set to **2 – vbAlignBottom**.

15. Double-click (Custom) in the Properties window to open the property pages for the StatusBar.

16. Click the Panels tab when the Property Pages dialog box appears.

17. Type **Sessions: 0** in the Text field.

18. Click the Insert Panels button to insert another panel. After the panel is added, change the Index field to **2** so you can modify the second panel.

19. Set the Bevel field to **0 – sbrNobevel**. Set the AutoSize field to **1 –sbrSpring**.

Skill 18

20. Click the Insert Panels button again. When the panel is added, set the index field to **3** to work on the third panel. Set the Style field to **6 – sbrDate**.

21. Insert one more panel and set the index field to **4** to work on the fourth panel. Set the Style field to **5 – sbrTime**.

22. After you have added all the panels, click the OK button to close the Property Pages dialog box. The form should look similar to Figure 18.7.

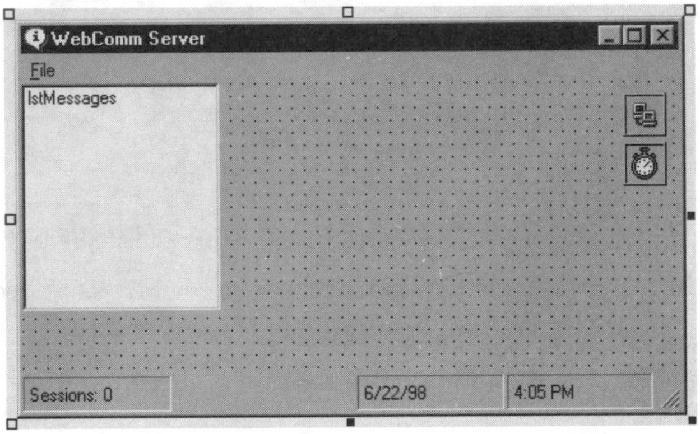

FIGURE 18.7: The WebComm Server in design mode

23. Save the project so you don't accidentally lose any changes.

You have now laid out the pieces of the application puzzle. Let's add some code to tie the pieces together.

1. Double-click frmMain to open its Code window.

2. Add the following lines of code to the (General)(Declarations) section of the form:

```
Option Explicit

Private Const WSK_LOCAL_PORT = 12345
Private Const MAX_SESSIONS = 11
```

The first constant tells the server to use local port number 12345. This is the port that the WebComm Client will need to talk to in order to chat. The second constant sets the maximum number of concurrent sessions to 11. This number is actually one more than the number of users that can chat simultaneously. The first session is utilized by the server to listen for connection requests. When it receives a connection request, the WebComm Server forwards the session to one of the other 10 Winsock controls and continues waiting for connection requests.

3.   Every time something happens to the server (for example, a user connects or disconnects), the interface is refreshed. This is the responsibility of the UpdateStatus procedure. Add this procedure to the (General)(Declarations) section of frmMain, as listed below:

```
Private Sub UpdateStatus()
    Dim i As Integer
    Dim actsess As Integer

    'Count the number of active sessions
    For i = 1 To MAX_SESSIONS
        With wsk(i)
            If .State = sckConnected Then
                'Increment the session count
                actsess = actsess + 1
            End If
        End With
    Next

    'Refresh the status
    With stsStatus
        .Panels(1).Text = "Sessions: " & _
            Trim$(Str$(actsess))
    End With
End Sub
```

The code in the UpdateStatus procedure checks the current state of each Winsock control in the array. If it sees that a control is currently connected to a client, it increments the actsess variable. When the loop is complete, the value in actsess is displayed in the first panel of the Status Bar.

4.   The code listed below creates a control array of Winsock controls and configures the protocol for each. Add this code to the Form_Load() event:

```
Private Sub Form_Load()
    Dim i As Integer

    'Configure the winsock receiver
    With wsk(0)
        .Protocol = sckTCPProtocol
        .LocalPort = WSK_LOCAL_PORT
```

Skill 18

```
                    .Listen
                End With

                'Load 10 more winsocks
                For i = 1 To MAX_SESSIONS
                    Load wsk(i)
                    wsk(i).Protocol = sckTCPProtocol
                    wsk(i).LocalPort = WSK_LOCAL_PORT
                Next

                'Update the status bar
                UpdateStatus
            End Sub
```

5. Add the following code to the Form_Resize() event:

```
        Private Sub Form_Resize()
            'Stretch the message list
            If WindowState <> vbMinimized Then
                lstMessages.Move 0, _
                    0, _
                    ScaleWidth, _
                    (ScaleHeight - stsStatus.Height)
            End If
        End Sub
```

6. Add the following code to the Click() event of mnuFileExit:

```
        Private Sub mnuFileExit_Click()
            'End the application
            Unload Me
        End Sub
```

7. We want the status to be refreshed every second, so add the following code to the tmrTimer_Timer() event:

```
        Private Sub tmrTimer_Timer()
            'Update the status bar
            UpdateStatus
        End Sub
```

The bulk of the work in the WebComm Server is completed by the Winsock control array. You will see from the sample code that many of the events of the wsk control array are used.

The first event to occur in the Winsock control is the ConnectionRequest() event. The following code is responsible for receiving the request, checking if any Winsock sessions are open, and routing the request to the available session.

8. Add the following code to the `ConnectionRequest()` event of the wsk control array:

```
Private Sub wsk_ConnectionRequest(Index As Integer, _
        ByVal requestID As Long)
    Dim msg As String
    Dim i As Integer

    'If this is the listening port...
    If Index = 0 Then
        'Let's find an open session
        For i = 1 To MAX_SESSIONS
            With wsk(i)
                If .State = sckClosed Then
                    'Connect to session i
                    .Accept requestID

                    'Break out of the loop
                    Exit For
                End If
            End With
        Next
    End If
End Sub
```

The `Index` parameter indicates which Winsock control triggered the event. Since we know that `wsk(0)` is the listening session, the code checks to make sure that it can forward the connection request to another control. The `RequestID` parameter is a unique value indicating the ID of the client requesting a connection. You use this parameter to accept a connection request on a specific Winsock control. After a Winsock control accepts a session, the `Connect` event for that control is fired.

9. Add the following code to the `Connection()` event of the wsk control array. This will force the interface to update itself when a new user connects to the server.

```
Private Sub wsk_Connect(Index As Integer)
    'Update the status bar
    UpdateStatus
End Sub
```

The next block of code does all of the work. It receives a message from a client and relays it back to all of the active sessions. This gives the application its "chat room" functionality. When data arrives from a session, it is buffered and a `Data-Arrival()` event is triggered to let the Winsock control know that there is data to be processed. You can then write a handler to get the data using the `GetData` method.

10.   Add the following code to the wsk_DataArrival() event:

```
Private Sub wsk_DataArrival(Index As Integer, _
        ByVal bytesTotal As Long)
    Dim msg As String
    Dim rc As Integer
    Dim i As Integer

    'Get the message
    wsk(Index).GetData msg, , bytesTotal

    'Add it to the list
    lstMessages.AddItem msg

    'Relay the message back to the other clients
    For i = 1 To MAX_SESSIONS
        With wsk(i)
            If .State = sckConnected Then
                'Relay the message back to the
                'selected client
                .SendData msg

                'Wait for the message
                'to go out
                DoEvents
            End If
        End With
    Next
End Sub
```

The code listed above is fairly straightforward. The line reading:

```
wsk(Index).GetData msg, , bytesTotal
```

retrieves the data stored in the buffer for the wsk(Index) control. Using the GetData method, it retrieves no more bytes of data than specified in bytes-Total, and it places them in the msg string. After the data is retrieved, the message is added to the list so an administrator can see who's saying what. If you wanted to, you could add code here to store each message in an ASCII file or a database using ADO code. After the message is logged, the server relays it to all of the active sessions, resulting in a broadcast event of sorts.

11.   The final event to occur in the life of the session is the Close() event. We simply want to refresh the screen when a user disconnects, so add the following code to the Close() event:

```
Private Sub wsk_Close(Index As Integer)
    'Update the status bar
    UpdateStatus
End Sub
```

12. Save the project so you don't lose any changes.

After the project is saved, press F5 to make sure the application starts without any errors. If it runs successfully, compile the project into an executable (.EXE) file by selecting File ➤ Make WebCommServer.exe from the Visual Basic menu. You will need to run the executable in the next section.

NOTE If you are unfamiliar with compiling your applications or building executables (.EXE) files, please refer back to Skill 14.

Although the application can be run locally, it is more impressive when you install it on a separate computer and watch it as the messages come in and get logged in the list. From the client's perspective, it is really cool knowing that the data is actually being sent over a network to another machine, and then relayed back. Continue with the next example. When you are finished, you will be able to start the WebComm Server and Client and start chatting!

Designing ActiveX Documents

As you learned in Skill 17, the ActiveX document allows you to bring the power of Visual Basic to the Internet or to your own intranet. An ActiveX document is a Visual Basic application that utilizes Microsoft Internet Explorer 3 (or a newer version) as an application container.

When you use ActiveX documents for your projects, you can create portable versions of your applications that can be used on laptops, at remote offices, or even from your home. Everything runs from a Web browser. An ActiveX document, however, is not a Web page; it is its own application. In addition, users can navigate between ActiveX documents and Web pages seamlessly through their browser.

To see how all of this works, let's continue developing the WebComm application by creating the WebComm Client using an ActiveX document instead of a Standard EXE project.

1. Start a new project by selecting File ➤ New Project from the Visual Basic menu.

2. Select ActiveX Document EXE from the New Project dialog box.

3. Set the Name property of the project to **WebCommClient**.

4. Open the Project Properties dialog box by right-clicking the project in the Project Explorer and selecting WebCommClient properties from the pop-up menu.

APARTMENT-MODEL THREADING

When the Project Properties dialog box appears, as shown below, take a look at the Threading Model section on the General tab. Threading is new to Visual Basic 6. Actually, it was previously released in a service pack for Visual Basic 5, but it is built into version 6. Some ActiveX components can now be multithreaded, meaning they can play nicely with other objects and not interfere with each other.

Visual Basic uses apartment-model threading to separate threads between objects. The way it works is each thread has its own copy of global data required for the object. As each thread is created, a new copy of the data is made, and any changes to it will not affect the global data for other threads. To oversimplify this concept, the result is a Visual Basic application that can perform limited multitasking.

If you are interested in learning more about multithreading, read Visual Basic's online help.

5. Click the Make tab and change the Title field to **WebComm Client**.

6. Click the OK button to close the dialog box.

7. Set the Name property of UserDocument1 to **docWebComm**.

8. Right-click the Toolbox and select Components from the pop-up menu.

9. Check the box next to Microsoft Winsock Control 6.0 and click the OK button to add the Winsock control to the Toolbox

10. Add a Winsock control to docWebComm and set its Name property to **wsk**.

11. Add a Label control to the upper-left of the document and set its Name property to **lblName**. Set its Caption to **Type your name here:**.

12. Add a Textbox control under lblName. Set its Name property to **txtName**. Delete the contents of its Text property.

13. Place another Label control below txtName and set its Name property to **lblTx**. Set its Caption to **Type your message here:**. Set its Enabled property to **False**.

14. Put a Textbox control under lblTx. Set its Name property to **txtTx** and delete the contents of its Text property. In addition, set its Enabled property to **False**.

15. Add one more Textbox a couple of grid lines below txtTx and set its Name property to **txtRx**. Set its Enabled property to **False** and delete the contents of its Text property.

16. Set the MultiLine property of txtRx to **True**, and set its ScrollBars property to **2- Vertical**.

After you have added all of the controls, the document should look similar to Figure 18.8.

Skill 18

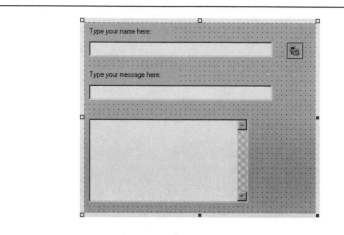

Type your name here:

Type your message here:

FIGURE 18.8: The WebComm Client in the Form Designer

17. Save the project so you don't lose any changes.

As you have probably figured out by now, visual design is only a minor part of developing applications in Visual Basic. Fortunately, the coding process is not that difficult either. Continue with the following steps to add the code that makes the application run.

1. Double-click the document in the Form Designer to open its Code window.

2. Add the following code to the `Resize()` event of the document:

```
Private Sub UserDocument_Resize()
    'Stretch the chat window
    With txtRx
        .Move 0, .Top, ScaleWidth, (ScaleHeight - .Top)
    End With
End Sub
```

3. Add the following code to the `Terminate()` event:

```
Private Sub UserDocument_Terminate()
    'Close the connection
    wsk.Close
End Sub
```

So other chat participants know who is online, the user should be required to enter his or her name. We can make sure of this by initiating the connection to the server when the contents of the Name field are filled in. After the user's name is entered and the Enter key is pressed, the document will connect to the server.

4. Add the following code to the KeyPress() event of txtName:

```
Private Sub txtName_KeyPress(KeyAscii As Integer)
    'Send data when user presses enter
    If (KeyAscii = 13) And _
            (txtName.Text <> "") Then
        'Connect to the server
        With wsk
            .Protocol = sckTCPProtocol
            .RemoteHost = "10.0.0.1"
            .RemotePort = 12345
            .Connect
        End With

        'Enable the chat boxes
        lblTx.Enabled = True
        txtTx.Enabled = True
        txtRx.Enabled = True

        'Prevent the user from changing
        'their name
        lblName.Enabled = False
        txtName.Enabled = False
    End If
End Sub
```

Notice how the transmission textbox (txtTx) and the chat window (txtRx) are disabled until there is some sort of text typed in the Name field.

NOTE   Before you run this application, you must change the RemoteHost property to the host name or IP address of the computer that is running the WebComm Server. In this example, RemoteHost is set to 10.0.0.1, which is the first available address in the TCP/IP test pool.

As in most chat rooms, the participant's message is prefixed by his or her name. This allows other participants to know who is saying what. Certainly our chat room should be no exception to this obvious courtesy. We can solve this problem by getting the value type in the Name field and appending the message text to the end of it. Then we can send the entire string at once.

5. Add the following code to the txtTx_KeyPress() event:

```
Private Sub txtTx_KeyPress(KeyAscii As Integer)
    Dim msg As String

    'Send data when user presses enter
    If (KeyAscii = 13) And _
        (wsk.State = sckConnected) Then

        'Add the sender's name to
        'the message
        msg = "[" & _
            UCase$(Trim$(txtName.Text)) & _
            "] - " & txtTx.Text

        'Send the message
        wsk.SendData msg

        'Clear the send box
        txtTx.Text = ""
    End If
End Sub
```

Now we need a handler to process incoming messages and display them in the chat window.

6. Add the following code to the wsk_DataArrival() event:

```
Private Sub wsk_DataArrival(ByVal bytesTotal As Long)
    Dim msg As String

    'Get the message from the buffer
    wsk.GetData msg, , bytesTotal

    'Add the message to the box
    With txtRx
        .Text = msg & _
                vbCrLf & _
                vbCrLf & _
                .Text
    End With
End Sub
```

7. Save your project!

As you can see, the code for the client is much simpler than the code for the server, yet both applications function in much the same manner. Each application must establish its side of the session and process incoming data appropriately. Data is processed in the `DataArrival()` event using the `GetData` method, and data is sent using the `SendData` method.

Well, enough of the theory. I'm sure you want to see the chat room work!

Using the WebComm Server

You can run the WebComm Server on the same computer you develop on, but to really see it shine, you should run it on a separate, networked computer. Choose the option that works best for you: running the WebComm Server on a separate computer, or running it on the same computer.

Running WebComm Server on a Separate Computer

If you want to run the WebComm Server application on another computer, follow these steps. Otherwise, skip this section and continue with the "Running WebComm Server on the Same Computer" section.

1. Create a setup program using the Package and Deployment Wizard as discussed in Skill 14.

2. Copy the completed setup program to the computer that you want to install it on. You could also copy the setup program to a central location on a file server that both computers have access to.

3. Run the setup application on the computer to act as the server.

4. After the setup has successfully completed, run the WebComm Server from the Start menu or Windows Explorer.

5. Skip the "Running WebComm Server on the Same Computer" section.

Running WebComm Server on the Same Computer

1. Run WebComm Server from Windows Explorer or the Run menu on the Start menu.

2. Make sure that WebComm Server starts up and says Sessions: 0 in the status bar.

Using the WebComm Client

Before you run the WebComm Client, make sure that the RemoteHost property set in the txtName_KeyPress() event matches the name of the computer that is running WebComm Server. If the Server is running on the same machine that the Client will, you can set the RemoteHost property to the IP address of your computer.

1. Start the WebComm Client application by pressing F5 in Visual Basic. Since the application is an ActiveX document, it needs a container to run in. In this case, it's Microsoft Internet Explorer. If everything starts up properly, your client will look like Figure 18.9.

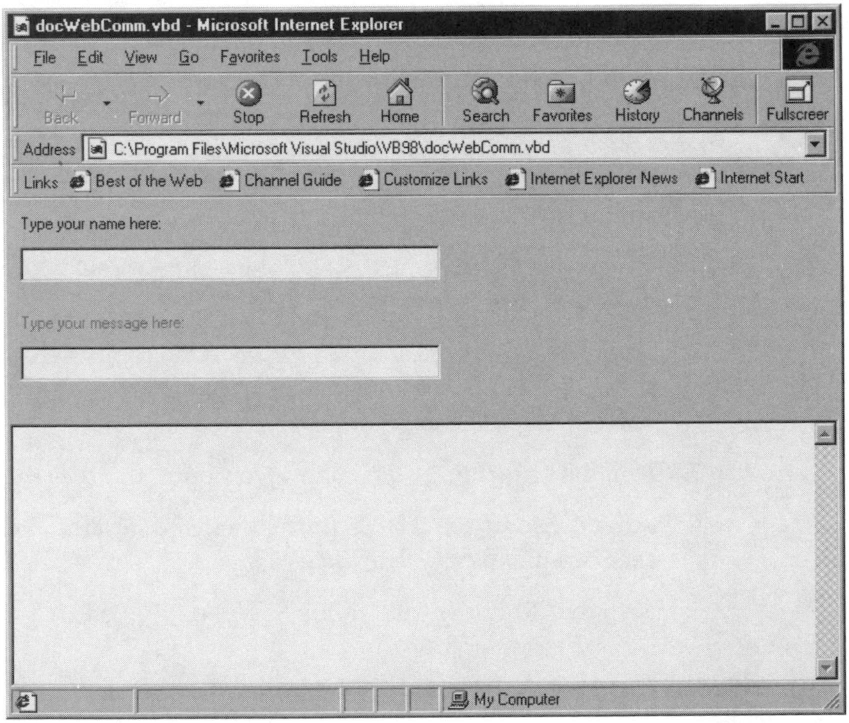

FIGURE 18.9: The WebComm Client running in Internet Explorer

2. Type your name in the Name field and press Enter. If your RemoteHost property is set properly, the Textbox txtTx should be enabled, and the Name field should be disabled. You are now locked in and connected to the WebComm Server!

3. Try typing **Is anyone out there?** In the field labeled Type your message here.

4. Press the Enter key to send the message. If everything works properly, you will see your message in the chat box, as shown in Figure 18.10.

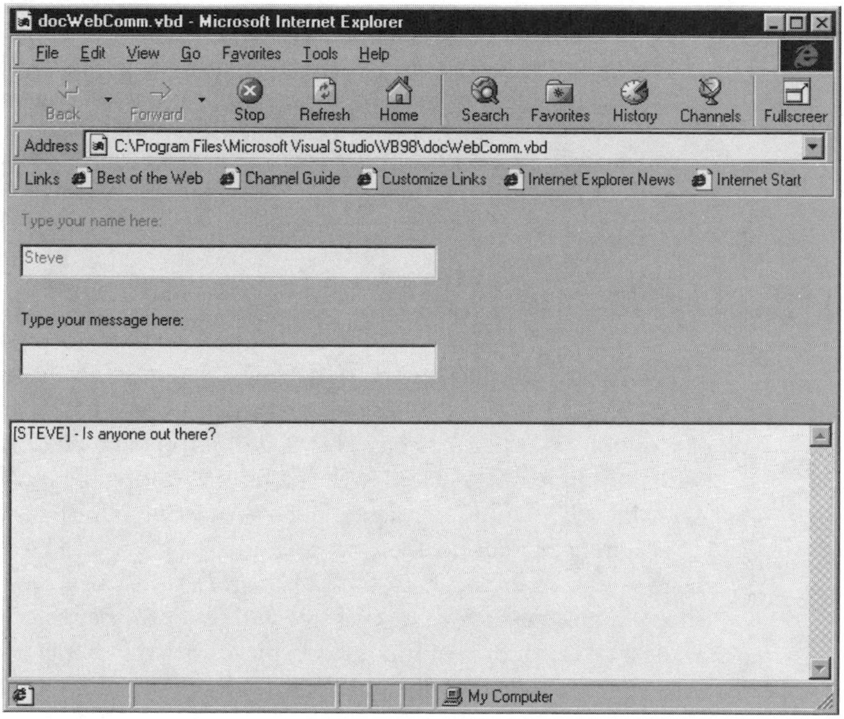

FIGURE 18.10: Now you're chatting!

You can continue chatting and watching the message arrive at your client. If you want, take a look at the WebComm Server. You will see a list of the messages you sent, and if you haven't disconnected, then the number of sessions should be at least one. When you are done playing in the chat room, close Internet Explorer. After it closes, be sure to stop the project in Visual Basic by selecting Run ➢ End from the Visual Basic menu.

As you can see, you can use Visual Basic to do some sophisticated things, and communications is one of the trickiest things to program! Visual Basic made it easy. There is a lot of room for improvement in the WebComm application. You may want to give the user the option of which server they would like to connect to. You could use a RichTextbox control instead of the plain Textbox control and add color to the message. If you wanted to be really adventurous, you could even modify the application to play wave files on the computers of people you're chatting with!

> **NOTE** Be sure to check the Sybex Web site at www.sybex.com. WebComm will be continually updated to include cool features. Not only will you be able to have a cool chat room of your own, but you can see the source code that makes it work. If you have any ideas on how the application can be improved, let us know!

Using Dynamic HTML

DHTML, or Dynamic Hypertext Markup Language, brings additional life to ordinary Web pages. Visual Basic 6 now enters the arena of what was once the domain of text editors and proprietary HTML editors, using its IDE and visual development paradigm to assist you in developing your own DHTML applications.

Since DHTML is a language of its own, it's beyond the scope of this book to cover it in detail. For detailed information on how to use DHTML, consult Visual Basic's online help, or check out *Dynamic HTML: Master the Essentials* by Joseph Schmuller (Sybex, 1998). Instead, we will cover the basics of using Visual Basic to create a DHTML project framework, place some elements in the page, and write some code to make the document come alive.

How DHTML Relates to Visual Basic

DHTML is based on the Document Object Model, which is a hierarchy of Web page elements. Elements are to DHTML what controls are to Visual Basic applications. In addition, a page in DHTML is like a Form object in Visual Basic.

This development paradigm makes it relatively simple to use your Visual Basic knowledge to develop smart Web pages. You can write Visual Basic code inside the events of DHTML elements, just like you do in your normal projects.

If you are familiar with creating Web documents in HTML, you might be better off to continue developing them with your own HTML editor, and importing them into your DHTML project. Then you can modify the elements to give your Web application that added flair.

Creating a DHTML Project

Now that you have seen WebComm run in Internet Explorer, we will create a DHTML page that will act as a start page for the WebComm Client application.

1. Create a new project by selecting File ➢ New Project from the Visual Basic menu.

2. Select DHTML Application from the New Project dialog box and click OK to create the project.

3. Change the Name property of the Project to **WebCommStart**. This will be the WebComm Start page.

4. Double-click the designer for DHTMLPage1 in the Project Explorer to open it in the Form Designer. The designer will look like Figure 18.11.

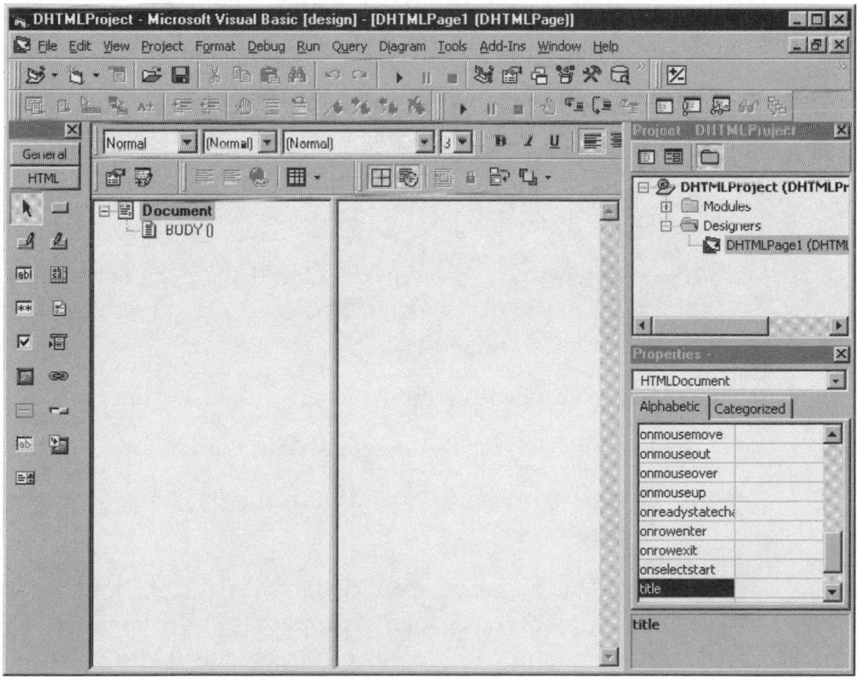

FIGURE 18.11: The DHTML Designer

As you can see, the designer is split into two panes. The pane on the left shows the list of components, called *elements* in DHTML. You can scroll down to view some of the properties of each element. The pane on the right represents the browser's representation of the page. You can type text or add more complex elements such as CommandButtons and TextBoxes. As you add elements to the page, you will see them appear on the left pane, where you can select them so you can modify their properties.

5. Set the ID property of DHTMLPage1 to **htmWebCommStart**.

6. Click in the right pane and type **Welcome to WebComm** and press the Enter key.

7. Highlight *Welcome to WebComm* and change the font to Arial, Bold, 6 using the toolbar at the top of the designer. Set its ID property to **pWelcome**.

8. Type **Brought to You by** and double-click the Hyperlink element in the toolbox. This will add a hyperlink after the text.

9. Type over the word Hyperlink1 and change it to **Sybex!**

10. Highlight *Brought to You by Sybex!* And change its font to Arial, Italic, 3. Set its ID property to **pSybex**.

11. Right-click the Sybex hyperlink and select properties from the Property Pages dialog box.

12. Type www.sybex.com in the Link field. Type **Look to Sybex for all of your computer book needs!** in the Pop-up Text field. Click the OK button to commit the changes.

13. In the Properties window, change the ID property to **lnkSybex**.

14. Double-click the Button element in the Toolbox to add it to the page.

15. Set the ID property to **cmdStart**, and its Value property to **Click Here to Start**.

When all the elements are added to the page, it should look like Figure 18.12. You can see all of the elements' properties in the left pane. The elements that are in bold are programmable, since you set their ID property.

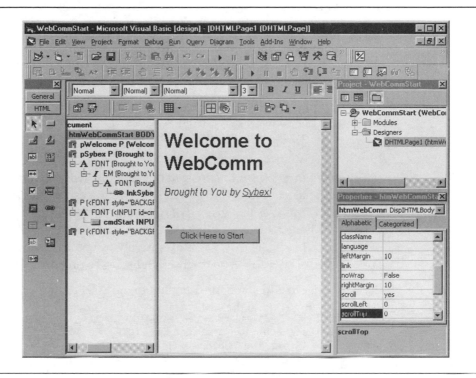

FIGURE 18.12: The page with the elements added

16. Double-click the page to open its Code window.

17. Add the following line of code to the (General)(Declarations) section:

```
Private Const LNK_WEBCOMM_CLIENT = " "
```

18. Type the complete drive and path to the WebComm.vbd file that you created in the previous example. This is the path that the page will look for when cmdStart is clicked.

Much like a Form object has a Load() event in Visual Basic, a DHTML application has an onload() event. You can place code in this event to configure the page before it is rendered in the browser.

19. Add the following code to the onload() event of the BaseWindow object:

```
Private Sub BaseWindow_onload()
    'Set the document properties
```

```
With Document
    .bgColor = "lightyellow"
    .linkColor = "blue"
    .vlinkColor = "blue"
    .alinkColor = "blue"
End With

'Configure the Welcome paragraph
pWelcome.Style.Color = "blue"
pSybex.Style.Color = "black"
End Sub
```

You may have noticed that instead of using intrinsic constants, the color values were text. That's because variables in DHTML pages are Variants by default. In addition, HTML uses text instead of constants.

You may have also noticed that the code changes the color of the Style property of the object. Since DHTML pages extensively utilize style sheets, you change the appearance, or style, of an object through its Style property.

20.   In order to add some functionality to the Start button on the form, add the following code to the cmdStart_onclick() event:

```
Private Function cmdStart_onclick() As Boolean
    'Start the WebComm client
    BaseWindow.navigate LNK_WEBCOMM_CLIENT
End Function
```

21.   To add a little flair to the Sybex link, let's make it change its color to red when the mouse moves over it. You can do this through the link's onmouseover() event with the following code:

```
Private Sub lnkSybex_onmouseover()
    'Change the link to red
    lnkSybex.Style.Color = "red"
End Sub
```

22.   And naturally, you want the link to reset its appearance when the mouse leaves the link. Do this by adding the following code to the onmouseout() event of lnkSybex:

```
Private Sub lnkSybex_onmouseout()
    'Change the link to blue
    lnkSybex.Style.Color = "blue"
End Sub
```

23.   Save and run the project.

Shortly after you tell Visual Basic to run the application, Internet Explorer will appear and show you your new DHTML page (shown in Figure 18.13).

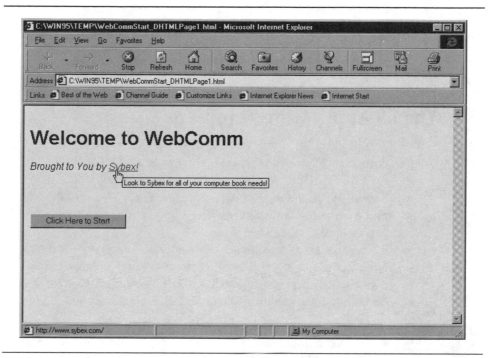

FIGURE 18.13: The WebComm Start page

If you move the mouse over the Sybex link, you will see it change its color to red. When you move the mouse away, it changes back to blue. If you rest the mouse over the link, a tool tip appears plugging Sybex computer books. When you are ready to go to the WebComm Client application, click the button on the page.

1. Close Internet Explorer and stop the application in Visual Basic by selecting Run ➢ End from the Visual Basic menu.

2. Compile the application by selecting File ➢ Make WebCommStart.dll from the Visual Basic menu.

3. Open the Web Index project you created earlier in this skill.

4. Add an item to lstSites using a command like the following, replacing the path with the one you used to save the WebComm Start page project:

```
lstSites.AddItem "d:\sybex\webcomm start page\" & _
        "WebCommStart_DHTMLPage1.htm"
```

5.   Save and run the project to test the new page.

Before you activate the WebComm Client application, be sure that the Web-Comm Server is running first. When you select the WebCommStart item from the list, the DHTML page should appear in the WebBrowser control. It will function just as it did when you tested it in Internet Explorer. If you click the button to start the WebComm Client application, it will display in the WebBrowser control as well!

The IIS Application Template

The final tool that you have to develop Internet-enabled applications is the IIS Application project template. This project template helps lay the framework for a DHTML-styled application that runs on Microsoft's Internet Information Server. It utilizes a combination of DHTML, Webclasses, Active Server Pages, and a scripting language such as VBScript or JavaScript to build sophisticated server-side applications.

Unfortunately, developing these applications is not for the faint of heart and is beyond the scope of this book. If you want to develop your own server-side applications, consider reading the Microsoft Developers Network or purchasing a good book that deals specifically with ISAPI, Webclasses, and Active Server Pages.

> **NOTE**   For more information on developing applications for Internet Information Server refer to *Mastering Microsoft Internet Information Server 4* by Peter Dyson (Sybex, 1997).

Are You up to Speed?

Now you can...

☑ **develop your own Web-browsing applications using the WebBrowser control**

☑ **use the Winsock control to enable your applications to communicate**

☑ **use ActiveX technology to write distributed Internet applications**

☑ **understand the basics of developing Dynamic HTML applications**

Using DLLs and the Windows API

- Introducing Dynamic Link Libraries (DLLs)
- Understanding DLL calling conventions
- Using the API Viewer
- Using the API in your application
- Creating a WavePlayer class
- Adding an application to the System Tray

Visual Basic allows you to program a great deal of functionality into your applications with a minimal amount of programming effort. However, there are times when you will need more functionality than Visual Basic provides. Fortunately, the kind folks at Microsoft spent a great deal of time building a great deal of functionality directly into the Windows operating systems. With a bit of creative coding, you too can tap the power of the Windows API and give your application that extra something you need!

Introducing Dynamic Link Libraries (DLLs)

Once in a while, you'll want to accomplish something that's quite simply beyond the capabilities of Visual Basic—or at least requires some very convoluted code. In such circumstances, you have three options:

- You can write the code in a language such as C and call the routines from Visual Basic.

- You can drive another application through OLE Automation.

- You can make use of existing libraries of routines that make up the *Windows Application Programming Interface*, or *API*.

NOTE   The Windows API is a set of files, called DLLs, that contain thousands of routines that programmers can access from their own applications. A great deal of the Windows operating systems are made up of these DLLs.

In this skill, we'll be talking about the last option, because it is beyond the scope of this book to go into the details of C and C++ programming. OLE Automation is also better left for when you have a good grasp of the Visual Basic fundamentals.

To access the Windows API, you link your programs to *Dynamic Link Libraries*, or DLLs. DLLs are components of applications that provide several functions in a file that can be linked to and used by a program when it is run. The functions are not built into your application. A DLL is a compiled version of code much like the classes discussed in Skill 4. DLLs are extremely useful if you want to reuse someone's code or you want your program to be smaller. The Windows operating systems work in much the same way. They are made up of several programs (called applets) and many DLLs that these applets use over and over. An example is the Open/Save File dialog boxes you use when opening or saving documents. Have you ever noticed they all look the same? Well, that's because they are. The dialog box is called from a DLL, so it can be used in many programs.

Many new programmers think of the Windows API as a great "black box" that is difficult to understand and use. In reality, the API is just a collection of DLLs that give functionality to the Windows operating system. The API as a whole serves as a compiled toolbox that exposes functionality that you can tap into if you know what you want, where to get it, and how to get it. Many of the DLLs making up the API can be found in the \Windows\System subdirectory, while others may reside in the Windows directory, or various subdirectories under it.

The most recent version of the API is the Win32 API. It contains functions that are all written in 32-bit code. This means that they can process much more information than previously written 16-bit code. For backward compatibility, there are also 16-bit APIs that can be called by older applications. Just think of an API as a function in a DLL with documentation that you can use to access the function.

DLL Calling Conventions

Calling DLLs can get quite complex (especially if you're unfamiliar with C language data types), but fortunately, the DLLs that make up the Windows API are well documented, and the code to declare them is provided with Visual Basic. In order to use a DLL's function with your application, you must declare the function before you call it from your code.

You tell Visual Basic how to access the DLL by declaring a procedure and specifying the appropriate parameters. Once this is done, you can let your program call the actual function in your code. Declaring the function lets the Visual Basic compiler know exactly how to pass data to and from the function. The Windows API is a very powerful and useful set of functions, but it is also very volatile. One mismatched parameter type can cause your program to hiccup, stop, or even crash your whole system. This is especially bad if you don't save your work often. A system crash is the most likely result of passing the wrong data type to or from a DLL.

TIP When working with DLLs, save your work before every test run. If the DLL is called improperly, you could crash the computer and lose your work!

The first step to accessing the Windows API is to determine which API function you want to use. Once you determine the name of the function, you must link it to your program. You do this by declaring it with the `Declare` statement. For example:

```
Private Declare Function sndPlaySound Lib "winmm.dll" _
Alias "sndPlaySoundA" (ByVal lpszSoundName As String, _
ByVal uFlags As Long) As Long
```

This command may look complicated, but actually it is fairly easy to understand once you are familiar with DLL calling conventions. What it does is call the `sndPlaySound` API, which plays a `.WAV` file. Let's dissect the declaration to understand better what it actually does.

Understanding DLL Calling Conventions

There are several similarities between declaration statements for the various APIs. Let's look at each of these so you can better understand what is actually happening.

Setting the API's Scope

The scope of the API function is determined just like it is for any procedures you write in Visual Basic. You can use the `Public` keyword to make the function available to the entire application, or use the `Private` keyword to make the function available only to the calling form.

In the previous declaration, the `Private` statement makes the API function local to the module it is in. This is just like creating a private function of your own, as discussed in Skill 4. You will not actually create the function, but you call it from your code just like any other function.

Declaring the DLL

The `Declare Function` statements tell Visual Basic to link to the `sndPlaySound` function that resides within the `winmm.dll` to your application. The keyword `Alias` specifies the name of the function as it is referenced in the DLL itself. The `Alias` keyword is used for compatibility between the standard 16-bit Windows API and the Win32 API.

Understanding Parameter Types

Parameters can be specified by value and by reference. If you pass a variable by value, using the ByVal keyword, you pass the actual contents of the variable to the function. When you pass it by reference, using the keyword ByRef, the function looks for the location in memory that the variable is stored and gets the value from there. This is used for compatibility with C and C++ because most of the API is written in those languages.

> **WARNING**   By default, parameters passed to DLLs are passed by reference. You must explicitly pass a variable by value using the ByVal keyword. If you omit this keyword, the value is passed by reference, and your routine will not function properly. In fact, you may crash your program.

After the Alias statement, you specify the parameter list that the function expects to see when it is called. We pass two parameters by value (ByVal). The two parameters are lpszSoundName and uFlags. The parameter lpszSoundName is a string variable that specifies the fully qualified path and filename of a .WAV file. The parameter uFlags is used to pass special handling parameters to the function. Don't worry about the prefixes lpsz and u. These are naming conventions commonly used in C and C++. Finally, the function returns a long integer to notify you if the function is successful.

Using the Return Code

The last statement of the declaration sets the return type. Because many of the APIs perform functions that you cannot see, they return a code to your program to indicate whether the function succeeded or failed, and why. This is important for you to know because as you work with the API your program will depend on the functions within it. If an API fails for whatever reason, and your application doesn't check the return code before it continues running, the program will possibly introduce a bug and crash.

This brings up another interesting point: You can code your own functions to set return codes for your program and others to utilize. This is good practice because it keeps your application communicating with its components. When you are programming, never assume that a procedure worked, but always check the return code if possible. This helps minimize the chances of your application going haywire due to a variable being set improperly, or not being set at all.

The Windows API is similar to the functions and sub procedures you create in your own applications but with one difference: The code is already written for you! Your only responsibility is to ensure that the API declaration is valid and you only use the proper variable types to move data to and from the API. If you are careless with these, you could very easily crash your program, or even worse, hang your system.

The API Viewer

Now that you understand the basics of DLL declaration, I want to show you a shortcut. Visual Basic ships with a utility called the API Viewer (see Figure 19.1).

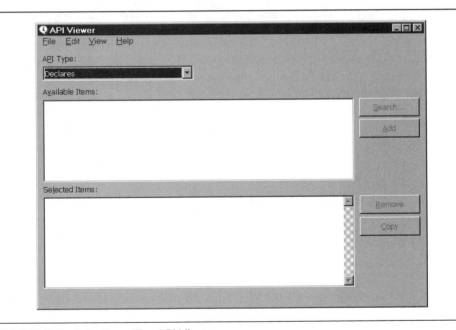

FIGURE 19.1: The API Viewer

The API Viewer is a browser that reads some files that contain most of the function declarations, variable types, and constant declarations that make up the Windows API. The viewer allows you to quickly search for the function you want to call and supplies you with the appropriate statements to include in your application.

To use the API Viewer, follow these steps:

1. From your Start menu, run the API Text Viewer, which is in your Visual Basic program group.

2. In the API Viewer, click File ➤ Load Text File.

3. Select Win32.api and click Open. The API Viewer will tell you that it can run faster if it converts the file to a database (see Figure 19.2).

TIP   The API Viewer will load the APIs faster if you convert the text file into a database. If you plan to make extensive use of the API, convert it to a database.

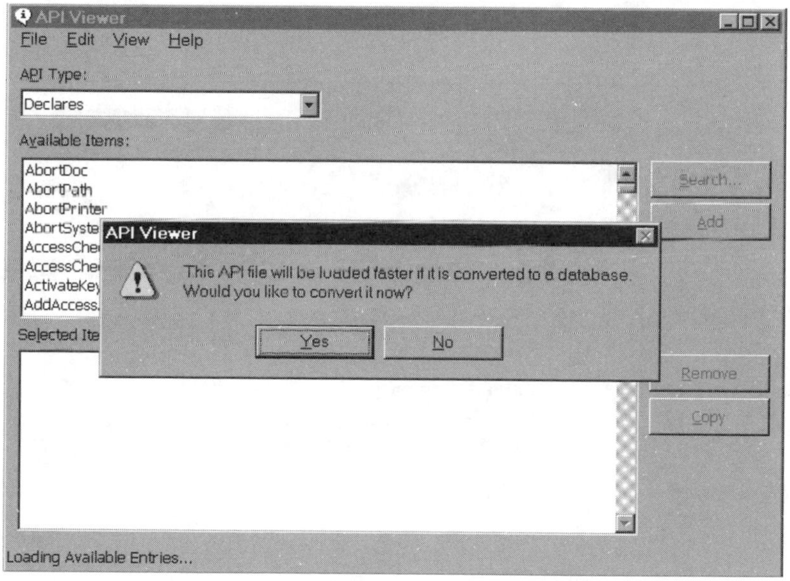

FIGURE 19.2:   Converting the API list to a database

---

4. Answer Yes to convert the file into a database.

5. After the list has been converted to a database, select Declares in the API Type list box at the top of the Viewer.

Skill 19

TIP   Another way to use the API viewer is to call it from the Add-Ins menu in Visual Basic.

Once an API file is loaded, you can scroll down the list, although it is quite long. This is not the entire Windows API, but it is a good subset and offers almost everything you could ask for. You can type the letters of the API you are looking for, and as you type, the list will scroll to it.

6. Scroll to the sndPlaySound function. When it is highlighted, click the Add button to copy the declaration to the Selected Items list (see Figure 19.3).

7. After the function declaration is added, click the Copy button. This will copy the declaration to the clipboard for you.

8. Close the API Viewer.

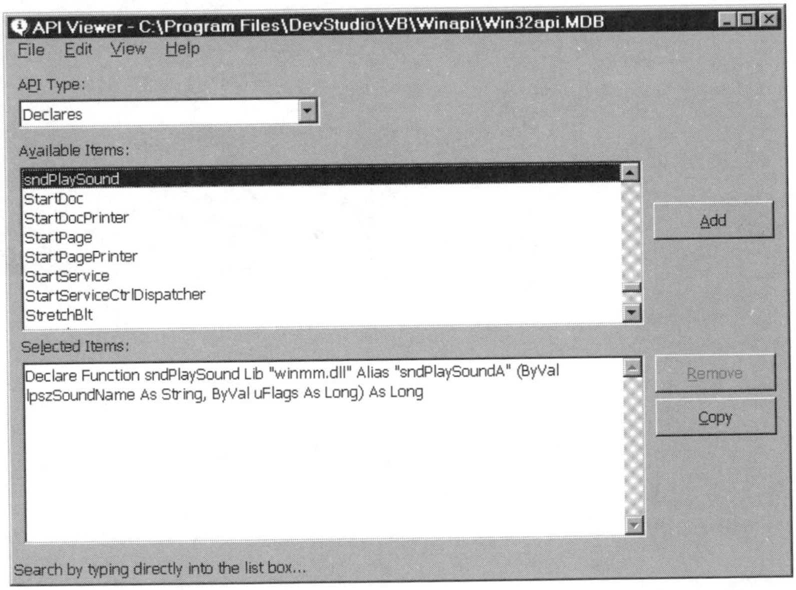

FIGURE 19.3:   The sndPlaySound declaration

Using the API in Your Applications

You now know how to use the API Viewer to retrieve the declarations you need for your programs. Now let's look at integrating the declarations with your applications. We will continue where we left off with our previous example:

1. In Visual Basic, start a new project. If the Project Wizard appears, select Standard EXE.

2. Double-click Form1 in the Project Explorer to open up the Code window.

3. Go to the (General)(Declarations) section and select Edit ➤ Paste. Your Code window should look similar to Figure 19.4.

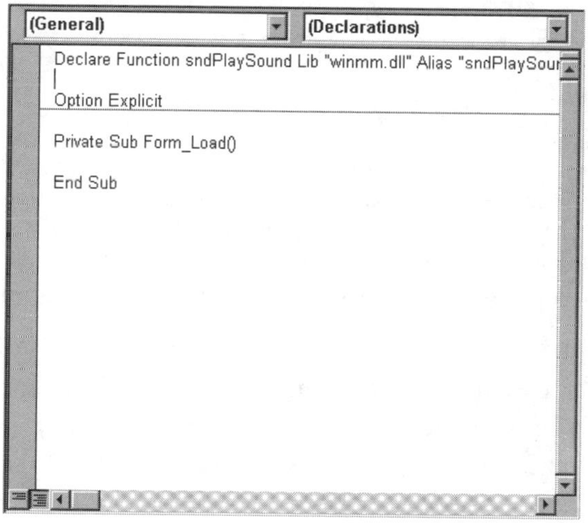

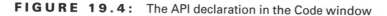

```
(General)                    (Declarations)

    Declare Function sndPlaySound Lib "winmm.dll" Alias "sndPlaySour
    |
    Option Explicit

    Private Sub Form_Load()

    End Sub
```

FIGURE 19.4:   The API declaration in the Code window

4. Insert the keyword `Private` in front of the `Declare` statement as follows:

```
Private Declare Function sndPlaySound Lib "winmm.dll" _
    Alias "sndPlaySoundA" (ByVal lpszSoundName As String, _
    ByVal uFlags As Long) As Long
```

Usually, API declarations should go into their own code module. However, you can place them in a form or a class by prefixing the `Declare` statement with a `Private` keyword. If you do not do this, you will receive an error message.

5. Next, add the following code to the Form_Load() procedure of Form1:

```
Private Sub Form_Load()
    Dim filename As String
    Dim rc As Long

    filename = "c:\windows\media\tada.wav"
    rc = sndPlaySound(filename, 1)
End Sub
```

 NOTE   You may need to change the filename parameter to point to another .WAV file on your computer. The path used above is just an example. Also notice that the return code (rc) is dimensioned as a long integer (Dim rc As Long). This must match the exact return type specified in the API declaration. The filename and the flags parameters must match as well. I set the flags parameter to 1 for this example.

6. If everything looks good, save the project and run it.

 WARNING   Always save your project before you run it if you are using the Windows API. One mismatched parameter can cause your whole system to crash. If you did not save your work, then it will be lost as well.

If you have a sound card installed and the volume turned up, then you should have heard the infamous Tada! sound. You can experiment by changing the filename parameter to play different sounds. As you develop your applications, you can use this API to spice them up. Maybe audio prompts are in order. If you are creating a screen saver or a video game, then sounds are practically a must.

Modifying the API Function

You can write your own functions to call API functions as well. These functions are called *wrappers* because you wrap code inside your function. If you want to turn off the sound, you can put the API function in your own wrapper so you can selectively turn the sound off and on. For example:

```
Public Sub PlayWav(filename as string, mute as Boolean)
    Dim rc as long

    If Not Mute Then
        rc=sndPlaySound(filename, 1)
    End If
End Sub
```

This is a useful procedure to add to your code library. You could possibly encapsulate it in your own .WAV file class if you want to. The important thing to remember is to give your users the option of having the sound on or off. While many like to have sound, the novelty can get old. When you allow the user to turn the sound on and off, you can capture this value and pass it to the PlayWav procedure. You can also disable sound if the user does not have multimedia installed on their system (although highly unlikely).

Creating a WavePlayer Class

Now that you know how to play a wave file using the Windows API, the next step is to make a reusable WavePlayer class that you can add to your future projects. The project is simple, but can be easily extended to accommodate volume controls as well. The class is simple, consisting of two properties and one method. Try the following example to create your WavePlayer class.

1. Start a new project by selecting File ➤ New Project from the Visual Basic menu. When prompted, select Standard EXE as the project type.

2. Set the Name property of Form1 to **frmMain**. Set its Caption property to **WavePlayer**.

3. Add a Command Button to frmMain. Set its Name property to **cmdPlay**, and its Caption to **&Play**.

4. Now we will add a blank Class module to the project. Right-click in the Project Explorer and select Add ➤ Class Module from the pop-up menu.

5. When the Add Class Module dialog box appears, select Class Module and click the Open button.

6. In the Properties window, set the Name property of the newly added class to **WavePlayer**.

7. Add the following lines of code to the (General)(Declarations) section of the WavePlayer class:

```
Option Explicit

Private mFilename As String
Private mFlags As Long

Private Declare Function sndPlaySound Lib "winmm.dll" _
    Alias "sndPlaySoundA" (ByVal lpszSoundName As String, _
    ByVal uFlags As Long) As Long
```

8. Add the following procedures to create the interface for the `Filename` property:

```
Public Property Get Filename() As String
    Filename = mFilename
End Property

Public Property Let Filename(ByVal vNewValue As String)
    mFilename = vNewValue
End Property
```

9. Now add the following procedures to expose the `Flags` property:

```
Public Property Get Flags() As Long
    Flags = mFlags
End Property

Public Property Let Flags(ByVal vNewValue As Long)
    mFlags = vNewValue
End Property
```

10. Finally, add the following code to add the only method to the class:

```
Public Sub Play()
    Dim rc As Long

    rc = sndPlaySound(mFilename, mFlags)
End Sub
```

11. Save your project now. If you created the code library in Skill 4, save `Wave-Player.cls` in the code library directory. This will make it easier to reuse it in the future. Keep this sample project in its own directory.

12. Open the Code window for `frmMain` and go to its `(General)(Declarations)` section.

13. In order to use the WavePlayer object, we must reference it. Do this by adding the following code:

```
Option Explicit

Private wav As WavePlayer
```

14. Now that we have a reference to the object, it must be instantiated. The best place to do this is in the `Form_Load()` event. Add this code to the `Form_Load()` event:

```
Private Sub Form_Load()
    Set wav = New WavePlayer
End Sub
```

15. Add the following code to the Form_Unload() event. This will destroy the WavePlayer object by setting it to Nothing, thus freeing memory when the application ends:

```
Private Sub Form_Unload(Cancel As Integer)
    Set wav = Nothing
End Sub
```

16. Finally, add the code to the cmdPlay_Click() event. This is the code that will make the WavePlayer actually play the file:

```
Private Sub cmdPlay_Click()
    With wav
        .Filename = App.Path & "\Tada.wav"
        .Flags = 1
        .Play
    End With
End Sub
```

WARNING   You will need to copy the appropriate wave file to the project directory before running this application. You could easily change the wave file to anything you would like to hear.

17. Save and run the application.

Although simple, this example shows you how easy it is to port stand-alone procedures to objects using class modules. In addition, this class can be reused in other projects you develop. Now you won't have to use the API viewer or remember which API to use to play sound bites. Just add the WavePlayer class to your projects, and your applications will be more entertaining than you ever imagined!

Adding an Application to the System Tray

Some applications written for Windows 95 or Windows NT version 4 allow themselves to be placed within the System Tray. The System Tray is the recessed box that sits on the right side of the Taskbar (shown here). Applications that monitor devices or run on schedules are often placed here when they run. Your system will most likely have a clock indicating the computer's time and possibly a speaker icon for your volume control.

Visual Basic comes with a sample program that you can compile to build an ActiveX control. You can use this control in your applications to place them in the System Tray.

Creating the *SysTray* Control

Before you can use ActiveX control in your application, you should compile it and store it in the \System subdirectory of the Windows directory. To build the control, follow these steps:

1. Open the Systray.vbp project in the \Common\Tools\VB\Unsupprt\SysTray directory on the Visual Basic CD.

2. In the Project Explorer, open the Modules folder and double-click mSysTray to open the code module in the Code window.

Examine the (Global)(Declarations) section of the file. You will notice several API declarations including CallWindowProc, GetWindowLong, and Shell_NotifyIcon (see Figure 19.5). These APIs, along with others, are used to place an icon in the System Tray. We won't go into the details of how the functions work, but you can browse the source code and read the comments to see what makes the control work.

```
(General)                              SubWndProc

Option Explicit

'-----------------------------------------------------------
' Api Declares....
'-----------------------------------------------------------
Public Declare Function CallWindowProc Lib "user32" Alias "CallWindowProcA" (
Public Declare Function GetWindowLong Lib "user32" Alias "GetWindowLongA"
Public Declare Function SetWindowLong Lib "user32" Alias "SetWindowLongA"
Public Declare Function Shell_NotifyIcon Lib "shell32.dll" Alias "Shell_NotifyIconA
Public Declare Sub CopyMemory Lib "kernel32" Alias "RtlMoveMemory" (pDest A:
Public Declare Function DrawEdge Lib "user32" (ByVal hDC As Long, qrc As RE

'-----------------------------------------------------------
' Api Constants...
'-----------------------------------------------------------
Public Const GWL_USERDATA = (-21&)
Public Const GWL_WNDPROC = (-4&)
Public Const WM_USER = &H400&

Public Const TRAY_CALLBACK = (WM_USER + 101&)
Public Const NIM_ADD = &H0&
Public Const NIM_MODIFY = &H1&
Public Const NIM_DELETE = &H2&
Public Const NIF_MESSAGE = &H1&
Public Const NIF_ICON = &H2&
```

FIGURE 19.5: SysTray API declarations

3. Select File ➤ Make Systray.ocx.

4. From the Make Project dialog box, set the Save In field to the \System sub-directory of the directory you have Windows installed on your hard disk. This will be C:\Windows\System on most systems.

5. Click the OK button to compile the control.

The SysTray control is now ready for use in your own applications.

Using the *SysTray* Control

Now that you have created the SysTray control, you can add it to your own applications just like any other controls. To try this out, let's create a simple program launcher that you can use to start some useful Windows utilities. Follow these steps:

1. Start a new project by selecting File ➤ New Project. Select Standard EXE from the New Project dialog box.

2. Once the project is created, change the Name property of Form1 to **frmMain**.

3. Right-click the Toolbox and select Components from the pop-up menu.

4. Click the check box next to C:\Windows\System\SysTray.ocx to add the cSysTray control to your Toolbox. Click the OK button.

5. Place the cSysTray control on frmMain and set its Name property to **clsSysTray**.

6. In the Properties window, set the InTray property to True and set the TrayTip property to **Application Launcher**.

7. Click frmMain to make it the active control. Select Tools ➤ Menu Editor to open the Menu Editor dialog box.

8. Create a menu by setting the Caption property to **&Apps**. Set the Name property to **mnuApp**. Click the Next button.

9. Click the right arrow button to create menu items.

10. Create the following menu items:

Caption	Name
C&alculator	mnuAppCalc
&Explorer	mnuAppExplorer
&Notepad	mnuAppNotepad
-	mnuAppSep1
&Close	mnuAppClose

Skill 19

11. Your menu should look similar to Figure 19.6. Click the OK button to close the Menu Editor.

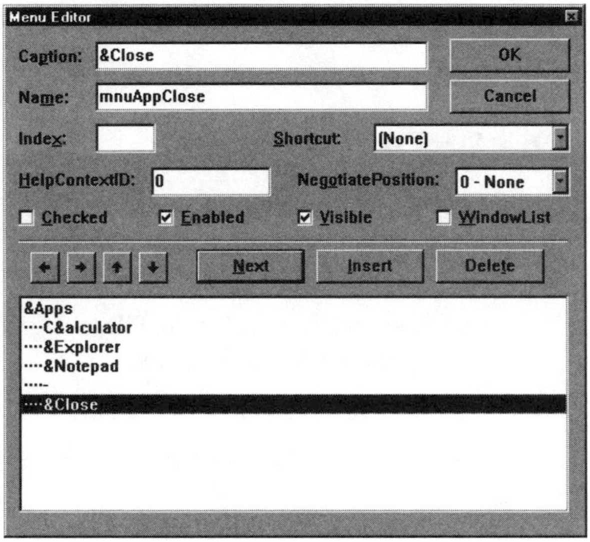

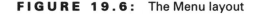

FIGURE 19.6: The Menu layout

12. Double-click frmMain to open its Code window.

13. Add the following code to the Load() event of the form:

```
Private Sub Form_Load()
    Me.Hide
End Sub
```

14. Open the MouseDown() event of clsSysTray and add the following code:

```
Private Sub clsSysTray_MouseDown(Button As Integer, Id As Long)
    If Button = 2 Then
        PopupMenu mnuApp
    End If
End Sub
```

15. Add the following to the Click() event of mnuAppCalc:

```
Private Sub mnuAppCalc_Click()
    Dim rc As Double
    rc = Shell("calc.exe", vbNormalFocus)
End Sub
```

16. Add the following to the Click() event of mnuAppExplorer:

```
Private Sub mnuAppExplorer_Click()
    Dim rc As Double
    rc = Shell("explorer.exe", vbNormalFocus)
End Sub
```

17. Add the following to the Click() event of mnuAppNotepad:

```
Private Sub mnuAppNotepad_Click()
    Dim rc As Double
    rc = Shell("notepad.exe", vbNormalFocus)
End Sub
```

18. Add the following to the Click() event of mnuAppClose:

```
Private Sub mnuAppClose_Click()
    Unload Me
    Set frmMain = Nothing
End Sub
```

19. Finally, save and run your project.

You should see a small toaster icon in your System Tray. If you rest the mouse pointer over it for a couple of seconds, you will see a tool tip that says Application Launcher. When you right-click the icon, you are presented with a pop-up menu that lets you select an application to launch (see Figure 19.7).

FIGURE 19.7:   The Application Launcher

You can modify this program to include your favorite and most used applications, or even link it to a database or ASCII file so you can customize the applications that appear on your menu. You should now have enough experience with Visual Basic 6 to take this application and make it as powerful as you like.

> **TIP**   System Tray applications usually offer a pop-up menu that allows the user to perform some action with the program. At a minimum, you should give the user the option to close the application. If you want to show a form or dialog box, place a Show method in the MouseDblClick() event of clsSysTray.

Looking to the Future

We have not even scratched the surface of what the Windows API can do. Here is a small list of interesting things you can do with the Win32API:

- Make forms "float" by remaining on top of the other forms
- Call network functions using the WNet functions
- Create a video capture application using the AVICap functions

There is no limit to what you can do when you put the right tools together with a little bit of imagination. Unfortunately, the entire Win32 API would fill volumes of text, so it is impractical to attempt to cover all of what you should know about it. Inevitably, as you develop applications and become more proficient in Visual Basic, you will learn more about its limitations. When you do, start searching the API. You can create almost any program using Visual Basic and the Win32 API.

Finally, go out and get yourself a book documenting the Windows API. Although the API Viewer gives you the declarations for the API, it does nothing to explain the parameters that the API functions require. A good API book will explain these APIs and their parameters. It is a wise investment, and if you plan to do any serious development, you will need one eventually.

> **TIP** Get a good book that documents the Windows API. You will be using it before you know it.

Now that you have learned the basics of Visual Basic, start playing with the sample applications included on the Visual Basic CD. In addition, start creating your own programs. Before you know it, you'll be a Visual Basic pro.

Are You up to Speed?

Now you can...

- ☑ **use the API Viewer to retrieve API declarations**
- ☑ **properly declare a procedure in a DLL**
- ☑ **use the API in your applications**
- ☑ **add your application to the System Tray**

Index

Note to the Reader: First-level entries are in **bold**. Page numbers in **bold** indicate the principal discussion of a topic or the definition of a term. Page numbers in *italic* indicate illustrations.

b

f

k

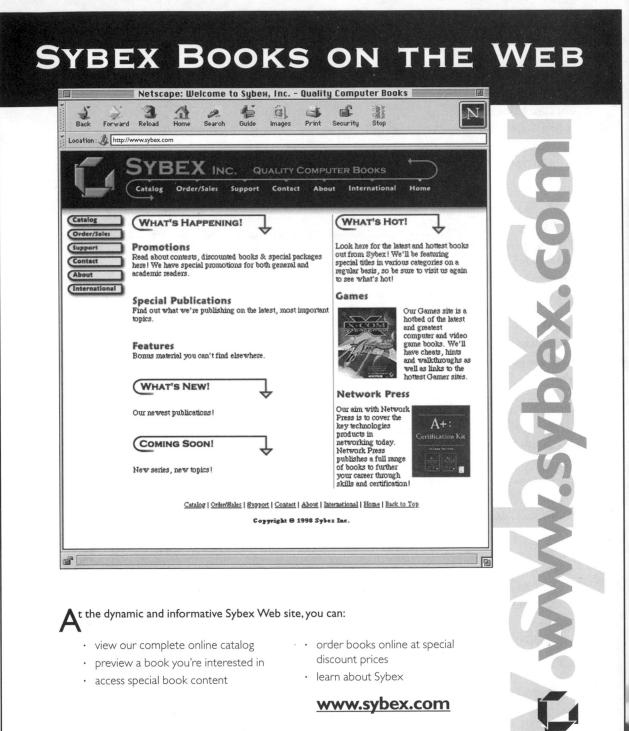